D1458575

70001358287 2

Europe

BRENDAN SIMMS

Europe

The Struggle for Supremacy, 1453 to the Present

ALLEN LANE
an imprint of
PENGUIN BOOKS

ALLEN LANE

Published by the Penguin Group
Penguin Books Ltd, 80 Strand, London WC2R 0RL, England
Penguin Group (USA) Inc., 375 Hudson Street, New York, New York 10014, USA
Penguin Group (Canada), 90 Eglinton Avenue East, Suite 700, Toronto, Ontario, Canada M4P 2Y3
(a division of Pearson Penguin Canada Inc.)
Penguin Ireland, 25 St Stephen's Green, Dublin 2, Ireland (a division of Penguin Books Ltd)
Penguin Group (Australia), 707 Collins Street, Melbourne, Victoria 3008, Australia
(a division of Pearson Australia Group Pty Ltd)
Penguin Books India Pvt Ltd, 11 Community Centre, Panchsheel Park, New Delhi – 110 017, India
Penguin Group (NZ), 67 Apollo Drive, Rosedale, Auckland 0632, New Zealand
(a division of Pearson New Zealand Ltd)
Penguin Books (South Africa) (Pty) Ltd, Block D, Rosebank Office Park,
181 Jan Smuts Avenue, Parktown North, Gauteng 2193, South Africa

Penguin Books Ltd, Registered Offices: 80 Strand, London WC2R 0RL, England

www.penguin.com

First published 2013
003

Copyright © Brendan Simms, 2013

The moral right of the author has been asserted

All rights reserved
Without limiting the rights under copyright
reserved above, no part of this publication may be
reproduced, stored in or introduced into a retrieval system,
or transmitted, in any form or by any means (electronic, mechanical,
photocopying, recording or otherwise) without the prior
written permission of both the copyright owner and
the above publisher of this book

Highgate
11/13 940.2 Sim
AMA

Set in 10.2/13.875pt Sabon LT Std
Typeset by Jouve (UK), Milton Keynes
Printed in Great Britain by Clays Ltd, St Ives plc

ISBN: 978-0-713-99427-8

www.greenpenguin.co.uk

Penguin Books is committed to a sustainable future for our business, our readers and our planet. This book is made from Forest Stewardship Council™ certified paper.

ALWAYS LEARNING

PEARSON

For Constance

A false balance is abomination to the Lord, but a just weight is his delight

Proverbs 11:1

You must in commanding and winning
Or serving and losing
Suffering or triumphing
Be either hammer or anvil

Johann Wolfgang von Goethe

Contents

Maps

Map 1. Europe in 1500

Sea
Estonia
Teutonic
Order
Riga
MUSCOVY
Moscow
Königsberg
Teutonic
Order
Prussia
Wilno
Lithuania
POLAND
Don
Warsaw
Vistula
Kiev
Cracow
Buda
HUNGARY
Transylvania
Black Sea
Danube
OTTOMAN EMPIRE
Constantinople
Rhodes
Cyprus
Crete
Mediterranean Sea
0 100 200 miles
0 200 400 km

Map 2. Europe in the Early Eighteenth Century

D E N
St Petersburg
Sea
Moscow
RUSSIAN EMPIRE
Don
EAST PRUSSIA
POLAND
Warsaw
Bug
MONARCHY
GARY
Black Sea
Danube
OTTOMAN EMPIRE
Constantinople
Mediterranean Sea
★ Barrier fortress
0 100 200 miles
0 200 400 km

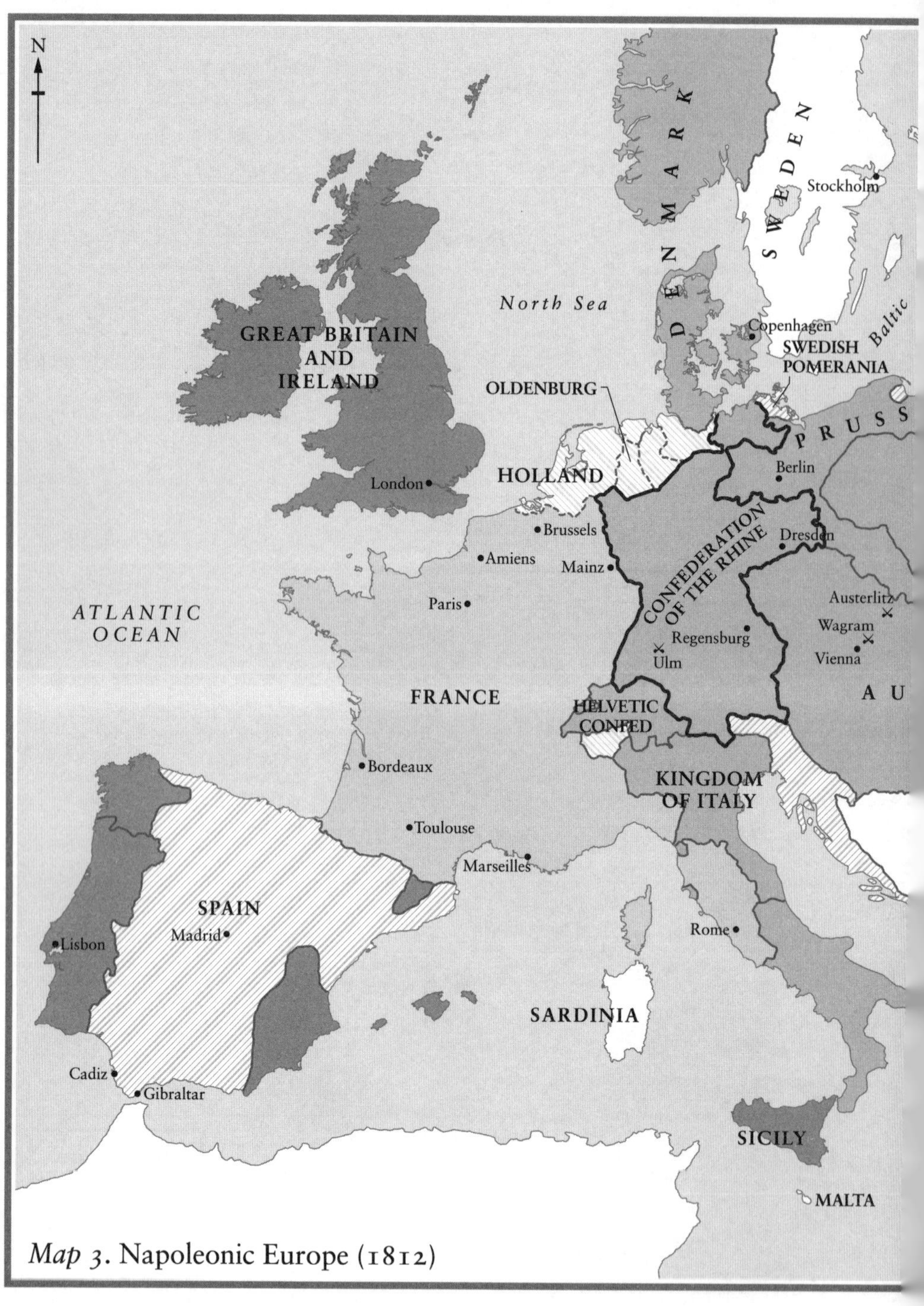

Map 3. Napoleonic Europe (1812)

France (frontiers of December 1809)
France (annexations 1810–12)
French occupation/administration
French satellites/allies
Great Britain and dependencies
St Petersburg
Sea
Moscow
Tilsit
I A
RUSSIAN EMPIRE
Warsaw
GRAND DUCHY
OF WARSAW
BESSARABIA
STRIA
Black Sea
OTTOMAN EMPIRE
Constantinople
Mediterranean Sea
0 100 200 miles
0 200 400 km

Map 4. Europe after the Congress of Vienna

St. Petersburg
RUSSIAN EMPIRE
Moscow
Sea
Riga
Dvina
Nieman
Wilno
EAST PRUSSIA
POLAND
Warsaw
Vistula
Kiev
Dnieper
Don
REP. OF KRAKOW
Dniester
THE HABSBURG EMPIRE
Pest
HUNGARY
WALLACHIA
Bucharest
Black Sea
SERBIA
Danube
BULGARIA
MONTENEGRO
Sofia
THRACE
Constantinople
OTTOMAN EMPIRE
ALBANIA
MACEDONIA
Morea
CYPRUS
Mediterranean Sea
Habsburg Empire
Boundary of German Confederation
0 100 200 miles
0 200 400 km

Map 5. Europe 1914

FINLAND
St Petersburg
ESTONIA
LIVONIA
Sea
COUR-
LAND
LATVIA
LITHUANIA
EAST
PRUSSIA
Tannenberg
Nieman
WHITE
RUSSIA
Warsaw
POLAND
Vistula
GALICIA
Moscow
R U S S I A N E M P I R E
Don
Kharkov
Donets
Kiev
Dnieper
U K R A I N E
Dniester
S T R I A -
Budapest
N G A R Y
Odessa
Sebastopol
Black Sea
ROMANIA
Bucharest
Belgrade
Danube
SERBIA
BULGARIA
Sofia
MONTENEGRO
Constantinople
ALBANIA
O T T O M A N
E M P I R E
Aegean
Sea
GREECE
Athens
CRETE
CYPRUS
(Britain)
PALESTINE
Mediterranean Sea
0 100 200 miles
0 200 400 km

Map 6. The Versailles Settlement and After

Territory lost by Germany
Territory lost by USSR
Austria-Hungary in 1914
Borders at start of First World War
1–4 Territory returned to Germany by plebiscite
FINLAND
Helsinki
Leningrad
Tallinn
ESTONIA
Moscow
Riga
LATVIA
RUSSIAN SFSR
LITHUANIA
Memel
Kaunas
Vilna
S O V I E T
WHITE RUSSIAN SSR
U N I O N
Warsaw
Brest-Litovsk
POLAND
Kiev
UKRAINIAN SSR
GALICIA
BESSARABIA
TRANSYLVANIA
ROMANIA
DOBRUJA
Black Sea
Bucharest
Belgrade
Danube
BULGARIA
Sofia
ALBANIA
Istanbul
Ankara
T U R K E Y
Salonica
Aegean Sea
GREECE
Izmir
Athens
DODECANESE
(Italy)
CYPRUS
(Britain)
Mediterranean Sea
0 100 200 miles
0 200 400 km

Map 7. The Destruction of the European Centre: Europe 1942

Greater Gemany
Powers co-operating with the Axis
Territories under German occupation
Italy and its territories
Neutral countries
FINLAND
Leningrad
Moscow
UNION OF SOVIET
SOCIALST REPUBLICS
REICHSKOMMISSARIAT
OSTLAND
Warsaw
GENERAL
GOVERNMENT
Krakow
Kiev
REICHSKOMMISSARIAT
UKRAINE
Stalingrad
HUNGARY
ROMANIA
SERBIA
BULGARIA
MONTE-
NEGRO
ALBANIA
GREECE
Black Sea
Istanbul
TURKEY
British mandate/occupation
SYRIA
IRAQ
CYPRUS
(British)
LEBANON
PALESTINE
CRETE
Mediterranean Sea
0 100 200 miles
0 200 400 km

Map 8. Contemporary Europe

EU Member States
EU New Members 2004
EU New Members 2007
EU Candidates
1949 Dates of NATO accession
FINLAND
Helsinki
Tallinn
ESTONIA
2004
Sea
Riga
LATVIA
2004
LITHUANIA
2004
Vilnius
KALININGRAD
(Russia)
Moscow
R U S S I A
Minsk
B E L A R U S
2004
Warsaw
1999
Kiev
U K R A I N E
SLOVAKIA
2004
MOLDOVA
Chisinau
Budapest
R O M A N I A
2004
G E O R G I A
Black Sea
Bucharest
Belgrade
SERBIA
B U L G A R I A
2004
Sofia
Kosovo
Skopje
Istanbul
MACEDONIA
2009
ALBANIA
2009
T U R K E Y
1952
Aegean
Sea
GREECE
1952
Athens
CYPRUS
Mediterranean Sea
0 100 200 miles
0 200 400 km

Preface

The position of a state in the world depends on the degree of independence it has attained. It is obliged, therefore, to organize all its internal resources for the purpose of self-preservation. This is the supreme law of the state.

Leopold von Ranke, *A dialogue on politics* (1836)

History is European ... it is quite unintelligible if treated as merely local.[1]

William Ewart Gladstone, British prime minister

Democracy refuses to think strategically unless and until compelled to do so for purposes of defence.

Sir Halford Mackinder[2]

We are often told that the past is another country, and they certainly did many things differently in the 550-odd years covered by this book. To western readers, religious wars, slavery, Nazism and even communism all seem quite alien today. By contrast, our ancestors would have been puzzled by the current western consensus on universal adult suffrage, racial equality and the emancipation of women. More than likely, much of what we take for granted today will seem odd to later generations. Some things, however, never change, or change only very little or very slowly. This book shows that the principal security issues faced by Europeans have remained remarkably constant over the centuries. The concepts, if not the language, of encirclement, buffers, balancing, failed states and pre-emption; the dream of empire and the quest for security; the centrality of Germany as the semi-conductor linking the various parts of the European balance; the balance between liberty and authority; the tension between consultation and efficiency; the connection between foreign and domestic policy; the tension between ideology and reason of state; the phenomena of popular hubris and national performance anxiety; the clash of civilizations and the growth of toleration – all these themes have preoccupied European statesmen and world leaders (insofar as these were not one and the same) from the mid fifteenth century to the present day. This book, in short, is about the immediacy of the past.

That said, it must be stressed that the past was once open. Our European story always contained the seeds of many futures. We will therefore have to pay as much attention as possible to the roads not taken, or those which led nowhere, as well as to the great highway which leads to the international state system of today, and the domestic order underlying it. We will have to treat the losers with a due degree of respect, however trying that might sometimes be. There was, after all, nothing inevitable about the defeats of Charles V, Louis XIV, Napoleon and Hitler. The coming of religious toleration, the abolition of slavery and the international slave trade, and the spread of western-style democracy in Europe were not preordained. Yet these outcomes were not random, either. As we shall see, the rise and fall of the great powers, the growth of freedom and the triumph of the west were closely linked. Whether they will remain so depends largely on what Europeans on both sides of the Atlantic do next. We shall have to make our own story, using history not as a manual, but as a guide to how these questions were approached in the past. It is for this reason that the final chapter ends not with a prediction, but with a series of questions. To have done otherwise would have made this a work not of history but of prophecy.

Introduction: Europe in 1450

Western and central Europe had enjoyed a sense of common identity since the high Middle Ages.[1] Almost everybody living there was a member of the Catholic Church, and acknowledged the spiritual authority of the pope in Rome; the educated classes shared a knowledge of Roman Law and Latin. Europeans were also united in opposition to Islam, which was on the retreat in the Iberian peninsula but fast advancing along Europe's south-eastern flank. Most European polities had broadly similar social and political structures. At the lower end of the spectrum, the peasantry paid feudal dues to the lords in return for protection, and tithes to the Church in return for spiritual guidance. The many self-governing cities were usually run by an elite of guildsmen and magistrates. At the top of the pyramid, the aristocracy, higher clergy and – in some cases – the cities entered into a security compact with the prince in which they pledged military service and counsel in return for protection and the confirmation or increase of their land-holding.[2] This 'feudal' contractual relationship was mediated through representative assemblies across most of Europe: the English, Irish and Scottish parliaments, the States General of the Low Countries, the Estates General of France, the *Cortes* of Castile, the Hungarian, Polish and Swedish Diets, and the German *Reichstag*.[3] The vast majority of princes, in short, did not wield absolute power.

Unlike the nearby Ottoman Empire or remoter Asian polities, therefore, European political culture was characterized by intense public or semi-public debate: about how much tax should be paid, by whom, to whom and for what purpose (almost always military). Although they were subjects rather than citizens in the modern sense, most Europeans believed in government by consent. Defending their rights – or 'privileges' in contemporary parlance – against princely encroachment was a constant preoccupation. Europeans did not live in democracies, but their elites were in an important sense 'free'. Moreover, there was an increasing desire for political freedom throughout late-medieval Europe, even if this was more aspiration than reality the further down the social scale one went.[4] This freedom was defended at home in the first instance, but sometimes a domestic tyrant could only be defeated with the help of neighbouring princes. For this reason, Europeans did not have a pronounced sense of sovereignty: many considered external intervention against 'tyrannical' rule not only legitimate, but desirable and even incumbent on all right-thinking princes.

It would be wrong to think of the principal European polities as 'great powers' or states in the modern sense. None the less, a process of 'state-building' was visible from the high Middle Ages, as princes sought to increase military mobilization in order to expand, or at least to survive.[5] Moreover, polities such as England, France, Castile, Poland and Burgundy had a clear sense of their own distinctiveness, strength and importance; in the English and French cases, at least, it is not premature to speak of a 'national' consciousness which had developed through political participation, a common language and war (mainly against each other). At the same time, however, Europeans were conscious of a common membership of 'Christendom' – a synonym for Europe – which still found expression in periodic crusades against the Muslims. Thanks to the travels of Marco Polo and others, they were aware of China and the east, but they were largely ignorant of the western hemisphere. Far from being 'Eurocentric', however, most Europeans still conceived of themselves cartographically as on the margins of a world centred on Jerusalem and the Holy Land.[6] It was for this reason that the early exploratory voyages were made along the west coast of Africa to find an alternative route to the east, and thus to attack the Muslims from the rear. The Portuguese prince 'Henry the Navigator', for example, hoped to outflank Islam and perhaps even join up with the imaginary kingdom of 'Prester John' in Africa or Asia (nobody was quite sure where). In 1415 Portugal took possession of Ceuta near present-day Morocco. Europe 'expanded', as it were, in self-defence.

Europe was also a profoundly divided continent. It had been engaged in internecine conflict throughout the Middle Ages: between emperor and pope, between the principal monarchs, between city states and territorial princes, between various barons, between rival cities, and between peasant and lord. Catholic unity had come under attack from Lollards in England, Hussites in Bohemia, Albigensians in the south of France and various other sects; there were also many voices within the Church highly critical of abuses which had developed over the Middle Ages. In the mid fifteenth century, Europe was perhaps calmer than it had been in the early Middle Ages, but it remained a violent and fragmented place. The Italian states, especially Venice and Milan, were at each other's throats, while Alfonso of Aragon was planning his own bid for predominance in the peninsula; Christians and Moors confronted each other in Spain, where the Muslims still held Granada; the Hungarians were about to embark on crusade against the Ottoman Turks; Philip of Burgundy was flexing his muscles, unsure of whether to go on crusade or to pick a fight closer to home; the Ottomans were gearing up to attack what was left of the Orthodox Christian Empire of Byzantium on the Bosphorus; and what would prove to be the Hundred Years War between England and France rumbled on.[7]

At the heart of this European contestation was the Holy Roman Empire, which stretched from Brabant and Holland in the west to Silesia in the east, from Holstein in the north to just below Siena in the south and Trieste in the south-east. It included all of present-day Germany, Austria, Switzerland, the Czech Republic and the Netherlands, as well as large parts of present-day Belgium, eastern France, northern Italy and western Poland. It was presided over by the emperor, who was chosen by seven electors – the Archbishops of Mainz, Cologne and Trier, and the ruling princes of Bohemia, the Palatinate, Saxony and Brandenburg. He ruled in consultation with the lay and ecclesiastical 'estates' of the Empire – the electors, princes, counts, knights and cities – assembled at the *Reichstag*, the German imperial parliament. Far from being a deferential herd, Germans were constantly arguing with authority, be it the princes with the emperor or the peasants with their lords, through local or imperial law courts.[8] The Empire was the fulcrum of European politics. More people lived there than in any other European polity. The cities of the Low Countries, the Rhineland, south Germany and northern Italy were – taken together – the richest, most vibrant and technically advanced in Europe. The Empire, or at least its most powerful princes, held the balance between England and France;[9] the English cause never recovered from the breach with the Duke of Burgundy, a member of the French royal family, with lands straddling the border between France and Germany, in 1435. Above all, because of its origin in the empire of Charlemagne, the imperial crown was a matter of intense interest not merely to German princes, but to neighbouring kings as well, especially those of France.[10] Uniquely among western European princes, its holder could claim universal authority as successor to the Roman Empire.[11]

Despite its critical importance and proud heritage, however, the Empire was in a state of acute crisis by the mid fifteenth century.[12] The power of the emperor, an Austrian Habsburg since 1438, had been whittled away through concessions made as a condition of his election, the *Wahlkapitulationen*. Private feuds were endemic, banditry rife and commerce subject to a slew of more or less criminal extortions. The imperial Church was sunk in a profound crisis and demoralized by abuses. Above all, the Empire was struggling to provide for the common defence. Unlike the English parliament, the *Reichstag* proved unable to agree a regular mechanism for taxation to fund imperial wars against the Hussites, the Turks and increasingly the French.[13] The Empire was also in the throes of an identity crisis. It aspired to represent Christendom as a whole, and it included people of many 'nationalities' among its subjects, including speakers of French, Dutch, Italian and Czech, but most of its subjects considered themselves German, or at least spoke dialects of German. They did not yet speak much of 'Germany', but from around 1450 contemporaries increasingly added the rider 'of the German Nation' to the term Holy Roman Empire.[14]

This book will show that the Holy Roman Empire, and its successor states, lay at the heart of the European balance of power and the global system it spawned. It was there that the strategic concerns of the great powers intersected. In friendly hands, the area could serve as a decisive force multiplier, in hostile hands it would be a mortal threat. What happened there mattered to England because it was the anchor of the 'barrier' in the Low Countries protecting its south coast from attack, and the hinge of the European balance; to Spain because it was the source of the imperial title and vital recruits, and served as the strategic hinterland to the Spanish Netherlands; to the Austrians later for the same reason; to the French because it was both a buffer and an inviting target for expansion; to Prussia because it ultimately provided the springboard for eastward and westward expansion; to early-twentieth-century Americans because of the Kaiser's intrigues in Mexico; and to the

Americans and Soviet Union, whose main objective was to either win that area or deny it to the enemy.

The Empire, and its successor states, has also been the principal source of political legitimacy for anybody who wants to speak for Europe. For hundreds of years, the major protagonists have sought the mantle of Holy Roman Emperor, to take up the legacy of Charlemagne. Henry VIII wanted it, so did Suleiman the Magnificent, Charles V had it, French kings from Francis I to Louis XVI sought it, Napoleon seriously thought about it, the echoes in Hitler's 'Third Reich' could not be clearer, and the European Union originated from the same area and in the same spirit, though with a very different content. In short, it has been the unshakeable conviction of European leaders over the past 550 years, even those who had no imperial aspirations themselves, that the struggle for mastery would be decided by or in the Empire and its German successor states. Queen Elizabeth I knew it; Cromwell knew it; Marlborough knew it; the two Pitts knew it; Bismarck knew it; the Allied high command in the First World War knew it; Franklin Delano Roosevelt knew it; Stalin knew it; Gorbachev knew it; the Russians who furiously resisted the eastward expansion of NATO after the fall of the wall know it; and the elites trying to keep the European Union together today for fear of allowing Germany to slip its moorings know it. Whoever controlled central Europe for any length of time controlled Europe, and whoever controlled all of Europe would ultimately dominate the world.

It is therefore not surprising that the struggle for mastery in Germany also drove the process of internal change in Europe. Englishmen revolted against Charles I because he failed to protect the Protestant German princes on whom their own liberties depended; Frenchmen broke with Louis XVI because of his alleged subservience to Austria; and Russians gave up on the tsar because he failed to get to grips with the Second Reich. Germany was also the crucible of the most important ideological changes in Europe: the Reformation, Marxism and Nazism were all incubated there, and shaped global geopolitics in decisive ways. The search for security and the quest for dominance also drove the expansion of Europe, from the first Columbian voyages to the nineteenth-century 'Scramble for Africa', and it lay behind the process of de-colonization as well. This was, to be sure, not always driven by German considerations, but the issue was never far from the surface, witness the attempts of seventeenth- and eighteenth-century English mariners to maintain the balance in the Empire by intercepting the supply of New World bullion to their rivals, William Pitt's remarks about 'winning America in Germany', the late-nineteenth-century French quest for imperial expansion to balance imperial Germany, and the attempt to mobilize Jews world-wide against the Kaiser through the Balfour Declaration, which culminated in the creation of the state of Israel after the Second World War.

I

Empires, 1453–1648

At last, empire has been conferred on me by the single consent of Germany, with God, as I deem it, willing and commanding . . . [T]he Spanish imperium, with the Balearics and Sardinia, with the Sicilian kingdoms, with a great part of Italy, Germany and France and with another, as I might say gold-bearing world [the Indies] . . . [a]ll these are hardly able to exist, or be maintained, unless I link Spain with Germany, and add the name of Caesar to that of King of Spain.

Emperor Charles V, 1520[1]

[T]he crown of Sweden had to pay close attention to Germany and protect itself, because it was a temperate and populous part of the world and a warlike people, that there was not a country under the sun in a better position to establish a universal monarchy and absolute dominion in Europe, than Germany . . . now, if one potentate wielded absolute power in this realm, all the neighbouring realms would have to apprehend being subjugated.

Johan Adler Salvius, Swedish negotiator
at Westphalia, 1646[2]

The year 1453 marked the start of modern European geopolitics, with the collapse of the Byzantine Empire in the east, followed shortly afterwards by that of the English empire in France. These two events had profound consequences for Europe as a whole, and especially for the Holy Roman Empire of the German Nation – usually known to contemporaries as 'The Empire' – which lay at its heart. The triumph of France over England soon led to increased French pressure on the western flank of Germany and an aspiration to control or at the very least influence the politics of the Empire. Further east, the Ottomans resumed their relentless advance into south-eastern and central Europe, which eventually took them twice to the gates of Vienna. The task of dealing with these threats fell to the Habsburg dynasty, which at the height of the reign of Charles V came to rule not only much of central, southern and north-western Europe, but large swathes of the New World as well. Crucial to the maintenance of that power was the imperial crown, through which a universal claim to lead Europe could be articulated, and which potentially provided a decisive voice in Germany. In the eyes of their opponents, on the other hand, the ambitions of Charles and his Spanish and Austrian Habsburg successors were part of a sinister plan to erect a 'Universal Monarchy' in Europe. The struggle of the Habsburgs to make good their imperial claims, and the determination of their rivals to deny them control of the Holy Roman Empire, dominated European geopolitics for the next 200 years.

The fall of Constantinople and the English defeat in France led to profound domestic changes across Europe. Over the next two centuries two different types of government, both of them direct responses to international challenges, began to emerge. On the one hand, there were the consultative systems of England and the Dutch Republic, whose remarkable resilience enabled both states not only to surmount all challenges but to maintain the European balance. On the other, there were the monarchical systems, ranging from straightforward despotisms such as the Ottoman Empire and Muscovy, to more mixed forms of government in France and Spain, in which representative assemblies continued to play an important role, but royal power was clearly in the ascendant. Meanwhile, the Empire, which lay in the middle both geopolitically and governmentally, struggled to give itself a constitutional structure capable of defusing internal tensions and keeping external predators at bay.

The first challenge came from the Ottomans. In the summer of 1453, Constantinople – capital of what was left of the Orthodox Christian Byzantine state – fell to the Turks after a long siege.[3] A brutal sacking followed, marked by thousands of murders and rapes, as well as the desecration of the city's ancient churches. Worse still from the Christian point of view, Mehmed II now adopted the title of 'Sultan I Rum' – ruler of Rome. He not only moved his capital to Constantinople – which the prophet Muhammed had thought the centre of the world – but retained the name of the city with all its European and imperial connotations.[4] It was now only a matter of time before the Ottomans launched a fresh offensive across the Mediterranean, or into the Balkans towards central Europe, in order to make good this claim to the Roman Empire, to achieve world domination through control of Europe, and to vindicate their universal mission to promote the spread of Islam. For this reason, the fall of Constantinople provoked a panic across Christendom.[5] Even in far-off Denmark and Norway, King Christian I declared that 'the grand Turk was the beast rising out of the sea described in the Apocalypse'.[6]

In the early sixteenth century, the Ottoman advance resumed under Sultan Suleiman the Magnificent. His aim was nothing less than Universal Monarchy: an inscription above the entrance to the Grand Mosque in Constantinople later proclaimed him 'Conqueror of the lands of the Orient and the Occident with the help of Almighty God and his victorious army, possessor of the Kingdoms of the World'.[7] Liaising closely with disaffected Spanish Moors and their exiled associates along the North African coast, he struck in the Mediterranean. After turning Algeria into an Ottoman vassal, crushing the Knight Hospitaller garrison at Rhodes, and securing most of the Black Sea littoral, the Sultan crashed into central Europe. In 1521, Suleiman took the great fortress of Belgrade, and five years later he shattered the Hungarian army at the battle of Mohacs. A huge swathe of south-eastern Europe, including nearly the entire fertile Danube Basin, fell under Ottoman control. Hungary – whose nobles had described themselves as the 'shield and rampart of Christianity' – was no more. In his self-proclaimed capacity as 'Distributor of Crowns to the monarchs of the world', Suleiman made his satellite John Zapolya 'King' of Hungary. The Sultan, the Greek historian Theodore Spandounes warned, was 'preparing an innumerable force to make war upon the Christians by land and sea', with 'no other thought but to devour' them 'Like a dragon with his gullet wide open'.[8] It was only with great difficulty that the Habsburgs repulsed a Turkish assault on Vienna itself in 1529.

In the late 1550s, Suleiman's successors pressed forward again. By 1565, the Turks had appeared before the strategically vital island fortress of Malta, which they very nearly captured. In the summer of 1570, Turkish troops landed on Cyprus, capturing the island a year later. As the Turks advanced in the late 1550s and early 1560s, Corsair and Morisco raids on the Spanish eastern seaboard, often penetrating far inland, mounted. At the same time, the Ottomans pushed further into Hungary, threatening the Holy Roman Empire. There was heavy fighting throughout the 1550s and 1560s, which resumed in the 1590s after a long truce. It was only in 1606, with the Peace of Zsitva, that the Ottoman threat to central Europe receded, at least for the time being.

If the Habsburgs were the main target of Ottoman schemes for Universal Monarchy, they soon developed ambitions of their own; indeed, they based their claim to leadership in Christendom partly on the need for western unity against the Turks. The election of Charles V as Holy Roman Emperor in 1519 determined the shape of European geopolitics for the next three decades.[9] He ruled not only over Spain, Naples, the Low Countries, Austria and Bohemia, but also a growing empire in the New World. A Spanish bishop therefore pronounced Charles 'by God's grace . . . King of the Romans and Emperor of the world'. A Universal Monarchy under Charles V, in which the Habsburgs ruled over a united and once again uniformly Catholic Christendom, seemed a realistic possibility.[10] It was only after some thirty years of campaigning against the Turks, France, the German princes and even England that Charles was forced to abandon his ambition to dominate Europe.

Within a few decades, however, his son, Philip II of Spain, showed himself to be every bit as formidable. He defeated the Turks at the sea battle of Lepanto, took control of Portugal and her overseas empire, colonized the Philippines, greatly increased the extraction of bullion from the New World, and was even the King-Consort of England for a while. Puffed up by success, Philip began to speak more and more openly about his European and global ambitions. The back of a medal commemorating the union of crowns with Portugal was inscribed with the words '*Non sufficit orbis*' – 'the world is not enough'. A Spanish triumphal arch carried a legend suggesting that the king was 'lord of the world' and 'lord of everything in east and west'.[11] Like his father, Philip ultimately failed, worn out by the battle against Dutch rebels in the Low Countries and winded by the disastrous Armada expedition against England. The Habsburg ambition to control Europe was no means over, however. During the Thirty Years War in the early and mid seventeenth century, it required the combined efforts of France, Sweden, the German princes and ultimately England to see off an Austro-Spanish attempt to dominate the continent.

At the heart of this struggle for mastery lay the Holy Roman Empire. Germany was weak – not quite a vacuum but never strong enough to resist being sucked into almost every major European conflict. Severe divisions between the component parts of the Empire – the emperor, the princes, the cities and the clergy – meant that Germans were unable to stop their territory from being marched over almost at will by foreigners. This mattered because the area corresponding roughly to present-day Germany, northern Italy and the Low Countries was the strategic centre of Europe. At some point or other, the interests of all the major protagonists intersected there.

For the Ottomans, the Holy Roman Empire was the main objective of their advance into central Europe. It was there that their main enemy, the Habsburgs, and the German princes who supported them, could be dealt a decisive blow. Moreover, it was only by occupying Germany that Suleiman could vindicate the Ottoman claim to the legacy of the Roman Empire.[12] The Holy Roman Empire was also the focus of Suleiman's 'leapfrog diplomacy', through which he exploited the hostility of the German princes to Charles V.[13] He even sent an agent to the Dutch rebels in Flanders. 'Since you have raised your sword against the papists,' he wrote, 'and since you have regularly killed them, our imperial compassion and royal attention have been devoted in every way to your region.'[14]

The Empire also lay at the core of Habsburg grand strategy. Charles V used his position there to box in his French rivals and provide a springboard for the recovery of Burgundy.[15] Increasingly, however, his authoritarian manner alienated the German princes. They were horrified to hear him announce in April 1521 that 'It is not my desire and will that there be many lords, but one lord alone, as is the tradition of the Holy Roman Empire'.[16] When Charles forced through the election of his brother Ferdinand as his nominated successor, these critics formed the Schmalkaldic League (1531), led by Hesse and Saxony, to oppose him. The emperor now began to pay more and more attention to Germany, turning his back on the Mediterranean.[17] By the early 1540s, Charles had all but crushed France, forcing her to renounce Milan and the Low Countries at the Peace of Crépy in 1544, and thus excluding them from Germany.[18] In 1546, he drew up plans to turn Germany, Milan, Savoy, the Low Countries and perhaps even Naples into a federation for mutual defence under his leadership, directed against both France and the Ottoman Empire.[19] A year later, Charles won a crushing victory in Germany at the battle of Mühlberg in April 1547. All this, however, provoked such furious resistance in the Empire and across Europe that the emperor was forced to back down and to divide his inheritance into a Spanish and an Austrian Habsburg line.[20] Charles might have won the battle for Germany militarily, but he lost it politically.

His successors as King of Spain, Philip II and Philip III, remained intensely engaged with the Empire, because it was the political framework within which the struggle against the Dutch unfolded, and because it encompassed or bordered the 'Spanish Road' by which Philip's armies in Flanders were supplied and reinforced. This lifeline ran from Spain, via north Italy, and across the Alpine passes, skirting the western edge of the Holy Roman Empire before reaching the Low Countries. Most of the route ran through Habsburg or Habsburg-controlled territory in the Mediterranean, Lombardy and Burgundy, but the last stretch through western Germany was vulnerable to attack. Moreover, Flanders could not be held unless Spain retained control of the river crossing points of the Rhine and Meuse. Without them, the early-seventeenth-century Spanish chief minister Gaspar de Guzmán, Count Olivares feared, Spanish Flanders would be 'locked in a cage'. Germany was thus the centrepiece of a precarious Spanish geopolitical edifice, the collapse of any part of which would trigger an unstoppable 'domino' effect. These priorities were reflected in seventeenth-century Spanish military expenditure, over half of which went on the Low Countries and Germany.[21]

Conversely, for France, a strong position in the Empire was vital in order to loosen the Habsburg 'encirclement' through the Low Countries to the north, the Free Duchy of Burgundy to the east, Milan to the south-east and Spain to the south. There were two mutually reinforcing strategies open to the French. The first was direct military intervention in the Empire. In August 1494, for example, Charles VIII led an army across the Alps with the avowed intention of vindicating his claim to Naples and thence to lead a pan-European crusade against the Turk. His real purpose was to seize the leadership of Christendom; to intimidate the pope into denying his Habsburg rival, Maximilian, an imperial coronation in Rome; and to break the ring of encirclement suffocating France.

More than fifty years later, Henri II intervened militarily in Germany, carrying out a famous 'March to the Rhine' and capturing Metz, Toul and Verdun for France along the way. During the Thirty Years War, the French chief minister, Cardinal Richelieu, intervened in Germany to curb the Habsburgs and to establish 'gateways' (*portes*) into the Empire.[22] Towards the end of that conflict, the French finally captured the south German town of Breisach, cutting the 'Spanish Road' and thus, as the French plenipotentiaries told Richelieu's successor, Cardinal Mazarin, 'this dangerous communication of the forces of the house of Austria, which our fathers feared'.[23]

The second French strategy was to form alliances with German princes against the emperor. Francis I, for example, was the earliest and most enthusiastic supporter of the Schmalkaldic League. Likewise, Henri II believed that the security of France depended on the defence of German 'liberties' – the independence of the German princes – against the emperor. In January 1552 he concluded the Treaty of Chambord in which he promised to prevent the princes 'from falling from their ancient franchise and liberty into a bestial, insupportable and perpetual servitude'; the banner of the alliance spoke of him as '*vindex germanicae et principus captivorum*' – 'avenger of Germany and of the captive princes'.[24] In 1609, Henri IV, fearing a Habsburg annexation of the north-western German territory of Cleves as yet another link in the surrounding chain of Spanish outposts, announced that he would show support for his 'ancient allies [in Germany] and for preventing the Emperor from augmenting himself at the expense of others'.[25] Weakening the Habsburg hold over the German princes was also the core of Cardinal Richelieu's grand strategy.[26] Spain, Richelieu wrote in 1629, wanted to 'make herself master of Germany and turn her into an absolute monarchy, overturning the former laws of the German Republic (*république germanique*) upon which the imperial authority is founded'. Like the two Henris, he believed that the French interest was to protect 'German liberties', the rights of the princes and representative assemblies, from the absolutist tendencies of the German emperor.[27] 'Weakening the excessive power of the House of Austria, and establishing the liberty of the princes of the Empire,' the French Secretary of State, Henri-Auguste de Lomenie, Count of Brienne, wrote in May 1645, after the Cardinal's death, was 'the main aim of the war'.[28] German freedoms and French security were thus inseparably linked.

Germany was also central to the security of the Dutch after they cast off Spanish rule in the late sixteenth century. The first priority of the new United Provinces was the defence of the 'garden' of Holland, a fenced-off area bounded by the North Sea to the west. But if the topography provided protection against attack from the north, south and west, the eastern border of the new republic, with the Holy Roman Empire, was extremely vulnerable. Here the Dutch strategy was to push outposts deeper and deeper into Germany, in order as the States General remarked in 1587 'to divert the war beyond the borders of our country'. From its very inception, therefore, the republic's security was based on a strategy of forward defence in the Holy Roman Empire.[29] Moreover, the rebel leader, William of Orange, was a prince of the Holy Roman Empire, and as the words of the Dutch anthem put it – 'of German blood'. There were nearly twice as many Dutch exiles in Germany as in England. It was to Germany that William fled in 1567, from there that William recruited most of his troops, and launched his principal attacks. His closest ally, John Casimir of the Palatinate, held lands in the strategically crucial area of western Germany. In the early seventeenth century, the Dutch were once again alarmed by events in Germany, this time by Habsburg designs on nearby Cleves. They promptly intervened militarily against the imperialists. The fate of the Dutch, in short, was intimately bound up with that of the Holy Roman Empire.

The Empire was also of vital strategic importance to England. When Henry VIII joined the scramble to contain Charles V in the 1540s, he dispatched missions in search of 'some league or amity with the princes and potentates of Germany'.[30] His short and disastrous fourth marriage to Anne of Cleves was primarily motivated by an interest in the Schmalkaldic League. Later, Germany took on a new significance as the outer defence works of the Low Countries, an area which Elizabeth I's adviser William Cecil described as 'the very counter-scarp of England', that is, a defensive position just outside the inner perimeter.[31] In 1572, Elizabeth paid John Casimir of the Palatinate to attack Spanish troops in Brabant.[32] It was against this background that Elizabeth finally intervened militarily in the Netherlands in the mid-1580s in order to prevent this critical area from being over-run by Spain. In the early seventeenth century, England was once again roused to action by fear of Habsburg penetration in north-western Germany. A substantial English force was duly sent to Cleves. In short, English grand strategy was increasingly driven by the assumption that the security of the realm depended on keeping the Low Countries and the Holy Roman Empire in friendly hands.[33]

Sweden, too, became more and more concerned with events in Germany. King Gustavus Adolphus and the Swedish parliament, the *Rijkstag*, observed the Habsburg advance there during the early stages of Thirty Years War with growing alarm. If nothing was done, the king warned the Diet in December 1627, the imperialists 'would soon be approaching our borders'. The *Rijkstag* agreed with Gustavus that it would be better to act pre-emptively in order to 'transfer the seat and burdens of war to a place which is subject to the enemy'. Moreover, true security could only be achieved by holding the Baltic German ports from which an attack could be launched. As Chancellor Axel Oxenstierna later remarked, 'if the emperor had once got hold of Stralsund the whole coast would have fallen to him, and here in Sweden we should never have enjoyed a moment's security'.[34] So in 1630, Gustavus landed forces at Usedom on the Pomeranian coast to establish a bridgehead. Their mission, according to the manifesto drawn up by his councillor, Johan Adler Salvius, was to prevent the creation of a Catholic Universal Monarchy in Christendom by defending 'the liberty of Germany'.[35] Not long afterwards, the Swedish king crushed an imperial force at Breitenfeld in September 1631. Swedish troops penetrated deep into southern Germany, even threatening Munich, capital of Ferdinand's closest ally. Many speculated that the Swedish king might attempt to seize the imperial crown himself.[36] Elector Johan Georg of Saxony even accused Chancellor Oxenstierna of wanting to become 'absolute master and *dictator perpetuum* in Germany'.[37]

The Holy Roman Empire was of profound strategic importance for another reason. Its untapped resources were believed to be so large as to tip the balance between Habsburg and Valois, Christian and Turk. The Empire's population in the early seventeenth century was 15 million, as compared to 8 million in Spain. Only France, with between 16 and 20 million inhabitants, was larger. In terms of sheer numbers alone, the manpower of Germany was an immense reservoir; qualitatively the skill of German mercenaries, especially heavy cavalry, was greatly prized. Germans formed the backbone of every army William of Orange had raised against Spain. By 1600, indeed, many Spaniards believed that the Dutch were more dependent on their German allies than on England.[38]

Spain, too, relied heavily on the military resources of the Holy Roman Empire, which from the late sixteenth to the mid seventeenth century, supplied some three quarters of 'Spanish' infantry in Flanders. The Empire, at least its western half, was also an immensely rich area, with vibrant merchant communities in Cologne, Frankfurt and other cities. Such was the demographic, military and economic potential of the Empire, the Swedish negotiator warned towards the end of the Thirty Years War, that 'if one potentate wielded absolute power in this realm, all the neighbouring realms would have to apprehend being subjugated'.[39]

The Empire was also of profound ideological importance in Europe and indeed beyond Christendom. The emperor outranked all other European monarchs, at least theoretically. For this reason, some of the most ambitious European potentates – Charles V, Francis I of France, Henry VIII of England – openly campaigned for the title; others, such as Henri II of France, did so implicitly. Even Ottoman rulers, such as Mehmed and Suleiman the Magnificent, laid claim to the imperial Roman heritage, further proof of their Eurocentricity. Most importantly of all, it was the emperor who was entitled to mobilize the resources of the Empire in conjunction with the imperial parliament, the *Reichstag*. Once again, therefore, European states were determined either to secure the imperial title for themselves or to prevent it from falling into hostile hands.

Despite his Muslim faith, Suleiman the Magnificent made a serious effort to appropriate the German imperial legacy. He pointedly stressed his monotheism, and adopted the western symbols of crown and sceptre in his iconography, with themes borrowed from Charles's coronation as 'King of the Romans'.[40] In the 1520s and 1530s a Venetian adviser helped Suleiman to organize western-style imperial displays in Hungary and occupied areas of Austria to impress the locals. To some extent, the Sultan succeeded: his sobriquet 'the Magnificent' was a European, not a Muslim honorific. Nor was Suleiman a completely implausible imperial contender. There were many German princes who thought that 'German liberties' would be better protected by the Turks than by the Habsburgs.[41]

To the Habsburgs, the imperial crown was a vital tool to hold their sprawling lands together. The emperor Maximilian used his position to mobilize Germany against France during the Italian wars of the late fifteenth and early sixteenth centuries. His successor, Charles V, was also in no doubt about the value of the crown of Charlemagne. 'It is so great and sublime an honour,' he remarked before the election, 'as to outshine all other worldly titles.'[42] Conversely, in the hands of the French the imperial title would spell doom, leaving the Burgundian lands dangerously sandwiched in between Germany and France itself. The imperial title would also provide rivals with a decisive advantage in resources and manpower. As the Habsburg Grand Chancellor, Mercurino Gattinara, said, 'if it were neglected, empire would be handed over to the French who by no means would reject such an opportunity but would pant for it with all their power and such would they be able to undertake with that empire that [Charles] would be able to preserve neither the lands of the Austro-Burgundian succession nor his Iberian kingdoms'.[43] For this reason, Charles threw huge resources – mainly bribes for the German princes – into the imperial election of 1519, and ultimately secured the title.[44]

Thereafter, Charles's claim to the leadership of Christendom rested on the German imperial crown, as did his hope of presiding over a Europe united and peaceful under his leadership. 'God the creator,' Gattinara announced in 1519, 'has given you this grace of raising you in dignity above all Christian kings and princes by constituting you the greatest emperor and king who has been since the division of the empire, which was realized in the person of Charlemagne your predecessor, and by drawing you to the right of monarchy in order to lead back the entire world to a single shepherd.' Time and again, Charles and his ministers would justify policies 'as much on account of the Empire as on account of our kingdoms of Spain'.[45] Charles proved unable, however, to persuade or force enough German princes to elect his son Philip King of the Romans, and thus his designated successor. While Philip succeeded as King of Spain, the imperial title devolved to the Austrian branch of the family. The Spanish Habsburgs and the emperor continued to work closely together, all the same. One way or the other, the German imperial crown was to be an important component of Habsburg power in Europe.

This fact drove France's preoccupation with the imperial title. In the late fifteenth century, Charles VIII lived in fear that the emperor Maximilian would tap into the resources of the German political commonwealth. He also sought to stake a claim to the imperial crown himself. To underline his aspirations, Charles minted coins with the unmistakable motto of 'Carolus Imperator' – 'Emperor Charles'.[46] Two decades later, Francis I made an unsuccessful bid for the imperial crown when he ran against Charles in the 1519 election. As the true heir of

Charlemagne, Francis claimed to be merely 'regaining' the title. Denying the Habsburgs the imperial crown was also essential to escape continuing encirclement. 'The reason which moves me to gain the empire,' Francis explained, 'is to prevent the said [Habsburg] King from doing so. If he were to succeed, seeing the extent of his kingdoms and lordships . . . he . . . would doubtless throw me out of Italy.' Moreover, Francis knew that possession of the imperial title would give him the right to lead Christendom, and therefore stressed his 'intention . . . to make war on the Turks more effectively'.[47] Some one hundred years later, Richelieu's mentor, Père Joseph, wrote that the principal war aim was to prevent the Spaniards from making 'the Empire hereditary in the House of Austria' and thus to achieve their 'pretensions of their monarchy over all Christendom [Europe]'.[48]

England, too, was profoundly concerned with the imperial title. In 1519, Henry VIII threw his hat into the ring against Charles and Francis. His candidature reflected a determination to rebuild the English empire in France and to assert herself in Europe more generally. The king was deeply conscious of the traditional French argument that England was subject to the pope, whereas the crown of France was subject to no one. If Henry wished to reassert his own claim to the French throne, then imperial stature was essential, as was a strong diplomatic position in Germany, which would threaten the French on their eastern flank. The path back to France, in other words, went through Germany. Imperial status would also increase the chances of Henry's (then) favourite, Wolsey, taking the papacy; for this reason, the king initially condemned Luther in the strongest terms.[49] There was some support for the English monarch in Germany, not least in the person of the emperor Maximilian, who was desperate to keep the French out, and not yet confident that a Habsburg candidate was viable. Henry's bid failed, but it is fascinating to speculate what would have happened if the king had won the imperial crown – making him Henry VIII of Germany as well as Henry VIII of England – and if his successors had kept it: history would have been very different. English forms of government might have spread to the continent: Calais enjoyed parliamentary representation, and even Tournai in Flanders, briefly held by Henry, sent a delegation to Westminster.[50] There would have been a very different British Empire, and perhaps also a more British Europe.

*

These geopolitical patterns were moulded, but not fundamentally transformed, by the religious and political cross-currents which roiled Europe from the mid fifteenth to the mid seventeenth centuries. In 1517, the German monk Martin Luther pinned his ninety-five theses to the church door at Wittenberg, attacking the Roman Catholic Church for its corruption and errors.[51] This 'Reformation' was not just a theological revolt, but a protest against internal disorder and external encroachments in the Empire. Luther, Ulrich von Hutten, Andreas Osiander and other reformers were profoundly concerned about the Ottoman advance and contributed several stirring calls to arms against the infidel.[52] They sought to revive the German nation through spiritual transformation, a call to repentance and prayer which would purge the Empire of the impurities which had weakened it in the face of attacks from east and west. Luther's message resonated not only among educated people, but also with the inhabitants of rural areas, especially in the south and west, who saw in the Reformation a chance to emancipate themselves from the control of the lords, and an opportunity to reform the Empire and restore German national 'honour' in Europe. The 'Peasant War' which erupted a few years later was thus no local *jacquerie*, but a popular demand to participate in the new *Reich*.[53] Many German princes, on the other hand, saw Protestantism as a shield against imperial encroachments and an instrument to extend their control over their subjects, emancipate themselves from the emperor and improve their finances by seizing Church property.

The political context was also a decisive factor in the English Reformation of the 1530s. A male heir was crucial not so much for the stability of England – where women could succeed – as for Henry's claim to France and the Empire, where they were disbarred by the Salic Law. When the pope refused to grant him a divorce to marry Anne Boleyn, Henry broke with Rome. Thereafter, Henry's despoliation of Church lands not only enabled him to buttress his rule at home, but provided a much needed boost to war-financing. His large-scale fortification of the south coast in response to the Franco-Habsburg Catholic threat, paid for by despoiling the secularized monasteries, and actually constructed from their stones taken from their ruins, epitomized the close link between the English Reformation and the security of the realm.

The Reformation encouraged the emergence of a 'culture of persuasion' and thus of European national and transnational publics concerned with religion, diplomacy and the common good.[54] The peoples of central, northern and north-western Europe were preached to, sung at, showered with printed pamphlets and bombarded with images, mainly cheap woodcuts. Over the next decades, varieties of Protestantism were embraced by rulers in all parts of Germany, but principally the north and east, in the Low Countries, in England and Scotland, in all of Scandinavia, and by many communities in Poland, Hungary and Bohemia. New fronts now opened up not merely within polities – where they could be exploited by their neighbours – but between states. To the existing solidarity between Christians against the Turk, and republics against princely tyrants, there was now added the fraternity of Protestants against Catholics and vice versa.

Nowhere were these divisions more keenly felt than in Germany, which was split down the middle by the Reformation.[55] There Catholicism, Lutheranism and Calvinism faced each other in grand array. In the 1590s, Calvinist diehards rallied around the Elector Palatine, determined to vindicate 'German liberty' against the emperor, and to achieve parity in imperial institutions.[56] They looked for help to their brethren abroad – the 'Calvinist International' in England and the Low Countries and they in turn strained every nerve to defend the cause in the strategically crucial German area.[57] The Dutch, the English and the Protestant German princes thus believed themselves to be tied together in a strategic community of fate. Elizabeth's principal adviser and effectively chief minister, William Cecil, for example, called for 'a conjunction with all princes Protestants for defence', especially with 'the princes Protestants of the [German] Empire'. So long as the Empire did not fall into hostile hands, in other words, the Dutch rebels, and thus England itself, would be safe.[58] Shortly after the turn of the century, the Calvinists went on the offensive. They repeatedly disrupted the imperial Diets culminating in the establishment of the Evangelical Union under the Elector Palatine. In 1609, the Duke of Bavaria responded by establishing the Catholic League, whose activities were subsidized by King Philip III of Spain. That same year, the Calvinists finally walked out of the Diet, precipitating a constitutional crisis.[59]

The critical issue was the future of the imperial crown, which had now become the subject of religious, as well as strategic, rivalry. The most plausible candidate, the Habsburg Ferdinand of Styria, was a nightmare for all Protestants. His absolutist pretensions and Jesuit training posed a direct threat to the Lutheran and Calvinist princes. Some of the more radical among them sought to pre-empt this danger by securing the election of a Protestant emperor.[60] This scheme was anathema, however, not just to the Austrian Habsburgs and German Catholics generally but also to Spain.[61] 'If the forces of a Protestant emperor were ever to be united with those of the [Dutch] heretics,' the senior Spanish adviser Don Baltasar de Zúñiga warned in September 1613, 'then the obedient provinces in Flanders will be lost, and with them the Duchy of Milan and the rest of Italy.' 'It is certain,' the Spanish diplomat Inigo Velez de Guevara, Count Onate, Spanish envoy to the Austrian Habsburgs, warned in 1618, 'that one would lose Flanders and Italy, upon which the whole monarchy rests, if one loses Germany.'[62]

Matters came to a head in May 1618 when the Bohemian nobility elected the Protestant Frederick of the Palatinate as their king, with the expectation that he would also bid for the imperial crown.[63] In March 1619, however, Ferdinand of Styria was elected emperor. He quickly moved to re-establish Habsburg control, defeating the Bohemian nobility at the battle of the White Mountain in 1620. Spanish troops occupied the Palatinate itself. Frederick was forced to give up his electoral title to Ferdinand's closest German ally and leader of the Catholic League, the Duke of Bavaria, thus copper-fastening the Habsburg grip on the imperial crown.[64] The balance of power within Germany had now shifted decisively to the Catholic side, and consequently was threatening to unhinge the whole European equilibrium.[65] As the Dutch States General wrote in February 1621, the final fall of the Palatinate would see 'the true religion extirpated, the universal liberty of Germany trampled under foot and, of greatest consequence, the imperial crown transported to the house of Spain'.

On the other hand, though religion often accentuated existing geopolitical divides, it did not always transcend them. To the Catholic French, for example, hatred of their fellow-Catholic Habsburgs trumped all other considerations. Francis I did not hesitate to ally with the Turks against Charles V. 'I cannot deny,' Francis remarked, 'that I keenly desire the Turk to be powerful and ready for war, not for himself, because he is an infidel and we are Christian, but to undermine the emperor's power, to force heavy expenses on him and to secure all other governments against so powerful an enemy.'[66] Nor did Francis's successors show any inhibitions about using the Protestant German princes to undermine the Habsburg emperor. Likewise, Cardinal Richelieu intervened in the Empire during the Thirty Years War in support of the Protestant princes and the Swedes, and against his Habsburg co-religionists. Sultan Suleiman, for his part, urged his Muslim supporters in Spain to coordinate their actions with the 'Lutheran sect' in the Low Countries and the Empire.

The struggle for mastery in Europe, and especially in the Holy Roman Empire, profoundly shaped domestic politics. It stimulated the emergence of a public sphere, mainly in the individual polities, but also on a pan-European basis. Argument about grand strategy was at the forefront of these debates, for which two illustrative examples will have to suffice. In the aftermath of the fall of their empire in France in the mid fifteenth century furious Englishmen wanted to know what had gone wrong, and who was to blame.[67] The resulting debate raged well beyond the confines of parliament in widely circulated hand-written texts.[68] Articles of impeachment drawn up against William de la Pole, the Duke of Suffolk, who was the Lord High Steward and King Henry VI's principal counsellor, which ultimately led to his execution, were dominated by allegations of betraying the English cause in France. In Kent, a band of agrarian rebels advanced on London complaining not only of local grievances but that the king 'has had false counsel, for his lands are lost, his merchandise is lost, his commons destroyed, the sea is lost, France is lost'.[69] Partisans of the house of York charged that royal ineptitude had led to the fall of France, questioned the readiness of the remaining English bases such as Calais, and accused their Lancastrian rivals of planning to surrender them to the French.[70] For most of the late fifteenth and early sixteenth centuries, therefore, English debate was focused on recovering the lost empire across the Channel. Over time, however, the attention of the English public sphere shifted to the Low Countries and the Holy Roman Empire. The Dutch rebels and the Protestant German princes were widely celebrated as bulwarks against Habsburg Catholic domination. At the start of the seventeenth century, many Englishmen condemned peace with Madrid as a capitulation to tyranny and an abandonment of the Dutch and continental Protestants generally.[71] Soon after, outrage at the treatment of German Protestants, the dynastic marriages with Spain and the failure of the Stuart monarchy began to dominate English political debate.[72]

In Germany, political discussion was greatly stimulated by the invention of the printing press by the publisher Johannes Gutenberg in the 1450s. Here the growth of Renaissance humanism drove the emergence of a proto-nationalist public sphere. It was primarily concerned with the decline of the imperial commonwealth and thus of the reputation of Germany in Europe. Germans saw themselves as the heirs to a universal Roman Empire in which they were the leading, though not the only, people; they were fully conscious of the fact that their polity contained a substantial Slav and Romance (*Welsch*) population. This imperial patriotism and nationalism defined itself through antagonism to the Burgundian and French encroachments in the west, and Hungarian and Turkish depredations to the south-east.[73] It was also expressed through increasing participation in imperial institutions, and the demand of humanists such as Johannes Avertinus that there should be greater efforts to defend 'German liberties' against the despotism of France and other predators.[74] There was a determination to tackle corruption in the German Church and a condemnation of endemic lawlessness, which was seen not just as a social scourge but a standing invitation to outside interference. In short, there was still plenty of life in the old Holy Roman Empire.[75]

Foreign policy also determined courtly politics throughout Europe, and sometimes even the rise and fall of whole dynasties. The issues varied from state to state, but by the early seventeenth century the common preoccupation was the situation in the Holy Roman Empire. Across the continent, failure or perceived failure in Germany during the Thirty Years War led to internal political change. Francisco Gomez de Sandoval, Duke of Lerma, Spanish chief minister, fell from power in Madrid in 1618 because he had proved unable to defend Spanish interests in Europe generally, and especially in the Holy Roman Empire.[76] His successor, Zúñiga, thrived on being able to deliver there and died in high favour in 1622. The man who took his place, Olivares, on the other hand, was criticized for the mounting costs of Spanish grand strategy, particularly in the Empire. Likewise, in Paris, the French chief minister, Charles d'Albert, Duke of Luynes, lost influence at court on account of his failed German strategy,[77] as did his successor, Charles, Duke of Vieuville. Cardinal Richelieu, on the other hand, waxed on the strength of his successes in the Empire.

It was in England, however, that foreign affairs led to the most spectacular domestic eruption. As the Austro-Spanish imperial tide engulfed Germany at the start of the Thirty Years War, parliamentary and popular outrage against the monarchy exploded.[78] To critics of the Stuart monarchy, the Bohemian conflict was not taking place in a far-off country between people of whom they knew nothing. As Sir John Davies told the House of Commons in 1620, 'the Palatinate is on fire; religion is on fire; and all other countries on fire ... this is dangerous to the Low Countries, the United Provinces and the whole Protestant interest'. Looking across to the continent, the king's parliamentary critics saw 'a mighty and prevalent party ... aiming at the subversion of all the Protestant churches of Christendom', and noted 'the weak resistance that is made against them'.[79] By 1642, the two sides were locked in a bitter civil war, which led to the defeat of the king in 1646, his execution in 1649 and the replacement of the monarchy by a Protectorate under Oliver Cromwell. The need to support the Palatinate and European Protestantism featured prominently in the major parliamentary statements of war aims. In short, the Great Rebellion against Charles was in its essence a revolt against Stuart foreign policy. Failure to grasp a foreign nettle led to the breakdown of consensus at home. In the end, Englishmen went to war with each other in 1642 because they had not gone to war effectively on behalf of the Protestant cause in Europe over the previous twenty years.

In order to remain competitive in the battle for Europe, states sought to consolidate internally, or to find security in larger unions. Charles V recognized the difficulty of coordinating the Austrian, Hungarian and Mediterranean fronts against the Turks in addition to his Italian, German and Burgundian theatres of war against the French and the Protestant princes of the Empire. He therefore subcontracted the defence of central Europe, and much of the management of the Holy Roman Empire, to his younger brother, Ferdinand. In 1522, Charles abdicated as archduke of Austria to make way for him, and nine years later he forced the German princes to elect him King of the Romans and thus his designated successor. This had profound implications for state formation in south-eastern Europe. Ferdinand rescued Bohemia and Silesia from the Hungarian wreckage, making his north-eastern flank more secure.[80] He told the *Landtag*, the assembled representatives of the nobility, at Linz in 1530 that 'the Turks cannot be resisted unless the

Kingdom of Hungary was in the hands of an Archduke of Austria or another German prince'.[81] After some hesitation, Croatia and the Hungarian rump joined the Habsburgs. In both cases, the link was essentially a contractual one, directly linked to Ferdinand's ability to provide protection against the Turks.[82]

The Dutch were even more successful in providing for the common defence. In the late sixteenth century they quickly overcame the 'particularism' which William of Orange warned was undermining the struggle to gain independence from Spain. In 1572, the States of Holland voted to make William *Stadholder* and supreme commander, granted him taxes to fight Philip, and proclaimed religious toleration to forestall civil war. Three years later the province of Zealand joined in: the very first joint measure was a declaration in October 1575 'that we should forsake the King [of Spain] and seek foreign assistance'. In 1579, Holland, Zealand, most of Utrecht, and the province of Groningen formed the 'Union of Utrecht'. A complex system of extraction, credit and war finance was agreed. All this probably made the Netherlanders the most highly taxed people in Europe. It was sustainable only because they had decided to take their destinies and security into their own hands. The Dutch now 'owned' their security policy. They started the revolt as a congeries of separate provinces, all fiercely attached to their privileges. It was only the pressures of conflict which created the United Provinces. The Dutch found ways to make war, but the war also made Dutchmen.[83]

In England, the demands of international politics produced some radical thinking about how the tension between metropolis and outlying areas could be resolved. The Tudors feared that, in the hands of a hostile power, Scotland and Ireland would be the 'back door' to England, or at the very least contribute to her encirclement. Elizabeth's early intervention and the triumph of Presbyterianism largely solved the problem north of the border, for the time being at least. Ireland, where the bulk of the population remained Catholic, and where the natives bitterly resented English colonists of whatever religion, was a much thornier issue. Spanish infiltration there had to be stopped, and the threat of Gaelic rebellion crushed for good. A durable solution would have to be found, especially in a context where rival states, as Elizabeth's chief minister, Cecil, warned in 1560, 'have of late so increased their estates that now they are nothing like what they were, and yet

England remains always one, without accession of any new force'. For this reason, he recommended 'united strength, by joining the two kingdoms [England and Scotland], having also Ireland knit thereto, is worthy consideration'. In the end, dynastic happenstance after the death of Elizabeth brought the Scottish and English crowns together under James I in 1603. A few years later, he launched the 'Plantation of Ulster', the expropriation of the native Catholic Irish landowners and their replacement by English and Scotch Protestant settlers. James thus secured the kingdom's westward flank once and for all, and ensured that England, Ireland and Scotland would act as one on the European stage.[84]

To the north and east, a similar process of consolidation was taking place. Here the decline of the Teutonic Knights and their territories on the Baltic sparked a partitionist cycle which threatened to engulf the entire area. In 1558, Tsar Ivan IV, 'the Terrible', grabbed Narva in northeastern Livonia. The Russians also seized parts of the northern Polish Commonwealth in the early 1560s. At around the same time, the Swedes annexed the northern half of present-day Estonia. Hemmed in on all sides by the Habsburgs, the rising Swedes, Muscovy and the Ottoman Empire, the weaker powers entered into a series of territorial mergers to stay competitive in an increasingly predatory neighbourhood. In 1561, the Teutonic Knights united with the Grand Duchy of Lithuania, and eight years later they both merged with the Polish Commonwealth in the Union of Lublin. The vast new Polish–Lithuanian conglomerate stretched from the Baltic almost to the Black Sea. It grew bigger still for a while when the King of Poland, Sigismund Vasa, succeeded to the Swedish crown in 1592, uniting the two monarchies. The union briefly provided some hope of holding back the Russians and Ottomans.

Central to the project of state formation and consolidation was the question of minorities, most of them religious. Throughout the sixteenth and early seventeenth centuries, European governments wrestled with the question of how they could be assimilated, or whether they should be suppressed or simply expelled. Again two illustrations will have to suffice. The Spanish experience represented one extreme. The collaboration of the local Muslim (Morisco) minority with the Ottomans drove Philip II to promulgate draconian new legislation in 1567. This required Moriscos to learn Spanish in three years; after that time, it would be a crime to speak, read or write Arabic in public or private. Morisco dress was forbidden as were their distinctive surnames. Philip even banned public baths, which were a front for covert Muslim ablutions. When protesting Moriscos drew attention to their large tax contributions, they were told by the king's representative that Philip 'valued religion more than revenue'.[85] The Moriscos promptly revolted in 1568, causing such extensive military problems for Philip that he had to draft forces from Italy before the rising was finally crushed.[86] He subsequently held all Moriscos, *whether or not they had been implicated in the revolt*, responsible for treason. Some 80,000 were deported inland to other parts of Spain in chains. About 10,000 remained in Granada, while those dispersed in other parts of the country became a constant security headache. In 1609, his successor, Philip III, moved to resolve the question once and for all, by expelling them *en bloc* – all 300,000 – to North Africa. Hundreds of years of Muslim civilization in Al Andalus had come to an end.[87]

In other cases, governments opted for religious toleration, because they genuinely believed in confessional co-existence, because they held that toleration strengthened state coherence in the face of the enemy, or simply because the groups involved were too powerful to be suppressed. Thus Emperor Ferdinand I tended to tolerate Protestants in order to mobilize his territories against the Ottomans.[88] The most systematic attempt at toleration was made by Ferdinand's son, Emperor Maximilian II. In 1571, he issued the *Assekuration*, which confirmed the right of Lutheran nobles in Austria to practise their religion on their own lands. Indeed, the emperor hoped to bury the confessional hatchet not only in Austria, but throughout the Empire. This was, Maximilian believed, his only chance of rallying the German princes against the Turks. In short, external threats led to very different approaches to religious toleration between the two lines of the Habsburg dynasty.

Europeans were divided as to whether autocratic or representative systems were best equipped to compete in the battle for Europe. The Florentine statesman and writer Niccolò Machiavelli made this question the focal point of his two seminal works, *The prince* and especially the *Discourses*. These books were the first systematic attempt to conceptualize the new geopolitics and its implications for the domestic structure of European states. In the preface to Book One of the *Discourses*, Machiavelli described states as communities which had banded together 'to live more conveniently and the more easily to defend themselves'. This, he stressed, they could not do without 'power'. Indeed,

Machiavelli admonished that 'Present-day princes and modern republics which have not their own troops for offence and defence ought to be ashamed of themselves.' The purpose of his ideal republic was thus not the articulation of civic virtue *per se*, but to make the best strategic decisions and mobilize the strength of the state behind them.[89] The key to success here was not simply resource extraction. 'Money,' he warned, 'is not the sinews of war as it is commonly supposed to be.'

Instead, the Florentine argued that the basis for a strong foreign policy was a sound domestic structure. In Book Six of the *Discourses*, Machiavelli spoke of the need to 'give the state a constitution which would put it in a position to enlarge itself if the occasion required it, and to preserve what it had conquered'. Here the crux was participation and debate, more important even than a large and efficiently exploited tax base. 'The masses are more knowing and more constant than is a prince,' Machiavelli wrote. Indeed, he argued that 'it seems as if the populace by some hidden power discerned the evil and the good that was to befall it'. The people would hold the executive to account in the great matters of state. Republics were thus stronger competitors in the international sphere. 'No cities have augmented their revenues or enlarged their territories but whilst they were free and at liberty,' he wrote. At the beginning of the sixteenth century, therefore, Machiavelli set out with unmistakable clarity the domestic and geopolitical issues which were to exercise European powers, be they autocracies or republics, to the present day.

The case of England suggested that Machiavelli was right. After the catastrophic loss of their French empire, Englishmen had concluded that the provision of 'good counsel' through parliament was essential.[90] Taxes would have to be paid on time – in other words the nation as a whole should take responsibility for the reconquest of France – but in return the king would have to listen to the advice of parliament and seasoned advisers. In time, Henry VIII was able to fund extensive campaigns in Scotland, Ireland and especially Europe thanks to close cooperation with parliament, which had to approve all past, current or imminent military expenditure. For more than thirty years the Lords and Commons stumped up largely uncomplainingly; there was no necessary link, therefore, between the pressure of war and the triumph of royal power.[91] This was because parliament was in broad agreement with the king's grand strategy: the vindication of the monarchy's rights in France, or at least the control of the coastline on the other side of the Channel, and the protection of the back door to England via Ireland and Scotland.[92] Likewise, Elizabeth I's position in Europe was greatly strengthened by her ability to work with parliament. Conversely, it was the divisions within Westminster and between parliament and crown which so fatally damaged early Stuart foreign policy.

In general, though, experience seemed to show that greater royal power was a prerequisite for strategic success. In France, for example, victory was attributed to the resurgence of the monarchy.[93] Reformist discourse tended to stress the need for strong central government with tax-raising powers. To be sure, the ejection of the English was a collaborative project in which the estates worked together with the king, but the emphasis was on execution, not consultation; on royal power, rather than baronial counsel. The French parliament, or Estates General, lost the right to assent to the important *taille*, a direct land tax, in 1439 and local estates in central France forfeited that privilege in 1451. They agreed not only to pay for the royal army, but to collect the tax for the king at a rate set by him. The various 'councils' which French kings consulted were a point of contact between monarch and nobility, but not a serious check on his power.[94] Above all, taxes were paid and troops raised without the consent of the Estates General. If parliamentary structures and national strength became increasingly synonymous in England, French political culture established a contrary but equally powerful connection between royal authority and France's place in Europe.

Moreover, the many polities in which representative assemblies remained strong appeared to suffer a resulting lack of internal cohesion and external leverage. Even the mighty Charles V had to cope with a profusion of parliaments: the *Cortes* of Castile, the Estates General of the Netherlands, and various smaller assemblies across the monarchy. The *Cortes* were happy to pay for operations in support of Spanish interests, such as the defence of Navarre, suppressing the Barbary corsairs, and fighting the Turks in the Mediterranean; they were not keen on wars in central Europe, however. A request to pay for an expedition to Hungary was refused in 1527, whereas one to attack Tunis in 1535 was granted. In 1538, rather than vote another payment, they even told Charles to make peace with France.[95] One of the reasons the burden fell so heavily on Castile was that very little money was raised from Aragon, Catalonia and Valencia, whose representative assemblies were distinctly uncooperative. The only other area where the shortfall could be made good was in the rich Low Countries, with their efficient taxation system. Here too, however, the estates were unhappy with royal foreign policy. 'What the Hollanders most complain about,' his Regent, Margaret of Parma, reported to Charles in February 1524, 'is that they always pay under colour of war, but one does not make war on their behalf.' In the 1540s and 1550s, the estates of the Netherlands paid only very grudgingly for the final stages of the wars against France.[96] Similar problems dogged later Habsburg rulers, in both Spain and Austria.

In eastern Europe, the connection between strong representative bodies and external weakness seemed particularly clear. When the Swedish nobility revolted against Sigismund Vasa of Poland–Lithuania–Sweden, the Polish Diet refused to vote him sufficient men to suppress the uprising. By 1599, Sigismund had been deposed by the Swedish parliament and the union with Poland was dissolved. In Russia, the experience of civil war followed by Polish occupation between 1598 and 1610 also made the case for greater autocracy. In 1613, the Romanov dynasty was installed on the throne, ending Russia's fifteen-year 'Time of Troubles' (1598–1613). To the Russian elite, the lessons of the past two decades seemed clear: too much 'liberty' led to chaos and national weakness; the terms 'free' and 'at will' suggested disorder and disturbance. For this reason, Russian society was organized around the principle of service to the state, especially the defence of its external sovereignty. To be sure, many Russians believed that they had a right of participation extending well beyond the 'bread and butter' issues of rudimentary economic security and social justice. Russians lacked, however, formal representative bodies – a States General, Estates General, *Reichstag* or parliament – on western lines. The assembly of Russian nobles (Boyars) – its name, *Duma*, taken from the Russian word for 'to think' or 'to consider' – did not have any control over taxation. Romanov power was thus more or less absolute, constrained only by the vast extent of the land. And so long as the new dynasty was able to deliver national greatness, or at least security, it would be safe.[97]

A similar process was taking place in Brandenburg–Prussia. The estates of Mark Brandenburg, however, did act as a brake on princely activism. They refused to support the elector's ambitions in Cleves, a major problem for John Sigismund, given their right to approve taxation and approve alliances. In his view, the estates had abdicated their responsibility for national defence. Confronted with the challenges of the early seventeenth century, they had effectively stuck their heads in the sand of the Mark. If Prussia was ever to become a major player on the European stage, or even the German one, this problem would have to be addressed. Later in the century, John Sigismund's successor, George William, was painfully conscious of being surrounded on all sides, and quite unable to protect his scattered territories, or even to persuade his estates to contribute to their defence. 'It pains me greatly,' he lamented in July 1626, 'that my lands have been wasted in this way and that I have been so disregarded and mocked. The whole world must take me for a cowardly weakling.'[98]

The greatest indictment of corporate political participation, however, was the Holy Roman Empire itself. It failed to mobilize effectively against either the Turks or the encroaching French. For example, when Emperor Frederick III of Habsburg convened an imperial Diet at Frankfurt in 1454, to launch crusade against the Turk, no action resulted. The frantic Hungarian emissaries were accused by the German princes of 'wanting to involve Germany in their calamities, since they were unable to defend their own kingdom'.[99] When the Turks resumed their advance in the summer of 1480, heading for the Austrian city of Graz, the *Reichstag* remarked sarcastically on the 'long speeches about the Turk' emanating from the emperor.[100] Likewise, Frederick's son and heir, Maximilian, was forced to give up Burgundy to France. One way or the other, the Empire was failing to respond coherently to the threats on its borders.

Unhappy with their treatment at the hands of outside powers, German reformers made repeated attempts to regenerate the Holy Roman Empire by increasing political participation in imperial bodies, especially the Diet, but these failed. In 1489, they assembled at the Diet of Frankfurt under the leadership of Berthold von Henneberg, Archbishop of Mainz.[101] Within a few years, he had established the 'common penny' (*der gemeine Pfennig*), a blended property, income and poll tax, payable to the emperor. In return, he was enjoined to uphold the general peace of the German lands (*der allgemeine Landfriede*) and reform the imperial law courts; Germany must be at peace at home in order to be formidable abroad. The emperor was constrained to accept the advice of an imperial 'council' – responsible to the Diet – on military matters. In other words, just as in mid-fifteenth-century England, the German imperial parliament was staking a claim to participation in matters of grand strategy. The next step was to put Germany's military house in order. At the Diet of Augsburg in 1500, the Empire was divided into ten regional 'circles' to which the task of internal order and mobilization against external enemies was to be devolved. This was not only an embryonic German collective-security system, but also a potential vehicle for national unity against outsiders.[102]

In the early sixteenth century, it looked for a moment as if the imperial council, which opposed Maximilian's military emphasis on Italy, would assert itself. They formed a 'Union of Electors', resolving to meet as a Diet in the absence of the emperor if necessary, and to push through a programme of reform. Germany looked set to find some form of greater national unity under either the emperor or the Diet. In practice, each side sought to block the other, producing stasis and stagnation. The estates proved adroit at clipping the emperor's wings. They were unable or unwilling, however, to create a truly national alternative: the experiment with the council soon petered out. None of the threats facing the Empire from the French, Turks or Hungarians, even taken together, were ever powerful enough to persuade the German estates to surrender their liberties to a powerful executive. On the other hand, by the early sixteenth century Germany had acquired enough of the characteristics of a state to ride out the storms ahead more effectively than it could previously have done.[103]

The Empire still made very heavy weather of the renewed Ottoman surge under Suleiman the Magnificent. The imperial Diet ignored repeated calls for help: from King Louis of Hungary to the Diet of Worms in 1521, and from the Croatian nobles at Nuremberg in 1522. In vain, Ferdinand of Austria called upon Germans to support 'the gallant Christian Croatian nation, which as a bulwark and a strong shield stands before our Inner Austrian lands'.[104] To the assembled princes, cities and clerics the danger seemed remote, and continued 'free-riding' on the Croats and Hungarians was a comfortable default option. A voluminous pamphlet literature agreed that the Turks were not an immediate threat to their liberties, suggesting instead that the Habsburgs were using the Ottoman spectre to pursue a tyrannical domestic agenda. Hungary's collapse at Mohacs did concentrate minds, but only briefly and very ineffectively. Throughout the 1530s and 1540s, the Empire sent several armies to Hungary, with mixed success. In the end, the Diet was never quite worried enough about the Turks, or sufficiently organized to do the job itself. Once again, an opportunity to unite Germany in the face of an existential external threat had been missed.

In the late sixteenth century, the chief imperial military commander, Lazarus von Schwendi, sought to get to grips with German military weakness. He feared that confessional and political differences would ignite a 'blaze of mistrust and division' in the 'poor fatherland', with Protestants and Catholics calling in outside powers to support them. In 1569, Schwendi warned that Spanish interference would lead to 'internal wars' and ultimately to the 'complete partition and destruction of the Reich and the total decline of German well-being'. For this reason, he demanded that Germany should mobilize all its potential to protect the integrity of the Empire. Indeed, if outside powers could be prevented from prostituting Germans through the untrammelled recruitment of mercenaries, Schwendi looked forward to a time when the *Reich* would be able to lay down the law to 'all foreign potentates' and erect a *Pax Germanica* in Europe. Failure to act, he warned, would condemn the Empire to 'pitiful downfall' on Byzantine lines. The proposals he produced at the Diet of Speyer in 1570 included a standing German imperial army, tasked with collective security, to be commanded by the emperor; Schwendi also hoped that the toleration of Protestants would rally German opinion behind a common effort against the Turks. The princes, who now distrusted the emperor more than they feared the Ottomans, shot down this attempt to unify Catholic and Protestant against the common foe. Germany would remain a military dwarf.[105]

The struggle for mastery also drove the expansion of Europe. In the late fifteenth century and the early sixteenth, Ferdinand and Isabella, and the Portuguese monarchs, continued their crusade against the Moors southwards into North Africa, capturing a number of enclaves there,[106] in order to deny the Ottomans a base to attack the southern flank of the peninsula. The same notion now lay behind the early exploratory voyages. From the mid-1480s, Christopher Columbus tried to interest the monarchs of Portugal and Spain in the idea of an Atlantic route to India. To be sure, a thirst for adventure, personal enrichment and glory were never far from his mind or that of other explorers and their sponsors. The ultimate purpose of the venture, however, was to launch an attack on the undefended Ottoman flank, leading to the recapture of Jerusalem, a task which Columbus described in more and more millenarian terms. Seizing new lands beyond the seas would not only open up a new front against the Ottomans; it would also secure the resources necessary for the recovery of the Holy Lands.[107]

Columbus set off in 1492, with charters signed by Ferdinand and Isabella. He took with him an Arabic interpreter (a Jewish convert to Christianity), and promised that 'all the gain of this my enterprise should be spent in the conquest of Jerusalem'.[108] Instead of reaching Asia and finding allies against the Muslims, however, or claiming a share of the riches of the orient, Columbus made landfall in the Caribbean, where a Spanish colony was soon established. The natives were described, logically enough, as 'Indians', an appellation which stuck until the late twentieth century. The initial European discovery of America, in short, was a consequence of the struggle for mastery against Islam, just as its subsequent colonization was driven by rivalries between the western powers. Meanwhile, the Portuguese probed down the west coast of Africa. To prevent the two Iberian powers from falling out in their crusading enterprise, in June 1494 the pope mediated the Treaty of Tordesillas, which divided the New World between them. West of a line beyond the Cape Verde Islands in the Atlantic was to be Spanish; east of the line Portuguese. In 1497–8, the Portuguese explorer Vasco da Gama sailed around the Cape of Good Hope and explored the eastern African coast, finding a more practical route to India.[109] When Colombus set off on his fourth voyage in search of India in 1502, he did so in the expectation of meeting da Gama in a kind of pincer movement. Within a few years, Portuguese raiders were harassing Muslim shipping in the Persian Gulf and the Red Sea, causing considerable economic dislocation. The planned encirclement of the Ottomans had now become tenuous reality.

The creation of the Spanish overseas empire was also driven by European imperatives, primarily the need to deploy the resources and prestige of the New World to tip the balance on the old continent. In 1519, Hernán Cortés conquered Mexico and its silver for the Spanish crown.[110] This made the Habsburg monarchy a kingdom – as the poet Ludovico Ariosto remarked – on which 'the sun never set'.[111] The New World was an increasingly important part of the balance of power, but it was completely subordinate to European considerations. The Spanish colonial empire took up relatively little of Charles V's time. Its principal function was to provide the resources to support his ambitions on the near side of the Atlantic: again and again, it was bullion from the Indies – usually about a quarter of total revenue – which either funded campaigns against the French, Turks and German princes directly, or provided the security against which the emperor could borrow from the great banking house of Fugger in Augsburg. For example, of nearly 2 million escudos' worth of treasure brought from Peru one year, the largest single recipient was Germany, followed by the Low Countries. Charles's travels throughout his reign also show his priorities quite clearly: he visited Italy on seven occasions, France on four, and England and Africa on two, and spent six long stays in Spain itself, but he travelled to Flanders and Germany on no fewer than nineteen occasions; he never visited the Americas. His imperial status stemmed from the *Imperium Romana*, not the global sweep of his lands.[112] In short, the Holy Roman Empire, not the emerging Spanish American Empire, provided the imperial context in which the ambitions of Charles V were played out.[113]

It was European considerations, too, which lay behind Elizabeth's naval offensive against Spain. The colonial balance, or lack of it, was conceived as part of the overall balance of power. 'Whoever commands the sea,' the English sailor and adventurer Sir Walter Raleigh argued, 'commands the trade; whosoever commands the trade of the world commands the riches of the world, and consequently the world itself.' The prestige and fiscal muscle Philip enjoyed as King of New Spain were an important part of his European leverage. Thus Richard Hakluyt, in his celebrated *Discourse of Western Planting* (1584), noted that 'with this great treasure' Charles V had 'got from the French King the Kingdom of Naples, the dukedom of Milan and all his other dominions in Italy, Lombardy, Piedmont and Savoy'. Elizabeth sponsored Drake's voyages between 1577 and 1580, not as the first step towards an overseas empire of her own, but to reduce the flow of bullion paying Philip's armies in Flanders. Likewise, as the Thirty Years War erupted in the Empire, the notion that American gold and silver subsidized not only Spanish endeavours in Europe, but also those of the emperor against German Protestants, was part of English strategic orthodoxy. Sir Benjamin Rudyerd told the House of Commons in 1624 'that Spain itself is but weak in men, and barren of natural commodities'; it was 'his mines in the West Indies' which fuelled 'his vast ambitious desire of universal monarchy'. No better way of helping the embattled Palatines, another argued, than to 'wast the Kinge of Spain's shipping upon his coast, [and] interrupt the retornes of his plate'. The connection made here between overseas empire, the security of England's continental bulwarks and ultimately the safety of the realm was to resonate in English strategic discourse for the next 150 years or so.[114]

The colonization of the New World was also very much an extension of the European conflict.[115] The Puritans who left England in the 1620s, and eventually arrived in Massachusetts, were not turning their back on the Old World, far from it. Despairing of England, and then of the increasingly exposed Dutch Republic, they saw America as a springboard from which they would prepare the defeat of the 'antichrist', that is the Habsburgs in Europe. They prayed for reform in England, for 'the miserable state of the churches in Germany' and the victory of the Protestant cause there; 'the news from Bohemia is very bad,' John Winthrop observed in 1621, some years before setting out for Massachusetts. The colonists followed the news from the continent closely, particularly that from Geneva, Frankfurt, Leiden, Heidelberg and Strassburg, as well as from England itself; they trembled for the Palatinate and rejoiced at the successes of Gustavus Adolphus. Some of them, such as Governor Winthrop's son Stephen, returned across the water to fight on the parliamentarian side in the Civil War, but the practical help they could render was limited.[116] Instead, the Puritans should be, as John Winthrop told them, 'as a shining city on a hill. The eyes of all people are upon us.' What was being celebrated here was not the apartness of the colonists but the opposite: their membership of Christendom, and the obligations deriving therefrom. They would help to redeem Europe as much through their example as by their efforts. American colonists, the parliamentarian cause in England and European Protestants were thus all bound up together in one greater community of fate.[117]

The centrality of Germany was reflected in the fact that the two most important European settlements revolved around the future of the Holy Roman Empire. Charles came to terms with the German Protestants at the Treaty of Augsburg in September 1555. He was forced to unravel the gigantic Habsburg dynastic trust into two separate Spanish and Austrian branches. Charles renounced his territories in reverse order of acquisition, abdicating as King of Spain in favour of Philip in 1555, and in the end laying down his most important title, the imperial crown, shortly afterwards. Two years later, Charles's long-suffering brother Ferdinand was elected Holy Roman Emperor. The Spanish Habsburgs had been uncoupled from the Empire. Not until the time of Napoleon would one man rule over such a wide stretch of Europe again. The Treaty of Augsburg also laid down the principle of *cuius regio, eius religio* – that territories should take the religion of the reigning prince. It sanctioned the 'secularization' of lands taken by Protestant princes from the Church before 1552, and established equality between Lutheranism and Catholicism, though not Calvinism. This was enough to restore peace to Germany, and thus to most of central Europe, at least for the time being.

Likewise, the Treaty of Westphalia (1648), which began to bring the pan-European contest involving France, Spain, Sweden, the Empire and many other powers, to an end, was a German settlement. It was much delayed because none of the antagonists felt able to conclude an 'honest' or honourable peace.[118] Spain tried very hard to maintain the unity of the *Casa de Austria*, and thus strategic cooperation with Vienna; this made them sceptical of a separate German settlement, especially one which left the French gains in the western part of the Empire intact.[119] The emperor hoped to make peace with Sweden and France, to keep them out of German affairs, and to hold on to as much imperial authority in Germany as he could.[120] France sought to eliminate Spanish influence in Germany and thus escape the longstanding 'encirclement', to reduce the power of the emperor by formalizing the right of the princes to conclude foreign alliances and, if possible, to unbolt the Habsburgs from the imperial crown by blocking their succession. In Germany itself, negotiations were long held up by the emperor's refusal to allow the estates of the Empire – whom he regarded as his vassals – to participate in discussions with the French. But if the German princes showed themselves as bitterly divided in the mid-1640s as they had since the turn of the century, they were also united by a consensus to restore the integrity of the Empire in the face of outside interference. For example, the Catholic Elector of Bavaria lamented that the 'spectacle' to which Germany had been reduced 'could have only one outcome, with various kings and potentates agreeing among themselves on the division of the Empire'.[121]

In the end, the deteriorating Habsburg military situation forced the imperialists to give way on key points, especially the right of the German princes to negotiate with foreign powers.[122] The French also compromised, failing to enforce a constitutional ban on the Habsburg succession to the imperial crown. In 1648, the German war finally came to an end with the signing of the treaties of Münster and Osnabrück; the Franco-Spanish conflict, however, continued. This settlement became known jointly as the 'Treaty of Westphalia', and has been seen by generations of international lawyers and international relations theorists as the breakthrough for the modern concepts of sovereignty and non-intervention in the domestic affairs of other states.[123] In fact, the whole purpose of the treaty was to guard against German princes exercising an untrammelled sovereignty which might jeopardize the confessional peace of the Empire and thus the whole European balance. It was also designed to ensure that Germany could not be united under an imperial authority, native or foreign, capable of aspiring to Universal Monarchy over the whole of Christendom. In short, the Empire was supposed to be strong enough to prevent Germans from falling out among themselves, and to keep out foreign powers, but not so powerful as to become a threat to the European order itself.

This tall order was to be achieved through a series of interlocking geopolitical, constitutional, ideological and confessional provisions. In territorial terms, the changes wrought – or ratified – by Westphalia transformed the European state system. Spain finally acknowledged the independence of the United Provinces, only holding on to Flanders and Wallonia (Spanish Netherlands). Sweden gained Western Pomerania – which protected her southern coastline from attack – as well as the bishoprics of Bremen and Verden, together with their three votes in the German Diet. The Palatinate was divided: the Upper Palatinate remained with Catholic Bavaria (which was permitted to retain its new electoral vote), but the critical Lower Palatinate, which lay astride the 'Spanish Road', was restored to the Protestant Charles Ludwig together with its old electoral vote. There were now eight electors in total. In a major concession on the part of the emperor, the treaty expressly permitted German princes, for the first time, to conclude alliances with foreign powers, but only 'provided . . . such alliances be not against the Emperor and the Empire, nor against the public peace of this transaction'.[124] French hopes of uncoupling the Habsburgs from the imperial crown were disappointed. On the other hand, the Austro-Spanish bid for Universal Monarchy, real or imagined, had been contained. The ghost of Charles V was laid to rest.

The treaty regulated the coexistence of the three major confessions, Roman Catholic, Lutheran and Reformed (Calvinist). In the new Holy Roman Empire religious matters – and thus effectively everything of substance – had to be settled by compromise between the Catholic and Protestant representatives at the Diet, rather than by majority vote. Within territories, rulers were bound to respect certain rights, including the right to convert; and if they themselves changed religion, they could not compel their subjects to follow suit. Those religious minorities who had enjoyed toleration in 1624, which was declared to be the benchmark year, were not only guaranteed it for the future, but could not be excluded from certain civic offices.[125] The geopolitical and the ideological clauses of the treaty were closely linked. Both Sweden and France had entered the war in defence of the 'German liberty' they deemed essential to prevent the Habsburgs from over-running the Empire and threatening their own freedom and security. This nexus was summed up by the Swedish negotiator, Johan Adler Salvius, who remarked, 'the Baltic sea will be the ditch, Pomerania and Mecklenburg will serve as counter-scarp, and the other Imperial estates will be, so to speak, the outer works' of Swedish security. The Swedish chancellor explained further that his aim was 'to restore German liberties . . . and in this manner to conserve the equilibrium of all Europe'.[126] Contemporaries thus saw a direct link between domestic liberty, the balance of power and the right to intervene. It was for this reason that both France and Sweden insisted on being recognized as 'guarantors' of the Empire and the liberties of its individual 'estates'. In short, the Westphalian treaties were nothing less than a charter for intervention: by fixing the internal confessional balance *within* German principalities, and by placing the whole German settlement under international guarantee, they provided a lever for interference in the internal affairs of the Empire throughout the late seventeenth and eighteenth centuries.[127]

Germany had been traumatized by the experience of civil war and humiliated by the march and counter-marching of foreign armies – Spanish, Danish, Swedish and French, to name only the most prominent – across her territory.[128] Other countries had suffered, to be sure, but none as badly as central Europe, where the German fate was considered to have been particularly gruesome.[129] The damage had been far from universal, of course, with some regions being devastated and others escaping almost unscathed.[130] All the same, the population of the Holy Roman Empire dropped from 21 to just over 13 million people, a far higher percentage loss than in any conflict before or since. Its central European location had nearly become a collective death sentence, which gained in the telling and retelling. By the end of the 1640s, princes, burghers and peasants alike were confronted by a nightmarish vista of devastated landscapes, razed crops, depopulated villages and poisoned wells. They were profoundly ambivalent, however, about the lessons to be drawn from all this. Everybody was agreed that the Empire should be maintained in order to protect Germany from foreign domination (and from themselves), but there the consensus ended. Should German principalities seek to appease their more powerful neighbours, and avoid conflict, or should they seek the domestic coherence and military muscle necessary to deter them? Were 'German freedoms' more at risk from the Germans themselves, or from the foreign powers which intervened to protect them?

By 1648, the great 200-year struggle for mastery in Europe had resulted in a stalemate. No one power proved capable of dominating the Holy Roman Empire and thus the continent as a whole. Charles V; Francis I; Henry VIII; Suleiman; Philip II and Philip III; and the France of Richelieu and Mazarin all failed; the Dutch and English saw their hopes of a Protestant emperor, or at least of knocking the Habsburgs off their imperial perch, dashed. There were, however, clear winners and losers. After its humiliating ejection from France in the mid fifteenth century, England had returned to European politics with a vengeance under Henry VIII and Elizabeth; after a long retreat under James I and Charles I, she was about to do so again under Cromwell. The French had emerged from a debilitating religious civil war as the principal state on the continent. Spanish power, by contrast, had passed the high water mark in central Europe and the Low Countries. The Austrian Habsburgs had embraced the 'German mission' against the Turks, but they had struggled to parlay this into a decisive position in the Empire. On the European periphery, the Swedes had suddenly burst on the German scene as a major force in the overall balance of power. Meanwhile, the Ottoman advance into central Europe had stalled, to be sure, but its resumption could be expected at any time. The rivalry of the great powers had also extended well beyond Europe itself, starting with Columbus's attempts to outflank Islam, and ending with the raising of new worlds in America and Asia to dominate, or to balance, the old.

All this had driven profound domestic transformations across Europe as states looked to increase their military capacity. In England and the United Provinces, this process stimulated the growth of political participation; it reduced it in France, Spain and many other states. By contrast, the polity at the heart of the European system, the Holy Roman Empire, made sporadic efforts to increase its military standing, but ended by being effectively neutralized, partly because Germans did not trust each other, and partly because neighbouring powers wanted to ensure that the resources of Germany would not be deployed against them. Internal and external factors were impossible to separate here. At Westphalia, therefore, the Empire was given a constitutional structure which sought to reconcile the political aspirations of Germans with the requirements of the international state system. The 'German freedoms' articulated in the *Reichstag* and in the various territorial estates had been preserved. It remained to be seen, however, whether further pressures generated by the European struggle for mastery would now turn Germany into a parliamentary system on Anglo-Dutch lines, or a more monarchical state on the French or Spanish model, or see a resumption of the tendency towards fragmentation, and outside interference, which it had experienced so extensively over the past 200 years.

2

Successions, 1649–1755

The [German] Empire is the main limb, Germany is the centre of Europe . . . Germany is the ball which [the powers] toss to one another . . . Germany is the battlefield on which the struggle for mastery in Europe is fought.

Gottfried Wilhelm Leibniz, 1670[1]

It is to be feared that the emperor's assaults on the authority of the imperial princes threatens to alter the government of the Empire to such an extent that it would become a monarchy, allowing the emperor to elevate himself to the absolute ruler of Germany, which would indeed overturn the balance of power in Europe.

First Commissioner of the French foreign ministry, 1729[2]

The Westphalian settlement brought peace to the centre of the European state system, but not for long. The Holy Roman Empire – and the imperial crown – continued to be the most important area of international contestation. Confessional differences remained important, in the Empire as in Europe more generally, and they repeatedly exploded into conflict.[3] At the heart of all these conflicts, however, was a complex of critical power-political and dynastic successions, most of which fundamentally concerned Germany. Over the next hundred years or so, Europeans fell out over how the vacuum left by Spain in the Empire should be filled, what to do about the succession to the Spanish crown itself, how to divide Sweden's lands in Germany and the Baltic after its rapid decline, and so on. More specifically, they battled over a series of disputed dynastic successions: to various small, but strategically crucial German principalities, to the imperial crown, to the thrones of England, Scotland and Ireland, to the crown of Spain, to that of Poland and finally to the whole Austrian Habsburg conglomerate. Each of these controversies ignited long and bitter wars, principally concerning, and fought on the territory of, the Holy Roman Empire.

After 1648, the German constitution established at the Treaty of Westphalia – the *Reichsverfassung* – became not merely *de facto* but formally the fulcrum of the European balance of power. The estates represented at the imperial Diet were subject to a system of double intervention. In order to prevent the Germans from falling out with each other, and thus either sucking in outside powers or exporting instability, the *Reichstag* had the authority to intervene against princes who violated the provisions of the Westphalian settlement, or who otherwise caused a disturbance likely to upset the peace of Germany and thus Europe as a whole. German princes were thus not formally sovereign, and the domestic room for manoeuvre of all but the very largest estates was heavily circumscribed in practice. Over the next hundred years, therefore, the Empire threatened and often actually carried out 'imperial interventions' – *Reichsexekutionen* – against princes who endangered confessional harmony, exercised 'arbitrary' power, or acted in any other way calculated to cause instability; in some cases, they were suspended or even removed from power.[4] The imperial constitution was also under the protection of the two named 'guarantor' powers, Sweden and France, who were supposed to protect the interests of Protestants and Catholics, respectively, and guarantee both against domination by the Habsburg emperor. In this way, Europe as a whole could rest easy that no one power would dominate the Empire and thus the whole state system.[5]

At the same time, having seen their country serve as a European thoroughfare for thirty years, the Germans themselves were determined to exclude outside interference as much as possible. They agreed that this required a more integrated form of imperial governance through the princes assembled in the imperial Diet. In theory, that was the body where the emperor and his estates exercised the sovereign power of the Empire. The territories represented there now sought to establish an imperial military organization which would keep the peace internally and keep out foreign powers. The design of this system was delegated, along with all the other matters left unresolved at Westphalia, to the next imperial Diet, which met at Regensburg in the mid-1650s. When King of the Romans (emperor-elect) Ferdinand died in 1654, the German electors agreed after some hesitation to elect Leopold of Habsburg as his successor, declining to encourage a candidature by the young Louis XIV, which French diplomats and some minor pro-Bourbon German princes had suggested informally. To be on the safe side, however, a large number of territories combined under the sponsorship of France to form the Rhenish League against imperial domination in 1658, the same year as Leopold I was crowned emperor. Egged on by the French envoys, they also ensured that Leopold's authority continued to be limited by 'capitulations' which he had to agree as a condition of his election.

There was some urgency to maintaining a peaceful balance in Germany, because conflicts continued to rage around her western and north-eastern borders. The Franco-Spanish war dragged on for another ten years after Westphalia, and unsettled the whole area from the Low Countries to the imperial fief of the Franche-Comté (Free County) of Burgundy. It was decided by the intervention of the English Commonwealth, where the Lord Protector, Oliver Cromwell, pausing only to subdue Ireland and the Scots, made his first priority the pursuit of the Protestant crusade in Europe which the parliamentarian side had so long demanded. Contrary to expectations, however, the Dutch refused to sink their colonial and commercial differences with London in the common cause. They even rejected England's offer to drop the Navigation Act of 1651, which stipulated that all commerce with the island should be carried by English ships, in return for an anti-Habsburg alliance, forcing Cromwell to crush them militarily in 1653–4. This triumph was followed by a successful diplomatic and naval humanitarian intervention on behalf of the Vaudois Protestants, who were groaning under the yoke of the Catholic Duke of Savoy. Then Cromwell finally launched his all-out assault on Spain, which he still considered the antichrist and Universal Monarch.[6]

Cromwell's crusade against Spain finally got underway in 1655, with an expedition to the Caribbean which captured Jamaica. The strategic purpose behind this 'western design' was not to carve out a new English empire overseas, but to deprive the Spaniards of the colonial resources to support a European hegemony. As the former West Indian planter

Thomas Gage observed, 'the flourishing condition of and strength of the House of Austria (Rome's chief strength and pillar)' was attributable to the 'American [silver] mines; which being taken away from Austria [meaning the Habsburgs more generally], Rome's triple crown would soon fall away and decay'. The main blow, however, would be struck in Europe itself. To this end, Cromwell concluded an alliance with France in 1657. At his insistence, Mazarin agreed to ease restrictions on the Huguenots. A year later, the joint armies inflicted a decisive defeat on the Spaniards at the battle of the Dunes. Madrid came to terms with London and Paris at the Peace of the Pyrenees in 1659. The treaty stipulated that those mountains, 'which anciently separated the Gauls from the Spains, shall henceforth form the division of those two kingdoms'; England annexed Dunkirk as a continental bridgehead through which it could pursue its interests in Europe. In 1658, Cromwell died and after a short interlude Englishmen, tired of internal strife and foreign war, restored the Stuart monarchy under Charles II.[7] The brief but decisive English eruption into Europe was over, and peace returned to the Low Countries.

To the north and east, the struggle for mastery in Scandinavia and the Baltic threatened to spill over into the Holy Roman Empire. Here Brandenburg–Prussia was in the front line. At Westphalia, the elector secured her northern flank through the acquisition of the lion's share of Pomerania, and rounded off her position in north Germany with the territories of Magdeburg, Halberstadt, Kammin and Minden. He now ruled a principality larger than Saxony, hitherto the premier German Protestant power. But Brandenburg also emerged from the conflict with a deep geopolitical trauma, having been powerless to stop the warring sides from traversing and pillaging the territory at will. Moreover, at Westphalia her main rival, Sweden, had gained a foothold in western Pomerania, on the very doorstep of the principality. Worse still, the Swedes were making good progress in their war against Poland, thus threatening to envelop Brandenburg on two sides.[8] Only in May 1660, when the war came to an end at the Treaty of Oliva, could the Great Elector breathe a sigh of relief. It was clear, however, that a showdown with the Swedes could not be averted in the long term. In his 'Political Testament', the Great Elector later warned that while peace was desirable, preparation and prevention were even better. 'One thing is sure,' he wrote, 'if you stand still and think that the fire is still far from your borders, then your lands will become the stage upon which the tragedy is performed.'[9]

The end of the war in Germany and the continued conflict in Europe had a profound effect on domestic politics across Europe. In the 1630s, Frenchmen had ceased to fight each other largely because their country had gone to war with Spain over control of the Empire. The conflict in Germany, however, sparked off a fresh round of domestic unrest in France. Richelieu's activist foreign policy, which was continued after his death in late 1642 by his successor, Cardinal Mazarin, had long been highly controversial in the French elite. Both men were accused of riding roughshod over traditional privileges in order to prosecute and fund the war; indeed, their hold on power was believed to be synonymous with permanent conflict in Europe. When Mazarin proposed to carry on the war against Spain, and conquer the Low Countries, even though the balance of power in Germany had been secured, the fragile domestic consensus disintegrated. Shortly after the signature of the Westphalian treaties in 1648, the *parlements* and large sections of the nobility erupted in a revolt known as the *Frondes*. They were reacting against both the direction of royal foreign policy, and the centralizing tax policies required to fund the continued military effort against Spain.[10] Mazarin was accused at one and the same time of failing to defend the frontiers of France, of 'continuing the war as a pretext for his tyranny and thefts', of alienating allies, and of losing territories 'which were left to us in treaties which he has broken'.[11] It was not until 1653 that royal forces had the situation completely under control. The French monarchy was forced to recognize that it needed a foreign threat to maintain internal unity, as much as it needed internal unity to contain external dangers.

Further east, the impact of war was having very different and varied effects. In the Commonwealth of Poland, the weakness of the crown in the face of outside pressure rendered it helpless to prevent the institution of the *liberum veto* in 1652, a constitutional convention by which the dissentient vote of a single Polish nobleman could paralyse the national parliament or *Sejm*. Because the nobility were very numerous, some 10 per cent of the population were entitled to vote, a greater proportion than elsewhere in Europe, including England. This could have given a participatory boost to the power of the state, as the Dutch and English assemblies had. In practice, however, Poland was nothing more than a cantankerous congeries of some fifty-odd semi-sovereign states, led by magnates many of whom could raise considerable independent military muscle. And because a single contrary vote sufficed to block a parliamentary resolution, the *Sejm* was effectively paralysed on all issues of substance. The result was incipient anarchy. If the *Sejm* had developed into a forum for the articulation of Polish national interest, and the mobilization of the necessary resources, the huge potential of a populous commonwealth stretching from the Baltic to the Black Sea would have been realized. Alternatively, a strong prince might have broken the constitutional logjam, and imposed some form of absolutism on French or Prussian lines. Either way, the resulting accretion of Polish power would have dwarfed neighbouring powers such as Sweden and Prussia.

Like the Great Elector, the tsars had emerged from the seventeenth-century troubles determined to create a domestic structure which would be both internally stable and capable of defending and expanding the boundaries of the state. In 1649, a new serfdom law code was promulgated creating a socio-economic order tying the peasantry to the land, and the nobility to state service. Under the direction of the visionary statesman Afanasin Ordin-Nashchokin, effectively the first Russian chancellor, a systematic plan for internal development was drawn up, including the simplification and abolition of tolls, and the creation of a merchant marine. The aim was to create a modern 'German'-style bureaucratic state capable of resisting encroachments from without, and serving as the vehicle for Romanov expansionist ambitions. Muscovy's representative institutions played an important role in all this, however. To be sure, the Boyar *Duma* – a council of the most notable families – was appointed by the tsar himself. Its members advised him on domestic and foreign matters, and served in the army, judiciary, diplomatic corps and administration. The *Zemskii Sobor*, or 'Assembly of the Land', on the other hand, was genuinely representative, and not only nobles but also clerics, traders, city-dwellers and even some state peasants were voted into it. The *Zemskii Sobor* played a crucial role in domestic and foreign policy throughout the century, electing a new tsar in 1613, raising taxes and troops for wars against Poland. It debated and approved the 1649 serfdom law, and in the 1650s the *Zemskii Sobor* was twice convened to consider whether the Ukrainian Cossacks should be put under the tsar's protection. As royal power stabilized, however, the

Zemskii Sobor was happy to take more of a back seat. Unlike seventeenth-century England and France, therefore, the Russian monarchy and its representative assemblies were not mutually antagonistic, but engaged in a common project of national self-assertion.

The most fundamental transformation, however, took place in Brandenburg–Prussia. The Great Elector argued that the exceptionally exposed nature of the Prussian polity, wedged between Poles, Swedes and the emperor, required an exceptionally rigorous domestic structure to support its defence. 'Alliances to be sure are good,' he wrote, 'but one's own forces are better still. One can rely on these with more security.' This had profound implications for the elector's relationship with his representative assemblies. On his reading, they had refused to resist the Habsburg drive for Universal Monarchy out of parsimony, parochialism and fear of princely tyranny at home; indeed, they had pointedly declined to fund his plans to take on the Swedes in 1649. Some of these bodies still maintained separate diplomatic representation in neighbouring capitals, and those of Ducal (East) Prussia tended to sympathize with the more relaxed Polish Commonwealth just across the border. None of them, in the elector's view, showed any sense of responsibility: they were, to quote one of his officials, 'indifferent to the defence of [their own] country'.[12] The security of the state required that their independence be eliminated.

In May 1653, the estates assembled in the shadow of the growing Swedish threat and increasing financial demands from the *Reichstag* to pay for the common defence of the Empire. The Great Elector demanded a system of state funding which would enable him to pursue a policy of 'armed defence' to safeguard his 'standing'. Under severe pressure, the estates finally acknowledged the demands of 'necessity' and agreed to surrender their right to approve taxation. They retained extensive feudal rights over the peasantry, and were awarded a privileged role in the army and administration, but their consultative role was severely curtailed. He had thus delivered on an earlier threat to exclude the estates from all 'important matters of life and death' (i.e. foreign policy and war). Two years later, the Great Elector set up the General War Commissariat to mobilize resources more effectively for war. Within two decades, he had increased his army tenfold.[13] Some of the more remote territories in the west, however, continued to defy the power of the prince; Prussian absolutism remained a work in progress.[14] In Sweden, likewise, the pressures of war eventually persuaded the political elite to restore monarchical power, reduce the influence of the *Rijkstag*, and agree a thoroughgoing domestic restructuring designed to increase the fiscal and military resources available for defence and external power projection.

In 1661, Louis XIV of France took over the reins of government on the death of Cardinal Mazarin. He was determined to achieve *gloire*, both personally and on behalf of France, partly as an end in itself and partly to buttress the standing of the monarchy at home; the *Frondes* had not been forgotten. To an extent often not realized by either contemporaries or posterity, Louis's policies were also driven by the quest for security. For the basic strategic situation of the monarchy had not changed: the Habsburgs still encircled France north, east and south. Huge Spanish armies remained in the southern Low Countries, the Franche-Comté and Lombardy, as well as below the Pyrenees. Louis responded to this predicament by trying to push the Spaniards further away from the northern frontier, expand steadily eastwards in Burgundy, Alsace and Lorraine, contest northern Italy, and pursue 'leapfrog' diplomacy with the Protestant German princes in the Empire, Sweden and the Ottoman Empire. He hoped to place a French claimant on the Polish throne and thus envelop the Austrian Habsburgs on both sides, offering to mediate between that country and Russia.[15] The 'historic' claims of the monarchy, not merely to adjoining French-speaking lands, but also to all territories once held by the French crown, were revived.

Above all, Louis had imperial ambitions. His 'Augustan' iconography harked back to Roman times,[16] while his grand strategy focused on the Holy Roman Empire, for ideological as well as strategic reasons. He expressed a strong interest in the German imperial title, even after his unsuccessful informal candidature in the late 1650s, if not on his own behalf then at least on his son and heir's, the Dauphin.[17] Louis was also determined to protect his northern and eastern border from attack by Spanish and allied forces based in the Empire. He therefore vowed in 1664 'to apply [himself] more than ever to German affairs'.[18]

Louis's ambitions required a thoroughgoing programme of domestic transformation to sustain them. In 1666, the energetic Marquis de Louvois became minister of war, and three years later he embarked on a round of military reforms, establishing commissioners of war, appointing quartermasters and standardizing weapons. Under his supervision the French nobility was effectively conscripted into military service, through a subtle blend of blandishment and coercion.[19] The royal army was transformed into a formidable fighting machine, enjoying a complete monopoly of force within the kingdom and a fearsome reputation throughout Europe. The aristocracy never again regained the position it had held as recently as the *Frondes*, and was forced to show obedience to the increasingly authoritarian king. In 1666, a pro-natalist policy was introduced in order to increase the population and thus the monarch's fiscal and military power.[20] Meanwhile Jean-Baptiste Colbert sorted out the royal finances, enforced the payment of taxes, stimulated manufactures and commerce. He also promoted the establishment of a 'New France' overseas, especially in Canada, designed to secure prestige and resources for the European struggle and to deny the same to the enemies of the monarchy. For Colbert economic activity was simply the continuation of conflict by other means. All this did not make Louis's power 'absolute' within France by any means, however. There were still many regional, corporate and other restrictions on his authority; the demographic and fiscal potential of France had not yet been fully harnessed.[21]

Not only was French society strongly shaped by Louis's great-power aspirations, but Louis knew that the European standing of the king was also a crucial factor in underpinning support for the monarchy at home. Even in remote Languedoc, for example, the dynasty's claim to defend France against Protestantism at home and abroad, and to frustrate 'the pernicious designs' of the Habsburgs, was central to its legitimacy. Local elites celebrated the unstoppable rays of the 'sun of France', and looked forward to the 'just punishment for their temerity' of those who dared defy it. 'Whenever the King wins a battle, takes a city or subdues a province,' one of Louis's critics lamented, the French people 'light bonfires, and every petty person feels elevated and associates the king's grandeur with himself; this compensates him for all his losses and consoles him in all his misery'.[22] All this could potentially backfire, of course, because perceived failure on the European stage would severely damage royal power within France.

The scene was now set for a concerted French diplomatic and military onslaught in the Empire. In September 1665, Philip IV of Spain died. Soon after, Louis – who was married to Philip's daughter – lodged claims to Habsburg territory in the Low Countries, based on the Brabantine 'Law of Devolution'. This was a local custom by which daughters enjoyed inheritance rights in private law; it was never intended to be applied to international politics. When these demands were rejected, Louis launched the 'War of Devolution' in May 1667, crushing Spanish forces and annexing some strategically important areas on his northern border. His northern and southern flanks were guarded by England, whose cash-strapped monarch, Charles II, had sold Dunkirk to Louis five years earlier. Moreover, because he was married to Catherine of Braganza, the English king supported the Portuguese bid for independence militarily, thus weakening Spain even further, and drawing off Spanish forces south of the Pyrenees. The Dutch did not intervene, partly because they were distracted by war with England, but mainly because the Grand Pensionary, Johann de Witt, sought to appease Louis rather than confront him. It soon became clear, however, that Louis's move against the Low Countries was only the overture to a much broader push into Germany itself. French security requirements demanded nothing less than what his envoy to Mainz called 'a barrier along the entire course of the Rhine as far as Cologne'.[23] All this was accompanied by expressions of renewed interest in the imperial crown: treaties concluded with allies such as Bavaria and Brandenburg now routinely included clauses committing them to support Louis's candidature at a future vacancy.

For the moment, however, there was not much the Austrian Habsburgs could do about it. From the beginning of the decade, it was clear that the Ottomans were about to resume their long-stalled advance into Hungary. In April 1663, with some covert French encouragement, they declared war on the Austrian Habsburgs. Their campaign ended in disastrous defeat at the battle of St Gotthard. The Austrians were prevented from exploiting their victory, however, by French diplomatic intervention on behalf of the Ottomans. Austria was once again fighting on two fronts, diplomatically and militarily.

The cumulative effect of the Franco-Turkish threat to the integrity of the Empire spurred the growth of constitutional structures in Germany. In February 1662 a new Diet had been summoned to discuss the looming Ottoman offensive. When it met in January of the following year, the emperor insisted that he could no longer bear the burden of the struggle alone. Leopold called upon the delegates to provide 'security for the Empire, our beloved fatherland of the German nation' through 'common discussion and a powerful unity'. Not long after, the Diet scrambled to address the danger from Louis, especially after his invasion of the Spanish Netherlands. It was at this point that the *Reichstag* began to sit continuously at Regensburg, which now became the constitutional capital of the Empire. The city grew into the communications hub of the Empire, in which measures were debated and resolved upon, albeit often not actually implemented; it was second only to London as a platform for the distribution of pamphlets, newspapers and other political media. Over the next two decades, the Diet asserted its right to declare 'imperial war' against external enemies, and began to discuss how best to mobilize the immense resources of the Empire to deal with them. As in England, the pressure of international events had led to an increase in the power of parliament.[24] It remained to be seen, however, whether the Diet would be able to use its new authority to provide for the defence of the German political commonwealth, or whether the divisions between its component parts would continue to block concerted action.

Meanwhile, the rest of Europe watched Louis's advance with growing unease. In 1668, England launched a belated attempt to contain him through a Triple Alliance with the Dutch Republic and Sweden, which was exercising its role as a guarantor power of the Empire. It soon collapsed. Thanks to French subsidies and English troops, Portugal achieved its independence from Madrid that same year, further weakening Spain. By the end of the decade, Charles was firmly in Louis's pocket, concluding the secret Treaty of Dover in June 1670, in which he undertook to support the French king against the Dutch in return for his military assistance in restoring Catholicism and monarchic power in England. Louis now took aim at the United Provinces, whom he regarded as a barrier to his ambitions in the whole of north-west Europe. In April 1670, he annexed the imperial fief of Lorraine, which cut the link between the Free County of Burgundy (Franche-Comté) and the Spanish Netherlands. Spanish power was now buckling all along the line: a Hispano-Dutch alliance in February 1672 underlined the extent to which the European scene had changed. Two months later, Louis struck: French troops punched through the Spanish Netherlands and swept into the United Provinces, scattering the defenders as they advanced. En route to attack the Dutch from the east, they contemptuously barged through Cleves, which belonged to their ally, Prussia. Louis seemed unstoppable.

It soon became clear, however, that the French king had gone too far. With their backs to the wall, the Dutch States General appointed William of Orange, an able commander and robust Francophobe, as *Stadholder*. His principal aim was to defend the 'liberties' of Europe – which he understood in the same way as the 'German liberty' of the princes of the Holy Roman Empire in the face of the overweening claims of the emperor – against Louis's attempts to disrupt the balance of power.[25] The de Witt brothers, architects of the policy of appeasement towards France, were murdered by an Orangist mob. The imminent fall of the Dutch Republic also galvanized the courts of Vienna and Berlin and the Empire more generally. In May 1674, the *Reichstag* declared an 'imperial war' against Louis – for the first time, France itself was condemned as 'an enemy of the Empire' – and by June of that year the Prussians were engaged in open hostilities with France. Louis hit back by supporting the Swedes, putting pressure on the Great Elector's northern flank. He also backed what was to prove to be the four-year Messina revolt against Spanish rule in Sicily, which erupted in 1674. That same year, England joined the attack on Holland. The young John Churchill, later Duke of Marlborough, was among those sent to Germany to support Louis against the imperial forces. In August 1674, the Dutch made a separate peace which guaranteed their independence. A year after that, Louis's Swedish allies were decisively defeated by the Great Elector at Fehrbellin and forced to sue for peace. By the late 1670s, however, the Spanish military position in the Low Countries began to crumble. At the Treaty of Nijmegen, which brought the war to an end in 1678, Madrid was forced to make further territorial concessions to Louis: Saint-Omer, Cambrai and Charleroi to the north, and, especially, Franche-Comté were lost. Louis for his part still felt vulnerable to attack from the Low Countries and particularly from Germany.[26]

All this administered a severe shock to the domestic politics of most western and central European states. A passionate transnational debate on how best to deal with the growth of French power erupted in the 1660s and 1670s. Thousands of pamphlets, sermons and broadsides flew back and forth, not just in England and Holland, where the political public sphere had always been vibrant, but also in the Empire.[27]

There the new genre of the *Mercure*, a monthly or annual review, contributed substantially to increasing the quantity and quality of argument on foreign and imperial policy. Not everybody agreed that Louis had to be stopped. Many English Tories, for example, felt that the Dutch were a greater commercial and ideological threat. In Holland, there were many who agreed with the de Witts that the French should be appeased, out of prudence, if not sympathy. There was also no shortage of German voices, which for one reason or another saw Louis as a useful tool against the local hegemon. By and large, however, Europeans, be they Catholic or Protestant, princes or parliament, concurred that the French king was aiming at a Universal Monarchy on the model of Charles V. For Protestants, there was even the ultimate horror of Louis's popery, and his aspiration to complete the work of the European counter-reformation.[28]

Germany was the key. It was control of the Empire that Louis wanted in order to draw on its resources and prestige. There was now widespread fear in Germany that Louis might make good a claim to the imperial crown, and perhaps even try to assassinate the emperor.[29] To English Whigs the notion that the European balance and English liberties should be defended in the Low Countries and the Empire was as axiomatic as it had been to parliamentarians in the 1620s.[30] Thus Sir Thomas Littleton warned parliament in April 1675 of the mortal danger stemming from the 'enlargement' which Louis 'had made of his empire in Flanders, Germany, the Franche-Comté and elsewhere'.[31] The Whigs now relentlessly battered Charles II's foreign policy, rising to a climax in the parliamentary sessions of 1677–8, and tried to curb the royal prerogative on the strength of his alleged failures.[32]

All this threw the condition of the Empire into sharp relief. The Diet had not intervened in support of the Spanish Netherlands during the War of Devolution.[33] It had also allowed the Duke of Lorraine's appeal for help in 1670 to go unheeded. The attack on the United Provinces, however, immediately jolted Germans out of their complacency. Louis's ravages in the Palatinate in the 1670s, and his treatment of Germany generally, inspired deep loathing and a passionate sense of national victimhood. Popular and pamphlet opinion decried him as 'the Christian Turk', the 'first-born of Satan', an Antichrist pure and simple. More generally, the French were condemned as corrupt and frivolous sexual deviants, slaves to the tyrannical whims of their monarch. German antagonism to Louis was not just based on primitive nationalism or xenophobia. His absolutist pretensions and religious intolerance stood in direct contradiction to traditional notions of *deutsche Freiheit* ('German Liberty'), the defence of the imperial estates in their dual capacity as executives at home and representatives at the *Reichstag*.[34] The wars against France were thus also very much wars of ideology. For many Germans, as much as for the Dutch and the English Whigs, Louis represented a mortal threat to the model of political and confessional co-existence they had so painstakingly developed by trial and error over many centuries. They were defending not just German 'soil' but also German 'liberties'.

The late-seventeenth-century strategic challenges stimulated calls for reform of the *Reichskriegsverfassung*, the imperial military constitution. Few could disagree with Samuel von Pufendorf when in a famous pseudonymous tract of 1667 he called for greater 'inner unity' in the Empire, and condemned the extent to which the Westphalian treaty gave 'strangers [foreign powers] an opportunity to mould Germany to their own particular wills'.[35] More controversial was Pufendorf's suggestion of an imperial council to advise the emperor on foreign policy, reviving an idea from the late fifteenth century. Others suggested that representation at the *Reichstag* should be tied to the number of men supplied for the common defence. The majority, however, were still wary of an imperial standing army. That, Pufendorf warned, would lead to 'military despotism'. For the moment, therefore, Germans willed the ends, but they were not yet ready to will the means.[36]

Increasingly, the battle for Europe was being fought out not only on the continent itself but also in the commercial and colonial spheres. According to the prevailing 'mercantilist' economic doctrine, trade was a zero-sum game. Colbert argued that a state 'could improve its commerce, its merchant marine, or its manufactures, only by taking away something from the trade, the shipping or the industry of another country'. Latecomers sought to 'emulate' their more successful competitors.[37] Capturing as many overseas colonies and as large a slice of world commerce as possible, or denying them to one's enemies, thus became a central part of grand strategy. This was never an end in its own right, but always a means to a larger purpose in Europe itself. In Madrid, for example, the loss of authority in central and north-western Europe after the Thirty Years War led to a greater effort overseas in order to secure the resources necessary to restore the Spanish position in the Low Countries and the Empire.[38]

Louis's advances had greatly improved French border security. His chief engineer, Sébastien de Vauban, had extensively fortified the new northern and eastern frontier after the Peace of Nijmegen. Yet the French king was determined not only to make himself invulnerable to attack but also to follow Richelieu by establishing 'portals' into neighbouring states to keep them in line. He already held the key north Italian fortress of Pinerolo, and in 1681 he annexed nearby Casale, effectively encircling Savoy. But Louis's main worry was the Empire. Due to the weakness of Spain, there was now little threat from Flanders, while the England of Charles II and his successor from 1685, James II, was friendly and domestically unstable. The chief threat came from the Austrians to the east, supported by the Dutch and, perhaps, the Prussians. It had been the German powers, Austria and Prussia, whose intervention had saved the United Provinces in the 1670s. So from 1680 Louis set up the Chambers of Reunion, courts designed to develop spurious historical title deeds which would allow him to 'reunify' – in other words annex – German territories on his eastern border. In October 1681, French troops occupied Strassburg on the Rhine. Louis, however, wanted more, because each advance simply created a new vulnerability to his north and east. The Chambers of Reunion escalated their work. Seeing the writing on the wall, Spain launched an unsuccessful pre-emptive strike in December 1683, but Louis ploughed on. By the middle of the following year, he had taken Luxemburg. All this put France on a collision course with the Empire. 'The Germans,' Louvois announced in June 1684, 'must from now on be considered our real enemies.'[39]

Louis was able to act in the west with relative impunity, because the Austrians were once again distracted by French 'leapfrog' diplomacy. In early 1683, the Turks resumed their drive north, with a substantial contingent of Christian Hungarian exiles in tow. By July they were at the gates of Vienna. Leopold fled his capital, to the derision of its inhabitants. He was saved by the papacy, for whom the war was essentially a clash of civilizations. Pope Innocent XI did not have many battalions of his own, but he was able to pledge the substantial diplomatic and financial resources of the Church in support of a crusade. The pope even engaged in a spot of leapfrog diplomacy of his own, sending an envoy to the Shah of Persia in 1683 with a view to attacking the Ottomans from the rear. This scheme, and another plan to persuade the Christian Abyssinians to distract the Sultan with an assault on Egypt, did not come off; the legend of Prester John died hard, evidently. More usefully, the pope negotiated a Russo-Polish understanding, allowing both powers to concentrate against the Ottomans. The Polish King, Jan Sobieski, needed little persuading to strike south, as the Ottomans were a huge threat to the Commonwealth's Black Sea provinces. Innocent also arranged and funded an Austro-Polish understanding. On 11 September 1683, Sobieski reached Vienna, united with imperial forces, and routed the Ottomans. Never again would the *Türkenglocke* sound across Germany. By the end of the seventeenth century it was clear that the call to Christian unity against the infidel, which had rallied Europeans since the crusades, and Germans to the emperor, had lost its force. In that sense, the Turks had been a kind of solution.

At this point, the 'easterners' won the upper hand in Vienna, and prevailed upon the emperor to press home his advantage against the Ottomans. In August 1684, Leopold signed a truce with Louis in order to have a free hand in Hungary and the Balkans. The pope, eager to avoid a divisive war between Christians in Germany, encouraged the emperor, and provided much of the finance for the 'rollback' campaigns of the 1680s and 1690s. The Hungarian and Croatian nobility now accepted an automatic right of accession to the throne for the Habsburgs. The subsequent campaigns to drive the Ottomans out of Hungary for good became a German national crusade. In 1685, the Hanoverians, the Bavarians, the Rhenish Circle, the Swabian Circle and Cologne sent nearly 30,000 men in total. These were the most impressive collective German military exertions ever seen. There were periodic Turkish revivals, but over the next decade and a half the general picture was one of progressive collapse. The Muslims of Slavonia were brutally expelled. Buda was taken, then Transylvania. At one point, Austrian troops penetrated as far south as Belgrade. Leopold even sent emissaries to the tsar in 1684 asking him to join the rampage. The Russians duly joined the Holy League against the Turk, and in 1687 moved into the Crimea. It would not be long before the Austrians would come to rue Leopold's injunction.

Meanwhile, the Empire lay open to further French encroachments. Matters came to a head, as they had so often in the past, over the Palatinate and the Rhine Valley. In 1685, Louis laid claim to part of the

Palatinate through his sister-in-law, Elizabeth Charlotte, whose brother, Charles, had died leaving a contested succession. To most members of the Empire, this demand represented a deadly challenge to their security. Leopold was finally forced to take cognisance of what was happening in the west, accepting the risk of a two-front war. In August 1685, moreover, the Great Elector of Brandenburg concluded an anti-French alliance with the Dutch.[40] The Prussians had learned a bitter lesson in the east. They could defeat the Swedes in battle, only to see them resurrected at the negotiating table by their powerful French sponsor. If Prussia was going to secure anterior Pomerania, it was going to have to become a major player on the European scene, or at least participate in the containment of France. Nobody had contributed more than Louis to the interconnection of the various parts of the European system, and nobody was to suffer more from it in the long run. So, in July 1686, Sweden, Spain, the Dutch Republic, the emperor, Brandenburg–Prussia and many other German princes united to form the League of Augsburg – later known as the 'Grand Alliance' – in order to confront France.

Louis tried to pre-empt the return of Austrian troops from Hungary by pushing further into the Empire. 'The news which the King has just received of the defeat of the Turkish army,' Louvois told Vauban, 'has made him judge it necessary to bring his frontier towards Germany to the last stage of perfection.'[41] In June 1688, the Elector of Cologne – an old French ally – died and Louis moved to impose a friendly successor over German protests. In late September 1688, he sent troops into the Palatinate, devastating that area once again and with it his reputation in Germany and Europe more generally. 'The pain of having to destroy cities as considerable as Worms and Speyer,' his veteran commander, the Duke of Duras, lamented, 'leads me to put before his Majesty the bad effect that such a desolation would have on his reputation and his *gloire* in the world.'[42] That same month Brandenburg–Prussia, Brunswick, Hesse and Württemberg all pledged specific numbers of troops in support of William of Orange. Not long after, the Empire declared war on the French king. In May of the following year, the Dutch agreed with Leopold to push the French back to their borders at the end of the Thirty Years War. They promised to help the emperor with the Spanish Succession, and to ensure that his son, Joseph, succeeded to the imperial crown. He was duly elected King of the Romans in January 1690 with a mandate to mobilize Germany to contain the French. In July 1690,

Spain entered the war against Louis, joined in October by Savoy. A new struggle for control of Germany and Europe had begun.

Louis's apparently limitless ambition set off another spate of internal transformations. In the Dutch Republic, William had had a hard time persuading the estates of the French threat even as late as the early 1680s. When Louis was crushing the Spanish garrisons in the Low Countries, for example, the assemblies of Groningen and Friesland, which were furthest away from the danger, recalled their troops, completely subverting the *Stadholder*'s attempts to mobilize a military deterrent. By the end of the decade, however, even the most sceptical oligarch could see that Louis would have to be resisted. In the United Provinces, therefore, the strategic situation resolved the longstanding deadlock between prince and estates in favour of the *Stadholder*. In England, it was the other way around. The anti-monarchical critique of English foreign policy building since the 1660s reached new heights with the fall of further bastions in Germany, especially Strassburg, which Whig pamphleteers described as a 'rampart' of German Protestantism, and thus of English liberty. Even some Tory pamphleteers lamented the loss of 'the Keys into Germany', though they tended to be more anti-Dutch than anti-French and preferred naval and colonial operations to costly continental land wars.[43]

Englishmen disagreed not just over the direction of policy, but also about the best form of domestic organization to defend the national interest. Many Tories wanted to resist Louis, but felt that it was necessary to support the monarch in order to give him the strength to do so. Charles II worked this theme for all it was worth. For example, at the opening of what was expected to be a particularly turbulent parliament in October 1680, he warned that 'our divisions at home [might] render our friendship less considerable abroad'.[44] Whig critics, on the other hand, increasingly took up the Puritan positions of the pre-Civil War period. They sought, in the words of one observer, 'not merely to compel the King to break the present alliance with France, but to bind him for the future to acquaint them with his intentions about the war, although hitherto such matters have always depended on his majesty's will, a prerogative of the crown'. When James II succeeded in 1685, his open Catholicism fuelled allegations of subservience to Louis; the suspension of parliament in November 1685 merely drove the critique 'out of doors', beyond Westminster. The king and his critics were agreed that the most pressing task was to re-establish England's European position, but whereas James believed that this was best achieved through a more monarchical and bureaucratic form of governance, directed primarily against the United Provinces, the Whigs championed parliamentary government against French Universal Monarchy. By the late 1680s matters had reached crisis point. In June 1688 a Catholic male heir was born to James, who would ultimately inherit over Mary and Anne, the two Protestant daughters from his first marriage.

A more immediate danger, however, was posed by Louis's move into the Palatinate. It was this impending coup which propelled William of Orange to invade England in November 1688. Only the restoration of constitutional government in England, the Dutchman believed, would enable the country to participate in the defence of European liberties against Louis. The new king saw himself as the leader of God's international forces on earth, and his English supporters such as Bishop Burnet called upon their countrymen not to skulk in their island but to act as a Protestant 'Israel', 'a light to the gentiles' in defence of liberty and true religion.[45] Likewise, it was the deteriorating European situation, rather than the still far-off prospect of James being succeeded by a Catholic male heir, which convinced the Whig grandees that they had no choice but to invite William as their 'deliverer'; when James fled, they made him their king as well. Louis failed to head the *Stadholder* off, because he was convinced until the last moment that William was bound for Germany. The English 'Glorious Revolution' of 1688, in other words, was a product of the state system, undertaken in order to restore England's weight in the councils of Europe.

The Nine Years War, which raged between Louis and much of central and western Europe from 1688 to 1697, was essentially a European war, fought principally in Flanders, the Rhineland–Palatinate and northern Italy. It was into these cockpits that the English, Dutch and imperialists poured the bulk of their resources. The Low Countries, in particular, were hotly contested, with the largest proportion even of the Spanish effort being invested there.[46] But the war also encompassed a series of regional conflicts, such as the War of the English Succession, which raged in Scotland and Ireland from 1689 to 1691, and, of course, the Turkish War. All these fronts were interconnected. Louis backed James II against his parliament. William pursued him to Ireland, inflicting defeats on James at the Boyne and Aughrim. William apologized to a German ally that he 'was obliged to go to Ireland' where he would be 'cut off from the civilized world', but once he crushed the Jacobites, he would soon be able 'to take action against the common enemy with all the more vigour' in the Low Countries and the Empire.[47] Louis also incited the Turks to draw off some of the heat in the west. By contrast Dutch and English diplomacy tried to keep them quiescent in order to free Leopold for greater efforts in the Empire. In 1692, George Ludwig of Hanover was elevated to the rank of elector as down payment for his future military services against the French and the Turks, proof once again of the close connection between the internal structure of the Empire and the broader European situation.

All this further stimulated the growth of a European public sphere. This was most vibrant in those places where the political nation had to be persuaded to vote men and money for military operations: England, the Dutch Republic and the North American colonial assemblies. It was at this point that an independent newspaper press emerged in London, to cater for the public's insatiable demand for news about the continent. But even in the Empire, where the connection between popular opinion and political or military action was less direct, literate people were determined to inform themselves about the events shaping their lives. 'They hurry to the post-houses and newspaper vendors,' the German writer Kaspar Spieler remarked satirically in 1695, 'and they are impatient to find out what the French King, the emperor, the pope or the Sultan in Constantinople is doing . . . and all this is really of so little relevance to them as knowing whether the moon is peopled by mere mortals or by Gods.'[48]

The great European struggle also drove a new round of extraction, mobilization and bureaucratic consolidation within many states. Far ahead of the pack were the two 'maritime powers', England and the United Provinces. Holland had shown the way in the late sixteenth century, when its superior fiscal-military organization allowed it to prevail against the much larger resources of Philip II. In the 1690s the English, partly drawing on imported Dutch ideas, established the strongest and most 'modern' state in Europe.[49] A funded national debt was created, supported by the new Bank of England (1694) and a sophisticated stock and money market.[50] An East India Company was established as a semi-state body.[51] Underpinning it all was a broad political consensus in favour of parliamentary government, and resisting tyranny at home and abroad. The Triennial Act of 1694 stipulated that parliamentary elections were to take place every three years, and the abandonment of censorship allowed political and commercial matters to be discussed freely inside and outside parliament. English politics throughout the 1690s were dominated by how best to wage the war, with the Whigs supporting William in his call for direct military intervention on the continent, while the Tories preferred a more indirect maritime and colonial strategy. There was little disagreement, however, about the fact that Louis had to be stopped, or that a free people required a strong, and thus expensive, state to protect them.[52] 'Do what is necessary to carry on the war,' the Commons proclaimed in the 1690s, 'but do nothing which may destroy the constitution.'[53] As a result, William III and his parliaments were able to raise the staggering sums needed to fight Louis, and managed to fund a huge proportion of the war, at least a third, out of long-term loans rather than income. Englishmen thus lived not only in the freest European state, but also the strongest in relation to its size and population.

Most European polities, however, took the absolutist path to increased effectiveness. Charles XI of Sweden pursued a policy of '*Reduktion*' – 'reclaiming' crown lands lost to the nobility – thus massively increasing the financial power of the monarchy. He also established the *Indelnighsverk*, a military-fiscal system of land-holding, which linked property-holding to taxation and army service; this took decades to implement, but by the end of the century it provided Sweden with a military weight out of all proportion to her population and wealth.[54] In the Habsburg monarchy, Emperor Leopold tried hard to reform the state apparatus, partly because the wars with France and the Turks required it, and partly because the capture of new lands in Hungary gave him an opportunity. In a striking contrast with England, Leopold's creditors refused all further loans in 1680 unless he promised to deal with his corrupt financial administration. Instead of working with his various estates, the emperor sought to push through a new financial system unilaterally from 1681. Eight years later, Leopold's commissioners recommended for Hungary the creation of a standing army, the raising of regular taxes and the dispatch of colonists to develop the land. Likewise, the middling and smaller German principalities engaged in active state building to increase their external power, in spite or perhaps because of their size.[55] Internal reform was by no means straightforward, however. There was often a big gap between aspiration and reality; many Europeans – even in Germany – continued to elude state attempts to register, regiment, improve, tax and recruit them.[56] Leopold was unsuccessful in his attempt to abolish the Hungarian nobility's *ius resistandi*, their traditional right since the Middle Ages to defy royal authority if they were denied justice, or felt they had been. He also had to concede Hungary the right to run its own separate and inefficient treasury. Likewise, Charles XI's policies drove the nobility in Finland and the Baltic into open revolt. The latter, under their dynamic leader Count Johan Patkul, established close links to outside powers such as Poland and invited them to partition Sweden in return for the restoration of their traditional liberties.

English North America became a particular site of contention between centralizers and representative assemblies. The royal governors and their Tory colonist sympathizers tended to see the French threat in largely secular terms and thought that they should try to 'out-absolute' Louis. They compared the military efficiency of French Canada, where most of a far smaller male population served in the militia, with the complete chaos in the much larger Dominion of New England. As matters stood, the English were in the words of one observer 'divided into so many petty, and separate governments, who minded themselves so much, letting the public interest sink'. Only a centralized colonial government, they argued, could mobilize all the local resources, strengthen the arm of the metropolis in Europe, and repel Franco-Indian attacks. Many of the Whig settlers, on the other hand, were religiously and politically radical. To them, Louis was an 'anti-christ' who enslaved the churches in Germany, he was the 'Tyrannous and treacherous Grand Seigneur of France [who] had fettered Europe'. As Cotton Mather, a New England minister and pamphleteer, warned in a sermon in 1686, 'The cup is going around the world. Tis come into America.' Far from supporting gubernatorial plans to make New England militarily better prepared, however, they condemned them as a covert assault on their freedoms. The colonists rejected all centralizing reform projects, especially conscription, and advanced the model of a loose federation of Protestant colonies instead.[57]

After nearly a decade of fighting, manoeuvring and mobilization, neither France nor the Grand Alliance was able to prevail. Louis scored some spectacular early successes in Italy, in Germany and at sea. By

1691, however, James had been decisively defeated in Ireland. The full force of England was now deployed against France in the Empire, the Atlantic and the Mediterranean. Yet William of Orange never succeeded in landing a decisive blow. The Austrians struggled to maintain themselves on two fronts. In 1690 the Turks recaptured Belgrade, and although the Habsburg advance resumed not longer after with substantial support from the Empire, the German effort in the Balkans was a distraction from the battle against France. Both sides became bogged down. The French invaded Catalonia in 1694, taking Barcelona three years later. Louis's resources, however, were now stretched to breaking point. Victor Amadeus of Savoy, always a reliable weathervane, if not a dependable ally, switched sides to Louis in 1696. The English and Dutch also began to run out of money. Both sides now looked for ways to end the conflict.

In September 1697, the Treaty of Ryswick finally brought the war to an end. Much to the disgust of German public opinion and many German princes, Louis managed to hold on to Strassburg. 'It is impossible,' the Margrave of Baden complained, 'that the liberty of Germany can be maintained if the city of Strassburg with all its fortifications . . . is not returned to the Empire.'[58] In most other respects, however, the French king was boxed in. From now on, the path into the strategically vital Low Countries was blocked by a 'barrier' of Dutch-garrisoned fortresses in the Spanish Netherlands, backed-up by an Anglo-Scottish guarantee. In Germany proper, the fulcrum of the whole European system, the Austrian Habsburgs continued to dominate, supported by the larger principalities and the resources of the Holy Roman Empire. George Ludwig of Hanover was awarded the title of elector in recognition of his services against the French and the Turks. As far as England was concerned, Ludwig promised to recognize William and Mary as King and Queen of England. Overseas, the treaty gave France Saint-Domingue in the Caribbean and confirmed her control of New France (Canada) including Acadia, but otherwise it said very little about the wider world, reflecting the general preoccupation with the European balance. Ryswick thus formalized the emergence of a new geopolitical system in Europe over the past thirty years, in which the Habsburg threat had completely receded, and the alleged pretensions of Louis XIV towards Universal Monarchy had moved centre stage.

A new order was also taking shape in northern and eastern Europe. In June 1696, Jan Sobieski died, bringing to an end a period of Polish revival. Much would ride on the choice of his successor. That same year, Tsar Peter I set off – notionally incognito – on a quest to observe the advanced states of western Europe at first hand, the better to modernize Russia on his return. The Tsarist Empire had only recently sloughed off its traditional isolation, with diplomatic representation in Austria, Denmark and the Dutch Republic; embassies to Britain and Prussia soon followed. A month later, Charles XI of Sweden died and was succeeded by the teenager Charles XII. Meanwhile the Austrians brought their war against the Turks to a triumphant conclusion at the Treaty of Karlowitz in 1699. The Ottomans were forced to cede most of what they still held of Hungary, Slavonia, Transylvania and parts of Croatia to the Austrians; Podolia, Kamenice and parts of the Ukraine were surrendered to Poland; and Azov to the Russians.

Both systems were thrown into deep crisis almost simultaneously by two dynastic wild cards that moved to the top of the deck at the dawn of the new century. The great powers were preoccupied by the question of who would succeed the slow-witted and childless Charles II of Spain. The prospect that he might be succeeded by the most plausible claimant – Philip of Anjou, Louis XIV's grandson – conjured up the horrific spectre of a huge Bourbon conglomerate comprising France itself, Spain, Sicily and Naples, the Spanish overseas empire and, of course, the Spanish Netherlands. This would be an empire more terrible still than that of Charles V. The next most serious candidate, Charles of Austria, would be only marginally less threatening, reuniting as he would the two Habsburg main lines. The only solution was partition, but in 1699–1700 various compromise schemes collapsed for one reason or another. No agreement had been reached before Charles II himself finally died in November 1700. His will made clear that the lands of the Spanish crown were to pass whole and undivided to the Dauphin's second son, Philip of Anjou, or, if he refused, to Charles of Austria.

This put Louis and the Austrian Habsburgs under unbearable pressure. In effect, the winner would take all. In February 1701, Anjou entered Madrid accompanied by French troops and advisers and took possession of his crown; Louis then pointedly refused to exclude him from the succession in France. 'There are no more Pyrenees,' he remarked in triumph. That same month, Louis moved into the Spanish

Netherlands, and expelled the Dutch garrisons of the 'barrier' fortresses. At stake was not so much the Spanish colonial possessions, or even Spain itself, but the vital strategic crossroads of the Low Countries and northern Italy. If held by a hostile power, particularly with a Habsburg prince south of the Pyrenees, they would re-encircle France. But if Louis controlled these territories, then neither England, the Dutch, nor the Austrian Habsburgs would be safe. With French troops firmly ensconced in the Spanish Netherlands, both the Dutch and the English political nations needed no further persuasion that Louis had to be resisted. In early September 1701, England, the United Provinces and the emperor formed a new 'Grand Alliance' to contain Louis. When James II died in exile shortly afterwards, Louis retaliated by recognizing his son – 'James III' – as King of England. A formal declaration of hostilities followed in May 1702.

The War of the Spanish Succession, as this epic new conflict came to be known, was really about control of the Low Countries, Germany and northern Italy. In Vienna, the 'war party' led by the emperor Leopold's eldest son, Joseph, was determined to purge the Holy Roman Empire of French influence. There was also a strong desire to keep the French out of Milan – which Leopold considered an 'incontestable part' of the Holy Roman Empire, and which might serve as the base for Louis to attack Austria itself. Finally, the Habsburgs wanted to maintain their claim to the Spanish crown.[59] The war against Louis in the west thus became something of a patriotic crusade of German princes led by the Austrians. In late 1700, the Prussians extracted a promise from Vienna to recognize Elector Frederick of Brandenburg as 'King in Prussia' in return for his support against France; he was duly crowned a year later.[60] The Empire declared war on France in October 1702, and the western imperial circles sent a substantial force under the renowned general Ludwig Wilhelm von Baden. Most of the other German princes, such as the Duke of Baden and the Elector of Hanover, also lined up against Louis. The big exceptions were Elector Joseph Clemens of Cologne and his brother Max Emanuel, Elector of Bavaria.

The main battle front was the Holy Roman Empire, to which all other theatres – Italy, Spain and overseas – were subordinate. Royal Navy warships attacked French convoys in order – as the Admiralty instructions stated – 'to depriv[e] them of the supply of money and plate which they seem to rely on for the support of the war'. In 1703, the raid on Spanish Havana was justified by the need to 'prejudice the family of Bourbon and advance the interests of the House of Austria'.[61] In 1704, Louis sought to deliver a knockout blow in Germany, by sending his main force, with a large Bavarian contingent, to attack Vienna. 'The poor Empire,' the English envoy to Berlin warned, now looked 'ripe for destruction'.[62] In August of that year, however, the Franco-Bavarian force was crushed at Blenheim in south Germany by a combined Anglo-Dutch-imperial army under the command of the Duke of Marlborough.[63] That same year, an English fleet captured Gibraltar, in effect sealing off the Mediterranean. When the emperor, Leopold, died in 1705, he was succeeded by Joseph, an ardent protagonist of the 'German' cause in the Empire, north and south of the Alps. By 1706, the Austro-Savoyard armies had expelled the French from northern Italy. Charles continued to hold his own in Spain, helped by risings against Philip in Catalonia and elsewhere. Most importantly of all, the Anglo-Dutch-imperial forces continued to pummel Louis in Germany and Flanders. In 1706, the French king was decisively beaten again at Ramillies, and his two most important German allies, the electors of Bavaria and Cologne, were placed under imperial banishment. Louis's hopes to dominate the Holy Roman Empire had never seemed more remote.

While the Spanish succession was disputed in central, western and southern Europe, northern and eastern Europe was roiled by the succession in Poland and Sweden. Neighbouring states feared their potential strength as much as they found their weakness provocative. The internal divisions of Poland invited outside interference and partitionist projects. Yet, as Jan Sobieski's reign had shown, Poland's potential was considerable: it had actually ended the seventeenth century with a substantial territorial increase at Ottoman expense. If the Commonwealth managed to reform itself, Prussia and Russia would face a much less pliable neighbour; even in its current chaotic state, it could not be allowed to fall into hostile hands. For this reason, Peter threatened the Polish nobility with war in 1697 were they to vote for the French candidate to the throne, Prince Conti. In the end, Augustus, the Elector of Saxony, was elected, partly because he paid the biggest bribes but also because he was believed to be most capable of recapturing the strategically important fortress of Kamenetz-Podolsk from the Ottomans, which he did shortly afterwards. Now the joint Russo-Prussian strategy was, as Frederick I of Prussia put it, to prevent the Saxons from establishing 'an arbitrary power over the Republic'. For Berlin, in particular, the Polish–Saxon union evoked the spectre of encirclement, wedged as Prussia was between the two territories. Polish 'liberties', in other words, would henceforth be central to Russian and Prussian security.[64]

It was the Swedish wild card, however, which really plunged the region into turmoil. Here the young and inexperienced Charles XII was believed to be easy meat for his neighbours. The Danes aimed to rebuild their western Baltic empire at his expense, the Russians sought the return of Novgorod, while the newly crowned King of Poland sought to expand into the Baltic province of Livonia. In September 1699, the Danes and Poles concluded a treaty directed against Sweden, joined two months later by Russia. The architect of this alliance was the renegade Livonian nobleman Count Johan Patkul, who sought to rid himself and his fellow countrymen of domination by the Swedish crown. In August of the following year, all three powers fell upon Charles. Much to their surprise, the new king turned out to be a military genius. In November 1700, he personally led his army to victory over the Russians at Narva. It was a bitter blow to Peter's great-power ambitions. Twelve months later the humiliation was still keenly felt by his ambassador at Vienna, who reported that the Austrians 'only laugh at us ... Our monarch needs without fail even a small victory, by which his name would win renown all over Europe.' For the next four years, though, Charles ran riot across Poland and the Baltic, inflicting a series of further defeats on his tormentors.[65]

At first, the War of the Spanish Succession and the Great Northern War, as it came to be called, ran their separate courses. By 1706, however, this seemed about to change. Charles's early victories had sparked a lively strategic debate on the Swedish side. Some, such as the royal adviser Nils Lillieroth, argued that the main enemy was Russia, and the first priority should be to secure the monarchy's first line of defence in the Baltic provinces. Failure to do so would allow Peter to threaten the Swedish province of Finland, the islands and eventually Sweden proper. Preventive action was therefore necessary, perhaps even the occupation of Russian lands around Pskow to increase the buffer zone. Charles, on the other hand, saw Poland–Saxony as the main enemy. He sought to place his own candidate, Stanislas Leszczynski on the throne there. In order to do that, however, he needed to deliver a decisive blow against Augustus. There was therefore no alternative to a direct attack on the

Saxon Electorate itself, which Charles launched in September 1706, using Sweden's Westphalian rights to intervene on behalf of Silesian Protestants as a pretext to traverse imperial territory. The primacy of Germany, which had characterized Swedish policy in Gustavus Adolphus's times, was thus reasserted.

When Charles hove into view in central Europe in the autumn of 1706, there was consternation in the Grand Alliance. 'I hope it is not true that the King of Sweden is marching towards Hungary,' Marlborough wrote to the Dutch chief minister in August 1706. 'If this is so, we shall be very embarrassed.' Charles, so the argument ran, would destabilize the Holy Roman Empire, and thus reduce its ability to prosecute the war against France. All those north German princes with troops in the west, such as Prussia and Hanover, now began to watch their backs nervously. Charles soon battered the Saxons into submission: at the Treaty of Altranstädt, concluded in October 1706 in the heart of his Electorate, Augustus made a complete capitulation, and forswore the Polish crown. The fear now, Marlborough warned, was that the Swedish king might 'find a pretext to advance further into Germany', bringing him 'further into the Empire, which is the only thing we apprehend and would avoid'. To this end, Marlborough met with Charles at Altranstädt in 1707, and persuaded him to turn east against the Russians; the emperor gave way on the Silesian Protestants. A collective sigh of relief was heard across Germany and the capitals of the coalition.[66]

The Great Northern War and the War of the Spanish Succession were not just some formalistic military-diplomatic minuet, but a desperate wrestling match. The outcome of these wars was a matter of life and death not merely for the men who actually fought the battles and civilians caught in the crossfire. Across Europe, governments, rebels and publics were locked in an existential struggle. France feared being caught in a renewed Habsburg vice-grip north, south, east and south-east. Louis, who remembered the 1650s well, was also determined not to see his kingdom thrown back to the times of the *Frondes*, or worse still to the turbulence of the late-sixteenth-century religious wars. German patriots fought to recover Alsace, or at least to prevent the further alienation of imperial territory in the west. Middling and smaller states like Savoy battled partly to move into the first rank of powers, but also to escape complete relegation. To the Dutch and English the question of the Spanish succession was central to the European equilibrium on which their freedoms, property and lives depended. Not only would control of the undivided Spanish inheritance make Louis the unchallenged hegemon in Europe, but his presence in the Spanish Netherlands constituted a direct threat to the safety of both England and the Dutch Republic. The English political philosopher John Locke summed up this ideological–geopolitical nexus in June 1701 as follows: 'how fond soever I am of peace I think truth [by which he meant Protestantism and parliamentary government] ought to accompany it, which cannot be preserved without Liberty. Nor that without the Balance of Europe be kept up.'[67]

In order to remain competitive in this perilous environment, European states sought greater domestic coherence through administrative, military and even constitutional reforms. The Habsburgs, for example, wanted to simplify the traditional system of separate administrations for the Austrian, Bohemian and Hungarian lands, with all the attendant duplication and friction. Joseph temporarily replaced the sclerotic 'Privy Conference' with a number of smaller bodies, most of them dedicated to a particular geographic area. He also drastically reduced the number of Privy Councillors, to reduce unwieldiness in decision-making, and improved the state finances. The formidable and unprecedented Austrian performance in the war, with huge deployments across numerous fronts, would not have been possible without these changes. Louis, too, tried to wrest even more out of his heavily taxed kingdom in order to meet the challenge of the Grand Alliance. During the Nine Years War, and again in 1701 with the renewed outbreak of hostilities, he introduced the *capitation*, the first direct tax which applied – unlike the traditional *taille* – to all subjects, irrespective of rank. It was followed a few years later by the *dixième*, another universal direct tax. Taken together these innovations generated about one quarter of the entire tax yield. Contrary to myth, therefore, French nobles did pay taxes. The problem was that they did not pay anywhere near to their full capacity. Had they done so, France would have packed a much greater military and diplomatic punch. Like the Habsburgs, Louis, however, had to tread carefully to avoid antagonizing the vested interests of the tax-farmers, office holders, tax-exempt nobles and other groups upon whom the monarchy ultimately depended. His power was, in fact, very far from absolute, reflecting instead a compromise between the crown and the nobility concerning the distribution of resources within, and the greater glory of the kingdom abroad.[68] In northern and eastern Europe, the pressures of the Great Northern War also had profound implications for domestic politics. In Russia, Tsar Peter disbanded the *Strelsy*, an over-mighty and militarily backward praetorian guard of musketeers, in 1699 and created a regular standing army. A central command followed a few years later and by 1718 he had set up a military college.[69]

Strategic pressures also drove profound constitutional changes within some European states. In 1701 the English parliament passed the Act of Settlement, which determined that Queen Anne would be succeeded by the Electress Sophia of Hanover – James I's granddaughter – and her heirs, providing they were Protestants. This explicitly excluded the Stuarts – Catholic *or Protestant* – and was designed to preserve the Revolution settlement of 1688 from them and their French backers. The parliament in Edinburgh, on the other hand, outraged at not having been consulted over the English measure, had soon after passed its own Act which only stipulated a Protestant succession. This left open the possibility that the Stuarts might abjure Catholicism and return, which raised the spectre of a separation of the crowns, and the re-encirclement of England. More generally, the war effort against France required ever greater coordination north and south. It made no sense at all to have two separate commercial and colonial policies, for example. Whig elites on both sides of the border agreed that whatever their differences, the containment of Louis XIV came first. So, in 1707, they concluded an Act of Union, in which Scotland received generous representation at Westminster, and retained its legal and educational system, but gave up its separate foreign and security policy. And as the Union was made in order to prosecute the war, so did the war make the Union. The common cause against popery and Universal Monarchy welded together the two halves more effectively than bribery, intimidation or crude commercial advantage ever could have done.[70]

In Spain, the demands of the war effort also led to profound constitutional change. At first, it seemed as if the conflict would increase political participation. When the allies captured Barcelona in October 1705, the resulting outcry against the mismanagement of the war prompted revolt of the nobility at the Council of State in Madrid. In November of that year they demanded that they be consulted on the direction of the war. On the contrary, Philip argued, it was not the lack of consultation which was undermining the national struggle but continuing regional divisions and jealousies. In 1707, he pushed through a union between the crowns of Castile and Aragon, which included Aragon itself, Valencia and Catalonia. Only Navarre and the Basque provinces held on to their autonomy. The rest of Spain was now a unitary state. Philip had achieved what had eluded Charles V, Philip II and most recently Olivares. Modern Spain, too, was a creation of the War of the Spanish Succession. But whereas in Britain Union had been achieved through parliament, in Spain it was effected at the expense of representative assemblies.[71] In France, the pressures of war failed to dislodge longstanding obstacles to constitutional reform. Reeling from the string of allied victories over the past two years, the French Marshal Vendôme suggested in 1706 that Louis rally popular support through the summoning of an Estates General, the first since 1614. The king refused to do so, possibly for fear of opening a Pandora's box of demands. For the moment, participation was largely limited to the legal functions of the *parlements*, which still enjoyed the right to register or reject new tax edicts.[72]

In the Ottoman Empire, the domestic consequences of the catastrophic strategic failure in the 1680s were dramatic. When Buda fell to the imperialists in 1686, the shock waves soon reached Constantinople. A Janissary revolt deposed Mehmet IV and replaced him with his brother, Suleiman II. The Grand Vizier was executed. In that sense, he, Mehmet and James II suffered varieties of the same fate for foreign policy misjudgements. The Ottoman Empire remained neutral during the War of the Spanish Succession. Memories of defeats at Vienna and Zenta were still fresh. All the same, the Turks saw the Treaty of Karlowitz not as the beginning of peaceful coexistence with Christian Europe but as a truce during which the empire caught its breath before resuming the advance. They found a theological justification for this in the *hudabiya* which Muhammed had concluded with the Meccans. This was a highly controversial policy domestically, however, and it was no coincidence that Sultan Mustafa II, who succeeded Suleiman II after a short interval, actually moved his capital to Edirne in order to conceal the calamity of the terms of Karlowitz as long as possible. In 1703, the Janissaries in Constantinople revolted, partly on account of local grievances, such as overdue pay, but mainly in protest against the Empire's declining international standing. They accused Mustafa not only of indolence and corruption – which were hardly hanging offences – but of having surrendered lands belonging to the 'House of Islam', which most certainly was. The Sultan was deposed and succeeded by Ahmed III.

When Charles XII finally withdrew from Saxony in 1707, the two wars which had seemed on the verge of becoming one great European conflagration ran their separate courses once more. The Grand Alliance now sought to extend the long run of victories it had enjoyed since 1704 and finally bring the French to heel. Defeating Louis in Germany, Flanders and the Po Valley was one thing; pressing the attack home into France itself, however, was quite another. Joseph was unable to persuade more than a minority of the princes to fight on to recover Alsace and Lorraine for the Empire, and create an 'imperial barrier' to further French expansion. Many of them were also sceptical of Joseph's claims to be conducting an 'imperial' rather than merely a personal war in Italy, the same issue which had dogged Maximilian around 1500 and other emperors since. There was no consensus even among the usually hawkish British and Dutch, among whom voices in favour of a compromise peace with Louis were beginning to be heard. The war stagnated. In 1707, the archduke Charles was badly beaten at Almansa in Spain, provoking a furious debate in the British parliament. A year later, the allies prevailed at Oudenaarde in Flanders, but it had not been an easy victory. Both sides began to think seriously about a compromise peace.

The Habsburgs were also worried about a new threat brewing in Germany. They had raised Prussia to the status of a kingdom in order to contain France, but, within a few years, Vienna began to have second thoughts. The ambitions of the new king were soon apparent: in 1702, Frederick I made an unsuccessful bid to succeed William as *Stadholder* of the United Provinces. A year later, the Prussians tried to assert their claims to the nearby south German territories of Ansbach and Bayreuth, and were blocked by the Austrian-dominated Aulic Council. For the moment, the Prussians still trod carefully: in his first Political Testament of May 1705, the king enjoined his successors to exercise 'extreme caution' about going to war because the new kingdom was surrounded by 'much more powerful and mostly hostile powers' who were 'jealous' of her success.[73] Vienna, however, was not deceived. 'The House of Austria,' Joseph's chief minister, Prince Salm, remarked in 1706, 'fears the power of the King of Prussia more than that of France, which is greater . . . the King of France only gnaws at the edges of those countries that border on it, but . . . the King of Prussia proceeds directly to the heart.'[74] It made sense, therefore, to reach an agreement with Louis.

Negotiations were begun in May 1709, and then continued in the Dutch towns of Gertruydenberg and The Hague throughout the winter of 1710. The sticking point proved to be not Spain, but Germany. To signal his flexibility, Louis had already pulled back the bulk of his men from the Iberian peninsula, and although he could never accede to allied demands to actually depose Philip, he might well have been able to persuade his grandson to abdicate Spain to Archduke Charles. What he refused to concede, however, was the coalition demand for the evacuation of Mons and Namur as pledges of good behaviour, the destruction of all French forts on the west bank of the Rhine, the return of Breisach to the Empire, and the banishment of Louis's closest German allies, the electors of Cologne and Bavaria. Taken together, these conditions amounted to, and were intended to constitute, nothing less than the complete destruction of the French position in the Empire so carefully built up by Louis and his predecessors. It would have left the monarchy open to attack from the north and east, and denied France the 'portals' through which she could exert influence beyond her borders. Louis therefore had no choice but to reject the terms on offer. The war would continue, at great cost.

Territorial demands and fortifications were one way of containing Louis, changing the nature of the French regime was another. Some of the allies began to wonder whether British and Dutch liberties might not best be protected through the promotion of liberty in Europe, and especially in France itself. Thus in order to win over the population of Brabant in 1706, Marlborough guaranteed that Vienna would honour traditional constitutional rights. That same year, a planned British amphibious expedition to Guyenne was to be accompanied by a proclamation in which the allies declared themselves the friends of French liberty, promising to revoke the Edict of Nantes and restore the moribund Estates General. Likewise, Marlborough wrote in June 1709 that, if they could, the powers of the Grand Alliance should demand that France 'again [be] governed by the three Estates, which I think is more likely to give quiet to Christendom than tearing provinces from them'. What the allies had in mind here was not the imposition of British-style parliamentary government, but rather the restoration of the traditional corporate liberties suppressed by the French monarchy. They expected these to exercise severe constitutional and fiscal constraints on Bourbon expansionism.[75]

Marlborough had put his finger on one of the great paradoxes of European history. He and many like him believed at one and the same time that while constitutional liberties were the bedrock of British national greatness, the encouragement of similar if not identical freedoms abroad would create allies rather than simply more effective competitors. In fact, the assumption that greater political participation would make for a more pacific France was highly dubious. For in June 1709, aghast at the harsh allied demands, Louis approached the French public directly, through his *intendants*, and the bishops, in order to explain why he was continuing the struggle. 'I share all the evils that the war has made such faithful subjects suffer,' the king announced, '[but] I am persuaded that they would themselves oppose the acceptance of conditions equally contrary to justice and to the honour of the name French.' This letter, which was read from parish pulpits throughout the monarchy, generated a wave of popular sympathy for Louis and galvanized the French war effort.[76]

As the peace negotiations stagnated, the war continued. In August 1709, the French repelled an imperial invasion attempt at Basel. A month later, the two sides battered each other into a costly draw at Malplaquet. In the face of continued expense and bloodshed, sceptical voices in the British public sphere and in parliament grew ever louder. In November 1709, the Tory Henry Sacheverell preached a fiery sermon at St Paul's, Westminster, against the government. The ostensible target was tolerance of Dissenters, but what really motivated the mob which rampaged afterwards through the city was foreign policy. 'Sacheverell and peace,' they cried, when attacking Dissenting meeting houses and the Bank of England. Worse news from the front followed. In 1710, the British expeditionary force in Spain was crushed at Brihuega, the Austrian-backed one at Villa Viciosa. A year later, French troops advanced deep into the peninsula. With the Whig policy of continental engagement now comprehensively discredited, Queen Anne dismissed her ministers and replaced them with a Tory administration under Robert Hanley and Henry St John, later Lord Bolingbroke, committed to a more maritime and colonial approach. Not long after, the Whigs were thrashed at the general election, primarily because the public had lost patience with their grand strategy.

In mid-April 1711, the emperor Joseph I died suddenly, leaving no son. Six months later, he was succeeded by his younger brother, Charles, the candidate of the Grand Alliance for the Spanish throne, who now hastily left the peninsula to secure his new titles and territories. This raised the spectre of a return of the empire of Charles V. As St John remarked, 'If the Empire and the dominions of Spain are to unite in the person of this prince [Charles], the system of the war is essentially altered.' The Whigs still argued that French power was so great that it required a combined Habsburg bloc to balance it; but the argument was being lost. Support for the land war in Europe ebbed away. British generals were openly censored by the House of Lords. Marlborough himself was sacked in December 1711. Flanders was progressively starved of men and money and resources were diverted overseas, though a much heralded expedition against Quebec ended in disaster in 1711. By the beginning of 1712, British forces in Europe had effectively ended operations, and the other belligerents were equally exhausted.[77] The Dutch, for their part, felt that France was as contained as it ever would be. Only Charles wanted to fight on until his Spanish inheritance had been secured. Peace therefore broke out by fits and starts, with the British and Dutch coming to terms with France at the Treaty of Utrecht in April 1713, and the emperor at the Treaty of Rastatt in March the following year.

The Utrecht settlement was designed to contain France. The fortress town of Kehl was returned to the Empire, shutting out the French on that part of the Rhine. The crucial Spanish Netherlands now passed to Austria, locking her more directly into the containment of France. Britain and the Dutch were expressly committed to defend the 'barrier' fortresses. It helped that the new King of England, George Ludwig of Hanover, who succeeded Anne in 1714 as George I, was a firm Francophobe determined to deliver on this commitment.[78] His own somewhat precarious position on the throne was in turn guaranteed by the Dutch. Thanks to the Hanoverian Succession, Britain was now also effectively a continental power, with a responsibility for the security of northern Germany. British constitutional freedoms were thus explicitly linked to the maintenance of the European balance. In Italy, Louis was boxed in by Habsburg gains in Lombardy. This was shielded by a buffer in Savoy, which was disappointed in its own ambitions for Lombardy, but strengthened instead by the addition of Sicily (later exchanged for Sardinia). The French position in the western Mediterranean was seriously weakened by Britain's retention of Gibraltar, which controlled the passage in and out of the Mediterranean, and the still more vital Minorca, whence it was supplied and from where the French Toulon squadron could be monitored. Philip was recognized as King of Spain – and the Grand Alliance abandoned its Catalan allies – but was forced to renounce all claims to the French throne.

The commercial and colonial aspects of the peace were significant, more because of their strategic importance than for any purely economic reasons. Britain annexed the whole of Newfoundland and Nova Scotia, and their fisheries, which were vital for the training of seamen. She also secured the coveted *Asiento*, the monopoly right to trade with South America, especially in slaves. This was now given to the British South Sea Company, which the Tories had set up in 1711 as a counterweight to the Whig-dominated Bank of England and the East India Company. Its purpose was to generate not merely personal profits for shareholders but also capital for governmental loans to pursue a vigorous foreign policy. This established a direct link between the slave trade and the European balance. The Dutch were awarded special trading privileges at the expense of the former Spanish Netherlands, and their new masters in Vienna. The River Scheldt was to remain closed to shipping in order to preserve the pre-eminence of Amsterdam; Dutch economic success was based at least as much on diplomatic coercion as competitiveness. The resulting economic gain was supposed to help the Dutch to garrison the barrier fortresses. Likewise, Bolingbroke sought a commercial treaty with France, not for pecuniary gain or to 'engage' the Bourbons, but because he thought that Britain would prevail in open economic competition. In this way, for both the Dutch and the British, the European commercial and strategic balances were closely connected.

Measured against his hopes in 1700–1701, all this was a bitter defeat for Louis. He held on to Quebec, but was excluded from the lucrative Spanish colonial trade. He was forced to expel the British Pretender from Saint-Germain in the Paris suburbs to Lorraine and later even further away. The fortifications of Dunkirk, from where French privateers had harassed Anglo-Dutch shipping, and which was an essential base for a descent on England, were to be dismantled. His hope that the Elector of Bavaria would be allowed to exchange his patrimony for the much richer Spanish

Netherlands was also dashed. Louis had, however, finally banished the 200-year spectre of encirclement. Henceforth, there would be – or so Louis believed – a friendly monarchy on the other side of the Pyrenees. At all events, now that the Netherlands had passed to the Austrians, France no longer faced the same potential enemy on both her northern and southern border. Germany, moreover, remained disunited: the vacuum on France's eastern boundaries was still unfilled. Charles, too, was bitterly disappointed. He had wanted to exchange the remote Spanish Netherlands for nearby Bavaria, and resented the economic restrictions which the maritime powers had inflicted on his new acquisition. Moreover, he still regarded himself as the rightful King of Spain. On the other hand, the Habsburg monarchy was now greater than ever, receiving the lion's share of Spain's European empire: not merely the Netherlands, but also Naples, Sicily and various north Italian lands.

It soon became clear that the Utrecht settlement was designed to address the challenges of the past, not those of the future. Its primary purpose, the containment of France, became redundant after the death of Louis XIV in September 1715. A series of weak regencies followed until his great-grandson, Louis XV, was old enough to ascend the throne. For the next twenty years or so, France would pursue a largely pacific policy, and reacted to changes in the European system rather than setting the agenda herself. The Jacobite Pretender 'James III' was banished to Avignon and ultimately 'beyond the Alps' to Rome. The real dynamism in the European system came from elsewhere, especially the continuing Great Northern War, where the future of the Baltic, eastern Europe and ultimately of northern Germany was at stake. In 1709, Peter the Great's unexpected but decisive victory over Charles XII at Poltava in the Ukraine signalled the rise of a new power centre in the east which was to have a fundamental impact on the balance across the continent. As the German philosopher Leibniz wrote that same year, 'The Tsar henceforth will attract the consideration of Europe and will play a big part in general affairs . . . It is commonly being said that the Tsar will be formidable to the whole of Europe, that he will be as though a Turk of the North.'[79]

The tsar's principal ambition was to eject the Swedes from northern Germany, gain a foothold there himself and secure a vote and voice in the *Reichstag*.[80] This would be the final nail in Sweden's coffin, the ultimate destruction of Gustavus Adolphus's legacy. In 1711, Peter besieged the Swedish garrison in the Pomeranian port of Stralsund, and married his son to the daughter of the Duke of Brunswick-Wolfenbüttel. A year later, the conflict spread still further along the north German coast when the Swedes invaded Mecklenburg, inviting a Russian riposte there. The northern war now threatened to unhinge the European balance as a whole. In May 1715, the Vienna Privy Conference warned that it 'would shortly plunge the whole German Empire into flames'.[81]

In April 1716, Peter concluded an alliance with Karl Leopold of Mecklenburg, and married another niece to him. Russian dynastic links now straddled the Baltic. A year later, Peter agreed the Siberian border with the Chinese, freeing his eastern flank. Large Russian forces camped at Copenhagen in preparation for an assault on Sweden proper; other units were ensconced in Pomerania and Mecklenburg. Unless something was done, the Russian tide would engulf the whole Baltic, swamp Sweden, and upset the German equilibrium on which the whole European balance ultimately rested. This was of intense concern to Sweden's traditional sponsor, France, to the Dutch, whose commerce dominated the Baltic, to the British, who drew their vital naval stores from the Baltic, and of course to the Holy Roman Emperor himself and all the territories of the Empire, including Hanover, whose elector had been King of England since 1714.

Russian ambitions threatened not only the security of many German states, but also their 'freedoms'. Duke Karl Leopold looked to the tsar for support in his brutal campaign against the privileges of the Mecklenburgian nobility; they in turn resented his 'tyranny'. So in 1719 the Diet mandated a Hanoverian-led imperial intervention – *Reichsexekution* – against Karl Leopold. The emperor's proclamation spoke of the duke's attempts to deprive the estates 'of their age-old privileges, freedoms and rights' through harsh measures, in order to 'force them into arbitrary subjection'. Karl Leopold's men and his Russian auxiliaries were quickly defeated at the battle of Waldmühlen. Nine years later, the imperial machinery swung into action once more. Karl Leopold was charged with undermining the local courts, and establishing a 'bloody assize'. The decree then drew up a long list of physical abuses inflicted on the duke's subjects, including a graphic description of the torture of a refractory magistrate. Once again Karl Leopold was accused of 'arbitrary rule'. There was also a broader fear that the duke's oppressive behaviour would cause a disturbance in the Empire. The imperial decree warned that it 'might involve the Roman Empire as a whole or its parts in dangerous disturbances'. In particular, the conflict gave the tsar an opportunity to fish in troubled waters. Here the ideological motivation was not simply a blind for some deeper strategic purpose, but inseparable from it. Geopolitics and good governance rhymed here. Only well-ruled neighbours would be good neighbours.[82]

Faced with a common front by so many European powers, Peter backed down in north Germany and sued for peace. All the same, the Treaty of Nystad, which brought the Great Northern War to an end in 1721, was a catastrophe for Sweden. She lost her entire eastern first line of defence in the Baltic: Livonia, Estonia and the Finnish province of Karelia. In Germany, she surrendered Bremen and Werden to Hanover, but held on to Western Pomerania. Stockholm, in other words, remained relatively immune to attack from the south, and could still theoretically influence affairs in Germany. To all intents and purposes, however, Sweden had ceased to be a great power, and had lost most of her influence in the Empire.

It was less obvious at the time, but the Great Northern War also fatally undermined the position of Poland. The Polish nobility – the *szlachta* – combined militant Catholicism and republican virtue at home with a determination to avoid foreign war at almost any price. Unlike the British and Swedish parliaments, therefore, the *Sejm* was not the vehicle for the articulation of a robust national interest, but a platform for curbing the ambitions of the Saxon kings and – in practice – for frustrating any kind of military mobilization whatsoever.[83] Given that the *Sejm* refused to address the question of national security with any seriousness, the best hope for Poland's continued independence lay with Augustus's plans to make the monarchy hereditary in the Wettin family. This would reduce both the role of the nobility – which had traditionally chosen the king – and that of outside powers, which had since time immemorial exploited the Polish constitution to interfere in the election process. For this reason both Russia and Prussia were determined to block it. In February 1720 Peter concluded an alliance with Prussia in which both parties committed themselves to guaranteeing the Polish constitution, and opposing any application of the hereditary principle to the crown. A month later, Augustus bowed to the inevitable, and informed Vienna, London and Stockholm that he was giving up his reform programme and submitting to Russian tutelage. This enabled

St Petersburg to destabilize the Commonwealth almost at will by backing religious dissenters, or supporting one of the many 'Confederations', in effect factions or parties, which periodically went into opposition on some issue or other. The result was that in Poland the protection of minority rights became inseparably merged in the popular mind with a sense of national inferiority.

The Treaty of Utrecht also failed to settle the struggle for mastery in the Mediterranean, particularly Italy. Spain emerged from the war greatly strengthened by the union between Castile and Aragon, and the other governmental reforms which Philip of Anjou and his French advisers pushed through between 1707 and 1715. He now ruled a kingdom which had shed its indefensible outlying provinces in the Netherlands, and commanded the largest fleet and army which Spain had seen for some time. This potential was now harnessed to the ambition of his second wife, Elizabeth Farnese, encouraged by the chief minister, Cardinal Alberoni, who was determined to recapture as much as possible of Spain's empire in Italy so as to provide an inheritance for her sons. Moreover, Philip still harboured claims to the French crown. Faced by an obvious Spanish intent to wreck the peace settlement, Britain and France – who were already collaborating in the Baltic and Germany – moved closer together. A formal entente between the powers followed in 1716. This did not deter Philip, who occupied the former Spanish territory of Sardinia in July 1717, and invaded Sicily a year later, expelling the Austrian garrison there. His next target was clearly Naples. Philip's aggression not only threatened to unravel the whole Habsburg position in the Italian peninsula, but also raised the spectre of a new Spanish hegemony in the Mediterranean more generally. So in October 1718, before the formal declaration of war, the Royal Navy launched a surprise attack on the Spanish fleet off Cape Passaro near Sicily and annihilated it. This was not only a pre-emptive strike to protect Naples from invasion, but also a preventive war to eliminate a potential Spanish naval threat further down the line.

Soon after, the British, Dutch, French and Austrians combined to form the Quadruple Alliance to contain Philip. By January 1719 both Britain and France were at war with Spain, and a few months later France invaded northern Spain. The Royal Navy attacked Galicia, and cleared the western Mediterranean of all Spanish shipping. In retaliation, Philip supported a failed Jacobite rising under the Earl of Mar in Scotland in April 1719. Before long, however, he was forced to dismiss Alberoni, rein in his wife and come to terms. At the resulting peace settlement Spain recognized the loss of her Mediterranean lands, at least for the moment. The only beneficiaries of the conflict were Savoy and Austria, who exchanged Sardinia and Sicily, each thereby gaining a more strategically manageable territory. At one level, therefore, the Utrecht settlement had worked.

The problem was that the Austrian Habsburgs now represented a potentially greater threat to the European balance than the French. They acquired Transylvania and the rest of Hungary in 1699; the Austrian Netherlands, Milan and Naples in 1714; and with the Treaty of Passarovitz, which ended a fresh war with Turkey in 1716–18, Belgrade, the Banat and part of Wallachia were added. Now the Austrians had even managed to round off their Mediterranean presence by jettisoning indefensible Sardinia, and gaining Sicily, which served as a bulwark for Naples. As it turned out, 1720 marked the high tide of Habsburg expansion, but at the time it seemed to many that the aspiration towards Universal Monarchy had migrated from Versailles to Vienna. These fears were stoked by the belligerence of Emperor Charles VI. He made little secret of his ambition to reclaim the Spanish throne and thus resurrect the empire of his namesake, Charles V – the very thing that the War of the Spanish Succession had been fought to prevent. Charles also began to throw his weight around in Germany, supporting the Catholic side in a series of bitter confessional disputes.

To George I and the British government, Austrian ambitions jeopardized not only the king's Hanoverian lands, and German Protestantism, but the security of the Empire more generally, and thus the very fundament of the European balance. The British Secretary of State, Charles Townsend, feared that the Austrians believed themselves 'so far above the rest of the human race' that they hoped to 'direct the affairs of this world according to their own wishes and without the assistance of any other power'.[84] The Regency government in Versailles, for its part, was concerned to contain the Austrian threat from the Netherlands, and to eliminate the various enclaves and exclaves which complicated the boundary with the Empire. Above all, the French were determined to deny the Habsburgs the resources of Germany. It was, as French diplomats never tired of warning throughout the early eighteenth century, an enormous reservoir of 'natural soldiers'. Indeed, the French foreign minister, Marshal Huxelles, was so fretful that 'the authority of the emperor was becoming every day more absolute' that he argued in March 1718 that defending 'the rights and liberties of the German states' was the only way of 'preventing the establishment of despotism in the Empire'.[85] For this reason, Versailles supported an Anglo-Hanoverian diplomatic intervention in 1719 to defend the rights of Palatine Protestants against their Catholic prince, and ultimately against the emperor himself.

Franco-British fears of another Habsburg Universal Monarchy came to a head in 1725. The crisis was a direct result of sudden dynastic permutations. Anxious to strengthen the monarchy through the rapid production of an heir, Louis XV renounced his longstanding intention to marry the still very young Spanish Infanta. Instead, he turned eastwards and married Maria Leszczynska, daughter of Stanislas, the sometime King of Poland. Philip and Elizabeth took this as an affront, and sought a rapprochement with the once hated Austrian Habsburgs. An Austro-Spanish alliance followed in May. The terms of that treaty constituted a direct threat to the general European balance. Charles VI promised not to obstruct Spanish demands for the return of Gibraltar and Minorca. He also agreed to the installation of Philip's eldest son, Don Carlos, by Elizabeth Farnese in some Italian duchies. Spain, for its part, granted the emperor trading privileges for his fledgling Ostend Company, which had been founded a few years earlier with a view to breaking into the lucrative colonial market. And if all this was not bad enough, there was talk of a marriage between Charles's eldest daughter, Maria Theresa, and one of the Spanish princes.

If the proposed dynastic merger took place, Britain and France would face an Austro-Spanish bloc stretching from Flanders on the English Channel to the heel of the Italian boot, and from Silesia to the Pyrenees and the walls of Gibraltar. 'Having the Austrian dominions joined to the vast territories of Spain,' Townshend warned, might make the new state 'more formidable to the rest of Europe than even Charles V was'.[86] Worse still, the emperor's German ambitions – which worried France and Britain far more than the colonial threat – would be funded by Spanish New World bullion, or perhaps even by his own Ostend Company. The British and French capitals now resonated to fears of imperial 'domination', 'intimidation' and 'absolute' power in Germany. The situation, one French diplomat complained, was worse than before 1648. For this reason, Britain and France came together at the Treaty of Hanover in September 1725 in a defensive alliance to contain Vienna and Madrid.

With France and Britain thus preoccupied, Russia was able to resume her push for complete domination of the Baltic. The key to the realization of these plans, as the Russian chief minister, Count Ostermann, argued in a series of memoranda in 1725–6, was an alliance with Austria. 'The Holy Roman Emperor can assist Russia not only' against the Swedes, Turks and Poles, he wrote, 'but may also deter other powers from attacking Russia'. So in early August 1726 the tsarina, Catherine I, finally threw off the mask and joined the Treaty of Vienna. Russian troops occupied Courland, to pre-empt a Polish annexation. To London and Versailles, the Russian plans were not merely a blow to the strategically vital Baltic area, still the principal source of naval supplies, but also threatened to revive Peter's plans to dominate north Germany and thus the Empire. Their countermeasures were hamstrung by the fact that there was no way of deterring Russia by threatening her western border. Instead, a Royal Navy squadron was sent to the Baltic, and Sweden was persuaded to join the Alliance of Hanover. At the same time, British and French diplomats at Constantinople tried to inveigle the Porte, as the Ottoman government was widely known, into attacking the Russians from the south. The plan, to quote Townshend, was to 'preoccupy . . . the Tsarina so much on the side of Asia that she may be less attentive and less enterprising to create trouble and uneasiness to the King on this side'. The interconnectedness between the various parts of the European 'balance' could not have been better illustrated.[87]

The great European standoff of 1725–7 thus spanned the continent from the Baltic to the Black Sea, and from the Channel to the Iberian peninsula, where Spain conducted a half-hearted siege of Gibraltar. But the principal point at issue was the Empire, including Flanders, where Charles threatened Hanover and – more to the point – where he could mobilize the resources and secure the bases to menace France and Britain directly. That is also why British naval efforts were so concentrated on the Spanish silver fleets: these attacks were not just crude smash and grab raids, but a calculated strategy to deprive the emperor of the funds to upset the balance of power in central Europe. That is why the bulk of Franco-British military preparations were focused on assembling a substantial land force in Germany, where they could contain Charles.

All this was not merely a dispute between the great powers but also a profound ideological conflict. Many contemporaries saw it as a clash between representative governments, of various stripes, and an equally heterogeneous group of absolutist states. The British parliament and the Dutch States General felt menaced by a Hispano-Austrian axis whose strength was at least partly based on the suppression of representative government at home. To use contemporary parlance, Europe was split into the camp of 'liberty', on one side, and that of 'despotism' on the other. These terms had long been bandied about by British and Dutch pamphleteers, and since the late seventeenth century they had become increasingly current in the growing central European public sphere as well. Newspaper readership in the Empire grew from about 250,000 overall, to about half a million by the middle of the century. Part and parcel of this critique was a growing unwillingness to accept the princely insistence on 'secrecy' in the discussion of political matters.[88] In satires, sermons, periodicals and 'political conversations', German rulers and especially the emperor were increasingly being held to account, particularly on foreign policy, which was the primary focus of 'imperial' patriotism. It showed a deep interest in the state not merely of German politics but also of the broader European balance of power upon which their security rested. As the author of the hopefully entitled *Friedens-Courier* (*Peace-Courier*) remarked, nobody could be so uninterested in the affairs of the world that 'even if he did not want to read about it himself, he would not at least ask his neighbour what was being said from time to time about the Peace [conference]'.[89] Many of these publications were state-sponsored, to be sure, but they showed that, far from being 'unpolitical', Germans were deeply interested in the world around them.

In the end, there was no general European conflagration. Neither Spain nor Austria was capable of sustaining a war in Germany and Italy against the Anglo-French alliance. Catherine preferred not to confront the Royal Navy in the Baltic. The Ottomans refused to attack the Tsarist Empire. The only shots actually fired were between the British and the Spanish on the high seas and before Gibraltar. War was averted through diplomacy and deterrence.

*

If Austrian strength was a threat, so was the inherent fragility of the Habsburg conglomerate. It soon became clear that the emperor, Charles VI, was unlikely to leave a male heir, raising the possibility of a contested succession and partition at the hands of neighbouring powers after his death. Charles had sought to pre-empt the issue by promulgating the 'Pragmatic Sanction' of April 1713, which laid down the principle that the Habsburg lands should pass whole and undivided first to his sons and daughters, and only thereafter to those of his late elder brother, Joseph. From May 1717, that heir-presumptive was Charles's eldest daughter, Maria Theresa. Charles did not take anything for granted, however. He knew that while the husbands of Joseph's daughters, the electors of Bavaria and Saxony, might have renounced any claims on behalf of their wives, these would be quickly resurrected if an opportunity presented itself. For this reason, Charles set about securing the agreement of the representative assemblies of the monarchy to the succession arrangements. By the middle of 1722, he had even persuaded the Hungarians to cooperate, in return, of course, for a recognition of their own privileges. Charles then shifted his attention beyond his borders, eventually signing up Spain in 1725, Russia in 1726, England in 1731 and the imperial Diet in 1732. At the same time, however, Charles was often forced to compromise, for example when he agreed to marry off one of Joseph's daughters to the Bavarians, in return for military support against the Ottomans in 1716. The overall effect of this anticipatory flurry, far from defusing the issue, was to encourage other European powers to think about how best to take advantage of Habsburg weakness.

This was especially true of France, which began to reassert itself on the European scene in the 1730s, after a long period of relative passivity following the death of Louis XIV in 1715. In part, this activism was driven by a greater sense of dynastic stability with the birth of the Dauphin – an heir to the throne – in 1729. In part also, it reflected increasing frustration at the diminishing returns from the alliance with Britain, whose commercial and German policies diverged more and more. France was already 'secretly' rebuilding the port facilities around Dunkirk, and investing heavily in her navy. Her economy was expanding at an impressive rate; so was her colonial footprint, especially in the Americas. But the main concern of French policy remained the growth of Austrian power in the Empire, which, as an official in the French foreign ministry remarked in 1729, threatened 'to alter the government of the Empire to such an extent that it would become a monarchy, allowing the emperor to elevate himself to the absolute ruler of Germany, which would indeed overturn the balance of power in Europe'.[90]

The revival of French power caught the rest of Europe unawares. Internal weakness and commercial decline made the Dutch Republic quite incapable of mounting a coordinated response. Austria was eager to contain France in the Empire and northern Italy, but felt hamstrung by her exposed position in Flanders, where she was loath to invest in defensive preparations. Alarmed by these sagging buttresses in the strategically vital Low Countries, and astonished by the evidence of economic growth in 'unfree' France, Britain now abandoned her hostility to Charles, and reverted to the traditional policy of bolstering the Habsburgs as a counterweight to France. In 1731, therefore, she entered into an alliance with Austria by the Treaty of Vienna and guaranteed the Pragmatic Sanction. Emboldened by British support, Charles now felt strong enough to ask the *Reichstag* to approve the Pragmatic Sanction, which passed the electoral college by six votes to three in January 1732.[91]

Far from deterring France, the British action made her more determined to face down Austria. In 1733, she concluded a 'Family Compact' with the Spanish Bourbons. This signalled, to be sure, an intention to cooperate against Britain overseas, but its main aim was a common front in Europe, where both parties planned to exploit the Austrian succession to despoil the Habsburgs. The most pressing concern, however, was to prevent Charles from gaining control of the Empire itself. Matters first came to a head over the question of the Polish succession, which shot to the top of the European agenda on the death of the King-Elector Augustus II in early February 1733. The French put forward Stanislas Leszczynski, who had briefly reigned during the Great Northern War and whose daughter had since married Louis XV. He was a popular figure, and left to their own devices the Polish nobility would almost certainly have elected him king. The Commonwealth was, however, far too weak to decide its own future. Moreover, what was at stake in 1733 was the whole geopolitical structure of Europe. To the Russians, the election revived the spectre of a reformist king who might transform chaotic Poland into a more dynamic power on their western border. For Austria, a French candidate in Warsaw threatened to wedge the monarchy in between Stanislas and his son in law, Louis XV. When the French tried to persuade the Ottoman Grand Vizier to support their candidate, the prospect of encirclement grew still more worrying. The Austrians and Russians therefore wanted another Saxon to succeed and maintain the status quo. The real issue, in short, was the future of the Habsburg monarchy, and its position in Germany.

It is therefore not surprising that so little of the War of the Polish Succession was fought in Poland. In September 1733, the Polish Diet elected Stanislas king. War between Austria and Russia on one side and France and Spain on the other soon followed. There was little that the French could do to help Stanislas, who was soon crushed in Poland. The real action took place to the west. Thanks to a Franco-Dutch treaty, the Austrian Netherlands were neutralized for the duration of the conflict. Almost everywhere else, however, the Habsburgs were on the defensive: in Lorraine, which the French occupied with ease at the start of hostilities; in northern Italy, where they were attacked by a Franco-Sardinian force in October 1733; in Naples, which was invaded by Spain in February 1734; and in Germany proper, despite having persuaded the Empire to declare war on France in April 1734. The emperor buckled under this onslaught. Britain refused point-blank to render Austria any assistance, despite the Treaty of Vienna. In the end, it was only the arrival of a substantial Russian expeditionary corps in the Palatinate in August 1735, after an epic march of more than 1,000 kilometres, which saved the Austrians from a more crushing defeat.[92] Charles was forced to sue for peace in October 1735. Naples and Sicily were ceded to Don Carlos, albeit with the proviso that they should never revert to the Spanish crown. France accepted the Saxon succession in Poland, and in return Stanislas was installed as Duke of Lorraine, with the understanding that it would fall to France directly on his death. It was a French triumph.

The continuing early-eighteenth-century international turbulence drove European states to strive for improved internal cohesion and resource extraction in order to increase their military capabilities. In 1715, for example, the Habsburg monarchy persuaded the Hungarians to fund some regiments of the standing army on a permanent basis. A year later, the Austrian Privy Council for Financial Affairs was created to improve fiscal coordination. Not long after that the president of the Court Chamber made the revolutionary suggestion that the monarchy should tailor its military establishment to reflect actual fiscal capabilities – not that anybody took any notice. The Habsburgs did not succeed in uniting their disparate provinces, and their various fractious representative assemblies, behind a project for the common defence. There was no 'Habsburg interest', only those of the individual component parts of the monarchy. Most territories, such as Naples, paid only for their own defence, and that grudgingly; the only substantial net contributor to the overall defence of the monarchy was Bohemia. In Bourbon France, on the other hand, the aristocracy had lost its formal veto on taxation. Direct levies and the reduction of privileges were stepped up, but not too much in order to avoid disturbing the fragile domestic consensus.[93] Though the *dixième* was reintroduced in 1733 to fund the War of the Polish Succession, the king was forced by noble and clerical opinion to abolish it after the fighting had finished, thus depriving the crown of valuable future revenue; this pattern was repeated throughout the century. The *parlements* – so long held at bay by the monarchy – increasingly asserted their right to 'register' and thus effectively to approve new taxes. Despite their considerable strength, therefore, both Austria and France were punching well below their weight for most of the century.

Russia, too, sought to maximize its power through internal reform. Peter the Great's programmes were not, however, about the importation of western and central European political norms such as consultation and 'liberty': the chaotic example of Poland put Russians off such experiments.[94] To the tsar, 'westernization' meant the creation of a modern absolutist state capable of increased economic growth and resource extraction. Indeed, the entire society and government of Russia was geared towards military mobilization. Aristocratic privilege and state service were directly linked. In 1722, the Table of Ranks spelt out the connection between noble ranks and those in the army or administration.[95] In return, the aristocracy were given virtually unrestricted control over their peasantry. In the parlance of today, early-eighteenth-century Russia was unfree, but meritocratic. Economically, the tsar failed. Though Russia was still – thanks to its huge population – the richest state in Europe cumulatively, it continued to lag far behind in terms of per capita wealth and all other indices of economic development. He succeeded politically and militarily, however. Russia entered the new round of the struggle for mastery in Europe with a comparatively large standing army of more than 100,000 men, which could be reinforced at any time from a virtually unlimited manpower reserve.

By contrast with the other major powers, Prussia commanded an influence well beyond what was warranted by her 'natural' or 'fundamental' strength. In the seventeenth century, the nobility had surrendered their right to be consulted on taxation and foreign policy, in return for princely support for serfdom. There had been periodic aristocratic demands for increased participation since then, prompting Frederick William to warn that he would do what it took to 'stabilize his sovereignty like a *rocher de bronze*'. In the next two decades he pressed ahead with governmental reforms designed to increase efficiency, creating the 'General Directory', the supreme administrative body, in 1722. A decade or so later, Frederick William introduced the famous 'cantonal system', which tied the peasants to a particular regiment and landholding. Under this arrangement, a veritable 'military-agrarian complex' developed, the nobility provided the civil servants and officer corps, while the peasantry worked the land and provided the rank and file.[96] It was underpinned by a system of dual-purpose state granaries designed both to supply the army and to increase the availability of grain in times of dearth; welfare and warfare were thus intimately linked.[97] This was a highly effective system, which guaranteed Frederick William a regular flow of recruits. It also made him less dependent on foreign mercenaries: about two thirds of his army was made up of Prussian subjects, a very high figure by contemporary standards. And yet there was some slack, even in Prussia, because a substantial proportion of the population, mainly town-dwellers, were 'exempted' from military service for one reason or the other.[98] Prussia's true potential had not yet been realized.

Common to the vast majority of these reform programmes was the assumption that absolutism delivered the best government at home and the most effective defence of state interests abroad. Parliamentary or corporate systems, on the other hand, were widely considered to be corrupt, chaotic and prone to outside intervention.[99] It was for this reason that the 'reform' party in Poland tried to curb the rights of the *Sejm* from the mid-1730s in favour of a more centralized government capable of resisting foreign powers; the 'patriots', by contrast, argued that only the restoration of their 'golden freedoms' would generate the necessary 'virtue' to resist external domination.[100] In Sweden, the monarchy made an unsuccessful attempt in 1723 to reduce external interference by moving from an elective to a hereditary succession. Similar problems were visible in the United Provinces, which were entering a period of long decline after the stupendous efforts of the struggle against Louis XIV. In 1716–17 the Secretary of the Council of State, Simon van Slingelandt, used the 'Great Assembly' of the States General to call for reforms to Dutch government and decision-making. In particular, he demanded that decisions should no longer be referred back to the provincial assemblies for ratification, and that central government be given the power to enforce legislation and taxation. Slingelandt's plan failed, primarily because the individual states no longer feared France enough to give up their jealously guarded autonomy, and because they regarded centralization as the restoration of the hated Stadholderate by another name. This had major implications for Europe as a whole, because a weak Dutch Republic would no longer be able to discharge its obligation to uphold the 'barrier' and generally help to maintain the 'balance of power'.[101]

In Britain, too, the parliamentary system was under increasing scrutiny. Ministers, or their spokesmen, argued that frequent elections gave 'a handle to the cabals and intrigues of foreign princes', and encouraged playing fast and loose with allies. For this reason, in mid-1716 government pushed through the Septennial Act, which increased the interval between general elections from three to seven years. Ministers also argued for the maintenance of a standing army, even in peacetime, 'both to suppress any insurrection at home, or to repel any insult from abroad; and to make good our engagements for maintaining the repose of Europe'. Tory and Whig radical critics, on the other hand, sought to hold the administration's foreign policy to account in parliament by demanding the release of diplomatic papers, as well as the right to approve treaties and subsidies to foreign powers. They saw in the standing army, as one outspoken MP put it, something quite contrary to 'the free execution of the laws of the land'. On this reading, external necessity was merely a stalking horse for domestic despotism. How many nations, he asked, 'had lost their liberties' on the pretence of countering 'the ambitious designs of their neighbour nations and the need to preserve the balance of power'.[102]

On the face of it, these debates would seem to bear out the general European belief that anything which tended to curb the authority of the crown at home inevitably weakened the state's ability to defend its interest abroad. In fact, the British system could boast two great advantages. First, the very high level of participation in the political process made the British state the most creditworthy in Europe, and thus enabled it to mobilize financial resources out of all proportion to its population, and even its 'underlying' economic strength.[103] Secondly, parliament and the public sphere provided a forum in which British interests could be articulated and refined, making for a more informed and flexible policy. There was thus a direct connection between domestic freedoms and foreign-political strength, but it was not a necessary or invariable one as the contrary case of the Polish Commonwealth made painfully clear.

Turkey, too, was driven by external threats to improve her internal cohesion. The Ottomans, the Janissary Hasan Kurdi lamented, were fiscally and technologically backward – they lacked 'treasury and artillery' – were too 'slow' in their decision-making, and suffered from exhaustion and 'disobedience'.[104] Unfortunately, the structure and traditions of the Ottoman Empire were totally inimical to the parliamentary and absolutist state forms in the rest of Europe. The Porte therefore devolved more and more power to the localities. Nor did the challenge lead to the emergence of an Ottoman public sphere: the 'advice books' which had been circulating for some time excluded foreign policy as a secret sphere not suitable for subjects.[105] Turkey therefore bucked the general European trend towards centralization, secularization and – at least in the west – ever-greater participation. Instead the late-seventeenth- and early-eighteenth-century Ottoman defeats sparked a deep yearning for moral and spiritual renewal. Many Muslims rejected any technical or political explanation for Muslim weakness in the modern world. They blamed Ottoman reverses on a lack of true piety, and the emergence of religious heresies right in the heart of the Dar ul Islam itself. The answer, these critics argued, was more Islam.[106] For this reason the eighteenth-century central Arabian preacher Muhammad ibn Abdul Wahhab (1703–92) called for an Islamic reformation, a return to the uncorrupted principles of medieval Islam. By the end of the century he had joined forces with the local tribal chief Muhammad ibn Saud, and raised most of the Arabian peninsula in revolt against the Ottomans. The religious radicalization of the Arab world, in other words, began in central Europe, before the walls of Vienna.

If domestic reform was one way of increasing external power, overseas expansion was another. Its most obvious, but increasingly marginal, benefit was straightforward resource extraction. Spain, in particular, had long funded much of her military effort with Central and South American bullion. Most other powers, however, derived more indirect advantages. Both Britain and France, for example, saw peacetime colonial trade and fisheries as a vital method of training seamen for naval service in war. More broadly, all colonial powers saw overseas trade, and indeed commerce generally, as an integral element of state power. 'If we can make commerce flourish,' the French political theorist and diplomat the Abbé de Saint-Pierre remarked, to the approval of Cardinal André-Hercule de Fleury, the French chief minister, 'we shall have as many troops as we want; if we allow commerce to languish, we shall have fewer soldiers, and less money wherewith to pay for their keep'. In Britain, such statements were routine from the late seventeenth century onwards. Not everybody was persuaded of this, however, especially in northern and eastern Europe, where interest in colonial enterprises remained low. Thus Frederick William sold Prussia's West African territory of Gross Friedrichsburg (in today's Ghana) to the Dutch because he had 'always regarded this trading nonsense as a chimera'.[107]

Austria had lost heavily during the War of the Polish Succession, but her humiliation was by no means complete. Russia's military support in Germany and her acceptance of the Pragmatic Sanction had come at a heavy price. Russia now expected Austria to support or at least to tolerate her southward expansion against the Ottomans. Russian war aims included the capture of the entire northern coast of the Black Sea, the annexation of the Crimea and the occupation of Moldavia and Wallachia. These were only to be the first steps, however. The crowning achievement would be a great push south culminating in the capture of Constantinople itself. As the author of this three-year plan, Field Marshal Münnich, put it in 1736, 'The Czarina will be crowned Empress of the Greeks in the oldest Greek church, in the renowned cathedral of Santa Sophia, and will bring peace – to whom? . . . to the whole world . . . Who will then question whether the Imperial title belongs to him who is crowned in Frankfurt, or to her who is crowned and anointed in Stamboul?' Russia's drive south, in other words, was intended in large part to create an alternative imperial legitimacy to that conferred by the Holy Roman Empire.[108]

Things did not turn out as either Austria or Russia intended. In April 1736, the Russians attacked Turkey, with the Habsburgs following suit in the following year. Instead of collapsing under this assault, however, the Ottoman Empire fought back effectively. The Austro-Russian attack was seen off, the lands lost to the Habsburgs in 1717–18 were recovered, and the crucial line of fortresses from Azov to Belgrade was re-established in more or less the form it had had at the close of the previous century.[109] For the second time in ten years, Vienna had been comprehensively humiliated. The roots of Habsburg weakness remained in the far-flung nature of the monarchy's possessions, and her extraordinarily cumbersome administrative and decision-making arrangements, which often led to paralysis. 'The least business,' the British envoy to Vienna remarked in 1735, 'produces a referate [memorandum], a referate produces a conference, and were the town on fire, there must be a conference to deliberate if the fire must be put out and how.' Monarchical governments, in other words, could be highly consultative, and they were not necessarily more decisive than the representative systems they so disdained. In fact, as the eighteenth century wore on, it became clear that the increasing bureaucratization of the continental European states hampered effective decision-making, while parliamentary Britain remained capable of extraordinary clarity of vision, resilience and determined action.[110]

At the same time, the British system was vulnerable to surges of irrationality. Ministers found this to their cost when colonial and maritime disputes with Spain provoked an outburst of popular xenophobia and belligerence in the 1730s. The case of a British seaman called Jenkins, who had had his ear cut off by the Spanish *guarda costas* on the high seas, brought matters to a head. Critics inside and outside parliament coupled their strategic demands with a call for broader political participation to counter the 'corruption' and weakness of the court and ministry. The opposition Whig MP William Pulteney claimed the right of parliament – 'His Majesty's great and chief council' – to scrutinize all diplomatic correspondence. A compromise treaty with Spain collapsed in a welter of public, pamphlet and parliamentary derision. In November 1739, Britain launched into the 'War of Jenkins' Ear' in the expectation of emulating the exploits of Sir Francis Drake, by pillaging Spanish shipping and despoiling her colonies; the more optimistic voices even hoped, as one influential peer put it, that intervention would 'enable [local populations] to throw off the yoke of Spain'.[111]

Sceptics doubted that Spain would roll over quite so quickly.[112] 'They are ringing the bells now,' the prime minister, Robert Walpole, warned, 'very soon they will be wringing their hands.'[113] So it proved: after some swift victories, including the spectacular capture of Portobello, British forces were soon bogged down in front of the Colombian fortress of Cartagena.[114]

Britain's intense naval and colonial preoccupation came at great cost to her position in Europe and the standing of the administration at home. France was now rampant on the continent, concluding a subsidy treaty with Sweden and even effecting a rapprochement with the bruised Habsburgs. In December 1738 plans for a Franco-Spanish double marriage were announced; at around the same time, the king and his ministers were rattled by a Prussian threat to Hanover. Most seriously of all, with their European flank secure, the French now began to think about concentrating attention and resources to deal with Britain at sea. London was acutely aware of this danger. 'If there is no diversion by a land war upon the continent and we have no security against invasion from France besides our own strength,' the British statesman Horace Walpole warned, 'I am afraid that by next spring or summer, the seat of the war will be in this island.'[115] The link between the European balance and the naval security of England was thus very clear to contemporaries.

As the decade closed, the future of Germany remained the unresolved major issue in London, in Versailles and across central Europe. Throughout 1738–9, Cardinal Fleury and other ministers repeatedly averred that maintaining their position in the Empire was the key to French security. Settling the Austrian succession in France's favour was thus as crucial to Fleury as the preservation of the entire Habsburg inheritance was to Britain. In order to make sure that the Habsburgs would never again pose a threat on France's eastern flank, the cardinal now planned to uncouple them from the imperial crown. This would prevent Vienna from concentrating the resources of Germany against the Bourbons. There was an urgency about this, because Versailles feared that if Maria Theresa's husband, Francis Stephen, became emperor, he would use his position to recover his lost Duchy of Lorraine. So when Charles VI finally died in October 1740, France was content to allow Maria Theresa to succeed him unopposed as ruler of the Austrian lands – leaving the other claimants with little choice but to follow suit. The real issue was who would succeed him as Holy Roman Emperor. It was thus clear, as 1740 drew to a close, that the struggle for mastery in Germany was about to enter a fresh and dramatic phase.

What nobody foresaw was that a dynamic new element was about to enter the equation: the Prussia of Frederick II.[116] The young king had succeeded Frederick William in 1740, and was widely believed to be a sensitive soul who had suffered at the hands of his brutish father. In fact, Frederick was determined to make a name for himself as a great commander and statesman on the European stage, not out of mere vanity, but as part of a calculated plan to rally the 'public' behind the monarchy through the pursuit of a glorious foreign policy. This was a new departure in Prussia, where his father had been so suspicious of the press that he had briefly banned all Berlin papers on his accession in 1713. For a long time the Prussian public sphere consisted of little more than the *Berliner Privilegierte Zeitung*, founded in 1722, which enjoyed, as its name suggested, a state-sanctioned monopoly. When Frederick ascended the throne, he encouraged the public sphere, albeit a highly controlled one, from the start: the *Haudesche Zeitung* was founded in 1740, the shortlived *Journal de Berlin ou nouvelles politiques et littéraires* first appeared that year, and 1742 saw the arrival of the *Spectateur en Allemagne*, edited by one of his confidants, Charles-Étienne Jordan. Most of all, however, Frederick was looking to make his mark among the broader German public in support of his ambitions in the Empire, and the quest for Prussian security.

Frederick's first priority was to address the Achilles heel of the monarchy: its geographic fragmentation. 'The worst thing,' he later remarked in his *History of my own times*, 'was the irregular shape of the state. Narrow and dispersed provinces stretched from Kurland [in the east] to Brabant [in the west]. As a result of this fragmentation (*Zerrissenheit*), the state had many neighbours but no inner strength and was exposed to far more enemies than if it had been rounded off more effectively.' It was clear to Frederick that simply working within the system of the Holy Roman Empire, as his predecessors had done, would only effect incremental improvements in Prussia's position. In this context, the disputed Austrian succession represented both a threat and an opportunity. Prussia had a vague claim to the rich and populous Habsburg province of Silesia, which abutted his core lands of Brandenburg. On the other hand, there was a real danger that one of the other claimants to the Austrian succession, the Elector-King of Poland–Saxony, would wind up with Silesia as compensation. The resulting encirclement of Prussia was something that Frederick wished to prevent at all costs.[117] 'If we wait for Saxony and Bavaria to make the first move,' he warned in early November 1740, 'we will not be able to prevent the Saxons from expanding.'[118]

So, in December 1740, Frederick struck. He invaded Silesia without warning and quickly occupied most of the province. Frederick had indeed chosen his moment brilliantly. Austria's traditional ally Britain was tied down in its costly colonial war with Spain. Her other backer, Russia, was in the throes of a succession struggle, after the death of the tsarina, Anne, in November 1740. Moreover, the Empire was preparing to decide who should succeed Charles as emperor, the Habsburg candidate, Francis Stephen, or the French-sponsored Charles Albert, Elector of Bavaria. These developments greatly facilitated Frederick's coup, but the invasion in turn set free the destructive forces which had been gestating in the Empire and across Europe throughout the previous decade.

Now all the solemn guarantees of the Pragmatic Sanction were set aside as the French, Saxons, Bavarians, Spaniards and others piled in to take advantage of what they believed to be the defenceless condition of Maria Theresa. In May 1741 Spain promised financial support for Charles Albert's imperial ambitions, in return for imperial recognition of her gains in Italy at Austrian expense. A month later, the French concluded a defensive alliance with Frederick. They agreed to his annexation of Lower Silesia and Breslau; in return, Frederick promised his electoral vote to Charles Albert in the forthcoming imperial election. In September, the Saxons attacked Maria Theresa, hoping to secure Silesia for themselves, and Charles Albert proclaimed himself King of Bohemia in December 1741. That winter, Spanish forces attacked the Habsburgs in northern Italy. And in January of the following year the imperial college of electors elected Charles Albert emperor. For the first time in many hundreds of years, a Habsburg was no longer at the head of the Holy Roman Empire of the German Nation.

The name given to this conflict, the 'War of the Austrian Succession', is thus a misnomer. It was really a 'War of the Imperial Succession': not just Austria but Germany was in contention. Britain feared that the succession of Charles Albert would – as the Duke of Newcastle, Secretary of State for the Southern Department warned – 'end in flinging the whole Empire into the hands of France'. This threatened not only to destroy the European balance, but also to unhinge the vital 'barrier' in the Low Countries on which the security of Britain and the United Provinces depended. In 1742, therefore, British troops were sent to Germany and the Low Countries, where they were joined by a Dutch corps in 1743. At the same time, the Royal Navy was sent into the Mediterranean to deter Spain, and in August 1742 a squadron appeared before Don Carlos's palace at Naples, compelling him to withdraw his troops from northern Italy or else face the destruction of his capital. Nor did Maria Theresa stand by quietly while her inheritance was partitioned. Despite early setbacks against Frederick, she mobilized a large army, and in January 1742 Piedmont weighed in on the Austrian side in northern Italy. A year later, an Anglo-imperial army crushed the French at Dettingen. The Bavarians, too, were soon in full retreat. The Habsburg monarchy had weathered the challenge.[119]

France now stepped up the pressure on Britain and Austria by concluding the Second Family Compact with Spain in October 1743. This stipulated cooperation between the two powers to instal the Spanish king's son by his second marriage, Don Philip, in Milan, Parma and Piacenza; joint action against Britain overseas; and the recovery by Spain of Minorca and Gibraltar. In the spring of 1744, Louis finally declared war openly on Britain and Maria Theresa. Shortly afterwards, French armies crashed into the Austrian Netherlands, driving allied forces – and the Dutch barrier garrisons – before them. An Austrian invasion of southern Italy was stopped by Spanish and Neapolitan forces in August 1744. In 1745, the French sponsored an invasion of Britain by Charles Edward Stuart, son of the Jacobite Pretender to the throne, designed if possible to knock London out of the war, but at the very least to distract her from the principal theatre of operations in Europe. It was only repelled with extreme difficulty. That same year, a joint operation by the Royal Navy and American colonial militia captured the key French fortress of Louisburg off the Canadian coast, while in May 1745 allied forces in the Low Countries were thrashed by the French at the battle of Fontenoy, not least thanks to the heroism of the 'Irish Brigade' of Jacobite exiles.

Amid this chaos, Frederick played his cards wisely. After defeating the Austrian armies at Mollwitz, he agreed to a British-mediated truce with Austria at Klein-Schnellendorf in October 1741, and subsequently concluded the Peace of Berlin in July 1742 with Maria Theresa, which left him in possession of Lower Silesia. 'One has to have the ability to stop at the right time,' he remarked. 'To force one's good fortune is to lose it, and to demand more and more is to sacrifice contentment.' His main task now, Frederick continued, was 'to acclimatize the cabinets of Europe to seeing us in the state which this war has accorded us, and a measure of moderation and equanimity will assist us in this goal. It is my hope that we would assert our position at the height of our rise to power with dignity.' The Austrian military resurgence, however, forced Frederick to re-engage in Germany. In May 1744, he combined with embattled Bavaria, the Palatinate and Hesse-Kassel to form the Frankfurt Union against Austria. In August of that year, Frederick rejoined the war by attacking Bohemia to establish a buffer zone between himself and the Austrians.[120]

The multiple threats facing the Habsburg monarchy in 1740–44 – principally in the Low Countries, Germany and Italy – forced Austria to prioritize. Her most radical strategic thinker, Wenzel Anton Count Kaunitz, then ambassador to Savoy, recommended concentrating on the Empire. By January 1744, he was advising Vienna to stop chasing Italian chimeras and to take 'care of affairs in Germany' instead. The main threat now was Prussia, so Austria's territorial aims should be the recovery of Silesia or perhaps an exchange of Bavaria for some of her more outlying territories. At one level, Kaunitz's emphasis on Germany was technical, almost 'algebraic'. It was geographically closer than Italy or Flanders, and its potential resources much greater. Yet his thinking also had a strong ideological component. The German national cause was still vibrant, and in promising to defend the Empire against threats from within – namely Prussia – and without – namely France – the Austrians could lay claim to a higher legitimacy. Austrian-sponsored pamphlets therefore demanded the recovery of 'German' Alsace from France, and generally appealed for a German patriotic response to the hereditary enemy. The Habsburg commander, Francis Stephen, became a German hero, not least on account of his lost – and formerly imperial – patrimony of Lorraine.

In November 1744, Prussian troops had been ejected from Bohemia. Two months later, in early 1745, Charles Albert of Bavaria fortuitously died, paving the way for the election of Francis Stephen as emperor.

Habsburg control over the imperial crown was re-established. That same month, Maria Theresa concluded the Treaty of Warsaw with Britain, the Saxons and the Dutch against Prussia. Military success, however, eluded her and after defeats at Frederick's hands at Soor and Hohenfriedberg in 1745 Austria was finally forced to cede Silesia to Prussia at the Treaty of Dresden. The necessary Habsburg focus on central Europe compelled them to neglect their traditional duties towards the 'barrier' in the Low Countries. Here the Anglo-Hanoverian army, and a half-hearted Dutch contingent, struggled to hold back the French advance. By February 1746, Brussels had fallen and it was becoming increasingly clear that the French tide would soon sweep into the United Provinces. Not since the time of Louis XIV had Dutch and British security been so imperilled.

All this had a powerful impact on the internal politics of the powers. In France, the successes of the 1740s bolstered the standing of the monarchy and helped to increase social cohesion. Underpinning this was a national consensus about the British danger and the even greater threat of Habsburg 'despotism'. The defeat of the allied army at Fontenoy therefore produced mass jubilation and, as Napoleon later remarked, gave the *ancien régime* 'another forty years'. This was because, as the Marquis d'Argenson wrote to the philosopher Voltaire just after the battle, 'The people can find happiness if only they can maintain the hegemony of France, for she is indeed in a position to dictate conditions, fair conditions, to Europe.' The unspoken corollary of this, of course, was that failure to sustain this position would make the French people extremely unhappy indeed.

In many other parts of Europe, by contrast, the war set off a series of domestic transformations. Maria Theresa was forced to make further concessions to the Hungarian nobility in order to keep them committed to the war effort. Wherever possible, however, she sought to limit the power of the estates, to centralize administration, increase taxation and recruitment, and generally mobilize the resources needed for the recovery of Silesia.[121] Her chief minister, Count Haugwitz, was less successful than she had hoped, but he still succeeded in raising much greater sums and armies than hitherto. Maria Theresa also embarked on a search for scapegoats, accusing the Bohemian nobility and the Jews of collaborating with the Prussians. She therefore ordered the expulsion of the Prague

Jews as a potential fifth column in 1744. This provoked the first general mobilization of trans-state Jewish opinion, producing a flood of petitions and protests from merchants and communities across Europe directed not only at the empress herself, but at the powers capable of influencing her. 'The case concerns the whole religious community of Jews,' the community in Hamburg argued, 'the scattered lambs. And one has always likened Israel to a herd of sheep. If one lamb is struck, it is felt by all lambs.' The empress's British ally did in fact intervene on their behalf, with the Secretary of State, Lord Harrington, condemning the expulsions to her ambassador as 'detrimental and prejudicial to the true interest of the common cause' against France. These pleas initially fell on deaf ears, but Maria Theresa soon relented and the Jews ultimately returned home. Europe had experienced its first – albeit only partially successful – humanitarian intervention on behalf of a non-Christian grouping.[122]

The war also had considerable consequences in Britain. Throughout the 1730s, popular and parliamentary opposition had been building to Walpole's policy of appeasement. Failures in the overseas war against Spain seriously damaged his administration, but it was the mismanagement of the European balance of power which proved fatal. In February 1741, parliament debated a 'Motion for the removal of Sir Robert Walpole', which charged that 'during the course of [his] administration, the balance of power in Europe has been destroyed; the House of Bourbon has been aggrandized . . . [and] the House of Austria has been depressed'. Over the course of the next two years, Walpole was battered by a series of such attacks, many of them designed not merely to depose him, but to pave the way for his impeachment, possible imprisonment and even execution. Once the imperial crown had fallen to the French-sponsored Charles Albert, Walpole's position became untenable and in March 1742 he resigned, only escaping an official enquiry and likely legal sanction by a tiny margin of votes. His successor, Lord Carteret, also fell over German policy, partly because of controversial payments made to Hanoverian troops in British service and partly for his failure to contain Frederick.[123]

In the Dutch Republic, the war was to have even more dramatic internal consequences. Ever since the death of the last *Stadholder*, William of Orange, in 1702, the United Provinces had been governed by an oligarchy of regents and regional assemblies who were determined not to surrender any of their autonomy, even if the foreign-political situation required it. As the French advanced from the south, the Orangist faction increased their agitation for the restoration of the Stadholderate in order to revitalize the British alliance and mobilize the nation for the common defence. Dutch pamphleteers began to remind the public of the lynching of the de Witt brothers in 1672 as a punishment for failing to contain Louis XIV. By mid-April 1747, the issue could no longer be finessed: a large French force crossed the border into Dutch Flanders and looked set to overrun the entire Republic. The domestic implications of this move were clear. 'You're ruining us,' one leader of the 'States' party complained to the French ambassador, 'you're making a Stadholder.' There followed a British-backed coup – begun in Zealand under the guns of a Royal Navy squadron – with strong popular support. Anti-French gangs roamed through Dutch towns; paranoia gripped the nation. William IV was duly installed as a *Stadholder* and the office was strengthened by making it hereditary in the House of Orange.[124] Neither Britain's best efforts nor the restoration of the *Stadholder*, however, sufficed to halt the French advance in the Netherlands. The key fortress of Maastricht fell in May 1747, and it seemed likely that the whole Republic would soon be overwhelmed.[125]

In the end, what decided the outcome in Germany and the Low Countries was the rising power in the east.[126] Frederick's attack on Maria Theresa and the subsequent coalition against her had infuriated the Russians. Given the interregnum in St Petersburg, the chief minister, Münnich, felt he had no choice but to appease Frederick, and a Russo-Prussian treaty was signed in December 1740. It was not until December 1741 that Tsarina Elizabeth secured the undisputed succession. Her first priority was to shore up the empire's northern defences. In March 1742, the Russians made a public though unsuccessful appeal to the Finns to break with Sweden and form a 'barrier' to protect St Petersburg. By August 1743, Sweden was forced to come to terms at the Treaty of Abo (Turku). A year later, Russia secured advance recognition of her candidate's right of succession to the Swedish throne and even landed troops outside Stockholm to deter Danish intervention. Only now could Russia turn her attention to events in Germany. In 1746, she concluded an alliance with Austria, together with a secret clause envisaging the partition of Prussia. An Austro-Russian military convention followed in November 1747, on which footing a substantial Russian army was sent to Germany.

The tsarina's intervention proved to be decisive across Europe. It was fear of the impending rapprochement between Maria Theresa and the tsarina which had driven Frederick to peace with the empress in late 1745, even though he still had the upper hand militarily. The Russian army bearing down on Germany – 'the best troops in Europe', as the British diplomat Lord Sandwich called them – also concentrated French minds. They were already embattled on the high seas, where the Royal Navy had massacred their merchant shipping, and overseas. The home front groaned under bankruptcies, shortages and inflation. In late 1747, the Marquis de Stainville lamented that French 'trade in general had diminished by one hundred millions'. Sugar, coffee and cod were all in short supply. To the south-east, the Franco-Italian armies had been expelled from Italy by 1746. Moreover, even the success of French arms in the Netherlands was a mixed blessing, because it alarmed much of the rest of Europe. And what use would the occupation of the entire Low Countries be, if the combined Austro-Russian forces flooded into France from the east? At the height of her military glory on land, therefore, France reluctantly agreed to make peace. For the second time in less than ten years and on both occasions without firing a shot in anger, Russian troops had acted as the arbiters of central and western Europe.[127]

In 1748, the Treaty of Aix-la-Chapelle brought the War of the Austrian Succession to an end. France withdrew from the Low Countries in exchange for the return of Louisburg, thus demonstrating the continuing centrality of Europe to British grand strategy. Maria Theresa managed to keep her husband on the imperial throne, and most of her territories intact. She failed, however, to recover Silesia, which remained in Prussian hands as a symbol of Frederick's new diplomatic standing. Austria was also compelled to surrender Parma, Piacenza and Guastalla, but maintained her grip on northern Italy. France grumbled, with the public using the phrase '*bête comme la paix*' as a regular term of abuse, and the first serious attacks on *ancien régime* foreign policy began, albeit still limited to peripheral issues such as the failure to support the Stuart Pretender more effectively against the Anglo-Hanoverians.[128] This made it all the more important to ensure that France emerged victorious from the next round with Britain.

*

In the hundred years or so since the Treaty of Westphalia, European geopolitics had been dominated by the imperial succession. Germany remained the principal concern of all the major powers. For Britain and the Dutch, the main focus was on maintaining the bulwarks which supported the 'barrier' in the Low Countries against France, and on preventing the French from dominating the Holy Roman Empire. For the Austrians, the Empire was their principal source of legitimacy and power. The French, for their part, sought to prevent Germany from being used as a base from which to threaten their eastern border, or being rallied behind a hostile power, especially the Habsburgs. Likewise, the two newcomers, Russia and Prussia, saw the Holy Roman Empire as the main area of international contention. These rivalries drove an intense colonial competition to gain resources and standing in the New World which could be leveraged in Europe. The Germans themselves, who lay at the heart of the system, had tamed their confessional divide and now coexisted in a geopolitical panopticon in which the members of the Holy Roman Empire and its guarantor powers exerted strong normative pressure for compliance with civilized rules of behaviour between *and within* territories. On the other hand, the Germans constantly sought but never found the collective voice which would turn them from objects into subjects.

By the middle of the century, the winners and losers were clear. Turkey never recovered from its defeat before the walls of Vienna; the Swedes proved unable to bounce back after Poltava, and the Dutch were in the grips of slow but inexorable decline. All three powers remained important for a long time, but we take our leave of them as major players in the struggle for mastery in central Europe. As with the Poles, the great powers now become concerned not with their strength, but with their weakness. The Habsburg monarchy had experienced some painful territorial surgery, but it remained largely intact and determined to wreak vengeance on its despoliators. The great beneficiaries were the rising powers of the east: Prussia, which had walked off with Silesia, and Russia, which had begun a seemingly unstoppable advance westwards. France, by contrast, had recovered from her defeat in the War of the Spanish Succession, but had failed to unbolt the Habsburgs from the imperial crown. Britain, for her part, had constructed an elaborate European security architecture to defend the overall balance and her south coast, but the decline of Dutch power threatened to undermine it. In short, the two central conflicts at the core of the system remained unresolved: the old Anglo-French struggle, the Second Hundred Years War spanning the continents, but centred on Germany, and the new Hohenzollern–Habsburg struggle for mastery, again centred on the Holy Roman Empire. These two struggles were about to merge in a clash which was to have revolutionary consequences for the whole state system.

3
Revolutions, 1756–1813

We are, [what] we have been for centuries; a puzzle of a political constitution, a prey of our neighbours, and object of their scorn outstanding in the history of the world, disunited among ourselves, weak from our divisions, strong enough to harm ourselves, powerless to save ourselves, insensitive to the honour of our name, indifferent to the glory of our laws . . . a great but also a despised people, a potentially happy but actually a very lamentable people.

Friedrich Carl von Moser, Imperial
German Privy Councillor, 1766[1]

The history of Germany is a history of wars between the emperor and the princes and states; of wars among the princes and states themselves; of the licentiousness of the strong, and the oppression of the weak; of foreign intrusions, and foreign intrigues; of requisitions of men and money disregarded, or partially complied with; of attempts to enforce them, altogether abortive, or attended with slaughter and desolation, involving the innocent with the guilty; of general imbecility, confusion, and misery.

James Madison and Alexander Hamilton,
Federalist Paper 19, 1787

We can see that the abrogation of this treaty [between Austria and France of 1756] is a revolution as necessary in foreign affairs, both for Europe and for France, as the destruction of the Bastille has been for our internal regeneration. Bravo! Bravo! Enthusiastic applause from the assembly and from the public galleries.

Pierre Vergniaud, speech to the French National Assembly, 1792[2]

In the mid-1750s, Europe was rocked by the 'Diplomatic Revolution' which saw the two arch-enemies, Bourbon France and Habsburg Austria – and later Russia – combine against Prussia and Great Britain. The resulting Seven Years War (1756–63) confirmed Prussia's rise to great-power status, ensured Britain's colonial supremacy, and inaugurated an irresistible surge of Russian expansionism which was to transform the politics of eastern and central Europe over the next decades. America was won in Germany; fighting on two fronts proved fatal to the Bourbons. By the later eighteenth century, all the major European powers were to be found in, or intimately involved in, the Holy Roman Empire: France and Russia as guarantors by virtue of the treaties of Westphalia and Teschen, Austria and Prussia as the largest states in the Empire, and Britain through the Hanoverian dynastic link as well as her role as guardian of the Low Countries, and its German hinterland. Below the surface, moreover, the Seven Years War laid two charges which detonated with spectacular effect in the last quarter of the century. For it was then that the first attempt to organize the thirteen colonies for war and expansion was made, and when the North Americans first began to think about taking their security into their own hands. This process, accentuated by Britain's neglect of her European position, especially in Germany, led directly to the creation of the United States of America. It was during the Seven Years War, too, that Frenchmen began the long national debate on Bourbon grand strategy, and the domestic arrangements necessary to support their great-power ambitions, which culminated in the Revolution of 1789. All this resulted in new geopolitical, constitutional and ideological fault-lines in Europe and across the Atlantic, as states canvassed different models of internal organization in order to make themselves more competitive on the international stage. *Reich* now contended with Republic; Empire against Union. The focal point of this struggle remained Germany and the Low Countries. Whoever controlled that space would dominate the continent and thus the world.

*

France was at a crossroads. If her policy had been firmly anti-Habsburg for hundreds of years, the main enemy was now Britain, whose colonial dominance was believed to give her the edge. The Marquis de La Galissonière, the Governor-General of Canada, warned in December 1750 that the resources Britain could draw from America 'to the exclusion of other nations, would most certainly give them superiority in Europe', especially in Germany and Flanders.[3] There was also growing concern at Versailles about Frederick the Great's Prussia. The German expert Louis-Augustin Blondel cautioned in January 1751 that a Prusso-British alliance – which was being avidly sought by London – would pose a mortal threat to the Empire and thus to French interests in Germany. 'The imperial constitution,' he wrote, 'is the basis of the grandeur of the King [of France] and secures the monarchy along the Rhine. The large number of small states, who have so many differing interests, ensures that the power of this mighty empire is never concentrated in one hand.'[4] There was also an increasing anxiety about the growth of Russian power, which had twice intervened decisively against France in Germany in the recent past. Hitherto the '*barrière de l'est*' – the alliances with Sweden, Poland and the Ottoman Empire – had largely served to contain Austria. Henceforth, they were designed, as the Count de Broglie later remarked, to push Russia 'back into her vast deserts and relegat[e] her to affairs outside the limits of [central] Europe'.[5]

Meanwhile, the Habsburgs and the Russians debated how to deal with Frederick. As the principal Austrian negotiator at Aix-la-Chapelle, Count Kaunitz, pointed out in a groundbreaking memorandum of March 1749, the old alliance with Britain and the hereditary enmity with France were now both redundant. Instead, he proposed an alliance with France, or at least an accommodation which would give Austria a free hand to deal with Frederick in Germany. St Petersburg, which had traditionally regarded Prussia as a subordinate power, was furious with Frederick for upsetting the balance in the Empire through the unilateral acquisition of Silesia. He was also seen as a threat to Russia's position in the north; in May 1747, the Prussian king concluded a defensive alliance with Sweden, and when Stockholm opened negotiations with the Porte, the threat of encirclement could no longer be ignored. So in April 1753 the Russians decided to curb Prussia through diplomatic means if possible and military action if necessary.

Britain, too, was undergoing a fundamental strategic rethink. The experience of the late 1740s had shown that the traditional pillars of her continental policy were in a state of terminal disrepair. The Dutch were too weak to defend the crucial barrier fortresses in the Low Countries, and the Habsburgs had suffered such heavy territorial losses in the 1730s and 1740s that their capacity to do so was also in doubt. Moreover, the French surge in America threatened Britain's maritime power and her European position. The thirteen colonies were a source of trading revenue, trained seamen and potentially also of naval stores. 'If we lose our American possessions or the influence and weight of them in time of peace,' Newcastle warned in 1750, 'France will, with great ease, make war with us whenever they please hereafter.'[6] Faced with these new realities, a substantial element of the British public sphere – pamphleteers as well as parliamentarians – demanded a vigorous 'blue water' policy, which eschewed costly continental commitments. The Whig administration, however, believed the key to containing France remained the Holy Roman Empire. A crucial strategic lesson of the War of the Austrian Succession had been the fatal results of allowing the alienation of the imperial crown from the Habsburgs. London therefore attempted to persuade the German electors to anoint Maria Theresa's son Joseph 'King of the Romans', thus ensuring his automatic succession to the imperial crown after the death of Francis Stephen. The resulting 'Imperial Election Scheme' dominated British foreign policy throughout the early 1750s.[7] It was an exercise in strategic pre-emption.

Across the Atlantic, the rising tension hastened the development of a lively American public sphere in which the colonists became more and more aware of their common identity and security interests.[8] Just like the British government, the settlers saw the colonial contest within the broader framework of the European struggle. The Bostonian William Douglass described the French as 'the common nuisance and disturbers of Europe, [who] will in a short time become the same in America, if not mutilated at home, and in America fenced off from us by ditches and walls, that is; by great rivers and impracticable mountains'.[9] Many colonists therefore demanded that Britain go on the offensive to eliminate the Bourbon threat once and for all by destroying Quebec and breaking out of the Bourbon encirclement through expansion. In his 1751 *Observations concerning the increase of mankind*, Benjamin Franklin argued new colonies to the west would save the existing settlements from being bottled up along the coast and provide the living space they so desperately needed. Thus Franklin praised 'the prince that acquires new territory, if he finds it vacant, or removes the natives to give his own people room'.[10]

The reality, however, was that the colonists were ill-equipped even to deal with the Franco-Indian threat on their own. They lacked a common purpose and vision. 'At present,' Franklin lamented, 'we are like the separate filaments of flax before the thread is formed, without strength, because without connection; but union would make us strong, and even formidable.'[11] This was illustrated in 1754, when the British summoned a Congress, which met at Albany in the colony of New York to discuss inter-colonial defence cooperation against the French and Indians. They proposed that individual colonies should no longer deal *ad hoc* and autonomously with the Indians, but pool resources and coordinate efforts instead. The meeting was a fiasco. All of the colonies present rejected the plan, even those, such as Pennsylvania, who had the most to lose from continued disunity. Governor Shirley of Massachusetts observed that the assemblies 'don't like the plan concerted by the Commissioners at Albany which all of 'em conceive to infringe upon their colony-liberties & privileges.'[12]

Throughout the early 1750s, the noose tightened around Britain and Prussia. At the Treaty of Aranjuez in 1752, the French, Spanish and Austrians agreed to bury the hatchet in Italy, leaving all three powers free to concentrate against London or Potsdam. Britain's Imperial Election Scheme petered out, not least because the Austrians did not want to alienate France. General Braddock's expedition of regulars and colonial militia was slaughtered by French-backed Indians on the Monongahela in 1755.[13] In May 1756, the Dutch declared themselves neutral, another blow to the 'Old System'. To the south, the Saxons were on the verge of declaring for Austria. They had long seen the Prussians as an irritating wedge between themselves and their Polish kingdom. Most worrying of all, the growing Austro-French rapprochement culminated in the Treaty of Versailles between the two powers in May 1756. This was truly a Diplomatic Revolution, which overturned more than two centuries of Habsburg–Bourbon/Valois enmity. It had radical implications for the balance of the Holy Roman Empire. For Frederick, a nightmare scenario now loomed in which Prussia would lose Silesia to Austria, Pomerania to Sweden, Magdeburg and perhaps more to Saxony, and East Prussia either to Poland (in return for the latter's ceding eastern lands to St Petersburg) or to Russia outright. Privately, Kaunitz looked forward to the '*destruction totale*' of Prussia.

Frederick's best chance of survival in this environment lay in an integrated domestic and foreign policy. 'I have seen small states able to maintain themselves against the greatest monarchies,' Frederick wrote, 'when the states possessed industry and great order in their affairs.'[14] The cantonal system provided a reliable stream of peasant recruits and aristocratic officers; in return the king regarded it as 'his duty to protect the nobility, who form the finest jewel in his crown and the lustre of his army'.[15] An efficient administration extracted ever more resources from the population: in the course of Frederick's reign the tax yield increased by a factor of three, of which some 83 per cent was spent on defence even in the peacetime years of 1745–56. Frederick also conciliated potential religious dissidents: he reached out to Catholics, especially those in strategically vital Silesia. The key for Frederick, however, was Germany. It was vital to prevent the Habsburgs from exploiting the imperial crown to mobilize the empire against him. 'From the time of Ferdinand I,' he wrote, 'the principles of the House of Austria tended to the establishment of despotism in Germany.' For this reason, the 'liberties of the Germanic body', that is, a balance between the emperor and the estates, had to be maintained.[16] Frederick also believed that the equilibrium within the Empire was the basis on which that of Europe as a whole rested. He was convinced that if the Habsburgs managed to overturn that balance, they would ultimately dominate the whole of Europe and thus eclipse Prussia. But the Prussian king failed to win substantial allies inside or outside Germany, with the exception of Britain, which was promised the defence of Hanover in return for subsidies at the Convention of Westminster in January 1756. Instead, paradoxically, Frederick's own actions were to enable Vienna to deploy the machinery of the Empire against him.

As open war in Europe and America drew closer in 1755–6, Britain and Prussia took pre-emptive action. London authorized ever more ruthless measures against internal security threats. In the Scottish Highlands, in a process which came to be known as the 'clearances', smallholders were encouraged or forced to emigrate, partly to allow more economic use of the land, but mainly to suppress Jacobitism and deny the French a local ally. Similarly, the French-speaking and Catholic Acadian population of Nova Scotia had long been a thorn in the side of the British government. In 1755, this nettle was grasped. Much of the troublesome Acadian population – about 7,000 of them – were deported to the thirteen colonies and dispersed, principally in Massachusetts, Virginia and Maryland, and ultimately to Louisiana. They now no longer posed a serious threat. In both cases, the British state had solved a pressing strategic problem through what would today be described as 'ethnic cleansing'.[17]

Frederick also resorted to drastic measures. After the Diplomatic Revolution he became increasingly concerned by the attitude of Saxony, that 'dagger pointed at Brandenburg's heart'.[18] His informant in the Saxon foreign office told him that the elector was just waiting for the opportune moment to throw off the mask and attack Prussia in conjunction with Maria Theresa, Louis and the tsarina. The Russians had wanted to strike at once, but the Austrians asked them to wait until the following year. Frederick decided to move first. In August 1756, he invaded Saxony and quickly overran the entire Electorate. Almost the first thing he did was to ransack the archive in the capital, Dresden, in order to find incriminating documents to justify his pre-emptive strike. These were published with great fanfare that same year, together with Frederick's claim that 'whoever anticipates a secretly planned attack, is perhaps engaged in hostilities, but is not the aggressor'.[19] The audience Frederick was addressing here was German: he was trying to dissuade the imperial Diet from issuing a banishment order against him for violating Saxon territory. He succeeded in averting the forfeiture of his lands, but failed to prevent the *Reichstag* from declaring war against him in January 1757. An imperial army was mobilized at a leisurely pace and sent to join the French.

The resulting conflict came to be known as the Seven Years War.[20] At first, things went badly for both Britain and Prussia. In the summer of 1756, a French force occupied Minorca, shrugging aside a British relief force commanded by Admiral Byng. To make the humiliation complete, Britain was rocked by an invasion scare at the end of the year and was compelled to hire Hanoverian mercenaries to defend the south coast. Things were only marginally better in 1757: there were further disasters in America while an expeditionary force sent to defend Hanover under the Duke of Cumberland got the worst of a brief battle with the French and promptly capitulated at the Convention of Kloster-Zeven. Prussia, for her part, soon got bogged down against the Austrians in Bohemia, suffering a stinging reverse at Kolin in June 1757. To the west, France committed herself by the Second Treaty of Versailles in May 1757 to maintain an army of 100,000 men in Germany against Frederick, and to pay subsidies to Austria until she had recovered Silesia. In the east, the Russians captured Memel and in late August 1757 won an important engagement at Grossjägerndorf. To the north, the Swedes advanced into Pomerania four months later. Frederick was completely encircled. It was only the king's military skill that enabled him to carry the day at Rossbach in November 1757, when the Franco-imperial army was resoundingly beaten. The German Imperial Army or *Reichsexecutionsarmee* – cruelly nicknamed the *Reissausarmee*, the 'army that bolts' – became the butt of universal derision; its commander announced that he would rather be 'shot' than lead it into action again.[21] Not long after, Frederick thrashed the Austrians at the battle of Leuthen. At around the same time, Britain repudiated the Convention of Kloster-Zeven, and began to fund a large army of British, Hanoverian and other German levies to defend north Germany against the French. By early 1758, its commander, Duke Ferdinand of Brunswick, had the French on the run.

The fortunes of war had major domestic political consequences across Europe. In Britain, the defeats of 1756–7 triggered a moral and political panic. In a widely read tract, the Reverend John Brown even attributed Britain's humiliation in Europe to a 'vain, luxurious and selfish EFFEMINACY'.[22] The road to salvation was a thoroughgoing moral regeneration, and the creation of a truly inclusive national militia to give expression to the new manly spirit. This military commitment was then parlayed into a claim for greater (male) political participation. 'Every subject, every Man,' William Williams sermonized in 1757, 'is a soldier.'[23] The Militia Bill of 1757 reflected this thinking. There was also an increasing sense that the state should take a closer interest in the medical welfare of scarce manpower, which suffered badly from disease in the campaigns overseas and 'rott[ed] piecemeal in the wilds of Germany'.[24] In France, the catastrophe at Rossbach – which Voltaire described as a humiliation worse than those of the Hundred Years War[25] – sparked a sense of national malaise about the 'corruption' of the nation through 'luxury' and neglect of manly tilling of the soil for 'effeminate' foppery.[26]

The most immediate impact of the war, however, was on high politics and grand strategy. France was shocked by news of the disaster at Rossbach – the monarchy's greatest military disaster since Blenheim.

The chief minister, Cardinal de Bernis, never really recovered from this blow to the nation's standing and his own reputation. 'The troops were totally undisciplined,' he later wrote. 'Treachery and incompetence were the orders of the day. Generals and nation were completely demoralized.'[27] Bernis fell from power within a year. In London, the early defeats led to the formation of a new government led by the opposition stalwart, William Pitt. The war also exacerbated longstanding divisions between the Whigs, who continued to favour a strategy based on military and diplomatic engagement in Europe, and the Tories, who wanted to abandon 'continental entanglements' and concentrate on beating France in the colonies and at sea. William Pitt managed to square these strategic circles. He invested heavily in both the 'German' and the overseas theatres, but he concentrated his main effort in the Empire, hoping to tie down French resources in Europe in order to press Britain's advantage overseas.[28] In 1759, Pitt's approach was vindicated in the 'year of victories'. The important French sugar island of Guadeloupe was captured in July; an Anglo-German force worsted the French at Minden in Westphalia at the beginning of August; later that month a French squadron was defeated in the Bay of Lagos; and in mid-September General Wolfe's army captured Quebec. 'Had the armies of France not been employed in Germany,' Pitt argued, 'they would have been transported to America . . . America [was] conquered in Germany.'[29] In other words, Britain's overseas empire was secured through her operations in the Empire.

In France, by contrast, no such synthesis was ever achieved. Instead, the great national debate on grand strategy begun in 1756 was to dominate politics for the next thirty years. At the heart of it was the Austrian alliance contracted during the Diplomatic Revolution. This rapprochement flew in the face of French diplomatic tradition, and was traduced almost as soon as it was effected by Jean-Louis Favier in *Doutes et questions*, a polemic commissioned by the anti-Austrian faction at court. He accused the treaty's supporters of abandoning the longstanding Bourbon allies of Sweden, Turkey and Poland. Worst of all, Favier continued, allying with Russia and Austria cast down Prussia in order to raise up the hereditary Habsburg enemy in Germany, and allowed the Russians to penetrate still further into the Holy Roman Empire, a policy which was also heavily criticized by serving diplomats. All this was couched in the classic language of moral panic, in which the 'unnatural alliance' was attributed to the feminine machinations of the king's mistress, Madame de Pompadour. The fiasco at Rossbach seemed to vindicate these critics. Popular opinion, which had initially been agnostic on the Austrian treaty, now swung decisively against it. It devoured Favier's tract, and similar philippics, which now circulated throughout Paris in manuscript.[30]

The new French chief minister, the Duc de Choiseul, reduced French commitments in Germany in order to concentrate on fighting Britain overseas, with Spanish help, if possible. This new strategy proved unable to turn the tide, however. Montreal fell in 1760, and when Spain finally came into the war on the French side in 1762, the result was another list of colonial disasters. British expeditionary forces swiftly captured Manila and Havana. Frederick the Great, on the other hand, was driven to the verge of complete extinction. He suffered a series of serious defeats at the hands of the Habsburgs, the Austrians even briefly occupying Berlin in October 1760. The most existential threat, however, was posed by the Russians, who fought him to a standstill at Zorndorf in 1758, and in 1759 inflicted Frederick's most crushing defeat at Kunersdorf. Only a 'miracle', Frederick thought, could save him now and in February 1762 one came to pass in the death of the Tsarina Elizabeth. She was succeeded by the strongly Prussophile Peter III, who abandoned his Austro-French allies in May and in June 1762 even made a treaty of alliance with Frederick.

Frederick was unable to press his advantage, however, because in July 1762 Peter III was deposed, murdered and succeeded by his wife, Catherine. She repudiated the treaty with Prussia but signalled her intention to cease hostilities. Britain, too, was war-weary, anxious about French advances in Germany, and determined to bank her colonial gains. In May 1762, London abandoned Frederick, after the new king, George III, his ministry, the public and parliament had tired of the 'German War'. Faced with this consensus, an embittered Frederick finally agreed to sheathe the sword. So, in 1763, the Anglo-Bourbon colonial war was concluded at the Treaty of Paris and the German war at the Treaty of Hubertusburg. On land, Prussia retained Silesia without 'compensation' to Austria for her loss. Overseas, the French ceded Canada, retaining only a tiny foothold in the islands of Saint-Pierre and Miquelon, the African colony of Senegal, and a string of territories in the Caribbean, including Grenada and Saint-Vincent. Spain recovered

Havana and Manila, but surrendered Florida to Britain. In recompense, she received Louisiana from France, a territory much larger than the present-day state of that name. The global balance now shifted decisively in favour of Britain, thanks to the success of her policy in the Holy Roman Empire, while the European equilibrium, on which the whole system rested, now adjusted to take account of the rise of Russia and Prussia and the relative decline of Austria and France.

The Seven Years War sparked searching inquests in the defeated Bourbon–Habsburg coalition.[31] To the French chief minister, Choiseul, the catastrophe was attributable to the decision to fight both in Europe and overseas. Henceforth, he argued, France should pursue no more than a holding strategy on the continent, using the Austrian alliance to prevent Britain from creating a diversion in Germany, and concentrate all of her resources on the navy. Critics, on the other hand, claimed that the whole basis of French strategy after 1756 had been misconceived. In their eyes, Austria rather than Britain remained the principal enemy. Continuing the Habsburg alliance after 1763, they argued, not only suggested that the monarchy had learned nothing from the war, but also signalled that the withdrawal from eastern and central Europe, and most crucially from Germany, would continue. Many French diplomats feared that this strategy left the path free for the Russian advance westwards. St Petersburg, as one official put it, aimed to 'encourage anarchy in Poland with the object of subjugating it', to 'gain influence' in Germany and ultimately to 'advanc[e] her troops to the Rhine, followed immediately by a swarm of Asiatic hordes . . . and thus overrun Italy, Spain and France, some of whose inhabitants they will massacre, some of whom they will enslave to re-people the deserts of Siberia'.[32] Germany, on this reading, was France's rampart against eastern despotism. As far as Austria and Prussia were concerned, the veteran French diplomat and German expert Louis-Gabriel du Buat-Nançay warned that France should not side with one of the German powers, but maintain a balance between them to prevent the 'formation of a [united] German monarchy which would overturn the [whole] European state system'.[33] In short, there was a growing elite view that the *ancien régime* was failing to defend French national interests, particularly in the Holy Roman Empire.

It was not just a particular policy which had failed at Rossbach, many critics felt, but the whole social and political system. Royal authority and aristocratic domination were both ultimately based on military performance; that had been the basis of the original feudal contract and its evolution since the Middle Ages. Defeat in the Seven Years War was a serious blow to both army and nobility; it made the case for merit over privilege. The resulting loss of monarchic and aristocratic legitimacy now began to work its way through the polity, generating a lively debate on which form of social organization would make France most competitive in the European state system. Most agreed that the existing system, with its jumble of hereditary nobles and sale of offices, was ineffective. Choiseul and most military reformers favoured the Prussian, or better still the Russian, model, with a state service caste where merit and function were rewarded. Others preferred a British-style 'commercial' nobility.[34] Others still called for a synthesis between the two systems. A small minority, such as Jean-Jacques Rousseau, favoured a citizen army. The cost of the war also drove many to demand greater political participation. The Abbé Mably argued that the nation should consent to taxation through the estates, but the crown's attempts to double the *capitation* on the nobility (and only on them) produced the first protests since the late seventeenth century. Their remonstrances claimed that the 'nation' had to approve all taxation. Taken together, all these critiques posed an opportunity and a threat to the *ancien régime*. The nation might rally behind a successful programme for national greatness, but it would not forgive another failure.

In Spain, defeat in the Seven Years War and the continued British threat after 1763 inspired a thoroughgoing programme of imperial reform.[35] This was a matter of vital importance to Spain's standing as a European power, for it was on her American empire that the security of the monarchy on the near side of the Atlantic rested. It was home to 9 million people, nearly as many as metropolitan Spain itself, and the source of vital bullion. For this reason, the Spanish government set up a secret committee to look into the defence of the Indies in 1763. It reported a year later that more Spanish regulars, local levies and fortifications were needed.[36] The necessary sums could only be found within the empire itself. Visitations were sent to the viceroyalties: to New Spain in 1765 and in the following decade to Peru and New Granada. Local officials were replaced with efficient and unpopular *intendants* from Spain proper. The government also began to investigate the introduction of large-scale plantation slavery into the Caribbean colonies, especially Cuba, in order to increase sugar production; by the end of the century the import of black African slaves was in full flow.[37] Slavery and Spain's place in the European state system were thus closely linked.[38]

The Habsburg inquest into the Seven Years War raged throughout the 1760s. One faction, led by the chancellor, Kaunitz, remained fixated on a war of revenge against Prussia. The other was led by Maria Theresa's son and heir, Joseph, who was her co-ruler, elected 'King of the Romans' in 1764 and succeeding his father as emperor in 1765. He was open to the idea of a rapprochement with Frederick, not least because he eyed the growing power of Russia with concern. The two men were also divided on the domestic implications of the defeat. Joseph demanded immediate increased military spending and a larger army. This necessitated thoroughgoing socio-economic reform. Kaunitz, on the other hand, wanted a strategy for sustained economic growth, producing higher tax yields and thus greater political-military clout in the long run. In neither case, however, was domestic policy the primary concern: for both Joseph and Kaunitz internal reform was the continuation of foreign policy by other means.[39] A reliable census was created in March 1770 in order to give the government a much clearer picture of the resources, human, animal and inanimate, available for mobilization in future.

The Seven Years War also ignited a passionate discussion about the future of the Holy Roman Empire.[40] Some, enthralled by Frederick's victory over the French at Rossbach, saw him as a national saviour against the 'mercenaries of Louis [XV]' who were trying to 'tear off' yet more parts of Germany.[41] Others, mindful of his attack on Saxony, were more ambivalent. There was general agreement about two things, however. First, Germans were genuinely fond and proud of their *Reich*, which they saw as an oasis of decency and legality in a desert of inter-state rapacity. The protection enjoyed by German peasants – even the most wretched – shielded them from mass expropriation on the scale of the Scottish highlanders or the French Acadians. Justice might come dropping slow from the sclerotic imperial courts, and the need for confessional consensus did nothing to invigorate the imperial Diet, but after the traumas of the Thirty Years War this was generally accepted as a price worth paying. Secondly, the events of 1756–63, in which foreign powers had marched the length and breadth of the Empire with impunity, had brought home to many Germans just how fragile their polity was. This feeling was summed up by the writings of Friedrich Karl von

Moser. What Germany needed, his tract *Vom deutschen Nationalgeist* (1765) argued, was a governmental structure which would contain internal tensions and deter outside aggression. 'Who would dare to attack Germany,' he wrote, 'if Germany were united.' The enthusiasm for imperial reform soon petered out, however. 'The deficiencies which are exposed in an Imperial War and an Imperial Army are so great, and so numerous and multifarious,' the frustrated Moser observed in 1768, 'that as long as the German Empire remains in its present constitution, it should for ever be forbidden to wage an imperial war, so long as at all possible.'[42]

Further east, tsarist Russia was mulling over her position in the state system. In purely military terms, Russia had performed well in the Seven Years War, but her rulers were painfully conscious that profound domestic change would be needed to remain competitive in the state system in the long run. 'Russia,' as Catherine the Great wrote in the very first line of her *Instruction* for government in 1767, 'is a European power.' The next paragraph went on to say that Russia had become a great power by being European, that is 'by introducing the manners and customs of Europe'. What Catherine had in mind here was not the Europe of representative institutions, but that of princely absolutism. This was because, as the second chapter of her 'instruction' explained, 'the extent of the [tsarist] Dominion requires an absolute power to be vested in that person who rules over it', in order to expedite decisions. The 'intention and end of Monarchy', she continued, 'is the glory of the citizens, of the state and of the monarchy', that is, territorial expansion and military success. 'From this glory,' Catherine added, 'a sense of liberty arises in a people governed by a monarch, which . . . may contribute as much to the happiness of the subjects as even liberty itself.' In other words, Russians would find compensation for their lack of freedom in the glory of their state as a European great power.[43]

The two victors, Prussia and Great Britain, responded to the end of hostilities with a mixture of strategic insecurity and domestic complacency. Frederick's principal preoccupation after 1763 was the rising power of Russia in the east, 'that mountain of snow' which threatened to engulf Prussia like an avalanche. An alliance with Russia in 1764 afforded him a breathing space, but no more. 'This state cannot maintain itself without a large army,' Frederick wrote in his Political Testament of 1768, because 'we are surrounded by enemies more powerful than ourselves against whom we may at any moment have to defend ourselves'.[44] The Prussian king did not think that this required broader political participation or social reform. On the contrary, he was convinced that it was only the strict exercise of monarchical authority which had enabled him to weather the storm. Frederick toyed with the idea of abolishing serfdom after the cessation of hostilities, but the success of the 'military-agrarian complex' gave him no incentive to embark on fundamental social reform. The efficient Prussian administration had managed to support the entire army on Silesian revenues, whereas the Habsburgs had previously struggled to pay for two cavalry regiments from the same area.[45] The Prussian army numbered 150,000 men in 1763: by 1777 it had grown to nearly 190,000, and at the time of Frederick's death in 1786 it almost stood at a colossal 200,000. All the same, the king lived in terror of his neighbours. Frederick told a senior diplomat that he should really have a monkey rather than a black eagle on his coat of arms, because Prussia could only ape the great powers.

In Britain, the end of the Seven Years War had immediate political and strategic implications. The chief minister, the Marquess of Bute, was so viciously attacked in the public sphere for 'deserting' Prussia and her 'magnanimous' King Frederick that he resigned in early April 1763.[46] At the same time, the sheer scale of the triumph in 1763 unleashed a wave of national self-satisfaction. Victory was attributed to the superiority of British commerce and virtue. This hubris was reflected in the direction of British foreign policy. Unilateral displays of naval muscle against France and Spain became routine. In 1763, for example, a naval force was dispatched to intimidate the French over Turks Island in the Caymans, and the Spaniards in the Bay of Honduras. These measures were seductive because they offered gratification without commitment, but they also gave Britain an international reputation for arrogance. More particularly, the new 'naval' approach allowed London to reduce its diplomatic and military presence in Europe, especially the Holy Roman Empire, leaving her dangerously isolated.[47] It rapidly became apparent, moreover, that the triumphs of the Seven Years War had not banished the Bourbon spectre for good, quite the reverse. Instead of a largely commercial agglomeration of trading posts and colonies, Britain was now responsible for a sprawling territorial empire, with a new and even more vulnerable perimeter line. To the west there was a miasmic border with the Spaniards and the increasingly unruly Indian tribes along the Mississippi Valley. To the north a large community of Québecois, too large to be deported, represented a potential fifth column. In 1763–4, British North America was racked by Pontiac's Indian revolt, which once again exposed the inadequacy of colonial defence structures.

The ministry now moved swiftly to put imperial defence on a stable footing. First, in October 1763 it issued a proclamation that there should be no settlement west of the Appalachians. This measure was designed to conciliate the Indians living there; to allay Franco-Spanish fears of untrammelled British colonial expansion; and to reduce the perimeter to be defended by the already overstretched crown forces. Secondly, plans were drawn up to double the overseas military establishment. About two thirds of these troops were to be deployed in North America, mostly along the western frontier; the rest were destined for the Caribbean. Britain was already heavily in debt as a result of the Seven Years War, so most of the costs would have to be met by the colonists themselves. 'Protection and obedience,' the British prime minister, Lord Grenville, remarked, 'are reciprocal ... The nation has run itself into an immense debt to give them their protection; and now they are called upon to contribute a small share towards the public expense.' To that end, he brought forward first a Sugar Act, and then a Stamp Duty on property, 'equally spread over North America and the West Indies'. It was designed to support the upkeep of a substantial regular force in the Ohio and Mississippi valleys. Similar measures were conceived for Ireland, and especially for India, where the East India Company was effectively an arm of the state.[48]

The legacy of the Seven Years War also resonated among the weaker powers, who were themselves desperately trying to stay competitive within the European state system. Poland, for example, reacted to developments in central and eastern Europe by trying to re-establish herself as an independent actor. Russian fiat had restricted the Polish army to 24,000 men in 1717, but the potential manpower reservoir was enormous. In the 1750s and 1760s, for example, individual magnates had been able to field large numbers of troops: the most powerful, Michael Radziwill, some 10,000. What prevented the Commonwealth from mobilizing a much larger army was not just outside interference but a chronic tendency towards internal division and anarchy. Thanks to the *liberum veto*, collective decision-making was virtually impossible. 'Poland,' the Russian chancellor, Count Mikhail Illarionovich Vorontsov, remarked in 1763, 'is constantly plunged in disorder; as long as she keeps her constitution, she does not deserve to be considered among the European powers.'[49] Indeed, Poles were so accustomed to seeing their country traversed at will by foreign powers that they referred to it as '*Karczma Europy*' – 'Europe's staging inn'. The new Polish king, Stanislas August Poniatowski, who was crowned in November 1764, set out to change this. He established a Polish diplomatic service, designed to prevent the magnates from pursuing separate policies, increased the army, and attempted to put the finances on a sound footing with a general tariff. Above all, Stanislas August planned to abolish the debilitating *liberum veto*, which made the Diet ungovernable.

Central to the post-Seven Years War debates, especially among the losers and smaller powers, was a preoccupation with which form of government and social organization was best suited to success in the international sphere. Here the record of the mid-century conflicts between 1740 and 1763 was ambiguous. Some felt that commercial parliamentary states had the edge, and they could point to the extraordinary ability of the British fiscal-military state to raise taxes and credits in support of a two-front war in Europe and America. Moreover, Britain had benefited from open debate on foreign policy, which had rallied the nation behind the common cause. Elsewhere, however, representative government had clearly underperformed, particularly in Sweden and Poland. The record of monarchical government was also distinctly mixed. For example, the restoration of the Stadholderate did not, as in earlier times, reinvigorate Dutch foreign policy; the slow decline of the United Provinces continued. Nor were the French failures at Rossbach, on the high seas and in America an advertisement for absolutism. On the other hand, the highly militarized and personalized monarchy of Frederick the Great had prevailed against all the odds. In his secret Political Testaments of 1752 and 1768, the Prussian king stressed the superiority of personal rule, which he claimed was better able to respond swiftly and secretly to an emergency than the cumbersome public representative or consultative bodies. This was the ultimate paradox of the Seven Years War: the two ideal types of European parliamentary and absolutist regimes, Britain and Prussia, had both emerged as victors.[50]

The pan-European wave of domestic and imperial transformations triggered by the Seven Years War and its aftermath soon led to a series of crises in the state system. First to erupt was the confrontation between settlers and metropolis in the thirteen colonies. There had already been considerable tension over the conduct of the war and the treatment of colonial officers by British regulars. Americans – especially the young George Washington, who was there – were particularly unimpressed by Braddock's defeat on the Monongahela, a veritable colonial Rossbach.[51] The 'Proclamation Line' of 1763 finally brought this resentment to the surface. American colonists expected to be awarded the Ohio Valley as the fruit of their struggles. No man or ministry, they felt, should set limits to the march of an empire. An 'expansionist' lobby now began to make its presence felt in the colonial assemblies of North America. They articulated a vision not just of territorial growth but of greatness: a single unified British geopolitical space on the continent, from sea to shining sea, from the Atlantic Ocean to the Gulf of Mexico.[52] Imperialist aggrandizement was thus part of the American project well before independence. It was in fact the reason why the Revolution took place.

Anglo-Spanish attempts at imperial reform both soon ran into difficulty. Grenville's Stamp Act of 1765, designed to pay for the new military establishment in America, provoked furious protests and had to be repealed. The Townshend duties of 1767 were devised with the same purpose in mind, and met a similar fate. Americans had been prepared – albeit grudgingly – to accept more government in pursuit of expansion, but few would dig into their pockets to defend the Proclamation Line. A fatal gap was emerging between the strategic and constitutional views of settlers and London. Imperial reform, so vital to maintaining the empire, now threatened to tear it apart. Spain's attempt to put imperial defence on a sounder footing, and to enable the colonies to support the monarchy's great-power ambitions in Europe, also met protracted resistance, provoking a revolt in Quito and Pueblo in 1765.

At around the same time, Stanislas August's reform programme was running up against vested interests inside and outside Poland. Prusso-Russian intervention stymied the proposed general tariff in October 1766, destroying any hope of providing the state with the independent revenue it so desperately needed for the common defence. Catherine also stirred up domestic resistance. About half the population of Poland, roughly 5 million, were Catholics; another 4 million were Uniates, that is Orthodox Christians who recognized the authority of the pope. The rest, about half a million Russian Orthodox and about the same number of Protestants, were known as 'dissidents'; the huge Jewish community defied classification. In 1767, a Russian-backed Confederation of Protestants and Orthodox demanded religious rights. Under duress, Stanislas agreed to the 'Perpetual Treaty' of 1768, which enshrined their rights, but also copper-fastened Russian domination of the Commonwealth. This provoked a patriotic Polish reaction in the Confederation of Bar, which dismissed Stanislas as a tsarist puppet. Civil war broke out. Russian troops moved in to 'protect' the dissidents. Fearing total Russian control of Poland, with the resulting danger to their northern border, the Ottomans decided to strike first. When Cossack bands violated Turkish territory in hot pursuit of Polish Confederates, the Porte declared war on St Petersburg.

Catherine made short work of the Ottomans. In July 1770, the Turkish fleet was crushed at Chesme. Russian troops occupied Moldavia and Bessarabia, and looked set to move into Wallachia. All this caused consternation in Potsdam and Vienna, where it was feared that unilateral gains by Catherine at Ottoman expense would further tilt the balance of power in favour of St Petersburg. The Russian tide would lap around the southern flank of the Habsburg monarchy. Frederick feared that 'the war against the Turks will decide the affairs of Poland', and thus clear the path for greater Russian interference in the Empire.[53] The only solution short of war was to split the territorial gains as evenly as possible. In August 1772, the three eastern powers announced that large areas of the Commonwealth would be partitioned between them. A huge chunk of eastern Poland went to Russia, the Austrians received the relatively prosperous province of Galicia, while Frederick annexed the much smaller but strategically crucial West Prussia linking East Prussia with the territories of the Prussian heartland. The naked rapacity of the move caused Maria Theresa some qualms, but the circumstances left her with little choice. She wrestled with her conscience and she won, or as Frederick put it, 'she wept, but she took'.

Two years later, Catherine bullied the Ottomans into the Treaty of Kutchuk Kainarji. Russian territorial gains were restricted to some lands around the Black Sea. Much more important was the informal influence secured by St Petersburg. The Ottomans surrendered the Crimean Khanate, which effectively became a Russian puppet. Catherine also forced the Porte to grant her the right to act as guarantor of the rights of Balkan Christians, just as Russia had long 'protected' Polish dissidents. Nearly a year later, in May 1775, the Austrians grabbed Bukovina, which rounded off their eastern border nicely.

All this had implications well beyond eastern Europe, Scandinavia and the Balkans. The bulwark keeping Russia out of central Europe had given way. 'Poland,' the Irish writer and British parliamentarian Edmund Burke noted, 'was the natural barrier of Germany, as well as of the northern crowns, against the overwhelming power and ambition of Russia.' The partition now threatened 'totally to unhinge the ancient system of Germany and the north'. Poland might now be 'the road by which the Russians will enter Germany'.[54] Further moves in that direction were to be expected. The struggle for the Holy Roman Empire had entered a new phase.

The impact of these international crises on domestic politics in western Europe was dramatic. In France, the most immediate effect was the increased urgency of putting the monarchy on a more stable financial footing. Higher taxes were unavoidable, but these were blocked by the *parlements*, which insisted on registering royal financial edicts before they became effective, and whose general fractiousness raised the borrowing costs of the regime on the international money markets. Conflict had been in the air for some time, because the costs of the Seven Years War, and the peacetime naval construction programme after 1763, had to be paid by someone. In 1768, full-scale confrontation erupted in Brittany, where the local *parlement* accused the governor of raising unconstitutional taxes to fund local defence. The *parlements* of Paris and other regional *parlements* backed Brittany. Deadlock ensued. A year later, the Comptroller-General of the finances warned that 'the finances of your Majesty are in the most frightful state of collapse'. The monarchy had no choice. So, in January 1771, Chancellor Maupeou dissolved the *parlements* in the teeth of furious opposition.

The international turbulence of the late 1760s and 1770s strengthened interventionist sentiment in Europe. In the 1770s no fewer than three German imperial counts were taken into custody for 'abuse of power'.[55] In Britain, prominent writers and parliamentarians such as James Boswell and Burke championed the cause of 'liberty' in Corsica, which the French had occupied in 1768 after expelling the charismatic patriotic leader Pasquale Paoli, and in Poland.[56] Many such interventions, of course, were driven by self-interested motives. Indeed, the effective defence of minority rights *depended* on a synergy between sentiment and strategy; the two were not always easy to separate. Sympathy for the cause of 'liberty' in Corsica, for example, was part of a broader concern for British freedoms and the containment of France on which these ultimately depended. On the other hand, it was also true that states intervened in defence of rights which they routinely violated themselves either at home or abroad. The French guarantee of the imperial constitution and Russia's professed concern for Polish 'liberties' are the most prominent examples. Many European states, or populations, could therefore be forgiven a certain ambivalence about interventions in the name of 'liberty' and 'toleration' which were transparently designed to keep them in a condition of permanent dependency.

All the same, humanitarian concern was not simply a matter of attacking the mote in the neighbour's eye, while ignoring the beam in one's own. This was demonstrated by the case of the Caribs of St Vincent, an island which had been annexed by the British from the French and was used for victualling Barbados. Some claimed that the Caribs were in league with the French on Martinique. Under pressure from local planters to colonize the island, London considered exterminating the Caribs, but rejected that as unethical. They accepted that deportation was impractical, and so recommended that the natives be decanted into what was effectively a reservation. When the Caribs resisted, a major campaign was launched against them in 1772. News of atrocities by crown forces provoked extensive parliamentary protests and demands for an inquiry into what was widely regarded as a cruel and unnecessary operation. The MP Barlow Trescothick spoke for many when he condemned war against 'innocent and inoffensive people'.[57] That same year, the Mansfield judgment effectively abolished slavery in Britain itself, though it remained widespread in British colonies and British ships continued to ply the slave trade across the Atlantic. Shortly afterwards, a parliamentary inquiry into the treatment of the Caribs was set up. A recognizably 'humanitarian' sentiment was abroad.

Across the Atlantic, a very different popular critique of British foreign policy was gaining traction. The North American colonists also lamented the defeat of 'liberty' in Corsica, and ostentatiously celebrated the vanquished patriot leader, Paoli.[58] At the same time, the settlers objected to the refusal of the British government to allow them to expropriate the native population west of the Proclamation Line. They criticized the progressive dismantlement (for reasons of cost) of forts beyond the Appalachians, which had been intended to deter Indian raids, and Franco-Spanish claims to the western territories. Matters came to a head when the East India Company, which London had hoped would finance imperial defence across the globe, effectively went bankrupt in 1772. The prime minister, Lord North, sought to put the company back on its feet in May 1773 with the hugely unpopular Tea Act. At around the same time, the long-awaited plan for a new western colony (in present-day West Virginia and eastern Kentucky) – to be named 'Vandalia' in honour of Queen Charlotte's Germanic ancestors – was finally abandoned by London. In May 1774, the Falkland Islands were evacuated, partly to save money and partly to appease Spain. To colonial critics, therefore, the British Empire was already collapsing, long before the Revolution; indeed, it was this sense of imperial collapse which prompted the colonists to rebel, not the other way around.[59]

The Quebec Act of 1774 was the final straw. This promised religious toleration to the French Canadians, and was widely believed by the colonists to be part of a popish plot against their Protestant liberties. Their main objection, however, was to the way in which the Act laid down the *external* borders of the province. All lands between the Ohio and the Mississippi – subject of furious debate between London and the expansionist settler lobby since 1763 – were now incorporated into Quebec. In the eyes of many North Americans this threatened an encirclement of the thirteen colonies by an absolutist government – a resurrected New France. So, in 1775, the colonists lurched into conflict with London over constitutional and strategic differences produced by the direction of British foreign policy. 'The first principle of the American Independence and Revolution that I ever embraced, advocated, or entertained' the founding father John Adams remarked looking back, 'was, *Defence against the French*.'[60]

British and patriot forces soon clashed at Lexington.[61] The shots fired there were famously 'heard around the world' not so much because they heralded the dawn of 'liberty', but because of their implications for the international state system. At stake was nothing less than the balance of power in Europe. Without America – so the consensus in London ran – Britain would be unable to face France and Spain on the near side of the

Atlantic.[62] Conversely, many European powers were convinced that if the British prevailed in America, they would gain such an accretion of power as to become insufferable. The Bourbon powers were conflicted because neither of them wanted to set a dangerous precedent of allying openly with rebels against lawfully constituted authority. This was particularly an issue for Spain, which was confronting very similar problems in her own extensive American colonies. The opportunity to take Britain down a peg was too good to be missed, however. Victory for the colonists, the French chief minister, the Count de Vergennes, observed in late 1775, would mean that 'The power of England will diminish and our power will increase to the same degree.'[63]

For their part, the American patriots were convinced that they could only survive by internationalizing the conflict. They had to persuade Europe that, as Benjamin Franklin put it, the American cause was 'the cause of all mankind [that they were] fighting for [Europe's] liberty in defending our own'.[64] Liberty here meant both constitutional freedoms and the 'liberties' of Europe, that is the balance of power. In March 1776, the Secret Committee charged with establishing foreign links and sourcing supplies abroad sent Benjamin Franklin as an envoy to France. The rebels also sent a representative to Vienna, to try to deny Britain access to German mercenaries for use in America. At least one third of the British troops in America, in fact, were hired from princes of the Holy Roman Empire; in the minds of the colonists the link between unfreedom in Europe and their own security was thus as clear as it had been in the times of Louis XIV and Louis XV.[65] These moves had an inexorable logic of their own, because full and open alliances with European states were not possible so long as the colonists regarded themselves as loyal subjects of the crown. Tom Paine's electrifying tract, *Common sense*, argued that only independence would enable the Americans to secure the foreign support necessary to defend the Revolution.

Diplomatic engagement was one way of protecting the Revolution and securing independence. Many Americans, however, already entertained a much broader conception of their security and their mission in the world; from the very beginning, they believed themselves and their state to be both exceptional and exportable. America, Paine argued, 'had made a stand, not for herself only, but for the world, and looked beyond the advantages she herself could receive' and her cause was 'in great measure the cause of all mankind'.[66] By representing the principles of self-determination in an age of empires, republicanism in a time of monarchy, written constitutions in a world of traditional corporatism and absolute government, and free trade against the prevailing mercantilism, the United States hoped to change the world through what it *was*.[67] An idea, he claimed, 'will penetrate where an army of soldiers cannot; it will succeed where diplomatic management would fail'; 'neither the Rhine, the Channel, nor the [Atlantic] ocean . . . can arrest its progress,' he predicted, 'it will march on the horizon of the world, and it will conquer.' Having done so, Paine believed, the spread of freedom would lead to universal peace as nations traded freely and disarmed. But if Paine was an internationalist, he was no interventionist. He was violently opposed to all international war, which he considered a conspiracy to subjugate and defraud peoples. In time, however, many Americans would come to believe that their own freedom could only survive by spreading it actively throughout the world, beginning with those areas closest to her. Once this belief established itself, the United States would increasingly change the world through what it *did*.

The American Declaration of Independence of 4 July 1776 did not create a unitary state. It spoke very clearly in the plural of united 'free and independent state*s*'. And yet, the United States had to acquire – very quickly – some of the characteristics of a single state in order to wage war against Britain. In November 1777, after a long and acrimonious debate, Congress agreed the Articles of Confederation. Rudimentary monetary, tax and credit systems were put in place. The states were dissuaded from issuing any more money, and they agreed to pay Congress a percentage of their state tax yield and individual land value. The Articles solved the problem of national cohesion only very imperfectly, however. Congressional taxes were voluntary and often not paid, the only recourse being the 'naming and shaming' of the defaulters. Americans therefore fought and won their war of independence as a 'Confederation', not as a single state or even as a union of states.[68]

Meanwhile Emperor Joseph II and his chief minister, Kaunitz, were determined to reshuffle the geopolitical hand they had been dealt by history. In late 1777, Joseph seized the initiative. His diplomats persuaded Karl Theodor of the Palatinate to agree a partial exchange of the Austrian Netherlands for his inheritance of Bavaria. In this way, Joseph hoped to trade a remote geopolitical liability for an asset which was contiguous with the main lands of the monarchy. His coup provoked an immediate response from Frederick the Great, who feared that it would change the balance of power within Germany. He aimed to keep the Empire in stasis, and thus deny the Austrians the opportunity of using the imperial crown to mobilize the potential of Germany against Prussia. Indeed, Frederick increasingly set himself up as a 'counter-emperor' to the Austrians in order to rally the middling and smaller territories in defence of the status quo. Given the continuing Habsburg–Bourbon alliance, therefore, it looked as if the American and German conflicts would merge into one great conflagration similar to the Seven Years War.

The resulting War of the Bavarian Succession put France on the horns of a dilemma. As Louis XVI observed in February 1778, he was committed by treaty to Austria, 'and we must maintain France's reputation in Germany, which has been under heavy attack for some time', not least because 'the guarantee of the Peace of Westphalia is inherent in the French crown'.[69] Weighed against that imperative was the obvious fact that intervention would open up a new front in Europe at the very moment when France had the opportunity to deal Britain a fatal blow overseas. In the end, the French decided to hold back and let events in central Europe take their course. Instead, long covert supporters of the colonists, and cheered by the US victory at Saratoga in 1777, they entered the American War openly in 1778, followed by Spain in 1779. Britain narrowly escaped a joint Bourbon invasion. A year later, the Dutch were so maddened by Britain's naval high-handedness that they entered the lists too. At around the same time, Catherine the Great, herself offended by the Royal Navy's treatment of non-belligerent shipping, founded the League of Armed Neutrality. Now Britain was, in the mortified expression of the head of the Admiralty, Lord Sandwich, practically 'at . . . war with the whole world . . . The powers united will dismember our state and make such partition among them as they see fit.'[70]

In the face of these challenges, the British state embarked on its most intense programme of mobilization so far. The Royal Navy increased its number of ships of the line by 50 per cent over the three years from 1778 to 1780; the number of seamen jumped by more than half in the same period. The British government also began to think about ways of tapping the vast manpower potential of Catholic Ireland, and overcoming the objections of the local Protestant Ascendancy to their recruitment.[71] In 1778, the first substantial measure of Catholic relief was enacted, and a bill to relieve Dissenters was introduced in the following year. All the same, many Britons feared that monarchy was gaining the edge over representative government. The past fifty years had shown that the 'free' polities of Poland, Sweden and the United Provinces were in terminal decline. The future seemed to lie with the central and eastern European autocracies, which had streamlined their societies for military mobilization and expansion. As the British Under-Secretary of State for War pointed out in mid-March 1778, 'the great military powers in the interior parts of Europe, who have amassed together their great treasures, and have modelled their subjects into great armies, will, in the next and succeeding period of time, become the predominant powers'.[72]

The stupendous performance of the British fiscal-military state did not suffice to turn the tide in America, or to uphold British naval supremacy when it was most needed. Britain's European isolation ultimately proved fatal. Undisturbed by a land war in Europe, the Bourbon powers outbuilt Britain at sea, as the Whigs had always feared they would. France not only gained temporary control of the waters around North America, but also succeeded in putting a land force ashore to support Washington. In 1781, a joint Franco-American effort boxed a large British force in at Yorktown and forced it to surrender. Lord North's government did not survive the blow for long. The new administration soon sued for peace.

The Treaty of Paris which brought the American War to an end in 1783 marked a revolution in the international state system. Britain was partitioned between France, Spain and the colonists. She was forced to recognize the thirteen colonies as independent states. Britain kept Gibraltar, but Florida and Minorca were surrendered to Spain, and France recovered Louisiana. France, in the triumphant words of Vergennes, had 'erased the stain of 1763'. Moreover, a new power had arisen in the western hemisphere, and far-sighted observers were already predicting that the baton would soon pass from Britain to the United States. 'This little island [England],' Horace Walpole had remarked on hearing of the Declaration of Independence, 'will be ridiculously proud some ages hence of its former brave days, and swear its capital was once as big again as Paris, or – what is to be the name of the city that will then give laws to Europe? – perhaps New York or Philadelphia.' When one Frenchman predicted that the thirteen states would become 'the greatest empire in the world', one member of the British delegation in Paris shot back: 'Yes Sir, and they will all speak English, every one of 'em.'[73]

The impact of the American War on European politics was dramatic. In France, it led to a resurgence of support for the *ancien régime*. As one observer later reminded Frenchmen, 'You yourselves, . . . in your homes, in your public places, in your cafés, and even in your taverns, saw in imagination the whole English navy swallowed up, and drank in long draughts, in advance, the pleasure of vengeance'.[74] But the sense of euphoria soon wore off. The financial cost of the war had been enormous, paid for largely through loans rather than new taxes, which put a particular premium on the creditworthiness of the *ancien régime*. The money markets, foreign and domestic, required transparency, and so increasingly did the French public. When, in February 1781, Jacques Necker published his famous *compte rendu* of the monarchy's finances, 100,000 copies were sold that year alone. The intent was to increase consultation and thus bolster credit, but the effect was to undermine confidence in the government. By autumn 1783, the crown was on the brink of bankruptcy.

The financial headache was compounded by a strategic one. French non-intervention in the War of the Bavarian Succession left the door open for increased Russian involvement in the Holy Roman Empire. Throughout the early 1770s, Catherine had expanded her influence, beginning with the marriages of her son and heir to German princesses, first from Hesse-Darmstadt in 1773, and upon that one's death in 1776 to another from Württemberg. Russian diplomatic representation, at the imperial Diet and among the smaller principalities, was massively increased. The tsarina wanted much more than just recognition of her own Russian imperial title. Catherine was staking a claim to nothing less than a decisive voice in the affairs of the Empire. She remarked in October 1779 that Russia 'had long desired the privilege of being a guarantor of the imperial constitution'. This was because, Catherine continued, it was this power which 'gave France its pre-eminent political influence' in Europe.[75] Her mediation led to the Treaty of Teschen, which brought the Austro-Prussian war over Bavaria to an end. Joseph was compelled to back down. The really crucial clause was that making Catherine a guarantor of the Holy Roman Empire. 'The Russians,' one British diplomat remarked, 'must now be considered the arbiters of Germany.'[76] In December 1778, the French envoy to the imperial Diet complained that the 150-year-old dominance of his country in German politics had been supplanted by that of Russia. This mattered intensely, because, as Vergennes observed the following year, 'Germany would in general be quite capable of harming France. Being the largest and most populous territory ... it is easy to see what advantage it would have over us if this formidable power were not limited by the form of its constitution ... We thus owe our superiority and our security to the forces of [German] disunity and to the vices of this constitution.'[77] France was in danger of allowing the Empire to fall into hostile hands.

In Britain, the American War provoked a furious debate about the cause of the disaster. Many agreed that the path to recovery would involve fundamental domestic transformation. Some believed that spiritual and moral renewal would be enough. Others argued that a broadening of the franchise was necessary to mobilize all the national energies in support of the common cause. Many supported the idea of 'economical reform' to put the finances back in order. Almost everybody accepted that a complete change of grand strategy was required. A 'second' and geographically even more extensive empire would be built, using the demographic reserve of American loyalists, many of them freed black slaves.[78] In 1788, the first settlers were put ashore in Australia, and new colonies were soon established or old ones developed in Africa, Asia and the Americas, especially Canada. The real task, however, was the rebuilding of Britain's alliances, especially in central Europe. The Tory 'blue water' approach, with its concomitant contempt for continental 'entanglements', had been widely discredited. 'To recover our weight on the continent by judicious alliances,' the seasoned diplomat and MP Sir James Harris remarked in December 1783, 'is the general wish of every man the least acquainted with the interests of this country.'[79] Never again should Britain find herself isolated in Europe.

In the mid-1780s, Joseph II stepped up moves to strengthen the Habsburg monarchy through a domestic reform programme.[80] All internal tolls except those between Hungary and the hereditary lands were scrapped. Some guild restrictions were lifted. Joseph also moved to break the dominance of the Roman Catholic hierarchy. In 1781, his Toleration Edict eased restrictions on Jews and Protestants; this was designed not only to mobilize dissenters more effectively in the service of the state, but also to pre-empt outside powers, especially Prussia and Russia, from manipulating them for strategic advantage. Joseph pursued liturgical reform, attempted to rationalize episcopal boundaries, dissolve purely contemplative orders, and generally to promote a slimmed-down, rational and less baroque Catholicism respectful of his authority and more relevant to the needs of his subjects (as he saw them). He tried to reduce the power of representative assemblies, especially in Hungary and the Austrian Netherlands, in order to enhance monarchical power. By the mid-1780s Joseph was gearing up to tackling the biggest issue of all: serfdom, and the triangular relationship between monarch, nobility and peasantry, which was, he believed, to be in urgent need of reconfiguration.

These measures were intended to make Austria a more formidable actor on the international scene, but they came at a considerable diplomatic price. Reform antagonized powerful domestic constituencies – such as the clergy and Hungarian nobility – which not only could be extremely disruptive but were also capable of entering into treasonable correspondence with rival powers. Joseph's reform of episcopal boundaries outraged the hierarchy of the Holy Roman Empire. His high-handedness convinced many German princes that the emperor, far from being the defender of the imperial constitution, now represented a serious threat to its integrity. Joseph's most controversial policy, however, was his determination to effect a territorial consolidation of the monarchy, riding roughshod over the imperial constitution, if necessary. In November 1784, he revived his plan to exchange the Austrian Netherlands for Bavaria. This provoked widespread fears of a new Habsburg Universal Monarchy in Germany which would unhinge the whole continental balance of power. This time – thanks to Joseph's open contempt for imperial conventions – Frederick was joined in his opposition by many traditional Habsburg allies, such as the Imperial Arch-Chancellor and Elector of Mainz. The resulting 'League of Princes' in 1785 showed that the Empire was still capable of mounting a concerted diplomatic response to internal threats. Once again, Joseph was forced to back down; the costs and failures of his foreign policy provoked widespread domestic criticism.[81]

Perhaps wisely, Russia did not press her advantage in the Empire. Instead, Catherine scaled back her German ambitions in return for an Austrian alliance to facilitate designs further south. The next Russian move, therefore, would not be in central Europe but in the Balkans and Black Sea, in order to secure an alternative 'Roman' legitimation.[82] The

Treaty of Kutchuk Kainarji in 1774 had given Russia the right to intervene on behalf of the Orthodox Christians in the Ottoman Empire, a privilege which Catherine ruthlessly exploited through her network of consulates. It also created a nominally independent Crimea, which immediately split into pro-Russian and pro-Ottoman factions. In November 1776, Catherine sent troops to intervene in the civil war; in 1783, she annexed the Crimea outright. All this was part of a much broader 'Greek Project' to capture Constantinople, restore Orthodox supremacy and vindicate Russia's status as the 'Third Rome'.[83] In this spirit, Catherine christened her newborn grandson Constantine in 1779 and the Russian base at Sebastopol boasted an archway inscribed with the slogan 'the road to Byzantium'.[84]

Seeing the writing on the wall, the Ottomans launched a pre-emptive strike on Russia in 1787. Once again, however, the Russians counterattacked, pushing south deep into the empire. This prompted an immediate response from the two central European powers. Failure to act could mean the total absorption of the Ottoman Empire, or at least its European parts, into Russia, and leave the Habsburg monarchy vulnerable to partial encirclement from the east. So, in late 1787, Joseph entered the war on Russia's side, to ensure that the spoils would be equally divided. This move, in turn, alarmed Prussia. Frederick the Great's successor, Frederick William II, believed that a successful Austro-Russian campaign against the Turks would leave him in a weaker position. Prussia was also threatened on her western side, where the Patriot Party – which was backed by Austria's ally France – was going from strength to strength in the United Provinces. A war on two fronts seemed a real possibility. When the Patriots seized the *Stadholder*'s wife – Frederick William's sister – the Prussian king decided to act. In 1787, he invaded the Dutch Republic and restored the House of Orange. A year later, he concluded the Triple Alliance with Holland and Great Britain. With his western flank now secure, Frederick William began negotiations with the Poles, Swedes and Ottomans. In January 1788, the Prussian chief minister, Ewald Friedrich von Hertzberg, unveiled a 'Grand Plan' for territorial reorganization which would ensure balanced gains for all three eastern powers. The Austrians would be allowed limited expansion in the Balkans, but would be forced to relinquish Galicia to Poland, which in turn would cede Danzig and Thorn to Prussia. Joseph was furious. He announced that he 'would rather fight a war to destruction' than 'allow the King of Prussia to possess a single village, much less realize this grand project in its entirety'.[85] That summer, Sweden attacked Russia in order to ease the pressure on the Turks. A broader European war seemed in the offing.

These events made a deep impression on the United States of America, the first independent European state established on the far shores of the Atlantic. 'A cloud has been for some time hanging over the European world,' Alexander Hamilton observed, '[and] [i]f it should break forth into a storm, who can insure us, that in its progress, a part of its fury would not be spent upon us?' Neutrality or restraint would not be enough. 'Let us recollect,' he continued, 'that peace or war, will not always be left to our option; that however moderate or unambitious we may be, we cannot count upon the moderation, or hope to extinguish the ambition of others.'[86] The capacity of even quite small actors to harm American interests was demonstrated when the withdrawal of British naval protection after the revolution immediately exposed US merchant shipping to vicious attacks by the Barbary corsairs operating out of North Africa. This was by no means just a matter of 'honour': the vigorous pursuit of commerce was regarded as essential to giving the young republic the strength to survive against Franco-British competition.[87] Thomas Jefferson and John Adams were informed by Tripoli's envoy to London in March 1785 that all nations which did not acknowledge the authority of the Koran 'were sinners, [and] that it was their right and duty to make war upon whoever they could find and to make slaves of all they could take as prisoners'. Initial attempts to strike a bargain with the corsairs simply led to an increase in their demands. In other words, the United States was forced to engage with the Muslim world, whether it wanted to or not.

There were also numerous threats to the new republic closer to home. Spain had closed the Mississippi to navigation in 1784, and maintained a menacing presence in Florida to the south, and was busy fortifying Texas. This provoked outrage among the colonists. 'Shall we be bondsmen of the Spaniards, as the children of Israel were bondsmen of the Egyptians?' asked one open letter circulated widely at town meetings and court openings in 1786.[88] The US Secretary of Foreign Affairs, John Jay, wondered whether the French were 'perfectly weaned from the desire of possessing continental colonies in America'. It was fears of being pre-empted by another European power, in fact, which drove the young republic to sponsor fact-finding explorations in the west.[89] Worse still, Britain had held on to Canada, and regained the command of the sea briefly lost during the War of Independence; she was strongly suspected not only of stirring up the native tribes but also of sponsoring Shays' rebellion in western Massachusetts. The net effect of all this, as Hamilton noted in mid-December 1787, was that 'the territories of Britain, Spain and of the Indian nations in our neighbourhood ... encircle the union from Maine to Georgia'.[90] In other words, all the issues which had originally led to the separation from Britain remained essentially unresolved.

Moreover, the constitutional arrangements inherited from the Revolutionary War were completely unsuited to deal with the challenges of the late 1780s. There was no real executive to speak of, Congress had no power to raise taxes to pay for national projects, and all international treaties had to be ratified by each and every one of the states before they came into force. The debts of the Revolutionary War were largely held by the individual states, with little prospect of being honoured, thus destroying all public creditworthiness. The United States lacked a proper military, because the states could not agree on how it should be paid for, and many Americans were fearful that it might be used to undermine their liberties. Indeed, so loose were the bonds which held the confederation together that many Americans feared the United States might fragment into its component parts, or even succumb to civil strife. This fear was particularly pronounced with regard to the all-important question of the west. Hamilton foresaw 'territorial disputes' over 'the wide field of western territory'.[91] Moreover, failure to pursue a strong line in the west would leave a vacuum for outside powers to exploit. There were real fears that the settlers between the Appalachians and Mississippi might petition to rejoin Britain, throw in their lot with Spain or even set up as an independent state. The choice was stark: either Americans moved closer together to create a state capable of waging war and conducting territorial expansion, or they would go to war against each other and ultimately become victims of expansion by an outside power.[92]

The representatives of the thirteen colonies therefore came together at Philadelphia in 1787 in order to revise the Articles of Confederation. The resulting debate, one side of which is immortalized in the exchanges between Alexander Hamilton, John Jay and James Madison in the *Federalist papers*, was largely driven by the primacy of foreign policy. 'Safety from external danger,' Hamilton wrote in November, 'is the most powerful director of national conduct.'[93] It was against this background that Madison and Hamilton looked at the 'federal system' of the 'Germanic empire', and found it to be 'a nerveless body, incapable of regulating its own members, insecure against external dangers, and agitated with unceasing fermentations in its own bowels'. 'Military preparations,' they noted, 'must be preceded by so many tedious discussions, arising from the jealousies, pride, separate views, and clashing pretensions, of sovereign bodies, that before the Diet can settle the arrangements, the enemy are in the field.' Even if the various obstacles to unity could be surmounted, Madison and Hamilton believed that none of 'the neighbouring powers would suffer a revolution to take place which would give to the empire the force and pre-eminence to which it is entitled'. As for Poland, they argued that it was 'equally unfit for self-government and self-defence [and] has long been at the mercy of its powerful neighbours who have lately had the mercy to disburden it of one third of its people and territories'.[94] Of all the European precedents, the only one which found any favour among the Federalists was the Anglo-Scottish Union of 1707, by which the two parties, formerly so divided, had come together to 'resist all [their] enemies'. Jay saw this form of 'entire and perfect union', to use the words he approvingly quoted from Queen Anne's letter to the Scottish parliament of July 1706, as the way forward for the American Republic.[95]

The constitution agreed at Philadelphia in 1787–8 showed that Americans had learned from their own experience and that of the British, Germans and Poles. Like the Scots and English, they determined as the preamble put it to 'form a more perfect union'. No state would have a veto on progress. All decisions at the Convention were by majority vote of the states: unanimity was not required. A strong executive was established in the shape of a presidency empowered to conduct foreign policy and conclude treaties, which were subject, however, to ratification by the two Houses of Congress. This was made up of the Senate, representing the individual states, and the House of Representatives. Mindful of what had happened in Poland, an electoral college was created on the suggestion of the Southern grandee Pierce Butler from South Carolina, to make domestic cabals and foreign bribery more difficult. All state war debts were 'federalized', restoring the 'public credit'. The existence of slavery was recognized in the clause giving 'other persons' three fifths of a representative but also a tax apportionment, and in the assumption that slave states and slavery could expand territorially.[96] At the same time, the signatories effectively agreed to abolish the slave trade within twenty years, and there was a general expectation at least in the north that the whole institution would be phased out gradually over time. That same year, the Northwest Ordinance laid down that territorial expansion was to proceed through the admission of new states to the Union on the basis of complete equality with existing states rather than the enlargement of existing ones. It also stipulated that the lands south of the Great Lakes and north of the Ohio River should be free, while the subsequent Southwest Ordinance permitted slavery in the states to be established to the south and west. The constitution came into force in June 1788. Like their European rivals, the Americans had remodelled their internal politics to make themselves more competitive in the international state system.[97]

Americans rejected the alternative solution to their strategic predicament, which was to create a 'service nobility' on Russo-Prussian lines dedicated to the defence of their independence. To be sure, some patriots experimented with the idea of creating such an American aristocracy based on the veterans of the Revolutionary War. The resulting 'Society of the Cincinnati' was a 'society of friends' committed to preserving 'inviolate those exalted rights and liberties of human nature for which they had fought and bled', to promoting 'union and national honour between the respective states . . . of the American empire [sic!]', and extending acts of beneficence . . . towards those officers and their families' in need.[98] Despite considerable interest from prominent founding fathers, especially George Washington himself, however, the Cincinnati never got off the ground, largely because it impaled itself on the crucial question of heredity. Instead, the new republic opted for a small standing army supplemented by a robust popular militia. This compromise was enshrined in the Second Amendment to the Constitution, which determined that '[a] well-regulated militia, being necessary to the security of a free state, the right of the people to keep and bear arms, shall not be infringed'.[99] Time would tell which of the two methods of mobilizing society for war, the continental European or that of the Continental Congress, would be more effective.

A very similar debate was raging in central and eastern Europe. The Poles watched the collapse of the Ottoman Empire in 1787–8 with trepidation, fearing they would be next. Determined not to succumb without a fight, the reformist King Stanislas August convened a four-year parliament in October 1788. Unlike previous sessions, this did not recess after six weeks but constituted itself into a confederation, resolved to sit until the Commonwealth had been put on a more secure footing. On the agenda were all the issues which would have to be addressed if Poland was to survive to the end of the century: army reform, the finances and the dreaded aristocratic veto. This programme was designed to forestall another partition, but it was also intended to make Poland a more effective alliance partner. Reform, Stanislas told Catherine at their meeting in May 1789, would enable the Commonwealth to send a substantial army to fight the Turks, and would even justify a share of the spoils. The Polish king demanded compensations for the losses of 1772 in the shape of Bessarabia, parts of Moldavia and a Black Sea port. The tsarina refused, but agreed reluctantly to pull her forces back from the Polish border. For the first time in more than two decades it looked as if Poland might once again become an independent actor on the European scene.

In Germany, fears of 'polonization' – partition at the hands of outside powers, or Austria and Prussia – injected new life into the debate on imperial reform. The *Reichstag* had been largely paralysed by regional and confessional divisions between 1760 and 1780, but the League of Princes showed that concerted collective action to defend the constitution was possible. In July 1787, Karl von Dalberg, the co-adjutor, deputy and designated successor of the Imperial Arch-Chancellor, launched a reform programme designed to restore coherence and a common purpose to the Empire. He argued that the constitution had become 'feeble', making the Empire 'contemptible to its neighbours'. The solution, Dalberg claimed, was a perpetual electoral capitulation, as a 'permanent constitution' for the Empire.[100] This, he argued, would lead to a stronger executive to carry out decisions agreed by the Diet. Some voices were also calling for broader political participation in imperial affairs. Christoph Ludwig Pfeiffer, a Habsburg propagandist, argued in 1787 that the imperial election should not just be a matter for the nine electors, but be decided by all the estates represented in the Diet. These initiatives led nowhere: unlike the American states, the component parts of the *Reich* had no intention of sacrificing their particular interests for the common good. The tension between the external security of the Empire and the 'German freedoms' of the individual princes remained unresolved.

The most spectacular response to the challenges thrown up by the European state system in the late 1780s took place in France. In August 1786, Charles Alexandre de Calonne, the French Comptroller-General of Finance, effectively admitted that the monarchy was bankrupt. Louis XVI was forced to convene an Assembly of Notables in February 1787. This dissolved three months later without having agreed any substantial fiscal reform. As a result, the monarchy was humiliatingly unable to intervene when the Prussians invaded Holland in September 1787. 'France has fallen,' Joseph remarked, 'and I doubt whether she will ever rise again.'[101] This was the last straw for a political nation whose patience with the failures of Bourbon foreign policy had worn thin and resulted in a profound crisis of legitimacy for the *ancien régime* at home.[102] Not only was the monarchy generally held responsible for the failure of French foreign policy, but hatred of the Austrian alliance placed the queen, Marie Antoinette, a Habsburg princess, in the firing line.[103] She personified Habsburg 'despotism', 'foreign' manipulation and 'unnatural' female influence. Not all of these attacks were unjustified: it was well-known that Marie Antoinette had pleaded her brother Joseph II's case diplomatically and dabbled in plans to partition France's old Ottoman ally. Marie Antoinette also became a lightning rod for a much broader sense of malaise. She was the principal target of a scurrilous, pornographic and often misogynistic assault from the 'lower' end of the public sphere. The nub of the critique, however, was fiscal-political. Noting the vast expense of the failed policy, one critic asked whether a royal minister should 'be able to spend in this way to further his plans? Not without the consent of the nation.'[104] The implication of this argument was clear: the increased taxation which French great-power ambitions required could only be effected at the price of more political participation.

Louis XVI and his ministers were now locked into a downward spiral. The political nation and the money markets, both foreign and domestic, had lost all confidence in Bourbon grand strategy. This meant that the monarchy found it difficult to borrow except at exorbitant rates of interest. This in turn reduced Bourbon diplomatic and military clout. In March 1789, the foreign minister, the Count de Montmorin, warned that no diplomatic initiatives were possible until the domestic crisis had been resolved and 'France would regain all its force and power'.[105] This further damaged the standing of the regime, creating a destructive cycle from which there was no escape. The various expedients adopted by successive ministries, increased taxation, coercion of the *parlements* and so on, only dug the *ancien régime* into a deeper hole. A successful war in support of Dutch liberty might have squared the circle. This, the strongly Austrophobic Comte de Ségur remarked, would have 'diverted the passions that were agitating and leading the country astray'. It never happened, Ségur continued, because the ministry was 'timid against our natural enemies, but bold against [the] nation'.[106] In other words, because the monarchy refused to go to war in defence of its strategic interests in Europe, it was forced into confrontation with its own people at home.

In mid-August 1788, Louis XVI finally agreed to summon an Estates General, for the first time since 1614. Petitions of grievances – *cahiers de doléances* – were drawn up. These accepted, for now, the monarchical system as 'the most conducive to its internal tranquillity and external security', and they did not oppose aristocracy *per se* so much as hope to make it serve the interest of the nation better.[107] The Estates General finally met in May 1789. By then, however, the political nation had lost confidence in the monarch and his ministers. The Third Estate now seized the initiative. Traditional conventions of voting by estate, which would have favoured the clergy (First Estate) and the nobility (Second Estate) were replaced by voting by head, which benefited the much more numerous Third Estate. This turned itself into a National Assembly in mid-June, and very shortly after it swore the 'Tennis Court Oath' that it would not dissolve before it had secured a new constitution for France. On 14 July a mob stormed the Bastille. In the countryside, the rural population was gripped by the *Grande Peur*, fear of an Austrian invasion and aristocratic reaction, which led to widespread attacks on nobles and their properties. As yet, however, the reformers did not mean to destroy the monarchy itself, quite the opposite. The lawyer Pierre-Louis Lucretelle put it this way: 'The august monarchy fits our physical situation and moral nature. Our aims and principles do not tend to weaken it, we wish only to regulate it in order to strengthen it.'[108] It was still possible for Louis to become a strong king through a vigorous foreign policy.

The wave of revolutionary change which swept France in late

1789 and throughout 1790 had many causes, but the principal driving force was a determination to make French society better able to support the re-establishment of national greatness on the European scene. Central to this was the role of the nobility. In the course of the year, reformers abandoned their hope that the aristocracy could be persuaded to embrace their martial destiny once more. Instead, in early August the National Assembly renounced all feudal privileges with a view to creating a social order based on merit rather than birth. The 'Declaration of the rights of man and the citizen' followed at the end of the month. In November it was the turn of the First Estate, which had also outlived its usefulness; the nationalization of Church property was decreed. The expected profits from the sale of Church lands were turned into *assignats* to fund government expenditure. Monastic vows were forbidden in mid-February 1790, and the nobility was finally abolished by formal order in June. A month later, the Civil Constitution of the Clergy subordinated the Church to the government, and in November the clergy were required to swear an oath of loyalty to that effect. The many national and linguistic minorities in the kingdom – Bretons, Flemings, Basques, Catalans and Germans – came under increasing pressure to adopt the French language and ways. So did the various dialect groups, especially in the south and west. The intent behind all these measures, as the revolutionary Emmanuel Sieyes argued, was to 'make all parts of France into a single body, and all the peoples who divide it into a single nation'.[109]

At first, all this made very little impression on the European great powers. There was considerable sympathy for developments in France. In Britain, many believed them to be inspired by the Whig 'Glorious Revolution', thus presaging the triumph of liberty in that country. In Potsdam and Vienna, the Prussian chief minister, Hertzberg, and Joseph II both welcomed what they saw as the victory for the principles of enlightened government. The forcible restoration of monarchical authority in France was not on the agenda of any European government. 'Without doubt,' Kaunitz stated unequivocally right at the end of July 1789, 'we cannot intervene in any manner.'[110] Germany itself stayed relatively quiet. There were a few risings in the west, which quickly petered out, and a revolt against the Prince Bishop of Liège. In the Habsburg monarchy, on the other hand, a truly revolutionary situation was developing in response to Joseph's reforms. By 1789, his plans to abolish serfdom had provoked massive disobedience in Hungary, while the attack on representative institutions in the Habsburg Netherlands led to a revolt there that same year. These disturbances were centrifugal tendencies, designed to reassert the dominance of local elites against a central authority determined to cut a more formidable figure in the European state system.

Only a tiny minority agreed with Edmund Burke's *Reflections on the Revolution in France* (1790), which spoke of an attack on tradition, religion, property and 'chivalry', 'a revolution in sentiments, manners and moral opinions'. 'It appears to me as if I were in a great crisis,' Burke writes towards the beginning of the *Reflections*, 'not of the affairs of France alone but of all Europe, perhaps of more than Europe. All circumstances taken together, the French Revolution is the most astonishing that has hitherto happened in the world.'[111] The *Reflections* were not merely a literary and political landmark but also a publishing sensation, selling between 17,000 and 19,000 copies (with a much greater readership) and provoking about another hundred pamphlets in turn.[112] Over the next years, Burke mounted a veritable crusade against the 'universal empire' of the Jacobins, bearers of an 'armed doctrine' which he considered every bit as dangerous as that of Louis XIV. In particular, he feared the impact of the Revolution on the 'centre of Europe' – Germany – 'that region which touches and must influence every other', where it was 'ruining the august fabric of the [Holy Roman] Empire'. Burke therefore invoked the 'law of neighbourhood' – or 'vicinage' – in support of his contention that European states were entitled to intervene in self-defence against France; he explicitly rejected the idea of non-intervention in the internal affairs of a sovereign state as 'a false principle in the law of nations'.[113]

The main reason why the outside powers paid so little attention to the crisis in France was because they were intensely preoccupied by events elsewhere. There was general agreement only that the Revolution had finally destroyed all French influence within the state system. 'I defy the ablest heads in England to have planned, or its whole wealth to have purchased,' the British Foreign Secretary, the Duke of Leeds, remarked shortly after the Bastille fell, 'a situation so fatal to its rival, as that to which France is now reduced by her own intestine commotions.'[114] The Prussians also welcomed the fall of the *ancien régime* as a blow to its Habsburg ally. In August 1789, scarcely a month after the fall of the

Bastille, the Prussian king resolved to take advantage of the new situation and to attack Austria by the beginning of the next year unless Joseph backed down in the Balkans. A few months later, he intervened against the revolutionaries in Liège, not to restore the old regime but in order to pre-empt the Austrians.[115] In January 1790, as France slipped further into chaos, Prussia concluded an offensive alliance with the Ottoman Empire, enveloping Austria on two sides. The general European war, which had seemed close on the eve of the French Revolution, now appeared imminent.

Meanwhile, Britain was debating intervention of a very different kind. In late May 1787, a group of parliamentarians, doctors, clergymen and others had met in London to form the 'Committee of the Society for the purpose of effecting the abolition of the Slave Trade'. Its supporters were driven by an often religiously inspired sense of humanitarian outrage at the whole concept of slavery, and especially the horrors of the 'middle passage', the transportation across the Atlantic. In mid-April 1791, William Wilberforce's parliamentary bill demanding the abolition of the slave trade failed, but put the issue firmly on the political agenda.[116] The slaves, of course, were not just passive recipients of western benevolence. In August 1791 a major counter-revolutionary revolt broke out in the French Caribbean colony of Saint-Domingue led by plantation slaves outraged not only by the Revolution's continued toleration of slavery and its failure to extend the rights of man to *gens de couleur* but also by its treatment of the king and revealed religion. Their leaders regarded themselves as African tribal chiefs rather than representatives of the people. Left to their own devices the revolting slaves would probably have set up a political system similar to the traditional slave-owning African kingdoms from which they had originally come; they regularly sold black captives to the Spanish and British.[117] The revolt was a major headache for the European powers, especially Britain and Spain, who drew much of their revenue, and thus their European leverage, from slave plantations in the Caribbean, and the Americans, who feared that the example of Haiti would inflame the black population of the Southern states. The relationship between slavery and the international balance was thus very close.

Events in France therefore did not command European attention until two geopolitical revolutions forced it on to the agenda. The first took place in the Empire. When Joseph II died in late February 1790 he was succeeded by Leopold II, who not only reversed his brother's confrontational domestic policies but was also determined to mend diplomatic fences with his northern neighbour. In July 1790, rather than go to war with each other over Joseph's expansion into Turkey, Austria and Prussia came to terms at the Convention of Reichenbach. Leopold agreed to halt operations in the Balkans without the expected territorial gains. Prussia in turn promised to support the Habsburg candidate as Joseph's successor to the imperial crown. If the terms of the agreement seemed innocuous enough, the very fact of an Austro-Prussian rapprochement was a geopolitical earthquake. It was pregnant with implications for the other German states, which feared a Habsburg–Hohenzollern partition of the Holy Roman Empire. Reichenbach also opened the way for Austro-Prussian cooperation against what was believed to be a weakened France. Prussia began to develop plans for the annexation of Jülich and Berg, and the compensation of their owners with territory in Alsace.

The other geopolitical transformation was a radical change in French grand strategy. To the revolutionaries, Austria, not Britain, was once again the main enemy.[118] France would once more look east, rather than across the Channel or the Atlantic. But whereas the Bourbons had worked with the grain of the imperial constitution to make incremental territorial gains, and provide the monarchy with more defensible borders,[119] the new French geopolitics stressed the necessity for the Republic to safeguard the 'natural limits' of France: the Pyrenees, the Alps and the Rhine. As the veteran anti-Viennese writer Claude-Charles Peyssonnel told the Society of the Friends of the Constitution in early March 1790, France's ultimate aim must be to secure 'her limits as far as the Rhine, which is the frontier marked out for her by nature'. This placed the western regions of the Holy Roman Empire, especially the Rhineland and the Palatinate, in the firing-line. The new men also stressed the importance of pan-revolutionary solidarity across Europe. In part, this was a matter of exporting the values of the Revolution, but it also reflected the deep-seated belief that the Revolution in France would never be safe in a Europe dominated by *ancien régime* states. As one letter to the Parisian Diplomatic Committee put it in July 1791, 'When there are no more tyrants in the world we shall have no more wars to fear.'[120]

These strands came together in revolutionary policy towards the Empire.[121] In ideological terms, the *Reich* represented everything the new order held in contempt: a reactionary hodge-podge of petty ecclesiastical territories and petty principalities. The revolutionaries reacted with derision when the imperial nobility and episcopate in Alsace protested to the Diet, and ultimately to the emperor, against the abrogation of their feudal privileges and diocesan rights through the abolition of feudalism and the Civil Constitution of the Clergy. To make matters worse, French émigrés plotting the restoration of the old order found comfortable billets in the courts of western Germany, especially nearby Koblenz. If they could persuade one or both of the German great powers to take on their cause, the Revolution would be in mortal danger. In August 1791, that moment seemed to have come, when the Austrians and Prussians concluded a Convention at Pillnitz in Saxony, by issuing a joint declaration of concern about the state of affairs in France.[122] The radical journalist and later foreign minister Pierre LeBrun called the document a 'declaration of war of despots allied against the freedom of nations'.[123] 'Should the campaign commence,' Thomas Paine wrote to the Marquis de la Fayette in February 1792, rather forgetting his earlier injunctions against the export of freedom, 'I hope it will end in a war against German despotism, and in establishing the freedom of all Germany. When France shall be surrounded with revolutions, she will be in peace and safety.'

External pressures also had a profound effect on the development of French domestic politics. Initially, the revolutionaries had been content to leave the running of foreign policy in crown hands. In the summer of 1790, however, an Anglo-Spanish crisis over Nootka Sound and ownership of the north-east Pacific coast brought about a change. The new foreign minister, Montmorin, informed the National Assembly in May that the king would honour the family compact and come to the aid of his fellow Bourbons. This caused outrage, partly because many felt that he had no right to do so without authorization from the Assembly, partly because not everybody was convinced that the new France should be honouring dynastic commitments entered into by the *ancien régime*, and in part because it was feared that the king would use war as a cover for the restoration of despotism. Most assumed that a republican France would be more peaceful, and would live in harmony with other republics; only a minority, such as the deputies Jean Sifrein Maury and Baron Malouet, warned that 'despotism and liberty have produced the same excesses'.[124] So at the end of the month, the Assembly passed a decree clarifying the relationship between the executive and the legislature.

The king was still to appoint ministers, diplomats and army officers but matters of war and peace would be decided by the nation, not the crown. No wars of conquest, or any measures which infringed the liberties of other people, were to be permitted; ministers who breached these guidelines would be liable to prosecution. More generally, the revolutionaries demanded greater transparency in foreign policy, to mark the breach with the secretive and incompetent practices of *ancien régime* diplomacy.[125] A new geopolitics had emerged, which questioned the very basis of legitimacy within the state system.

In early November 1791, the National Assembly decreed that all émigrés must return or face confiscation of their property. The king vetoed the measure. Then the National Assembly demanded a pre-emptive strike against the émigrés, and instructed the king to demand their expulsion by the German princes hosting them along the western border of the Empire. Otherwise, France would carry out the operation herself, even if it meant infringing imperial sovereignty. The king now went along with this measure, because he saw in it a last resort to restore his former power. A successful war would rally people behind the crown, whereas a lost conflict would at least destroy the Revolution. Secretly, however, Louis was urging the great powers to intervene and restore him to his former authority. The queen and the Baron de Breteuil encouraged him in this strategy, and maintained a clandestine correspondence with Vienna. At the end of January 1792 the French issued an ultimatum to Austria, and in early March the hawkish revolutionary General Charles-François Dumouriez became foreign minister. In the middle of the following month, war was declared on Austria, citing the emperor's interference in the internal affairs of France, especially 'his wish to support the pretensions of the German princes owning lands in France', which was a direct affront to 'the sovereignty of the French nation'. Prussia joined in on 13 June. In late July 1792, the coalition commander, the Duke of Brunswick, issued a manifesto which listed the defence of the 'German princes in Alsace and Lorraine' and 'of Germany' in general, even before the 'equally important' aim of terminating 'anarchy in the interior of France'; the two objectives were, of course, inseparably linked.[126] The French Revolutionary Wars had begun.[127]

For France, the struggle was both an ideological and a strategic contest; the two considerations were inseparable in the minds of many Frenchmen. The Declaration which accompanied war with Austria renounced any 'view to making conquests' and stressed that force would never be employed 'against the liberty of any people'.[128] In mid-November 1792, the Convention, which had succeeded the legislative Assembly, issued its public Decree of Fraternity and Help to Foreign Peoples, in which it undertook to 'grant fraternity and aid to all peoples who wish to recover their liberty; and it charges the executive power with giving the generals the orders necessary for bringing aid to such peoples and for defending citizens who have been, or who might be, harassed for the cause of liberty'.[129] Here the most pressing issue was Belgium, which was the closest staging post for an Austro-Prussian attack, where the lie of the land did not allow for any obvious 'natural limits', and where local revolutionaries were begging for help. The answer, according to Charles-François Dumouriez and Pierre LeBrun, who were successively foreign minister from March 1792 to April 1793, was to eject the Habsburgs from the Netherlands and instal a united friendly Jacobin republic in their place. 'If the people do not have the means to carry out the revolution by their own efforts,' Pierre-Joseph Cambon argued, 'then it will be necessary to supplement them and to act in their own best interests by exercising temporarily the revolutionary power.'[130]

Russia remained aloof, at least for now. Catherine made no mention of her guarantor role in Germany after 1791.[131] The tsarina was preoccupied by affairs nearer to home; indeed, her moral support for the Austro-Prussian intervention in France was largely driven by the desire to exploit the weakness of Poland. There was some urgency in doing so, because the Polish reform programme culminated in May 1791 in a constitution designed to ensure the continued survival of the Commonwealth in a dangerous international environment. Far from being an outgrowth of French revolutionary principles, as Catherine claimed, this document provided for a hereditary Saxon monarchy. The *liberum veto* was abolished, as were confederations and the anarchic 'right of resistance'; the army was increased and reformed. Indeed, the tsarina opposed the constitution precisely *because* it was trying to give Poland a powerful monarchy which would protect her from being held to ransom by her neighbours. So, in late January 1793, Catherine persuaded Frederick William II to abandon Stanislas and participate in a second partition of Poland. Huge swathes of western Poland were annexed by Prussia, while Russia grabbed another enormous belt of territory in the east. The *liberum veto* and the elective monarchy were restored. A sullen but compliant 'dumb session' of the Polish Diet ratified these decisions in September 1793. A year later the Poles rose in vain to reassert their independence under the charismatic leadership of Tadeusz Kościuszko. At the end of that campaign the Austrians, Russians and Prussians agreed the final partition of Poland (1795). It was a brutal illustration of the fate in store for those states which failed to find the inner cohesion to survive.[132]

Nowhere was this more keenly noted than in neighbouring Germany. On the one hand, most Germans felt that the superstitious, degenerate, lazy, backward, brutal and bigoted Poles had got no more than they deserved; religious and national minorities were generally better treated after the partition. On the other hand, the parallels between their two situations as divided commonwealths surrounded by predatory great powers were unmistakable. 'The recent fate of Poland,' one pamphleteer warned, 'will also be that of Germany', unless it embarked on a timely programme of imperial reform.[133] 'When Poland has been completely partitioned', the imperial reformer Johan Jacob Moser warned, 'then it will be our turn to be eaten.'[134]

Meanwhile, the advance of the Austro-Prussian forces under the Duke of Brunswick was halted at Valmy in mid-September 1792. Within a few months the French counter-attack had swept the allies out of France and back into the Austrian Netherlands and western Germany. Savoy was annexed in late November 1792. The revolutionary advance into the Low Countries immediately led to serious tensions with Britain. In February 1793, the National Convention declared war on Britain and the Dutch Republic. Conflict with Spain followed a month later. All this further radicalized French politics. The onset of war sparked a wave of popular paranoia. A failed French invasion of Belgium in late April 1792 was blamed on the king and a mysterious 'Austrian Committee' supposedly directing French policy from behind the scenes. At the end of May priests who refused to swear loyalty to the Civil Constitution were deported as a potential security risk. This mass hysteria culminated in the 'September massacres' of prisoners accused of giving comfort to the enemy. It was not long before suspicion fell on the royal family, who were believed – rightly – to be in league with the enemies of the Revolution abroad. The monarchy was overthrown in early August and by the end of the year Louis XVI himself was on trial for his life; he was executed in late January 1793. Henceforth, domestic politics were to be dominated by trials and debates on the conduct of the war. In April, a decline in military fortunes led to the creation of the Committee of Public Safety, and in September the fall of Toulon to British forces sparked the mass executions of the 'Terror'.

Surrounded on all sides by hostile powers, the revolutionaries steeled French society to meet the challenge. In late February, the Convention decreed the conscription of 300,000 men, and the next few months saw the creation of revolutionary armies funded by *assignats* – the paper bills drawn on confiscated Church lands – which became the sole legal tender, and a forced loan on the rich. At the end of August 1793, at the instigation of Lazare Carnot, minister of war and 'Organizer of Victory', the National Convention proclaimed that 'all Frenchmen are to be permanently requisitioned for the service of the armies'. Not all of French society responded positively: conscription provoked anti-revolutionary revolts by the royalist Chouans in Brittany and the peasants of the Vendée; 'federalists' in many parts of the country, and various southern rebels also defied the authority of Paris for many years.[135] These groups soon entered into correspondence with Britain, which dispatched a series of unsuccessful expeditions to the western and southern coasts of France throughout the 1790s. The authorities moved to crush insurrection with extreme violence. 'Soldiers of Liberty,' the Convention instructed the Army of the West in October 1793, 'the brigands of the Vendée must be exterminated.'[136] The region was subjected to a sustained campaign of suppression by the revolutionary *colonnes infernales*, which resorted to large-scale executions, burnings and even mass drowning. More than 100,000 people, mostly civilians, were killed and about one fifth of the total housing stock was destroyed. In part, the Convention's announced aim to 'destroy' the Vendée reflected metropolitan concern about the links between the rebels and outside powers, and fears for the unity of France, but it also reflected a utopian vision from which all 'reactionary' elements had been purged.

The internal energies unleashed by the Revolution made France once more the first power in Europe. To many contemporary observers, the French had developed the ideal form of domestic organization for external power projection, which was not only superior to absolutism, but also trumped Britain's ability to punch above its weight through its consultative fiscal-military state. Tom Paine, for example, predicted that

Britain's mixed monarchical-parliamentary system would eventually destroy her national greatness, just as the European monarchies were being laid low by their parasitic aristocracies. By contrast, he argued, modern republics, such as the United States and France, could wage 'a war of the whole nation'.[137] In the course of the next three years revolutionary forces flooded into the Low Countries, western Germany and northern Italy. The underlying motivation here was not just the establishment of the 'natural limits' but the hope of banishing war through the elimination of reactionary governments; designs for continental hegemony were not, as yet, evident. 'The French nation declares,' said the National Assembly in mid-December 1792, 'that it will treat as an enemy of the people anyone who, refusing liberty and equality, or renouncing them, might wish to preserve, recall, or treat with the prince and the privileged castes.'[138] It promised not to lay down arms until these peoples shall have adopted the principles of equality and established a 'free and popular government'. Under its various revolutionary governments from the National Assembly, through the Legislative Assembly, the National Convention to the Directory, France sought not so much absolute power in Europe as absolute security through universal peace.[139]

Very soon, however, the revolutionaries found that each expansion made them less rather than more secure. Once Belgium had been occupied, many Frenchmen began to argue that they should press on into the Dutch Republic, partly in order to prevent her from joining, as Dumouriez put it, 'a formidable league that could crush us' and partly because 'without Holland, our position in Belgium will become untenable'.[140] The first thrust into the Dutch Republic in February 1793 miscarried, but towards the end of the following year a second attempt succeeded, and by mid-January 1795 Amsterdam had been occupied. Four months later, France established the 'Batavian Republic' with the collaboration of local Jacobins. In Italy, the advance of the revolutionary armies – commanded from 1796 by a remarkable young general, Napoleon Bonaparte – spread like a rash right down the peninsula to the heel of the Italian boot, turning out improvised new political structures as it went: the Cispadane Republic in 1796, the Cisalpine and Ligurian in 1797, the Roman in 1798, and the Parthenopean in 1799. In March 1798 Switzerland was occupied and reorganized as the 'Helvetic Republic'. This was a dynamic driven by fear as much as greed.

The principal preoccupation of the new geopolitics, however, was Germany. Ever since the spring of 1791, French diplomats had been pondering a reorganization of the Empire, involving the abolition of the imperial crown and the consolidation of the smaller principalities into larger entities, which would then confederate into a buffer state to protect France's western border. Accompanying this geopolitical agenda was a profound ideological antipathy. 'The Holy [Roman] Empire,' as one revolutionary put it in 1795, 'that monstrous assembly of small and large despots ... must also disappear by the effects of our incredible revolution. The kingdom of France supported it, the French Republic shall work for its destruction.'[141] At the same time, the French were anxious – as one of the Directory's experts put it – that 'Germany would become, by a series of usurpations, a kingdom under a single head'.[142] The 'natural limits' were established though the elimination of all imperial enclaves within France – such as Montbéliard – and the annexation of all territory on the left bank of the Rhine. The French also experimented with local Jacobin regimes, and a short-lived republic was established in Mainz.[143] Many German intellectuals and administrators sympathized with the apparently more 'rational' and efficient French who freed them from feudalism.[144] It was not long, however, before the revolutionaries realized that these movements lacked popular legitimacy and were thus ineffective agents of French foreign policy. Far from being useful allies, they proved to be liabilities which had to be propped up. For this reason, plans for further republics, such as one in south Germany, were soon shelved.[145]

On the other side of the Rhine, the German princes observed all this with mounting horror. The threat of 'polonization' at the hands of Austria and Prussia was now aggravated by the reality of French annexationism. Maddeningly, the lesser German powers could not guard against the one without risking the other. Some, such as Duke Frederick of Württemberg, spoke defiantly of their determination not to let their territory become a 'toy' of the great powers. In practice, however, their room for manoeuvre was painfully limited. 'It depends entirely on Russia, England and France,' the Bavarian envoy to Vienna remarked in 1795, 'what the fate of the Empire will be.' And by the late 1790s it had become abundantly clear to the German princes that nobody was going to haul their chestnuts out of the fire for them.[146] All this produced a last great debate on the reform of the imperial constitution. Many agreed with Renatus Karl von Senckenberg's claim in 1790 that if only the Empire could present a common front to the outside world then 'no other empire in Europe' would be as powerful.[147] The Austrian chief minister, Baron von Thugut, even suggested arming the people in a *Volksbewaffnung*, the German equivalent of the *levée en masse*. But when the smaller and middling princes assembled at Wilhelmsbad in late September 1794 in a final attempt to combine in defence of the Empire, their efforts were blocked by Vienna. The Austrians saw the meeting as a constraint on Habsburg power in the Empire and feared that it would be hijacked by the Prussians.

Most German states now sought to make their peace with France. At the very end of 1794, the Diet asked the emperor to sue for peace on the basis of Westphalia. The Empire, in other words, was prepared to accept Revolutionary France as a guarantor power. First to jump ship were the Prussians. By the Treaty of Basel in April 1795, they promised to observe strict neutrality in the imperial war against France. The French, for their part, undertook to honour a neutrality zone in northern Germany, which would be dominated by Prussia. All German territories west of the line were left to fend for themselves, and a secret clause envisaged the eventual French annexation of the left bank of the Rhine. Only the Austrians battled on wholeheartedly. The problem was that the Empire was increasingly unwilling to shoulder the burden against France. Thugut recognized that no such arrangement would last, but continuing the war damaged Austria's standing within the Empire. Brutal requisitioning policies in south Germany antagonized people and rulers alike. Moreover, the costly Italian campaigns of 1795 and 1796, designed to reduce French pressure in Germany, backfired. They exposed the Emperor Francis (who had succeeded after the premature death of his father, Leopold) to the same charge that his ancestor Maximilian had faced 300 years earlier, of abandoning German interests for Italian ones.

To make matters worse, the new French general in Italy, Napoleon Bonaparte, was driving all before him, and criticizing the poor performance of the Parisian government on other fronts. In September 1797, he translated military fame into domestic political capital and together with his allies took control of the Directory in the coup of *Fructidor*. Napoleon does not seem to have started with a grand strategic blueprint; subsequent rationalizations by him and others need to be treated with scepticism.[148] 'Napoleon never had a plan,' his long-serving foreign minister, Charles-Maurice de Talleyrand-Périgord, later remarked, 'it was always what had just happened that told him what to do next.'[149] The pursuit of 'glory' and 'destiny' – two constants in Napoleon's rhetoric – does not constitute a strategy in itself, beyond that of perpetual motion and conflict.[150] All the same, certain recurring assumptions and policies can be identified. First and foremost, Napoleon wanted to dominate Europe, uniting it on French terms and for the benefit of France. The execution of this design required him to control Germany in order to secure its resources and to appropriate the legacy of the Holy Roman Empire for his own imperial project. This approach in turn brought Napoleon into prolonged conflict not merely with Austria and Prussia, but also with the ultimate arbiters of the Empire, Russia and Great Britain. Containing Russia meant taking a forward position well beyond Germany, especially in Poland, the Balkans and the Mediterranean. And striking at the bases of British power meant either an invasion of England itself, or a blow against the overseas empire from which London drew so much of its strength.[151] To quote Napoleon himself – albeit in rueful retrospect from St Helena – his aim at this time was 'to re-establish the kingdom of Poland as a barrier against the Muscovite barbarians, divide Austria, establish client states in Italy, declare Hungary independent, break up Prussia, form independent republics in England and Ireland, control Egypt, drive the Turks out of Europe, and liberate the Balkan nations'.[152]

Faced with all this, the Habsburgs finally made peace with France at the Treaty of Campo Formio in October 1797. Its terms marked a fundamental shift in European geopolitics: the Austrians exchanged remote Belgium and anterior Austria for the more proximate Venetia, whose independence was thus extinguished. They had effectively been banished from western Germany and the Low Countries. There were more profound changes to come, however. The future of the Holy Roman Empire was referred to a Congress at Rastatt, which met from November 1797 to consider how the princes who had been expropriated by the French on the left bank of the Rhine were to be 'compensated'. This cleared the way for a whole-scale territorial reorganization of the Empire arbitrated by Paris, the final shift from a traditional Bourbon policy of maintaining the complex balance in Germany towards a partition which would create a smaller number of larger states.[153] That same year, Napoleon set the tone for what was to come when he referred to the Holy Roman Empire as 'an old whore who has been violated by everyone for a long time'.[154] Campo Formio was therefore at best only a truce before the struggle for mastery in Germany resumed. It lasted hardly more than a year because, as the new ruler of France, Napoleon Bonaparte proved to be an even more subversive actor in the European state system than his revolutionary predecessors. He came to power on the back of his personal military prowess, and with the promise to wage the conflict against *ancien régime* Europe more effectively than the Directory had done. This project underlay Napoleon's domestic pledge to 'complete the Revolution' and in so doing to 'end' it. The huge energies unleashed by the fall of the French monarchy would now be turned outwards.

In 1798–9, Napoleon went on the offensive across several fronts. In Germany, his diplomats pushed ahead ruthlessly with territorial reorganization. Switzerland was occupied in January 1798 in order to round off French territory and secure the important Alpine passes. An abortive expedition was sent to Ireland in the summer and autumn of 1798 to support a rebellion by the United Irishmen against British rule. At around the same time, Napoleon landed in Egypt, leading to war with the Ottoman Empire, and in the following year he invaded Palestine. This operation did not signal a turn to the 'orient', but was intended to strike at the bases of British power in India and thus reduce London's influence in Europe.[155] 'To truly destroy England,' Napoleon remarked to Talleyrand, 'it is necessary for us to seize Egypt.'[156] In Italy, French troops advanced steadily down the peninsula, capturing Naples in January 1799. In the Caribbean and on the high seas, France stepped up the pressure on British shipping, and the sugar colonies which financed so much of the British war effort and that of her European allies. Napoleon also began to think about ways of recovering France's overseas possessions. All of these operations, though tactically aggressive, were justified as strategically defensive in character. In practice, there was little difference between defensive and offensive here: the absolute security of France could only be achieved through the absolute insecurity of all her neighbours far and near.

The resumption of the French advance under Napoleon produced an instant response from the European great powers. In Vienna, Thugut watched the attacks on Switzerland and the Ottoman Empire with deep concern, but his principal anxiety was Germany. 'If the French continue to hold Switzerland,' he wrote in July 1798, 'revolution in the Swabian circle first and then in all of Germany is inevitable ... whose ruin will lead to the upheaval of all of Europe.'[157] Once Germany went, he feared the rest of Europe would go with it. That was also the view of Paul I, who succeeded Catherine as tsar in 1796. He was not only ideologically more hostile to the Revolution, but also deeply worried about Napoleon's push into the Mediterranean and the Levant. Above all, Paul wanted to re-establish the balance of power in Germany, which Catherine had rather neglected in her final years. In the words of one Bavarian diplomat, Russia, passive for so long, now threw 'herself into the middle of the fray as a principal protagonist' in the Empire.[158] So in 1798–9, Austro-Russian troops attacked the French in southern Germany and northern Italy with the help of British subsidies; and an Anglo-Russian force landed in Holland. The War of the Second Coalition had begun.

Faced with this new round of international conflict, the British sought to reduce their strategic vulnerabilities and maximize internal cohesion. The 1798 rising in Ireland and the accompanying French expedition had demonstrated once again the dangers of an open flank to the west. The government of William Pitt the Younger therefore introduced the Act of Union between Great Britain and Ireland in 1800, which merged the parliaments of both countries. This was supposed to be accompanied by Catholic emancipation, in order to reconcile the majority population to the British link, and to facilitate their recruitment in large numbers into the armed forces to fight against France. 'Supposing there were no other reasons which rendered the union of the sister kingdoms desirable,' the British Under-Secretary for Ireland, Edward Cooke, remarked, 'the state of Europe, and especially of France, seems to dictate it.' The measure failed because George III blocked it for religious reasons.[159]

By contrast, the people at the centre of the storm, the Germans, remained divided. Their political commonwealth, the Holy Roman Empire, failed to find the unity and cohesion necessary to keep outside powers at arm's length. No wonder then that one pamphleteer looked forward around the turn of the century to the day of a 'national union, in which the German people would finally control German lands and German energies', and no more be exposed to the 'pillage of foreign armies, the daily despoliations of internal tyrants', nor be 'the constant victim of foreign powers'.[160] Some still looked to one or other of the

German great powers to provide that direction. Johann Gottfried Herder, for example, hoped that Prussia would become the 'central power ... which would preserve the lands of all German peoples ... from oppression by foreign nations and languages'.[161] The reality of Prussian foreign policy since 1795, however, had been a steady retreat from 'German' commitments to a much more narrowly northern and eastern focus.[162] This meant that the full potential of Germany around 1800, the nearly 16 million people who did not live in either Austria or Prussia (about two thirds of the total) was still unrealized.

The impact of the Napoleonic challenge was also felt on the other side of the Atlantic, where the United States watched events with rising alarm throughout the 1790s. Hostility to London surged as the Royal Navy interfered with American shipping as part of the blockade against France and it took all of John Jay's ingenuity to hammer out a compromise treaty in 1794. At the same time, French ambitions also posed a direct danger. News that France was seeking to buy Florida, and take over the whole Spanish Louisiana territory, which she did by the Treaty of San Ildefonso in October 1800, provoked alarm in Washington. These threats and US–French naval tensions led to an 'undeclared war' – a 'semi-hostility' as Hamilton termed it – between the two states in 1797–1800. All this meant that American domestic politics were completely dominated by the question of how to deal with the international impact of the French Revolution.[163] It was a period, as President Monroe later remarked, 'during which the policy of the Union in its relations with Europe constituted the principal basis of our political divisions'. The Jay Treaty only passed the Senate after a brutal debate, and – along with foreign affairs more generally – became the principal issue in the 1796 election.

Meanwhile, the Second Coalition was coming apart at the seams. Prussia refused to join the effort, despite intense British lobbying. The Austrians and the Russians quarrelled over the conduct of operations in Germany and Italy. Britain and Russia fell out violently over the future of the Mediterranean, in particular the strategically vital island of Malta, and more generally over the Royal Navy's treatment of neutral shipping. Relations deteriorated to such an extent that the tsar set up the second League of Armed Neutrality – which eventually included Russia, Prussia, Denmark and Sweden – to contain Britain's maritime unilateralism. Nearly a decade after the start of the Revolutionary Wars, in other words, much of Europe was united, not against Napoleon but in defiance of Britain. As the French *Bulletin of the Army of the Reserve* declared following Bonaparte's crushing victory at Marengo, 'the generals, officers and soldiers of the Austrian army . . . appear convinced that we only fight each other so that the English can sell their sugar and coffee at a higher price'.[164] Some voices in St Petersburg, such as Fedor Rostopchin, were urging the tsar to turn his back on central Europe again, to drop the preoccupation with the balance of power, confront Britain and partition the Ottoman Empire with Austria and France. At the beginning of 1801, Paul even prepared to send a large Cossack force to attack British India, a project only called off after his assassination a few months later by court conspirators opposed to his plans for a Franco-Russian alliance. By February 1801, the exhausted Austrians concluded a peace settlement with Napoleon at Lunéville; the British eventually followed suit at Amiens in late March 1802.

The two treaties gave Napoleon the chance to rebuild France's overseas empire, partly to secure the resources necessary for European hegemony and partly to deny them to Britain, making it more difficult for London to fund future coalitions against him. Central to this project was taking possession of the American territories ceded by Spain, and the recovery of the rich island of Haiti. Bonaparte's plans to create a new 'New France' were doomed to failure, however. His attempt to reoccupy Haiti ended in failure due to disease and determined local resistance. Napoleon's plans to develop Louisiana also came to nothing. Washington was determined to prevent the revival of a French presence on the southern and western flanks of the Union, through diplomacy if possible and pre-emptive military action, if necessary.[165] 'France possessing herself of Louisiana,' President Jefferson warned the French negotiator, 'is the embryo of a tornado which will burst on the countries on both sides of the Atlantic.' In the face of this implacable American opposition, Napoleon decided to sell the whole territory to the United States for the huge sum of 80 million dollars, or about four cents an acre. He ploughed the money back into military preparations for the next round with Britain, drawing a loan from the London bank of Baring on the strength of the Louisiana bonds; British capitalists were selling him the rope which would hang them. The strategic implications of the deal were enormous. Napoleon had given up his claims to the western hemisphere for good. The United States, by contrast, had doubled in size to include all or parts of the future states of Arkansas, Missouri, South and North Dakota, Minnesota, Nebraska, Montana, Iowa, Kansas, Montana, Wyoming and Oklahoma.[166]

Napoleon's real empire was in Europe. The treaties of Lunéville and Amiens left him in complete control of western and southern Europe. Belgium had long since been annexed, and the Batavian Republic was a French satellite; the traditional 'counterscarp' of England had been comprehensively torn down. Italy was also totally under his thumb: Piedmont was directly incorporated into France, while the rest of the peninsula was divided into a congeries of puppet republics. Iberia, too, had been entirely overawed. Spain, an ally since 1796, had been forced into a conflict with Britain's ally Portugal in the 'War of the Oranges'. The crucial unresolved issue, however, was the future of central Europe, where the bulk of the Empire was tottering but still intact, where Austria and Prussia stood bruised but yet unbowed, where the new tsar was determined to make a stand against French encroachments, and where the British still hoped that diplomacy and gold would mobilize another coalition against France. It was there that the vital interests of all the major protagonists would converge for an epic showdown once the distribution of territory had been agreed at the Imperial Recess. 'Germany', as the staunch anti-Napoleonic propagandist Friedrich von Gentz remarked, 'is the central point. There can be no more independence in Europe, if that of Germany is not assured.'[167]

In 1803, the Imperial Recess finally pronounced on how the spoils of the 1790s were to be divided. It soon became clear that the greatest damage to the fabric of German politics had been done not by the French themselves, but by the partitionist tendencies they had unleashed among the larger and middling German states. Despite stinging military defeats, Austria and Prussia were actually major beneficiaries of the first ten years or so of the French wars, having in both cases traded exposed western territories for larger, more contiguous lands. In relative terms, however, it was the middling states who gained most. Thanks to their 'compensation' for losses on the left bank of the Rhine, Baden, Württemberg and Bavaria all increased substantially in size and coherence, swallowing up the smaller principalities. In recognition of their new benefactor all three began to transfer their allegiance from the Empire to Napoleon. At the same time, many Germans now saw the Frenchman as a surrogate emperor. Napoleon himself encouraged these expectations by proclaiming himself Emperor of France in May 1804, and crowning himself with the crown of Charlemagne in Paris in December 1804.[168] Napoleon was careful to validate his imperial title with a referendum: French coinage now bore the contradictory motto of '*République française – Napoléon empéreur*'. The Habsburgs reacted by proclaiming their own imperial crown of Austria. There were now four potential empires in contention in central Europe: French, Russian, Austrian and the Holy Roman.

The outcome of that struggle was a central concern for all European powers. Ostensibly, the cause of the renewed outbreak of hostilities between Napoleon and London in 1803 was the future of Malta, but the real issue was British fears about French ambitions in Europe more generally. Pitt had given up trying to eject the French from Belgium, but he still hoped to persuade them to evacuate Holland. In particular, Britain was determined to keep Napoleon out of northern Germany, partly to defend the eastern flank of Holland, partly to safeguard the king's patrimony of Hanover, but mainly to protect the integrity of the Empire, upon which the whole European balance rested. Likewise, Tsar Alexander I reiterated in September 1801 that the 'independence and security' of the Holy Roman Empire were central to the 'future security' of Europe as a whole.[169] He therefore hoped to establish a Franco-Russian joint control over Germany and had agreed in June 1802 to the Imperial Recess on that basis. His adviser Alexander Borisovich Kurakin claimed that this understanding with France made him 'the protector of Germany and the angel of peace for the universe'.[170] But the resumption of the Napoleonic advance in Germany with the occupation of Hanover in late 1803, the kidnapping of the British diplomat George Rumbold in north Germany a year later, and many other indications that the French intended to violate the integrity of the Empire gave Alexander pause. Thugut, now no longer in office, but a keen observer of events, described Napoleon in 1804–5 as a 'new Charlemagne' who had amassed in the Holy Roman Empire and in 'the most essential countries of Europe . . . the means more than sufficient to rule the world'.[171]

So in 1804–5, a new 'Third Coalition' of Austria, Russia and Britain slowly assembled against Napoleon. The allies discussed ways not only of constructing effective geopolitical barriers to contain France, but also of promoting domestic political principles which would sustain these structures. Alexander envisaged the right of self-determination for all peoples liberated from the French yoke, which as he put it in September 1804 was a principle 'founded on the sacred rights of humanity'. More concretely, the tsar planned to box Napoleon in with an enlarged Piedmont-Sardinia, Holland and Switzerland; the non-Austrian and non-Prussian parts of Germany should be amalgamated into a credible federation buttressing the entire edifice. Pitt presented a very similar 'Plan for the Reconstruction of Europe' four months later, albeit one largely shorn of any ideological connotations. Piedmont, he suggested, should be strengthened by the acquisition of Genoa, with a view to keeping the French out of northern Italy. Most important of all, however, was the north-western barrier, which was to be defended by a resurrected Holland, a new system of barrier fortresses stretching from Basel to the Ehrenbreitstein fortress at Koblenz, and a Prussia enlarged by significant parts of the former Austrian Netherlands and Luxemburg, and further lands in western Germany. All this was to be sealed by a joint British–Russian guarantee of the European territorial status quo.

The key was Prussia. If she could be persuaded or intimidated into joining the coalition, Napoleon's position in Germany might well become untenable. Throughout 1805–6, therefore, a succession of allied and French envoys made the voyage to Potsdam to tempt – or push – Frederick William off the fence. Caught between the neutralist counsels of his principal minister, Baron Haugwitz, and the pro-Russian 'war party' headed by Barons Hardenberg and Stein, the king vacillated fatally. He took a stand against Napoleon in October 1805, only to be confronted by the defeat of the Austrians at Ulm, and then that of the Austro-Russian army at Austerlitz in December. The tsar retreated eastwards, leaving the Austrians to make the best peace they could at the Treaty of Pressburg. Shortly afterwards, the Prussians not only were forced into line by the French at the Treaty of Schönbrunn but occupied, and then annexed, Hanover at Napoleon's invitation.

Having effectively shut the Habsburgs out of Germany, Napoleon was now well placed to appropriate the imperial tradition.[172] Within the Empire important voices were encouraging him to do so. The Imperial Arch Chancellor, Karl von Dalberg, who had attended Napoleon's coronation in 1804, implored Bonaparte to save Germany from anarchy and restore its constitution. He looked forward to the moment when 'the occidental [Roman] world empire revives under Emperor Napoleon, as it was under Charlemagne made up of Italy, France and Germany'. In February 1806, Napoleon wrote to Pope Pius VII that he was now effectively Charlemagne, as he held the crown of France as well that of the Lombards. He also let it be known through his mouthpiece, the *Moniteur*, that he would soon recognize only those European dynasties which were linked by blood to his own. In May 1806, Dalberg appointed Napoleon's uncle Cardinal Fesch his deputy and successor and three months later he approached Napoleon with a formal plan in which the Empire was to become a federation under his protection. A few months later, Prussia belatedly woke up to the Napoleonic threat, suddenly went to war with France, was routed at the battle of Jena in October 1806, and only survived as a much-reduced independent state thanks to the intercession of Alexander.

Napoleon was now the undisputed master of Germany and thus of Europe as a whole. Prussia had to disgorge her holdings in northern Germany, as well as most of the gains from the Polish partitions. Austria lost Venetia, Istria and Dalmatia to the new Kingdom of Italy, and the Tyrol to Bavaria, which – along with several other middling German states – had sided with Napoleon in 1805–6. Talleyrand's advice that the relative power of Austria be maintained in order to keep Russia out of Germany and central Europe was ignored. Napoleon now planned to rally Germany against the tsar under his direct leadership. The foreign minister eventually resigned in opposition to Napoleon's German policy, increasingly convinced that the emperor's hubris would provoke an overwhelming coalition against France.[173] Poland was partially reconstituted as the Grand Duchy of Warsaw. The new satellite states of Berg and Westphalia were established in western and northern Germany. Württemberg, Bavaria and Saxony became kingdoms; Baden a Grand Duchy. To the disappointment of many in Germany, however, Napoleon did not take over the imperial crown himself. Instead, he set up the Confederation of the Rhine, which eventually included almost all the German states apart from Austria and Prussia. A month later he commanded the Habsburgs to surrender their imperial German title. They acceded to his request, but unilaterally proclaimed the dissolution of the whole Holy Roman Empire in early August to pre-empt any attempt by Napoleon to seize the discarded crown. Nearly 800 years of German political commonwealth had come to an end. A myriad of German statelets was reduced to around forty. A long French diplomatic tradition of maintaining the imperial constitution had been overturned. The territorial consolidation of Germany had begun.[174]

This geopolitical earthquake sent tremors right through the European system. Alexander came to an arrangement with Napoleon at the Treaty of Tilsit after his defeat at Friedland in June 1807, forswore any ambitions in Germany, and announced that the area between the Elbe and Niemen would serve as a buffer to 'cushion the pinpricks that precede the cannon shots'.[175] A year later, the Russo-French consensus on Germany was reaffirmed at a meeting between the two emperors in the Thuringian town of Erfurt. The senior Austrian diplomat, Count Metternich, was painfully conscious of being the meat in the new strategic sandwich between Napoleon's German and Polish allies. 'The confederation of the Rhine,' he wrote in July 1807, 'embraces us on both sides. Any war with France would begin at the same time on the borders of the Inn and the Wieliczka.'[176] The same was more or less true for Prussia, which was jammed between the Grand Duchy of Warsaw and the French satellite Kingdom of Westphalia from 1807. Faced with these realities, both German great powers had no choice for the time being but to pursue a policy of accommodation. Napoleon, in short, was left in possession of virtually the whole of Germany, whose resources were channelled to him through the Confederation of the Rhine. Hundreds of thousands of Bavarians, Württembergers and other recruits were pledged to the French imperial project, making Germany the principal reservoir of manpower and resources to sustain Napoleon's later campaigns. The greatest impact of the fall of the *Reich*, however, was on the German political psyche. The title of a pamphlet published in 1806 by the Nuremberg bookseller Johann Philipp Palm – 'Germany in her deepest humiliation' – spoke volumes about how most Germans viewed the fate of the Empire, and Palm's execution by Napoleon only increased the resentment. As the geographer August Zeune remarked bitterly in 1808, the Germans were being treated 'like animal[s], exchanged, given away, ceded, [and] trampled down . . . like a ball . . . passed from one hand to another'.[177]

Napoleon's conquests had won him a European pre-eminence much greater even than that achieved by Louis XIV or Charles V, but complete security eluded him. He was now compulsively driven to ever more conquests abroad, and ever greater militarization within his empire. Both

Russia and Great Britain were still forces to be reckoned with. For the moment, Napoleon was content to leave the tsar a sphere of influence in eastern Europe, while he dealt with Britain. After the catastrophic naval defeat at Trafalgar in October 1805, a seaborne descent was temporarily out of the question, so Napoleon attempted to destroy Britain economically through the 'Continental System', proclaimed in the Berlin Decrees of November 1806, which shut her out from mainland Europe. Britain responded in January 1807 with Orders in Council that forbade trade between French ports by neutrals, a measure which hit North and South American commerce very badly. In October 1807, Napoleon forced the Spanish to allow French troops to cross their country to attack Portugal in order to deprive Britain of her last remaining ally on European soil. This strategy marked a shift from Napoleon's earlier attempts to bring Britain to heel through naval and colonial operations. In March 1808 a palace coup against the French-backed minister Manuel de Godoy provoked a full-scale French invasion of Spain.

The continuing war in Europe also shaped Napoleon's domestic policy, and that of his clients. During the 1790s, the revolutionaries had sought to create an efficient and egalitarian French society capable of re-establishing the European standing lost by the *ancien régime*. Napoleon, on the other hand, saw the creation of a new nobility as the key to the maintenance of French military superiority. He therefore embarked on a programme of re-feudalization within the empire, and encouraged allied states to do the same. He created the Legion of Honour in May 1802 to reward faithful service in the army and, more sparingly, administration. He set out to repair relations with the Catholic Church by concluding a Concordat, in which he agreed to pay clerical salaries in return for a high level of control over the hierarchy and papal blessing for his imperial ambitions; Pius VII attended the French imperial coronation at Notre-Dame. In March 1808, however, he went a step further and created a fully fledged imperial nobility, in which status reflected public service and could be passed from father to son. In order to ensure that lineage did not displace merit over time – as tended to happen in all feudal societies – there was provision for noble status to lapse if future generations failed to do adequate service for the state. The huge lands captured in Italy, the Low Countries and Germany provided the fiefs for this new aristocracy.[178]

Similar imperatives underlay domestic reforms in French-dominated

Europe which were principally designed to maximize resource extraction and military mobilization in support of Napoleon's ambitions. The content of these measures, which often picked up where eighteenth-century reformers had left off, varied from state to state, but they usually included the abolition of internal tariffs in order to stimulate economic development and generate more revenue from taxation, the dismantlement of noble assemblies and other 'intermediary powers', fiscal reforms to deal with the spiralling state debt, an end to guild restrictions, religious toleration to ensure the peaceful integration of new lands with diverse populations, and the secularization of Church property. Common to all of the states in the French orbit was the introduction of conscription to meet Napoleon's constant demand for more soldiers.[179] All this amounted to the 'integration' of Europe into one coherent system.[180] It was, of course, a case of uniformity rather than unity, in which the French nation was explicitly dominant.[181] For example, in the Trianon decrees of August 1810, Napoleon granted French ships the exclusive privilege of trading a limited number of colonial goods with the British and selling these on to the rest of Europe. 'What is good for the French,' he claimed, 'is good for everybody.'[182] 'There is not enough sameness among the nations of Europe,' Napoleon argued. 'There must be a superior power which dominates all the other powers, with enough authority to force them to live in harmony with one another – and France is best placed for that purpose.'[183]

Inevitably, the overweening power of France provoked a reaction across Europe. In those areas directly occupied by Napoleon or under his effective control, popular resistance erupted. The French revolutionary armies had already driven the peasantry of southern Italy into rebellion in the late 1790s; in the first decade of the nineteenth century, they were joined by Tyroleans and Spaniards. There were almost as many motivations as there were rebels. Much of the Neapolitan, Spanish and Tyrolean opposition was driven by local factors, outrage at French anti-clericalism, and the oppressive regime of taxation and conscription which the Napoleonic war machine required. In the case of some insurgents, such as the German bandit Schinderhannes, the dividing line between patriotism and criminality was very fluid. One way or the other, Robespierre's warning that Europe would not welcome 'armed missionaries'[184] was vindicated: the 'reason', 'fraternity', 'equality' and 'liberty' offered by France were rejected not only because they were an outside imposition, but because they were highly oppressive in practice. 'I attest,' Napoleon's foreign minister, Talleyrand, cautioned, 'that any system which aims at taking freedom by open force to other peoples will only make that freedom hated and prevent its triumph.'[185]

Among the remaining independent European states, Napoleonic hegemony forced the elite to take a long hard look at domestic structures. In Prussia, the old military-agrarian complex, which had served Frederick the Great so well, was completely discredited by the catastrophe of Auerstedt and Jena. A thoroughgoing programme of reform was launched under the aegis of Barons Stein and Hardenberg. As Hardenberg argued in his Riga Memorandum of September 1807, the 'geographical situation' of the monarchy meant that she had to 'concentrate her strength, and organize and systematically co-ordinate all aspects of her internal affairs', or else risk 'becom[ing] the prey of her powerful neighbours'.[186] So, between 1807 and 1813, the Prussian reforms improved decision-making by replacing the Byzantine system of unaccountable royal councillors with 'responsible' ministries; opened the officer corps to bourgeois candidates according to the merit principle; abolished the guild system to liberalize the economy; emancipated the peasantry to create a free market in land and consequently abandoned the old cantonal system in favour of a French-style universal military service; and lifted restrictions on the Jews. Prussia's external vulnerability, formerly used to justify noble privileges and the separation of the army from society, was now advanced as an argument for a 'real military state' in which they formed an indissoluble unity.[187] There were also calls for greater popular participation through a 'national representation' to mobilize the entire population behind the struggle against Napoleon.[188]

The Napoleonic advance also sparked an intense debate about domestic reform in Britain. Pitt had resigned in 1801 when the king refused to countenance Catholic emancipation, but the issue returned to the agenda after the shocks of 1805–7. The Earl of Selkirk wrote in a pamphlet of 1808 that there had been 'so vast a change in all the surround[ing] countries' that 'our arrangements, internal as well as external, must be adapted to our new circumstances'. With the loss of her European allies, the only way in which the nation could hope to survive against the vastly superior population of France was 'by exertions unprecedented in the improvement of our internal resources'.

Increased taxation and recruitment was only part of the answer: the hidden energies of British society would have to be set free. 'In order to save this land from foreign subjugation,' the radical Whig MP Sir Francis Burdett argued, 'we must get rid of domestic oppression; we must have arms and reform.' Britain thus had, as the veteran electoral reformer John Cartwright argued in 1809, 'naught . . . but this alternative – either parliamentary reformation under George the Third, or national subjugation under Napoleon the First.'[189] For the moment, the British government resisted demands for franchise reform, and although the ministry made a fresh attempt to push through Catholic emancipation, it was defeated in parliament in 1807.

The defeat of the Third Coalition also provoked intense domestic argument about the direction of British grand strategy.[190] It temporarily discredited the advocates of intervention in Europe. The 'Ministry of All the Talents' headed by William Pitt's long-time rival, Charles James Fox, sought peace with Napoleon in 1806–7, and concentrated on overseas expansion. Part and parcel of this more 'global' reach was the abolition of the international slave trade, which the London parliament passed into law in 1807. The United States followed suit that same year, in accordance with the constitutional agreement of 1787 to end the trade after twenty years, and banned the carriage of slaves under its own flag. This marked the beginning of a subversive new abolitionist geopolitics, based on the coercive power of the Royal Navy, which made full use of its belligerent right to search to harass slavers on the high seas. The new government under Lord Portland also returned to the attack in Europe. British troops were dispatched to Stralsund in a last-ditch attempt to breathe life into Prussian and Russian resistance. Nor did London despair after Tilsit, which seemed to array the entire continent against her. When the Danish fleet was in danger of falling into French hands in September 1807, Britain carried out a pre-emptive naval strike on Denmark, destroying her ships and inflicting numerous civilian casualties at Copenhagen. A year later, British troops were dispatched to the Iberian peninsula to support the Portuguese and Spanish struggle against Napoleon. Throughout the length and breadth of the continent, especially in Germany, British agents pursued covert action against Napoleon, subsidizing propaganda and supplying arms to guerrilla groups.[191]

Taking heart from the French distraction in the Iberian peninsula, the Habsburg monarchy now girded its loins for one last push against

Napoleon. A graded income tax was introduced in 1800 to cope with the deficits caused by the cost of war in the 1790s, and loss of traditional capital markets in the Low Countries, northern Italy and Germany. To address the chaotic state of Austrian decision-making, a State Council (*Staatsrat*) of ministers was created in 1801.[192] After the disasters of 1805, the Habsburgs set up a national militia, the *Landwehr*, based on a moderated principle of universal service. Above all, the Austrians sought to tap into the growing sense of German nationalism against France. The Hungarians, however, refused to pull their weight. Instead, they used the French threat as a lever to extract concessions from Vienna. No new funds or men were voted at the acrimonious Diet of Pressburg in 1807–8. Faced with this belligerence, Vienna backed off from extending the *Landwehr* from the German and Slav provinces to Hungary. The Austrian bureaucracy had had its fingers badly burned during the reign of Joseph II. Risking a domestic revolution to contain the revolutionary power of Napoleon seemed a cure worse than the disease. The Habsburg reform programme was also short-circuited by the ill-judged decision to take on Napoleon again in 1809. Austria did win an important victory at Aspern-Essling, but it soon became clear that Vienna had massively miscalculated. The Russians, preoccupied with events in the Baltic, Black Sea and Balkans, did not move; the Prussians refuse to budge without them. In July 1809, Napoleon routed the Austrians at Wagram. The resulting peace settlement left them a landlocked rump, hemmed in by Illyria to the south, now directly ruled from Paris, the *Rheinbund* (Confederation of the Rhine) to the west and the Grand Duchy of Warsaw to the north. Austria was now effectively a French satellite, 'forced' as Metternich told the emperor 'to seek its security in adaptation to the French system', at least until 'Russian help' was on the cards.[193] A humiliating forced marriage between Bonaparte and the emperor's daughter Marie Louise followed.

Control of Germany was the key to Napoleon's next step: shutting Russia out of Europe for good, a goal which had so long eluded eighteenth-century French strategists. The emperor believed that it was not enough to remain within the ramparts of the economic and military fortress which he had constructed. The economic integration of Europe envisaged by the Continental System – a structure based on French national selfishness which could only function on the basis of reciprocity – failed.[194] Across the continent, but especially in formerly prosperous French provinces such as Alsace, markets began to contract and economic distress grew. The Continental Blockade was no longer watertight, with an active illicit British trade along a coastline which the weak French navy could not possibly police. Napoleon now moved to close a gap in the blockade by occupying most of the north German littoral, including Hamburg, Bremen and Lübeck in 1810; one of the territories affected was Oldenburg, whose ruling family was closely connected to the tsar. The resulting outrage at St Petersburg was accentuated by Napoleon's apparent intention to resurrect Poland as a buffer against the tsar. Austria was forced to cede Galicia to the Grand Duchy of Warsaw, and the Polish army was massively increased. Very soon, however, the French emperor came to the conclusion that Russia would have to be crushed militarily. It was the old Napoleonic security dilemma: each conquest required another to safeguard it in a destructive dynamic which could only end in failure.

In St Petersburg, the French presence on her western frontier inspired an intense debate on Russia's grand strategy. Some argued that a preemptive strike on Napoleon was the only way to head off the danger. Alexander, however, was deeply opposed to this option. So unwilling was Alexander to provoke Napoleon that he forbade the construction of border fortifications and artillery emplacements on the right bank of the Niemen. What decided the tsar in the end was Germany. In April 1812, Alexander demanded that Napoleon withdraw from Prussia and Swedish Pomerania altogether, that he reduce his garrison at Danzig, and compensate the Duke of Oldenburg. That same month, the tsar concluded an alliance with Sweden by which they would conduct a joint descent on the north German coast; Stockholm was to receive Norway in return, to compensate her for Russia's absorption of Finland. War between France and Russia was now inevitable.

Washington also had to face the consequences of Napoleon's domination of Europe. Britain was determined to compensate for the growth of French power on the continent through colonial expansion and naval assertion. In particular, Washington was alarmed by British expeditions to Buenos Aires in 1807, the Orders in Council of 1808, which seriously disrupted American trade, the repeated impressment of US sailors into the Royal Navy, and British involvement in pan-Indian uprisings in 1811. These issues alone might not have been enough to precipitate a breach between the two countries, had it not been for irreconcilable territorial disputes. The United States was determined to stop any other power from moving into the vacuum left by Spain. So in early 1811 President Madison asked Congress to occupy any such lands pre-emptively, in particular West Florida. There was also the perennial problem of the west, which had dominated American domestic and foreign policy since the middle of the last century. In 1806, these nightmares dramatically resurfaced, when the former vice-president, Aaron Burr, was accused of trying to set up an independent settler state in the Louisiana territory with British support and charged with treason. Washington's collision course with London was furiously controversial at home, and domestic politics was dominated by the divide between voices counselling caution and the expansionist 'war hawks'. Eventually, however, the Americans, infuriated by the arrogance of the Royal Navy, still wary of the British presence in Canada with its many former loyalists,[195] and now anxious about the future of the west, the south-west, the Caribbean and the whole of Latin America, decided to break out of the looming encirclement. In June 1812, the United States declared war in order to settle the question of hemispheric dominance between them and the British once and for all.

That very same month, Napoleon's *Grande Armée* crossed the Niemen into Russia to decide the struggle for mastery in central Europe. Only about half of this 600,000-strong force were Frenchmen (itself a very elastic description given the greatly inflated boundaries of the empire, which now included the Rhineland and many other parts of western Germany), the rest coming from Holland, Italy, Poland and of course Westphalia, Bavaria, Saxony and the other *Rheinbund* states. Prussian and Austrian auxiliary corps guarded the northern and southern flanks of the *Grande Armée*. Without control of Germany, in fact, Napoleon's attack on Russia would not have been possible. At first all went well, and by the beginning of winter the tsar's army had been heavily defeated at Borodino and Moscow was occupied. The failure to stop the French advance early on prompted considerable unrest, and it is possible that further setbacks might have sparked a palace revolution against Alexander. Within a few months, however, the rigours of the Russian winter had forced Napoleon to withdraw. By the end of the year, his shattered army had been completely expelled from tsarist territory.

The whole of Germany was now forced to make a decision. A Russian army was in hot pursuit of the French, and could be expected to cross through Poland into central Europe at any moment. Napoleon's distress was further increased by defeats in Spain at the hands of Wellington's Anglo-Iberian coalition forces. Few, however, were willing to write off the emperor yet. He had bounced back from seemingly inevitable ruin in Egypt in 1798 and on countless other occasions. 'Rattle your chains if you will,' the poet Goethe warned, 'the man is too strong for you.'[196] A mis-step now could cost the surviving German powers their very existence. 'All the considerations of Austria and other poor intermediaries,' Metternich warned, 'must be directed at how not to be wiped out.'[197] Prussia – which lay directly in the path of the Russian advance – would have to make up its mind first. Throughout the winter of 1812–13, Frederick William vacillated. Competing factions urged the king either to honour his commitments to Napoleon or to throw in his lot with the allies; some officers even considered a putsch to replace him with a more decisive member of the Hohenzollern family. Not even the defection of General York von Wartenburg's corps, which had been guarding the northern flank of the *Grande Armée*, to the Russians at the Convention of Tauroggen in 1812 could move him. Frederick William's hand was finally forced when the estates of East Prussia assembled without his permission and authorized a *levée en masse* to fight the French. The Prussian political nation, or part of it, had taken ownership of foreign policy.

Russian opinion was divided on whether to press on into Germany. Prussian exiles serving with the tsar, such as the reformer Baron Stein, called on Alexander to reorder central Europe under Russian leadership in order to keep Napoleon out. Many Russian officers and nobles, fearful of being sucked into a central European morass remote from the empire's traditional security concerns closer to home, counselled restraint. Alexander, however, was determined to deal with Napoleon once and for all, and to vindicate the German mission begun in the eighteenth century. When Frederick William came off the fence in February 1813, he concluded the Treaty of Kalisch with Russia at the end of that month. This effectively reconstituted Prussia as a great power, by promising to restore the borders of 1806. The purpose of these restorations, as Alexander told the Russian ambassador to Berlin in March 1813, was to make Prussia the '*avant garde* of Russia', that is a buffer against attack from the west.[198] Towards the end of March 1813, Frederick William issued the Proclamation of Kalisch in which he and

Alexander pledged their support for a united Germany. A Russian-backed Central Administrative Council under Baron Stein was set up to recruit on a pan-German basis and prepare the 'reorganization' of southern and western Germany. All this was accompanied by a ringing appeal from Frederick William – '*An mein Volk*' – in which he called upon the population of each of his provinces to rise up and expel the French. In May 1813, the Swedes landed in north Germany. In June 1813, at the Treaty of Reichenbach, Britain pledged to support the Russo-Prussian war effort with increased subsidies.

Austria still hesitated. Metternich feared that too rapid and comprehensive a defeat of Napoleon would upset the balance of power in Germany for good. There was no point in simply exchanging French hegemony for a Russian one, nor was Metternich prepared to allow the Prussians to steal a march on him. He therefore sought to build alliances with the *Rheinbund* states, which were in search of a new sponsor after the French defeat in Russia. Between October 1812 and November 1813 Bavaria, Baden and Württemberg were all detached from Napoleon in return for territorial guarantees. One way or the other, Metternich reassured them, the 'Third Germany' would be reconstituted. Metternich was less successful with regard to France, which he hoped would remain as a strong counter-weight to tsarist power in central Europe. During a memorable meeting at Dresden in late June 1813, Napoleon not only resolutely refused to moderate his demands, but callously announced his intention to wade through the blood of millions to regain his position of pre-eminence. So, in early September 1813, Austria joined Prussia and Russia at Teplitz to agree the 'dissolution of the Confederation of the Rhine, the complete independence of the intermediary states between Austria and Prussia',[199] and the repartition of Poland. The final showdown in Germany could now begin.

The forces now arrayed against Napoleon were formidable: not only the Russian army which had defeated him in 1812, but the Austrians, Prussians and virtually the whole of Germany, now almost entirely united for military purposes for the first time in its history. Prussia, in particular, was able to field a higher proportion of the population – just over 10 per cent – than any of the other combatant powers, and lost a smaller ratio through desertion.[200] The *Freikorps*, or 'free corps' of patriotic students and artisans, mobilized many nationalists not represented in the regular forces; although relatively few in number, they took on a disproportionate totemic importance. Only the Saxons remained loyal to Napoleon, partly because the Prussians, who hoped to annex them, would not allow their king to change sides. Napoleon put up a stiff fight all the same, winning victories at Dresden and Bautzen. In mid-October 1813, however, the two sides finally met in a climactic battle at Leipzig. This 'Battle of the Nations' ranged Frenchmen, Poles, Italians and Germans against Prussians, Russians, their German allies and all the peoples who made up the Habsburg Empire. Eventually, after three days of epic struggle, Napoleon was utterly defeated. The great battle for supremacy in central Europe was over. It was now only a matter of time before Napoleon was defeated in France. A new European order was about to be born.

Late-eighteenth-century geopolitics was dominated by three revolutions. The American and French Revolutions both originated as revolts against *ancien régime* grand strategy, be it London's territorial restraint in the west or the diplomatic retreat of the Bourbon monarchy in central Europe. The new states pioneered new forms of domestic organization to maximize their leverage in the international system: the American Constitution and Revolutionary and Napoleonic France. A clash between them was averted, partly because the United States regarded Britain as the greater threat, but mainly because the French gave higher priority to control of the European continent, especially of Germany. This produced the third revolution, a geopolitical upheaval in which the revolutionary regime and Napoleon destroyed the balance in the Holy Roman Empire, and ultimately the Empire itself, thus upending the entire equilibrium. French annexations, the partitionist frenzy they unleashed, the reforms they undertook and those that they provoked, fundamentally changed the face of the continent, especially Germany. The United States, meanwhile, moved closer to complete hegemony over her own continent by preventing Britain from moving into the vacuum left by France and Spain. Her attention remained, moreover, firmly riveted on developments in Europe, which represented both a geopolitical and an ideological threat to the young republic. In time, a confrontation between the heirs to the Continental Congress and those of the continental European autocracies was inevitable.

The losers in this revolutionary roller-coaster were first and foremost the smaller German states, who were swallowed up by the new territorial arrangements. Prussia and Austria survived, and indeed expanded, but they were made painfully conscious of the essential fragility of their situation. Britain suffered terribly through the loss of America, but managed to re-establish her position in the European balance by the end of the period. French power waned, waxed and finally collapsed in the face of an overwhelming European coalition. First and foremost among the great beneficiaries of the great transformations following the Seven Years War were the American colonists who carved a new state out of the British North American Empire, and formed a mighty union to defend it. Tsarist Russia, meanwhile, continued her meteoric ascent, pushing deep into the Ottoman Empire and central Europe and, above all, acting as the arbiter of Germany. Both powers, however, also suffered from acute vulnerabilities. Their undisguised expansionism clashed with the interests of the other great powers. Moreover, both Russia and the United States were saddled with peculiar domestic arrangements in the form of serfdom and slavery which prevented them from rallying all internal forces in support of their external ambitions. In the minds of many European governments and publics, all this made resisting Russian and American ambitions not only a matter of strategic interest but ideologically imperative. The stage was set for a new geopolitics of emancipation: from national bondage, from autocratic rule, from serfdom and from slavery.

4
Emancipations, 1814–66

As far as the fate of our [German] Fatherland is concerned, the dice have not fallen in accordance with the forces of light. We can only build [the Fatherland] from within through courageous and loyal attitudes and through disseminating real hatred against all things foreign [Waelsch]. There will be no lack of storms from without which will drive us more and more towards unity.

Ernst Moritz Arndt, 1814[1]

What is the great mission of our times? . . . It is emancipation. Not merely the Irish, Greeks, Frankfurt Jews, West Indies blacks and such oppressed peoples, rather it is the emancipation of the world, Europe in particular, which has come of age and now tears itself loose from the iron leading strings of the privileged, the aristocracy.

Heinrich Heine[2]

The Germanic Confederation is not a Union formed solely by the voluntary association of the states that compose it, and which therefore can be altered and modified at the absolute will of these states without reference to a consultation with any other parties. The German Confederation is a Union of a different character and kind. It is the result and creation of a European treaty concluded at Vienna in 1815, and it forms part of the general settlement of Europe which that Treaty established and regulated.

Lord Palmerston, 3 December 1850[3]

The treaties which brought to an end to the Revolutionary and Napoleonic Wars and the struggle between Britain and the United States transformed European geopolitics. In Europe, they reconstituted the old Holy Roman Empire under a new guise, and reordered northern Italy and the Low Countries in order to contain France. Russia held on to most of her gains. Austria and Prussia made substantial territorial acquisitions which reoriented both powers: south and south-east in the first case, and westwards in the second. The impact of these changes on European geopolitics over the next fifty years was profound, nowhere more so than in the fulcrum of the system, Germany. In North America, the United States shut Britain out of the west, but her claims in Central America and the Caribbean were still contested by the major powers. Moreover, the domestic provisions of the treaties were full of geopolitical implications on both sides of the Atlantic. Thanks to the provisions on Jewish emancipation, the international slave trade and constitutional arrangements, the battle lines were now drawn within polities, dividing the United States and most European states down the middle, especially Germany. The classic geopolitical themes of buffers, encirclement and expansion were now seen through the prisms of national, political, religious and slave emancipation. By the end of this process, both the Americans and Germans were well on the way to finding, albeit at great cost, the national unity they needed to survive in a world of predatory great powers.

Once Napoleon had lost control of Germany at the battle of Leipzig in October 1813, his position in Europe quickly crumbled. The allied armies – swelled by contingents from the defecting *Rheinbund* states – now advanced inexorably westwards into France, while the Duke of Wellington crossed the Pyrenees from Spain and headed north. Despite plucky resistance on home territory, the French were soon overwhelmed. Napoleon abdicated at the Treaty of Fontainebleau in mid-April 1814, and was sent into exile on the Mediterranean island of Elba. The Bourbon monarchy was restored under Louis XVIII, and, by the relatively generous First Treaty of Paris, France was permitted to keep the territory she had acquired between the Revolution and the outbreak of the Revolutionary Wars in 1792, in particular Savoy. In September 1814, the victorious powers sent representatives to Vienna to establish a stable post-war order. Shortly after, Europe was convulsed by the return from Elba, during the 'Hundred Days', of Napoleon, who gave his guards the slip and was welcomed back by a French population which had tired quickly of the Bourbons and sought to regain the hegemony they had enjoyed for the past two decades. Britain, most of whose best troops were in America, was caught badly off balance. After some early successes, however, Napoleon was beaten at Waterloo in June 1815 by an allied army made up largely of Germans of one sort or another.[4] Napoleon was exiled once again, this time to St Helena, from where he did not return.

Meanwhile, the Anglo-American struggle over the Great Lakes was reaching a climax. The expectation of the Congressional 'war hawks' that Canada would soon be 'liberated' from British rule was soon dashed. A prolonged slugging match on land and sea followed, as London was able to deploy troops released by the defeat of Napoleon. The war caused deep fissures within the Union: the mainly Republican south and west largely supported Madison's decision, but Federalist New England was solidly opposed. Several northern states refused to send their militia to Canada or withdrew them soon after the outbreak of hostilities. The Massachusetts Senate roundly condemned a war 'waged without justifiable cause, and prosecuted in a manner which indicates that conquest and ambition are its real motives' and announced that 'it is not becoming a moral and religious people to express any approbation of military or naval exploits which are not immediately connected with the defence of our sea-coast and soil'. Secession seemed on the cards.[5] A spate of belated US successes then supervened, forcing London to sue for peace. Thanks to the communications lag in the pre-telegraph age, the last and most spectacular American victory – the battle of New Orleans – was fought some days after peace had been agreed. An inter-American civil conflict had been narrowly averted through a victorious war over the common British enemy.

By then, the Vienna Congress was in full swing. Right at the top of the agenda was the containment of future French expansionism through territorial reorganization – the British Secretary of State for Foreign Affairs, Viscount Castlereagh, argued that 'to keep France in order, we require great masses . . . Prussia, Austria and Russia ought to be as great and powerful as they ever have been',[6] if not more so. The establishment of a moderate regime in Paris would also curb French adventurism. Hardly less urgent was the issue of how to deal with the explosion of

Russian power, which had erupted into central and western Europe to the consternation of all.[7] The tsar's new role as the arbiter of Europe was epitomized by a massive review of some 150,000 Russian troops and 540 artillery pieces which he staged on the plain of Champagne, not far from Paris, in early September 1815. This spectacle made a deep impression on the attending allied leaders, who included the King of Prussia, the Emperor of Austria and the Duke of Wellington.[8]

All these concerns merged in the central issue at Vienna: the 'German Question'. In February 1814, the allies committed themselves to a central European framework 'composed of sovereign princes united by a federal bond which will assure and guarantee the independence of Germany'.[9] Eight months later, Castlereagh elaborated that Germany should constitute 'an intermediary system between Russia and France',[10] which would contain both states without threatening them. Britain was determined to prevent Russia from filling the vacuum in central Europe. A resurrected Poland which was 'really Russian', Castlereagh's diplomat-brother, Charles Stewart, warned, would 'advanc[e] the Russian frontier . . . almost into the heart of Germany'.[11] At the same time, the Austrian chancellor was anxious to stop the Prussians from gaining hegemony in Germany, and from helping themselves to too much territory, especially at the expense of Napoleon's defeated ally Saxony, which was an important buffer between the two powers, and in Poland. So in late 1815 the great powers came up with a settlement designed to keep the British in, the Russians out and the French down.

The Treaty of Vienna forced France to disgorge all lands acquired between 1789 and 1792, and to pay a crippling indemnity. Poland remained partitioned between Russia, Austria and Prussia; part of the tsar's share was turned into a kingdom with its own army and parliament. Alexander retained most of the massive gains of the past decades, including Bessarabia, taken from Turkey, and Finland, ceded by the Swedes. Stockholm was compensated with territory to the west. The treaty ending the war between Denmark and Sweden in January 1814 had already decided the struggle for mastery in Scandinavia in favour of Sweden, which wrested Norway from Denmark, thus depriving it of 40 per cent of its population and nearly 85 per cent of its territory. Piedmont-Sardinia recovered Savoy from France and was enlarged with a view to blocking French designs on Italy. Strategic depth in the peninsula was provided by the Austrians, who were granted Lombardy and

Venetia, along with the old Venetian Republic's coastal strip in Dalmatia, as well as collateral Habsburg branches in the smaller principalities of Tuscany, Modena and Parma. Switzerland was guaranteed perpetual neutrality within its traditional cantonal system.

The most profound changes, however, took place in the lands of the former Holy Roman Empire. Austria ceded Belgium to Holland to form the Kingdom of the United Netherlands, intended as a bulwark against French expansion into the Low Countries; the scattered territories in the west known as 'Anterior Austria' were also given up for good. Prussia's hopes of rounding off her borders with neighbouring territory were largely disappointed; she had to make do with the northern half of Saxony, rather than the entire kingdom. Instead, Prussia was awarded the enormous prizes of the Rhineland and Westphalia with the express intention, as Castlereagh put it, of putting her 'more in military contact with France', in order to 'provide effectually against the systematic views of France to possess herself of the Low Countries and the territories on the left bank of the Rhine'.[12] It was only with some difficulty that Potsdam managed to fend off the British offer of a large slice of southern Belgium as well. The myriad of smaller principalities which had been such a feature of German politics before the 1790s were not restored for the most part, whereas Bavaria, Württemberg, Baden, Hanover and a number of other states survived the fall of Napoleon greatly enlarged. Britain made no large-scale territorial gains in Europe, though she did retain her colonial booty (including Ceylon and the Cape Colony) and a number of bases, including Malta; the personal union with Hanover was restored. This restraint was deliberate. 'Our reputation on the continent as a feature of our strength, power and confidence,' Castlereagh argued in mid-April 1814, 'is of more real moment than any acquisition.'[13] He parlayed this standing into the Quadruple Alliance of 1815 between Russia, Prussia, Austria and Britain. Article 6 of this agreement pledged the parties to meet regularly in order to maintain the European balance of power and other matters of pressing common concern. This arrangement has become known as the 'Congress System'.

Castlereagh's determination to collaborate with, rather than dictate to, the European powers had implications for the question of slavery. British abolitionists bombarded the Congress, including the tsar and the King of Prussia, with demands for the banning of the trade. Thomas

Clarkson's suggestion that Britain should cede France 'some little territory in Germany' in order to sweeten the pill of ending its slaving was rejected.[14] To the fury of British abolitionists, the final treaty did not stipulate an immediate and complete end to the international slave trade, or – failing that – permit Britain to annex the French colonies with which it was carried out. 'We were masters of the negotiation,' the Whig Lord Grenville lamented, '[i]n this cause the example of Great Britain was all-powerful . . . her determination final.'[15] Most European powers, including many opposed to slavery, feared that the issue was really a stalking horse for British naval dominance, and a pretext to continue with the right of search even after the end of hostilities. France, in particular, regarded the enforced end to her slave trade as an unbearable national humiliation. As a compromise solution, the Russian tsar proposed a maritime league to suppress the trade. Castlereagh, anxious not to undermine the domestic standing of the restored French Bourbon regime, did not press the point. In the end, the powers agreed a common statement that the slave trade was 'repugnant to the principles of humanity and universal morality'. For the moment this was mere aspiration, but the potentially huge international ramifications of the issue were already clear.

The Vienna Settlement regulated not only the borders but also the internal structure of the new Europe. Britain and the eastern powers both rejected republicanism in favour of the 'monarchical principle', the former preferring constitutional monarchies, the latter insisting on 'corporate' or absolutist systems. 'Congress Poland' was given a parliament and a constitution; many of the southern and western German states, such as Bavaria and Württemberg, held on to or were granted constitutions; and in Prussia the promulgation of a constitution was much discussed in 1814–15. In France, the allies restored the Bourbon monarchy, whose authority was balanced by a charter of rights and a parliament elected on a very narrow franchise. The intention was to defuse popular tendencies towards military adventurism, but to be on the safe side allied governments vetted legislation beforehand; they even demanded to see an advance copy of Louis XVIII's opening speech to parliament. An army of occupation was deployed to keep an eye on residual Bonapartism, to ensure that the indemnity was paid in full and to assist the Dutch in protecting against French attempts to revise the Vienna Settlement.[16] The general intention of the allies was to promote governments which would be robust enough to withstand revolutionary pressures from below, and sufficiently effective to deter external aggressors, but not so strong as to menace their neighbours.

At the heart of this new order was the German Confederation – *Deutscher Bund* – which replaced the defunct Holy Roman Empire. It was designed to maintain the European balance by being strong enough to contain Franco-Russian ambitions, yet not sufficiently powerful to develop hegemonic ambitions of its own. The preamble to the constitutive German Federal Act therefore called for a 'strong and durable union for the independence of Germany and the peace and equilibrium of Europe'.[17] This was envisaged as a commonwealth of parts as well as the whole; sacrificing any individual state for strategic reasons was expressly prohibited. The eleventh article of the Confederation bound members to provide mutual assistance in the event of an invasion, not to make separate peace with the aggressor and not to conclude agreements which threatened the integrity of the *Bund*. To this end, the defence of Germany was entrusted to federal military contingents from Prussia, Austria and the middling and smaller states, also known as the Third Germany, and a number of 'federal' fortresses in the west: Mainz, Landau, Luxemburg, and later Rastatt and Ulm. Political coordination was to be provided by the Diet at Frankfurt, under the presidency of Austria. At the same time, the *Bund* was charged with maintaining the internal political balance in Germany, both between and within the member states.[18] This was essential to prevent outside powers from being sucked into the resulting conflict, or exploiting German quarrels to gain unilateral advantage. The whole arrangement was guaranteed by all the signatory powers to the Vienna Final Act; indeed, the constitution of the *Bund* was written into the Vienna Final Act, which thus became a new European Treaty of Westphalia.[19]

All this amounted to a geopolitical revolution in Europe. The inexorable eighteenth-century Russian march westwards continued: Congress Poland jutted perilously into Prussia and the Habsburg Empire. Denmark had been destroyed as a Baltic and Scandinavian power; her attention was once more turned southwards. But the greatest shift had taken place in Germany. Prussia, a power of increasingly 'eastern' orientation during the past hundred years, now became the guardian of the gate against France in the west. Austria, for centuries a western power intimately involved in the politics of the Rhineland, Burgundy and the Low Countries, now acquired a largely Balkan, eastern European and especially Italian focus.[20] There was also a fundamental transformation in the way the great powers did business. They had learned the virtues of cooperation and restraint during the final stages of the struggle with Napoleon, and this culture continued to permeate diplomacy after 1815. At the same time, the great powers were agreed as never before that what happened inside European states – questions of slavery, toleration, political oppression and radical subversion – had profound implications for relations between states. The fifty or so years following the Treaty of Vienna are the story of how these contradictions played themselves out, of how Europeans unlearned the habit of consensus, at differing speeds and at differing times, with consequences which were as fatal to the stability of Europe as they were conducive to political and social change.

Meanwhile, the Treaty of Ghent brought the war between Britain and the United States to a formal close in December 1814. Its implications were no less revolutionary. The United States had survived its first major trial of strength with a great power since independence. Both parties agreed to work towards the abolition of the slave trade, though the institution of slavery itself was now not challenged. Britain returned the disputed territory around the Great Lakes and promised to return slaves who had run away from their American masters. London failed to fulfil the latter clause, instead making a substantial cash payment in compensation. The future battle lines between Britain and the young republic were now clear. The two powers would continue to jockey for influence, partly in North America – where the final border between the United States and Canada had not yet been clearly determined – but especially in Central and South America and the Caribbean.[21] The pan-European commitment to the abolition of the slave trade entered into at Vienna clashed directly with the increasing determination of the United States to exclude outside intervention of any kind in the western hemisphere. The intertwined issues of territorial expansion and slavery were an explosive charge which brought Americans into conflict with Europe on more than one occasion, and ultimately drove them to go to war against each other.

With Napoleon safely incarcerated in the South Atlantic, many European governments now attempted to cash in their 'peace dividends'. In Britain, the traditional 'fiscal-military state' gave way to the 'laissez-faire state'.[22] An army of more than 600,000 was cut to about 100,000, half of them serving overseas. This was in part driven by financial considerations, but it also reflected a politico-cultural shift. In 1816, the young Whig Lord John Russell spoke against expenditure on the army on the grounds that it would transform Britain from 'a naval into a military nation, and, instead of continuing a mighty island, into a petty continental state'.[23] In Prussia and Austria, governments also sought to get to grips with the debts of the Napoleonic Wars by reducing their armies, and state spending more broadly. The Habsburgs were desperate to avoid having to summon a Hungarian Diet to raise the necessary money for the army. In Prussia the king broke his promise to promulgate a constitution and 'national representation'. On the other hand, the Prussian government accepted that it could not increase taxes or take out substantial fresh loans without consulting its population, in effect forswearing all great-power ambitions. For this reason, the Prussian *Staatschuldengesetz* (State Indebtedness Law) of 1820 promised to do neither without summoning a general representation of the people. In 1823, as a stopgap, Frederick William III set up a regionally based system of noble-dominated assemblies, the *Provinziallandstände*. These were consultative bodies only, with no fiscal powers, and during the early years they suffered from apathy and low turnouts. For now, the social and political order in the eastern monarchies was safe, but only so long as developments in the European state system did not disturb these fragile domestic compromises.

Across the Atlantic, Americans watched European developments closely. The 'monarchical principle' enunciated at Vienna was seen as an ideological threat to the young republic. There were also two pressing geopolitical problems requiring immediate action. The Barbary pirates had resurfaced during the war with Britain. So in 1815 an American fleet was dispatched to chasten Omar Pasha of Algiers, destroying his fleet and occupying his harbour. Closer to home, the vacuum created by the loosening Spanish imperial grip made a decision on Florida urgent. The territory itself was considered next to worthless, but it could not be allowed to 'fall into the hands of an enemy possessing a superiority on the ocean', especially Britain. That would leave the republic encircled north and south. So in 1819 Florida was bought from Spain, and in 1820 the northern frontier of the Union was buttressed by the creation of the state of Maine.[24] All this required considerable state intervention to put the United States on a military footing to guard against European interference, and to take advantage of opportunities for territorial expansion. In 1816, Congress passed a large naval expansion bill designed to remedy defects that had become evident during the war of 1812. Even Andrew Jackson, who is often mythologized as a doughty individualist, did not doubt that it was necessary. In March 1817, he criticized Congress's 'mania for retrenchment', accused it of losing 'sight of the safety of our country at home, and its character abroad'. 'Every man with a gun in his hand,' he thundered, 'all Europe combined cannot hurt us.'[25] Europe, indeed, was the central preoccupation of much of Andrew Jackson's presidency: between a third and a half of his annual messages to Congress were devoted to foreign affairs.[26]

The challenges to the settlement of 1814–15 came quick and fast. French power revived quickly: the army was reconstituted, albeit on a much smaller basis. In 1818 the indemnity was paid off, the allied army of occupation was withdrawn, and selective conscription by ballot was introduced. For the moment, French intent was clearly defensive. That summer, a defence commission met to discuss the threat to France's eastern border and concluded that only a large-scale programme of military expansion and fortress construction could guarantee security against the German Confederation. Indeed, Germany remained the principal preoccupation of French planners and strategic debate until the Prussian invasion of 1870.[27] Likewise, for all its imperial preoccupations, the primary British strategic concern throughout the fifty years after 1815 remained Europe: the security of the British Isles, and especially the protection of the south coast and London against French invasion.[28] There were restless powers to the east and south too. Tsar Alexander showed remarkable restraint after 1815,[29] but the extent of Russia's power continued to unsettle her neighbours not least because the bulk of her army – more than two thirds – was stationed in Poland or along the western border. In Italy, the enlarged state of Piedmont-Savoy was looking for ways to guard against her continued vulnerability. The best way of achieving this, the Savoyard diplomat Joseph de Maistre continued, was for the monarchy to 'embrace', and thus 'stifle', the revolutionary nationalist currents in the peninsula. 'The King', in fact, 'should make himself chief of the Italians.'[30] A new Piedmontese geopolitics, based on the assumption that the territorial buffers necessary for dynastic security could only be achieved by appropriating the national cause, was in the making.

European stability was also challenged by the emergence of domestic critiques and revolutionary movements on both sides of the Atlantic after 1815. The greatest potential threat came from the growth of revanchism in the French parliament and public sphere. Nearly 40 per cent of the deputies elected under the constitutional charter introduced by the Bourbons in 1817 had been Bonapartists during the Hundred Days, and even many royalists believed passionately that France should be the arbiter of Europe. They relentlessly hammered the Bourbon government for its toleration of allied interference in French domestic politics, its acquiescence in the unjust 'treaties of 1815', for permitting the encirclement of France by a hostile coalition, and for its failure more generally to articulate a vision for French greatness. In particular, critics demanded the return of the Rhineland and Savoy, the natural borders which could serve both as buffers and as sluice gates through which French power could inundate Italy and Germany at will. As yet, these tendencies were kept in check by Bourbon repression and by the restricted franchise of 100,000 voters; and for the moment the regime resisted the temptation to compensate for its unpopularity through an adventurous foreign policy. There was every likelihood, however, that increasing popular pressures at home would lead to a more assertive policy abroad.

A similar debate was taking place across the Rhine. Here, too, the emerging national and liberal public sphere was deeply dissatisfied with the Vienna Settlement.[31] Many critics had wanted the creation of a German nation state on French lines, which would have facilitated the implementation of liberal reforms, and would have been robust enough to withstand external aggression. They got neither, and were profoundly unhappy with the loose ties offered by the Confederation. At the heart of this critique was continued fear of France. 'In the Bourbon lilies,' the veteran nationalist Joseph Görres warned, 'there remain Napoleonic bees and wasps seeking honey.'[32] For the moment, though, the resulting frustration was channelled inwards against the local barriers to German unity. Liberal nationalist agitation soon grew from a few hundred students in duelling fraternities to mass rallies such as the Wartburgfest, held in 1817 to mark the 300th anniversary of the posting of Luther's theses. In 1819, matters came to a head when the Russian agent and reactionary playwright August von Kotzebue was murdered by a student radical. Fearful of imminent revolution, and anxious to pre-empt outside intervention, Metternich persuaded the Prussians to agree the repressive Karlsbad Decrees that same year. What would happen, however, when the force of German liberal nationalism burst these fetters, or when one or the other power sought to harness that energy for its own ends, was anybody's guess.

South of the Alps, Italian liberal nationalists also took aim at the Vienna Settlement. This was accompanied by the cultural and patriotic nationalist surge of the *Risorgimento* unleashed by the great social and administrative upheavals of the Revolutionary and Napoleonic period.[33] Illegal secret societies such as the *Carbonari* attacked the dominance of Austria, and the subservience of repressive local dynasties to its dictates. Above all, critics lamented the continuing territorial fragmentation of Italy and demanded national unification. This reflected partly a burgeoning sense of common identity, and partly the belief that Italians would have to stick closer together if they were to survive in an increasingly predatory world where the trend was towards ever larger state formations.[34]

In Russia, too, discontent with the established order, and especially with tsarist foreign policy, was stirring. A myriad of secret and semi-secret societies sprang up, their ranks swelled by returning officers. Underpinning this was the development of a public space in which political questions could be debated: the first quarter of the nineteenth century saw the founding of over 120 new magazines in Russia, and the rate was increasing with each passing year. The principal bone of contention was Poland, which some Russian liberal nationalists – especially the 'Southern Society' of 'Decembrists', as they later became known, founded in 1817 – saw as a potential ally, and others regarded with the deepest suspicion. When Alexander proclaimed the Kingdom of Poland in May 1815, and referred to the possible future 'internal aggrandizement' of the new polity, many Russians interpreted this as a signal that territories lost to the Tsarist Empire in 1772 were to be returned. Critics also felt that he was not doing enough on behalf of the Orthodox Christian cause in the Ottoman Empire.

It was against this background that a series of revolutionary crises erupted on both sides of the Atlantic. In 1819, a former Russian officer, tsarist confidant and Greek patriot, Alexander Ypsilanti, led a revolt against Ottoman rule in the Danubian provinces of Moldavia and Wallachia, which are today part of Romania. By 1821, the fighting had spread to the Peloponnese and Greece proper, and in January of the following year a Greek national assembly elected a president of the Hellenic Republic, agreed a constitution, and declared the independence of the 'Greek Nation'. Turkey reacted with extreme brutality. Patriarch Gregorius V of Constantinople was hanged in public, and in 1822 the Ottomans murdered or deported the entire population of the island of Chios. Meanwhile, Spain was confronting independence movements in America.[35] To Spaniards, including liberals, these revolts threatened their plans to use the empire to recover their European stature, or at least to support them against renewed external aggression. So, in January and February 1820, King Ferdinand VII assembled a large force to recapture Buenos Aires. As they waited in Cadiz for transportation to South America, however, liberal officers rebelled and established constitutional government. A few months later, in July 1820, *Carbonari* and liberal officers in southern Italy combined with liberal officers against Ferdinand I of Naples and Sicily. He was forced to adopt a constitution on the Spanish model. Shortly after, the same happened in Portugal. By the spring of the following year, the revolutionary spirit had travelled northwards. In early March 1821 elements of the Piedmontese army rebelled, and called upon King Victor Emmanuel I not only to grant a constitution, but also to rescue Italy from the Habsburgs.

All this was accompanied by the emergence of a pan-European liberal humanitarian public sphere. This was most pronounced in Britain, where the anti-slave trade movement was dominant. In 1817, however, the cause experienced a serious setback when in the *Le Louis* judgment, the British courts rejected the Royal Navy's right to stop suspected slave ships belonging to powers which had not given it permission to do so. 'Forc[ing] the way to the liberation of Africa by trampling on the independence of other states', it was held, was tantamount to 'pressing forward with a great principle by breaking through every other great principle that stands in the way of its establishment'. For this reason, the British government sought to build a diplomatic consensus for abolition, and to avoid unilateral action. Even when such agreements were forthcoming, however, attention to legal norms made them difficult to enforce; a vibrant multiculturally run illegal slave trade continued across the Atlantic for much of the early nineteenth century.[36]

For this reason, activists and their parliamentary sympathizers were constantly pressing ministers to deploy the Royal Navy more vigorously against slaving stations off West Africa and the ships carrying their human cargo across the Atlantic.[37] In the early 1820s, the geopolitics of empathy was extended to include the Greeks, whose plight struck a chord among liberals and romantics, particularly in Britain, Russia and the United States – often for very different reasons – but also across much of western and central Europe. There were widespread calls for intervention to halt Ottoman atrocities. Some, such as the British poet Byron, volunteered to fight on behalf of Greece.

The Greek, Latin American, Spanish and Italian crises sparked a debate which dominated European diplomacy – and often domestic politics – throughout the early and mid-1820s. At one level, most of the great powers were agreed, most of the time, that these eruptions were the expression of some deeply subversive streak in European and colonial society which might unhinge the established order and the state system. Metternich, in particular, was obsessed with the idea of an international revolutionary conspiracy orchestrated by a mythical central *Comité Directeur*. Alexander, who had previously dallied with liberalism, was shocked into agreement with him by events in Spain and Italy. The Prussians, at this stage very much in Metternich's thrall, tended to go along with him on all broader European questions.[38] In Paris, the restored French monarchy was also deeply uneasy about revolutionary activity, especially in bordering Spain and Piedmont. Britain was more cautious about interfering in the domestic affairs of a foreign power, but even Castlereagh announced in January 1821 that 'no government can be more prepared than the British government is, to uphold the right of any state or states to interfere, where their own immediate security or essential interests are seriously endangered by the internal transactions of another state'.[39] He was not opposed to the principle of intervention as such, merely to its exclusive application in support of the reactionary interest in Europe.

At the same time, the great powers interpreted the revolutionary crises in the context of post-1815 geopolitics. For France, intervention in Spain or Italy would provide a vehicle to escape the constraints of the Vienna Settlement, and to rally domestic opinion behind an unpopular regime. For Britain, France and the United States, the Spanish American eruptions were an opportunity for territorial and commercial expansion. For

Russia, the Greek revolt was a chance to resume Catherine the Great's steady southward advance. At the same time, European powers were concerned to deny these opportunities to their rivals. Russia was anxious that her western rivals would establish a monopoly position in the former Spanish Empire. Alexander even speculated that the revolts were part of a design to put 'all the treasure of the Americas at the disposition of Britain'.[40] Metternich, for his part, feared a Russian advance into the Danubian principalities, which would further encircle the empire's south-eastern flank. He was also far more concerned about French penetration of Italy than about the revolutions themselves. Metternich was deeply ambivalent about a French intervention across the Pyrenees for similar reasons, and the thought of Alexander leading a restoration of the Bourbon monarchy there filled everybody with even greater horror. Castlereagh warned that a universal principle of interventionism would give the Russians 'an almost irresistible claim to march through the territories of all the Confederate states to the most distant point of Europe'.[41] Very often, in short, the fear of allowing one power a unilateral strategic advantage exceeded the ideological common ground against revolutionary tendencies.

In November 1820, the Russians, Prussians and Austrians met at Troppau and agreed that 'States which have undergone a change of government due to revolution, the results of which threaten other states' needed to be brought back into line 'by peaceful means, or if need be by arms'. On this basis, the powers met again at Laibach in 1821 to authorize Austrian intervention in Naples and Piedmont. Once the revolutionary outbreaks in Italy had been dealt with, another Congress was convened at Verona ostensibly in order to discuss the implementation of reforms in the pacified areas to forestall further eruptions. Very soon, however, the meeting became embroiled in debate about what do about Greece and especially Spain; tempers flared, not least because the French delegates used the occasion to demand revision of the Rhine frontier. This time, no agreement was reached and the French intervention in Spain in April 1823, which crushed the revolution and reinstated Ferdinand, was a unilateral action heartily disapproved of by Metternich. The elephant in the room at the Congresses and throughout the intervention debate was the German Confederation. Castlereagh argued that '[t]he general security of Germany' was 'inseparable' from that of 'Europe' as a whole. He was adamant, however, that the threat from revolution had to be 'direct and imminent' as well as 'military in character, actual and existent'; otherwise it would provide the Russians with a pretext to move into Germany.[42]

The most robust opposition to the principle of intervention, however, came from across the Atlantic. Public and governmental opinion saw Spain and Greece, especially the former, as ideological bulwarks against the advance of European absolutism. Matters came to a head when France not only crushed the Spanish revolution, but offered to provide naval support to ferry Spanish and French Bourbon princes across the Atlantic to establish conservative monarchies in the former Spanish Empire in place of local radicals. John Quincy Adams suspected European powers of an intention to 'recolonize' the Spanish lands and 'partition [them] out among themselves'. An appalling vista now presented itself: 'Russia might take California, Peru [and] Chile; France [might take] Mexico – where we know she has been intriguing to get a monarchy under a Prince of Bourbon. And Great Britain, as her last resort, if she could not resist this course of things, would take at least the island of Cuba for her share of the scramble. Then what would be our situation – England holding Cuba, France Mexico?'[43] The United States, in other words, would be encircled by hostile European powers.

This was the context in which President Monroe famously addressed Congress in his 'Seventh Annual Message' in early December 1823. He observed that Europe was the 'quarter of the globe, with which we have so much intercourse and from which we derive our origin', and of whose events 'we have always been anxious and interested spectators'. He warned that while the United States was pledged to respect 'existing colonies', it would 'consider any attempt [by European powers] to extend their system to any portion of this hemisphere', by 'oppressing' the new Latin American republics, 'as dangerous to our peace and safety'. He also announced unambiguously that 'the American continents, by the free and independent condition which they have assumed and maintain, are henceforth not to be considered as subjects for future colonization by any European powers'. In other words, the 'Monroe Doctrine' reflected not a turn towards hemispheric isolationism, but a continuing American belief that events in Europe were of profound relevance to the security of the republic.

*

The international turbulence of the 1820s resonated across Europe. The huge costs of intervening in Italy forced the Habsburgs to summon the Hungarian Diet again in 1825. A stand-off ensued: the Magyars under their leader, István Széchenyi, failed to have Hungarian adopted as the official language, while the Austrian government went away empty-handed. In Britain, the international situation – and especially the legacy of the struggle against Napoleon – shaped the debate on reform. When Roman Catholic emancipation was finally passed in 1829, the argument in its favour owed much to the Duke of Wellington's famous speech in which he reminded parliament that his victories would not have been possible without the contribution made by Catholic Irishmen. The Tsarist Empire, too, was rocked by internal disturbances brought on by strategic factors. A 'war party' at court felt that Alexander was not doing enough to help their Greek brethren;[44] so did the Union for Salvation, a liberal nationalist clandestine organization. Infuriated by the failure to act in the Balkans, and determined to exploit the power vacuum left by the death of Alexander in December 1825, the conspirators launched the unsuccessful revolt from they have since taken their name. They ensured, however, that Nicholas I ascended the throne with a consciousness that Russian grand strategy would henceforth have to take these voices into account.

It was in this context that the European powers contemplated the next phase of the Greek crisis. In February 1825, frustrated by the continuing resistance of the Hellenes, the Sultan called upon his nominal Egyptian vassal Mehmet Ali to suppress the rising. He agreed, in return for the promise of Syria, and very soon his powerful army was advancing inexorably – and bloodily – through Greece. Pro-Greek committees lobbied furiously for intervention against the Sultan. The new tsar, too, felt the force of popular sentiment on Greece. In April 1826 he concluded the Convention of St Petersburg with Great Britain, at which both parties agreed to mediate in Greece, and forswore any commercial or territorial gains. At the Convention of Akkerman six months later, Britain, France and Russia further agreed that Greece should become a semi-autonomous vassal state of Turkey. Both Paris and London hoped that a strong Greece, far from being an agent of tsarist expansionism, would actually function as a barrier to St Petersburg; in any case, the British prime minister, Earl Grey, was more concerned to keep the Russians out of Germany than the Balkans. Humanitarian concerns about Turkish atrocities also played a role.[45] The initial intervention was carried out by an Anglo-French naval force, which – following a misunderstanding – completely destroyed the joint Ottoman and Egyptian fleet at Navarino in October 1827. Right at the end of that year, Sultan Mahmud II decided to pre-empt the looming coalition against him by declaring a jihad on Russia. After a short campaign the Turks were forced to come to terms at the Treaty of Adrianople in September 1829. Greece became independent, Wallachia and Moldavia received autonomy, while Russia made only very modest territorial gains in the Caucasus.

The international controversy over Spain, Italy, Greece and Latin America temporarily distracted attention from the principal issue in European politics: the future of Germany. Here Prussia regarded the revival of French power in the 1820s with growing concern. Frustrated by what he saw as Austrian apathy, the new Prussian foreign minister, Count Bernstorff, began to cultivate the middling and smaller German states, many of whom feared renewed French aggression. At the heart of his more assertive policy was the creation of a Customs Union, whose primary purpose was political and strategic, rather than commercial.[46] The Prussian finance minister, Friedrich von Motz, predicted that 'political unity' would be 'the necessary consequence of commercial' union. The ultimate aim, he concluded, was a 'united, internally and externally truly free Germany under Prussian leadership and protection'. The link between German unity and Prussian security was thus articulated for the first time.

Across the Rhine, French observers watched the growth of German military capacity with anxiety. There were many voices inside and especially outside parliament that took the monarch and his ministers to task for failing to revise the hated 'treaties of 1815' more quickly. It was for this reason that King Charles X speculated that 'perhaps a war against the court of Vienna would be useful to me in terminating the internal debates and occupying the nations *en grand* as it desires'.[47] Rather than take on the Habsburgs, the French government picked on the ailing Ottomans in North Africa. In early July 1830, it seized Algiers, partly to root out the Barbary pirates once and for all, partly to secure the looming vacuum on her southern flank before it was occupied by another power, but mainly in order to revive the popular standing of the ministry. It was too late. Later that month, the accumulated resentment at the restored monarchy's domestic policies, and its inability to reclaim France's rightful role in Europe, exploded in revolution. The main line of the House of Bourbon was deposed, and Louis-Philippe, Duke of Orleans, ascended the throne as the 'citizen king'.

Over the next two years, revolutionary discontent spread across Europe in response to or at least in tandem with events in France. In late August 1830, the Belgians revolted against King William IV of the United Netherlands, and declared their independence; Luxemburg also rebelled and was claimed by Belgians, in defiance of the German Confederation. Three months later, the Poles rose in Warsaw against Russian rule. Most German states remained relatively quiet, but there were revolutionary eruptions in Saxony and Brunswick. The beginning of 1831 saw revolts in Italy, in Parma and Modena. Meanwhile, domestic unrest bubbled in Britain as demands for franchise reform grew. And, in late 1831, Mehmet Ali – whose relations with the Ottoman Empire had been sour since the failed intervention in Greece and the refusal to award him Syria in compensation – finally broke with his overlord and advanced on Constantinople. In December 1832, he inflicted a heavy defeat on the Turkish army at the battle of Konya. Tsar Nicholas began to fear that Mehmet would over-run the whole of Turkey and lead the Crimean Tartars into an Islamic crusade against Russia. From the Atlantic to the Bosphorus and beyond, Europe was in turmoil.

The implications of these upheavals for European stability were far more serious than they had been in the 1820s. This time, revolution had struck France itself, and to diehard reactionaries such as Metternich the subsequent reverberations across the continent were too numerous, and apparently similar, to be entirely coincidental. He suspected, as he had for a long time, that dark forces were orchestrating the violence from the shadows. 'The directing committee of Paris will triumph,' Metternich warned a Russian diplomat in August 1831, 'and no government will remain standing.'[48] The main threat to the system was not ideological, however, but geopolitical. There was every sign that the new regime in Paris would pursue the activist foreign policy its supporters demanded. 'The cannon of Paris,' General Lamarque declaimed to the French parliament in mid-January 1831, 'has silenced the cannon of Waterloo.' Radicals now routinely called for a pre-emptive war of liberation in Europe, or at the very least for a crusade to help the Belgians, Italians and Poles. This reflected not just a desire to spread freedom for its own sake, but a belief that the French revolution would only be safe in a Europe that was also 'free'. Pro-Polish rioters rampaged through the streets of Paris. In January 1832, troops were landed at Ancona to keep an eye on Austrian troop movements in the Papal States. Most worryingly of all, from the point of view of the rest of Europe, were the demands for union with Belgium, which reached a climax when the Belgians themselves offered Louis-Philippe's younger son, the Duke of Nemours, the crown in place of William.

In short, the revolutions of 1830–32 hit at the very core of the European states system in Germany and the Low Countries. A union between France and Belgium would destroy the barrier erected in 1815, expose the southern coast of England to attack and rip open the western border of the Confederation. Unlike recent tsarist advances, it would also be a unilateral French territorial gain large enough to unhinge the European balance. Any internal or external threat to the *Bund* was a mortal threat to international stability and thus British security. 'Our real interest in Germany,' the British ambassador to Austria argued in September 1832, 'is that it should be strong, united, monarchical and federal, under these conditions, incapable of aggression itself, and repelling it from the East and from the West, it becomes the key stone of the peace of Europe.'[49] The political unification demanded by the German national movement would destroy the balance of power. For this reason, the British ambassador to the Confederation warned against the 'extravagant doctrine of the Unity of Germany'.[50] A European conflict seemed inevitable. 'Perhaps [all] this looks very much like a general war,' one left-wing Parisian newspaper wrote breezily in August 1831, 'but the opposition does not mind a general war.'[51]

Faced with these challenges, the great powers did not embark on a counter-revolutionary crusade as both Metternich and Nicholas had initially suggested. Instead, they agreed to contain, not to crush, France; they would not interfere with the revolution, but any French attack across the Rhine would be instantly repelled. The crucial future of Belgium was settled at the London Conference in December 1830. It was to be separated from Holland, but only on condition that it was neutralized and accepted an uncontentious – that is non-French – monarch. To add credibility to their diplomacy, Austrian forces put down the Italian revolutions, while a much larger, Prussian-led confederal force was assembled in Germany to deter France. The German revolutions were also quickly suppressed. Belgium was more complicated: William IV refused to accept the loss of Belgium and, in early August, Dutch forces attempted to recapture it. This provided France with a pretext to intervene in turn, and to besiege William's men in Antwerp amid great patriotic fanfare, and under the watchful eyes of Britain, Prussia, Austria and Russia. It took until the very end of 1832 to subdue the Dutch and guarantee the integrity of a new neutralized Belgian state; French troops withdrew shortly afterwards. Meanwhile, the tsar suppressed the Poles in September 1831 and in February 1833 sent troops to the Straits at the Sultan's behest, where they stopped Mehmet Ali in his tracks. The resulting Treaty of Unkiar Skelessi in July 1833 was a clear victory for the tsar. It left the Straits open to Russian ships in time of war, but closed them to the navies of other powers.

When all the smoke had cleared in 1833–4, the contours of a new European geopolitics were visible across the continent. In this way, the Ottoman Empire was turned into a massive barrier defending Russia's southern flank, with Constantinople functioning as a sally-port into the Mediterranean. For the moment, the Russians exercised their new-found influence with restraint, partly because they had internalized the rules of the Congress System, and partly because they feared provoking a balancing coalition against them. When Alexander Menshikov called for further advances south some years later, he was told by the foreign minister, Charles de Nesselrode, that this would simply provoke the British and French to establish naval bases in the Black Sea.[52]

The liberal nationalist challenge had been checked but not contained. The formal foundation of Greece by the Treaty of London in 1830 signalled the emergence of a restless power on the western flank of the Ottoman Empire. Most Greeks, about three quarters, still lived outside the boundaries of the state, in Macedonia, Thessaly, the islands, Asia Minor and of course in Constantinople. Uniting them all now became the 'Great Idea' – or '*Megale Idea*' – of Greek foreign policy, and the dominant subject of debate in Greek domestic politics for the next ninety years or so; indeed, it was the only uniting principle in an otherwise fragmented society.

A more immediate issue was the continued growth of Italian nationalism, reflected in the 'Young Italy' movement under the leadership of the liberal nationalist Giuseppe Mazzini. As he put it in his 'General instructions for the members of Young Italy' (1831), the peninsula needed unity because without it 'there is no real strength; and Italy surrounded as she is by powerful, united and jealous nations, has need of strength before all things'. It rejected federalism: 'by reducing her to the political impotence of Switzerland, [it] would necessarily place her under the influence of one of the neighbouring nations'. Mazzini embedded his programme for Italian unity within a broader vision for European unity, which was 'the great mission Italy [was] destined to accomplish towards humanity'. He was confident of ultimate victory, because he believed that 'Europe [was] undergoing a progressive series of transformations, which [were] gradually and irresistibly guiding European society to form itself into a vast and united mass'. In April 1834, these sentiments found expression in the foundation of 'Young Europe' in Berne by Italian, German and Polish delegates. For the moment, at least, the group planned to avoid conspiratorial activity and intended to subvert the established order by the power of their ideas alone.[53]

Most importantly of all, the revolutions of 1830–32 accelerated the transformation of German geopolitics which had begun in 1815. Austria showed herself too preoccupied with events in Italy to pay much attention to the defence of the Confederation generally or of Luxemburg in particular. The middling German states, for their part, were manifestly unable to provide for their own security. Bavarian military expenditure, for example, had fallen by over one third annually between 1819 and 1830.[54] The chief minister of Bavaria, Karl August von Wangenheim, even prided himself on 'doing the minimum' for the common defence. The confederal fortresses either had not been built, or were in a state of disrepair. It was Prussia, not Austria, which pleaded the cause of Luxemburg before the timid Diet at Frankfurt. She did so not just out of a sense of German patriotism, but because of a growing belief that the security of Prussia in the European state system depended on rallying the whole of Germany to her cause. At the same time, the realization was setting in throughout Baden, Württemberg and even Bavaria that only Berlin could protect them against France. 'I know no south Germany and no north Germany,' King Ludwig of Bavaria wrote in March 1831, 'only Germany. I am convinced that safety is only to be found in firm connection with Prussia.' Not long after the crises subsided, most of Germany agreed to join Prussia in the famous Customs Union – *Zollverein* – in 1833. The chief minister of Hesse-Darmstadt, Freiherr von Thil, was quite open about the political implications. 'I do not hide the fact,' he wrote, 'that once we are bound in a commercial way to a great power, we will also be bound in a political sense.'[55]

The revolutionary crisis also gave nationalist and liberal sentiment a massive boost. In 1832, the 'German patriotic association for the support of the free press' was set up. It soon commanded a membership of more than 5,000 across state boundaries, and played an important role in organizing the Hambach Festival that same year. Well over 20,000 Germans turned up there to show their patriotic colours. Liberal sentiment inside and outside the south German parliaments, particularly in areas directly neighbouring France such as Baden, began to look to Prussia for their security.[56] The Palatine democrat and Bavarian subject Johan Georg Wirth even called for a league of German constitutional states to be led by Prussia. In Prussia itself, the Rhenish liberal David Hansemann called for constitutional reforms in order to 'maintain and increase the power of the state both internally and with respect to its external relations', in particular the containment of France. A German liberal national public sphere had been born, whose primary preoccupation was the achievement of national unity against the French threat.[57] This link between internal political reform and external defence was spelled out by Prince Joseph zu Salm-Dyck, a delegate to the Rhenish provincial Diet. 'It is precisely the creation of a unified representation,' he wrote to the Prussian governor of the Rhineland in late January 1831, 'which will overcome harmful differences [between the various regions of the state] and allow the merely aggregated parts of the monarchy to dissolve into a unified whole.' He also noted that 'the power of France and the influence which it exercises on its neighbours derives from its liberal institutions' and claimed that 'Prussia can claim the same power and influence' but only by 'putting itself at the head' of the constitutional movement.[58]

Developments in Germany were watched closely, west and east. The speed and size of the Prussian mobilization deeply impressed the French military establishment. Henceforth, they considered Prussia rather than Russia the principal threat. More generally, France feared the force of German nationalism. 'We must have the Treaty of Vienna,' the diplomat Adolphe de Bourqueney remarked in July 1832. 'The independence of the small German princes is what must be the foundation of our policy in Germany. Do with your subjects what you please ... we cannot consent to the disappearance of a single German state, no matter how small it is.'[59] The Russians, for their part, saw Austria and Prussia as a counter-revolutionary dam or breakwater which would halt, or at least slow down, subversive currents before they reached Poland, and ultimately Russia itself. It was with this in mind that the tsar exerted pressure on Berlin to disavow ministers who wanted to cooperate with liberal nationalism. He got his way after the death of Motz and the replacement of Bernstorff by the conservative Friedrich Ancillon as foreign minister in the early 1830s. In 1833, the three eastern powers came together at Münchengrätz, to agree a joint policy of stability on conservative principles in central Europe and the Ottoman Empire. Two years later, Berlin and St Petersburg advertised their solidarity by holding joint military manoeuvres in Poland. The counter-revolution was closing ranks across Europe.

In the west, liberal and constitutionalist powers were quick to pick up the gauntlet. British foreign policy, in particular, manifested an emancipatory and at times almost messianic streak. This reflected a strong sense that European peace and Britain's own security depended, as the Foreign Secretary, Lord Palmerston, put it, on the 'maint[enance] of the liberties and independence of all other nations'. On his reading, the survival of freedom in Britain required its defence throughout Europe: constitutional states were thus her 'natural allies'. There was also a broader feeling that Britain should, as Palmerston argued in August 1832, 'interfer[e] by friendly counsel and advice', in order to 'maintain the liberties and independence of all other nations' and thus to 'throw her moral weight into the scale of any people who are spontaneously striving for . . . rational gov[ernmen]t, and to extend as far and as fast as possible civilization all over the world'.[60] In other words, Britain would not 'interfere' in the internal affairs of other countries, or impose her values on unwilling populations, but she pledged her support to those who were willing to take the initiative – who were 'spontaneously striving' – to claim their liberal birthright.

Globally, the main battlefront was the international slave trade, and, increasingly, the institution of slavery itself. In 1833, slavery was finally abolished throughout the British Empire, which led a year later to the establishment of a French abolitionist society.[61] A cross-Channel Franco-British agitation against the slave trade now began, and a joint governmental programme for its eradication became a real possibility. This cleared the way for a more robust policy against the international slave trade, which the Royal Navy had been battling with varying success since 1807.[62] The newly independent Central and South American states had just abolished slavery, while Britain forced Madrid to give up the legal importation of slaves in 1820, and was increasing the pressure on Spain to abolish slavery altogether in her only remaining large colony of Cuba.[63] In 1835, London and Madrid concluded a treaty to limit the slave trade; for the moment this agreement was not honoured on the Spanish side, but it was a further step in the international de-legitimation of the trade. The British and Foreign Anti-Slavery Society was founded in 1838, and two years later the World Anti-Slavery Convention took place in London. Tensions with Portugal, whose ships still carried the lucrative human cargo to Brazil, rose.

In the United States, on the other hand, the issue of slavery became increasingly contentious in domestic and foreign policy, at the very moment when the new cotton economy was taking off in the South.[64] In January 1820, the Missouri Compromise determined that – with the exception of the state of Missouri itself – there should be no slavery north of the 36° 30´ parallel, but this agreement was under attack from both sides of the divide. William Lloyd Garrison founded his abolitionist newspaper, *The Liberator*, in 1831. Public opinion in the Northern states became more and more radical in opposition if not to slavery in the South, then at least to its extension in the west. Southerners, for their part, eyed not only the domestic but also the international scene with misgivings. Further west, French influence in Mexico was on the rise, reflected in their temporary occupation of Veracruz, ostensibly in order to enforce the repayment of Mexico's international debt; they were also active in California. It was clear that if the United States did not move into the vacuum to her west and south, another power would. And yet, so long as slavery divided North and South, no domestic consensus on expansion was possible. The inexorable westwards march of the United States therefore ground to a twenty-year halt.

The main focus of the new geopolitics, however, was Europe. With liberal – but not radical – governments in Paris after 1830, and in London from 1832, France and Britain were now ideologically aligned. In 1834, both powers responded to Münchengrätz by coming together with liberal-constitutionalist Spain and Portugal to form the Quadruple Alliance. 'The Triple League of despotic governments,' Palmerston exulted, 'will now be counter-balanced by a Quadruple Alliance in the west.' The continent was now split into two ideologically divided camps. Once hopeful of Alexander's intentions, liberal opinion saw the Tsarist Empire of Nicholas I as the bulwark of reaction across Europe. The British writer Robert Bremner noted at the end of the decade that the European press was teeming with books painting Russia as the 'most boundless, irresistible ... most formidable, and best consolidated [power] that ever threatened the liberties and rights of man'.[65]

This cold war was hottest in the Iberian peninsula, the principal battleground in the confrontation between west and east. Portugal had been convulsed by civil war ever since the late 1820s; Spain erupted in 1833, when the death of Ferdinand led to a succession struggle between the governing liberals who supported the infant Queen Isabella, and her conservative uncle, Don Carlos. The eastern powers supported Iberian conservatives with arms, money and diplomatic assistance. Spanish and Portuguese liberals, for their part, sent no fewer than six requests for international intervention in the next decade and a half; Britain and France responded with naval support, diplomatic leverage and the loan of the Foreign Legion. The French interior minister, Adolphe Thiers, claimed that it was in the French national interest that the internal government of Spain should correspond to that of France. This made the defence of Spanish liberalism imperative. Moreover, Thiers argued, the law of 'neighbourhood' – '*voisinage*' – gave France the right to intervene;[66] this was the same argument from 'vicinage' which Burke had advanced in the 1790s. To Palmerston, the first task of his 'western confederacy' was the protection of constitutionalism in the Iberian peninsula, which he saw as the first line of defence for freedom closer to home.

The western European liberal international consensus began to fragment towards the end of the decade. It came under increasing attack domestically in both countries. In France, the restive parliamentary and public sphere felt that not enough was being done to help the cause of liberty across the continent, and – for this amounted in their eyes to the same thing – to re-establish France's position within the state system. Louis-Philippe was battered not only over his cautious policy towards Spain, but also for tolerating the Austrian military repression of riots in the Free City of Cracow. In Britain, the liberal camp was split between Palmerstonian interventionists and the orthodox economic liberal followers of Cobden. Breaking with the Russophobe consensus – which embraced Britons of all stripes, but particularly liberals – Cobden rejected intervention ('no foreign politics'). Not only did he minimize the tsarist threat, but Cobden also believed that an activist foreign policy necessitated a backward domestic policy complete with a large standing army, spiralling national debt, colonies, and Corn Laws designed to entrench aristocratic supremacy in state, society and armed forces. For him, the repeal of the Corn Laws and the promotion of international free trade were instruments to secure liberalism at home and thus peace abroad – and vice versa.[67]

In the end, it was events, not opinions, which shattered the liberal geopolitics of the 1830s. Even at the best of times, France and Britain had competed as much as they had cooperated in the Iberian peninsula, overseas and elsewhere. Their relations were thrown into turmoil, however, by the renewed outbreak of war between Mehmet Ali and the Ottoman Empire. In 1839, Mehmet declared the independence of Egypt, provoking a disastrous invasion by the Sultan.[68] Encouraged by France – where opinion regarded Mehmet as a liberal modernizer – the Egyptians advanced deep into the Ottoman Empire. In the middle of this drama, another crisis erupted from Damascus, where news reached Europe in early 1840 that leading Jews of the city had been convicted of ritual murder by Mehmet's authorities on the basis of evidence supplied by the French consul. Liberal public opinion in Britain – already excited over slavery – was outraged by the treatment of the Jews, and prominent anti-slavery campaigners such as Sir Thomas Fowell Buxton and the Irish parliamentary leader Daniel O'Connell took up their cause. More importantly, the London government and politicians of almost every stripe were deeply concerned about French penetration of the Near East. So was Metternich, and on this matter he was assured of Prussian diplomatic support. The Russians, needless to say, regarded the prospect of a French-backed dynamic modernizer in Constantinople with horror. So, in mid-July 1840, all four powers agreed to prop up the Ottoman Empire and protect the Straits from occupation by a third party. In September 1840, the Royal Navy was dispatched to the Lebanon, where it landed a force of British and Austrian marines north of Beirut, to force Mehmet to relinquish Syria. Palmerston told the British consul to leave Mehmet in no doubt about 'the extreme disgrace' which the barbarities of Damascus 'reflected upon his administration'.[69] Faced with this united front, Mehmet released the Jews, and evacuated Syria. Not for the first time in European history, the west had produced not only the disease but also the cure.

In France, the eastern crisis detonated a popular and parliamentary explosion. Enthusiasm for Mehmet – who was seen not only as a modernizer, but also as a Russophobe and opponent of British 'maritime despotism' – ran high in 1839, so the government had no difficulty in securing monies that July to increase the Mediterranean fleet. The real aim of the exercise was not so much the promotion of French influence in the Middle East, however, as to secure a bargaining counter which could be traded for progress on the Rhine frontier. Against this background, it is hardly surprising that the exclusion of France from the four-power agreement of July 1840 on the Straits struck Paris like a thunderbolt. Press, parliament and popular opinion erupted in outrage at the humiliation. The French political writer Alexis de Tocqueville warned that 'there is no government, indeed no dynasty, that would not be exposing itself to destruction if it wished to persuade this country to stand idly by'.[70] The outraged masses demanded war and electoral reform; the Beirut landings provoked yet another assassination attempt against the king. Thiers felt he had no choice but to raise the stakes, and demand 'compensation' for France's disappointment in the Near East through a revision of the Rhine frontier. He ostentatiously decorated his office with military maps of the Rhineland, threatened the Austrians on their 'weak side' in Italy, and generally talked up the prospect of a European war in order to keep domestic opinion at bay. 'I prefer to fall on the banks of the Rhine or the Danube,' the Duc d'Orléans announced, 'than in a gutter of the Rue Saint Denis.'[71] In other words, either the French would go to war in Germany or they would go to war with each other.

Across the Rhine, the French eruption produced a corresponding German reaction. A surge of nationalism engulfed the country, especially in the south and west, where the prospect of a second French occupation in a lifetime did not appeal. Once again, however, the inadequacy of the confederal defence arrangements was cruelly exposed. Between them, Württemberg, Baden, Bavaria and all the other middling or smaller states could only muster a fraction of the forces required. The Austrians, afflicted by a cantankerous Hungarian Diet, heavily committed in Italy and crippled by debt, were in no position to act either. Once again, it was Prussia which rose to the challenge, and within a very short period of time had not only put the western confederal fortresses in order but also mobilized nearly 200,000 men. In the end, Louis-Philippe lost his nerve, Thiers resigned, France climbed down, and war was averted.

The Eastern and Central European Crises of 1839–40 triggered a series of transformations in European foreign and domestic politics. They accelerated the tendency of the Third Germany to look to Prussia for protection against French revanchism. Even if they still stubbornly refused total military subordination to Berlin, the smaller German states were forced to concede that the idea of an independent military deterrent was unrealistic. For every step back towards a particularist past, they now took two steps forward into the Prussian future. The Rhine Crisis also gave a powerful boost to the emergence of a German liberal nationalist geopolitics which transcended state boundaries. 'The German [empire] must be mighty and strong,' the Rhenish liberal David Hansemann wrote in a widely distributed memorandum in 1840, 'for we have dangerous neighbours.' In the east, he wrote, there lay Russia, 'the most consistently expansionist state since Roman times, which has already taken up a threatening position in the heart of Prussia [i.e. in Poland]', and was threatening East Prussia. To the west lay France, 'a state which is dangerous because of its internal cohesion, the warlike and excitable nature of its inhabitants and because of their tenacious and unhappy belief in the need to control the Rhine border sooner or later'. It therefore fell to Prussia to unite Germany and save it from being the 'cockpit of all major European wars'.[72] Similar views were expressed by liberals the length and breadth of Germany, even including the south. The French had thus scored an own goal with fateful consequences. Metternich remarked in November 1840 that it taken Thiers 'only a short time to lead Germany to a place where Napoleon had brought it by ten years of oppression'.[73]

Like their monarchic predecessors, German liberal nationalists agreed that domestic structure should reflect the needs of foreign policy. Unlike them, however, they took this as a mandate for constitutional government. Prussia, as Hansemann noted, was made up of 'widely dispersed' provinces. It needed a 'correspondingly vibrant, general and national' patriotism to hold them together; 'only freedom,' he averred, 'can create such a patriotism in Prussia'. German liberal nationalists therefore sought to compensate for their geopolitical vulnerability between east and west through a programme of internal reforms. 'If you unify and liberate the nation at home,' the liberal Robert Prutz argued, 'you will also make it great and powerful externally.' In particular, liberals wanted to harness the power of the middle classes: only public opinion, a popular militia and 'homogeneity of principles' could guarantee security; traditional monarchic power was no longer enough. It was in this context that liberals renewed their demand for a Prussian, and ultimately a German, 'national representation', as the only vehicle which could mobilize the nation against external enemies.[74]

The events of 1839–40 also led to profound geopolitical shifts in the Balkans. Russia had frustrated a French coup at the Straits, but the London Convention between Britain, Austria, Prussia, France, the Ottoman Empire and herself, which took place in the summer of 1841, was in most respects a defeat. The agreement explicitly forbade the passage of Russian ships, and those of all other foreign powers, through the Dardanelles and Bosphorus in peacetime. Even more worrying was the sense that the Ottoman Empire was on the verge of internal collapse, or dismemberment at the hands of Mehmet Ali and other local potentates. In January 1844, the tsar raised the problem on a visit to London and urged the British government to consider how to react if 'unforeseen circumstances' led to a power vacuum at Constantinople.[75] Rather than join in the scramble to despoil the Ottoman Empire, Britain tried to encourage the Sultan's reforming efforts, in the hope of making Turkey less prone to internal explosions and less vulnerable to external attack. Central to this endeavour was the defence of minority religious rights. London wanted the transformation of the Ottoman Empire not to humiliate or dominate it, but to strengthen it against external predators and reduce the danger of internal unrest. 'There is no reason,' Palmerston remarked of the *Tanzimat* reforms, 'why [Turkey] should not become a respectable power.'[76] She was being asked to join the west, not to submit to it.

It was across the Atlantic, however, that the impact of the renewed west European liberal geopolitics was most keenly felt. In 1839, the French government announced its intention to abolish slavery, which it finally did six years later (allowing a transitional period in her colonies), drawing the net ever tighter around slavery and slave-trading. Palmerston refused to recognize the independent state of Texas – which had broken away from Mexico – until it had abjured slavery in 1841. In

May of that year, Palmerston signalled his intent to bring the long campaign to an end with a treaty between the five European great powers. American slave-owners observed these developments with mounting concern. In August 1843, the US Secretary of State, Abel P. Upshur, predicted that 'England is determined to abolish slavery throughout the American continent and islands'.[77] Southern strategists increasingly drew the conclusion that, in order to survive, slavery would have to expand, and in order to expand the slave lobby – far from barricading itself behind the principle of 'states' rights' – would have to take over the apparatus of US foreign policy, ending nearly two decades of relative strategic restraint. In 1844, the Tennessee Democrat James Polk was duly elected president on a platform of further territorial expansion after a contest in which relations with neighbouring states and with the great powers, and developments in Europe more generally, featured prominently.[78]

Back in Europe, new transnational ideological and geopolitical fault-lines were opening up within European societies. The Damascus Affair, and the accompanying western and central European outbreaks of anti-Jewish sentiment, hastened the growth of an international Jewish public sphere from 1840. 'We have no country of our own,' Rabbi Isaac Leeser told a meeting of Jews in Philadelphia in August 1840, 'we no longer have a united government under the shadow of which we can live securely' and yet 'we hail the Israelite as brother, no matter if his home be the torrid zone or where the poles encircle the earth'.[79] Financially and morally supported by the wealthy diaspora in France and Britain, activists began to target governments and organizations which pursued openly anti-Jewish policies. Thus Moses Montefiore and the Frenchman Adolphe Crémieux went to Damascus to demand the release of the accused, while the Rothschilds intervened on behalf of Jews threatened with expulsion from the Russian Pale of Settlement. The Jewish international locked horns with individual states, especially the Tsarist Empire, but its main focus was on the transnational enemy, Roman Catholicism. Of course, the Jewish response also helped to create the very phenomenon which it was trying to combat. 'The Hebrew nationality is not dead,' the French Catholic newspaper *Univers* thundered in 1840. 'What religious connection is there between the Talmudists of Alsace, Cologne or the East, and Messrs. Rothschild and Crémieux.' It went on to speak of 'a sense of unity [that] binds Jews together, making them act as one man in all parts of the world [so that] by means of their money they can, when it suits them, control almost the entire press in Europe'.[80] This was the paradox of Jewish internationalism: it raised the cost of discrimination, but it also left Jews everywhere more vulnerable to paranoia and oppression.

This Jewish internationalism was universalist rather than nationally exclusive. Most Jews believed that their own freedom would only be possible as part of a broader process of European social and political emancipation; they had not yet grasped that it might also free anti-semites from state restraint, or that their own national rights might have to be secured at the expense of the rights of others. Just before Montefiore set off for Damascus in 1840, he announced that he was vindicating 'the claims of [the whole] of humanity', which was 'outraged in the persons of our persecuted and suffering brethren'. Montefiore explained that his visit therefore had a purpose much wider than that of purely Jewish solidarity, which was 'to infuse into the governments of the east more enlightened principles of legislation . . . and in particular to prevail on those governments to abolish the use of torture, and to establish the supremacy of law over undefined and arbitrary power'.[81] The purpose behind these 'humanitarian' endeavours was not to colonize the states in question, but to make them better places for their populations and ultimately more viable members of the state system.

The 1840s also marked the emergence of another European transnational geopolitics, reflecting the massive social and economic changes of the past fifty years or so. Britain had already seen an 'industrial revolution', and many other states, particularly in the west, were on the verge of following suit. Industrialization, urbanization, the railway boom, the growth of the bourgeoisie, the emergence of the embryonic 'working classes' – these were all, to a greater or lesser degree and at different speeds, pan-European developments. So were alienation, industrial protest and class conflict. Observing all this in the early 1840s was the radical young journalist Karl Marx. He was living and writing in the Prussian Rhineland, a rapidly industrializing area in which many of Germany's first railways were being built. It was in this environment that he began to develop his materialist conception of history as a process of class conflict based on socio-economic interests. In 1844, he met up with the like-minded Friedrich Engels and both men started work on *The German ideology*. The only answer to the prevailing capitalist system of injustice, they argued, was 'communism ... an ideal to which reality [would] have to adjust itself'. This could only be realized if European workers recognized that they had more in common with each other than with their oppressors. In late September 1845, a group of left-wing British Chartists, German workers and artisans, and various other European revolutionaries convened in London to found the Fraternal Democrats; though Marx and Engels did not attend themselves, they were instrumental in preparing the event. Socialist internationalism had been born.[82]

The international scene remained relatively stable until mid-decade, but from 1845 on all hell broke loose. In December of that year, faced with the threat of British and French penetration of Mexico, and the relentless advance of the anti-slave trade movement around the periphery of the republic, the United States annexed Texas as a slave state. It did so partly to pre-empt a European power, and partly because the Southern lobby required the extension of slavery to new territories in order to maintain their domestic position against the abolitionist threat in the North. Border tensions soon escalated into a war which Mexico lost decisively.

Europe was also entering a phase of severe domestic unrest and international tension. It took place against the background of escalating Anglo-French colonial differences, and the fear that the advent of steam would undermine British naval supremacy; the first of many invasion scares along the south coast followed in 1844–5. 'The Channel is no longer a barrier,' Palmerston warned the House of Commons in June 1845. 'Steam navigation has rendered that which was before impassable by a military force nothing more than a river passable by a steam bridge.'[83] In 1846, the Franco-British entente was crippled by a row over the marriage of Queen Isabella's younger sister – and expected heir – to Louis-Philippe's son. This coup infuriated London, which had hoped that she would marry a cousin of Prince Albert. Britain was rocked by another invasion scare which lasted into 1847. At around the same time, a Polish revolt in Habsburg Galicia was put down by the Austrian authorities with some difficulty and considerable bloodshed. The really important developments, however, took place in Germany. In early August, King Christian VIII of Denmark issued an 'open letter' declaring the Duchies of Schleswig and Holstein to be an integral part of the Danish monarchy. This was an affront not only to the German Confederation, of which Holstein was a member, but also to the German national movement, which claimed both duchies for their planned united German nation state.

These events interacted with the geopolitical discourses within European states. The French invasion scare drove a debate about British military preparedness, which was widely believed to have declined since 1815, and precipitately during the 1840s. The London government responded to this challenge innovatively, embracing Cobden's call for international peace through free trade. Often seen as a reflection of shifts in British society, the abolition of the Corn Laws in 1846 actually had its roots in foreign policy. It was expected not merely to destroy the domestic bases of British militarism by crushing landlord power, but also to link states commercially through what we would today call 'interdependence', thus making war all but impossible. Free trade, Cobden predicted, would inaugurate 'the greatest revolution that ever happened in the world's history', destroy 'the antagonism of race, and creed and language', and make 'large and mighty empires ... gigantic armies and great navies' redundant.[84] In France, the continuing failure of the Orleanist regime to overturn or at least revise the Vienna Settlement led to a terminal crisis of legitimacy. 'It is above all the mistrust caused by the government's handling of the foreign question,' the socialist Étienne Cabet remarked in 1840, 'that makes us desire the reign of democracy so strongly: that is the main cause of our internal agitations.'[85] The resulting tension between the administration, the small and largely pacifist electorate and the much larger group of nationalist republican hawks began to tear the country apart. Foreign policy featured prominently in the 1846 election campaign, which mobilized far more people than were actually entitled to vote.

Across the Rhine, German public opinion erupted in fury over Schleswig-Holstein. The Confederation fumbled; Metternich remained studiously inactive. In Baden, the radical Friedrich Hecker threatened to send volunteers to the duchies if the Confederation and the princes refused to act. All eyes now turned to Berlin. 'Prussia must put herself at the head of Germany,' the liberal Heidelberg historian G. G. Gervinus argued. 'This requires three things,' he continued, 'Prussia must promulgate a constitution, it must allow freedom of the press and it must attempt a forceful foreign policy.'[86] After a prolonged period of vacillation, Berlin was forced to concede that Prussia's exposed geopolitical position between west and east required a military and logistic mobilization which only greater domestic political participation could guarantee. This was not possible, however, because raising new taxes or taking out substantial new loans required the consent of a national representation, something which the king and conservatives were desperate to avoid. The question became acute after the autumn of 1845, when the French government began a network of strategic railways threatening the western border of the Confederation. When, in April 1846, a federal commission stressed the need for an equivalent German system of strategic railways, the issue could no longer be deferred.

Once again, the Confederation dithered. Austria, preoccupied by escalating revolutionary violence in Italy, did nothing; the southern German states were unable even to agree the gauge of an integrated rail network. If Germany was to have the system of strategic railways she so desperately needed, Prussia would have to act alone, or at least take the lead. In order to do so, however, she would have to submit to a fundamental reform of her political economy. The only way out of fiscal-political gridlock was to call a national representation in order to sanction the extraordinary taxation required for railway construction. So, in 1846, Frederick William finally bit the bullet and summoned a United Diet to meet in the following year. When this assembled in the summer of 1847, it provided a national forum at which liberal grievances could be articulated. This growing confidence and activism of the liberal nationalist public sphere found expression in the founding of the *Deutsche Zeitung* in May 1847. Its programme consisted of three main demands: a competitive position for German goods in foreign markets, an end to the diplomatic dependence on Russia, and an active 'German' foreign policy in pursuit of political unity; these were to be achieved through an alliance between the Prussian state and the nationalist movement.

The Prussian Adjutant-General, Ludwig von Thile, met these concerns halfway in his opening address to the Diet. Prussia, he argued, was 'called by its geographic location to be the champion of Germany', because its 'lands everywhere comprise the vanguard of Germany and enemies first have to step over our bodies before they can penetrate further into Germany'.[87] To this end, the government argued, a railway linking the two halves of the monarchy was not only commercially desirable, but strategically vital. The majority of the mostly liberal delegates agreed with this analysis. 'If our brothers cannot hurry to our aid,' one remarked, 'then we shall be . . . flooded by Cossacks, Kalmuks and Kirgizians.'[88] They were sceptical, however, as to whether the government had the backbone to deliver on nationalist demands. This concern merged with their determination to use the monarchy's financial embarrassment to promote constitutional change. The United Diet refused to vote Frederick William the monies for the *Ostbahn* until he agreed to the establishment of a permanent national representation across the monarchy. They forced him to agree to various other reforms, such as extending the emancipation of the Jews to all provinces. Soon after, Hansemann demanded Prussian action in support of German interest in Schleswig-Holstein. Meanwhile, in central and southern Germany, deputies from the representative assemblies met to debate how best to achieve national unification, as well as social and constitutional reform.

In Austria, Metternich faced fiscal-political gridlock. Huge sums were required to fund the programme of railway construction started in 1842, and to keep a lid on revolutionaries in Italy. These could not be found in Hungary, where a new radical leadership under Lajos Kossuth was emerging. Raising taxes still further in some of the other territories risked provoking unrest unless it was accompanied by obnoxious constitutional concessions. The only alternative, borrowing on the international money markets, depended on maintaining Habsburg credibility at home and abroad. For when the Vienna syndicate agreed to advance substantial loans to the government, it did so on condition that the level of public bonds did not fall below par. To cap it all, the opposition triumphed in 1847 elections to the Hungarian parliament. In the late 1840s, therefore, the Austrian state found itself being slowly strangled by the very same fiscal-political vice which had destroyed the French *ancien régime* in 1787–8. Something would have to give.

Matters were brought to a head across central and western Europe by two interlocking crises. There been a poor harvest in many European countries in 1845–6. Impoverished artisans became progressively more restive. A collective credit crunch, rocketing unemployment and rising interest rates – in many ways the first crisis of the capitalist system – added to government woes in 1847. What gave the established order the *coup de grâce*, however, was its failure in foreign policy. The final straw was the Swiss crisis of 1847, triggered by the victory of the liberal

Protestant cantons, led by Berne, over the smaller conservative Catholic cantons of the *Sonderbund*. According to the Vienna Settlement, the great powers were guarantors of the Swiss constitution, and there was every prospect that Austria, which sympathized with the conservatives, and France, which backed the liberals, would soon find themselves engaged in a proxy diplomatic and ideological struggle. At stake here was not so much Switzerland, as the stability of Germany and the whole European system. Metternich feared that the liberal victory would act as a magnet for revolutionary tendencies in south Germany, from where events in Switzerland were being closely watched. Indeed, German liberals launched a massive petition campaign in support of the Swiss liberals; they were particularly impressed by the performance of the liberal militia, which they wished to adopt as a model for themselves. Metternich failed, however, to impose his will on Switzerland, not least because he lacked the financial resources to do so.

Taken together, the socio-economic and politico-diplomatic crises of late 1847 rapidly destroyed the remaining legitimacy, and thus the financial credibility, of the *ancien régime* in France, Austria and Prussia. François Guizot, the French prime minister, was on his last legs. Anxiety about the growth of Prussian power and the security of the eastern frontier had been mounting from the mid-1840s, and the administration was also under heavy radical fire for acquiescing in the annexation of Cracow, and abandoning Italian nationalists. In parliament, Victor Hugo extolled Napoleon and condemned materialism. Across Paris, 'banquets' – in reality opposition demonstrations of up to 20,000 people – were held to demand a broader franchise and a more active foreign policy to destroy the treaties of 1815 and support nationalist revolutionaries in Italy, Poland and Germany. In Austria, Metternich – who had been so determined to learn from Joseph II's mistakes – found himself locked into an ever-tightening vicious circle of foreign-political confrontation, domestic unrest and fiscal constraint. In early March 1848, as the public bonds plummeted, the banks finally pulled the plug. The government was forced to summon the estates to dig itself out of the financial morass. As in France in 1789, therefore, the strength of the established order had been comprehensively eroded by a searing fiscal and foreign policy critique from the vibrant public sphere long before the first protestors took to the streets in Paris, Vienna or Berlin. 'The government was not overthrown,' Tocqueville remarked, 'it was allowed to fall.'

The revolutionary virus struck first at the weakest point of the old order: Palermo.[89] It quickly spread from Sicily to the mainland, and very soon the King of Naples and Sicily was forced to grant a constitution. The rulers of Piedmont and Tuscany, seeking to pre-empt revolution in their territories, followed suit. These events were not enough, however, to provoke a European upheaval. The revolution in Paris, which erupted in February, was another matter. The flight of Louis-Philippe, the proclamation of the Republic and the emergence of a coalition of radicals, socialists and moderates were a profound challenge to the whole Vienna Settlement. There was an immediate war scare in southern and western Germany, especially Baden and the Prussian Rhine Province, where a French attack was imminently expected, and where the continuing failure of the established authorities to provide for the common defence undermined their legitimacy still further. In Italy, revolutionaries seized power in Venice and Milan, the Habsburg forces retreating into a network of fortresses; later that year, they took over Rome as well. At around the same time, revolutionaries took control of Berlin, and compelled the king to agree to a constitution and sign up to German unification. Liberals and nationalists also grabbed power in Schleswig-Holstein, Baden, Bavaria and various other German territories. In the Habsburg Empire, liberal insurgents forced Metternich into exile and formed a coalition government with conservatives in Vienna. Liberals and nationalists also took control in Hungary, Prague and Cracow.

All this already represented a huge ideological challenge to the Vienna Settlement, but it was the potential geopolitical impact of the revolutionary takeover which most concerned the two remaining great powers, Great Britain and Russia. The liberal nationalist foreign policy programme in France, Germany and Italy was effectively a declaration of permanent war against conservative Europe. A crusade to free the Poles and Italians, to unify the Germans, and generally roll back Tsarist despotism seemed on the cards. An intervention to support Italian revolutionaries was right at the top of the list of radical demands in Paris. The new Prussian liberal government sent troops to support German nationalists in Schleswig-Holstein against the Danes. It openly considered war with Russia on behalf of the Poles. In Italy, the revolutionaries looked to not only the creation of a unitary state, but also the export of their principles. 'The end which I pursue,' Mazzini announced, 'is Italian unity, the Italian thought concentrating itself in the Rome of the people, and radiating from there across Europe.'[90] His revolutionary agenda coincided – in part – with that of the Piedmontese ruler, Charles Albert, who was seeking to expand at Habsburg expense. Appealing to Italian national sentiment, he vowed to 'do it alone' and attacked the Austrians, threatening to overturn the carefully constructed balance in the peninsula. The proliferation of nationalist revolts within the Habsburg Empire also had profound implications for the European system, because they seemed to presage Austria's collapse as a major power.

There was much that was impractical and utopian in the liberal nationalist vision, but it was also grounded in a keen sense of strategic priorities. The main enemy in France and Germany was not the Habsburg Empire but the tsarist colossus, which was seen as the reactionary lender of last resort. Not even the most optimistic radical thought that it could be destroyed; it would have to be contained. At this point, in fact, the French favoured a German federation to block Russia – the foreign minister, Édouard Drouyn de Lhuys, called for a Franco-German fraternal pact to reconstruct a 'free and independent' Poland as a buffer in the east.[91] They also wanted to keep Austria as strong as possible for the same reason. To that end, the new French prime minister, Alphonse de Lamartine, offered to compensate the Habsburgs for the loss of Italy with the Danubian principalities. In July 1848, the French foreign minister, Jules Bastide, explained that an expanded Austria would serve as 'a barrier between Russia and the complete domination of east Europe'.[92] Paris sought to square these national and strategic circles by recommending a 'Danubian federation'. In the same vein, the German liberal nationalists assembled at Frankfurt looked to a restored Poland as the bulwark of European liberalism against tsarist despotism.

Disagreements over foreign policy radicalized the revolutions. This was particularly the case in France, where irritations with Lamartine's cautious policy quickly surfaced. In mid-May 1848, the Constituent Assembly was invaded by leftist demonstrators calling – unsuccessfully – for an army to be sent to Germany to deter Prussia and help the Poles, all to be financed by a tax on the rich. Not long after, Napoleon Bonaparte's nephew, Louis Napoleon, was elected to the National Assembly, and in December he won the presidency in a landslide. This was a vote if not for immediate then certainly for urgent revision of the Vienna Settlement. 'The name of Napoleon,' he himself boasted a year later, 'is a programme in itself',[93] a clear wink at a territorially revisionist agenda.

On receiving news of the election, King Frederick William IV of Prussia told a group of German parliamentarians that 'You can see Germany threatened on the Rhine. I hope that when I call my people to arms it will show itself worthy of its fathers and will gloriously protect her borders as in 1813'; he even called for the erection of a 'bronze curtain' (*mur d'airain*) against France in the west.[94] In the short term, however, Louis Napoleon contented himself with sending an expedition to Rome in April 1849, in order to pre-empt an Austrian attack on the Roman Republic. He restored the pope, partly to appease Catholic opinion at home but mainly to reassert French power in the peninsula and thus rally the public more generally behind the new regime.

The revolutions also saw the articulation of an even more radical geopolitics. In late January 1848, the League of Communists reacted to news of revolution in Naples and Sicily with a request to Karl Marx and Friedrich Engels to speed up their planned programmatic statement. The result, after a mad scramble, was *The communist manifesto*, which appeared in February, the same month as Paris erupted. 'A spectre is haunting Europe,' the authors announced, 'the spectre of communism.' It existed, they claimed, because it 'was already acknowledged by all European powers to be itself a power'. Unlike all other working-class or socialist parties, Marx and Engels claimed, the communists 'point out and bring to the front the common interest of the entire proletariat, independent of all nationality'. Indeed, they continued, 'working men have no country ... [because] national differences and antagonisms between peoples [were] daily more and more vanishing, owing to the development of the bourgeoisie, to freedom of commerce, to the world market, to uniformity in the mode of production and in the conditions of life corresponding thereto'. In this interconnected world a new geopolitics which pitted the common interest of the exploited against their oppressors was the only answer. It would render state and national conflict redundant because 'in proportion as the exploitation of one individual by another is put an end to, the exploitation of one nation by another will also be put an end to'.[95]

All this posed a massive challenge to Britain and Russia. Liberal and socialist plans for the reconstitution of Poland threatened the very core of the Tsarist Empire. 'Poland as understood by the Poles,' the Russian diplomat Baron Peter von Meyendorff warned in March 1848, 'extends to the mouth of the Vistula and Duna, as well as to the Dniepr at Kiev and Smolensk.' 'Such a Poland,' he continued, 'enters Russia like a wedge, destroys her political and geographical unity, throws her back into Asia, [and] puts her back two hundred years.' Stopping this, Meyendorff concluded, was the cause of 'every Russian'.[96] The British were also worried about Italy, because it destroyed the southern bulwark against the expansion of French power. The region was, as Palmerston put it in June 1848, no longer 'the shield of Ajax', but 'the heel of Achilles'.[97] Recognizing that the Habsburgs had had their day in the peninsula, he and Russell now began to search for a new solution to the barrier problem.

But the central battleground for all the parties in 1848–9, conservatives, liberals, radicals, socialists and communists, and the great powers, was Germany. Here the revolutions threatened to overturn the whole basis of the Vienna Settlement, ideologically and geopolitically. The British, for their part, observed the collapse of the Habsburg position in 1848–9 with deep concern. 'The exclusion of Austria from the organization of Germany,' the British ambassador to Munich, Sir John Milbanke, cautioned in late April 1848, 'appears, if examined in connection with the balance of power in Europe, only in the light of an aggrandizement of Prussia. It completely alters the balance. It destroys the treaties which form the basis of European national law. The great powers would be fully justified in declaring it a casus belli.'[98]

On the other side of the divide, there was a corresponding sense of expectation. 'The communists turn their attention chiefly to Germany,' Marx and Engels wrote in the *Communist manifesto*, 'because that country is on the eve of a bourgeois revolution.' This, they argued, was bound to take place 'under more advanced conditions of civilization, and with a much more developed proletariat' than the revolutions in seventeenth-century England and eighteenth-century France. Indeed, Marx and Engels were convinced that 'the bourgeois revolution in Germany [would] be but the prelude to an immediately following proletarian revolution'.[99] The German liberals at Frankfurt, for their part, wanted a united constitutional Germany in place of the loose confederal conglomerate established at Vienna. They were divided, however, on the question of whether this should be a *Kleindeutschland* – a 'small Germany' excluding the Habsburg lands – under Prussian leadership, or a *Grossdeutschland* – a 'greater Germany' which included them – under Austrian leadership.

Both London and St Petersburg were aware that a united Germany would have profound implications for the overall balance, particularly if allied to a dynamic liberal nationalist movement. 'Our whole system,' Nesselrode, the Russian foreign minister, remarked in April 1848, 'must change because a new power is arising in Germany which, united, democratic and ambitious, has the means to make considerable difficulties for us.'[100] In particular, St Petersburg was worried about the situation in Schleswig-Holstein, which affected the security of the Baltic.[101] Neither Britain nor Russia objected to the idea of greater German unity *per se*, but they both had very different conceptions of what the ideological complexion of the new state should be. As early as March 1848, Palmerston welcomed any initiative that aimed 'to consolidate Germany and give it more unity and political vigour', as 'productive of additional security of the balance of power in Europe'.[102] A moderate liberal Prussian-led united Germany, Palmerston remarked in July 1849, 'would be ... a solid barrier between the powers of the continent',[103] which would contain France and exclude Russia. The Tsarist Empire, on the other hand, wanted a strong conservative Germany under Prussian or Austrian leadership, or managed as a condominium, which would suppress revolutionary activity in the confederation, cease to interfere in Poland, and act as a bulwark against the spread of revolutionary ideas from France. Russia was therefore firmly opposed to German unity as a 'democratic project'.[104]

The Austrians came up with the most radical plan for central Europe. The Habsburgs were determined to maintain their position in Germany, and to make their empire more effective through greater centralization. Right at the end of 1848, Prince Schwarzenberg, the chief minister, advanced a scheme to create 'a great, united, powerful'[105] Germany incorporating the existing lands of the Confederation as well as all the Habsburg Slav, Hungarian, Polish and Italian territories. Although the ostensible purpose of this 'Empire of Seventy Millions' was to enable Germany to deter external aggression by great powers, it was rejected by the great powers as a threat to the European balance. The French warned that a huge territorial expansion of the Confederation – which would greatly increase the military power that could be brought to bear on their eastern border and particularly by the Habsburgs in Lombardy – would not be tolerated. Britain took the same view, as much for ideological as geopolitical reasons. 'The whole mass,' Russell warned in mid-November 1850, 'might in the name of the Confederation be employed against France or Belgium. This is a serious matter ... inconsistent with the balance of power in Europe.'[106] Both powers argued that the territorial and constitutional order of the Confederation formed an integral part of the European balance and 'public law', and could therefore not be altered unilaterally. The Russians welcomed the idea of a strong conservative Germany, but were not prepared to fight a European war to implement it. Isolated, Austria was forced to back down and Schwarzenberg's plan was quietly shelved.

The European revolutions had failed for many reasons. Revolutionary unity was fractured by divides between town and country, liberals and radicals, Protestants and Catholics. In most cases, the peasantry were bought off with concessions at an early stage and became a largely conservative force; in Italy, this helped the Habsburgs in their struggle against the largely bourgeois and artisanal revolutionaries. After the initial period of shock had worn off, conservatives in Prussia, Austria, France and across Europe rallied, founded newspapers and went on the offensive. The King of Prussia refused to accept a crown offered – 'from the gutter' – by the liberal nationalists at Frankfurt. He would not countenance a united Germany except by the consent of all the powers involved. The armies, which had proved so unreliable in 1847–8, were purged of subversive elements and deployed to devastating effect by General Prittwitz in Berlin, General Cavaignac in Paris and Marshal Radetzky in northern Italy. In eastern and central Europe, where 1848 had dawned with hopes of a 'springtime of the peoples', the nationalities were soon at each other's throats.

The really decisive factor, however, was the strategic failure of the European revolutionaries. Lamartine issued a circular to the great powers in March 1848, abjuring any intent to subvert the Vienna Settlement by force. The republic celebrated 'her reinstatement in the rank she is entitled to occupy among the great powers of Europe', but she accepted that the existing 'territorial limits' were 'facts which the Republic admits as a basis ... in her relations with foreign nations' and she promised not to 'pursue secret or incendiary propaganda among neighbouring states'.[107] This made clear that the pan-liberal crusade so frequently invoked in the late 1840s would not materialize. Moreover, many Frenchmen were uneasy about German unity, even under liberal auspices: the *Gazette de France* warned against a '*colosse allemand*' in 1848, and Jules Bastide, the minister of foreign affairs, feared for France if all 45 million Germans followed a 'single impetus'. He therefore advocated a policy of 'division and balance of power' towards the eastern neighbour.[108] When Britain and Russia, concerned for the balance in the Baltic, imposed the armistice of Malmo on the Prussian troops supporting the German national cause in Schleswig-Holstein, there was nothing to stop them. Lacking any military force of its own, the Frankfurt parliament was helpless to intervene and never recovered from the resulting humiliation. More generally, German revolutionaries took fright at the national aspirations of Poles, Czechs and other minorities.[109] In Italy, Charles Albert was crushed – twice – by Austrian troops and was forced to abdicate in favour of his son, Victor Emmanuel. Piedmont itself survived largely unscathed due to its value as a buffer state. Finally, in 1849, the Russians intervened militarily in Hungary to restore Habsburg power in Budapest. In the end, contrary to what liberals, socialists and communists had proclaimed, counter-revolution proved to be international, while revolution remained national and even regional in scope. Liberals and workers had not united, but conservatives and reactionaries had.

Despite their failure, the revolutions wrought huge domestic and geopolitical changes. The election of Prince Louis Napoleon as French president in November 1849 led to vigorous, if ultimately futile, negotiations with the Russians, Prussians and Austrians about French expansion into the Rhineland in return for balancing gains by the eastern powers elsewhere. He combined this activist foreign policy with a populist domestic stance in support of a broad franchise. At the beginning of December 1851, he seized power in a largely bloodless coup, won elections in February 1852 and in November of that year carried a plebiscite for the restoration of the empire. The new constitution created a monarchy with near-absolutist power, which monopolized the right to introduce legislation, for example, but one buttressed by popular support. Napoleon was 'responsible before the people, to whom he has always the right of appeal',[110] through plebiscites. This was a formula for a highly activist foreign policy, driven by Napoleon's neo-Bonapartist ambitions and the revisionist sentiments of French public opinion. The Rhine border and the Italian settlement, and the 'grandeur' of France more generally, were firmly back on the international agenda.

Austria reacted to the traumas of 1848–9, and the humiliation of rescue by the Russians, with a programme of 'neo-absolutist' state-sponsored modernization. The Sylvester Patent of 1851 attempted some long-overdue agrarian reform; peasants now became equal before the law. At one level, the measures were a success: foreign trade doubled, state revenue was increased by two thirds, and Hungary was finally compelled to pull its fiscal weight.[111] Unfortunately for the Habsburgs, centralization alienated the Hungarians (who paid four times more in taxes under the new system), Poles and Italians, and it found few takers among the increasingly vociferous Slav populations. To the north, the new Prussian *Landtag* elected on a limited three-class property franchise lost no time in demanding both greater efforts in support of 'German' interests and control of the budget. The same was true of the parliaments of the southern and western states. Moreover, many German liberals were taking a long hard look at their failure in 1848–9, and were increasingly unnerved by Louis Napoleon's revival of French claims to the Rhine border. There were widespread fears that – as the Augsburg *Allgemeine Zeitung* put it in November 1850 – 'our land will once again become the arena in which cocky foreigners will fight out their quarrels with our blood' as they had during the Thirty Years War; there was a huge upsurge of interest in the mid seventeenth century as a site of national trauma, massacre, division and humiliation. Around Christmas 1853, the *Kölnische Zeitung* warned that Germany 'could not consider itself safe from Poland's fate'.[112] These liberals began to accept that some sort of grand bargain with the Prussian state might have to be struck in order to achieve German unity. They would have to choose not only between Austria and Prussia, but between freedom (*Freiheit*) and unity (*Einheit*).[113]

For the moment, though, Prussian conservatives and the government kept nationalist groups at arm's length, partly for fear of contamination by the liberal virus but also because – as Otto von Bismarck told the *Landtag* in March 1851 – parliamentary control of the budget would make a coherent foreign policy impossible. 'Prussia's greatness,' he argued in a memorandum to the crown prince two years later, 'was by no means achieved through liberalism and free-thinking, but through a series of strong, resolute and wise rulers, who carefully nourished and saved the military and financial resources of the state.' For this reason, he laid down that 'every Prussian should [only] enjoy the degree of freedom which is consonant with the public welfare and with the course which Prussia has to take in European politics, but no more'. 'One can have this freedom,' Bismarck remarked pointedly, 'without parliamentary government.'[114]

In the mid-1850s, the European and global system was roiled by a fresh round of crises. Unsettled by the manifest weakness of the Porte in the face of Egyptian aggression and western European interference, the Tsarist Empire moved pre-emptively to secure its share in the expected breakup. 'We have on our hands a sick man,' Nicholas I famously remarked, 'a very sick man. It will be ... a great misfortune if, one of these days, he should slip away from us, especially before all necessary arrangements were made.'[115] In February 1853, the Russian foreign minister, Menshikov, delivered an ultimatum demanding that the Sultan grant the tsar sovereignty over the Orthodox populations in the Ottoman Empire, and five months later Russian troops occupied the Danubian principalities, provoking the Sultan to declare war. In November 1853, the tsar demanded the independence of the Danubian principalities, Serbia, Bosnia and Bulgaria, and an expanded Greece; all this was accompanied by a call for a general Christian rising against Ottoman rule. That same month, the Russian navy destroyed an Ottoman squadron at Sinope on the Black Sea. A Franco-British ultimatum demanding that Russia withdraw from Moldavia and Wallachia was ignored. On the contrary, in March 1854, Russian troops poured across the Danube and pushed south.

All this sent shock waves across Europe. The real issue was not the Ottoman Empire, but Germany and the whole balance of power. To Vienna, the presence of Russian troops in Moldavia and Wallachia extended the ring of encirclement around the empire's eastern border; it was imperative to get them out as quickly as possible. That was also the view in France and Britain, where central European concerns took priority over very real worries about Turkey and – in the latter case – the security of India.[116] Coming after Russian military intervention in Hungary and diplomatic intervention in Germany in 1848–9, the occupation of the principalities seemed to signal the tsar's intent not merely to partition the Ottoman Empire but to dominate Europe as a whole. In the great parliamentary debate in February 1854 on the eve of the declaration of war, Russell argued that Britain should confront Russia in order to 'maintain the independence, not only of Turkey, but of Germany and of all European nations'.[117] Likewise, the Foreign Secretary,

Lord Clarendon, emphasized that 'Germany by its geographical position must be the principal bulwark against Russian aggression'.[118] The French agreed.

Britain, France and – a little later – Piedmont therefore declared war on Russia and sent a substantial expeditionary force to attack the tsar on his southern flank in the Crimea. For the next two years, the conflict raged with fluctuating fortunes. After initial disasters, the western powers captured Sevastopol in September 1855, inflicting a humiliating defeat on the tsar. The really decisive blow was struck in Germany, however. Vienna persuaded the Prussians – though neutral – to support their demand that the Diet commit itself to the defence of Austria on the Danube. This meant that the tsar would potentially face the combined power of Germany on his western front. The Habsburgs issued an ultimatum to the Russians to withdraw from Moldavia and Wallachia. Gnashing their teeth, the tsarist forces made way for an Austrian garrison for the duration of the conflict. This deprived the Russians of their forward base for an attack on the Ottomans, and the opportunity to deliver a knock-out blow on land by the shortest route. In December 1855, the Austrians even joined the French and British in an ultimatum to the new tsar – Nicholas I had died in March of that year – to end hostilities or face combined action against him. Isolated in Europe, Alexander II sued for peace. The resulting Treaty of Paris in 1856 was a devastating blow to Russian ambitions. Not only was the tsar forced to back off from plans to partition the Ottoman Empire and co-opt the Balkan Christians, but he was forbidden from maintaining ships or arsenals in the Black Sea. More generally, the preamble to the treaty stated that the independence and integrity of Turkey were central to 'the peace of Europe', while its second article called on the Porte to 'take advantage of public law and the European concert'. The Ottoman Empire was being invited to join the state system on an equal basis, because its stability and strength were considered vital to international peace.

The reverberations of the Crimean War were felt across the world. In the United States, there were fears that the victory of France and Britain would lead to increased interference by the western powers in 'their' hemisphere. If London and Paris could send an army by sea to the other end of Europe and impose their will on Russia, there was nothing to stop them from crossing the Atlantic. For this reason, most Americans,

North and South, had cheered on the Russians. The anxiety was strongest, however, among the slave interest, which was further isolated by the Ottoman abolition of slavery in 1856 as part of its entry fee to polite international society, and feared an Anglo-French crusade against itself. These concerns came at a time when domestic tension over slavery was steadily increasing. Southerners had long resisted the formation of non-slave states in the Nebraska Territory north of the Mason–Dixon Line. They feared, as the Missouri senator David R. Aitchison put it, that they would be 'surrounded by free territory',[119] and exposed to constant attack by abolitionists. The Kansas–Nebraska Act of 1854 was therefore a Southern victory, which broke with the Missouri Compromise by creating two states, in which 'popular sovereignty', that is the will of the white settlers, would determine the question of slavery. At the same time, the slave interest sought to expand southwards, perhaps in order to counter-balance the steady increase in 'free' states by increasing Southern seats in the House of Representatives, and to pre-empt the spread of abolitionist British and French influence in those areas.[120] In the Ostende Manifesto in the autumn of 1854, issued while Britain was distracted in the Crimea, US diplomats warned Europe not to force emancipation upon Cuba. In 1856, as Britain and France triumphed in the Crimea, President Buchanan was elected on a platform of acquiring Cuba by purchase, and three years later he eventually approached Congress with a request for 30 million dollars to that end. United States foreign policy had been well and truly captured by the slave interest.

It was in central Europe, however, that the Crimean War had its greatest geopolitical impact.[121] Hitherto, the Tsarist Empire had tried to stay on good terms with both Prussia and Austria, but tilted strongly towards the latter on ideological grounds. During the war, both powers had blotted their copybooks in St Petersburg, but Austria's humiliating ultimatum had given far more offence than Prussia's timid neutrality. Henceforth, the Russians saw the Austrians as the principal barrier to their Balkan ambitions, and the idea that the path to Constantinople ran through Vienna – a common slogan in later decades – began to gain currency in St Petersburg. Even more crucially, the Russians were determined that they would never again face the full force of the German Confederation under the aegis of Austria. Vienna would have to be unbolted from the leadership of Germany. So in late August 1856 the new Russian foreign minister, Alexander Gorchakov, announced in a widely discussed circular that the tsar would no longer support his fellow monarchs. The message was clear: the Habsburgs would face the next revolutionary challenge on their own.

The Crimean War provoked a sustained round of domestic reform in Russia. Defeat had shown that the traditional social forms were not up to the challenge of mid-nineteenth-century western powers. The problem lay in the fact that, thanks to the constraints of serfdom, most of the empire's vast population was not pulling its weight militarily, with perhaps a tenth of those eligible actually available for military service.[122] The choice facing the tsarist regime was stark. Either the agrarian system had to be reformed, or the empire risked further defeats in the European state system. So, in March 1856, Alexander II told an audience of Moscow gentry that serfdom should be abolished, sweetening the pill with the observation that it was better to do so 'from above' before it took place spontaneously 'from below'. He eventually signed the legislation into law in mid-February 1861. What the tsar was determined not to concede, however, was any sort of political participation on the western model. The resulting imbalance between socio-economic modernization and political stasis was remarked on by contemporary observers: the revolutionary activist Alexander Herzen famously spoke of Russia being 'Chingis-Khan with telegraphs'.[123]

The Crimean War also had a profound impact on domestic politics in the British Empire.[124] News of the military and organizational fiascos in the peninsula provoked widespread consternation in parliament and the public sphere. Lord Aberdeen's government fell in January 1855 over his defeat in a vote to establish a parliamentary select committee to look into the conduct of military operations; Palmerston replaced him as the man who could win the war. There was disagreement, however, over how best to bring British society into line with the needs of the European state system. Some such as Samuel Morley, a Nottingham hosiery manufacturer and later MP, argued in June 1855 that failure in the war reflected a lack of popular legitimacy and that 'the people themselves' should take more responsibility for their own security through the militia and franchise reform.[125] Others pointed to the conservatism and unprofessionalism of the army, where officers bought their commissions rather than acquiring them through merit. To liberal and radical critics, all this was evidence of continuing 'aristocratic' dominance of British institutions which enfeebled the nation in its struggle with external enemies. In order to prepare for the challenges ahead, Britain embarked on a round of internal and imperial reforms. Over the next few years, a Royal Commission into the defences of the United Kingdom was set up, the Foreign Office was reformed, and military expenditure was substantially increased. London also attempted to put India in a better state of readiness against Russian attack by modernizing the East India Company's forces. These reforms provoked the Mutiny of 1857, which was brought under control only with great difficulty.

It was in Italy, however, that the impact of the Crimean War was most acutely felt. The prime minister of Piedmont, Count Cavour, was now able to exploit the goodwill he had built up in London and Paris through participation in the war. To Cavour, the security of Piedmont could only be guaranteed by embracing the Italian national cause. His efforts chimed with those of the disparate radicals in the National Society such as the Venetian Daniel Manin, the Sicilian Giuseppe la Farina and (from July 1856) the Savoyard defender of the Roman Republic, Giuseppe Garibaldi. These men had undergone a fundamental rethink after the failure of the revolutions of 1848–9. They would have preferred a confederation of republics or better still a unitary republic, but, like German nationalists and Prussia, they came to see a powerful Piedmont as their only hope of getting rid of the Austrians.[126] Cavour played to this sentiment brilliantly. 'Events have led Piedmont to take up a definite and firm position in Italy,' he wrote in 1857. 'Since Providence has willed that Piedmont alone in Italy should be free and independent, Piedmont must use her freedom and independence to plead before Europe the cause of the unhappy peninsula.'[127] When he met with Napoleon III at Plombières in July 1858 to discuss the expulsion of the Habsburgs, the circumstances were uniquely favourable. Russia, still furious about Austrian 'betrayal' during the Crimean War, had signalled her intention to stand aside; in a secret Franco-Russian treaty of early March 1859, the tsar agreed to changes in Italy and to neutralize the German Confederation, in return for an implicit pledge to revise the hated 'Black Sea' clauses. In Britain, public sentiment was strongly pro-Italian and government opinion was increasingly convinced that a strong Italy would be a more effective barrier to the French than the ramshackle Habsburgs. Neither Cavour nor Napoleon III, in fact, desired a united Italy. What they agreed at Plombières were the cession of Nice and Savoy to France, large-scale compensatory Piedmontese annexations in northern Italy, the continued independence of Rome itself (which was important to appease French Catholic opinion at home) and Naples, while Tuscany and the Papal States were to be combined into a Kingdom of Central Italy. All these territories were to be linked through an Italian Confederation.[128]

Vienna decided to pre-empt the looming attack by issuing an ultimatum in April 1859 demanding that Piedmont cease military preparations. This turned out to be a serious mistake, because the failure to explore diplomatic avenues to war cost Austria valuable goodwill in Europe. This was especially true for the German Confederation, where most states feared being dragged into a war with France on account of Habsburg ambitions in Italy; Prussia initially observed a strict neutrality. Austria was quickly and decisively beaten in costly battles at Magenta and Solferino. At this point, however, the Confederation began to stir under Prussian leadership in order to prevent a complete Austrian collapse. A large force was mobilized threatening France on her eastern border. Napoleon lost his nerve: fearing Prussian intervention, he came to an agreement with the emperor Francis Joseph at Villafranca on terms which fell far short of those outlined at Plombières. Lombardy was ceded by Austria to Napoleon III, and by him to Piedmont, but the central Italian principalities were to be restored. Nationalist opinion was outraged; Cavour resigned in disgust. For the second time in less than a decade, the German card had been played in Europe to decisive effect.[129]

It was too late, however, to stop the rush to Italian unity. Popular movements took advantage of the vacuum left by the departing Austrians to seize power in central Italy, followed soon after by Piedmontese troops under the pretext of 'restoring order'. The occupations were swiftly ratified by plebiscites. Not long afterwards, Garibaldi occupied the Bourbon Kingdom of the Two Sicilies on his own initiative with a band of nationalist volunteers. Once again, Piedmontese soldiers arrived hot on his heels partly to complete the unification of Italy and partly to ensure that the masses did not get out of hand. In October 1860, the new Kingdom of Italy was proclaimed under King Victor Emmanuel II. It included all of the peninsula, with the exception of Nice and Savoy, which were ceded to France as a reward for military assistance, and Venetia, which remained Austrian for the time being. The first great breach in the Vienna Settlement had been made.

The Italian war had a major impact on European domestic politics and the states system. In Austria, the first loss of territory since the Napoleonic Wars drove the authorities to abandon 'neo-absolutism' and attempt a liberalization to shore up the empire. To Napoleon, the victory, and the recovery of some of the lands lost in 1815, was a vindication of his view that the reorganization of Europe on 'national' lines was fully compatible with French interests. For the moment, he had silenced internal critics who rallied to the cause of national 'glory'. In Britain, the events in Italy were regarded with ambivalence. On the one hand, the annexation of Savoy, the defeat of Austria and French naval ambitions produced another invasion scare, and a fresh 'volunteering' movement.[130] On the other hand, the Italian victory promoted a sense of liberal triumphalism: the conviction that the tide of events in Europe was heading inexorably towards nationalist and constitutionalist modernity on English lines. Gladstone, when asked what had turned him from a Conservative into a Liberal, replied succinctly: 'Italy.'[131]

The most profound impact of the Italian war, however, was felt in Germany. It further reduced Austrian prestige, partly because of the defeats at Magenta and Solferino but also because of fears that the Confederation would be dragged into alien Habsburg conflicts. It also produced a fresh wave of German national feeling.[132] This was sympathetic to the Austrians, who were – when all was said and done – still Germans deserving of solidarity, and imitative of the Italians, who had blazed the way for national unification. In mid-August 1859, nationalist liberals set up the *Nationalverein* to agitate for the unification of Germany under a single national parliament.[133] It demanded the abolition of the Confederation, the creation of a central authority and the transfer of all political and military powers to Prussia until this had been achieved. The Hohenzollerns were once again being offered the liberal-constitutionalist 'German mission' which they had refused to accept in 1848–9. Adolphe de Bourqueney, a veteran French diplomat, warned that Napoleon III had opened a Pandora's box in central Europe. 'We have played too much with the empty pompous words of nationalism,' he wrote in 1859. 'The only serious nationalism which we have brought to light is that of Germany. Without a single afterthought we have restored to German opinion its antipathy for France.'[134]

The mobilization of 1859 had certainly intimidated Napoleon, but it also exposed the profound military unpreparedness of Germany, and even of Prussia. This belief sparked two intertwining reform debates which were to set the agenda for the next decade. Prussia now sought to ensure a more effective response to the next French challenge, but her attempts impaled themselves immediately and predictably on the objections of the other German states, led by Austria, which feared a loss of sovereignty. Inside Prussia itself, the government now had to address the fact that financial constraints were preventing the size of the army from reflecting the growth in population. Only half of those eligible for conscription in the 1850s were in fact recruited. The army, and the regent, Prince Wilhelm, wanted to expand the regular army through the introduction of a three-year training period for conscripts, rather than relying on the traditional *Landwehr*. This was fiercely resisted by the strong liberal faction in the Prussian parliament, the *Landtag*. They, and the German liberal nationalists in the *Nationalverein* generally, required no persuading of the need for greater military preparedness against France. The society's paper announced in early June 1860 that 'No-one doubts any more that the German Rhine frontier is threatened with a French attack.'[135] There was widespread unease, however, about the cost of the proposed reforms and the political implications of breaking with the concept of a citizens' militia. Liberals argued instead that constitutional change would give the monarchy the internal coherence necessary to deter external predators.[136] The result was deadlock, in Prussia as in Germany as a whole.

Meanwhile, the core problem of Prussian and German geopolitics had not gone away – if anything, it had got worse. The Hohenzollern monarchy and the Confederation still felt marooned in the centre of Europe, wedged between the Tsarist Empire and a France rampant after victory in the Crimea and Italy. Ever since she had taken on the role of guardian of the gate in the west in 1815, Prussia had sought to rally Germany behind her. These schemes hit an immovable object in Austrian opposition and the continuing refusal of the Third Germany to compromise her sovereignty in return for increased security; economic integration did not lead inexorably to political unity. Reform of the German Confederation seemed more remote than ever, and yet Conservative dynasticism was no longer a sufficient basis of legitimation for the Hohenzollern monarchy. So, by the end of the 1850s, the Prussian leadership faced a series of interlocking and seemingly intractable problems at home, in Germany and in the European states system.

Otto von Bismarck, however, saw how these liabilities could be turned to Prussia's advantage. The idea that the security of Prussia required her to take the lead in Germany was not new. 'There is nothing more German,' Bismarck observed in 1858, 'than Prussian particularism properly understood.' Bismarck also believed that Prussia could only survive if it secured 'safe borders', either through leading a reformed German Confederation, or though straightforward territorial annexation.[137] In 1859 he described these 'natural frontiers of Prussia' as nothing less than the Baltic, the North Sea, the Rhine, the Alps and the Lake of Constance. This was a programme for Prussian dominance which would bring the independence of the Third Germany to an abrupt end. It could only be achieved if Bismarck could secure the acceptance of the other powers to a massive change in the European territorial order, or isolate those who objected; sideline or at least gain parity with Austria; win over the Third Germany, or crush those elements who refused to cooperate; co-opt the German national movement; and either persuade or bypass the liberals in the *Landtag*, in order to secure the funds to pay for the necessary military action. A few months before taking office as Prussian chancellor in late September 1862, Bismarck announced privately that 'My first care will be to reorganize the army, with or without the help of the *Landtag* . . . As soon as the army shall have been brought into such a condition as to inspire respect, I shall seize the first best pretext to declare war against Austria, dissolve the German Diet, subdue the minor states and give national unity to Germany under Prussian leadership.' His interlocutor, the future British prime minister Benjamin Disraeli, afterwards remarked to the Austrian ambassador: 'Take care of that man; he means what he says.'[138]

As Prussia prepared to give herself and Germany the cohesion it needed to survive in an unstable Europe, the confrontation in North America came to a head during the presidential campaign of 1860. At issue were not Northern demands for the abolition of slavery; all but the most ardent abolitionists accepted that some form of gradual and consensual emancipation was the only way of avoiding a secession which would damage the Union beyond repair. It was the Southerners who took the offensive. They demanded territorial aggrandizement – and thus the extension of slavery – as the price of remaining in the Union. By contrast, the Republican candidate, Abraham Lincoln, promised to frustrate the absorption of Cuba as a slave state. Following his victory at the polls, the negotiations for the purchase of Cuba collapsed. 'In the Union,' the Georgian state senator Philemon Tracy warned just after the election, 'you cannot have an inch of new territory.'[139] Worse still, slavery was now completely isolated internationally. Britain made its fierce opposition to the annexation of Cuba clear, and was increasing pressure on Madrid to promulgate a decree of emancipation there. After the Russian abolition of serfdom in mid-February 1861, the 'peculiar institution' of slavery stood entirely alone in the civilized world. Having failed to coerce Washington into an expansionist policy on its own terms, and observing the deteriorating global situation, the South launched a pre-emptive strike.[140] In April 1861, Southern artillery shelled Fort Sumter, signalling the start of hostilities with the North. The seceding states set up a Confederacy explicitly designed not only to keep the abolitionist North at arm's length, but also to facilitate territorial expansion. Its constitution looked forward to the acquisition of new lands, which could only be slave states. The South thus went to war with the Union over the same issue which had driven London and the thirteen colonies apart: territorial expansion.

To Britain and France, the American Civil War seemed a heaven-sent opportunity to cripple a global rival. 'England will never find a more favourable occasion,' Napoleon III told the British ambassador to Paris in 1862, 'to abase the pride of the Americans or to establish her influence in the world.'[141] London, however, preferred to wait until the Confederacy had landed a military blow; and although slavery did not deter even many Liberals – such as Gladstone – from sympathizing with the Confederacy, it did incline public opinion firmly against active intervention in support of the South. France seized the chance to meddle openly in Mexico, where Napoleon III wanted to establish the Habsburg Archduke Maximilian as emperor under his protection. A substantial military force was sent to back him, including several thousand men from France's ally, Egypt;[142] this was proof, once again, that non-intervention in the Middle East was no guarantee that the Middle East would not attempt to interfere in the affairs of the western hemisphere. These initiatives provoked an allergic reaction in Washington. 'The people of the United States can never regard with indifference,' the Republican platform in the 1864 election campaign warned, 'the attempt of any European power to overthrow by force or to supplant by fraud the institutions of any Republican government on the western continent.' Indeed, they would view 'with extreme jealousy, as menacing to the peace and independence of their own country, the efforts of any such power to obtain any such footholds for monarchical government sustained by foreign military force, in near proximity to the United States'.[143] For the moment, however, the Union had its hands full fighting the Confederacy and had to bide its time.

Taken together, the inability to mobilize more effectively, the North's slave emancipation proclamation and the failure to secure outside intervention doomed the Confederacy. Public opinion in Britain was not opposed to cutting the Americans down to size, but it was passionately opposed to a war in support of slavery. Tension between the two countries continued, not least because British-built ships, such as the *Alabama*, played havoc with Northern shipping. In autumn 1863, Lincoln went so far as to warn that the construction of ships which could break the Union blockade would lead to war. Napoleon III remained obsessed with Mexico, where his imperial ambitions were already running into difficulties. So the Confederacy was left to soldier on alone, and was gradually choked by the weight of Northern numbers and industrial superiority. In 1865, General Robert E. Lee surrendered at Appomattox courthouse. The war of American reunification was over.

In Europe, the struggle for German unity was by then in full swing. This pitted Bismarck's radical project against the liberal geopolitics of Britain and France, and Austria, a conservative power in both the ideological and geopolitical sense. The decisive factor was Russia, which the Prussian chancellor was able to win over through luck and good judgement. For, in January 1863, the Poles, emboldened by Russia's defeat in the Crimea, spurred by the triumph of nationalism in Italy, hopeful of French aid, and taking advantage of a more liberal regime designed to conciliate them, rose in revolt against the tsar. There was momentary panic in St Petersburg, where Alexander feared a revival of the 'Crimean Coalition'. British and French publics were strongly sympathetic to the Poles, and both governments provided powerful rhetorical support. Since military intervention was out of the question, this only had the effect of prolonging the agony, until the final victory of Russian forces. 'If the British government do not mean to fight,' the British ambassador to St Petersburg remarked in frustration, 'let them say so, and stop the loss of life and the suffering attendant on a rising, which unaided cannot succeed.'[144] The Austrians, anxious to appease liberal, Catholic and Polish opinion at home, remained uneasily neutral, compounding the offence they had caused during the Crimean War. Bismarck, by contrast, came out strongly in support of the tsar, concluding a convention to seal off the border between Prussia and Russian Poland.

The chancellor was now in an excellent position to exploit the next opportunity to promote his Prusso-German agenda. In March 1863 the Danes announced the incorporation of Schleswig into the monarchy. The Diet of the German Confederation, under heavy pressure from outraged nationalists, declared war on Denmark. Most German liberals, including those outside Prussia, cheered Bismarck on. The old Prussian doctrines of encirclement, in other words, had gained wider currency throughout the nation. Unlike 1848, Russia stood aside; so did France, planning to use the resulting international turbulence to reopen the Vienna Settlement. Prussian and Austrian troops crushed the Danes in the spring and summer of 1864. Schleswig and Holstein were taken under the joint administration of Vienna and Berlin. Once again, Britain was forced to watch impotently from the sidelines.[145] German liberals and nationalists, on the other hand, exulted in the first victory for their cause under Prussian leadership. Despite commanding a large majority in the *Landtag*, they decided to swallow their objections to the fact that the war had been fought by troops paid for by taxes levied without parliamentary approval. Bismarck had hit on a formula which solved his domestic and foreign policy difficulties in one fell swoop.

While Bismarck was striking at the roots of the Vienna Settlement from without, the stability of the European order was being threatened from within. Industrialization had led to a huge growth in the proletariat, to class consciousness and ultimately the establishment of international political organizations. In July 1863, anarchists and socialists had met in support of Polish independence. Like their liberal counterparts, they saw the Tsarist Empire as the principal reactionary force in Europe, and consequently regarded all its opponents as progressive elements. German nationalism was particularly favoured: 'Germany takes Schleswig,' Karl Marx had earlier announced (in August 1848), 'with the right of civilization over barbarism, of progress against stability.' In September 1864, various leftist groups came together to form the International Working Men's Association, to work for international socialist revolution across state boundaries.[146] Thus was born a new European power, 'The International', which was to feature in the rhetoric and policies of conservative statesmen and on the agenda of

European summits throughout the decade and those following. It created fresh geopolitical fronts, cutting across traditional alignments.

For the moment, however, the pace was being set by state-sponsored radicalism. In 1865, Bismarck turned to deal with Austria, the principal obstacle both to Prussian territorial expansion and to the realization of German national aspirations. Vienna was on the back foot, having only just kept up with Prussia in the Danish war and suffering from a new round of Hungarian obstructionism. The Magyars were firmly opposed to a forward policy in the Confederation, especially not if it involved military action. 'Their wars are not our wars,' the Hungarian patriot leader, Ferenc Déak, warned in 1861.[147] Hungary's unwillingness to pull its weight had always been the Achilles heel of the Habsburgs, and in the mid-1860s it was particularly fatal because Hungary could have covered Austria's entire state deficit if it had only met its obligations. Russia would continue to observe a benevolent neutrality towards Prussia. 'Our current relations with foreign powers,' Nesselrode's successor as Russian foreign minister, Alexander Gorchakov, reminded one interlocutor in September 1865, 'have been shaped by the period of the Polish crisis.'[148] Russia, he continued, was opposed to France's revolutionary 'nationality principle', in which 'Germany was the path to Poland'. Germany was the key, as always, and Russia was determined that ideologically congenial Prussia should dominate there.

In this context, the attitude of France was decisive. Napoleon III was the great victor of the past decade, and he planned to use the showdown between Austria and Prussia to assert his own interests in Germany. He was once again, however, under severe domestic pressure to broaden political participation and defend French national interests more vigorously. Failure to protect the Poles had dented Napoleon's reputation at home, but what really worried critics was Germany. By promoting nationalism Europe-wide, undermining Austria and encouraging Prussia, so the argument ran, the emperor had broken the first rule of French foreign policy, which was to prevent the emergence of a strong Germany on her eastern flank. 'One of my greatest reproaches against Italian unity,' the veteran Thiers warned the *Corps Législatif* in mid-April 1865, 'is that it is destined to be the mother of German unity.'[149] In August 1865, French opinion and Napoleon himself were shocked by the Convention of Gastein, at which Austria and Prussia settled the administration of Schleswig and Holstein without reference to Paris. Despite these warning signs, Napoleon failed to support the Austrians in the looming showdown. He was distracted by the situation in Mexico, where Maximilian's fortunes began to decline spectacularly after the defeat of the South in the Civil War. Britain, too, was preoccupied with overseas matters. 'England is no longer a mere European power,' the Chancellor of the Exchequer, Benjamin Disraeli, explained, 'but the centre of a great maritime empire . . . she really is more an Asiatic power than a European.'[150]

In 1866, Bismarck struck. He refused to support proposals for confederal reform from Vienna and the Third Germany. In April, the Prussian chancellor concluded an alliance with the Italians, promising them Venetia in return for opening up a front on Austria's southern flank; he also encouraged Hungarian separatism in order to weaken Francis Joseph at home. That same month, Prussian troops occupied Holstein, which was supposed to be under Austrian administration. Austria – supported by virtually the whole of the rest of Germany – mobilized for war, partly to divert attention from her multiplying national problems, but mainly to head off the Prussian challenge to her position in Germany.[151] To the surprise of many, Prussian forces used the new rail network to assemble rapidly in Bohemia and crushed the Austrians at the battle of Sadowa in June 1866. The armies of the Third Germany secured some local successes against the Prussians, but were quickly shrugged aside. In August, Austria accepted her exclusion from Germany at the Treaty of Prague; two months later, she ceded Venetia to France, who then gifted it to Italy at the Treaty of Vienna. Prussia annexed Schleswig-Holstein, Hanover, Hesse-Cassel and Frankfurt. Much of the rest of Germany, some twenty-two states in all, was corralled into the North German Confederation under the leadership of Berlin. The south German states retained their independence, but were forced to sign secret military agreements which tied them ever closer to Prussia. For the first time ever in modern European history, most of Germany was now organized as a single power centre. The struggle for mastery in Germany was over; a new phase in the struggle for supremacy in Europe was about to begin.

In the fifty years after the Vienna Congress, European geopolitics had remained as globalized as ever. The great powers contended over Egypt,

Syria and the Ottoman Empire in general. A new humanitarian geopolitics centred on slavery and protection of the Jews merged with longstanding beliefs about the link between good governance and international stability. Britain and France faced off against the United States, and each other, in Central America and the Caribbean. They went to the brink of intervening in the American Civil War. The central contestation, however, was in Europe: in the Iberian peninsula, Italy and, above all, Germany. It was in the German Confederation that geopolitical interests clashed most loudly, and where the liberal and national sentiments roiling the whole continent had the profoundest implications for the whole European balance; these stresses ultimately destroyed the central European order and paved the way for a completely new geopolitics based on an independent united Germany rather than a loose confederation under international supervision.

The losers in all this were some of the most backward actors in the state system. By the end of our period the American Confederacy had been destroyed, tsarist Russia defeated in the Crimea, and the Austrian Habsburgs ejected from Germany. Britain, by contrast, had prevailed diplomatically across Europe through the adoption of anti-slavery as an international norm, and support for the survival of the Ottoman Empire, the emergence of a united Italy and the progressive unification of Germany. France had enjoyed more mixed success, but overall she could be well satisfied with the containment of Russia and the destruction of Austrian influence in Italy. The most successful polity by far was Abraham Lincoln's United States, which had not only crushed secession but deterred outside intervention. Bismarck's Prussia, which had co-opted constitutional nationalists, also did remarkably well. Moreover, although the unification of Germany and the United States was far from complete, both states seemed well on the way towards great power status based on representative government of one sort or another. To liberals, all this seemed to suggest the dawn of a new era. Little did they know that popular participation would take European geopolitics in unanticipated directions in the years ahead, leading eventually to a confrontation between these two mighty unions.

5
Unifications, 1867–1916

His Majesty the King of Prussia in the name of the North German Confederation, His Majesty the King of Bavaria, His Majesty the King of Württemberg, His Royal Highness the Grand Duke of Baden, His Royal Highness the Grand Duke of Hesse . . . conclude an everlasting federation for the protection of the territory of the federation.

German Constitutional Treaty, 1871[1]

Gentlemen, if the war which has hung over our heads for more than ten years like a sword of Damocles – if this war were to break out, no one could foresee how long it would last nor how it would end. The greatest powers in Europe, armed as never before, would confront each other in battle . . . Gentlemen, it could be a Seven Years' War; it could be a Thirty Years' War; and woe to the man who sets Europe ablaze, who first throws the match into the powder barrel!

Helmuth von Moltke, May 1890[2]

The end of the German and American civil wars in the mid-1860s left the European and global scene utterly transformed by two great national unifications. In North America, the long struggle for mastery between North and South was resolved with the Confederate surrender in 1865. A year later, the struggle for mastery in Germany was decided at Sadowa, and the subsequent Treaty of Prague. In both cases, the result was an unprecedented accretion of political, military and economic strength with huge implications for the balance of power. Despite their massive resources, however, neither the Americans nor the Germans were at ease with the outside world or, indeed, with themselves. The united Germany inherited Prussia's preoccupation with encirclement, and even after reunification US leaders still saw threats all around them. Both societies were profoundly divided at home: culturally, regionally, politically and economically, and this affected their sense of place in the world. All the same, the established powers – Britain, France, Austria and Russia – now faced new threats to which they reacted both internally and diplomatically. This led to an explosive growth of popular interest in geopolitics in Europe and across the Atlantic. The rising power of Berlin, in particular, set the agenda for the next fifty years, first in the European capitals and then in Washington as well. By the end of the period covered in this chapter, therefore, the two unified colossi were on collision course. The question of which of these two great-power centres would prevail in Europe and across the world was not to be decided until the middle of the following century.[3]

The victory of the North in the American Civil War led to a more active US foreign policy. The long domestic deadlock on expansion was broken. In December 1868, President Johnson told Congress that 'Comprehensive national policy would seem to sanction the acquisition and incorporation into our federal union of the several adjacent continental and insular communities.'[4] All this was bad news for the Indians who inhabited the great space between the core area of the Union and its outliers on the Pacific Ocean. Over the next thirty years, they were progressively expropriated, marginalized and in many cases simply killed, as the Union moved westwards in a cascade of new states.[5] The renewed US sense of purpose also spelt trouble for European powers with major interests on the far side of the Atlantic. The most pressing issue was Mexico, where Washington saw the French-sponsored imperial forces, and the Egyptians whom the Khedive had sent to oblige Napoleon III, as a strategic threat and ideological affront to the United States. Emperor Maxmilian was the personification of what the Monroe Doctrine had been designed to prevent: monarchical institutions in America's backyard, supported by a European power. In September 1865, the Egyptians were warned by the Secretary of State, William Seward, that with the Civil War over Congress and Presidency were now 'united in a concern for the safety of free republican institutions on this continent'. More directly, the Khedive Ismail was cautioned by the US envoy that what he had 'done in Mexico at the request of another power, the United States *might* do in Egypt at the request of some friendly power'.[6] After a brief war scare French and Egyptian forces abandoned Maximilian, who was soon after captured and executed by Mexican republicans.

Washington now turned to face Britain, which blocked territorial expansion to the north, and with whom there were unresolved maritime disputes from the Civil War, especially concerning compensation for the depredations of the British-built Confederate commerce-raider *Alabama*. An Anglo-American compromise convention in January 1869 was thrown out by the Senate. That May the Republican senator and chairman of the Foreign Relations Committee, Charles Sumner, even demanded the cession of British North America. At the same time, tension flared along the south-eastern border of the Union, where Spain feared that the United States would use the persistence of slavery as a pretext to annex Cuba, anxieties that were increased when the island erupted in a revolt against Madrid from 1868.

On the near side of the Atlantic, the revolutionary power in the system was Bismarck's Prussia, the directing spirit of a North German Confederation which included Saxony, the northern part of Hesse, the Mecklenburgs and a number of smaller states; King Wilhelm described the German Confederation as 'the extended arm of Prussia'.[7] The confederal parliament was elected by universal direct male franchise – a concession Bismarck intended to outflank the bourgeoisie. But the Prussian writ ran further still, because those members of the *Zollverein* outside the Confederation, such as Baden, Württemberg and Bavaria, sent deputies to a joint 'Customs Parliament'. Bismarck hoped that these could be used to mobilize popular support for the next stage of the unification project, and to force the hands of the state governments. It remained his belief that the security of Prussia could only be ensured by establishing firm ramparts to the south and west, that is by bringing Baden, Württemberg and Bavaria into closer association with Prussia.

Left to their own devices, however, the southern states had no intention of submerging themselves in a united Germany. Not even the economic incentives offered by the *Zollverein*, and cooperation with a rapidly industrializing Prussia, could persuade the elites to surrender their hard-won sovereignty, or their populations to submit to Prussian tutelage. Economic cooperation did not lead inexorably to political union. All the independent middling states had sided with Austria in 1866, and Vienna's withdrawal from Germany did not automatically cause them to seek shelter with Prussia.[8] On the contrary, the Customs Parliament elections of March 1868 produced southern majorities against union. Liberal nationalists also did badly in the Bavarian and Württembergian elections of 1869. As the prominent liberal writer Gustav Freitag lamented a year later, 'It is not true that the South German states are being drawn gradually closer to us. They are of necessity becoming more distant from us the more legislation progresses in the North. And what then? Division for eternity.'[9] Throughout the late 1860s, nationalist deputies in the north German *Landtag* battered Bismarck's administration for its failure to protect Baden from France by admitting her rapidly to the new Confederation, and for its failure to promote German unity more generally. This prompted National Liberals such as Karl Twesten to use the approval of the budget in April 1869 as a lever to demand a more open presentation and discussion of 'the principal objects of foreign policy'.[10] Only a powerful external threat would generate the necessary momentum for a popular geopolitics to complete the unification project, and consolidate the chancellor's position at home.

The sudden explosion of American and Prusso-German power in the mid-1860s had a profound impact on grand strategy and domestic politics in Europe, and around the world. As far as Germany was concerned, Britain showed little anxiety for now. The Foreign Secretary, Lord Stanley, remarked in August 1866 that 'to us there is no loss, rather gain, in the interposition of a solid barrier between the two great aggressive powers of the continent [France and Russia]'.[11] All the same, the events of the late 1860s convinced many that Britain needed to mobilize fresh resources to defend her position in the state system. Gladstone argued in April 1866 that the Union triumph in the Civil War demonstrated the advantages of a broad franchise so that 'augmented power can be marshalled on behalf of the government and increased energy given to the action of a nation'.[12] In 1867, the franchise was extended in the Reform Act, a measure which had deep domestic roots to be sure but one which was also enacted with a strong sense of its importance for Britain's international position.

At the same time, London began to explore ways in which the growing overseas empire could be made to contribute to imperial defence.[13] British North America, which was most threatened by the post-war American expansionist surge, and the sheer gravitational pull of US greatness, began discussions for federation in 1865, and in 1867 the existing settler colonies there formed the Dominion of Canada.

In Vienna, an impassioned debate now broke out between those who wanted to cut their losses in Germany to concentrate on the Balkans, and those who demanded that the Prussian unification project should be stopped or at least slowed through cooperation with France and the southern German states. 'We shall get out of Germany altogether,' Franz Joseph vowed after Sadowa, 'whether it is demanded of us or no, and after the experiences with our dear German allies I hold this to be a blessing for Austria.'[14] His new foreign minister, Count Friedrich Ferdinand von Beust, on the other hand, announced that he 'would not shrink from any ... possible consequence' of an alliance with Napoleon III to curb Prussia, 'not even French aggrandisement in Germany'.[15] The Prussian victory also had a profound impact on Habsburg domestic politics. Constitutional reform now became imperative, partly because the empire's defeat had weakened Franz Joseph's hand against Hungarian demands, but mainly because the long-running sore of Magyar resentment made a strong foreign policy impossible. In 1867, Vienna finally came to terms with Budapest in the *Ausgleich*, or 'Compromise', agreement. Hungary not only retained its own parliament with substantial fiscal and legislative powers, and acquired its own army, the *Honved*, but was formally accorded equality of status with the Austrian half of the empire. The new state was a dual monarchy – Austria-Hungary – and the dynasty hoped that the energies set free by the new constitutional structure would make the empire more competitive in the European state system.

In St Petersburg, the prevailing view remained that Bismarck's advance in Germany was the best method of weakening France, thus allowing Russia to revise the hated Black Sea clauses.[16] Critical voices, however, were beginning to make themselves heard beyond governing circles. In 1865, pre-emptive press censorship was abolished in the major cities, immensely boosting the nascent public sphere. Taking advantage of these new freedoms, the Slavophile I. S. Aksakov and the Moscow newspaper magnate M. N. Katkov argued that Russia's main enemy was now Prussia, whose advocacy of the 'German' cause represented a mortal threat in the Balkans and closer to home.[17] Just as Bismarck was uniting Germany, Russia should rally the Slavs. Like Britain, Russia sought to increase her European weight through imperial expansion in central and east Asia. 'Like the United States in America, France in Africa . . . and England in . . . India,' Gorchakov remarked in December 1864, Russia was compelled to expand 'less out of ambition than [by] absolute necessity' in a world 'where it is extremely difficult to stand pat'. Many inside and outside government were sceptical of eastern expansion, which they viewed as a distraction from Russia's core interests in Europe, especially the Balkans. 'Whatever makes Russia greater' in Asia, Katkov complained in March 1865, 'weakens her in Europe. Russia's role as a great power is not based there but on her rule over the western marchlands and in her position on the Black Sea. Our history is played out in Europe and not in Asia'.[18]

In France, the rise of Prussia dominated foreign and domestic politics after 1866. Napoleon sought to counter the twin embarrassments of defeat in Mexico, and the unilateral victory of Bismarck over Austria, by staking claims to 'compensation' in western Germany, Luxemburg and even Belgium. His foreign minister, the Marquis de la Valette, justified these claims in September 1866 with the argument that '[a]n irresistible power . . . pushes peoples to unite in large agglomerations and makes the intermediary powers disappear'.[19] The emperor's diplomatic ambitions forced him into concessions at home to shore up support for his activist policies abroad. In mid-January 1867, ministers were allowed to address parliament, and to be questioned by deputies. A year later restrictions on the press and parliamentary debate were lifted. The opposition promptly stepped up its attack on the regime's incompetence. Thiers charged in parliament that Napoleon had allowed the consolidation of Germany and thus the establishment of a major power, 'young, active, bold and devoured by ambition', right on France's eastern border. Hundreds of years of French strategy had thus been overturned. 'There is not,' Thiers thundered in March 1867, 'a single mistake left to make.'[20] As the decade drew to a close, it was clear that Napoleon III would either have to score a spectacular foreign policy victory, or yield further ground to his domestic critics.

The Prussian chancellor now broke the deadlock in a series of masterstrokes. Bismarck secretly encouraged French demands for Luxemburg in 1867, only to disavow them when the inevitable public outrage set in. He squared the tsar in March 1868, thus ensuring that the Russians would keep Austria-Hungary in check. In March/April 1869, Bismarck exploited international controversy over French attempts to take over parts of the Belgian railway system. That same year, Prussia supported the candidature of a Hohenzollern to the Spanish throne. This was furiously opposed by France. The foreign minister, the Duc de Gramont, swore that France could never allow Leopold of Hohenzollern-Sigmaringen to assume the 'throne of Charles V',[21] a direct reference to France's traumatic sixteenth-century encirclement by the Habsburgs. Across Paris and the provinces the cry went up that the Prussians were now not only on the other side of the Rhine, but also south of the Pyrenees as well. Napoleon decided to pre-empt this perceived danger – which rested on the highly questionable assumption that Leopold would be willing and able to subordinate Spanish foreign policy to Bismarck's aims – by confronting Prussia. The government, as the chief minister, Émile Ollivier, freely admitted, also hoped to use the crisis for domestic purposes; it 'must show firmness and spirit or we shall not be able to cope with revolution and socialism at home'.[22] When Bismarck manipulated the record of a meeting between the Prussian king and the French ambassador in the notorious 'Ems Telegram', the mutual feeling of outrage in France and Prussia led to war.

Napoleon's best chance of victory was a rapid advance into Germany, to capitalize on the supposed superiority of his field army before the Prussians could mobilize their reserves. As the chancellor had expected, this aggressive intent drove German nationalists, and especially the governments of the southern German states, into Bismarck's arms. Even many who had remained sceptical of German unity – or at least of its Prussian-led variant – now took sides against France.[23] Bismarck now had the necessary popular and princely mandate for a national war against the hereditary enemy. In mid-July, Franz Joseph, disgusted by Napoleon's abandonment of his brother Maximilian to Mexican vengeance, announced his neutrality. The southern German states, carried along on a wave of nationalist enthusiasm, lined up behind Prussia, and once the victories mounted the rest of Germany – initially hesitant – soon followed. Even those who had been brutally annexed by Prussia in 1866 – such as the Hanoverians – joined in the struggle against the 'hereditary enemy'. Within a few months the French army had been defeated at Sedan, and Napoleon was taken prisoner. In May 1871, the German Empire was proclaimed in the Hall of Mirrors in Versailles.

The united Germany was by any standard a colossus. With a population of 41 million people, it was larger than France (36 million), Austria-Hungary (about 36 million) and Britain (31 million). Only the vast Tsarist Empire could boast an even greater number of subjects (77 million).[24] By comparison, the population of Prussia in 1850 had been only 16 million. Moreover, unlike its stagnating French rival, the German population was rapidly increasing. Harnessed to this demographic motor was a rapidly industrializing economy, the best educational system in the world, and an army which was second to none. Contemporaries compared Germany to the recently reunited United States. 'The adoption in Europe,' President Ulysses S. Grant told Congress in February 1871, 'of the American system of Union under the control and the direction of a free people, educated to self-restraint, cannot fail to extend popular institutions and to enlarge the peaceful influence of American ideas.'[25] Popular journals celebrated Bismarck as a 'founding father', and even as the 'Washington' of the new empire.[26] Unlike the United States, however, this vast new entity was located at the heart of Europe. The consolidation of the European centre had eliminated the buffer of 'intermediaries' which had so long separated the great powers; Austria had been shut out of Germany for good.[27] Where there had for hundreds of years been a plethora of smaller states, and as recently as seven years previously there had still been nearly forty distinct entities, a single power ruled supreme. Over the next decades, this fact would dominate the foreign and domestic politics of the major European states.

The defeat at Sedan, and the capture of Napoleon III, destroyed the Second Empire. Many Frenchmen now believed that only a revolutionary transformation at home could save the nation from total defeat. The Third Republic was proclaimed and a Government of National Defence with the charismatic Léon Gambetta as minister of defence. The National Guard was revived. Because they were following the script of 1792, many Frenchmen were convinced that the resulting wave of nationalist, liberal and radical enthusiasm would sweep the Germans out of the country.[28] By the beginning of the following year, however, the Germans had forced the new government to sign an armistice, the terms of which included the cession of Alsace and Lorraine and the payment of a huge indemnity. The peace party under Thiers won the subsequent elections overwhelmingly, the Bonapartists were wiped out, and after a bitter debate the assembly which met at Bordeaux soon agreed to Bismarck's terms. The parliamentary vote for peace provoked the revolt of the Paris 'Commune' in March 1871 by those who wished to fight on, partly in order to vindicate the national honour but also because they regarded the decision as a Trojan horse for the restoration of the monarchy. Two months later, the Commune was crushed by the government before the occupiers could do so.

All this forced Frenchmen back to the drawing board.[29] The principal strategic challenge after 1871 remained Germany. According to the influential *Revue des deux mondes* in January 1872, 'The House of Hohenzollern is condemned to perpetual war, like Napoleon, because it refuses to limit its gains . . .'[30] Likewise, domestic politics was dominated by the question of how to recover Alsace-Lorraine, or at least to restore France's rightful place in the European states system.[31] The right now gave up its long opposition to universal service; on the left, former doves were transformed into hawkish advocates of the *levée en masse*. A series of military laws in 1872, 1873 and 1875 increased the length of military service to five years, making France – for all the shortcomings of her system of conscription – the most highly militarized society in Europe. A strong executive was set up, with a directly elected quasi-monarchical president who was not responsible to parliament.

In eastern and south-eastern Europe, the collapse of France also led to a major geopolitical reconfiguration. The Austro-Hungarian chief minister, Beust, finally gave up on Germany, and decided to seek Bismarck's help against Russia abroad and revolution at home. He also sought to create a more unified 'Central Europe' – '*Mitteleuropa*' – to balance the loss of French support against St Petersburg.[32] This was partly in recognition of the new power-political realities, partly a response to Russian support for Panslavist agitation in the empire, especially Bohemia, and partly a gesture towards domestic sentiment. For Russia, the French defeat provided an opening for a renewed push south towards Constantinople. In November 1870, the tsar unilaterally revoked the hated Black Sea clauses, signalling his intention to resume the advance into the Ottoman Empire. It soon became clear, however, that there were still serious obstacles to the realization of the 'historic mission'. The Habsburgs, recently extruded from Germany and Italy, were more than ever determined to prevent the tsar from outflanking them to the south-east. 'The road to Constantinople,' Russia's General Rostislav Fadeyev wrote in his famous *Opinion on the Eastern Question* (1870), '[now] lies through Vienna.'[33] There was a growing view, however, that the real barrier to Russian ambitions, and Panslavist aspirations, was Germany. The two major Russian newspapers, Mikhail Katkov's *Moscow Gazette* and the *The Voice*, exploded with anti-German vitriol in 1870–71. They condemned 'the dictation of Prussia to Europe' and claimed that 'an unrestrainable and natural tendency impels Germany on the path of conquest'.[34] For the moment, however, this rhetoric was still contained by official tsarist policy, which remained favourable to Bismarck on ideological grounds and welcomed German unification as a breach in the hated Crimean system. For him, and for most tsarist statesmen, the main enemy was still London not Berlin.

In Britain, the epochal significance of German unification was immediately recognized, but there the consensus ended. Some believed that the annexation of Alsace-Lorraine had revealed the new Germany to be a potential threat to the European balance. Gladstone cautioned in late November 1870 that 'so soon as Germany begins the work of aggrandisement ... she steps out of her own bounds and comes to us upon a ground where every country is entitled to challenge and discuss the title', just as the great powers had done with Russia over the Crimea.[35] Three years later the British ambassador to Berlin, Odo Russell, cautioned that Bismarck aimed not only to hold down France in perpetuity but to achieve the 'supremacy of Germany in Europe and of the German race in the world'.[36] Most Britons, however, held that German unification was a good thing and posed no threat to British security; indeed, Napoleon III's defeat actually reduced the danger to the south coast.[37] Many diplomats and commentators, such as the long-serving Robert Morier, were highly enthusiastic about the emergence of a Protestant, powerful and potentially liberal state in the centre of Europe, capable of containing both France and Russia.[38] Besides, most sceptics – including Russell – gradually accepted Bismarck's assurances that Germany was a 'satiated' power. The real reason the events of 1870–71 mattered, however, was not because they led to the unification of Germany, but because they marked the collapse of French power. Disraeli described this development – in a much misunderstood speech – as the principal result of the 'German Revolution'.[39]

Britain felt French weakness most acutely with respect to the Americas and the Tsarist Empire. The revocation of the Black Sea clauses was greeted with alarm, as were the Russians' advances in central Asia which would soon put them within striking distance of Afghanistan and shortly after of India. Likewise, the new situation after the defeat of France made it, as the British ambassador, Lord Loftus, put it, 'of incalculable importance to England . . . to find herself shielded from all embarrassments on the side of America'.[40] London duly did so in the Treaty of Washington of May 1871, and in the summer of 1872 agreed to pay the substantial compensation awarded to the United States by the arbitrators in the *Alabama* controversy. Against this background, German unification posed a peculiar problem. 'Whatever be the faults of French ambition,' Lord Loftus remarked, 'she has rendered and is capable of rendering Great Britain services in hemispheres' such as the Americas, India and China. 'Germany,' by contrast, 'is powerless as an ally to serve in those regions.'[41] In short, it was not the colonial ambitions and naval capabilities of the new *Reich* which Britain initially worried about, but their absence.

The French collapse also had a profound effect on British domestic politics. First, the unmistakably brutal process of German unification shattered the liberal belief in the ameliorative power of trade and the inexorable advance of international law.[42] The idea that liberal values would prevail without war, or did not need to be defended militarily, was no longer credible. As the former Conservative prime minister Lord Derby crushingly remarked in July 1870, 'Gladstone really believed in Cobden's theory that men were growing too civilized for war', which was why the Franco-Prussian War 'found [liberals] astonished and perplexed'.[43] A war scare now gripped the country. Futurist tracts predicting the invasion and conquest of Britain sold in their hundreds of thousands. One famous example, *The battle of Dorking*, penned by the army officer and subsequent MP G. T. Chesney in May 1871, posited a Prussian attack bulldozing aside ill-trained local militias while British regulars gnashed their teeth impotently overseas. 'Europe' suddenly seemed very near.

Many Britons now felt that more government was needed to deal with the new threats to their security. Reform of the army, long a preoccupation for liberals and radicals critical of the 'unmanly' aristocrats who still ran it, became imperative. The Franco-Prussian War convinced enough conservatives that noble privileges and traditional practices in the army could no longer be justified, and sufficient liberals that their own freedoms depended on an effective army to defend them. In 1871, Gladstone's minister for war, Edward Cardwell, finally pushed a military bill through parliament in the teeth of intense opposition. His reforms put an end to the worst abuses, such as the purchase of commissions, and began to haul the British army into the late nineteenth century. It was now not possible for Gladstone to cut military expenditure as planned, and thus, as he had hoped, abolish the income tax. In April 1871, the chancellor, Robert Lowe, presented a budget in which greater costs for the army were to be covered by an additional 1 per cent on the income tax, a tax on matches and twice the previous succession tax on landed estates. This was intended as a pan-social contribution to national defence, but the ensuing outcry forced Gladstone to increase the income tax instead. When the army and navy later refused to agree to the spending cuts which Gladstone wanted in order to abolish the income tax, he called a general election in January 1874. His defeat, and replacement by the Conservative leader, Disraeli, was thus to a very large degree a result of the Franco-Prussian War.

At the same time, Britain sought to make up in global weight for what she lacked in European military power.[44] In July 1871, the supporters of 'Imperial Federation' met in London, in the shadow of German unification.[45] There was widespread agreement that the colonies should be more closely integrated to defend British interests; the laying of transatlantic cables now made this technically possible for the first time. In 1872, the South African Cape Province was granted self-government, in the hope that it would not only pay for its own defence but act as the motor of further expansion into the interior. Four years later, Disraeli made Victoria 'Empress of India', a move designed to keep pace with the old empire of Russia and the new German Empire; Britain was now effectively a dual monarchy.[46] Imperial expansion also provided an opportunity to reassert the universality of British liberal and humanitarian values, which had been badly battered by the Prussian victories in Europe. The historian James Anthony Froude, for example, saw the colonies as an instrument to 'recover ... the esteem of the world'.[47] The principal vehicle here was the campaign to abolish slavery and the slave trade within Africa. This received a huge boost when news of David Livingstone's rescue by Stanley, and his horrific accounts of the treatment of the black population, reached London in 1872. By the following year, a full-scale parliamentary and press campaign was calling on the government to take the struggle to the enemy by intervening in East Africa, and there was also pressure on Egypt to deliver on its commitments against slavery.[48]

Meanwhile, a formidable challenge to the state system was building in the very heart of Europe. The International Working Men's Association grew exponentially during the period of German unification, and it had also secured the allegiance of about 100,000 North American workers; in this and other respects, the United States was effectively part of the European system. As the 'Internationale', Eugène Pottier's rousing anthem of 1871, made clear, class solidarity across state borders was the key to victory. The lines 'Peace between us, war to tyrants' struck terror not only into the hearts of property-owners but also of European strategists who were depending on working-class recruits to defend their national sovereignty. Though it began as a loose association of the followers of Marx, Pierre-Joseph Proudhon, Mazzini and Auguste Blanqui, the First International was increasingly dominated by the Marxists. At the Hague Congress in 1872, Bakunin was kicked out. This was not simply spite or sectarianism. The defeat of the Commune had served as a warning that mere enthusiasm was not enough. The forces of revolutionary socialism would have to be united and centralized if they were to take on the forces of capital and reaction. 'Only when the forces of the labouring masses are thus tightly bound centrally, nationally as well as on a world-wide scale,' the German Marxist organ *Sozialdemokrat* argued, could 'the working class ... unleash all its might. Democratic centralization – that is the key to the victory of the working class.' Time would show that what was envisaged here had very little to do with democracy and everything to do with centralism.[49]

Bismarck proclaimed the new Germany to be a 'satiated' power with no further territorial ambitions. The *Reich* was still threatened on two flanks, however: in the east by Russia, which was on the move again after a long period of passivity, and in the west by France, which remained completely unreconciled to her defeat in 1870–71. In the next two decades, Bismarck referred frequently to his '*cauchemar des coalitions*', the revival of the 'Kaunitz Coalition' of Austria, Russia and France. To make matters worse, this potential diplomatic encirclement was heightened by a sense of ideological envelopment. As a staunch Protestant conservative, Bismarck saw enemies on all sides: Gladstonian liberalism in Britain, royalist and Catholic revanchism in France, revolutionary Panslavism, not to mention the socialists, anarchists and assorted radicals assembled in the First International. Because French revanchism throughout the 1870s had a distinctly Catholic and royalist colouring, the chancellor eyed the millions of German Catholics, many of whom were ambivalent about Prussia and unification, with deep suspicion. He also regarded the papacy, which had just proclaimed itself infallible on matters of doctrine, as at best a dangerous alternative focus of loyalty, and at worst the nerve centre of a Jesuit plot to revive the French Empire and destroy his Protestant *Reich*. He lumped them together with Social Democrats, Hanoverian monarchists and Poles, as *Reichsfeinde* – 'enemies of the empire' – and thus a potential security risk.

The new German Empire of 1871 was ill-equipped to deal with these real and imagined threats. Its constitution was really a unification treaty of the various kingdoms and principalities for external defence, a 'United States of Germany', in effect. The guiding spirits of this effort were the German emperor – the erstwhile King of Prussia – and his appointee, the chancellor. According to the constitution, 'the emperor determin[ed] the effective strength of, the division and the arrangement of the contingents of the Reich army' in wartime. In peacetime, however, the constitution stipulated that 'the effective strength of the army . . . will be determined by legislation of the Reichstag',[50] a national parliament elected by direct universal male suffrage. This meant that the external defence of the empire would become the subject of domestic political debate. The direct connection between foreign policy, budgetary control and the growth of popular political participation was thus maintained; there was plenty of scope for further 'democratization'.[51] On the other hand, the federal structure of the united Germany allocated direct taxes to the regional parliaments, and only indirect revenue to the central government, which was responsible for overall defence. As a result, the *Reich* could only afford a much smaller army than her population size warranted, with by no means all eligible recruits being conscripted every year. The military high command and Prussian conservatives connived in this, because it enabled them to exclude socialist agitators, real or imagined, from the ranks. All this meant that for almost all of its forty-year existence, the second German Empire would be punching well below its fiscal and economic potential.

Bismarck responded to the external pressures on the *Reich* with a two-pronged strategy. At home, he pursued a cultural war, or *Kulturkampf*, against German Catholics with the support of anti-clerical liberals. Priests were jailed, Catholic publications were harassed and an atmosphere of fear and intimidation poisoned parliament and the public sphere. Abroad, Bismarck relied on clever management of the European state system. Unlike Britain, France and Russia he was content to leave overseas expansion to others: 'The Chancellor,' one of his interlocutors noted, 'refuses all talk of colonies',[52] partly because Germany did not have the means to protect them, partly because they were a useful tool to distract Paris from her losses closer to home, but mainly because the European security of the *Reich* was his principal concern. 'My map of Africa,' he once remarked, 'lies in Europe. Here is Russia and here is France and we are in the middle. That is my map of Africa.'[53] This overseas restraint reassured the United States. In December 1871, Bismarck told the German ambassador to Washington that 'We have no interest whatsoever in gaining a foothold anywhere in the Americas, and [that] we acknowledge unequivocally . . . the predominant influence of the United States' there.[54] The key, Bismarck believed, was to be one of two in a Europe of three powers, and one of three in a Europe of five. This meant being allied to either Austria-Hungary or Russia over eastern European matters, and with both against the British and French over matters of broader importance. The Three Emperors' League he brokered between Wilhelm, Alexander and Franz Joseph in 1873 was both an attempt to reduce Austro-Russian tensions which might force Bismarck to choose sides, and a signal that the conservative powers were united to defend 'considerations of a higher order'[55] against the threat of liberalism, socialism and anarchism. The ultimate aim of all this was the permanent isolation of the irreconcilable 'hereditary' enemy, France. 'I am convinced,' he wrote in late February 1874, 'that the danger which threatens us from France starts from the moment when France appears to the courts of Europe to be capable of making an alliance again.'[56]

The French army laws, and the Third Republic's huge defence expenditure, made this question acute by the mid-1870s. In March 1875, a journalist widely believed to have been briefed by Bismarck speculated in a newspaper article that if the French did not rescind the law 'War [would be] in sight.' The plan here was to humiliate France, force her to abandon her military preparations, and render her an implausible ally to the other great powers. Bismarck's sabre rattling was no mere macho posturing, or attempt to distract domestic critics, but part of a calculated policy of deterrence. 'One does not casually attack somebody,' he wrote in late May 1875 at the height of the 'War in Sight' crisis, 'whose sword lies loosely in the scabbard.'[57] The effect of Bismarck's gambit was, however, the opposite of what he intended. Far from isolating France, the German threats caused the other powers to fear for the European balance. Ominously for the chancellor, Russia refused to support him and expressed public opposition to a further decline in French power. In Britain, Disraeli tilted perceptibly towards Paris on European affairs in defence of the balance of power.[58] The French military law stood; Bismarck was forced to back down. His attempt to ensure the absolute security of Germany, at least on her western flank, had created a sense of insecurity throughout Europe.

In 1875, the Orthodox Slav peasants of Bosnia-Herzegovina rose in revolt against their Muslim overlords. A year later, the fighting spread to Bulgaria. The Turks responded with extreme brutality, sending irregular soldiers to burn villages. Tens of thousands of civilians were murdered in scenes redolent of the Greek atrocities. The 'Bulgarian horrors', as they soon became known, touched off a passionate debate in Britain. Appealing to 'our common humanity', Gladstone, the Liberal opposition leader, called upon the government to 'apply all its vigour to concur with other states of Europe in obtaining the extinction of the Turkish executive power in Bulgaria'. Events in the Balkans also hastened the emergence of popular geopolitics in Russia. News of the Bosnian and Bulgarian massacres sent the press and public – including many usually apathetic peasants – into a patriotic frenzy. There was an almost unanimous demand for military intervention from the press, huge demonstrations, a proliferation of proclamations and flood of volunteers for active service in the Balkans.[59] By April 1877, the Russians were at war with Turkey, forswearing all territorial claims, putting herself at the head of an intervention guided by the principle, as Prince Gorchakov put it, 'that the independence and integrity of Turkey should be subordinated to the guarantees demanded by humanity [sic],

Christian Europe and the interests of peace'.[60] By January 1878, the tsar's men had reached Constantinople. Not long after, the Porte sued for peace. The resulting Treaty of San Stefano in March 1878 did not aggrandize Russia directly, but hacked a large chunk out of Turkey's European empire. It created a huge Bulgaria stretching from the Danube in the north to the Aegean in the south, the Black Sea in the east as far as (but not including) Albania in the west. The strategic map of the Balkans had been fundamentally transformed.

This further blow to the integrity of the Ottoman Empire deeply alarmed the great powers. Austria feared that she would be next. Britain was equally horrified by the Russian advance. Her main aim, as Disraeli put it in December 1876, was not to support the ambitions of Balkan Christians but to keep the Russians out of Turkey. If the Greater Bulgaria created at San Stefano under her tutelage was allowed to stand, Russia would possess a convenient base from which to mount the capture of Constantinople. A Royal Navy squadron was therefore sent to the Straits. The issue for Bismarck, on the other hand, was not 'the welfare of Turkey', or that of her subjects, but the 'calamity of a [possible] breach' between Russia and Austria-Hungary. The German chancellor was desperate not to be forced to choose between the two powers. Neutrality was no answer, since that would simply deprive him of any leverage. In his famous 'Kissinger Diktat' of mid-June 1877, Bismarck stressed that the result of all this instability might well be a revival of the 'nightmare of coalitions', the 'kind of nightmare [which] will long (and perhaps always) be a legitimate one for a German minister'. German security, in other words, was inextricably bound up with the fate of the overall European balance.

Bismarck's strategy as 'honest broker' was therefore 'not one of gaining territory, but of a political situation as a whole, in which all the powers except France had need of us, and would thus be deterred as far as possible from coalitions against us by their relations with each other'.[61] This meant taking charge of developments well beyond Germany's immediate sphere of interest in order to reduce tensions between her allies, and to remove any instability which could be exploited by France. The resulting Congress of Berlin – which Bismarck chaired – drastically scaled back the territory awarded to Bulgaria at San Stefano. Macedonia was restored to Turkey, and the southern half of the country – known as Eastern Rumelia – was made autonomous. Greater Bulgaria was no more. Austria-Hungary was permitted to occupy and administer Bosnia-Herzegovina, though not to annex it outright. Britain acquired Cyprus, and thus a base in the eastern Mediterranean from which to support the defence of the Straits. Underpinning these arrangements was a great-power commitment to prevent the perpetration of grave human rights abuses, partly in pursuit of a broader desire to uphold 'civilized' norms of behaviour, but mainly to deprive neighbouring powers of a pretext for intervention. The new states, Bulgaria, Montenegro, Serbia and Romania, were compelled to subscribe to a policy of non-discrimination, especially against the Jews, who were – as one British diplomat put it – 'under the protection of the civilized world'.[62] Only well-governed polities, the argument ran, would be stable and peaceful members of the European system. In this way, the man who famously thought the entire Balkans worth less than the bones of a 'Pomeranian musketeer'[63] became the co-guarantor of human rights in the Balkans.

German mediation at the Congress of Berlin shaped European politics for the next decade. The Russian public erupted in fury at the brutal emasculation of Greater Bulgaria. The Panslavist publicist Ivan Aksakov condemned the Congress as 'nothing other than an open conspiracy against the Russian people . . . with the connivance of Russia's own representatives'.[64] Some critics now took aim at the very institution of tsarism itself, which had proven incapable of defending the national interest. Nervous police reports referred to revolutionary whispers 'that only two countries still lack constitutional government: the Russian Empire and the Celestial Kingdom of China'.[65] In Britain, Disraeli's perceived failures over the Bulgarian horrors, and his subsequent imperialist escapades in Africa and Afghanistan, played a substantial role in his political travails of the late 1870s. The immorality of Conservative foreign policy was the centre-piece of Gladstone's famous Midlothian campaign, which emphasized the 'common humanity' and the 'brotherhood of man'. His criticism was not just of the immorality and expense of killing blacks or Afghans for naked colonial gain, but of the consequent neglect of Britain's mission to spread liberalism and constitutionalism, especially in Europe. The export of British values, in other words, not vain swagger, was the proper role of foreign policy. The Liberal election victory in

1880, a verdict on Disraeli's international performance as much as anything else, showed this view to have traction among the British public.

The most important effect of the Bulgarian and Bosnian imbroglios, however, was their impact on Bismarck's strategic thinking. It was clear that the fundamental choice between Vienna and St Petersburg could no longer be delayed. The chancellor now opted for an Austro-German rapprochement which would rally the combined force of central Europe against attack from east and west. 'If Germany and Austria were united,' Bismarck remarked in 1879, 'they would be, together, a match for any enemy, France or Russia.' An important part of Bismarck's decision was his recognition that opting for Austria was much more palatable to German domestic opinion than closer collaboration with St Petersburg. The chancellor even spoke of the need to establish between 'the German Empire and Austria-Hungary an organic connection which should not be published like ordinary treaties, but should be incorporated into the legislation of both empires, and require for its dissolution a new legislative act on the part of one of them'. Nothing ever came of this scheme, which would have amounted to Schwarzenberg's plan for an empire of 70 million on a constitutional basis.[66] Bismarck did, however, abandon the *Kulturkampf*, as a gesture to Catholic opinion, and in early October 1879 he concluded an agreement with Austria-Hungary, later known as the Dual Alliance, which committed both powers to help each other in the event of a Russian attack. This move, the details though not the general thrust of which remained secret, was also intended to drive the tsar back into the chancellor's arms. One way or the other, the German chancellor believed that he had pre-empted the emergence of a 'Kaunitz Coalition'.[67]

Bismarck was still one of two in a world of three, but would he remain one of three in a world of five? This depended on keeping France isolated from Britain, and both powers separate from Russia. Here Bismarck could turn a potential liability into an asset. Once the Catholic threat had waned in the late 1870s, largely due to the electoral retreat of the right in France, the German chancellor became increasingly concerned with the threat of socialist and anarchist subversion. A spate of laws directed against the Social Democrats followed, and Gladstone's vocal international promotion of liberal values after his re-election in 1880 was observed with mounting concern. Bismarck now parlayed this alleged threat to all monarchies into diplomatic gain at St Petersburg. The Russian government, traumatized by the assassination of Tsar Alexander II in mid-March 1881, was uniquely receptive to the idea that pan-European conservative solidarity needed to be maintained against threats from below. So long as all parties kept a lid on their domestic critics, good relations could be maintained. It was with this in mind that the chancellor pushed through the *Dreikaiserbund* with Austria and Russia in June 1881, claiming that 'the danger for Germany of a Franco-Russian coalition [was now] completely removed'.[68] To be on the safe side, though, he concluded the Triple Alliance with Austria and Italy in mid-May 1882 mainly to secure the Habsburgs' southern flank in order to allow them to concentrate against Russia.

The new international alignments of the 1880s also had a profound effect on European domestic politics. As relations with Austria-Hungary and Germany declined, the tsarist government became increasingly concerned about the security of the western borderlands, with their large non-Russian populations. The 'Russification' of Poles, and increasingly of Germans, was stepped up. Particular attention was now paid to the Jews of the Pale, who were caught between traditional peasant anti-semitism and government-inspired panics about their reliability in strategically important regions. The minister of war, for example, announced that henceforth only 5 per cent of army medics could be Jewish, because their co-religionists had allegedly shown 'deficient conscientiousness in discharging their duties and an unfavourable influence on the sanitary service in the army'.[69] To be sure, the pogroms of 1881–2 in Kiev, Odessa and Podolia began spontaneously from causes which had nothing to do with security considerations, but the administration did nothing to stop them. Count N. P. Ignatiev, the minister of the interior, accused Poles and Jews of being behind 'the secret organization of the Nihilists'. Hundreds of thousands of Jews fled the Pale into Germany and Austria-Hungary.[70] Across Europe and the United States, humanitarian groups and Jewish organizations mobilized to express their outrage: the Tsarist Empire now became the quintessential oppressor in the minds not only of the central and western European publics, but also of American opinion.[71]

All the while, a fierce argument raged across Europe about the domestic structure best suited to guarantee external security. Bismarck continued to claim that the precarious geopolitical situation of the empire required a strong executive, and should place clear limits on the power of the *Reichstag*. In Britain, Lord Randolph Churchill regretted that 'capricious' public and parliamentary opinion made a consistent grand strategy impossible. This stress on monarchical or executive power over that of popular sovereignty was based on the widespread elite and radical assumption that electorates were less belligerent than their governments. The British reformer John Morley fervently believed that a parliament elected on universal suffrage would refuse to go to war. Increasingly, however, domestic critics were calling for a greater parliamentary involvement in external affairs partly in order to exercise oversight, but mainly because they believed that greater popular political participation was necessary to mobilize the nation for the defence of its vital interests. Moreover, the rise of humanitarian concerns about minority rights, and especially slavery, tended to encourage interventionism. In short, the growth of popular geopolitics tended to produce greater belligerency in the state system.

Throughout the late nineteenth century, the great powers engaged in imperial expansion and reorganization to secure manpower, economic resources, territory and prestige which could be deployed against European rivals. In France, imperialism was seen as necessary either to provide Germany with lands to be exchanged for Alsace-Lorraine, as Gambetta advocated throughout the 1870s, or to even the odds with her much stronger neighbour. The cabinet minister Paul Bert spoke of them as 'a means of bolstering national energy so that when the time is ripe we can win back the two provinces'.[72] Tunis was annexed in 1881, not least to pre-empt Italy, and an expedition was dispatched to Tonkin in Indochina in 1885. Meanwhile, support for 'Imperial Federation' grew in the British Empire. In a famous Melbourne lecture in late August 1885, the Australian writer Edward Morris argued that 'The future belongs to the big states. Germany at least has not reached its full size,' he warned, and would 'continue to expand'. His prognosis was for 'three great empires, the United States and Russia, with Germany not far behind them'. If Britain was not to risk 'complete effacement', she would have to integrate her empire more effectively into imperial defence.[73] The governmental architecture Morris proposed was a 'union' between the Australian provinces, and comparable lands in other parts of the empire, but 'federation' between those unions and Britain itself. Failure to tighten the imperial bonds, many feared, would lead to a repeat of the traumatic American experience when the thirteen colonies broke away from London, thus precipitating a crisis in Britain's European position.[74]

Imperialism was not just a geopolitical but also an ideological project: the two motivations were inseparably intertwined, especially in Africa. The existing colonies were constantly threatened by the instability of neighbouring states and tribes. Colonial powers now applied a principle which they had long practised on their own continent. When a state became 'permanently anarchical and defenceless', the long-serving Foreign Secretary and prime minister, Lord Salisbury, remarked with reference to Europe, neighbouring states were obliged to impose either a 'tutelage of ambassadors' or 'partition'.[75] French colonialists, for example, believed that their hold on North Africa would never be secure, until the nomads on its southern periphery had been pacified and the entire territory from the Mediterranean to the French footholds on the Ivory Coast was under their control. Likewise, British strategists sought to neutralize the predatory Zulus, and the equally restive Afrikaners to the north of the Cape Province. Above all, the great powers wanted to fill the vast 'vacuum' in the African interior, partly to secure their existing colonies against attacks from that quarter, partly to secure its resources and partly to pre-empt their rivals. Central to this project was the campaign to abolish the East African slave trade, which was seen not only as a moral imperative by many Europeans, but also as necessary to the establishment of good government and stability across the continent. Here British naval measures had proved unsuited to stopping the Arab trade, which was carried on in thousands of small boats across the Red Sea and Gulf of Aden.[76] If the Africans were to be freed from the curse of bondage, and civilized norms were to prevail, there would have to be a robust 'continental' expansion into the belly of the beast, to smash the Arab slave emirates and their local black African auxiliaries. British public opinion would accept nothing less.[77] The alternatives for the local populations were Arab slavery or European colonialism and the choice would be made for them, either way.

All this made central Africa briefly the fulcrum of European geopolitics. The French pressed in from the north-west, the British from the south and north-east. Bismarck feared that the Congo Basin would become the source of coloured soldiers which the French would use against him in Europe. The map of Africa was closing in on him. He therefore called a conference of European powers in Berlin, which met from December 1884 to late February 1885 to discuss the future of the area, and to ensure the neutralization of the Congo Basin in the event of war.[78] In the resulting 'scramble' most of the continent was divided up. London got Bechuanaland, British East Africa and British Somaliland. France received Benin, Gabon, Madagascar. and various West African territories. Bismarck walked off with South-West Africa, German East Africa, Togo and Cameroon. Together with the Pacific territories in New Guinea, the Marshall and Solomon Islands, these made up the new German overseas empire. The vital Congo Basin itself, whose huge potential resources could not be allowed to fall into the hands of a major European power, was awarded to inoffensive Belgium. It was generally expected that her liberal young monarch, Leopold, would abolish the slave trade there and give its unfortunate inhabitants a fresh start in life. Once again, Bismarck had been forced to engage with events far from the German borders to ensure the security of the *Reich*. Events in central Africa and central Europe were thus closely linked.[79]

The process of imperial modernization provoked stubborn resistance from local forces. When the Egyptians tried to demonstrate their European credentials by expanding their empire in the south, and especially by fulfilling their treaty obligation to extirpate the slave trade there, they soon drove the Muslim grandees in the Sudan, who were culturally attached to and economically dependent on slavery, to revolt in 1881 under the 'Mahdi'. In 1883, the Khedive's army, commanded by Hicks Pasha, was massacred; two years later, in February 1885, the rebels captured Khartoum after a long siege and killed its legendary defender, General Gordon. The victorious Mahdi then proclaimed a jihad, condemned the Khedive as a traitor to Islam, reinstated slavery and vowed to restore the caliphate. At around the same time, the Boers saw off a British attempt to push north from the Cape Province, defeating a British army at Majuba Hill in 1881. Three years later, the discovery of gold on the Witwatersrand gave the Boers the resources to buy weapons from Europe.

Colonial expansion was also highly controversial in the west. There were strong humanitarian reservations about the ethics of imperialism.[80] There was also profound disagreement over whether European values could or even should be exported to the extra-European world. '[W]e think,' one radical anti-imperialist wrote, 'all experience is against premature attempts to introduce our peculiar civilization into the existence of tribes at a much lower stage', and as for slavery it was 'enough if Western Europe prevents all exportation of Africans, leaving it as a domestic institution to their own development'.[81] Another objection was that the preoccupation with Asia and Africa distracted statesmen from more pressing security concerns closer to home. German Social Democrats relentlessly battered colonialism as an expensive luxury which would divert resources from the looming showdown with tsarist despotism. In Russia, the Panslavists were prepared to tolerate expansion into central Asia, but only so long as it did not detract from the 'historic mission' in the Balkans. This critique was most pronounced in France, where most felt that the chief purpose of national policy should be settling of accounts with Germany, not the pursuit of overseas baubles. These tensions burst into the open over the failure of the Tonkin expedition in 1885, which brought down Jules Ferry's government. The main radical newspaper lamented that 'For a couple of dubious mines in Indochina, Ferry is pawning off to Germany our security, our dignity, and our hopes.'[82]

The great powers were abruptly reminded of the primacy of Europe when, in September 1885, Bulgarian nationalists – acting independently of Russia – suddenly announced the reunification of Eastern Rumelia with Bulgaria proper. Russia was deeply unsettled by events because the Bulgarian national movement had largely emancipated itself from her control. In the autumn of 1886, therefore, Tsar Alexander III tried to force Sofia to accept a pro-Russian heir to the throne. When that failed, Russian agents resorted to kidnapping and forced abdication, provoking violent Austrian protests. By late 1886 and early 1887 Vienna and St Petersburg were on the verge of full-scale war. A major conflagration was only averted when Bismarck mediated. He feared both an Austro-Russian conflict, with Germany caught in the middle, and a total humiliation of his new Habsburg ally. In the end, Bismarck persuaded the Russians to back down and accept the Bulgarian parliament's election of the 'neutral' Ferdinand of Saxe-Coburg-Gotha as king. Once again, the chancellor sought to embed German security in the settlement of issues far removed from central Europe itself.

Over the next two years, the aftershock of the Bulgarian crisis fundamentally recast European geopolitics. In London, the Bulgarian emancipation from tsarist tutelage made it realistic for the first time to think of Balkan nationalisms as a possible constraint on St Petersburg, rather than as a mere Russian cat's paw. This permitted the British to reconcile the otherwise conflicting demands of ideology, which dictated opposition to Turkish misgovernment, and *Realpolitik*, which required a blind eye to the same in the interests of blocking the tsarist advance. In Vienna, the events of 1885–7 were a timely reminder of the continuing dangers of Russian expansionism. In Russia, Bismarck's claim to impartiality was roundly rejected by the public sphere. The Panslavists loudly lamented that, when all was said and done, Russian influence in Bulgaria had been comprehensively reduced, and a further barrier to the realization of the 'historic mission' at the Straits had been erected. The Germanophobic discourse, which had begun in the late 1860s, now not only dominated the press but gained increasing traction within tsarist circles. In France, too, there was an anti-German lurch in public opinion. Throughout 1886–9, Parisian politics were dominated by the charismatic and belligerent figure of General Georges Boulanger, the war minister, who promised to heal domestic divisions in preparation for a showdown with Bismarck.

In Germany, the Bulgarian crisis greatly boosted public and parliamentary criticism of Bismarck's foreign policy. In August 1886, the influential *Berliner Tageblatt* demanded action against Russia, which it regarded as both an ideological and a strategic threat. Bismarck was also attacked for allowing the French threat to grow on his western flank. The leading National Liberal Rudolf von Bennigsen called for a 'second war' with France over Alsace-Lorraine in order to guarantee the 'permanent security of the German national state'.[83] Influential voices in the military began to revive the call for a pre-emptive strike. Instead, Bismarck negotiated a defensive Reinsurance Treaty with the tsar in mid-June 1887, by which he agreed in principle to allow Russia to take control of the Straits. The content of the treaty would have been so unpopular in both countries, however, that the chancellor and the tsar were forced to keep it secret. In February 1888, the terms of the Dual Alliance were finally published, making the contradictory promises to Russia and Austria a matter of public debate. Matters came to a head four months later during a renewed Austro-Russian war scare over Bulgaria, which continued into 1889. As the demand for 'clarity' echoed across the imperial chancelleries, the newspaper columns and the *Reichstag*, Bismarck's policy of equidistance between St Petersburg and Vienna had become untenable.

It was in this context that the young Wilhelm II came to the throne in 1888. The new Kaiser shared the majority view that Germany would now have to choose between Austria and Russia, and that for ideological, domestic and military reasons she should opt for Vienna. In 1889, the Kaiser forced Bismarck to announce that the Reinsurance Treaty would not be renewed, a move which reflected rather than caused the Russo-German estrangement. That same year, Russia took offence at the Kaiser's first visit to the Ottoman Empire, which signalled that the promises concerning the Straits in the lapsed Reinsurance Treaty were now completely null and void. In March 1890, Bismarck resigned. A year later, Russia began the construction of the Trans-Siberian railway with French capital. Various naval exchanges and other visits culminated in a full defensive alliance in 1893, and a military convention in January 1894. It was a triumph of common security concerns over countervailing cultural, economic and ideological interests. In Britain, the Franco-Russian rapprochement was viewed with great alarm. In response, the Royal Navy proclaimed a 'two-power standard' in 1889, which laid down that Britain should build 'to a standard of strength equivalent to that of the combined forces of the next two biggest navies in the world'. It was in Germany, however, that the Franco-Russian alliance really struck like a thunderbolt. The 'nightmare' which had haunted Bismarck since 1871 – military encirclement by France and Russia – had come to pass.

Germany reacted sharply to the new threat. The first drafts of the famous Schlieffen Plan were drawn up in 1891–2. It was predicated on the assumption that France would have to be defeated quickly in the event of war, before the combined numerical superiority of the enemy alliance could make itself felt.[84] For the rest, Germany relied increasingly on the Austrian alliance, not least because, as the new chancellor, Count von Caprivi, admitted disarmingly, he 'could not play with five glass balls' like Bismarck but was only capable of 'simultaneously keeping two glass balls in the air'.[85] It was not simply incompetence or want of choice, however, which drove Caprivi closer to Vienna. Rather, his post-Bismarckian 'New Course' was based on a radically different understanding of how German security was to be guaranteed. Instead of the nerve-wracking juggling of balls, which would end in tears sooner or later, the chancellor sought to create a powerful German-Austro-Hungarian trading bloc of 130 million in central Europe, which could compete economically with the United States and with the French and British overseas empires and compensate for the military and territorial might of tsarist Russia. This was an innovative exercise in spatial thinking to escape Germany's traditional predicament in the middle of Europe (the *Mittellage*).[86] The alternative for a power without viable colonies, Caprivi feared, was massive emigration – a strategic demographic threat of major proportions. 'We must export,' he warned, 'either we export goods or we export people.'[87] German emigration not only hugely benefited the United States, but also the British Empire, especially Canada, both potential rivals. Moreover, the Americans were beginning to discriminate against foreign trade with the McKinley tariffs, which came into force in the 1890s. With all this in mind, Caprivi embarked on an active foreign trade policy, concluding treaties with Austro-Hungary, Italy, Belgium and Switzerland in 1891. Further agreements were planned with Spain, Serbia, Romania and even Russia in 1893–4. The purpose behind this policy was not primarily economic, nor was it a quest for global commercial dominance, but rather it was to ensure the security of Germany in Europe.

The Franco-Russian rapprochement had a profound impact on domestic politics. In Germany, the increased military threat put an even greater premium on mobilizing national energies for external defence through reform. 'I am looking for soldiers,' Kaiser Wilhelm remarked in connection with education reform, 'vigorous men who will also be intellectual leaders and servants of the Fatherland.'[88] The tension between the internal diversity of Germany – with its disparate groups of Catholics, socialists and others – and the external security of the state also needed to be resolved. This was necessary, because the doubling of military expenditure in the late 1880s and early 1990s had to be approved by the *Reichstag*. Caprivi sought to address this through his *Sammlungpolitik*, a strategy of rallying as many parties and groups behind the government as possible. For example, the government gave way in 1891 to demands from the Catholic Centre Party for concessions on schools in order to pass an army bill. When the Kaiser wobbled in the face of a Protestant backlash, Caprivi resigned, citing the need for domestic unity for security reasons. A year later, the army bill was rejected by the *Reichstag*, forcing new elections. Another crisis broke out in March 1895, when the Prussian war minister and the Foreign Secretary once again argued that the Centre Party had to be appeased to get the army estimates through. In this way, the strategic requirements of the united Germany, which had once militated against broader popular political participation, now drove a process of greater parliamentarization.

German society and politics were not simply a passive actor in all this. On the contrary, Catholics and socialists not only welcomed the domestic gestures made in their direction, but shared the fundamental strategic assumptions – especially fear of Russian aggression – on which German policy was based. Indeed, most Germans, be they bourgeois nationalists or internationalist workers, were if anything more robustly anti-tsarist than the elites. This found expression in the creation of popular militarist associations and leagues. In 1894, radical nationalists set up the Pan-German League. The ambition of the bourgeois nationalist project, and its irritation with the restraint of government policy, was summed up by the rising German sociologist and economist Max Weber. 'We must realize,' he announced in his famous Freiburg Inaugural Lecture of 1895, 'that the unification of Germany was a youthful prank which the nation played in its dotage, and should have avoided on account of its cost, if it was to have been the completion rather than the starting point of a bid for German global power.'

The alliance against Germany shaped internal politics in Russia and France. In St Petersburg, the finance minister, Sergei Witte, appointed in 1892, was convinced that the transformation of economy and society was central to the restoration of Russia's international standing.[89] He argued that protectionism was the key to economic development; he rejected free trade as a device of more advanced rival powers to keep the empire in economic subjection. In 1894, Russia authorized a large increase in defence spending to match Germany. Anxieties about the security of the western border areas did not cause, but certainly aggravated, another round of anti-semitic riots in 1893, especially in Kishinev. It was in France, however, that the domestic consensus came under the greatest strain. As relations with Russia improved, those with the small Jewish community declined. In 1886, Édouard Drumont wrote *La France Juive*, which called for the state to confront the Jews, who supposedly constituted a German fifth column. The recovery of Alsace-Lorraine would therefore have to begin with a purification at home. His ideas soon gained widespread acceptance not only on the right, but also among many radicals and socialists as well. This became evident in the autumn and winter of 1894, when the discovery that top secret military documents were being leaked to the Germans resulted in a witch-hunt against an army officer, Alfred Dreyfus. As a Jew and an Alsatian with potential links to Germany, he was deemed to be doubly guilty of treason, convicted in a show trial and banished to a penal colony. Yet the leaks continued. By January 1898, the rumblings that Dreyfus was innocent had exploded in a famous letter – '*J'accuse*' – by the novelist Émile Zola, in which he charged that the officer was the victim of a conservative conspiracy to pervert the course of justice.

Faced with the growth of anti-semitism across Europe, Jews began to strike back. At a local level, they formed self-defence organizations or political parties such as the *Bund*, founded in 1897 as the General Union of Jewish Workers in Russia and Poland. Jews also sought to bring financial and diplomatic pressure to bear on behalf of their co-religionists. In the early 1890s, the Rothschilds, Bismarck's confidant Gerson Bleichroeder and other Jewish bankers boycotted loans to Russia in protest against the 1881 pogroms, the 1886 expulsions from Kiev, the 1891 deportations from Moscow and St Petersburg, and other discriminatory measures. Some Jews, however, were beginning to think of a more radical solution to the growth of international anti-semitism. The breakthrough came when the Austrian Jew Theodor Herzl published *Der Judenstaat* in 1896, a manifesto for the creation of a Jewish national state. Part and parcel of the new movement was a conscious attempt to toughen the moral and physical fibre of Jewry, by turning nervous 'coffee house Jews' into what Max Nordau called 'muscle Jews'.[90] The more effectively Jews rallied in their own defence, however, the more anti-semites became convinced that they were facing an international conspiracy; these fears soon found expression in the forged 'Protocols of the Elders of Zion', published in 1903 at the instigation of the tsarist secret police, which purported to show a Zionist plot to control the world. This was the Jewish 'security dilemma'.

The 'Zionist' movement – which held its first congress at Basel in 1897 – was not only secular but very much German in character and orientation. Herzl himself was a fervent admirer of Bismarck, German was the working language of the Zionist movement, and Berlin soon became the informal capital of the World Zionist Executive. Zionists did not expect to be able to achieve their state on their own: they would need a great-power sponsor, and Herzl expected and hoped that that would be what he regarded as the most progressive polity in late-nineteenth-century Europe, Imperial Germany. 'The character of the Jewish people,' Herzl wrote, 'can only become healthier under the protectorate of this great, powerful, moral Germany, with its practical administration and strict organization. Zionism will enable the Jews once more to love Germany, to which, despite everything, our hearts belong.'[91] 'We owe it to the German in us that we are Jews again,' the German Zionist Moses Calvary wrote. 'Here,' Calvary concluded, 'is the living proof of the extent of Germany's nurturing of our own creative being: political Zionism is Europe's gift to Judaism.'[92]

From the mid-1890s, the focus of the great powers shifted to the global arena, where they sought to gain or protect the prestige and resources which could be leveraged to sustain their European position. In China, the main area of interest, they tried to secure exclusive commercial concessions from the ailing Manchu dynasty. In Africa, the principal battleground was the vacuum left by the Mahdists in the greater Sudan area, and the apparent weakness of neighbouring states.[93] British and French expeditions pressed in from all sides from the mid-1890s. In 1896, the Italians attacked Abyssinia in the hope of quick territorial gain. There was also increased tension in southern Africa, as Cecil Rhodes colonized what was to become Rhodesia. It very soon became clear, however, that the great powers were not going to have it all their own way. Italy's invasion of Abyssinia ended in a humiliating defeat at Adowa. In 1895–6, the 'Jameson Raid', a Rhodes-sponsored attempt to topple the Boer leadership, ended in complete fiasco. Above all, in the Far East, European ambitions in China clashed with those of Japan. To Tokyo's great chagrin, however, she was forced by the great powers to return the crucial Liaotung peninsula to China after victory in the Sino-Japanese War of 1895. The fate of the Far East, clearly, would be decided not by its inhabitants but by the European great powers, and those Asians willing to learn to play by their rules and beat them.

On the other side of the world, the United States was also flexing her muscles. The process of western expansion and consolidation now largely – though not entirely – complete, Americans increasingly turned their attention outwards once more. That same year, the publication of Alfred Thayer Mahan's *The influence of sea-power upon history* led to a renewed awareness of the importance of the global maritime balance for the United States. More pressingly, Cuba was once more in American sights. In 1895, the island erupted in full-scale revolt against Spain. Very soon the American public was appalled to learn not only of the scale of Spanish repression – 100,000 dead from famine, disease and war – but also of the policy of *reconcentración*, or 'resettlement', by which many islanders were herded into brutal camps. A huge petition campaign was mounted in December 1895 to demand that the Republican Congress support Cuban freedom. Resolutions calling for the recognition of Cuban independence passed both houses of Congress by huge margins. President Cleveland, a Democrat, prevaricated.

The problems raised by Cuba were not just ideological and humanitarian, but also strategic. Many Americans believed that the defence of 'freedom' abroad was vital to prevent 'despotic' powers from threatening the United States. The continuing instability on the republic's southern flank threatened to draw in outside powers. That said, Americans who wished to project their values abroad, or at the very least protect their flanks, were confronted by some sobering facts. The United States was not only much weaker in naval terms than Britain, but would also struggle to match Spain, and even Chile. Her army was tiny, large enough to deal with Indian tribes, but no more. Washington was an economic giant to be sure – her manufacturing output was the largest in the world by 1890 – but she remained a military pigmy. All this had implications for American domestic politics. A great effort abroad was only possible if the various immigrant communities were successfully integrated, and left their national allegiances behind them. More broadly, the supporters of American great-power ambitions argued for a larger military and a stronger state – with all that this implied for the provision of education, infrastructure and thus increases in taxation – which would realize the full potential of the nation for its global mission. In the November 1896 presidential elections, the Republican Party under William McKinley won on a platform based on reform at home, US naval expansion and a more activist policy abroad.

Meanwhile the German Empire tried to escape her encirclement by France and Russia. The key was Britain, the only uncommitted major European power. If Germany could secure a British alliance, she would remain one of three in a world of five, and French military pressure on her western border would be hugely reduced. London, however, was still largely focused on her overseas empire, and sought to avoid specific continental entanglements. When Britain cancelled a trade treaty with Germany, Wilhelm remarked bitterly that 'If we had had a strong, respect-inducing fleet, then this abrogation would never have happened.'[94] The Kaiser became convinced that Britain would only take Germany seriously as a European partner if the *Reich* possessed naval and 'global' clout of her own. More generally, German strategists and important sections of the public began to subscribe to the *Weltreichlehre*, or 'doctrine of world empire', according to which the geo-economic power of the global empires would crush the weaker central European bloc.[95] 'Three enormous empires of conquest,' the prominent academic Gustav Schmoller warned, 'who with their greed for territory, their sea and land power, their trade, their export, [and] their expansionist power threaten to grind down, indeed to destroy all other smaller states, to box them in economically, and to starve them of the light they need to live.'[96] In mid-January 1896, therefore, Wilhelm proclaimed that 'the German Empire has become a world empire',[97] and a year later he announced a naval programme under the leadership of Admiral Tirpitz. The first naval law followed in 1898.

The 'global' turn in German grand strategy also reflected a sense that the security of the *Reich* was affected by the emergence of new power centres outside Europe. Wilhelm fretted about American power and its 'arrogant' Monroe Doctrine, which cut across his own global plans. In 1895 he floated the idea of a 'continental league' of Germany, France and Russia to contain the 'Anglo-Saxon' powers, Britain and the United States. In September 1896, at a meeting with the tsar in Breslau, the Kaiser even suggested that the whole European continent should unite to balance the rising power of Washington. That same year, Wilhelm ostentatiously sent the Boer president, Paul Kruger, a telegram congratulating him on defeating the Jameson Raid. The Germans began to take a keen interest in the affairs of South Africa more generally.[98] In November 1897, Germany moved into the Chinese port of Kiatschou. A year later, the Kaiser made a second highly publicized visit to the Ottoman Empire, stopping off in Palestine. Shortly afterwards, a German company was given the task of building a railway to Baghdad and down to the Gulf, the start of the 'Berlin–Baghdad railway'. The real point of all this global posturing, however, was to frighten London into an alliance against Paris and St Petersburg. In essence,

Weltpolitik was not a bid for world domination but a cry for help in Europe.

In Britain, all this heightened the sense of alarm which had been building ever since the Russo-French rapprochement. The empire was already under threat from the tsar in central Asia and the Far East; the French in the Sudan; the Boers in South Africa; and the United States across the Americas. Now British official and public opinion was outraged at the 'Kruger Telegram': one British diplomat spoke of 'a determination on the part of the German government to make their influence felt in South-east Africa'.[99] The announcement of Tirpitz's naval programme in 1897 further heightened tensions. In a secret Anglo-German agreement in August 1898, Berlin left the Boers to their fate in return for an option on Portugal's African colonies, but the damage had been done. Henceforth, a strain of Germanophobia was distinctly audible among the many other antagonisms. Beneath the splendour of Queen Victoria's Diamond Jubilee celebrations, there lurked a feeling of deep unease, captured by the poet Rudyard Kipling in his famous 'Recessional'.

> Far-called our navies melt away;
> On dune and headland sinks the fire:
> Lo, all our pomp of yesterday
> Is one with Nineveh and Tyre!
> Judge of the Nations, spare us yet,
> Lest we forget – lest we forget![100]

The two-power standard, scarcely a decade old, was no longer enough. Britain would need allies to survive the challenges ahead, and it would have to find them either in the New World or in the traditional European system on which it had turned its back for so long.

In 1898–1903, global tensions exploded in a series of crises which were to transform the international system. First to erupt was Cuba, where the deteriorating humanitarian situation, mounting US popular demand for intervention and escalating fears that the island might fall into the hands of another power eventually drove Washington into action. 'It is no answer to say,' President William McKinley told critics, 'that this is all in another country, belonging to another nation, and is therefore none of our business.' On the contrary, he argued, 'it is specially our duty, for it is right at our door'.[101] This was the Burkeian right of intervention by 'vicinage'. In late April 1898, the president pre-empted a threatened binding Congressional resolution for military intervention, and the unilateral recognition of Cuban independence, by declaring war on Spain. It was, as McKinley argued six months later, a 'war for humanity', a time to 'take occasion by the hand and make the bounds of freedom wider yet'.[102] Spanish forces on land and at sea were soon defeated. A far more vexed question was what to do with the Spanish American empire. Left unattended, the Republican leader, Henry Cabot Lodge, warned, Cuba would become 'like Haiti or Santo Domingo . . . with no Monroe Doctrine [of their own] to prevent other nations from interfering'.[103]

Meanwhile, the long struggle for mastery in central Africa between Britain and France reached its climax. Both powers moved rapidly into the vacuum left by the Italian defeat at Adowa, the collapse of the Egyptian Empire and the subsequent steady disintegration of the Mahdist state. At the beginning of 1898, the French explorer and army officer Jean-Baptiste Marchand reached Fashoda; a fortnight later, he was confronted by the British general Herbert Kitchener, fresh from routing the Mahdist army at Omdurman. The war of the Egyptian succession, which had raged since the fall of Khartoum to the Mahdi, seemed about to erupt into a full-scale European conflagration. France had to choose between fighting to expand its colonial possessions to balance Germany, or to achieve the same end by reducing its colonial footprint in order to conciliate London. Paris backed down, selling her central African stake at the height of the market. Fashoda, and the French overseas empire more generally, had served its purpose. It was traded for the possibility of an entente with Britain on which the security of France in Europe depended.

British attention now shifted to southern Africa, where tension with the Transvaal and the Orange Free State had been escalating since the Jameson fiasco. Simple mineral wealth, the fabled gold and diamond deposits, was not the main issue. South Africa was of vital geopolitical importance because it served as the crucial hinterland of the naval base at Durban from which the route to India was defended. It could not be allowed to fall into the hands of another European power, especially Germany, which was already ensconced to the north-east (in present-day Tanzania) and north-west (in present-day Namibia). Knowing that annexation was on the cards, Kruger decided to strike first. In October

1899, he launched a lightning attack into the Cape Province. It took a serious effort by London and the rest of the empire to throw him back. Thereafter, the critical issue was whether outside powers would intervene on behalf of the Afrikaners and cut the British Empire down to size, just as France and Spain had done during the American War of Independence.[104] Pro-Boer feeling ran high throughout Europe, especially in France, Germany and Ireland, and there was joint military planning between Paris and St Petersburg in 1900 about a possible French descent on Britain, and a Russian invasion of Afghanistan. There was even talk of a partition of the British Empire, with Spain taking Gibraltar, France making gains in Africa, and Russia in central Asia. But the 'Saratoga' moment came and went, and by May 1902 the Boers had been crushed.

Important as events in Africa were for the European and global balance, they were dwarfed by the struggle for mastery in the Far East. 'The storm center of the world has shifted to China,' the US Secretary of State, John Hay, remarked, 'whoever understands that Empire . . . has a key to world politics for the next five centuries.'[105] Here the void left by the weakness of the Chinese Empire sucked in powers searching for resources, prestige and markets and seeking to deny them to their rivals. The Russians pressed in from the north, outraging the Japanese by, in March 1898, leasing the Liaotung peninsula, which Tokyo had handed back to China under international pressure three years earlier. The Germans, French, British and others all pressed their claims on the Celestial court. Chinese nationalists saw the 'Middle Kingdom' under attack from all sides and rose in revolt against foreign domination. This 'Boxer Rising' provoked an international intervention to suppress it, not because the powers were united in occidental outrage against the orient, but because they feared that their competitors might seek unilateral advantage. The widely expected complete partition of the Chinese Empire never actually happened, because the balance of power in the region did not permit it.

The global crises of the turn of the century had a profound effect on European foreign and domestic politics. In London, the experience of diplomatic isolation during the Boer War triggered a passionate debate on grand strategy. The Foreign Secretary, Lord Landsdowne, now condemned the 'musty formulae' and 'old-fashioned superstitions' against continental entanglements. '*Prima facie*,' he wrote in 1902, 'if there be no countervailing objections, the country that has the good fortune to have allies is more to be envied than the country that is without them.'[106] But an alliance with whom against which power or powers? The hatchet with France was slowly being buried, but there were still serious differences to be ironed out over North Africa. Russia remained a huge threat, and it was against her that Britain's first major diplomatic initiative of the new century, the Anglo-Japanese alliance of 1902, was directed. The main worry, however, was Germany, which had shown unconcealed sympathy for the Boers and whose naval ambitions were seen as a direct challenge to British maritime supremacy.[107] Sir Edward Grey, soon to be Foreign Secretary, remarked in January 1903 that Berlin was now 'our worst enemy and our greatest danger'. The discussion at the highly influential 'Co-efficients' club, at which Grey spoke, summed up the widespread feeling in late April of that year. 'As regards Germany,' the minutes reported, 'it was felt that her overseas ambitions, her economic development, and the rapid increase of her population made her a serious rival for this country.'[108] By the end of 1903, in short, the German threat had replaced the Russian menace as the principal concern for British foreign policy.[109]

This had profound implications for maritime strategy and imperial governance. Over the past two decades, Britain had assumed that her global status depended on the empire. 'As long as we rule India,' Lord Curzon, the viceroy, remarked in January 1901, 'we are the greatest power in the world. If we lose it we shall drop straightaway to a 3rd rate power.'[110] Now a large army capable of intervening on the continent would be needed, and the Army Reform Bill of 1901 was a first step in this direction. The creation of the Committee of Imperial Defence, a body which despite its name was firmly focused on the military situation in Europe, followed in 1902. That same year saw the establishment of the new 'Home Fleet' in response to the German naval challenge and which soon absorbed most of the Admiralty's attention and resources.[111] If Britain was going to do less on the global stage, however, then the empire would have to do more. The white settler colonies were already coming to this conclusion themselves. Australia and New Zealand observed German advances in the Pacific, and especially the Japanese victory over China in 1895, with concern. The New South Wales statesman Sir Henry Parkes therefore stepped up the negotiations for federation begun in 1889. In 1900, New South Wales, Victoria, Queensland,

Tasmania and South Australia finally came together to form a federation. This reflected not the rise of separatist nationalism, but the opposite: a determination to keep the British connection as security provider of last resort, and a realization that the burden of imperial defence would have to be shared more equally. Britain was to remain the global sheriff, but Australia would serve as her deputy in the South Pacific.

The Boer War and the rising German threat also provoked a debate about the state of British society. If the military had made such a meal of a few farmers toting rifles, how could Britain expect to match a real European adversary equipped with modern artillery? There were also severe doubts as to whether the population was fit for a long struggle: the poor physical condition of many urban recruits suggested that the national stock had 'degenerated'. These sentiments gave rise to the 'national efficiency' movement, designed to make Britain a more productive, rational and thus more powerful society.[112] In February 1902, the National Service League was set up to agitate for the introduction of conscription, thus 'distributing the burdens of national defence equally among all classes, instead of allowing them to weigh crushingly upon the proletariat'.[113] A year later, Joseph Chamberlain, the Secretary of State for the Colonies, and his Tariff Reform League sought to bind the empire more closely to Britain through 'imperial preference' against 'unfair' foreign imports, even if this resulted in reduced competition and thus in higher prices for consumers, especially with regard to agricultural produce.[114] Its aim was the transformation of the British Empire into a consolidated trading bloc which could compete on equal terms with Germany and the United States. The money from high import duties, so the argument ran, could be used to fund the social reforms necessary to rally the population for the great tasks that lay ahead. Tariff reform soon split the Conservative Party between protectionists and free traders.

Germany's global ambitions were also causing intense anxiety in the United States.[115] During the Spanish–American War a large German squadron had appeared in Manila Bay, giving rise to fears of German ambitions in the Pacific. German ships also began to patrol the Caribbean and South Atlantic from 1901. A year later, the German ships in an international force sent to collect unpaid debts had shelled Venezuelan ports until forced to stop by a US ultimatum; Berlin also refused to guarantee that she would not seek territorial aggrandizement at her expense. President Theodore Roosevelt had no objection, he warned a German diplomat, to outsiders 'spanking' any South American state that misbehaved, but he was strongly opposed to any country, including the United States, gaining 'additional territory' there.[116] In 1904 Washington was rocked by news that Germany had demanded the cession of a port in Santo Domingo. Roosevelt now spoke of the 'extreme desirability of keeping Germany out of this hemisphere', as 'the only power with which there is any reasonable likelihood or possibility of our clashing within the future'.[117] The waves caused by the geopolitical revolution in central Europe in 1866–71 had finally reached American shores.

Roosevelt's response to the security challenges facing the United States was not merely diplomatic and military but also ideological. 'Chronic wrongdoing, or an impotence which results in a general loosening of the ties of civilized society,' he told Congress, 'may in America, as elsewhere, ultimately require intervention by some civilized nation.' He insisted that the object was always to 'develop the natives themselves so that they shall take an ever-increasing share in their own government'. He also believed that the promotion of American values, 'speaking softly' if possible but wielding a 'big stick' if necessary, was the best guarantee of international peace and stability in the long run, and thus of US security.[118] After the Kishinev pogroms of 1903 in Russia, for example, the president protested to St Petersburg. The growing British–American understanding was based partly on a sense of geopolitical common ground – against Russia and especially Germany – but also on shared values, and here it was the tsarist autocracy and the alleged absolutism of the Kaiser they had in their sights.[119] These 'Anglo-Saxons' despised the red, yellow and brown races – to be sure – and they feared the 'Slav', but their principal preoccupation was the 'Teuton'. 'The *Vaterland*,' the US Secretary of State, John Hay, remarked in 1898, 'is all on fire with greed and hatred of us.'[120] Several years later, Roosevelt told a British diplomat that 'nowadays . . . no-one in America thinks of England as a possible enemy. Germany is the chosen foe of the [US] Navy.'

This activist foreign policy required strong government at home, Roosevelt argued, 'applied in a progressive spirit to meet changing conditions'. He was painfully aware that 'civic lawlessness, brutal corruption and violent race prejudices . . . at home' embarrassed the United States abroad. Moreover, although Roosevelt celebrated the entrepreneurial spirit of most Americans, he feared that unfettered capitalism would not only lead to enslavement by the 'great corporations', but would also 'sap' the 'vitality of . . . the working classes'. For this reason, the president supported labour unions 'in order the better to secure the rights of the individual wage worker'; he launched a programme of infrastructural investment; and he embarked on a campaign of determined 'trust-busting' because he believed that national government alone could 'deal adequately with the great corporations'. Roosevelt celebrated immigration and naturalization, so long as it was of the 'right kind'. This he defined not 'by birthplace or creed', but according to the criteria of 'Good Americanism': 'a matter of heart, of conscience, of lofty aspiration, of sound common sense'. He did all this not only because he thought that Americans deserved no less, but also because he believed that it was necessary to defend Americans' security by projecting American values abroad.

Germany therefore emerged from the global turbulence around 1900 with little reason for satisfaction. *Weltpolitik*, designed to boost the *Reich*'s resources, prestige and diplomatic room for manoeuvre, had actually increased her insecurity. An expeditionary force, dispatched with great fanfare in June 1900 to fight the Boxers and deployed to cries of 'Germans to the front', infuriated the Russians and Japanese. The desired British alliance remained elusive: negotiations in 1898–1902 collapsed because London was unwilling to commit to the defence of Germany in Europe, and Berlin baulked at supporting Britain militarily in Asia. As we have seen, the naval programme, far from impressing the British and Americans, merely antagonized them. On the other hand, the US victory over Spain and Britain's defeat of the Boers showed the Germans the price of maritime weakness. Berlin therefore decided to press ahead with the naval programme, taking care not to precipitate a pre-emptive strike by London. This 'Copenhagen Complex' – named after Britain's destruction of the Danish fleet in 1807 to stop it from falling into French hands – led the German foreign minister, Count von Bülow, to warn that 'in view of our naval inferiority we must operate so carefully, like the caterpillar before it has grown into a butterfly'.[121]

In February 1904, Japan pre-empted further Russian expansion in China by launching a devastating surprise attack on the tsarist fleet in Port Arthur. Over the next year and a half, the two powers slugged it out in Manchuria and on the high seas. To general surprise, the tsar quickly found himself on the back foot, outfought by the well-trained and well-equipped Japanese, friendless with the exception of little Montenegro (which declared war on Japan in Panslavist solidarity), and unable to raise enough money internationally because of a boycott by Jewish bankers. The defeat of the Russian army at Mukden in late February and the complete destruction of her Baltic fleet at Tsushima in May 1905 finally forced St Petersburg to sue for peace. The tsar evacuated Manchuria, surrendered the strategically vital Port Arthur and acknowledged Japanese supremacy in Korea, which Tokyo formally annexed five years later. Russia's humiliation was almost complete; she was spared only the indignity of paying an indemnity to Japan. The consequences of her defeat were now to resonate across the globe and through the international state system.

To most westerners, the Russian defeat was the result of her political backwardness. They argued that whereas Japan enjoyed constitutional government, the Tsarist Empire did not; the Japanese victory was therefore seen as a vindication of western values, which seemed to augur well for the progress of civilization and good governance across the world. The Japanese, Roosevelt wrote at the height of the war in July 1904, were 'a wonderful and civilized people, entitled to stand on an absolute equality with all the other peoples of the civilized world'.[122] He expected nothing of Russia, on the other hand, 'until her people begin to tread the path of orderly freedom, of civil liberty, and a measure of self-government'. In Russia itself, critics of the tsarist regime were coming to the same conclusion. The policy of eastern expansion had always been controversial among the broader public, especially when it resulted in neglect of the empire's 'natural' sphere of influence in the Balkans.[123] As the news of the defeats in the east mounted, popular opinion grew more restive. In July 1904, the interior minister, Plehwe, was assassinated. In November 1904, there were calls for mass banquets – in conscious imitation of Paris in 1848 – to rally against the autocracy, and large-scale protests broke out in January 1905. The following month, the tsar finally agreed to a consultative assembly, the *Duma*. The resulting parliament was chosen on a restricted and indirect franchise and did not satisfy liberal demands, but it was a start. In October 1905, the tsar issued a manifesto guaranteeing civil liberties such as freedom from arbitrary arrest, of speech, religious observance and association. Laws were to be approved by the *Duma*. At the same time, the state sought to create a more reliable and effective conscript army.[124] The purpose behind this programme of limited political modernization was to harness the potential of Russian society to the great project which lay ahead: rebuilding Russia's international position and vindicating her strategic interests.

As Russia's global policy collapsed in Manchuria and at Tsushima, Britain and France contemplated the continued rise of German power with alarm. The escalating Anglo-German naval race was a symptom rather than the fundamental cause of the antagonism, which lay in London's perception that the Kaiser sought to upset the European balance of power.[125] Irrespective of how many ships the Germans could build in the short term, it was a longstanding axiom of British strategy that the Royal Navy would never be able to contain an enemy who controlled the bulk of the resources of the continent. Moreover, it was assumed that the Russian defeat in the Far East would make her more dependent on Germany, and possibly even open to an alliance. The result was the *Entente Cordiale* of April 1904 between Britain and France. This was an understanding rather than a military alliance, and the specific terms amounted to little more than a colonial deal, with Morocco falling to France, while Paris finally gave up on its share of Egypt. The *Entente* did not as yet involve any official cooperation between the two armies, still less concrete war plans against Germany on the lines of the Franco-Russian alliance. Cleverly, the French did not insist on this, at first, but sought to suck the British in ever more deeply by creating a moral obligation towards a continental commitment.[126] For Britain, the hope of French support in moderating Russia still played an important role. But for all that the signal was clear: if Britain and France were not yet jointly pledged to contain Germany, their new friendship had profound implications for the European balance of power generally, and in particular for Germany.[127]

News of the Franco-British rapprochement was greeted with consternation in Berlin. Bismarck's *cauchemar des coalitions* – the fear of being crushed between the mills of a powerful hostile alliance – was a step closer to realization. The Kaiser wrote that the situation reminded him of Frederick the Great's predicament before the Seven Years War; press voices spoke once again of being 'surrounded on all sides', in language reminiscent of the popular geopolitics of the 1850s and 1860s.[128] The imperial leadership now sought to find ways out of what the Kaiser called the 'gruesome Gallo-Russian vice'. In 1905, the German general staff drew up the final version of the Schlieffen Plan, designed to enable Germany to cope with encirclement. If she failed to do so, Schlieffen warned, 'the gates will be opened, the drawbridges let down, and armies of millions of men will pour into Central Europe across the Vosges, the Meuse, the Königsau, the Niemen, the Bug, and even across the Isonzo and Tyrolean Alps in a wave of devastation and destruction'.[129] Rather than just sitting back and awaiting the enemy attack some influential voices argued for an active policy. The German foreign minister, Count von Bülow, rejected these demands, as Bismarck had before him.[130] He did, however, try to take advantage of Russian weakness by putting pressure on the weakest link in the surrounding chain: France. This was the thinking behind the Kaiser's intervention in Morocco in 1905–6. He was not so much staking a belated claim to North Africa as trying to make Germany more secure in Europe by prising open the encircling coalition.

At first, all went well. In March 1905, the Kaiser landed in Tangier and demanded an international conference to safeguard the integrity of Morocco, which the French were progressively turning into a protectorate. Paris, exposed by the lack of effective Russian support and not yet able to call on Britain, backed down publicly in June 1905; the foreign minister, Théophile Delcassé, was forced to resign. In late July, the Kaiser pressed his advantage by concluding a defensive alliance with the tsar at Björkö. Within a very short time, however, St Petersburg drifted back to France after the Russo-Japanese War ended and the tsar was forced by his ministers to repudiate the alliance with Germany. Meanwhile, Britain reacted sharply. In January 1906, the British Foreign Secretary, Sir Edward Grey, authorized the first Anglo-French staff talks. The naval race with Germany, now focusing on a new, more advanced class of battleship called the 'Dreadnought', escalated.[131] Those who knew the extent of German industrial superiority, such as the former prime minister Arthur Balfour, warned that Britain would be outclassed in terms of 'dockyards', 'manufactory', 'great guns' and 'armour': 'If the Germans think it worth their while, I do not think we can count upon building battleships quicker than they can.'[132] By the time the international conference demanded by the Kaiser actually convened in January 1906, Germany was completely isolated. The French were put in charge of the Moroccan police and thus firmly in control of the whole territory.

Germany's strategy to break open the ring of encirclement had merely welded the links closer together.

The emerging British view of Berlin was summarized by the Foreign Office German expert, Eyre Crowe, in his famous 'Memorandum on the present state of British relations with France and Germany' of January 1907. Far from being invulnerable behind its maritime moat, he argued, Britain was actually 'in the literal sense of the word, the neighbour of every country accessible by sea'. It therefore followed that the overriding interest of the British state, greater still than its concern for 'free intercourse and trade', was to make sure that there was no 'general combination of the world' against it, which would very quickly result in the loss of naval superiority. This in turn meant that it was 'almost a law of nature' that London should intervene to maintain the European balance of power. This, Eyre claimed, was now endangered by Germany. After a long listing of Berlin's alleged provocations in South Africa, in China and in the naval race, Crowe pointed out that 'the edifice of Pan-Germanism, with its outlying bastions in the Netherlands, in the Scandinavian countries, in Switzerland, in the German provinces of Austria, and on the Adriatic, could never be built up on any other foundation than the wreckage of the liberties of Europe'. If that was what Berlin was aiming for, he concluded, then this 'general political hegemony and maritime ascendancy' threatened the 'independence of her neighbours and ultimately the existence of England' and had to be stopped.

There was worse to come for Germany. Defeat in the Far East encouraged the Russians to turn their attention back to Europe, and especially the Balkans. Here St Petersburg had long since come to regard Germany as the principal obstacle to her ambitions. It was the Kaiser who protected the Sultan in Macedonia, was pressing ahead with the construction of the Berlin–Baghdad railway, and generally propped up Ottoman power throughout the Near East. In this context, the Russians looked again at Great Britain, whose enmity was still keenly felt in Persia and central Asia, but whose interest in the Balkans and the eastern Mediterranean had decreased considerably since the 1870s. On the crucial issue of Constantinople, London and St Petersburg were no longer so far apart. So, in late August 1907, the two powers reached an agreement which divided Persia into a Russian zone of influence in the north, a British one in the south and a neutral area in the middle. A *modus vivendi* was reached on Tibet and Afghanistan. As with the Anglo-French entente, a colonial entente had been concluded in order to secure more vital European interests. 'This necessity for a close unit [between Britain, France and Russia],' the German chargé d'affaires in St Petersburg remarked drily, 'is a compliment, though a troublesome one, for the German army, the German navy, our merchants, and the general capacity of the German people for development.'[133]

The domestic and international ripples of the diplomatic revolutions of 1904–7 – the Japanese victory in the Far East and the formation of the Triple Entente between Russia, France and Britain – now spread across Europe. A vigorous debate erupted in the Ottoman Empire about the domestic transformation necessary to rescue Turkey from destruction. In late July 1908 a group of 'Young Turk' officers forced Sultan Abdul Hamid to reinstate the 1876 constitution and call elections, and eventually ousted him altogether. The principal aim of the new Committee for Union and Progress was to restructure Ottoman society at home and project power more effectively abroad. At the very top of their agenda was the recovery of Bosnia-Herzegovina, which had been under Austro-Hungarian occupation since 1878, but remained under nominal Ottoman suzerainty. This suddenly exposed the southern flank of the Austro-Hungarian Empire. The Bulgarians took the chance to declare full independence; Serbia began to agitate for control of Bosnia. Baron Aerenthal, the Habsburg foreign minister, moved into the resulting vacuum by announcing the unilateral annexation of the two provinces. Russia, which thought she had at least secured a *quid pro quo* for the passage of her warships through the Straits, could only fume impotently. In Berlin, the issue was seen as a test of the Anglo-Russian entente. 'Austria,' the senior diplomat Friedrich von Holstein, widely known as the 'grey eminence' of the empire, argued in early October 1908, 'is today fighting for its own selfish reasons, [but it is also] our battle against the European Concert – alias English hegemony, alias encirclement.'[134]

This cascade of ententes, annexations, and arms races dominated European domestic politics throughout the second half of the decade. In Germany, public opinion was growing restless at the bleak international situation and about the conduct of foreign and imperial policy in general. This critique took on humanitarian, strategic and constitutional forms. In November 1906, for example, the Centre Party launched a ferocious attack on the indemnity bill to pay for the suppression of the

Herero rising in South-West Africa, on the grounds that the commanding general, von Trotha, had used excessive force.[135] In 1907, the government actually fell over the army estimates, and there was another row over the naval estimates in 1908. In general, the objection was not so much to military spending *per se*, as how it was to be paid for and the uses to which it was being put. As Germany became more and more isolated, particularly after the Anglo-Russian convention, parliamentary and press patience wore thin. In early December 1908, Philip Scheidemann, a delegate for the Social Democratic Party (SPD), lamented that the 'iron ring' was closing around Germany.[136]

In St Petersburg, too, foreign policy remained at the centre of domestic politics. The new *Duma* held the government's feet to the fire on the defence of Russian interests. The moderate constitutional Octobrist and Kadet parties demanded a voice in foreign policy, and argued that Russia could never realize her full potential on the European stage without a thorough programme of social and political reform.[137] Their sense that Russia was losing ground internationally turned parliament into a forum for an attack on the autocracy. Here the central issue was how to handle Germany. Many conservatives – hostile to British and French liberalism – sympathized with the Kaiser. They wanted to return to the era of the Three Emperors' League, or even the Holy Alliance. The prevailing opinion, however, was strongly anti-German. The Octobrists spoke of the 'inevitable struggle with the Germanic races', and the Kadet leader, P. N. Miliukov, saw himself locked in confrontation with 'Germanic civilization'.[138] The autocracy had been put on notice: if it failed once again to defend Russian greatness abroad against Germany, a new liberal regime would.

In Britain, disagreements about how best to marshal the nation and the empire to meet the German challenge remained central to domestic politics. Tariff reform was fiercely resisted by Liberals and many Conservatives on the grounds that it violated the principle of free trade, and drove up the price of basic foodstuffs. In December 1905, the Conservative government of Arthur Balfour finally collapsed under the strains of this issue. The resulting January 1906 election resulted in a large Liberal majority under Henry Campbell-Bannerman. Tariff reform was shelved. Instead, the new government resorted to classic liberal methods to strengthen Britain. In 1907, the Secretary for War, Lord Haldane, introduced the Territorial and Reserve Forces Act with its provision for military training in schools and universities. This was seen as an alternative to conscription and 'militarism', and was intended to stiffen the moral and physical sinews of the nation against Germany. At the same time, the Liberals sought to reconcile the working classes to the state through a programme of social and welfare reform, especially through the introduction of health insurance and pensions. The trouble was that while the policy of strength abroad and justice at home was complementary in conceptual terms, it appeared to be contradictory from the fiscal point of view. Budget hawks demanded to know what it would be: 'Dreadnoughts or old-age pensions', guns or butter.

Matters came to a head in 1909, when intelligence reports suggesting that the Germans were pulling ahead in naval construction were made public; these were aggravated by wild rumours that German spies were staking out East Anglia and the south coast.[139] In October of that year, the government set up the Secret Service Bureau (which later developed into MI5 and MI6) specifically to deal with German penetration.[140] The navy estimates were a more controversial matter. In his famous Limehouse Speech of late July 1909, David Lloyd George, the Chancellor of the Exchequer, embraced the need for more Dreadnoughts and attacked the landed elites for refusing to agree to the necessary new taxation to pay for them. Radical liberals, in other words, argued that the traditional social structures were no longer in the national interest. Rather like continental European reformers, Lloyd George claimed that 'the ownership of land is not merely an enjoyment, it is a stewardship. It has been reckoned as such in the past; and if they cease to discharge their functions, *the security and defence of this country* [my italics], looking after the broken in the villages and their neighbourhoods which are part of the traditional duties attached to the ownership of land ... the time will come to reconsider the conditions under which the land is held in this country.'[141] So when the House of Lords threw out the budget in late November 1909, the resulting general election was not just about the constitutional question of whether the House of Lords had acted properly, or the question of wealth redistribution, but also the issue of how national security was to be funded, and how British society should be reshaped to meet the challenges of the new era. Two elections in 1910 showed Liberals and Conservatives to be neck and neck; the

Liberals, who were very slightly ahead, eventually formed a coalition government with the Irish nationalists. Lloyd George got his pensions, and the navy got their ships.

The pressure of international events also led to a change in the role of women. In central and western Europe, patriotism became the vehicle through which some women could articulate a claim to political participation. Of course, greater female engagement in patriotic politics and charitable organizations did not necessarily involve a 'progressive' or feminist agenda; very often, it was accompanied with a stress on feminine self-sacrifice and reaffirmation of existing relations between the sexes.[142] Increasingly, however, women used their contribution to the national cause to argue for greater rights and even the granting of the franchise. It was no accident that these claims were first staked in Britain, the only developed European country which had fought a (almost unsuccessful) major conflict in decades. In 1903, just after the Boer War, Emmeline Pankhurst founded her Women's Social and Political Union (WSPU); two years later, her daughter Christabel disrupted a Liberal meeting in Manchester to demand votes for women. In 1912, Millicent Fawcett founded the National Union of Women's Suffrage Societies (NUWSS) to agitate for the franchise. All this was registered with alarm by governments, Conservatives and most Liberals. There was little initial enthusiasm for women's rights *per se,* but there was widespread recognition that the female population represented a vast new source of energies to be tapped. Moreover, there was a consensus that the vitality and size of the 'national stock', and the provision of sturdy young males for military service, was linked to women's health. This sentiment was particularly strong in Britain, where fears of a eugenic decline had become rampant during the Boer War. Motherhood, rather than women, was their concern. The training of midwives was instituted in 1902, and eight years later the Midwives Act required their legal certification. In 1907, Lloyd George sponsored National Baby Week, with its slogan 'It is more dangerous to be a baby in England than to be a soldier.'[143] For the moment, however, European governments and European males could not quite make up their minds whether they wanted to keep women confined to the home to nurture new soldiers, or to mobilize them more comprehensively for the challenges which lay ahead.

*

In Germany, traditional geopolitical anxiety gave way to paranoia after the Anglo-Russian convention in 1907. The diplomatic 'encirclement' of Germany, as the Kaiser lamented in October of that year, was taking its 'calm, unalterable, inevitable course'. She was now one of two in a world of five. Whether this would also lead to her being surrounded in the military sense was still an open question, however, and opinion in Berlin was furiously divided on how to proceed. All were agreed with the Kaiser and his new chancellor, Theobald von Bethmann-Hollweg, that Germany needed to 'break up' encirclement. Some, such as Bülow, speaking in June 1907, argued that Germany could weather any storm so long as it maintained the 'firm bloc, which we constitute with Austria in central Europe'.[144] Others, such as the Kaiser, pushed for greater naval spending; this was formally proposed in November 1907 and the bill passed the *Reichstag* in 1908. Others still, such as Bethmann, argued from 1909 that Germany should scale down her naval programme and colonial ambitions to conciliate London. All three approaches were tried in combination, but none made Germany more secure. Austria-Hungary was domestically too divided to balance the Triple Entente, even if Italy remained neutral, which was doubtful. The Kaiser's increased naval spending simply provoked the mammoth British Dreadnought programme of February 1909. Bethmann's overtures to London got nowhere because Britain was not prepared to provide concrete military guarantees against either France or Russia.

In May 1911, the French shattered the fragile consensus in Morocco by occupying Fez, at the request of the Sultan and in response to escalating civil unrest. Germany therefore decided to make one last attempt to break open the ring of encircling powers by attacking its weakest link, France. Berlin demanded 'compensation' for the French gain, and at the beginning of July the armoured cruiser *Panther* appeared off the Moroccan port of Agadir to back up the claim. The result was simply to drive Paris and London closer together. Lloyd George made a strong speech supporting France. Austria-Hungary remained on the sidelines. By early November, Germany had been forced to accept a French protectorate in Morocco in return for a face-saving slice of the French Congo. Once again, Berlin's attempts to loosen the stranglehold had only led to the noose being tightened around her neck.

The Second Moroccan Crisis sparked a fresh cycle of international and domestic turbulence across Europe. In November 1911, the Italians booted the Turks out of Libya and the Dodecanese islands. The prospect of a complete Ottoman collapse in turn triggered a shift in Balkan geopolitics, which had been in uneasy equilibrium since 1908. Russia fretted that the Straits were now under threat from the south, and offered to guarantee them against Italy. Austria-Hungary was so worried about the growing threat on her flank that the military chief, Count Franz Conrad von Hötzendorf, demanded a pre-emptive strike to cut Rome down to size. Above all, the local powers saw their chance to destroy the Ottoman Empire in Europe once and for all. At the end of 1911, Serbia, Bulgaria and Greece had begun negotiations to sink their differences and unite against the Turks. A major Balkan crisis was in the offing. All this took place against a background of global instability. In the Far East, Japan finally annexed Korea in 1910 in order to strengthen her buffer to the west. This move caused outrage in China, and it also accentuated growing American unease – it was not yet full-scale anxiety – about a looming struggle for dominance in the Pacific. The general feeling that the Manchu dynasty was powerless to prevent partition inspired a revolution in October 1911, and the proclamation of the Republic under Sun Yat Sen. On the other side of the world, Mexico began to slip into civil war with the outbreak of a revolt against her longstanding president, Porfirio Díaz, and became a running sore on the southern flank of the United States.

To Washington, the Mexican and the Moroccan crises were closely linked, because of the highly exaggerated fear that the vacuum below the Rio Grande would be filled by a hostile power. Many Mexicans did indeed seek a counterweight to their northern neighbours, only this time it was not the Paris of Napoleon III but the Kaiser's Berlin. 'Mexico's foreign policy,' President León de la Barra informed the German ambassador in 1911, 'will aim at reliance on Europe and especially on Germany.'[145] Washington therefore knew that a shift in the European balance in favour of Berlin would soon make itself felt in the western hemisphere. For this reason, the United States supported London's attempts to maintain it. 'As long as England succeeds in keeping the balance of power in Europe,' Theodore Roosevelt wrote, 'well and good. Should she . . . fail in doing so, the United States would be obliged to step in, at least temporarily in order to re-establish the balance of power in Europe.' Far from being mired in isolationist ignorance, therefore, the US diplomats were keenly aware of European dynamics; they regularly warned of a potential German pre-emptive strike.[146] Taken together, a rising state with naval ambitions on the far side of the Atlantic and a weak state on her doorstep spelt danger for the United States. After the Second Moroccan Crisis, in short, the Americans feared that the next 'leap of the *Panther*' would be across the Atlantic.

The German imperial leadership now backed away from *Weltpolitik*, and began to concentrate on security closer to home. As Bethmann remarked to the *Reichstag* in November 1911, 'Germany can only pursue a strong policy in the sense of world policy if it remains strong on the continent.'[147] The navalist slogan 'Our future lies on the water' was abandoned. As the publicist and longtime critic of the emperor, Maximilian Harden, remarked, 'Now our future lies on the continent. This awareness has returned to the German people.'[148] The result was an increased elite and popular consciousness of 'encirclement'. As the Chief of the General Staff, von Moltke, remarked in December 1912, Germany remained 'surrounded on three sides by its enemies', and the relative military balance with Russia was steadily deteriorating, thanks to her increased armaments and railway construction.[149] Faced with this predicament, important voices in the imperial leadership, and the public sphere, began calling once again for a preventive war to forestall an attack by the enemy coalition further down the line. At a Crown Council in 1912 the Kaiser and his advisers rejected this option, but agreed that war was 'inevitable' in the long run, 'the sooner the better'.

The *Entente* also concentrated ever more closely on Europe. A *réveil national* ('national awakening') swept France, as public opinion was reminded of the fact that the real enemy lay just across the border. In August 1911, the Chief of the High Command, General Joffre, inaugurated 'Plan 17' for a thrust into Germany. The question of Alsace-Lorraine, long submerged by colonial concerns, shot back to the top of the agenda. In January 1912, Poincaré was elected prime minister with a mandate to face down Germany. In Britain, the security of France and the Low Countries moved back into focus. The new Germanophobe Director of Military Operations, Sir Henry Wilson, began to plan openly – and with considerable political encouragement – for a continental military commitment.[150] In June 1912 a naval agreement gave France the lead role in the Mediterranean, allowing Britain to concentrate on the North Sea; the bulk of the fleet was now concentrated in home waters.[151] Europe, the First Lord of the Admiralty, Winston Churchill, told the

Australians and New Zealanders in April 1913, was 'where the weather came from'.[152]

The growing threat of war dominated domestic politics. In Germany, the humiliation of the Second Moroccan Crisis provoked a barrage of popular and parliamentary assaults on the weakness of imperial foreign policy.[153] The Pan-Germans demanded war, so did the National Liberal leader, Basserman. In a turbulent session of the *Reichstag* in November 1911, the chancellor was accused of allowing Germany to drop 'out of the ranks of the great powers'. In the centre and on the moderate left, which represented the largest proportion of the population, concern focused on the vulnerability of the *Reich* to Russian attack, and the waste of resources on frivolous colonial adventures. In Russia, too, impatience with tsarist foreign policy was mounting in the *Duma*. The principal critic here was Aleksandr Ivanovich Guchkov, leader of the dominant Octobrists. A longstanding critic of inefficiency and lack of coordination in national security matters, Guchkov called for increases not in the navy, which would have signalled a renewed commitment to the Far East, but in the army, which was needed to defend Russian ambitions in the Balkans and central Europe.

Across the continent governments were now faced with the problem of how to maximize their military capability. At the heart of these debates were defence and its social and economic implications. In June 1912, the Russian *Duma* authorized a huge increase in expenditure on the Baltic fleet, which was largely directed against Germany. A month later, the critical international situation enabled the Austro-Hungarian government to push through an increase in the army against Magyar obstructionism, the first in more than twenty years. In France, the government sought to balance German superiority by introducing a law lengthening the military service to three years. When Berlin responded with an army bill it immediately ran into difficulties. Conservative aristocrats in the army were reluctant to dilute its social exclusivity by admitting working-class recruits to the ranks, and middle-class candidates to the officer corps. There was also a broader anxiety on the right that direct wealth taxes might be required to pay for the increases. To make matters worse the *Reichstag* was dominated by the Social Democrats, now the largest party after the huge turnout in the January 1912 elections; this made more indirect taxation, which tended to fall disproportionately on the working classes, very difficult. German Social

Democrats, centrists and liberals were not opposed to greater military preparations, however, on the contrary. 'Social Democracy,' the SPD leader, August Bebel, asserted in 1913, 'has always realized that the geographical and political situation of the *Reich* makes a strong defence necessary.'[154] Indeed, with regard to tsarist Russia, their bitter ideological enemy, the Social Democrats and liberals were in many respects more hawkish than the imperial leadership itself. The left–liberal critique also lambasted the '*Dekorationsmilitarismus*' – its alleged obsession with parades and other flim-flam – of the old officer class for its obsolescence; Social Democrats wanted to make war not traditionally, but effectively. The young liberal Gustav Stresemann demanded that 'the German *Reich* should be outwardly great, and free at home; that is the objective we are fighting for'.[155] In June 1913, the German army increases, funded by progressive direct taxation, went through the *Reichstag*. The 'creeping parliamentarization' of Germany was going hand in hand with its preparation for war.

There was one crucial deadlock, however, which no amount of cooperation at national level could break. Imperial Germany might have been the product of the 'wars of unification', but it was by no means a unitary state. It was a federation in which extensive cultural, educational and – above all – fiscal powers were devolved to the individual states. The Prussian parliament, which represented some two thirds of the population of the empire, could be relied on to vote the direct taxes to pay for the army but in Bavaria, Württemberg and Baden the position was much less clear. This placed an artificially low ceiling on the sums which imperial Germany – a very rich country – could spend on armaments, and explains why less well-off but more centralized polities such as France and Russia could spend a much larger sum in relative terms, and in the Russian case in absolute figures as well. German statesmen and planners were well aware of the problem, which left their poorer rivals pulling ahead in the arms race. The paradoxical effect of all this was to make imperial Germany more likely to go to war, not because she was spending too much on armaments, but because she was able to spend so little.[156]

The tsarist government was also trying to integrate Russian society into the great national project, albeit less successfully. To be sure, the *Duma* was an enthusiastic supporter of the 'historic mission', and supported more defence spending, at least in principle. The problem was that the *Duma*, which was elected on a narrow property franchise, was violently opposed to the progressive direct taxation necessary to pay for the military increases. Only 7 per cent of taxes were directly levied, compared to 30 per cent in Britain. At the same time, many parliamentarians were arguing that the government should involve the middle classes, if not the peasant masses and the workers, in foreign policy. To Guchkov, indeed, Russian greatness and the survival of the bourgeoisie were linked. The only way forward, he argued in November 1913, was to marshal 'those circles and groups of the population whose political faith lies primarily in Russia's role as a great power'.[157] By the beginning of 1914, therefore, Russia had reached an impasse. The political nation demanded a more active foreign policy, but refused to give the executive the means to pay for it; the government wanted to raise taxation to fund armaments but would not countenance the political reforms which would have persuaded the *Duma* to agree to it. A successful war might save the tsarist regime, but failure would surely destroy it.

Britain's domestic deadlock was of a different nature. Ever since the 1910 elections, the Liberal government had been dependent on the Irish Parliamentary Party for a majority in the House of Commons. The Irish were worth conciliating not just out of political opportunism, but also because their cooperation in any forthcoming European conflict was highly desirable. Their leader, John Redmond, was a keen imperialist, who wished for nothing more than self-government and participation in the empire on equal terms, with defence and foreign policy remaining firmly under the control of Westminster. In 1912, the Third Home Rule Bill was duly passed, and looked set to come into force two years later after the Lords veto had lapsed. The measure provoked furious resistance among Irish Unionists, and in 1912 Northern Protestants signed the Ulster Covenant pledging to oppose Home Rule by force of arms if necessary. At the beginning of 1913, they founded the Ulster Volunteer Force; the nationalists responded by setting up their own paramilitary formations. Both sides imported arms from Germany. British officers in Ireland, egged on by Sir Henry Wilson, announced that they would not help the civil power to enforce Home Rule. By the beginning of 1914, Britain was on the verge of civil war. The potential strategic implications of this were clear: Irish nationalists had never hesitated to intrigue with Britain's enemies in time of war, and even the 'loyalists' suggested that if the king was not 'loyal' the Kaiser would be.

The national question posed a serious threat to most of the European great powers, but it was of existential importance to the socialists. Their strategy against a European war rested on the solidarity of the proletariat across borders as expressed in the concept of the 'general strike', by which workers would paralyse the rival capitalist war machines. Nationalism was a mortal challenge to this approach, but while some dismissed the phenomenon as a form of 'false consciousness', others were more open to its 'progressive' potential, particularly where class differentiation was not far advanced. Thus the Austrian Otto Bauer, the leading socialist expert on nationalism, argued that personal and cultural autonomy were necessary, but that the state would have to be a unitary organization for all its citizens on an equal basis. A young Bolshevik later known as Stalin, on the other hand, wrote in his 'The national question and social democracy' (1913) that nationalities should have the right of 'self-determination up to the point of secession',[158] though they should not be allowed to weaken any state they remained a part of through demands for self-government or other special rights. This tension between class and nationality was to run through socialist and later communist geopolitics to the end of the century.

Meanwhile, the implications of the Moroccan and Mexican crises continued to reverberate in Europe and across the Atlantic. In October 1912, the Balkan League attacked the Ottoman Empire, bringing the Porte to its knees within two months. The Treaty of London, which formally concluded the First Balkan War in May 1913, marked the end of the Ottoman Empire in Europe, now reduced to a tiny toehold just outside Constantinople. In Mexico, meanwhile, the democratic reformer Francisco Madero was murdered in February 1913 and replaced by General Victoriano Huerta, who soon enjoyed close German support. To President Woodrow Wilson, this posed both a strategic and an ideological challenge. In late November 1913, he sent a circular note to the great powers announcing that 'Usurpations like that of General Huerta menace the peace and development of America as nothing else could', by making 'the development of ordered self-government impossible'.[159] Above all, Washington was determined to prevent the growth of German influence on her southern flank, epitomized by the unilateral dispatch of German cruisers to protect her nationals. The United States imposed an arms embargo on Huerta's forces, in which Britain participated. Only Germany refused to abide by the measure, providing the

Mexican military dictator with diplomatic, moral and even some logistical support.

The questions of how the space created by the collapse of the Mexican Republic and the Ottoman Empire should be filled came to the boil simultaneously in early 1914. For Turkey, defeat in the Balkan Wars proved traumatic. It lost 80 per cent of its European lands and 16 per cent of its total population (4 million); about 400,000 refugees crowded into Anatolia. Worse still, Constantinople was now dangerously exposed to attack and there were real fears for the integrity of the Ottoman heartland, Anatolia, where about one fifth of the population was non-Muslim. If the same principles were applied there as in the Balkans there would soon be nothing left of the empire. The war finally destroyed the traditional reliance on the great powers. Britain and France, now preoccupied with keeping Russia locked into the containment of Germany, had long since abandoned the defence of Constantinople. The Ottoman Empire had played by the rules of the international community, only to be told by the great powers that it must capitulate to the demands of the Balkan nationalists. 'We must now fully recognize that our honour and our people's integrity cannot be preserved by those old books of international law,' one Turkish journal remarked in mid-October 1912, 'but only by war.'[160] Putting Turkey back on the European map would require a new and more reliable great-power ally, and that could only be Germany.

In Serbia, the Balkan Wars also led to a strategic redirection. The Belgrade security apparatus, together with the clandestine nationalist 'Black Hand' organization, began to plan how a confrontation with Austria-Hungary, with Russian support, could be engineered. The Tsarist Empire supported the Serbian campaign because it regarded Austria-Hungary, and its sponsor, Germany, as the ultimate obstacle to the realization of Russia's 'historic mission' at the Straits. There was now, moreover, a pressing need for pre-emptive action before German penetration of the Ottoman Empire became irreversible and Turkish military preparations were complete. For this reason, the Russians reacted violently to the announcement in late 1913 that the German General Liman von Sanders was to command the garrison at the Bosphorus. The foreign minister, Sergei Sazonov, now demanded a 'programme of action' to ensure a 'suitable solution of the historic problem of the Straits'; detailed plans for the seizure of the Straits by *coup de main* were drawn up. He also warned that 'it should not be assumed that our operations against the Straits could proceed without a European war'.[161] The Austrians, and particularly the Germans, would have to be subdued first. 'The shortest and safest operational route to Constantinople,' the Russian Quartermaster-General Yuri Danilov argued, 'runs through Vienna . . . and Berlin.'[162] Berlin remained the roadblock on the path to Constantinople.

The crises which had been building on both sides of the Atlantic suddenly erupted in the late spring and summer of 1914. When President Wilson heard that the Huerta regime in Mexico was about take delivery of a consignment of German arms at Veracruz he ordered the occupation of the port. The capture of the city in late April provoked a Mexican nationalist backlash against the United States. It was not Wilson's intention, however, to occupy any part of Mexico permanently; this would have met stiff resistance from anti-imperialists and Southern whites at home. Nor, on the other hand, could he simply withdraw and allow the vacuum to be filled by a German-backed repressive regime. The solution to this ideological and strategic dilemma, Wilson believed, was democratization. 'They say the Mexicans are not fitted for self-government,' he wrote in a newspaper article of May 1914, 'and to this I reply that, when properly directed, there is no people not fitted for self-government.'[163] Within a few months, Huerta had been ousted and the leader of the Constitutionalists, Venustiano Carranza, was installed as president. US troops withdrew not long afterwards. It later turned out that the weapons were in fact from an American manufacturer and had merely been routed through Hamburg to avoid the embargo, but the incident reinforced US fears of a German presence on her southern flank.

In late June 1914, Archduke Franz Ferdinand, who was expected soon to succeed the ailing emperor Franz Joseph, was assassinated in the Bosnian capital, Sarajevo, by agents of the Black Hand, in an operation planned in Belgrade, almost certainly with the knowledge of senior members of the Serbian government, and very possibly with Russian support as well. To Vienna, the murder was both a challenge and an opportunity.[164] The Habsburg heir to the throne had been murdered by terrorists sponsored by the security apparatus of a neighbouring state. Failure to respond would simply encourage further attacks, and would amount, as

Count Leopold Berchtold, the Austro-Hungarian foreign minister, put it, to a 'renunciation of our great power position'.[165] Serbia would have to be severely punished, and prevented from launching future provocations. The resulting stiff ultimatum, which one contemporary observer described as the most formidable document ever addressed from one sovereign state to another, was designed to do just that. It was undoubtedly a challenge to Serbian independence, and reflected the Austrians' view that past behaviour had shown the sovereignty of Belgrade to be incompatible with regional stability and their own security. The Austro-Hungarians were also pursuing a much broader agenda. Berchtold was determined to 'use the horrible deed of Sarajevo for a military clearing up of [the] impossible relationship' with her southern neighbour.[166] In short, a strike against Serbia would break the ring of encirclement which had been tightening around the monarchy over the past few years.[167]

Germany was determined to back her ally to the hilt. An Austrian collapse would leave her totally isolated against the Entente and expose her hitherto secure southern flank. The crisis was also a welcome opportunity to prise open the Franco-Russian stranglehold. If St Petersburg failed to back Serbia, or better still failed to secure Anglo-French support, then she would suffer a humiliation even greater than during the Bosnian crisis with possibly fatal consequences for the Entente. If Russia did come to Serbia's aid, then Germany was willing to risk war on the grounds that it was in any case inevitable under much less favourable conditions further down the line. It was, as the Kaiser argued in early July, 'now or never ... The Serbs must be dealt with and quickly.' Even the generally moderate Bethmann now favoured preventive action because, as he warned around the time, 'The future belongs to Russia which grows and grows and becomes an even greater nightmare to us.'[168] Whatever happened, the Moroccan fiascos had shown that Germany must not fight without Austria-Hungary at her side. Moreover, German public opinion, especially the sceptical Social Democrats, would have to be brought on board. With this in mind, Germany committed herself to support Austria-Hungary unconditionally, hoping that war could be localized but taking a 'calculated risk' that it could not.

All this made confrontation between Austria and Serbia highly likely, and a European crisis inevitable, but the conflict only turned into a general conflagration as a result of Russian actions. It was St Petersburg which took the first irrevocable steps towards military action between the great powers. This was partly because it could not afford another Bosnian crisis: Sazonov warned that 'Russia [would] never forgive the Tsar' if he surrendered to the Germans and 'heaped shame on the good name of the Russian people'.[169] For this reason, Belgrade would have to be backed. The crisis was also a chance, however, to pursue the 'historic mission' at the Straits, by locking Britain and France into a general war to reduce German power and thus clear the way for an advance to Constantinople. France quickly signalled its willingness to support Russia, believing it had no other way of containing Germany and avoiding isolation; Britain equivocated, still hoping that the war could be localized. On 28 July, the Habsburg monarchy declared war on Serbia. A day later Russia announced partial mobilization, against Austria only, and two days after that general mobilization, against Germany as well.

St Petersburg had thus taken the first fatal step after which the logic of 'war by timetable' played itself out. Russian mobilization threatened the premise on which the Schlieffen Plan was based. Germany now had to mobilize immediately in order not to find herself caught in the Franco-Russian vice and to exploit her superior railway network to eliminate one of her rivals before the other arrived on the scene. On 1 August, Germany ordered general mobilization and declared war on Russia; this provoked a French mobilization, as the Russians had expected. This in turn forced Germany to attack France, and on 2 August she demanded free passage through Belgium; a day later, she declared war on France and a day after that German troops invaded Belgium as they began to execute the Schlieffen Plan. In Britain, Sir Edward Grey spent anxious weeks wondering whether the private military promises to France, which went well beyond the formal *Entente* treaty obligations, would be honoured by parliament. Making 'a bargain with Germany at the expense of France', he warned, 'would be a disgrace from which the good name of this country would never recover'.[170] The issue was decided, in any case, by the violation of Belgium neutrality, which London was pledged to protect. On 5 August, the British Empire declared a state of hostilities with Germany. *Pace* Cobden, and his liberal pacifist follower Norman Angell, who had famously argued in the *Great Illusion* (1913) that commercial links made war impossible, economic interdependence had failed to keep the peace.[171] Investors and bankers despaired. Europe was at war.

Germany and Austria-Hungary took up arms in order to escape

decades of worsening 'encirclement'. Berchtold spoke of the need 'to weaken Russia lastingly'.[172] In September 1914, no doubt rendered expansive by initial German military successes, Bethmann demanded 'security for the German Reich in west and east for all imaginable time. For this purpose France must be so weakened as to make her revival as a great power impossible for all time. Russia must be thrust back as far as possible from Germany's eastern frontier and her domination over the non-Russian vassal peoples broken.' To this end, Belgium must be turned into a 'vassal state', Holland must be made 'dependent', while *Mitteleuropa* was to be a single economic space under German tutelage. In other words, European geopolitics should be completely reordered so as to guarantee total German security in perpetuity.[173] Britain, France and Russia, on the other hand, went to war to contain Germany. 'Our primordial objective is the destruction of German power,' the French ambassador to St Petersburg, Maurice Paléologue, said.[174] This was because he wanted to eliminate the last remaining great-power block to the realization of Russia's 'historic mission' at Constantinople. By the London Treaty in March 1915, Britain and France formally committed themselves to the Russian annexation of the Straits, the Sea of Marmara and the islands of Imbros and Tenedos, which formed Aegean outworks of the Dardanelles. They did so because they were determined to lock St Petersburg into the war against Germany, which the British Foreign Secretary, Sir Edward Grey, called 'the issue . . . on which all other issues depend'. Failure to do so, the French minister for foreign affairs warned, would risk 'throwing' the tsar 'into the arms of Germany'.[175]

The outcome of this struggle was not predetermined. Defence spending and military establishments in 1914, which reflected pre-war decisions rather than underlying strength, give a misleading sense of the actual balance of forces. In 1913, Britain, France and Russia spent in total more than twice as much on armaments than Germany and Austria-Hungary. With regard to raw industrial potential, the Triple Entente also had the edge over the central powers, but far from a decisive one. In terms of GNP, where Germany's was not much bigger than Britain's, while that of Austria-Hungary lagged behind France and Russia, the disparity was admittedly greater.[176] In terms of population, the gulf was greater still: the combined population of the three Entente powers was about twice that of the central powers.[177] Germany, however, had the more effective army to begin with. It swept through

Belgium more or less as efficiently as Schlieffen had intended; the French attacked much less successfully in the south. The 'swing door' would have trapped the French armies but for two things. First, the Russians moved more swiftly than expected into eastern Prussia; they were crushingly defeated by Field Marshall Paul von Hindenburg and General Erich Ludendorff, but the need to contain the tsar had drawn off men desperately needed in the west. Secondly, the German planners had not made sufficient allowance for the British Expeditionary Force, which the Kaiser had dismissed – either on account of its small size or for its assumed fighting qualities – as a 'contemptible little army'. An important part here was played by the Indian contingent, which, as Curzon wrote, 'helped to save the cause both of the Allies and of civilization' in autumn 1914.[178] As a result, the right wing was not strong enough to envelop the Anglo-French armies, and a French counter-attack at the battle of the Marne brought the German advance to a halt. After some further sparring the two sides settled down into trench warfare.[179]

The resulting conflict was not static, nor did it take place in a geopolitical vacuum. As the fronts in Flanders, Picardy and the Vosges solidified, the protagonists sought to outflank the enemy or lever open his position by military and diplomatic means. The main area of confrontation remained the western front, where both sides sought to deliver a decisive blow in a series of costly offensives over the next four years. In the east, the war remained essentially one of movement. These facts dictated the two opposing strategies. The central powers sought to break open the ring of encirclement, and knock at least one of their major enemies out of the war. In November 1914, Turkey entered the war on the German side with a view to pre-empting Russian designs on the Straits and rebuilding her European position. In October 1915, Bulgaria joined the central powers in the hope of reversing her losses during the Second Balkan War. Berlin's attempt to starve out Britain through unrestricted submarine warfare, however, had to be abandoned after loud protests from neutrals, especially the United States. In the east, the Austro-Hungarians made very heavy weather of the Serbs, and soon got into difficulties with the Russians as well. German reinforcements, by contrast, did much better: by the end of 1915 they had eliminated Serbia, the remnants of whose forces withdrew to Corfu. That same year, after suffering a shattering defeat at Gorlice-Tarnów, the Russians were pushed back hundreds of miles, and the school of 'easterners' in the

German high command, led by Ludendorff and Hindenburg, argued that a decisive offensive there could drive the Russians to the negotiating table, and thus permit resources to be transferred for the final showdown in Flanders. The Chief of Staff, Erich von Falkenhayn, on the other hand, insisted with the support of the Kaiser that the main effort should be made against the British and French on the western front. Here, the Germans mounted a series of massive offensives, culminating in the huge Verdun campaign of 1916, designed as Falkenhayn put it to 'bleed France into seeing sense'[180] and force her to sue for peace.

The Allies were initially no more successful in outflanking the enemy through diplomatic manoeuvre. Japan joined the Entente shortly after the outbreak of war, but despite Bethmann's fears that she would send forces to Europe, Tokyo confined herself to mopping up Germany's Pacific possessions. Italy was a more promising prospect. She was still formally committed to the Triple Alliance, but her territorial ambitions could only be satisfied at Austrian expense. Moreover, Italy wanted to use the opportunity to secure what her prime minister, Antonio Salandra, defined as 'frontiers on land no longer open to annexation'. This involved a claim to the South Tyrol, Trieste and Dalmatia, to contain the Austrians north of the Alps and shut the Russians out of the Mediterranean as much as possible. In some of these territories, Italians were in a minority. When the Allies guaranteed these aims at the Treaty of London in April 1915, Italy joined the war shortly afterwards. In theory, this exposed the soft underbelly of the central powers. The overall military balance hardly shifted, however. Within a very short period of time the Italians too were bogged down in trench warfare along their northern border. The next diplomatic coup, which was the entry of Romania into the war against Austria-Hungary in the hope of annexing Transylvania, also failed to turn the tide. After a lightning German campaign, Romanian forces were soundly beaten in the summer of 1916 and forced to withdraw from virtually their entire country.

Militarily, the Entente powers sought to tighten the ring of encirclement around Germany and Austria-Hungary, to crush them by force of numbers or starve them out through a close maritime blockade.[181] The allied powers not only surrounded Germany and Austria-Hungary, but thanks to their colonial empires they also enveloped the Ottomans. Meanwhile, the British and French sought to wear down the enemy through constant pressure on the western front, which the Allied high command agreed should be the principal theatre of operations. Indeed, the First Lord of the Admiralty, Winston Churchill, conceived his ill-fated campaign to capture the Dardanelles in 1914–15 not just as a device to knock Turkey out of the war, and clear a path to southern Russia, but primarily to prevent Germany from constructing a submarine base at Constantinople, to stop her from expanding into the Middle East, and as a dummy run for more important operations against Germany in the Baltic and North Sea.[182] The heavy casualties among Australian and New Zealand troops at Gallipoli caused tensions between their publics and the metropolis. All the while, Britain and France launched a string of offensives in the west, designed as Marshal Joffre wrote in his Chantilly Memorandum in December 1915 to ensure 'the destruction of the German and Austrian armies', but the main target was Germany. Far from launching a mindless series of massed assaults, the Allies pursued a coherent multi-front campaign against the central powers from the start.[183] These offensives reached a peak in July–September 1916 with the huge British attack along the Somme. The desired breakthrough was not achieved, but the rate of attrition began to wear down the Germans.[184]

Both sides also sought to undermine their enemy at home or in their imperial possessions. 'Our consuls in Turkey and India,' the Kaiser remarked on the eve of war, 'must inflame the whole Mohammedan world against this hateful, lying, conscienceless people of hagglers.'[185] The US ambassador to Constantinople, Lewis Einstein, described this relationship – spearheaded by the German-Jewish diplomat Max von Oppenheim – as '*Deutschland über Allah*'. In tandem with these efforts, German propagandists sought to excite Hindu nationalism against the British in India, though with little success.[186] Berlin also sponsored Irish nationalists, sending arms to support an insurrection against British rule at Easter in 1916. At the same time, Germany and Austria-Hungary promoted the political and ethnic fragmentation of the Tsarist Empire by supporting the Union for the Liberation of the Ukraine, agreeing to the creation of a Polish state – albeit under German tutelage – in August 1916, and generally backing subversive movements in Russia.[187] 'Victory and the first place in the world is ours,' one German statesman argued, 'if we succeed in revolutionizing Russia in time and thus splitting the coalition.'[188]

On the far side of the Atlantic, Germany sought to tie down the United States through a programme of subversion and infiltration. A covert operation was launched to plant bombs in factories and ships supplying arms to the Allied war effort. Very little damage was actually done by these agents, but their discovery did serious harm to German–US relations. A more promising field was Mexico, where civil unrest had broken out again shortly after US troops had withdrawn in 1914. Here Berlin sought to deny the British navy access to vital supplies of Mexican oil. The main German aim, however, was to suck the United States into the Mexican morass. 'It would be highly desirable,' the German foreign minister, Gottlieb von Jagow, stressed, 'for America to become involved in a war and be diverted from Europe, where it is clearly more sympathetic to England.'[189] In early March 1916 the Mexican warlord 'Pancho' Villa attacked the town of Columbus in New Mexico, not necessarily at the direct instigation of Germany but certainly with her approval.

The Entente, for its part, supported separatist elements in the Habsburg monarchy.[190] In May 1915, Britain sponsored the creation of the Yugoslav Committee in London, designed to rally Slovenes, Croats and Serbs behind the establishment of a new South Slav state at Vienna's expense. The Croat leader, Frano Supilo, explained that without such a framework 'Italy would gobble us up like macaroni.'[191] The British also encouraged Czech and Slovak nationalists to combine against German domination under the leadership of the charismatic T. G. Masaryk. In the Middle East, Britain entered into negotiations with Arabs and other peoples seeking to throw off the Ottoman yoke. The Armenian card seemed particularly promising, because if a separate state was established in 'historical Armenia' (which was much larger than the independent state of the same name today) it would cut the Berlin–Baghdad railway, link up with the Russians in the north and perhaps with the British marching up from Egypt, hammering another rivet into the ring of encirclement around Turkey and the central powers. In early 1916, the Sherif of Mecca, Hussein bin Ali, and Sir Henry McMahon, the British high commissioner in Egypt, corresponded about the creation of an independent Arab state. Later that year, the French and British concluded the Sykes–Picot agreement which divided the Middle East into a British sphere of influence in Palestine and Mesopotamia and a French one in Greater Syria. But by the end of 1916 none of these promising endeavours had decided the war one way or the other.

For the moment, the United States remained neutral, but she followed events in Europe, especially German behaviour, very closely.[192] Washington tilted strongly towards the Entente, allowing her to profit from their greater creditworthiness by drawing on American financial and industrial resources.[193] She almost came to blows with Germany over her unrestricted submarine warfare, especially after the sinking of the passenger liner *Lusitania*. She also remained deeply concerned about challenges to hemispheric stability. As early as November 1914, Wilson's confidant Colonel (sic) Edward House fretted that Brazil was 'the main object of Germany's desires', and that the Kaiser no longer regarded the Monroe Doctrine as applicable below the equator.[194] But the main problem was Mexico. Washington was well aware that Berlin, as Secretary of State Robert Lansing put in October 1915, wanted 'to keep up the turmoil [there] until the United States is forced to intervene', and hoped to avoid doing so as long as possible. 'Our . . . relations with Germany,' he continued, 'must be our first consideration; and all our intercourse with Mexico must be regulated accordingly.'[195] After Villa's raid on Columbus, however, Wilson was forced to respond. In late March 1916, a punitive expedition under General Pershing crossed the border in pursuit. It failed to apprehend Villa, caused widespread Mexican outrage and was withdrawn without achieving its objectives. The United States, having forsworn annexation, was now condemned to perpetual intervention in Latin America. In all these cases, the aim was not only to reduce instability in America's backyard but also the perennial imperative to prevent another power from establishing a presence there and thus threatening the Union on its southern flank.

The war dominated European domestic politics. At first, it served to heal internal rifts. In Austria-Hungary, the government used the opportunity to suspend parliament altogether. Irish Home Rulers and Unionists alike went off to fight the Germans rather than each other. The Conservatives rallied to support the Liberal government's war effort, not so much in order to protect Belgium as to prevent France from being crushed by Germany and thus the destruction of the whole European balance.[196] On the left, the Independent Labour Party reconciled support for the war, opposition to capitalism and suspicion of Germany through hatred of 'Kruppism'.[197] In France, left and right joined to form the '*Union Sacrée*' to fight the invader. Russian public opinion also rallied around the tsar, now that he had decided to take on the Teuton and fight to realize the 'historic mission' at the Straits. The *Duma* voted the necessary taxes and war credits. In Germany, the socialists signed up to the *Burgfrieden* – 'peace within the fortress' – for the duration of hostilities; the Kaiser proclaimed that he no longer recognized 'any parties, only Germans'. All of the major parliamentary parties voted their governments the necessary credits to wage war in 1914; without them, the conflict would have ground to a halt very quickly, or resulted in the defeat of the state where the consensus had broken down. The principal reason why German and French socialists fell into line was not nationalist false consciousness, but a fear that failure to do so would put them at the mercy of tsarist despotism or the Kaiser's absolutism. In these circumstances, the Second International's concept of a general strike to strangle an imperialist war at birth and start the revolution never got off the ground.

The conduct of the war dominated French and British high politics throughout 1915–16.[198] At issue was the appointment of military commanders, the extraction of resources and the question of whether some new innovative strategy – such as the Dardanelles campaign – could shorten the war, or whether, as the generals insisted and most politicians reluctantly agreed, the key to victory was a crushing blow against Germany on the western front. In May 1915, the 'shell crisis', a shortage of artillery ordnance, so damaged the prime minister, Herbert Asquith, that he was forced to bring in senior Conservatives to form a coalition government dedicated to prosecuting the war more effectively. Five months later it was the turn of René Viviani's French cabinet, which had lost the confidence of the National Assembly for its failure to secure a quick victory. All the while, the French parliament encroached more and more on the running of the war effort, so that in June 1916 the delegate André Maginot, crippled at Verdun, stood up in a secret session to excoriate the 'unpreparedness and inertia of the High Command'.[199] And, in December 1916, Asquith's continued failure to win the war brought in the Liberal radical Lloyd George as the man who could deliver the 'knock-out blow' to end the war.[200] Of the two powers, Britain proved better able to combine an intense war effort with openness and parliamentary supremacy. For example, the failure at Gallipoli effectively destroyed Churchill's career for the time being, and led parliament to set up a committee of inquiry in mid-1916. Even at the height of a global conflict, therefore, British politics maintained its capacity for public strategic critique.

In America, opinion on the war was deeply divided. The internationalist, largely east coast elite – such as the Republican leader, Henry Cabot Lodge – sympathized with the western allies ideologically and regarded Germany as a threat to the balance of power. They regularly charged that Wilson had left the nation 'defenceless' before German aggression, demanded inquiries into military preparedness and supported the lobbying efforts of the pro-Entente National Security League. The US Navy Act, which authorized a huge increase in naval expenditure in 1916, reflected a sense of alarm about German intentions. In the first two years of the war, several thousand Americans volunteered for service in Europe, most of them in British or French formations.[201] By contrast, the German-American lobby tended to sympathize with the central powers. So did most American Jews, largely because of Russia's record of anti-semitism. Most Americans, however, were determined not to be sucked into a European conflict, and Woodrow Wilson won re-election in 1916 on a promise to maintain US neutrality.

The war also had a profound effect on societies and economies. The main issue confronting the belligerents from 1914 was how best to extract the human and economic resources available to them.[202] Conscription was already in place in France, Germany, Austria-Hungary and the Tsarist Empire, but Britain fought the opening stages of the conflict with an all-volunteer army.[203] This state of affairs could not be sustained, and was condemned by Liberals – many of them social radicals – as well as Conservatives. In the summer of 1915, the Manifesto for National Service demanded that 'every fit man, whatever his position in life, must be made available, as and when his country calls for him'. In mid-1916 conscription was finally introduced in Britain; politically sensitive Ireland was exempted, for the time being at least. Lloyd George supported the bill on the basis that 'every great democracy which has been challenged, which has had its liberties menaced, has defended itself by resort to compulsion'.[204]

Few European states went to war expecting a short contest, but even so governments were soon overwhelmed by the problems of supply. Britain's 'shell crisis' was only resolved by the creation of the Ministry of Munitions, headed by Lloyd George. A year later, the French government set up state consortia to run the war economy more efficiently, and eventually not only took over the supply of raw materials but also set prices and regulated capital movements; one of these thrusting young bureaucrats was Jean Monnet. All across Europe, principles of free capitalism gave away to the *dirigisme* and corporatism which the management of the war effort demanded. The increase in state power, even in formerly 'liberal' polities such as Britain, was enormous. It was Germany, however, under the capable leadership of Walther Rathenau, which made the transition most effectively.[205] In 1916, the Hindenburg Programme mobilized the entire society for war: in December of that year the 'Law for patriotic auxiliary service' recruited all men between the ages of seventeen and sixty not already serving as workers or agricultural labourers. This 'war communism' ensured that the *Reich* was able to go on fighting even though it was outnumbered, surrounded and cut off from global sources of raw materials and foodstuffs.

In one respect, however, the Entente powers had a head start. France was able to bring the 50 million inhabitants in her colonial empire to bear; eventually about half a million of them served on the western front against Germany or in the Middle East against Turkey.[206] Britain was even more successful in playing the imperial card. About 400,000 men served in the Canadian Expeditionary Force, mainly on the western front. Hundreds of thousands also came from Australia and New Zealand; the Australian prime minister undertook to support the mother country 'to the last man and the last shilling'.[207] More than 70,000 South African whites, the vast majority English-speaking, and about 40,000 blacks were deployed in Europe. About a million Indians served beyond the subcontinent, many on the main European battlefronts. Instead of the Germans 'setting the east ablaze' against Britain, they found themselves fighting Asians and other imperial troops on the battlefields of Flanders. The economic value of the imperial contribution was also enormous. By the end of 1916, Canada alone was producing about a quarter of Britain's total munitions needs and, with the partial exception of South Africa, the entire imperial war effort was paid from local revenue or loans.[208] The struggle against German domination of the continent was thus the dominant issue not merely in Europe but across much of the globe as well.

Confronted by what it called a 'world of enemies', Imperial Germany looked to its salvation in mobilizing new resources closer to home. In effect, as Falkenhayn stated brutally, this meant that Austria-Hungary would 'have to give up her sovereignty' and become, to quote Jagow, 'merely a Germanic *Ostmark*'.[209] Vienna, wracked by nationalist subversion on the peripheries and crucified by the poor performance of its armies, had no choice but to comply. The Magyar elite went along with this, because, as the Hungarian prime minister, István Tisza, put it in April 1915, 'Hungary can serve as a bulwark against the Slav tide that is threatening the western coast of the Adriatic only if it is united with Austria . . . Hungary's fate is linked to the existence of Austria-Hungary as a Great Power.'[210] By early September 1916, Austria-Hungary had agreed to a unified high command with Germany under Hindenburg, and thus effectively ceased to exist as an independent state. At around the same time, the German liberal politician Friedrich Naumann published his hugely influential tract *Mitteleuropa*, a plea for Berlin to organize the Danubian Basin under its control to sit out encirclement. Germany would only be secure, in other words, if it controlled the demographic and industrial potential of central Europe.

The pressures of war accentuated the paranoid strain in European domestic politics. States and publics saw enemies around every corner; censorship and police surveillance became the norm even in the western democracies. In Britain, mobs smashed shop-windows with Germanic names; nearly 30,000 'aliens' were interned. Patriotic feminists constructed the Germans as 'masculine', and therefore predatory.[211] The monarchy, too, felt the heat and was prevailed upon to rename itself the 'House of Windsor'. The Kaiser remarked on hearing the news that the British should now really re-title Shakespeare's play the 'Merry Wives of Saxe-Coburg Gotha'. An attempt to introduce identity cards, however, failed due to widespread opposition. Spy-fever also gripped France, where German agents were believed to be everywhere, leading to the internment of thousands of people, and the Tsarist Empire, where riots against 'foreigners' became frequent. Paranoia was taken to extremes with regard to the Jews. In 1916 nationalist anti-semites in Germany insisted on an official census to establish whether or not Jews were serving at the front in appropriate numbers, or skulking in the rear and indulging in war profiteering, as their detractors claimed. The tsarist authorities, convinced that the Jews of the Pale were all German agents, encouraged Ukrainian pogroms throughout the war, and even deported thousands of Galician Jews as a potential security risk.[212] Though brutal, the Jewish experience was dwarfed by the treatment meted out to the Armenians by the Ottomans. Convinced that they were in cahoots with the Russian forces advancing steadily through the Caucasus, and determined to rid themselves of a long-running ethnic sore, the Turkish authorities embarked on a systematic programme of deportation and killing.[213]

In other ways, however, the demands of war had a profoundly emancipatory effect. Working-class women soon found paid work in the burgeoning munitions factories, while middle-class and aristocratic women threw themselves into various voluntary activities or nursing. All across Europe, millions of women felt empowered by the fact that their country now needed them. They rejected the claims of a small minority that conscription should be opposed, and that the international women's movement should stick to its largely pacifist pre-war stance. 'Could any woman face the possibility,' the veteran Suffragist Emmeline Pankhurst asked, 'of the affairs of the country being settled by conscientious objectors, passive resisters and shirkers.'[214] She and the majority who thought like her believed that the citizenship they demanded also implied patriotic duties. More generally, the pressures of war accelerated welfarist tendencies. This was most obviously the case in France, where wages were linked not only to productivity but also to the number of dependants. These pro-family and pro-natalist policies were designed not only to keep the peace but to maintain the birth rate at a time of severe national blood-letting. The principle of equal pay for equal work was thus violated for reasons which had nothing to do with gender politics and everything to do with national security imperatives.[215]

The social and political challenge of the war was most keenly felt among the central and eastern European powers. 'The old class and caste system has had its day,' Admiral Tirpitz predicted shortly after the outbreak of hostilities, 'win or lose, we will end up with pure democracy.'[216] Though Imperial Germany remained a deeply stratified society throughout,[217] many cultural and social boundaries were transgressed in the course of the conflict. The officer corps became less exclusive as lower-middle-class and even working-class men filled the gaps left by dead aristocrats. More pressing still was the question of political participation. At the end of 1916, the National Liberals, Centre Party and Social Democrats came together to form the Constitutional and Budget Committees. Their aim was to articulate a parliamentary voice in foreign and strategic policy, and thus assert some sort of control over the life and death struggle in which they were engaged.[218] These men were no pacifists: if the annexations the right-wing parties demanded were realistic, and necessary for German security, then they would support them. If unrestricted submarine warfare was required to bring England to her knees, and get the blockade off their backs, so be it. Popular geopolitics in Germany as elsewhere tended to be more robust than that of the elites, but in return it demanded the abolition of the Three-Class Electoral Law in Prussia and its replacement by universal suffrage, in order to mobilize the entire people against the Entente. This was the primacy of foreign policy taken to its logical conclusion. 'Only he who sees internal politics from the perspective of its inevitable arrangement according to the needs of foreign policy,' Max Weber warned Prussian conservatives, 'is a politician. Those who do not like the "democratic" consequences which follow from this should do without the great-power policy for which they are required.'

In Russia, the constitutionalists also used the war to stake a claim to greater political participation. From early February 1915 the *Duma* won the right to meet in secret session on the budget and hear a report from the war minister. Parliamentary pressure increased with news of defeats. In early June 1915, the Conference of Kadets called for a 'government possessing the confidence of the public',[219] and not long after the war minister and interior minister were replaced by figures more acceptable to the *Duma*. The demand for a 'government of public confidence', and for a change in the army high command, was repeated in the autumn of 1915 after the Kadets and Octobrists united to form the Progressive Bloc, which commanded a majority in the *Duma*. Instead, the tsar prorogued the *Duma* and rather than appoint a new supreme commander, he took over the running of the war himself. By linking the standing of the dynasty so closely to the fortunes of the war, the tsar was pursuing a highly risky strategy. Fresh defeats in the summer of 1916 led to popular and parliamentary charges that the autocracy was failing to defend the national interest. 'Is this stupidity or treason?'[220] Miliukov asked the *Duma* in mid-November after the latest round of military fiascos. Rather like the dying days of the French *ancien régime*, this critique focused on the alleged corruption of the royal family, as evidenced by the sinister influence of the Russian monk Rasputin, confidant to the tsar and especially to his wife, and its allegedly German sympathies. Right at the end of December 1916 patriotic conspirators murdered Rasputin. It was clear that if the next year did not bring better news from the front, the autocracy's days would be numbered.

As 1916 drew to a close, therefore, it was still too early to tell which of the great powers were the winners and losers of the huge transformations which roiled Europe and the world after American and German unification. These two events had dominated grand strategy and domestic politics in France, Russia and Great Britain, inspired more popular, press and parliamentary participation even in autocratic societies, drove colonial expansion and powered the process of imperial reorganization in the British Empire. After two years of war, it appeared as if the central powers and the Triple Entente were more or less evenly matched; the massed power at the heart of the continent was too great to be defeated by the combined force of the British, French and Tsarist Empires, and yet it was not strong enough to prevail either. It would take a new European geopolitics, a confrontation between the two powers that had unified in the 1860s, to break the deadlock.

6

Utopias, 1917–44

[Civilization] will be swept aside by the consuming fire of Bolshevism. Out of this terrible devastation new governments will arise . . . and the first people to come to their senses . . . will be the Germans . . . With their power of efficient organization backed by the almost endless resources of Russia, Germany will dominate Russia, and, if she unites with Japan, Asia will be subject to her will.

Robert Lansing, US Secretary of State, 1919[1]

[I]f we would take the long view, must we not still reckon with the possibility that a large part of the Great [Eurasian] Continent might some day be united under a single sway, and that an invincible sea-power might be based upon it? . . . Ought we not to recognise that that is the great ultimate threat to the world's liberty so far as strategy is concerned, and to provide against it in our new political system?

Sir Halford Mackinder, 1919[2]

Whoever controls Europe will thereby seize the leadership of the world. It must therefore remain the objective of our struggle to create a unified Europe, but Europe can only be given a coherent structure through Germany.

Adolf Hitler, 1943[3]

The year 1917 marked a watershed in European and global geopolitics, beginning with the Russian Revolution, followed by the American entry into the world war, and finishing with the Balfour Declaration promising the establishment of a Jewish national home in Palestine. Over the next thirty years or so, the geopolitical and domestic consequences of these developments worked themselves out in a period of unprecedented turbulence in Europe and around the world. It was marked by the clash between two unifications, American and German, and three Utopias: democratic, communist and National Socialist. The fulcrum of the struggle was Germany, which Wilson's new international order was designed to contain and convert; which was the main focus of Soviet revolutionary geopolitics; against which the Balfour Declaration was directed; and from where the Nazi challenge later emerged. German power was also the focal point of European internal politics: in the preoccupation of the Weimar Republic with the constraints of Versailles; the central question of containment in France and other European countries; and in the Soviet hopes for revolution in central Europe, which were followed by the urgent need to contain Hitler. For Germany's neighbours, far and near, the key objective remained preventing Germany from falling into hostile hands, while ensuring that she herself did not develop hegemonic ambitions of her own. For the Germans themselves, the question was how to structure their grand strategy and domestic politics to prevent themselves from being crushed by the global great powers, without in turn inviting an overwhelming coalition against them. Both projects failed, with catastrophic consequences.

As the third year of war dawned, Germany strained every nerve – militarily, diplomatically and domestically – to force the issue. In order to starve Britain out, she resumed unrestricted submarine warfare in February 1917. Given the feeble American response to Pancho Villa's raid on New Mexico, Berlin did not fear adverse reaction from Washington. To be on the safe side, though, the German foreign minister, Arthur Zimmermann, sent a telegram promising Mexico the return of Texas, Arizona and New Mexico, if it sided with Berlin in the event of the outbreak of war between the *Reich* and the United States. The navy was instructed to think about ways of supplying arms to the Mexicans. Meanwhile, Germany sought to mobilize all remaining economic resources to prevail against the enemy coalition, no easy task given that she was surrounded on all sides and cut off from her traditional sources of raw materials. Rathenau partially solved this problem by rationalizing the production process to maximize output and minimize the effects of the blockade. There was a limit, however, to what could be achieved by straightforward extraction. It was becoming clear that the *Reich* would only be able to survive against a 'world of enemies' if it could generate increased popular political participation. It was for this reason that the Kaiser's Easter Message of 1917 signalled his intention to repeal the discriminatory Three-Class Electoral Law after the end of the war.

In the British Empire, the need to mobilize ever more manpower to contain Germany forced London to look again at its relationship with the empire. Conscription, which had long been ruled out to avoid inflaming nationalist sentiment, was put back on the agenda in Ireland, and this prospect reopened the wounds left by the suppression of the Easter Rising. As a result, the moderate Home Rule party was increasingly eclipsed by the radical separatist Sinn Féin movement. In most of the empire, by contrast, the price of continued military support was the demand for increased political consultation in the direction of the conflict, and greater political equality more generally. Colonial leaders, outraged at what they believed to be British military incompetence on the western front, called for a voice in grand strategy. The British government bowed to these demands by creating an Imperial War Cabinet in the spring of 1917, promising 'continuous consultation' and an 'adequate voice in foreign policy . . . and foreign relations' for 'autonomous nations of an Imperial Commonwealth' after the end of the conflict. A few months later, the India Secretary, Edwin Montagu, held out to the subcontinent 'the gradual development of self-governing institutions [and] the progressive realization of responsible government' within the British Empire on a vague timetable at some point after the war.[4] The demands of war against Germany, in short, hastened the emergence of political consciousness in Canada, Australia, New Zealand and India; and they profoundly shaped debates in Ireland, where this consciousness was long-established.

In Russia, the autocracy's failure to achieve the promised decisive victory over the Germans strengthened the supporters of greater political participation. Only true parliamentary government, the Kadets and Octobrists argued, could mobilize the whole of Russian society against the enemy. This critique merged with a broader popular paranoia about Jewish- and German-sponsored 'treachery' behind the lines and in high places, especially the royal family with its 'German' consort and her sinister favourite, Rasputin. By the beginning of 1917, therefore, the Romanov dynasty had undergone a loss of legitimacy similar to that of the Bourbon monarchy before 1789. Just as the 'Austrian' Marie Antoinette became the scapegoat for the strategic failures of her cuckolded husband, so was Nicholas's inability to defend the true Russian national interest attributed to the machinations of a courtly clique of 'Germans'. A series of strikes and military mutinies finally brought down the autocracy in late February 1917, bringing to power a ministry under Prince Lvov, with Paul Miliukov as foreign minister, determined to resume the offensive against the Germans at the next available opportunity. The 'first' Russian Revolution, in other words, was a protest not against the war as such, but against the failure of the tsar to prosecute the conflict against Germany more vigorously.

Shortly after this earthquake, the European scene was transformed by developments on the other side of the world. Relations between Germany and the United States were already strained thanks to the resumption of unrestricted submarine warfare. At the end of February, Washington first saw the decoded secret 'Zimmermann Telegram', which had been intercepted by the British intelligence service. American opinion was outraged by the news that Berlin had offered the recovery of Texas, New Mexico and Arizona in exchange for an alliance. Not long after, news of the first sinking of US ships hit the headlines. There was also widespread alarm about the Germans' plans for the integration of *Mitteleuropa* under their leadership, which Wilson claimed was a scheme to 'throw a broad belt of German military power and political control across the very centre of Europe and beyond the Mediterranean into the heart of Asia'.[5] Taken together, these developments convinced many Americans that developments in Europe, particularly the threat of German hegemony, had profound implications for their security in the western hemisphere. They had the potential to threaten not only the commerce of the United States, but its very territorial integrity. The danger could only be contained through direct intervention in the European state system. To stand aside, President Wilson warned, would be to risk a map in which the '[German] black stretched all the way from Hamburg to Baghdad – the bulk of German power inserted into the heart of the world'. In April 1917, the United States declared war on Germany.

In the view of President Wilson, Imperial Germany also represented a profound ideological challenge to American political values. 'The world must be made safe for democracy,' he told Congress in his speech in support of war with Germany. 'Its peace must be planted on the tested foundations of political liberty.'[6] German aggression, he explained, was the product of Wilhelmine despotism: 'German rulers have been able to upset the peace of the world only because the German people . . . were allowed to have no opinion of their own.' It was the belief of the American government that the defence of US democracy at home required its defence abroad. Wilson's aim was not so much to make the 'world safe for democracy', as to make America safer in the world through the promotion of democracy.[7]

By the summer of 1917, therefore, the strategic situation was becoming critical for Germany. The French and British maintained a steady pressure in the west with attacks around Arras, Ypres and Soissons from late May. At around the same time, the Italians started a fresh offensive on the Isonzo against the Austrians. In late June, the new Russian government authorized Brusilov to launch a large-scale attack on the eastern front. Caught between the Russo-Italian pincers, Austria-Hungary began to buckle under the strain. To the south, the British resumed their advance through Palestine and Mesopotamia. The long-term perspective for Berlin was even grimmer, thanks to the expected arrival of American forces in large numbers. A 'peace resolution' of the Centre Party leader, Matthias Erzberger, which forswore annexations, and passed the *Reichstag* with a substantial majority in July 1917, reflected these sober new realities. That same month, Bethmann-Hollweg was forced out and replaced as chancellor by Georg Michaelis. When he in turn lost the confidence of the *Reichstag* in October, Count von Hertling was drafted in as a replacement. The 'creeping constitutionalization' of the *Reich*, visible even before 1914, was rapidly speeding up under the pressure of war.

The German high command quickly regained the initiative. In late October 1917, a joint German–Austrian offensive pulverized the Italian defences at Caporetto and nearly forced Rome to sue for peace. The real coup, however, was landed in the east. 'Russia appeared to be the weakest link in the enemy chain,' the German State Secretary in the foreign office, Richard von Kühlmann, observed. 'The task therefore was gradually to loosen it, and, when possible, to remove it. This was the purpose of the subversive activity we caused to be carried out in Russia behind the front – in the first place promotion of separatist tendencies and support of the Bolsheviks'; regular payments were made to the Bolsheviks in support of this strategy.[8] Lenin, the Bolshevik leader, was conveyed in a sealed train across German territory from Switzerland, via Sweden and Finland, to Russia. His faction eventually gained the upper hand in the debates following the collapse of the costly second Brusilov offensive in July 1917. They predominated in the soldiers' and workers' councils that seized power in October–November promising 'peace and bread'. A fierce debate now broke out in St Petersburg on the future direction of Russian foreign policy. Some still strongly supported the war, or at least opposed a precipitate and disadvantageous peace. In November 1917, the Bolsheviks seized power. The All-Russian Congress of Soviets of Workers', Soldiers', and Peasants' Deputies now passed a 'Decree on peace'. It proposed 'to all belligerent peoples and their governments' immediate negotiations for a 'just and democratic peace . . . without annexations . . . and without indemnities'. The decree also announced the abolition of 'secret diplomacy'.[9] A Russo-German armistice was signed in December 1917. In short, not only did Lenin espouse an ideology originating in Germany, but he brought it to Russia as part of a scheme devised by the German high command to knock her out of the war.

By the end of 1917, therefore, the western allies suddenly found themselves at a disadvantage, not only in Russia but on other fronts as well. After some promising developments in 1917, Allied forces were once more bogged down in the Middle East and on the western front. The Italians needed substantial support just to hold the line. Russian forces were falling back before the Ottomans in the Caucasus.[10] As for the eastern front, once Berlin cut a deal with the Bolsheviks, large numbers of German troops would be transferred for a final showdown in the west. If they arrived before the Americans put in an appearance, the war would be lost. To make matters worse, Germany now controlled the entire resources of eastern and central Europe. The *Reich* was also moving towards still closer integration with Austria-Hungary. Germany, Wilson warned an audience in Baltimore in early April 1918, was trying to dominate the whole of Eurasia.[11] Similarly, the British imperial statesman Lord Milner feared that 'the Central bloc under the hegemony of Germany will control not only Europe and most of Asia but the whole world'.[12]

It was now imperative for the Entente to wrest the initiative back from the central powers. In early November 1917 the British Foreign

Secretary, Arthur Balfour, issued a Declaration promising the creation of a 'Jewish National Home' in Palestine. Regionally, this was conceived of as a pre-emptive strike to prevent the Turks – and their German backers, who were in Palestine in increasing numbers – from cutting the British Empire in half by attacking the Suez Canal. A strategically placed colony of Jewish settlers would guard the approaches to Egypt. More broadly, the Balfour Declaration was a political and ideological bid for the support of Jews world-wide; 'I do not think it is easy to exaggerate the international power of the Jews,' the Foreign Office minister, Robert Cecil, remarked.[13] While Jewish communities had for the most part demonstrated enthusiastic support for their respective national causes, Jews generally tended towards the central powers, partly because of Russian anti-semitism and partly because many Jews, especially those in central and eastern Europe, looked to Germany for the defence of civilized values. Jewish leaders such as Chaim Weizmann routinely suggested that if the Entente failed to provide them with a national home in Palestine, the Kaiser would.[14] One way or the other, it was the British who sought out the Zionists, rather than vice versa. The Balfour Declaration was driven not by concern for what the Entente powers could do for the Jews, but for what world Jewry could do for the struggle against Germany.

Not long after, President Wilson announced his famous 'Fourteen Points' in January 1918. These were designed to prevent the emergence of a German-dominated bloc in Europe, and to establish a new order based on democracy and self-determination, qualified by geopolitics. Point six demanded the 'evacuation of all Russian territory'; point eight called for the evacuation of all French territory by Germany, and the return of Alsace-Lorraine; and point nine requested that the Italian borders be 'readjusted on national lines'. Point ten spoke for the 'autonomous development' of the peoples of Austria-Hungary; it left open, however, whether the empire should not remain united for external purposes to act as a counterweight to Germany. According to point eleven, Romania, Montenegro and Serbia – then under Austro-German occupation – were all to be restored; the last was to receive access to the sea, guaranteed by the great powers. The Arab lands, with the exception of Palestine, were to be granted self-government – but their foreign policy was to be under British control. Point thirteen called for the establishment of an 'independent Polish state', with access to the sea guaranteed by the great powers, containing 'indisputably Polish populations'. Finally, the fourteenth point called for a 'general association of nations' to safeguard world peace and the territorial integrity of states. The driving force behind these demands was not any abstract principle, but a concern to reduce German power in Europe to manageable proportions.

Bold action was also required over Russia. While the Entente powers were strongly opposed to the threat the revolution posed to the liberal capitalist and democratic order, the real issue was how the eastern front could be restored. Far from being determined to stamp out Bolshevism above all else, Balfour announced in April 1918 that 'if the Bolshevik government will cooperate in resisting Germany, it seems necessary to act with them as the *de facto* Russian government'. Two months later, the Chief of the Imperial General Staff, Sir Henry Wilson, warned that if Germany dominated the continent, 'with no preoccupation in Europe, she could concentrate great armies against Egypt or India by her overland routes'.[15] In early July 1918, therefore, the Allied Supreme War Council resolved to intervene militarily against the revolutionaries, primarily in order to pursue the war against Germany more vigorously.

All this sparked a debate among the Russian revolutionaries which went to the heart of the whole revolutionary project.[16] 'If the rising of the peoples of Europe does not crush imperialism,' Leon Trotsky warned, 'we will be crushed . . . that is unquestionable.' According to Marxist theory, the forces of counter-revolution would either cancel each other out – the waves would be, as Lenin put it, 'destined in the end to break on each other' – or else the mature post-capitalist working class would repel them, assisted by revolutions across the world. Reality now intervened. The working classes in western and central Europe did not rise in solidarity, or at least not yet; the revolutionaries were on their own. Moreover, whereas Marx had expected the triumph of communism in an advanced society such as Britain or Germany, the Bolsheviks had seized power in a backward state with a tiny working class, populated largely by peasants.[17] It was a case of revolution in the wrong country. Lenin now conceded that there was no choice for the moment but to 'remain at our post until the arrival of our ally, the international proletariat, for this ally is sure to arrive . . . even though moving much slower than we expected and wished'.

In March 1918, the Bolsheviks concluded a punitive peace treaty at Brest-Litovsk, 'clenching our teeth', as Trotsky later remarked, 'conscious of our weakness'.[18] Huge swathes of Russian territory were surrendered, in return for peace and thus a 'breathing spell', as Lenin put it, to consolidate the revolution at home. Not only, however, did the Germans continue to advance despite Brest-Litovsk, but Allied intervention got underway and various separatist movements proliferated in the Ukraine, in the Baltic provinces and across the former Russian Empire.[19] In this context, the domestic policy of the revolutionaries was largely shaped by the foreign-political situation. The Mensheviks, a minority faction of the party opposed to the more exclusive approach of the Bolshevik majority, argued that the only way to protect Russia from external attack was to re-establish the Constituent Assembly, replace communist dictatorship with democracy, and mobilize the entire country for the struggle.[20] Lenin, on the other hand, argued that 'the defence of the socialist fatherland . . . requires the waging of a merciless war . . . against the bourgeoisie in our own country'.[21] Mass shootings, arrests and deportations – many of them personally initiated or approved by Lenin himself – now became the order of the day in Soviet Russia.

The deteriorating strategic situation also shaped domestic affairs in the Entente and associated powers, albeit less drastically. French politics throughout 1917–18 were dominated by arguments about the conduct of the war. Aristide Briand's government fell in March 1917 over the issue of whether parliament had the right to discuss strategy in secret session. That summer, after a renewed offensive had collapsed amid heavy casualties, French soldiers mutinied *en masse*. The military failures and the mutinies provoked an outbreak of mass paranoia about German agents and treachery at home. Right-wingers accused the interior minister, Louis-Jean Malvy, of being a spy on account of his failure to arrest potential subversives at the beginning of the war. In July 1917, the Radical leader Georges Clemenceau openly taxed him in parliament with 'treason'. A month later, the government of Alexandre Ribot resigned after a merciless battering of its military record. Its successor, headed by Paul Painlevé, did not last long: it was forced out in November 1917 after the collapse of the Italian and eastern fronts. His replacement, Clemenceau, was made of altogether sterner stuff. He not only arrested the former Radical Party leader and supporter of a negotiated peace, Joseph Caillaux, on suspicion of treason in January 1918, but assured parliament in March 1918 of his absolute determination to see the conflict through to the end. 'Internal policy, I wage war,' he said, 'foreign policy, I still wage war.'[22]

On the other side of the Channel, and on the far side of the Atlantic, the final stages of the war likewise shaped domestic politics. The huge casualties of the British army's Passchendaele campaigns from July 1917 finally drove the Labour leader, Arthur Henderson, to demand an international peace conference, and tender his resignation from the government when it was refused by Lloyd George. Early in the following year the prime minister saw off, with some difficulty, a public attack on his manpower policy by two powerful generals, worried that Britain lacked the troops to stop the final German offensive; it was the Chief of the Imperial General Staff, Sir William Robertson, who had to resign instead and was replaced by Sir Henry Wilson. The United States also threw herself into the business of domestic mobilization. In 1916, she possessed the seventeenth-largest army in the world; within a very short time the imposition of conscription had produced 4 million men, half of whom were sent to France. War expenditure, which exceeded all federal spending since the establishment of the constitution, was funded by aggressively marketed 'Liberty Bonds'. The Committee of Public Information, headed by Wilson's nominee and former journalist George Creel, dispatched more than 70,000 'minute men' to convince the public in town hall meetings across the nation – totalling 7.5 million events in all – that the 'very future of democracy' was in the balance.[23] Americans of German descent were ostracized; *sauerkraut* was rechristened 'victory cabbage'. Domestic criticism was muzzled through the Espionage Act (1917) and Sedition Act (1918). Police and vigilantes targeted socialists and anti-war protestors, many of whom were only released by Republican governments after the conflict had ended. On the other hand, mobilization for war allowed certain minority groups, such as African-Americans, to prove their patriotism and to articulate claims for full citizenship on the strength of their military service.[24]

The final act in the struggle for mastery in Europe opened with a great German offensive on the western front in March 1918. At around the same time, German aircraft and Zeppelins stepped up their attacks on British cities, hoping to wreak maximum damage with new *Elektron* incendiary bombs. In the east, German forces continued to advance deep into the Ukraine. On the high seas, the U-boats wrought havoc on Allied shipping. For several months, the outcome of the war hung in the balance. The Germans were never able to prevent the Americans from crossing the Atlantic in large numbers, however, and the aerial offensive soon petered out. The British and French reacted to the crisis on the western front by appointing a joint Supreme Allied Commander, Marshal Foch, the first example of successful Anglo-French military integration. By the summer of 1918, the Germans had been halted at the second battle of the Marne. American troops intervened decisively at Belleau Wood in June 1918. By the beginning of August, the British and French scored a decisive victory near Amiens in an engagement described by General Ludendorff as 'the black day of the German army'.[25]

In early October 1918, the liberal Prince Max von Baden was made German chancellor as a concession to President Wilson's democratic agenda. Shortly afterwards, the Allies breached the formidable 'Hindenburg Line'. At around the same time, Allied forces finally broke through on the Salonica front, forcing Bulgaria to surrender in late September. British forces punched through the Ottoman defences in Palestine. At the end of the following month, the Italians routed the Austrians at the battle of Vittorio Veneto. By then, the Austro-Hungarian Empire was in a state of disintegration as its constituent parts began to rebel against Habsburg rule. The new German government, hopeful that it would be able to negotiate a settlement based on Wilson's Fourteen Points, put out peace feelers to the Allies. At the end of October, German sailors at Kiel mutinied against the order to attack the Royal Navy in a desperate attempt to turn the tide, and the unrest spread rapidly across the country. Germany erupted in revolution, the Kaiser abdicated and on 11 November the Germans signed an Armistice which amounted in effect to a surrender.

The Allied victory had many causes. In part, Germany was simply crushed by the weight of the Entente's superiority in manpower and economic resources. The controversial strategy of attrition certainly wore the central powers down until Foch and the Americans delivered the *coup de grâce* in 1918.[26] It is also true that the German home front was subjected to extreme privations due to the blockade. Metrics alone, however, do not explain the outcome. Big battalions, for example, did not save tsarist Russia. Indeed, of the original belligerents of 1914, only British and French society proved able to take the strain until the bitter end. To be sure, the French army mutinied in 1917, but the nation rallied and deserters were shamed back to the front. Russia, by contrast, was forced out of the war through revolution that same year, and in 1918 both Germany and Austria-Hungary disintegrated from within, in the first case because the social inequalities aggravated by the Allied blockade had worn down the civilian population and in the second case because the monarchy was no longer capable of keeping the lid on national antagonisms. The western democracies were slow to start the war, but only they survived it intact.[27] All the same, it had been close-run thing.

The war *against* Germany was over; the struggle *over* Germany now began. The debate on its future divided not only the victorious coalition, but the political leadership within France, Britain and the United States. Nowhere was the discussion more bitter than in Paris, where the cost of the war was being counted. 1,300,000 men had been killed in the trenches, and another 3 million wounded, many of them left crippled for life. Well over a million French women and children had been widowed or orphaned, and were totally dependent on the state. The birth rate, never high, had plunged during the war and looked unlikely to recover. The ideal solution would have been the division of Germany into several smaller states. 'In order to secure a lasting peace,' one French foreign ministry memorandum argued in October 1918 as the end was in grasp, 'the legacy of Bismarck must be destroyed.'[28] At the very least, many demanded a larger buffer on France's eastern border. Her supreme military commander, Marshal Foch, mounted a massive press campaign arguing that this could only be guaranteed through control of the Rhine frontier.[29] The political leadership under Clemenceau argued that to insist on this would destroy the crucial alliance with Britain and the United States. He eventually prevailed, but only with difficulty and on the understanding that the terms imposed on Germany would be so severe as to prevent her from embarking on fresh conquests for the time to come.

The British and the Americans, on the other hand, were not only suspicious of traditional French ambitions in central Europe, but convinced that the best way of dealing with Germany was by changing her behaviour rather than her capabilities. There was agreement in London and Washington that the aggressiveness of the Wilhelmine Empire abroad had been a product of her illiberalism at home. The obvious solution, therefore, was the destruction of 'Kaiserism' and the introduction of liberal democracy. Austen Chamberlain, the Chancellor of the Exchequer, argued shortly after the war that 'if Germany remains or becomes democratic, [it] cannot repeat the folly of Frederick the Great and Bismarck and his later followers'.[30] This should be achieved by local actors if possible, and by outside pressure if necessary. 'The tragic fact remains,' the British historian and political adviser William Harbutt Dawson argued, 'that the German nation cannot by its own will shake off one of its political fetters.' He spoke for many in Britain and the United States when he added that it would require external intervention to remove 'that system, which for fifty years has proved a plague centre in the life of Europe'.[31]

Moreover, the German Question was aggravated by the problem of Bolshevism. The outbreak of revolution in Germany suggested to the Russian revolutionaries that the general rising of the proletariat which they had expected in 1917 was now at hand. 'The crisis in Germany has only begun,' Lenin exulted. 'It will inevitably end in the transfer of political power to the German proletariat ... Now even the blindest workers in the various countries will see that the Bolsheviks were right in basing their whole tactics on the support of the world workers' revolution.' He warned that 'The Russian workers will understand that very soon they will have to make the greatest sacrifices in the cause of internationalism', and that 'The time is approaching when circumstances may require us to come to the aid of the German people.' This was because, as Lenin explained in his 'Letter to the workers of Europe and America', 'The revolution in Germany – [was] particularly important and characteristic as one of the most advanced capitalist countries.'[32] Once the *Reich* fell to the revolution, the rest of Europe would follow, but if reaction regained the upper hand, the Russian Revolution could not hope to survive for long. So when the Comintern was established in March 1919 to take on the 'international bourgeoisie', the official language of the new organization was not Russian or even English but German.

The western allies, for their part, were locked in combat with the Bolsheviks in Russia itself, and desperate to stop them from moving into the emerging vacuum in central Europe. Britain and America soon came to believe that the best way of effecting this was by recruiting Germany to the struggle against revolution, or at least denying her to the Bolsheviks. Bolshevism, the US Secretary of State, Robert Lansing, warned in October 1918 even before the war had ended, 'must not be allowed to master the people of Central Europe, where it would become a greater menace to the world than Prussianism'.[33] For this reason Churchill called for 'the building up of a strong yet peaceful Germany which will not attack our French allies, but will at the same time act as a moral bulwark against Bolshevism', and thus 'build a dyke of peaceful, lawful, patient strength and virtue against the flood of Red barbarism flowing from the east'.[34]

The Treaty of Versailles, which settled the future of western and central Europe in late June 1919, five years to the day after the assassination of Franz Ferdinand, was a compromise between the various Allied demands and strategic concerns.[35] It was designed to guard against a revival of German expansionism while maintaining the *Reich* as a bulwark against the spread of Bolshevism. Germany gave up all of her colonies. Alsace-Lorraine was returned to France and north Schleswig to Denmark; Eupen-Malmedy was ceded to Belgium. The future of the Saar was to be decided by plebiscite. In the east, Germany surrendered West Prussia and the Wartheland to a reconstituted Poland, and Memel initially to French administration, before it was seized by the new state of Lithuania. Danzig was made a 'free city'. The future of the important industrial area of Upper Silesia and the southern half of East Prussia, both hotly contested between Polish and German armed bands, was to be decided by a plebiscite. In all, the *Reich* lost about 13 per cent of its territory and about 10 per cent of its population. Germany was also subjected to a regime of disarmament, occupation and reparation payments. The Rhineland and the Palatinate were to be occupied by British, French, American and Belgian forces for up to ten years, partly to contain the *Reich* and partly to keep an eye on each other.[36] Germany was forbidden to erect fortifications close to the borders. The new German army, the *Reichswehr*, was not to exceed 100,000 men and was to be made up entirely of professionals; conscription and all other forms of short-term service were outlawed. No aircraft or tanks were permitted, and most of the navy was to be surrendered. Germany was thus completely defenceless militarily. Her most important rivers – the Rhine, Danube, Oder and Elbe – were placed under international control. Finally, Germany was deemed by article 231 of the treaty to be responsible for the costs of the war and therefore presented with a massive reparations bill in cash and kind totalling 226 billion Marks. The centre of Europe, in effect, was to be neutralized, and monitored by the victorious coalition.

Underpinning this new territorial dispensation in Europe was the League of Nations, whose Covenant was written into the first twenty-six articles of the Versailles Treaty. The League was based in Geneva and consisted of an Assembly, to which all recognized states belonged, and a Council, which was made up of the five victor powers, Britain, France, Italy, Japan and the United States. Neither Germany nor the Soviet Union was admitted to the League. On the contrary, its primary purpose was the containment of Germany, and to a much lesser degree of the Soviet Union, through the guarantee of the territorial settlement at Versailles and its disarmament clauses. According to article 10 of the Covenant, members undertook 'to respect and preserve ... against external aggression the territorial integrity and existing political independence of all members of the League. In case of any such aggression or in case of any threat or danger of such aggression the Council shall advise upon the means by which this obligation is to be fulfilled.' In short, the League of Nations stood or fell with the Versailles Treaty and the containment of the *Reich*.[37]

President Wilson did not want the League, as he put it, to become merely a 'Holy Alliance' directed against Germany.[38] He always intended that Berlin should be admitted to full membership once it had demonstrated democratic credentials, not least in order to contain the Russians. Wilson therefore sought to embed the central European settlement in a broader transformation of international behaviour. At the heart of this was universal disarmament: the Versailles Treaty explicitly stated that the restrictions on Germany were '[i]n order to allow for preparation for general arms limitation by all the nations'.[39] Moreover, the League sought to change not only relations *between* states, but also behaviour *within* states through the establishment of a Commission for Refugees, a health organization, a slavery commission, a Committee for the Study of the Legal Status of Women, and various other transnational bodies. Most importantly of all, the League guaranteed a series of bilateral 'Minority Treaties' to protect the basic religious, civil and cultural rights of all inhabitants. Thanks to the efforts of Lucien Wolf, the Anglo-Jewish human rights advocate, European Jews now appeared to enjoy a comprehensive, internationally sanctioned and enforceable system of civil rights, embedded in a programme of similar rights for all.[40] In part, these provisions reflected a free-standing progressive agenda pursued for its own sake, but the principal motivation was to reduce domestic tensions which might lead to international tension and even war.

If the League of Nations was designed primarily to secure the European balance of power, it also had profound implications for the wider world. Germany and Turkey were divested of their empires, but the victor powers did not just want to cut these territories adrift as independent states, partly because some of them would instantly collapse into anarchy, partly because the precedent would create a subversive dynamic within the other empires, but mainly because the resulting vacuum would quickly become the subject of great-power rivalry. Nor could these lands simply be partitioned among the victors, because President Wilson would not allow this for ideological reasons. The result was the 'mandate' system, by which the League authorized one of the Allied or associated powers to administer the forfeit colonies and provinces until they were ready for full independence. Despite strong resistance from France, which wished to use its new territories as a source of manpower to contain Germany, mandatory powers were explicitly forbidden from fortifying their territories or raising armies there, thereby seeking unilateral advantage which might affect the balance of power. On this basis Mesopotamia (present-day Iraq) and the Transjordan fell to Britain; so did Palestine, where London was tasked by the League with implementing the Balfour Declaration there. Syria (present-day Lebanon and Syria) was awarded to France. Wilson and many Arabs were disappointed in their hopes for a united Arab state, or confederation of states as envisaged in the Sykes–Picot agreement. Once it became clear that she was not going to be assigned any territories herself, Germany became a firm opponent of the whole mandate system and a passionate supporter of early independence for the states concerned.

The Treaty of Versailles and League of Nations Covenant dominated domestic politics across Europe and the far side of the Atlantic after 1918 among winners and losers alike.[41] In Germany, defeat, territorial losses and the prospect of a huge reparations bill put unbearable pressure on the Weimar Republic. It was henceforth indelibly associated in the public mind with national humiliation comparable to that experienced during the Thirty Years War or at the hands of Napoleon. The Social Democrat president, Friedrich Ebert, lamented that 'Versailles conditions with their economic and political impossibilities are the greatest enemy of German democracy and the strongest impetus for communism and nationalism.'[42] Quartermaster-General William Groener warned that the League was designed for 'the maintenance of the political encirclement of Germany'.[43] Max Weber counselled repudiation of the treaty, even at the price of an Allied occupation of the whole country, on the grounds that the young republic would be crippled at birth by the stigma of Versailles. The German military leadership, however, ruled out a resumption of the war which would have risked total defeat, followed by an Allied invasion and possibly partition. Their first priority, and that of the Social Democrat-led government, was to keep the *Reich* intact. This meant dealing with regional movements which threatened its integrity, and revolutionary eruptions which might give the Allies an excuse to intervene. A left-wing Spartacist uprising under Rosa Luxemburg and the younger Karl Liebknecht was put down with severity; the Bavarian Republic of Kurt Eisner met a similar fate. Gritting her teeth, Germany signed the Treaty of Versailles.

Yet if defeat and revolution were mortal threats to the *Reich*, they also represented an opportunity to break with the federal traditions which had prevented Germany from realizing her true fiscal and military potential for so long. At the top of the agenda was the permanent unification of the Prussian, Bavarian, Württembergian and Saxon armies, which had hitherto been under unitary command only in time of war. In October 1919 the new *Reichswehrministerium* not only amalgamated the war ministries in Stuttgart, Munich and Dresden with that in Berlin, but took on the functions of the Prussian general staff.[44] Likewise, in the debates preceding the Weimar constitution, the constitutional lawyer Hugo Preuss, who drafted most of it, argued that 'The outward strengthening of the Empire so that the outside world is faced only by a single Empire rather than individual tribes is necessary for the [continued] existence of Germany.' The resulting constitution created a much more centralized Germany, in which the regions lost many of the federal powers, especially in the fiscal sphere, they had retained in 1871. Taken together with the creation of a single German army, the centralization of fiscal powers would inevitably transform the European balance. The German Republic of 1919 was therefore potentially much more powerful than the Empire of 1871 had ever been.

Versailles brought little joy to the victors, moreover. France was unable to insist on the Rhine border, accepting instead the demilitarization of the Rhineland, and an additional weak bilateral promise of support from Lloyd George against 'unprovoked aggression by Germany'. Marshal Foch therefore loudly condemned the treaty as a 'capitulation' and even 'treason'. It received a bumpy ride in the National Assembly. All the same, the November 1919 elections were widely regarded as a verdict on the war and the settlement: Clemenceau and his *Bloc National* won handsomely. From then on, French politics were driven by the quest to consolidate the victory and to effect the domestic reconstruction and transformation necessary to repair the war damage. Particular emphasis was placed on reparations, both to keep taxes down and to persuade the electorate that the German threat was being contained. Another priority was to make up the demographic shortfall, which would leave France militarily exposed in the future. The labour force was buttressed by encouraging Spanish, Italian and Polish immigration. Work-place nurseries, social housing and other state or state-mandated benefits were introduced not in deference to some socialist or feminist agenda, but with the specific purpose of increasing the birth rate.[45] In the economic sphere, the minister of commerce, Étienne Clémentel, proposed integrated national planning with Britain and the United States for the distribution of raw materials, energy resources and foodstuffs. This was designed to raise French productivity and protect it from the ravages of the free market. The minister for the colonies, Albert Sarraut, drafted an ambitious plan for the development of France's overseas colonies, to compensate her for the weight she now lacked in Europe.

In Italy, critics spoke of a 'mutilated victory', which had denied them rightful gains in the Adriatic. 'Let us put it bluntly,' the republican newspaper *L'Italia del Popolo* argued, 'we have been defeated. Defeated as Wilsonians, defeated as Italians. We have won the war and lost the peace.' The government of the prime minister, Vittorio Orlando, was hounded out of office. His successor, Francesco Nitti, was almost immediately confronted by a challenge from the radical nationalist poet and adventurer Gabriele d'Annunzio, who seized the Istrian port of Fiume – now Rijeka in Croatia – from Yugoslavia in September 1919. At the same time, Italian democracy struggled to deal not only with the fallout from Versailles, but also the huge social and economic divisions which bubbled up after the end of the war. In the Italian general elections at the end of the year, the liberal governing coalition did badly while annexationist parties of various stripes were rampant. The great beneficiary of all this was the former socialist, strong interventionist and war veteran Benito Mussolini, whose fascist 'Blackshirt' movement (founded in March 1919) now began to gain more and more adherents. He effectively substituted the promise of an assertive Italy abroad for radical change at home.

The British victory celebrations did not last long, either. Lloyd George's coalition swept back to power in the general election immediately following the end of the war on a platform of, as one candidate put it, 'squee[zing] Germany until the pips squeaked'. In Ireland, however, the radical nationalist Sinn Féin party completely routed the more moderate Home Rulers, and eventually embarked on an armed struggle leading to independence. Across Britain, millions of demobilized men flooded back into the workforce and an uncertain future. As passions subsided, sickened by the cost of the war, and repelled by what they saw as French vindictiveness, many Britons began to feel that the conflict had been a tragic mistake and that Germany needed to be rehabilitated. So when John Maynard Keynes published *The economic consequences of the peace* in 1919, he was pushing at an open door. Keynes, who had been a member of the British delegation at the Versailles Conference, argued that the punitive reparation clauses were economically completely self-defeating. He pointed out that the general European recovery, on which the world and particularly the British economy depended, could only begin on the Rhine. Forcing the Germans to export their way to paying reparations would undercut British products. Moreover, 'The treaty includes no provisions for the economic rehabilitation of Europe,' he warned, 'nothing to make the defeated Central empires into good neighbours, nothing to stabilise the new states of Europe, nothing to reclaim Russia.'[46]

In the United States, President Wilson made the Versailles Treaty and the League the cornerstone of his campaign for re-election in 1920. 'Dare we reject it,' he asked, 'and break the heart of the world?'[47] Praising article 10 of the Covenant, which committed signatories to the defence of the territorial integrity of all members, as 'the very backbone of the whole covenant', Wilson called upon the United States to assume 'the leadership of the world'.[48] This repelled 'isolationists', but the most serious resistance to ratification came from the Republican Party, the traditional standard-bearer for American internationalism. Critics such as the former Secretary of War, Elihu Root, were concerned that the rhetorical flourish masked a weak and ineffective treaty. Likewise, the former Republican president, William Howard Taft, vigorously supported article 10, but only if it entailed an absolute obligation to go to war in its defence, rather than the vague 'moral obligations . . . binding in conscience only, not in law' that Wilson had in mind. In particular, the Republicans demanded concrete security guarantees for France against Germany, which Wilson refused to give.[49] The Republican criticism, in other words, was not that the League of Nations embroiled Americans too much in the outside world, but that it failed to do so comprehensively and effectively enough.[50]

In the end, the League treaty was defeated in the Senate, where it failed to secure a two-thirds majority, and Wilson himself was worsted in the 1920 presidential election. The United States would become neither a member of the League of Nations, nor a signatory and thus a guarantor of the Versailles settlement. The American people may not have broken the heart of the world, but they certainly wrecked the complex geopolitical architecture designed in 1919 to contain the revival of German power.

So when the dust settled in the early 1920s, a fundamental geopolitical revolution had taken place in Europe and more globally. The British Empire was now the undisputed hegemon in the Middle East and central Asia, as well as in Africa and Australasia. She was now at the pinnacle of her power, with a formidable military apparatus and a vast military-industrial economic base to fall back on in time of war. In the Far East, Japan had emerged as the new hegemon, confronting not so much Russia as the European empires, the perennially weak China, and ultimately the United States. In Europe, the Ottoman, Habsburg and Tsarist Empires had all disappeared. A series of successor states had taken their places in central, eastern and south-eastern Europe: Poland, Czechoslovakia, Hungary and Yugoslavia. Above all, while Germany had shed substantial territorial feathers and was hedged about by the restrictions of the Versailles Treaty, she remained not only the largest state in Europe outside the Soviet Union, but in relative terms she was even more formidable than before 1914.[51] She was no longer balanced by powerful empires to her east and south-east. Moreover, in 1921 Germany produced three times as much steel as France, and the demographic gap between the two was increasing. Worse still, as Sir Halford Mackinder warned in his 1919 book *Democratic ideals and reality*, the 'heartland', which included the former German Reich, Austria-Hungary and the Tsarist Empire, was a 'vast triple base of man-power' that remained beyond the control of 'sea-power' and was thus a potentially mortal threat to the western democracies.[52]

The challenges to the Versailles system mounted in the course of the new decade. In February 1920, close to victory in the Russian Civil War and with the withdrawal of the interventionist powers in the offing, Lenin approved plans for a Red Army attack on her western neighbour, Poland. The Polish head of state and army commander, Joseph Pilsudski, therefore decided on pre-emptive action.[53] In late April, Polish armies crossed the border and quickly advanced deep into the Ukraine, capturing Kiev a month later, while 'White' forces under Marshal Wrangel thrust northwards from the Crimea. In the summer of 1920, however, the Red Army under Marshal Mikhail Tukachevski went on the offensive and pushed the Poles all the way back to Warsaw. If they could punch through their final defences, hastening a revolution by the Polish proletariat, the Bolsheviks would have Germany firmly in their sights. The forward ramparts of the revolution against the Entente would then lie along the Rhine and Ruhr, rather than in the Ukraine.[54] In late July, the Red Army crossed the Bug. German workers refused to handle war material for the Poles, and even conservatives rejoiced that Pilsudski was getting his comeuppance. On orders from Moscow, German communists became ever more nationalistic in their rhetoric.

Seriously alarmed, the Entente powers sent a military mission to Poland. The French, in particular, feared that a Polish defeat would allow the Germans to restore their pre-1914 borders in the east without firing a shot, and to leverage their new position as sole bulwark against Bolshevism in order to revise the disarmament clauses of Versailles.[55] Their primary objective was not to prevent a Polish revolution, but to keep the revolutionary tide out of Germany. In the end, the Polish workers did not rise but backed Pilsudski against the Russian invaders, and in late August 1920 Entente-backed Polish forces decisively defeated the Red Army in the 'Miracle on the Vistula'. The subsequent Treaty of Riga in March 1921 settled the borders in eastern Europe, at least for the time being. The Soviet Union had to accept the independence of Finland and the Baltic states, but it reasserted control over White Russia, the Ukraine and most of the former Tsarist Empire in the Caucasus and the Far East. Poland remained in possession of Vilnius, which it had seized from the Lithuanians. The War of the Tsarist Succession was over.

By far and away the most serious challenge, however, was German revisionism. The *Reich* had gone from being an imperial power to being a victim – as she saw it – of colonization herself. Germany had not merely been stripped of her own overseas possessions, but had sacrificed large swathes of German-populated territory, as well as being subjected to debt servitude by an Anglo-American 'cartel'.[56] Over the next ten years or so, Berlin sought to reduce reparations payments or even evade them altogether, demanded territorial revision, the right to rearm for self-defence, and membership of the League with overseas mandates as a symbol of equality. In the short term, given the absence of any substantial military muscle of her own, Germany tried to leverage her weakness, arguing (on the whole speciously) an inability to pay reparations, her centrality to the world economy, and the danger that a complete collapse of German power would turn central Europe into a battleground. Over time, Berlin hoped to use her huge economic potential to force a revision of Versailles. The only other trump Berlin held was Russia: cooperation with the Soviet Union encircled Poland, might persuade Moscow to reduce interference in German domestic politics, and would force the western allies to treat the *Reich* with more respect. Playing these two cards simultaneously, as Germany tried to do, was fraught with difficulties. The tension between opting for the west on economic and ideological grounds, and for the east on strategic grounds, made for a highly ambivalent German geopolitics in the years ahead.

The Soviet Union, for its part, remained convinced that an encircling capitalist world was in league for her destruction. She responded with a twin-track strategy. To keep the enemy off-balance, Moscow instigated a number of insurrections in central Europe, especially Germany, between 1920 and 1923.[57] At the same time, the Soviet government pursued a policy of rapprochement with Berlin to keep it out of the Allied camp, and to put pressure on Poland. Secret Russo-German military collaboration to evade the disarmament clauses of Versailles began in 1920 and really took off in the middle of the decade. Two years later, in 1922, Germany and the Soviet Union concluded a friendship treaty at Rapallo, sending a collective shiver down spines in London, Washington and especially Paris.[58]

By then, the Versailles system was buckling along its southern periphery. In October 1922, Mussolini marched on Rome and took power. He promised not only to resolve the country's deep economic, social and political problems, but more importantly to make Italy great among the powers. His ambition was to make the Mediterranean a '*mare italiano*' by 'expelling those who are parasites' and smashing 'the chains of hostility that surround Italy in the Mediterranean'. Mussolini argued that the nation needed to carve out its own '*spazio vitale*', not just through the acquisition of a critical land mass, but by gaining access to the Atlantic and Indian Oceans. This strategy threatened the French in North Africa, required 'the demolition of the British Empire', which strangled Italy by holding the exits to the Mediterranean in Gibraltar, Malta and Egypt, and challenged the territorial integrity of Yugoslavia and Greece. It could only, as the Italian dictator admitted, be executed 'at Germany's side'.[59]

There was broad agreement between the Entente powers on how to respond to Russia. Bolshevism must be contained. The French encouraged Romania, Czechoslovakia and Yugoslavia to create the 'Little Entente' in 1921; this was primarily designed to counter Hungarian revisionism, but Paris hoped that it would also serve to deter the Soviet Union. Hopes that some of Russia's former borderlands could be organized into a 'United States of Eastern Europe' had to be abandoned, however.[60] There was also a consensus that Mussolini's Italy was a menace to both powers in the Mediterranean particularly, but also in Africa and to the stability of the Balkans. This soon led to the 'Corfu Incident', when the Royal Navy was mobilized to stop Italy from taking over the island in 1923. Mussolini was forced to back down, but it all left planners in London and Paris with yet another military headache to cope with.

Germany was quite another matter. France interpreted events in the Soviet Union, the Mediterranean and the Middle East within a Germano-centric framework which saw Berlin behind the tide of global unrest against the colonial powers.[61] The main threat, however, came from directly across the Rhine. The most senior French military commander, Marshal Foch, cautioned that so long as Germany retained a nucleus of trained officers, she could rearm in a very short period of time. In 1920, France concluded a military agreement with Belgium, and in 1921 with Poland, thus threatening the *Reich* on its eastern flank. At around the same time, French troops responded to German default on reparations payments by temporarily occupying three towns in the Ruhr. Britain and the United States, on the other hand, pursued a more conciliatory policy towards Germany. In March 1922, the Americans signalled their intention to withdraw their army of occupation from the Rhineland within a year.[62]

In the Soviet Union, the continuing tension with the capitalist world led to a radical domestic change of course. In the absence of world revolution, the Soviet Union would have to reconcile the peasantry, grow her economy and generally achieve the inner cohesion necessary to fend off outside attack. The result was the New Economic Policy after 1921, which allowed the peasants to produce for a limited free market, and paved the way for outward investment in and technological transfer to the Soviet Union. 'Considering . . . that further interventionist attempts' were to be expected, the All-Russian Soviet Congress resolved in January 1922 that 'the restoration and rehabilitation of the national economy . . . the quickest and widest possible development of trade with other countries, the attraction of foreign capital and technical personnel to exploit the natural wealth of Russia, and the receipt from other states of cooperation in the form of loans', were so essential to Soviet security that it was prepared to honour the tsarist debts to the western bourgeoisie.[63] As Lenin put it in a probably apocryphal remark, 'the capitalists themselves will be happy to sell us the rope which we will use to hang them'.

France and Britain sought to increase their leverage in Europe by defending and developing their overseas empires.[64] 'France does not stop at the Mediterranean, or at the Sahara,' General Mangin remarked in January 1919, 'she extends to the Congo . . . she constitutes an empire vaster than Europe, and which in half a century will number one hundred million inhabitants.' The real value of these colonial troops lay in their use against Germany. Tens of thousands of West and North Africans served in the army of occupation in the Rhineland, a move which sparked widespread condemnation across the former Entente powers, where it became a matter of racist, pacifist and feminist concern. Mrs H. M. Swanwick of the British section of the Women's International League for Peace and Freedom spoke for many when she moved that 'In the interest of good feeling between all the races of the world and the security of all women, this meeting calls upon the League of Nations to prohibit the importation into Europe for warlike purposes, of troops belonging to primitive peoples, and their use anywhere, except for purposes of police and defence in their country of origin.'[65] The experience also left a lasting trauma among the German population. 'French militarism,' the Social Democrat chancellor, Hermann Müller, told the *Reichstag* in April 1920, 'has marched across the Main as into enemy country. Senegal negroes are camping in Frankfurt University, guarding the

Goethe House.' In the minds of German nationalists, there could be no better illustration of the mortal threat which the French colonies represented not just to the sovereignty of the *Reich* but to its cultural and 'racial' integrity.[66]

By the beginning of 1923, the French had given up on waiting for an Anglo-American security guarantee, or the improvement in German behaviour which London and Washington forecast from a policy of restraint. Paris could not accept the status quo, because this had an inbuilt economic and demographic dynamic that was inexorably shifting to France's disadvantage. So in January 1923 the French once again used a (probably deliberate) shortfall in reparations payments to send in the troops. This time, however, they and their Belgian allies occupied the entire Ruhr area. That same month, the Lithuanians occupied Memel in the east. A large proportion of Germany's industrial potential, and millions of its inhabitants, fell under foreign rule. France resumed her policy of sponsoring separatist movements in the Rhineland and the Palatinate. Chancellor Wilhelm Cuno's government responded by proclaiming a policy of 'passive resistance'. This was designed to wear the French down through a thousand cuts of civil disobedience, especially strikes, while denying them the opportunity to deploy their crushing military superiority. France was pilloried internationally for her behaviour, but the cost of paying the salaries of the striking employees and the general economic disruption quickly led to hyperinflation and widespread misery, especially among members of the middle class who had lost their life's savings. In August 1923, the discredited Cuno was replaced as chancellor by Gustav Stresemann. By the end of September, the *Reich* government was forced to call off passive resistance and admit defeat. The German Communist Party, trying to take advantage of the widespread sense of national humiliation and severe economic distress, launched another abortive rising. An attempt by an obscure right-wing agitator, Adolf Hitler, to exploit the government's capitulation to France by launching a *Putsch* in Munich also failed in November 1923, leading to his arrest, trial and imprisonment.

The Ruhr Crisis prompted a strategic rethink across Europe and on the far side of the Atlantic. Yet another failed uprising in Germany finally tipped the balance in Moscow away from world revolution, and towards building socialism in one country. This gave the advantage to Stalin in the struggle to succeed Lenin after his death in January 1924. Unlike his rivals Trotsky, Grigory Zinoviev and Nikolai Bukharin, he had been a long-term sceptic of world revolution. In the short term, the Soviet Union turned towards a policy of accommodation with the west, which secured diplomatic recognition by Britain in 1924, followed by Japan and various other states in 1925. In Germany, Gustav Stresemann, now foreign minister in the cabinet of his successor, Wilhelm Marx, came to recognize the political and economic bankruptcy of the established *Revisionspolitik*. Though a strong nationalist, and a former annexationist, Stresemann knew that Germany was too weak to overturn the Versailles Treaty through military means or diplomatic confrontation.[67] For this reason, Stresemann sought to overcome Versailles not through rearmament, or financial chicanery, but through embedding German security and economic prosperity in a wider European settlement. He planned to use financial interdependence to promote European cooperation and effect German strategic equality through peaceful means. 'One must simply have . . . so many debts that the creditor sees his own existence jeopardized if the debtor collapses,' Stresemann argued a few months later.[68] The victorious allies, in other words, had to be persuaded that they needed a stable, prosperous Germany as much as she did herself.

Meanwhile, Paris was forced to accept that the kind of direct military intervention pursued in 1920–23 was no longer viable. The diplomatic and economic costs of using reparations to contain Germany were simply too high. Hawks such as Poincaré, who relentlessly argued the need for permanent strategic preponderance over Berlin, emerged from the Ruhr Crisis with their standing reduced; conciliators such as Aristide Briand were correspondingly strengthened. The result was a new French grand strategy. To be on the safe side, plans were drawn up for the construction of a line of fortifications within France to replace the concept of forward defence in the Rhineland. There was a much greater emphasis now, however, on a more multilateral approach designed to tie Germany into a web of legal, economic and political constraints which would inhibit or dilute her residual revisionism.[69]

The emergence of a more collaborative spirit in Europe, especially among German and French elites, found expression in the birth of the Pan-European Union in late 1923.[70] In the following year, its founder, Count Richard Coudenhove-Kalergi, set up the journal *Paneuropa* to agitate for 'a non-party mass movement for the unification of Europe'.

Together with many other similar organizations and publications, it called upon Europeans to sink their differences, forswear nationalism, to celebrate their common heritage and values, and band together to protect them against Godless communism and, in some cases, American materialism. Coudenhove-Kalergi's own vision was pro-European rather than anti-American: he sought to imitate the US model politically and economically, while preserving as much of Europe's cultural traditions as possible. Within a couple of years the movement had gained many adherents in Germany, including the president of the *Reichstag*, the chairman of the Democratic Party and a former economics minister, and in France, where the socialist leader, Léon Blum, was an enthusiastic supporter and the foreign minister, Aristide Briand, served as honorary president of the *Paneuropa Union*.[71]

In Britain and the United States, the Ruhr Crisis of 1923 served as evidence of the need to re-engage on the German Question. The prime minister, Ramsay Macdonald, saw the French occupation of the Ruhr in 1923 as evidence of a 'historical craving' to dominate central Europe. Likewise, Curzon accused France in early October 1923 of seeking 'the domination of the European continent'. For this reason, London refused to recognize the 'so-called autonomous governments of the Palatinate',[72] which it regarded as mere French puppets. On the other hand, the British Foreign Secretary, Austen Chamberlain, wrote in January 1925, 'We cannot afford to see France crushed, to have Germany, or an eventual Russo-German combination, supreme on the continent, or to allow any great military power to dominate the Low Countries.'[73] A much broader settlement was therefore required, which addressed French security concerns, recognized Germany as an equal, and locked her into a web of mutual cooperation and constraints. These developments coincided with a profound shift in US policy towards Europe. There was a growing consensus among agricultural and industrial lobbies in the United States that, as one spokesman put it in February 1922, 'our interests are indissolubly united with the interest of Europe, and until we have a reorganized, a sound condition of affairs in Europe . . . we shall not have normal healthy times at home'.[74] Moreover, the Ruhr Crisis threatened to create a vacuum in central Europe which the Soviet Union might fill.

The Republican internationalists in charge of American foreign policy now sought to stabilize the situation through a strategy of economic intervention. In early April 1924, the administration proposed a plan drawn up by the banker Charles Dawes which was designed to lighten the German reparations burden by revising the schedule of payments, to give the *Reich* access to American credits and thus ignite a European boom in which all boats would float with the rising tide. This would put an end to the sterile strategic zero-sum games of the immediate post-war period. The policy was not intended to dominate Europe: in June 1924, Charles Evans Hughes, the US Secretary of State for Foreign Affairs, spoke for many when he abjured any desire to act as 'the world's policeman' there. Nor was US policy simply designed to create an economically dependent German client state. When the major Ruhr industrialist Hugo Stinnes asked the American ambassador to Berlin to support a Mussolini-style right-wing putsch against the Republic in late September 1923, Washington recoiled in horror. Nothing, the US administration feared, would be more likely to promote a communist revolution than backing a unrepresentative conservative *coup d'état.* Instead, Republican internationalists aimed to create a viable democratic state in Germany which would be strong enough to maintain stability in central Europe, and keep the Bolsheviks at bay. They sought not to control Europe, but to prevent the continent, and especially German militarism, from endangering world peace once again.

A year later, Chamberlain, Briand and Stresemann concluded the Locarno agreement of October 1925, a non-aggression treaty between Paris, Berlin and Brussels, guaranteed by London and Rome. Germany accepted the territorial settlement in the west, including the loss of Alsace-Lorraine. In return, Germany was to be admitted to the League of Nations on an equal basis, albeit without a commitment to participate in any collective military action against the Soviet Union. To be on the safe side, Stresemann concluded a reinsurance treaty with Russia in late April 1926. Taken together with the Dawes Plan, these arrangements were a comprehensive attempt to settle the problem of German power and put the stability of the continent on a sound footing. A new spirit of cooperation was hailed, and found expression in the award of the Nobel Peace Prize to two of its architects, Briand and Stresemann. In Locarno, Briand announced, '*on a parlé européen*'.[75] The settlement only held in the west, however; Britain had refused to extend her commitment to France and Belgium to cover eastern and central Europe. 'No British government,' Chamberlain announced in a tone redolent of Bismarck, 'would even risk the bones of a single British grenadier' to defend Poland. Indeed, Germany pointedly declined to guarantee its borders with Poland and Czechoslovakia, signalling its intention to seek revision at some stage in the near future. Only time would tell whether the peace of Europe was divisible as the contractants at Locarno believed. The US ambassador to London, for one, was unhappy with the creation of different classes of boundaries, which he predicted would merely 'fix the point where the next great war will begin', that is, on the Polish–German border.[76]

The Dawes Plan and the Locarno agreement dominated European foreign and domestic politics for the rest of the decade. In Germany, Stresemann got both measures through the *Reichstag*, but he was accused by the right-wing opposition of having sold out the national interest to the Entente powers, especially American and Jewish financiers; the communists charged him with making the country a slave to international capital. In this context, Adolf Hitler's manifesto *Mein Kampf* – 'my struggle' – portrayed international politics as a struggle for space, which was 'the chief support of . . . political power'. On his reading, the German *Reich* was in danger of being dwarfed by the huge landmasses of the Soviet Union, China, the United States and the French and British Empires. 'All,' he pointed out, 'are spatial formations having in part an area more than ten times greater than the present German Reich.' Indeed, Hitler argued that 'From the purely territorial point of view, the area of the German Reich vanishes completely as compared with that of the so-called world powers.' For this reason Hitler dismissed calls for 'the restoration of the frontiers of 1914', as 'a political absurdity [because] the Reich's frontiers in 1914 were anything but logical. For in reality they were neither complete in the sense of embracing the people of German nationality, nor sensible with regard to geo-military expediency.' To restore them would simply put Germany back in the impossible position she had been in before the war, globally encircled by territorially vast world powers.

The solution, Hitler argued, was to 'creat[e] a healthy viable natural relation between the nation's population and growth on the one hand and the quantity and quality of its soil on the other hand'. Germany, led by the National Socialist party, 'must strive to eliminate the disproportion between our population and our area'. This meant that 'land and soil' in the east, on the territory of 'Russia and her vassal states' – the Soviet Union – should be 'the goal of [German] foreign policy'. It was there that the Germans could acquire the necessary *Lebensraum* to match the vast spaces open to their global rivals. Hitler also laid out the domestic preconditions for this cosmic struggle for living space: the need to unite the *Volk* behind the project of national reassertion, in particular by isolating the 'harmful' elements which corrupted and confused the people. Here Hitler especially had the Jews in mind, whom he regarded both as a domestic threat to the purity of the race and as the directing mind behind an international plutocratic and communist conspiracy against Germany. For Hitler, even more so than for most Germans, therefore, foreign and domestic politics were inseparably intertwined.[77]

The Soviet Union and Poland were also deeply unsettled by the Dawes Plan and Locarno. Viewed from Moscow, the rapprochement between the principal European powers amounted to a conspiracy against them. Meanwhile the situation in central Europe went from bad to worse. In particular, the Soviet Union feared, as *Izvestia* put it in May 1925, that 'Germany's choice of a definitively western orientation and entry into the League of Nations can objectively lead only to the deterioration of relations between Germany and the Soviet republic.'[78] All this served to strengthen Stalin's position within the Soviet elite. His doctrine of 'socialism in one country' allowed him to consolidate the power of the party at home and his own personal position in Moscow. Locarno also provoked a crisis in Poland, which the western powers seemed to have abandoned to the tender mercies of German revisionism. Warsaw was only too aware that Germany would use membership of the League to deploy the robust minority-rights provisions of the charter against her. 'Every honest Pole,' the retired Polish army commander and former head of state Marshal Pilsudski, remarked, 'spits when he hears this word [Locarno].' The final straw came in April 1926, when Stresemann's reinsurance treaty with Russia confirmed the encirclement of Poland. A month later, Marshal Pilsudski launched a coup designed primarily to provide the strong leadership which Poland would need to survive in an ever more dangerous international environment. The nation was wracked by paranoia against minority groups suspected of disloyalty such as Germans, Ukrainians and Jews. One of those fleeing the 1926 pogroms was a young man called Menachem Begin, who made his way to Palestine.

The new European settlement profoundly shaped the British Empire.

When the question of a European security pact was discussed at the Committee of Imperial Defence in 1925, it soon became clear that it could not be concluded without consulting the dominions. There was therefore a strong risk that British defence policy would be 'paralysed'. In January 1926, the secretary to the committee, Maurice Hankey, penned an influential memorandum arguing that a new form of 'Pan-Britannic' imperial organization was required to cope with the revival of German power, the 'Balkanization of Europe' and the rise of Japan in the Far East. The resulting Imperial Conference at Westminster in October–November 1926, attended by the prime ministers of Britain, Canada, Newfoundland, Australia, New Zealand, South Africa and the Irish Free State recognized the equality of the dominions, and indeed their implicit right of secession from the empire. In return, all of the prime ministers present, except W. T. Cosgrave of the Irish Free State, promised to help Britain in time of war. Not long afterwards, the consultation of the dominions in foreign affairs was put on a formal footing, and in due course the Statute of Westminster proclaimed the official equality of the dominions with the mother country. The new, 'third' British Empire would speak with one voice in world affairs.

The new cooperative framework of international politics promised by Locarno reduced tensions in western Europe. In 1926, Germany was admitted to the League of Nations and, after some wrangling, given a permanent seat on the Council. A year later, the International Military Commission in the Rhineland was finally withdrawn. It soon became clear, however, that French security concerns and German demands for equality were impossible to reconcile. The Versailles Treaty explicitly linked the immediate disarmament of Germany to a general reduction of military establishments worldwide. France, in particular, had made few moves in that direction, and showed every sign of wanting to ensure Germany's strategic inferiority for time immemorial. There was no other way, Paris argued, of preventing her neighbour from realizing her huge demographic and military-industrial potential. The logical conclusion of this argument was that French security and European stability required that German economic power *as such* be reduced. This was anathema not only to Berlin but to London and Washington as well. As one State Department official remarked, one 'could hardly ask the Krupp factories to go out of the business of making ploughs because in war, they might make guns'.[79] Moreover, the world at large was not disarming – on the contrary. In the summer of 1927, the major naval powers – especially Britain and the United States – failed to reach agreement at the Geneva Conference. It was no surprise, therefore, that Germany now began to demand the return of her occupied territories and the recognition of her military equality with ever greater insistence.[80]

Alarmed by the breakdown of his relations with Stresemann, and concerned at the disengagement of the United States from Europe, Briand approached Washington in April 1927 with a suggestion of a Franco-American non-aggression pact. The Frenchman was really after a US guarantee of the European status quo, but Washington insisted on a much broader treaty to which all powers could subscribe. This initiative resulted in the Kellogg–Briand Pact of August 1928, which outlawed war 'as an instrument of national policy', except in self-defence. This agreement, which almost all European states joined, was very much in line with the classic American notions of non-coercive international cooperation. At the behest of the Secretary of State, Frank B. Kellogg, the pact contained no enforcement mechanism, and everybody who signed it was well aware that the right to self-defence could be so broadly interpreted as to render its provisions nugatory. What, for example, if France occupied parts of Germany to prevent her from rearming, as she had done in 1920 and 1923, and what if Berlin used force to reassert her national sovereignty? Once again, Washington had flunked the German Question. That same year, the French minister of war, André Maginot, authorized the construction of a ring of fortifications on France's eastern border. It was that same year, too, that the French returned to the Gold Standard, pressing ahead with the establishment of a substantial gold reserve – the second-largest in the world by the beginning of the next decade – in order to provide them with greater economic leverage against Germany.[81]

The Kremlin, too, was highly sceptical that the Kellogg–Briand Pact would lead to an outbreak of international peace and goodwill. Instead, it believed that if the revolution was to survive over the long term, then the Soviet Union would have to mobilize the necessary domestic resources to repel all comers. At the July 1928 Party Congress, Bukharin proclaimed war to be 'the central problem of our time', for which the Soviet Union had 'little time' to prepare.[82] Youth militarization was stepped up. The directive for the First Five Year Plan, in 1928, specifically cited the prospect of another war of intervention as justification for a crash programme of industrialization. The New Economic Policy, with its free market in agricultural produce, was abandoned. Dependence on foreign experts and suppliers was to be eliminated. The collectivization of farms would generate the surplus food to feed the workers building the factories to produce the armaments which would keep the Soviet Union safe. Collective farmers were effectively 'bound to the land'; many were shot for failing to cooperate. What the peasants called the 'second enserfment' began: a new 'service class' was created to meet the external needs of the state. To that extent, 1927–8, and not 1917, marked the start of the social transformation of Russia under the primacy of foreign policy.[83] 'Stalinism' was born.

The Dawes Plan and the Kellogg–Briand Pact were the context in which Hitler penned his *Second Book* in 1928. This volume, which was not published until after the Second World War, was exclusively devoted to foreign policy and it showed how Hitler's strategic conceptions had developed since writing *Mein Kampf* in late 1923. Influenced by the recent extensive American economic intervention in Europe, and her growing industrial and cultural strength, he was now much more conscious of the power of the United States.[84] He pointed out that whereas Germany had reached the limits of her internal demographic development, the sheer size of the United States meant that the 'American Union', as he called it, 'can continue to grow for centuries.'[85] 'Americans', he went on, were 'a young, racially select Folk' – effectively 'a Nordic German state' – who maintained their stock through 'special standards for immigration' which elevated them above the racially degenerate 'Old Europe'. This was 'slowly leading to a new determination of the world's fate by the Folk of the North American continent'. In a direct rebuff to the 'pan-Europeans', Hitler attacked those 'who want to propose a European Union to the American Union in order thereby to prevent a threatening world hegemony of the north American continent'. In the absence of the right racial 'values', he argued, this would be nothing more than a 'Jewish Protectorate' subject to 'Jewish impulsions'. The creation of a 'European great power' on these lines would involve the 'racial submersion of its founders', and would thus never survive against the 'American Union'. This was Hitler's answer to Stresemann, Briand and Coudenhove-Kalergi. There was nothing for it: the German *Volk*'s 'prospects' of matching those of the 'American *Volk*' would be 'hopeless' unless the territory of the *Reich* were 'considerably enlarged' to the east.

German nationalists were reminded of US influence in Europe in August 1929, when Washington announced a new scheme for the settlement of German reparations drawn up by the bankers J. P. Morgan and Owen Young. Within a few months, however, the Wall Street Crash of late October 1929 struck at the heart of the American economy. Its geopolitical consequences were profound. US interest in Europe was radically reduced; many of the American loans which underpinned the boom in the Weimar Republic and the reparations programme on which the territorial settlement rested were now recalled. The International Bank of Settlements set up by the Young Plan was crippled by the resulting credit crunch. America moved towards protectionism. European economies, dependent on American markets and capital, suffered a sharp downturn. Damaging though the Crash and the following slump were, however, they were not enough to plunge Europe and indeed the United States into a deep depression. Instead, it was the contest for supremacy in central Europe which administered the fatal blow to the world economy.

Towards the end of 1929, German domestic politics lurched to the right not because of the fallout from Wall Street, but in response to the announcement of the Young Plan.[86] Critics such as Hitler and the press baron and conservative nationalist politician Alfred Hugenberg condemned the projected repayment schedule – which stretched until 1988 – as a 'new Paris diktat' which would 'enslave' the German people for the rest of the century. They lost the resulting referendum by a large margin, but the debate had served to focus nationalist energies and galvanize the substantial constituency for whom the return to great-power status was the principal issue. The plan was eventually approved by the *Reichstag* in March 1930, but the intervening controversy put Hitler firmly on the German electoral map. In the *Reichstag* elections of six months later, which were dominated by reparations and rearmament rather than the economic situation, the Nazis became the second-largest party with nearly 20 per cent of the vote. Germany was now virtually ungovernable, driving Chancellor Heinrich Brüning to rule by presidential decree.

France watched all this with alarm. Aristide Briand now made one last attempt to lock Germany into a stable balance which would guarantee French security. He proposed to trade French sovereignty in return for permanent restraints on German power in a united Europe. In May 1930, Briand unveiled a detailed plan for a 'European Federal Union', which would be assembled in a 'European Conference' boasting its own permanent executive. Economic cooperation was central to the whole endeavour, but Briand stressed that 'any progress in the sphere of economic unity was strictly determined by the security question'.[87] London refused to participate. These schemes garnered some support among Social Democrats, but the German response was generally cool. Berlin saw the plan as an attempt to impose 'new coils' upon them, as State Secretary von Bülow put it.[88] Instead, Berlin preferred to press ahead with its plan for the consolidation of German power in central Europe, especially through cooperation with Vienna.[89] In early July 1930, the German government rejected the Briand plan.

Matters came to a head between Paris and Berlin soon after. In late August 1930, the German foreign minister, Julius Curtius, launched a plan for a customs union with Austria, designed to draw ever wider swathes of eastern and south-eastern Europe into the orbit of Berlin: first Austria, then Hungary, Czechoslovakia, Romania, Yugoslavia and possibly even Poland. This would thus not only lead to European partial economic integration under German leadership – something which Briand had been frantic to prevent – but also to the *de facto* unification of Germany and Austria, which the Versailles Treaty expressly forbade. In mid-March 1931, Curtius signed the agreement in Vienna. A month later, one senior German diplomat looked forward to the 'forced' entrance of Czechoslovakia to the union; the resulting 'encirclement' of Poland, he added, would enable Germany to challenge the disputed eastern borders from a position of strength.[90] In retaliation, France deployed her considerable economic muscle – which had increased in relative terms compared to the US and Britain after 1929 – to bring down the largest Austrian bank, the Wiener Kreditanstalt, in May 1931. This led to a German banking crisis, which tipped the country into economic collapse and ultimately deepened the Depression in the United States. In the year before the French destroyed the Kreditanstalt, German unemployment stood at 3 million; a year after it had jumped to more than 5 million and was to rise still further. Likewise, the US unemployment rate was a high 9 per cent in 1930, but it had risen to a crippling 16 per cent by late 1931 and 24 per cent in 1932. In other words, it was the European geopolitical crisis of the early 1930s which caused the Great Depression, not the other way around.

All now depended on whether the next round of the disarmament conference at Geneva, which opened in early February 1932, could reach a settlement that would satisfy both Berlin and Paris. The French refused to agree to German equality without satisfactory guarantees; if the talks failed, the *Reich* government stood by to implement a large-scale programme of rearmament. The race to see whether the Weimar Republic could deliver on military equality now entered its final stretch. Chancellor Brüning made no secret of his hope that he could bridge irreconcilable domestic divides through foreign policy success. France's sabotage of the Austrian Customs Union, and then her obstructionism at Geneva left him defenceless against the onslaught of the nationalist right. Brüning's government fell in May 1932, largely because the *Reichswehr* and President Hindenburg had given up on him, only a few months before the French, British and Americans conceded German military equality in principle at Geneva in July. When the chancellor had begged not to be brought down 'one hundred metres from the finishing line', it was rearmament he was referring to, not economic recovery.[91]

The resulting elections in July 1932 made Hitler's National Socialists – capitalizing on growing unemployment and discontent with Versailles – the largest party. Because there was no parliamentary majority for any candidate, Hindenburg appointed Franz von Papen chancellor. Rearmament was his highest priority. Papen made overtures to France and Poland, offering the regional guarantee of the eastern border withheld at Locarno, cooperation against the Soviet Union, and a customs union, in return for a complete end to reparations and total 'equality' of armaments. In June–July 1932, the Lausanne Conference announced the end of reparations with a final payment, but the French refused to budge either on armaments or on allowing the Germans to remilitarize the Rhineland. The nationalist right – led by Hitler – and the communists lambasted Papen's alleged 'surrender'; his defence minister, General Kurt von Schleicher, spoke contemptuously of a German 'defeat'. In early December 1932, Hindenburg sacked Papen, but fresh elections only produced further parliamentary deadlock. Hitler's National Socialists lost several million votes but remained the largest party; the communists made substantial gains. Hindenburg appointed Schleicher chancellor, with a view to continuing government by presidential decree.[92] To the fury of nationalist opinion and the *Reichswehr* ministry, however, Schleicher refused to embark on full-scale rearmament even after the Geneva Conference allowed Germany to do so in principle. In January 1933, Hindenburg sacked the general and replaced him as chancellor with Adolf Hitler. He was supposed to rally domestic opinion behind the new government, while tried and trusted conservatives in key positions oversaw the revival of the *Reich* as a great power. The Nazi takeover in Germany, therefore, was a product not so much of the economic depression as of the failure of disarmament and the persistence of revisionism.

Adolf Hitler took power with a popular and elite mandate to overturn the Versailles Treaty. He shared the prevailing view that Germany's central position in Europe, surrounded as she was on every side by potential enemies, required more defensible borders than the 1919 settlement provided. To that extent, the new chancellor was part of a Prusso-German strategic tradition going back hundreds of years. Ultimately, however, Hitler was proposing a radical break with traditional German geopolitics. The relatively minor territorial revisions demanded by the nationalist right would not make Germany more secure. Only the capture of 'living space' in the east would provide the critical landmass to enable the *Reich* to survive in a world dominated by the French and British Empires, the Soviet Union and especially the 'American Union', all of them manipulated by the Jews. This was a grandiose vision, certainly, but it was hardly limitless. Hitler was not aiming for global hegemony, but the eastwards territorial expansion which alone would enable Germany to maintain her independence among the world powers. His contention that Germany would be a world power or nothing was therefore not mere nihilistic hubris, but reflected his belief that the *Reich* would have to achieve a critical global mass or risk being swallowed up. He expected the final showdown with the United States and 'world Jewry' to take place at some point in the remote future, probably after his own death.[93]

Hitler now moved to reshape German government and society for war. After a lone communist burnt down the *Reichstag* building, Hitler used the ensuing outrage to push through a range of repressive measures aimed at political opponents, many of whom disappeared into concentration camps. The Communist Party was banned. Fresh elections held in an atmosphere of fear and intimidation in early March 1933 resulted in a greatly increased Nazi vote, but still no majority. Hitler was already sure of the support of substantial sections of the nationalist right, however, and soon the Catholic Centre Party yielded to his embrace, albeit reluctantly. In late March 1933, the *Reichstag* voted him far-reaching powers under the Enabling Act. This effectively made Hitler the supreme lawmaker, and authorized him to conclude treaties with foreign powers without reference to parliament. Over the next few months, the regions and all administrative and social institutions were brought into line in a process known as *Gleichschaltung*. The party's paramilitary formations, the SA and SS, fanned out across the *Reich* suppressing opposition. By the middle of 1933, Hitler's power was by no means absolute in Germany, but his regime was so firmly entrenched that it could not be dislodged by any means other than an outright invasion.

The rearmament of Germany, which had already begun in the late Weimar period, was now speeded up. Hitler expanded the *Reichswehr* and pressed ahead with the development of weapons forbidden by the Versailles Treaty, such as tanks and aircraft. In 1934, Hitler ordered the killing of the SA leader, Ernst Röhm, thus signalling his intent to increase and modernize the traditional armed services, rather than replace them by a mass militia. Underpinning all this was a much broader process of social mobilization and transformation. Hitler believed passionately that Germany would only survive the forthcoming struggle if she could achieve inner unity and racial purity. A compulsory Labour Service was established for purposes of ideological indoctrination and military mobilization.[94] Class distinctions were to be transcended by national solidarity. German society was to be a '*Volksgemeinschaft*', a 'racial community', and instead of aristocrats, bourgeois and workers, there should be only '*Volksgenossen*', or 'people's comrades'.[95] Women were encouraged to marry, stay at home and raise the next generation of German warriors. 'Every child that a woman brings into the world,' Hitler announced, 'is [equivalent to] a battle, a battle waged for the existence of her people'; a celibacy tax was introduced for unmarried men and women.[96] Hitler also sought to heal the rift between Catholic Germany and the Protestant mainstream by concluding a Concordat with the pope. Above all, Hitler moved decisively against the Jews, whom he regarded as the principal threat to the cohesion which Germany society needed to cope with the challenges ahead. Jews were rigorously excluded from the civil service, and subject to an economic boycott. It was only a concern for public opinion in Britain and the United States, and fear of reprisals orchestrated by 'world Jewry', that restrained the chancellor from taking more extreme measures right away.

At first, Hitler trod carefully in the international sphere. He was anxious not to provoke an attack before his rearmament programme had taken effect. In a speech to the generals of early February 1933, Hitler expressed concern that the French and their 'eastern satellites' would attack before the domestic transformation was complete. 'If it were to be learned that Germany was planning a war,' he stressed later that year, 'this could have highly damaging consequences.' Intelligence reports suggested that a Polish invasion was on the cards.[97] Hitler therefore relied on a mixture of bluff, conciliation and manoeuvre. The military dimensions of the Labour Service were played down in order to confuse the watching Allies. France and Britain were duped into believing that German air power was much further advanced than it actually was.[98] In January 1934, Hitler broke out of the Franco-Polish encirclement by concluding a non-aggression pact with Warsaw. All the same, the aggressive thrust of German policy was clear. Hitler ended the secret military cooperation with Moscow. He announced his intention to withdraw from the League of Nations, and shortly after he crashed out of the Geneva disarmament talks. Hitler also used the large Nazi party in Austria to agitate for *Anschluss* with Germany. By July 1934, they felt strong enough to launch a *Putsch* attempt that failed but during which the Austrian chancellor, Engelbert Dollfuss, was murdered. Hitler's determination to resurrect German power, to dominate central Europe and to destroy the Versailles settlement generally was now plain for all to see.

German policies caused consternation among the other European powers. In 1934, responding to Hitler's lunge towards Vienna, Mussolini sent troops to the Brenner Pass on the Austro-Italian border. Hitler immediately backed off. The Soviet leadership was equally if not more alarmed by the victory of National Socialism. They had read *Mein Kampf*, especially the bits about 'Russia and her vassal states', took Nazi ideology seriously, and were in no doubt about what it meant for them. Hitler, the veteran communist Karl Radek warned in 1933, was 'overturning Versailles'. Stalin and his Commissar for Foreign Affairs,

Maxim Litvinov, therefore sought to tie Hitler into a system of mutual guarantees if possible, and to contain him through collective international action if necessary.[99] The Soviet Union therefore joined the League of Nations in 1934. That same year, the Comintern abandoned its traditional hatred for Social Democrats and called upon 'anti-fascist' parties across Europe to unite against Hitler. Diplomatic feelers were put out to Britain and France. At the same time, however, the Soviet Union fretted that the western powers would come to terms with Hitler over her head. Moscow would have to tread carefully between the imperial rivals and prevent them from getting too close to each other.

There was also no doubt in Paris, Warsaw and London that the new Germany posed a threat. The Poles put down a strong marker by occupying the Westerplatte near Danzig in March 1933, and serious thought was given to the idea of a joint pre-emptive strike with France against Germany before her rearmament was complete. There was no appetite for such a course of action in Paris, however. Joseph Paul-Boncour, the French foreign minister from December 1932 to January 1934, unsuccessfully sought a pact between France, Britain, Italy and Germany to guarantee the peace. He was followed by Louis Barthou, who saw a Soviet alliance directed against Germany as the solution. In mid-September 1934 he even helped Stalin to secure a seat on the Council of the League of Nations. In London, the Defence Requirements Sub-Committee pronounced unmistakably in February 1934 that while both Japan and, to a lesser extent, Italy were serious threats, the 'ultimate potential enemy' was Germany.[100] The defence of the wider empire was a much lower priority. Britain decided in July 1934 to establish a substantial 'Field Force' for deployment to the continent in time of war. Yet there were very few in Whitehall and Westminster who were advocating out-and-out military resistance to Hitler at that point. One of them was Winston Churchill, now in the political wilderness, who argued from the start that the Germans – 'this mighty people, the most powerful and most dangerous in the western world' – had voluntarily subjected themselves to Hitler, and should be resisted without delay.[101] The perceived strength of the Luftwaffe greatly increased anxiety about Hitler. For this reason, the prime minister, Stanley Baldwin, warned parliament in July 1934, during a debate on the expansion of the RAF, that 'since the day of the air, the old frontiers are gone'. 'When you think of the defence of

England,' he continued, 'you no longer think of the chalk cliffs of Dover; you think of the Rhine. That is where our frontier lies.'[102]

On the far side of the Atlantic, Hitler caused relatively little alarm for the moment.[103] President Franklin Delano Roosevelt, who was inaugurated in January 1933, did not want to jeopardize his programme of internal recovery through external distractions. Moreover, his Secretary of State, Sumner Welles, was strongly sceptical that any fundamental US interests were at stake in Europe. The only initiative that Roosevelt launched to balance Germany, and to a lesser extent Japan, was the recognition of the Soviet Union in November 1933.[104] One way or the other, the great powers failed not only to take preventive action against Hitler in 1933–4, when it would have been militarily straightforward, but even to form a common front against him. Regime change or the forcible restoration of German democracy was never considered.

All the same, the Nazi threat had an immediate effect on domestic politics across Europe. Stalin was conscious that failure to deal with it would undermine his authority at home. 'No people,' he remarked in 1933, 'can respect its government if it sees the danger of attack and does not prepare for self-defense.'[105] He therefore tightened his grip on party and population even further. Even though the origins of the policy pre-date Hitler's takeover of power, collectivization was stepped up, resulting in a huge famine in the Ukraine in 1933. That same year, Stalin unleashed a series of 'Treason Trials', which led to the execution of Lev Kamenev, former deputy chairman of the Council of People's Commissars, and Zinoviev on charges of conspiring against the Soviet Union with fascists and Trotskyites abroad. At the same time, a concerted campaign was launched against national groups suspected of collaborating with the external enemy, especially in the Ukraine and White Russia.[106] In Moscow, high politics polarized around the question of how to respond to Hitler. Figures such as Vyacheslav Molotov, chairman of the Council of People's Commissars, and the collectivization supremo, Lazar Kaganovich, challenged Litvinov's policy of trying to create a European alliance against Hitler through the League of Nations. For the moment, Stalin went along with Litvinov, but nobody knew better than he that the power he had won promising to defend the Soviet Union against external attack could just as easily be lost on the same grounds.

British and French domestic politics after 1933 were also substantially shaped by the rise of Hitler. The bitterly contested East Fulham by-election in October 1933 was dominated by the question of rearmament and won by the candidate opposed to greater military expenditure.[107] In the 1935 general election both major parties were opposed – Labour bitterly so – to large-scale rearmament, and the victorious Conservative prime minister, Stanley Baldwin, later notoriously admitted that any other position would have led to his defeat. At the heart of this hesitation was widespread fear of aerial bombing, which it was widely believed would cause hundreds of thousands if not millions of civilian casualties. The subject dominated Commons debates on foreign policy and rearmament with the result that press, parliamentary and public interest in national security largely exhausted itself in demanding increased provision for air defence; it was expected that Hitler would be contained and in the end defeated by naval blockade. There was hardly any popular concern at all for the state of the European balance, and the huge continental commitment which would be required to uphold it. In public opinion, the 'blue water' policy of an earlier generation of navalists had become a 'blue skies' strategy designed to minimize British involvement in Europe as much as possible.

In France, there were huge right-wing riots outside the Chamber of Deputies in Paris in February 1934. The left saw this as a Nazi- or Mussolini-style attempted takeover, and therefore responded positively to Moscow's suggestion of a Popular Front against 'fascism'. In June 1934, the communists and socialists formed a unity pact; the Radicals joined a month later. In France, unlike in Britain, leftist parties thus quickly came around to the view that the Nazis would have to be resisted by force. The problem was that French society was in a state of abject moral and physical decline. Pacifism, or at least a 'war anxiety' induced by the traumatic memory of the trenches, was the dominant discourse. Large sections of the press were in German and Italian pay, teachers and trade unionists were strongly opposed to confronting Hitler militarily, and nearly a third of males eligible for the army were deemed unfit for service, nearly twice as many as in more vigorous Germany.[108] In both countries, therefore, there was widespread pessimism about whether democracy would be strong enough to prevail against the dictators, or indeed whether it deserved to do so. There were many on the European right, especially in France, who sympathized with fascism and felt that it was better able to give expression to the national will. They felt that if they could not beat Hitler they should join him.

The challenge of the dictators also affected the relationship between London, Paris and their overseas empires. The imperial priority, as the British Permanent Under-Secretary to the Treasury, Warren Fisher, remarked in the mid-1930s, was to contain the 'Teutonic tribes, who century after century have been inspired by the philosophy of brute force'. On the other hand, the support of the empire, especially self-governing British dominions, could not be taken for granted. There was still considerable doubt among the Canadians, Australians, New Zealanders and South Africans that confronting Germany militarily was necessary or wise, not least because anxiety about Italian and especially Japanese power often loomed larger overseas.[109] Some constituencies, such as the Afrikaners and the French Canadians, could not be relied on at all: the *Québecois* leader, Henri Bourassa, warned that 'British imperialism must not be allowed to drag Canada into any more wars.'[110] In 1935, the India Act sought to deliver on earlier promises of self-government and meet the demands of the Congress Party halfway. The subcontinent was to remain an imperial strategic reserve, paid for in part by London, poised to deploy troops or labour forces to operate east and west.

American politics in the first years after 1933, by contrast, were largely unaffected by the changing geopolitical situation. To be sure, the economic trauma of the Great Depression meant that US anxiety about the future of democracy was widespread, but only a tiny minority saw Nazism or Italian fascism as a viable alternative. Nor were the dictators popularly regarded as a threat, at least for the time being.[111] There were as yet relatively few calls to show solidarity with the European democracies or to protect the Jews from discrimination. President Roosevelt's 'New Deal', a huge experiment in state intervention into the economy, was not driven by a concern to prepare American society for the next conflict. He spoke of a 'war' on depression, not on neighbouring powers. The radical measures taken in the early 1930s, the creation of the Tennessee Valley Authority, the Works Progress Administration and other programmes designed to take the United States out of depression, or at least to ameliorate its effects, were perhaps the first undertaken by any government of a major power *without* an explicit strategic agenda.

In March 1935, Hitler announced the introduction of conscription, and the replacement of the old 100,000-man *Reichswehr* by a *Wehrmacht* of more than half a million men. The existence of a growing air force, the *Luftwaffe*, was made public. This was the most serious Nazi breach of the Versailles settlement so far. The complete rearmament of Germany, and thus the transformation of the whole European balance of power, was now on the cards. This time, the powers reacted quickly. In mid-April, the British, French and Italians formed the 'Stresa Front' to uphold the Locarno Treaty, defend what was left of Versailles, and resist any further German encroachments. In early May, France and the Soviet Union concluded a treaty of mutual assistance albeit without any meaningful military protocols. Germany was now much more effectively surrounded than at any point since 1917. Hitler would have to act quickly before the ring drew tighter around the *Reich* and strangled in its infancy the domestic transformation he had inaugurated. He would have to prise open the encircling coalition and throw this first sustained attempt to contain a resurgent Germany off-balance.

In late June 1935, Hitler made a significant breach in the hostile front. He persuaded the British to conclude a Naval Agreement in which he renounced the return of German colonies, explicitly acknowledged British maritime superiority by agreeing to limit German construction to one third of that of the Royal Navy, and undertook not to engage in unrestricted submarine warfare. In Britain, locking Hitler into an arms control agreement while she still held the advantage was reckoned a great success. It was also seen as a way of escaping a continental commitment and concentrating on imperial defence. In return, Hitler had subverted British commitment to the Stresa Front. All the same, Germany's position remained extraordinarily precarious until October 1935. That month, Mussolini – misunderstanding the spirit of Stresa – sought to draw on his credit in Paris and London by invading Ethiopia, thus underlining Italy's claim to great-power status. Much to his surprise, the British and French governments – under pressure from outraged public opinion – strongly opposed the move. They did not, however, press the League of Nations to impose effective sanctions – especially a crucial oil embargo – on Mussolini. Hitler, on the other hand, expressed not only public sympathy for Italian ambitions in Africa, but also signalled his willingness to resolve the thorny question of the South Tyrol by accepting Italian sovereignty there. The Stresa Front, and with it the prospect of a pan-European coalition to contain a resurgent Germany, disintegrated.

Hitler now moved quickly to exploit the opening by occupying the demilitarized zone in the Rhineland in late March 1936. This was another hammer blow to the Versailles system, and a direct challenge to the Stresa powers. Hitler later pronounced the subsequent forty-eight hours as 'the most nerve-wracking my life. If the French had then marched into the Rhineland we would have had to withdraw with our tails between our legs, for the military resources at our disposal would have been wholly inadequate for even a moderate resistance'.[112] Paris, however, did not move and nor did London. The 'Führer' also speeded up the mobilization of German society and the economy. In August 1936, he conceived a 'Four Year Plan' – the choice of words suggested a quicker pace than Stalin's 'Five Year Plan' – to prepare for war by 1940/41. Hermann Göring was put in charge of this effort. 'Autarchy' – self-sufficiency in foodstuffs and raw materials – became the watchword. The costs of rearmament were to be borne in full knowledge of their distorting effect on the economy. 'The confrontation we are heading towards,' Göring remarked at the end of the year, 'requires huge capabilities. There is no end to rearmament in sight. The only decisive thing here is victory or defeat. If we win, business will be compensated sufficiently. One cannot be guided here by actuarial considerations of profit, but only by the demands of politics.'[113]

The geopolitical and domestic consequences of the re-militarization of the Rhineland were enormous. Other powers now scrambled too. In October of that year, Belgium abandoned the Franco-Belgian military accords of 1920 to pursue an 'exclusively and completely Belgian' policy, in effect to become neutral.[114] Hitler's coup also provoked a passionate debate within Britain and France. Some British observers argued that Hitler was merely moving into his 'back yard'. Most were concerned that the staff talks with the French would provoke Hitler, and drag them all into another continental European war. In France, by contrast, the German move contributed substantially to the election of a Popular Front government under Léon Blum in April 1936, which was pledged to unite the country against fascism at home and abroad. His administration embarked on an ambitious programme of social transformation, designed to make France not only more equal, but also more resilient in the face of Hitler and Mussolini.[115] The school-leaving age was raised, the Bank of France was placed under partial state control, fixed prices for wheat were introduced, and in August 1936 the arms industry was nationalized. Édouard Daladier's defence ministry was permitted to increase expenditure radically to nearly one third of the entire budget. France was preparing for the worst.

Battle between the Popular Fronts and the emerging German–Italian alliance was soon joined. In July 1936, Spanish nationalist forces under General Francisco Franco revolted against the left-wing Popular Front government elected earlier that year, plunging the country into civil war.[116] Many perceived this proxy conflict between European fascism and the international Popular Front as an ideological war between dictatorship and democracy. It was the geopolitical issues at stake, however, which made the Spanish Civil War such a crucial front in the battle for mastery in Europe. Hitler sent an expeditionary force to help Franco, in order to put pressure on France's southern flank and re-create the pattern of encirclement which had threatened Paris in the time of Charles V. More importantly, Hitler was determined to pre-empt a communist victory which would spill over into France, allowing both powers to collaborate with the Soviet Union in the encirclement of Germany. Mussolini sent an even larger force to support the nationalists. Stalin dithered for some time, but eventually backed the Republicans. The French Popular Front government of Léon Blum, by contrast, declared a policy of non-intervention in August 1936. Britain followed suit. Both powers imposed an arms embargo on the whole country, which tended to favour the better-equipped nationalist forces. Thousands of volunteers from France, Britain, Germany, the United States and many other parts of the world flocked to Spain in the 'International Brigades' to fight 'fascism'.

As Europe was sucked into the Spanish vortex, another crisis was brewing on the other side of the Mediterranean. In 1936, encouraged by the Grand Mufti of Jerusalem, the Palestinian Arabs launched a three-year revolt against the British mandate designed to drive out the Jewish population. Zionist settlers retaliated and set up clandestine organizations such as the *Irgun* and *Betar*; for the first time, Jews would now take the fight to the enemy militarily. Bitter guerrilla warfare resulted. London eventually deployed about 10 per cent of the British army in the late 1930s to secure this crucial piece of the geopolitical jigsaw in the Middle East. In 1937, at the height of the disturbances, the Peel Commission recommended a partition of the area between Arabs and Jews with an exchange of population between the two states. Arab leaders feared that they were too weak to prevail against British imperialism and world Zionism on their own; for this reason, they looked to Nazi Germany for ideological inspiration and practical help.[117] For the time being, however, the Arabs were much more interested in Hitler than he was in them. The Führer was still experimenting with the idea of deporting German Jews beyond the boundaries of Europe, perhaps to Africa; in 1938, he approved the idea of sending them to Madagascar. A Jewish state in Palestine was therefore not a threat, but an opportunity to dump more refugees.

By the end of 1936, Hitler was back in control of events. He had not only broken out of Franco-Polish encirclement, but he had stymied a serious attempt by France, Britain and Italy to contain him at Stresa. The United States – his ultimate enemy – had hardly stirred. He had restored full German sovereignty over the *Reich* itself, the Saar and the Rhineland; rearmament was proceeding apace. Mussolini – who had been such a bone in the throat over Austria – increasingly came round after the Abyssinian crisis. From July 1936, his new Italian foreign minister, Count Ciano, sought to 'faschistize' Italian diplomacy and to steer his country in a more 'revolutionary' and pro-German direction. A formal alliance – the 'Axis' – followed in October. A month later, Hitler concluded the Anti-Comintern Pact with Japan, and – in due course – Italy. This was directed principally against the Soviet Union, which was now menaced west and east by the Axis, but it was also intended as a global 'encirclement' of the British Empire in order to deter it from intervention in continental European affairs. A new global geopolitics, pitting the Axis dictatorships against the western democracies, and both against Soviet communism, had emerged.

Stalin reacted violently. He became increasingly paranoid about foreign subversion and embarked on a prolonged round of 'purges' to consolidate his control over party and state.[118] The most capable army commander, Marshal Tukachevski, was executed on suspicion of treasonable contacts with the German secret service; tens of thousands of Red Army officers perished with him. Hundreds of thousands of ordinary citizens were also shot. Countless more were sent to the Gulag, an archipelago of more than one hundred labour camps mainly in Siberia. Kulaks, an independent larger farmer class, were accused of being in league with the Japanese through an imagined 'Russian General Military Union'. There was also a strong ethnic component to the persecution, in which 'enemy nations' were systematically targeted. Koreans were deported from the Far Eastern provinces in case they might collaborate with the Japanese. About 100,000 Poles in the Ukraine and White Russia considered to be a potential security risk were shot in 1937–8. It was, at one level, the politics of the permanent pogrom and at the other the logical conclusion to the long Russian tradition of coercive modernization in the face of an external threat. About 4 million men and women were affected in all, of whom about 800,000 were killed.

On the other side of the world, President Roosevelt also reacted sharply to the new Axis geopolitics. Looking west and east, he saw forces gathering which would threaten the security of the United States in the long term. In Europe, the dictators were on the march; in Asia, emboldened by the Anti-Comintern Pact, the Japanese launched a full-scale invasion of China in early July 1937. That year the journalist Livingston Hartley published *Is America afraid?*, arguing that the domination of Europe by a single power such as Germany, and Asia by Japan, threatened to encircle the United States. This would be, moreover, the envelopment of democracy by dictatorships. In early October 1937, Roosevelt gave voice to these sentiments in a much-publicized speech at Chicago. 'Let no one imagine that America will escape,' he cautioned, 'that America may expect mercy, that this Western Hemisphere will not be attacked.' 'When an epidemic of physical disease starts to spread,' Roosevelt continued, 'the community approves and joins in a quarantine of the patients in order to protect the health of the community against the spread of the disease.'[119] At the same time, Roosevelt had not completely given up hope that Germany might be contained through a new 'general settlement' in Europe at which her reasonable demands were met. To this end, he authorized his Secretary of State, Sumner Welles, to tour the continent and mediate between the great powers. Whether it was to be the carrot of the 'Welles Plan', or the stick of 'quarantine', one thing was clear. The United States had re-engaged with European geopolitics.

In Berlin, the shift in American policy towards Europe struck home like a thunderbolt. Hitler's strategy had been to establish German dominance in central Europe, preparatory to destroying the Soviet Union and securing the *Lebensraum* in the east without which the *Reich* could not hope to contain the overwhelming power of the United States. Roosevelt's shot across his bows in early October 1937 rendered the original timetable obsolete. Henceforth, Hitler had to reckon with American hostility. This meant that the domestic transformation of Germany and the consolidation of central Europe under his leadership would have to be speeded up. For this reason, Hitler summoned a meeting of his political and military leaders in the Imperial Chancellery in early November 1937. A sudden urgency now entered the Führer's discourse. 'It [is my] unalterable determination,' Hitler announced, 'to solve Germany's problem of space by 1943–1945.'[120] Only the acquisition of 'greater living space' and raw materials in Europe, adjacent to the *Reich*, would suffice. The first step in this direction, he ordained, was the annexation of Austria and Czechoslovakia.

At the same time, Hitler stepped up the pace of domestic change. In February 1938, he pushed out the war minister, Werner von Blomberg, and the Chief of the Army, Freiherr von Fritsch. Hitler replaced them with the Supreme Command of the *Wehrmacht* under the utterly subservient Wilhelm Keitel, and the equally pliable Walther von Brauchitsch as Chief of the Army. He also used the opportunity to remove the conservative nationalist Konstantin von Neurath and replace him with the radical Nazi Joachim von Ribbentrop as foreign minister. The German national security apparatus was now completely in Hitler's hands. His next target was Austria, control of which would not only give the Reich a substantial demographic and economic boost, but also expose Czechoslovakia to attack on its southern flank. Here Hitler exploited another opportunity; indeed, events forced his hand. In early March 1938, the Austrian chancellor, Kurt Schuschnigg, announced the holding of a referendum on unification with Germany. He intended to skew the wording of the question, and the composition of the electorate, in such a way as to ensure a rejection of *Anschluss*. Hitler immediately moved to preempt this and occupied Austria amid scenes of wild enthusiasm from the local population. This time, Mussolini stood aside. At the beginning of the following month, Hitler ordered the traditional imperial insignia to be moved from Vienna to the party city of Nuremberg. This highly symbolic move was intended to suggest a synthesis between the old Holy Roman Empire and National Socialism.

All that now stood between Hitler and total control of central Europe was Czechoslovakia, with its large and restive German minority in the Sudetenland, who made up more than one third of the population. There was no appetite in either London or Paris to defend its integrity.

This reflected a widespread belief that Berlin had a legitimate grievance against the Czechs over the treatment of the Sudeten Germans, and residual hopes that Hitler's aims were essentially limited. The principal reason, however, why the two western powers refused to intervene was fear of a rearmed Germany. Nobody who remembered the *Reich*'s extraordinary military performance in the world war wanted to risk another conflict if it could possibly be helped. In particular, general staffs in both Britain and France strongly opposed a land war against Germany in 1938. They ruled out simultaneously fighting Hitler in central Europe and Mussolini in the Mediterranean; London also had the Japanese to worry about. Cooperation with Stalin's Soviet Union was ruled out on ideological and practical grounds. The dominions were resolutely against fighting over Czechoslovakia. Doing so would shatter the very unity of the British Empire upon which London depended as a force multiplier in Europe. Even ardent resisters such as Sir Robert Vansittart baulked at taking on Hitler openly and this weakened their hand against the dominant 'appeasers'. 'It is easy to be brave in speech,' the Permanent Under-Secretary in the Foreign Office, Sir Alexander Cadogan, asked him at the time of Hitler's ultimatum over Austria, '[but] will you fight?' Vansittart replied: 'No.' 'Then what is it all about?' Cadogan rejoined. 'To me it seems a most cowardly thing to do to urge a small man to fight a big [man] if you won't help the former.'[121]

For this reason, western leaders were anxious to refute not only the idea that Hitler represented a fundamental threat to European peace, but the notion that there was an irreconcilable gulf between Nazism and the west. 'We shall never get far' in the work of mediation, the British prime minister, Neville Chamberlain, told parliament in early November 1938, 'unless we can accustom ourselves to the idea that the democracies and the totalitarian states are not to be ranged against one another in two opposing blocs'. Much better, he argued, for Britain to 'work together' with its rivals and thereby 'facilitate the international exchange of goods and the regulation of international relations in various ways for the good of all'.[122] While Hitler was consciously waging an ideological war, the western democracies continued to pursue a strategy of engagement in the spirit of Locarno. They rejected Stalin's frantic attempts to create a common diplomatic front against Germany. The effect of this approach was the opposite of what was intended. Instead of entering into constructive cooperation, or allowing themselves to be enmeshed in a web of mutual obligations, the dictators simply pocketed all concessions and made further demands.

So when Hitler confronted Czechoslovakia in the autumn of 1938, brandishing the minority-rights legislation of the League on behalf of the Sudeten Germans, Prague faced the onslaught alone. It was unable to take up Stalin's offer of military aid because neither the Poles nor the Romanians – fearful that the Red Army would refuse to leave – would grant transit through their territory. Mussolini strongly backed Hitler. Britain and France instructed Prague to capitulate to Hitler's demands; despite having a strong army the Czechs decided not to fight. Chamberlain flew to Germany in late September to arrange the Czech surrender. In the Munich agreement, he allowed Hitler to annex the entire Sudetenland, an industrially and strategically vital semi-circle around the Bohemian periphery. Czechoslovakia was not only territorially mutilated but rendered militarily defenceless. The rest of Bohemia was there for the taking. Returning to Britain, Chamberlain proclaimed 'peace in our time'.

The Munich agreement had a profound effect on European domestic politics and geopolitical alignments. In late 1938, French opinion polls showed that 70 per cent of Frenchmen wanted to resist any further German encroachments. In Britain, the longstanding debate between 'appeasers' and 'resisters' on how to deal with Germany became the central political issue. More and more members of the Labour Party moved away from pacifism and towards the view that Hitler had to be stopped; the left-wing press, led by the *Daily Mirror*, now relentlessly battered appeasement.[123] The Conservatives remained a 'class divided' between those such as Churchill, Harold Macmillan and Anthony Eden, who believed that concessions simply encouraged further demands, and the Chamberlainite majority, which held that another war against Germany would destroy civilization as they knew it and open the door to a communist takeover of the whole of Europe. Some such as the Foreign Secretary, Lord Halifax, even saw Hitler as a 'bulwark of the west against Bolshevism'. Matters came to a head during the bitter by-elections held in late October and early November 1938 when Liberals, Labour and Conservative dissidents rallied to support anti-appeasement candidates. In Oxford, their campaign literature announced that a vote for the official Conservative candidate was 'a vote for Hitler'; he squeaked in with a greatly reduced majority. Three weeks later, however, a Conservative majority at Bridgwater was overturned in a result that was widely regarded as a popular rejection of appeasement. The message was clear: Chamberlain's policy of appeasement had now lost its popular backing.[124]

In Germany, on the other hand, Hitler's triumph at Munich effectively silenced critical voices within the elite. Carefully laid plans by General Ludwig Beck and other military critics to topple Hitler before he plunged Germany into a ruinous war were called off. The conspirators received little encouragement from abroad: Chamberlain dismissed the German resistance as 'Jacobites' who lacked legitimacy at home. Hitler now stepped up his campaign against the enemy within. On 9 November 1938, the SA and the mob were let loose on synagogues and Jewish property across Germany in the *Kristallnacht* pogrom. A month later, Ribbentrop insisted that all representatives of Jewish descent be excluded from his diplomatic receptions. In late January 1939, Hitler escalated his rhetoric still further. He prophesied to the *Reichstag* that 'If International Finance Jewry within Europe and abroad should succeed once more in plunging the peoples into a world war, then the consequence will not be the Bolshevization of the world and therefore a victory of Jewry, but on the contrary, the destruction of the Jewish race in Europe.'[125] In other words, Hitler regarded his struggle against the Jews as part not of domestic politics but of grand strategy.

In March 1939, Hitler took advantage of a crisis in Czech–Slovak relations to occupy Prague. Once again, the British and the French gave way; the League of Nations took no action and neither did the United States. Bohemia and Moravia became a German protectorate; Slovakia declared its independence as a German satellite. Czechoslovakia ceased to exist. Hitler's military and economic preparations for war received a powerful boost from the absorption of the Czech army, which included many advanced armoured fighting vehicles, and the industrial potential of Bohemia. Rather than rallying to contain Germany over Czechoslovakia in 1938–9, the smaller and middling powers now rushed to make their peace with Hitler. Romania, Yugoslavia and Bulgaria sought German protection. Some states even joined in the feeding frenzy themselves, partly in order to indulge longstanding ambitions, but also because they believed that restraint would only be rewarded by unilateral gains on the part of their rivals. Poland seized the disputed territory of Teschen from Czechoslovakia in late 1938, and Hungary annexed a substantial strip of southern Slovakia populated largely by Magyars. Mussolini, too, was anxious to 'compensate' for Hitler's gains with acquisitions of his own. He responded to Hitler's annexation of Bohemia and Moravia by occupying Albania in April 1939. One way or the other, the European map was being changed as much by reactions to Hitler as by the man himself.

Within British and French domestic politics, however, opinion shifted sharply against appeasement. Hitler's occupation of Prague effectively destroyed popular and press confidence in government strategy towards Germany; the parliamentary rumblings grew greater. Chamberlain was relentlessly attacked from the opposition benches and, more worryingly for him, was confronted with calls from Conservative resisters for an all-party government. In effect this would have lined Britain up in a 'popular front' against Hitler. Similar developments were taking place in France. The appeasers led by the foreign minister, Georges Bonnet, were losing ground to the resisters around the prime minister, Daladier. British and French society was preparing to resist Germany.

London and Paris were now forced to recognize that Hitler not only totally dominated central Europe – something they tolerated with severe misgivings – but intended to overturn the whole European balance on the strength of it. In late February, the cabinet agreed to go to war in the event of a German attack on Holland, Belgium or Switzerland, and issued a public guarantee of French security. The continental 'Field Force' was mobilized in the first months of 1939, and the first really intensive Anglo-French staff talks followed soon after. The *Entente Cordiale* had been revived. It was not enough, however, just to draw the line in the west. Further German gains in eastern Europe – and rumours of a descent on Poland or Romania were already circulating – would have to be prevented. Moreover, Hitler could only be defeated – or better still deterred – if he was forced to fight on two fronts; keeping the Poles in play was therefore vital. For this reason, the western powers issued a formal guarantee of Polish and Romanian independence in March 1939, though not necessarily of their territorial integrity. This was designed to allow some room for a Polish–German territorial settlement, but to deter Hitler from outright annexation, thus denying him the resources to wage a successful war against them.

Hitler's actions had also made a deep impression on the United States. Roosevelt told his civilian and defence chiefs that for the first time since the Holy Alliance in 1818 the United States now faced the possibility of an attack 'on the Atlantic side in both the Northern and the Southern hemispheres'. If the Germans could defeat or seize the Royal Navy that would result in a substantial shift in the maritime balance of power to America's disadvantage. Furthermore, as Roosevelt pointed out in a press conference at around the same time, technological advances – especially air power – had brought a potential attack 'infinitely closer' than in previous decades.[126] Moreover, the dictators posed not merely a strategic but also an ideological threat; indeed, the two considerations fused in the president's mind. For much of the late 1930s, he feared that Hitler or Mussolini might 'do in Mexico what they did in Spain', which was to 'organize a revolution, a fascist revolution'.[127] Roosevelt therefore saw the struggle against the European dictators as a cosmic battle between two world views, in which the security of the United States was inextricably linked to that of the world beyond the western hemisphere.[128]

Stalin, however, was now convinced that the western European powers were not interested in a common front. On the contrary, there was every sign that they hoped that Hitler could be used to contain him. In March 1939, therefore, the Soviet dictator warned publicly that the USSR would 'maintain vigilance and not allow those who would provoke war to draw our country into a conflict', nor would he 'pull others' chestnuts out of the fire'.[129] His suggested Franco-British-Russian alliance to guarantee the territorial settlement in eastern Europe – in effect simply an extension of the promise London and Paris had already made – led to desultory negotiations which dragged on through the summer. The delay was partly due to Polish refusal to countenance Soviet military help – which would have fatally undermined Warsaw's hold on its White Russian and Ukrainian provinces – and a mistaken Anglo-French belief in the strength of the Polish army. Radical action was needed to break out of the vicelike grip in which Tokyo and Berlin now held the Soviet Union. That same month, the Russians decisively defeated Japanese forces in Mongolia at the battle of Nomonhan. His eastern flank secure, at least for the time being, Stalin could now concentrate on Hitler.

For his part, Hitler was feeling more and more boxed in. Deeply worried by Roosevelt's increasingly belligerent rhetoric,[130] and convinced that the showdown with the United States was much closer than he had expected, Hitler ordered the implementation of the 'Z-Plan', the construction of a large ocean-going surface fleet – the *Weltmachtsflotte*,[131] capable of projecting German air power across the Atlantic, not just against the British Empire but also the United States. In March, Hitler resurrected his colonial demands in Africa and brought Spain into the Anti-Comintern Pact, a move directed much more across the Atlantic than at Moscow. In April 1939, he abrogated the Anglo-German naval treaty, partly as a reaction to the Polish guarantee, but also in recognition of the fact that the maritime confrontation with the Anglo-Saxon powers was moving closer.

It was in eastern Europe, however, that Hitler's new timetable really made itself felt. The only way of balancing the world powers, especially the United States, lay through the conquest of living space in the east. To this end, Hitler approached Poland in late October 1938 – shortly after the Sudeten crisis – with an offer of a joint campaign against the Soviet Union.[132] In return for Danzig and military cooperation – including transit across Polish territory to attack Russia – Warsaw would receive lands in the Ukraine. Poland, in other words, was to be co-opted as a junior partner in the *Lebensraum* project, not eliminated; it would rank somewhere between an ally, such as Mussolini, and a complete satellite, such as Slovakia. To Hitler's surprise and immense irritation, however, the Poles refused his overtures. Worse still, the Anglo-French guarantee both 're-encircled' Germany – the phrase was on everybody's lips in Berlin from March 1939 – and created an immovable obstacle to the Führer's grand strategy. The Poles stood between him and the ultimate security he craved: spatial depth in the Russian interior. If the Soviet Union were to be attacked, Poland would have to be crushed. With breathtaking audacity, Hitler now turned to Stalin to eliminate the last barrier to attacking him.

The resulting Molotov–Ribbentrop Pact of August 1939 was thus very much a sudden German initiative, but it offered Stalin at least a chance of a managed territorial reorganization in the east. Without agreement, Hitler would simply take the lot, and he might even ally with the French and British against Russia. Stalin was also playing a long game, hoping – as he told the Politburo in mid-August – for a 'Sovietized Germany', the ultimate prize, after a Franco-British victory over Germany. For all these reasons, he explained, it was 'in the interests of the USSR ... that war breaks out between the Reich and the capitalist

Anglo-French bloc'.[133] Stalin's main concern was not Poland, but the Baltic states: he feared that Hitler would move into Lithuania, Latvia and Estonia. The first clause of the pact dealt with Lithuania, only the second with Poland, and the intention seems to have been to mark the eastern limit of German expansion into Poland, rather than necessarily a zone for direct Soviet occupation. So when Hitler attacked Poland on 1 September 1939, he fired the opening shots of a Soviet–German war of coalition against the established European territorial order. Neither dictator got the war, or the partner, he had originally wanted, however. Hitler had intended to invade the Soviet Union in alliance with Poland; Stalin would have much preferred to have joined an Anglo-French front against Nazi Germany.

Britain and France eventually declared war on Germany on 3 September 1939, with great reluctance, and made no effort to attack Hitler's exposed western border. They still hoped for a compromise peace which would leave Germany intact as a bulwark against Bolshevism.[134] Stalin now, for his part, feared that a German defeat would upset the European balance and expose him to a concerted attack by the capitalist powers.[135] In the event, Warsaw's resistance crumbled quickly, and so on 17 September – the day after he finally vanquished the Japanese forces at Khalkhin Gol in Mongolia – Stalin sent Soviet troops into her eastern provinces. The fourth partition of Poland was complete. An intense period of Russo-German cooperation now followed, during which Stalin sent Hitler vital raw materials to wage war against the western powers; the NKVD returned escaped German communists to Hitler; and the SS handed Ukrainian nationalists over to the Soviet Union. Both intelligence services ruthlessly suppressed the Polish intelligentsia and officer corps. In November 1939, Stalin attacked Finland with a view to securing a buffer to defend Leningrad. A full-scale Russo-German territorial reorganization of eastern and northern Europe was underway.

The war had profound, but very different, effects on domestic politics. Unlike 1914, France did not experience a new *Union Sacrée* bringing together all parties and classes of society, however briefly and superficially. On the contrary, the divides between left and right, and between right-wing and left-wing appeasers and right-wing and left-wing resisters deepened. The position was further complicated by the Hitler–Stalin pact. The Communist Party was instructed by Moscow to refuse all cooperation with the government; its leader, Maurice Thorez, deserted from the army and fled to the Soviet Union. Armament production was sluggish, primarily because the economically liberal government left it in the hands of private enterprise. The war was prosecuted timidly, both in military and in propagandistic terms. French forces lulled themselves into a false sense of security behind the Maginot Line, while Hitler and Stalin reordered eastern Europe.

In Britain, the outbreak of war and the failure to contain Hitler nearly destroyed Chamberlain's government. In the end, the prime minister was pushed into taking action by a popular, press and parliamentary determination to confront Germany. As a result, Britain entered the war unenthusiastically but united, the only major state of the subsequent victorious Grand Alliance which took on Hitler directly rather than being attacked by him. Moreover, Australia, Canada, New Zealand and South Africa all rallied to the cause, in the last case only after a very bitter parliamentary debate; Ireland remained neutral. The war economy worked efficiently from the start of hostilities, thanks not least to government-sponsored cooperation between industry and trade unions in order to boost arms production.[136]

The totalitarian powers, on the other hand, pursued much more radical internal policies. Stalin revolutionized the occupied Polish territories, uprooting the bourgeoisie; fearful that they might form a pro-Allied fifth column, he ordered the murder of thousands of captured Polish officers in Katyn Wood in April–May 1940.[137] Likewise, Hitler tightened his grip on the German home front and the occupied territories. In late September 1939, all the security and surveillance organizations were united under Heinrich Himmler in the formidable *Reichsicherheitshauptamt*. A month later, Hitler authorized the start of a 'euthanasia' programme designed to eliminate 'unworthy life' and strengthen the biological fibre of the nation for the struggle ahead. Baltic and Russian Germans were brought 'home' into the *Reich*. He repeated his warnings that the Jews would be punished for plunging Europe back into war. The Jews in Poland were herded into ghettos; tens of thousands were summarily shot. For the moment, however, the German Jews were left alive, primarily to deter the United States. In July 1940, Hitler referred to them explicitly as 'hostages' in German hands. For all the rhetoric, however, Hitler did not yet order the total mobilization of German society for war. He was much slower than the British to draft women into the workplace, and more concerned to maintain the supply of consumer goods. Germany was still arming in breadth rather than depth: it would have difficulty sustaining a long war against Britain and France. Hitler was determined that there should be no repeat of the experience of the First World War, when the home front had collapsed as a result of the blockade.

With Poland crushed, Hitler was anxious to wind down the war in the west, and to secure *Lebensraum* in the east, before the United States intervened. In late September 1939, he opened a 'peace offensive' designed to achieve a compromise peace with Britain and France. He would then almost certainly have launched his attack on the Soviet Union as originally intended. London and Paris were not prepared to leave him in control of Poland, however, and so the overtures were rejected. Worse still, from the Germans' point of view, the British and French were preparing to cut off their supply of iron ore through Norway. So in April–May 1940, Hitler was forced to improvise again. He pre-empted the Allied occupation of Norway with his own invasion; Denmark was also occupied to secure the line of communication. Shortly afterwards, Hitler launched a lightning invasion of Holland, Belgium and France. This operation – which he feared might take several years – succeeded beyond his wildest expectations. Within a few weeks, the Low Countries had been completely over-run, the French army crushed, and the British Expeditionary Force so comprehensively beaten that it was lucky to escape in such large numbers from the beaches of Dunkirk.

The German victory in the west transformed European politics.[138] From June 1940, Hitler controlled not only the whole of central Europe, but also most of Poland, the entire northern half of France, the Low Countries, Denmark and Norway. What was left of France was dominated by Germany. The new, nominally independent 'Vichy' regime under Marshal Pétain and his chief minister, Pierre Laval, in the south sought to carve out a role for itself in Europe through 'collaboration' with Berlin.[139] The traditional European balance of power was no more. It had been replaced by German hegemony. This unleashed a territorial scramble which did as much – if not more – to change the European map than Hitler's direct actions. For the remaining powers, Hitler's geopolitical threat was both a threat and an opportunity. The Soviet leader was determined to 'compensate' for Hitler's gains, and pre-empt further German advances close to his borders, through annexations. Shortly after the fall of France, therefore, Stalin occupied the Baltic states, and a month later he forced Romania to hand over Bessarabia and the North Bukovina. He began to penetrate the Balkans, not only to pre-empt the Germans but also to keep out the British, whom he regarded as the principal capitalist world power and a standing threat to Soviet security. The net result of all this was that by the end of the year Stalin had invaded, occupied or territorially despoiled about as many independent states as Hitler.

Mussolini reacted to the collapse of France by pushing ahead with his plans for a fascist empire in south-eastern Europe and the Mediterranean.[140] In June 1940, he launched a belated and completely unsuccessful offensive in the south of France; he was rewarded with a zone of occupation nonetheless. Shortly afterwards he attacked the British in North Africa, and was ignominiously repulsed. Finally, in late October, Mussolini invaded Greece hoping at least to establish a Balkan hegemony to balance Hitler's dominance of central and western Europe. Once again, Italian forces became hopelessly bogged down as the Greeks put up a much stiffer resistance than expected. As if all this were not bad enough, the British sank much of the Italian fleet at anchor at Taranto in November 1940. Mussolini's humiliation was now complete. The string of defeats undermined the regime at home, where the first cracks were beginning to appear; foreign policy, long a tool of fascist governance in Italy, was now threatening to undermine it.[141] The Spanish dictator also hoped to take advantage of the collapse of French power. He occupied the International Zone in Tangier in mid-June 1940, not least in order to pre-empt the Italians. In October 1940, Hitler met Franco at Hendaye, but failed to persuade him to abandon his neutrality. At issue was not the Spaniard's refusal to attack Britain; he was eager to do so. The problem was that Franco presented a long list of territorial demands including not just Gibraltar but Oran and Morocco. This not only cut across Hitler's policy of trying to win over Pétain for the anti-British coalition, but would also have offended Mussolini.[142] In short, it was not Franco's restraint which kept Spain out of the war, but Hitler's.

The German invasion of the Low Countries precipitated a parliamentary revolt against Chamberlain in May 1940 (sometimes misleadingly described as the 'Norway debate'). The new government under Winston Churchill was determined to fight on and to make whatever military, economic, social and constitutional sacrifices necessary to achieve victory. In mid-June 1940, Churchill made an unsuccessful offer of union with France – involving joint citizenship and a common government – designed to lock the French into the war effort against Germany, or failing that to secure their fleet.[143] The Nazi threat was so existential, in other words, that it justified the surrender, or at least the pooling, of British sovereignty. Not long after, once the French had capitulated, Britain rejected Hitler's peace overtures. That summer, the Royal Air Force repulsed the *Luftwaffe*'s attempt to gain control of the skies over England, and even with air superiority Germany's ability to get past the Royal Navy would have been highly doubtful.[144] In any case, Hitler had never intended to fight Britain, if it could be avoided, and he was sucked into hostilities only by London's refusal to let him dominate central and eastern Europe. He called off 'Operation Sealion', the projected invasion of the south coast.

The fall of France had a major impact on the British Empire. It was now the last line of defence against Hitler – Churchill planned to carry on the struggle from Canada if Britain itself was conquered – and a reservoir of strength on which London could draw. Britain, therefore, never 'stood alone'.[145] Hundreds of invaluable 'imperial' pilots flew in the Battle of Britain.[146] New Zealand battle casualties were the highest among all belligerents as a proportion of the population, with the single exception of the Soviet Union.[147] Factories in Canada, Australia and India actually produced more rifles than Britain itself, as well as tens of thousands of aircraft; the Canadian economy alone was equal that of Italy. Over the next five years or so millions of Canadians, Australians, New Zealanders and South Africans served in one capacity or another, mainly against the Germans in the first instance. So did many Indians, who were in the war whether they liked it or not. After May 1940, the Indian army was doubled to 2 million men, and the resources of India were deployed systematically in support of the war effort. The combined industrial output of the British Empire soon exceeded that of German-occupied Europe in every category with the exception of rifles.

Hitler was no longer focused on fighting the British Empire, however. Shortly after the fall of France he signalled to his military leadership that he planned to attack the Soviet Union at the next opportunity. The failure to subdue Britain that summer and autumn, and Churchill's refusal to countenance an amicable division of the world between them, added to his determination to deal with both enemies before the Americans could intervene. In late September 1940, he brought together the Italians and Japanese to form the Tripartite Pact. At the end of the year, he issued a detailed instruction on how the attack on the Soviet Union – 'Operation Barbarossa' – was to be executed. First, however, Hitler had to secure his southern flank in the Balkans. Here Mussolini's failed Greek adventure brought British troops to help the Greeks. Worse still, the Italian offensive in North Africa not only failed but provoked a devastating British counter-attack in early 1941. To cap it all, Yugoslavia was convulsed by a Serbian nationalist coup widely interpreted as a rejection of alignment with Germany. So, in February 1941, he sent the *Afrikakorps* under Rommel to stem the tide in North Africa and to secure the area as a staging post from which to threaten America;[148] within a very short time, the British army there was in severe difficulties. Two months later, he overran Yugoslavia and Greece, both of which fell under joint Italo-German occupation; a Croatian puppet state under Ante Pavelić was established in the north, and a Serbian one in the south under Milan Nedić. Hitler had not originally intended to occupy so much of Europe, so quickly, and these snap strategic decisions were to have unexpected consequences.

Italian failure and Rommel's success in North Africa forced Hitler to think systematically about the Middle East. He now envisaged a massive pincer strategy, in which the *Afrikakorps* advanced east through Egypt and Palestine towards Mesopotamia, while another army wheeled south from the Ukraine, through the Caucasus, to join up with Rommel. Arab nationalists now saw Hitler as their best hope of expelling Zionists from Palestine and the British from the whole region. In January 1941, the Grand Mufti of Jerusalem, Amin al-Husseini, offered Hitler a strategic partnership against the 'Anglo-Jewish coalition'. This would also end 'the exploitation and the export of petrol for England's profit'. He subscribed wholeheartedly to the Nazi policies against the Jews, including physical extermination. The Nazi foreign minister, Ribbentrop, was enthused by the possibilities of the Middle East, especially after the pro-German Rashid Ali took power in a coup in Baghdad and launched pogroms against the Jews. Rashid Ali was soon crushed by the

British, however, and the two *Luftwaffe* squadrons deployed to Mosul with the help of the Vichyite authorities in Syria were shot down in a few days. For Hitler, however, the Middle East remained essentially a sideshow: local leaders were much more interested in him than he in them.

What really preoccupied the Führer was the United States. President Roosevelt had reacted to the fall of France with horror. He regarded the German victory as a fundamental shift in the European and thus the global balance of power, not least because Hitler might now inherit French possessions in South America and the Caribbean. Roosevelt feared that Hitler's real objective was to gain access to the Atlantic, probably by gaining a foothold in the Iberian peninsula, or even the Azores and Cape Verde.[149] US domestic opinion – where interventionists were still heavily outnumbered by sceptics and outright isolationists – meant that Roosevelt had to hold back. The president therefore framed his support for Britain as a strategy to pre-empt German penetration of Latin America. In early September 1940, he negotiated a deal by which the Royal Navy received elderly American destroyers in return for the lease of British bases. This move was directed against Hitler, to be sure, but it could also be defended in traditional terms as a diminution of the power of the British Empire in the western hemisphere. That same month, Congress agreed to the introduction of conscription, the first peacetime draft in US history.

In November 1940, Roosevelt secured a third term of office as president, and with it the room for manoeuvre he had lacked. He could now begin the containment of Hitler in earnest. At the very end of December 1940, he told the nation in one of his famous 'fireside chats' that the United States would act as the 'arsenal of democracy' against the dictators. In March 1941, Roosevelt introduced 'Lend-Lease', by which the United States 'leased' – in practice gave – huge quantities of war materials to the cash-strapped British and Chinese. This was, as the Secretary of War, Henry Stimson, pointed out, effectively 'a declaration of economic war' on Hitler and Japan; in a radio speech the day the Lend-Lease Bill passed the Senate, Roosevelt spoke openly of 'The Second World War', which 'began a year and a half ago.'[150] Later that same month, the president and his chiefs of staff agreed that, in the event of conflict with the Axis powers, the United States would concentrate on dealing with 'Germany first'. All the war plans focused on the Atlantic, Germany and the *Reich*. With this in mind, the Americans conducted the 'Washington conversations' with Japan in April 1941 designed to hold Tokyo in check while Germany was sorted out. Hitler was not privy, of course, to US military planning but the general direction of US policy – which he attributed to the power of 'world Jewry' in Washington – was unmistakable. That same month, desperate to avoid a Japanese defeat, which would leave him facing the full might of the Americans alone, and convinced that open conflict with Roosevelt was only months away, he made a fateful promise to Tokyo that he would support them in a future war against the United States.

So, on 22 June, the Führer invaded the Soviet Union. Next to the *Wehrmacht* itself, the invading army included, or came to include, national contingents from allied Italy, Finland, Romania, Hungary, Slovakia and neutral Spain (whence Franco supplied the Blue Division) as well as volunteers from almost every part of Europe, France, the Low Countries and Scandinavia. Hitler had mobilized almost the whole of Europe in support of his strategy. His aim was not just to eliminate Bolshevism, or at least to push it beyond the Urals, but to secure the *Lebensraum* which Germany needed to survive the looming showdown with the encircling Jewish Anglo-American coalition. To this end, the lands conquered were to be ruthlessly colonized and purged of all Jewish and communist influences. Right from the beginning, the army executed Soviet commissars as suspected agents of world Jewry, while SS *Einsatzgruppen* advancing behind the front line slaughtered hundreds of thousands of male Jews; the women and children were generally spared, for the moment.

Stalin now oversaw the total mobilization of Soviet society. He announced that the struggle 'cannot be considered a normal war . . . between two armies', but a 'fatherland war' of 'freedom against slavery'.[151] Critical industries in danger of being overrun by the Germans were dismantled and reassembled in safe locations beyond the Urals. Very soon, these were turning out tens of thousands of tanks, aircraft and artillery pieces. Millions of soldiers were drafted; many officers languishing in the Gulag were released to serve on the front line. Russian national sentiment was encouraged. Stalin was slow, by contrast, to appeal to popular religious sentiment. This seems to have developed spontaneously as a reaction to invasion, and the regime revived the Moscow patriarchate not so much to promote it as to manage a wave of enthusiasm which might otherwise be directed against the regime.[152] Dissent, potential and actual, was still brutally suppressed: about 2.5 million people were sent to the Gulag during the war, and hundreds of thousands of Germans and Chechens were deported pre-emptively for fear they might collaborate with Hitler. Towards the end of 1941, based on vital intelligence that the Japanese did not plan to attack in the east, and were in fact about to attack the United States, Stalin authorized the transfer of powerful Siberian divisions westwards. By the end of the year, the Red Army had stopped the *Wehrmacht* from reaching Moscow. The outcome of the war was still entirely open, but it was clear that the chance of a quick German victory had passed.

Roosevelt now stepped up the pressure on Hitler still further. He did not accept Stalin's astonishing offer to deploy American troops under US command anywhere on the Russian front. Public opinion was still strongly opposed to formal belligerence. The president did, however, send Stalin substantial military aid, unfroze Soviet assets and freed Soviet shipping from the restrictions of the Neutrality Act. He met with Churchill at Placentia Bay off Newfoundland in mid-August 1941 and agreed what came to be known as the 'Atlantic Charter'. This announced a 'better future for the world' on the basis of the rejection of 'territorial changes that do not accord with the freely expressed wishes of the people concerned' and the establishment of a peace '[a]fter the final destruction of Nazi tyranny'; and the disarmament of nations 'which threaten, or may threaten, aggression outside of their frontiers'.

The crucial phrase was the reference to 'the final destruction of Nazi tyranny'. The Charter was a strategy for the defeat of Hitler, a super-Versailles which would once again disarm Germany. It was a remarkable document from a non-belligerent power, issued without Congressional authority. In the following month, the president instructed US destroyers to shoot at German raiders or submarines on sight. 'When you see a rattlesnake poised to strike,' Roosevelt warned the nation in another of his 'fireside chats' on 11 September 1941, 'you do not wait until he has struck before you crush him.' Nobody listening to this address – including the Nazi leadership in Berlin – could have been in any doubt that the president was putting the German dictator on notice. In effect, Germany was *already* at war with the United States.

Against this background, both leaders made fateful decisions. As German armies thrust deep into Russian territory, Japan made ready in

August 1941 to abandon her neutrality and move against Stalin in the east. Roosevelt feared that this would administer the *coup de grâce* to Russia and hand her huge resources to Hitler. He therefore imposed an oil and steel embargo on Tokyo, partly to help the Chinese, but mainly to deter an attack on the Soviet Union. This set the clock ticking: the Japanese needed to secure alternative sources of energy in the Dutch East Indies or they would have to cave in to American pressure and abandon all their ambitions for Asian predominance. At around the same time – we do not know exactly when – Hitler decided on the complete annihilation of European Jewry: men, women and children, north, south, east and west. The planning heads of the relevant economic, administrative, diplomatic and police authorities were summoned to Berlin to work out the practical implementation of that policy. Not long after that, at the very beginning of December 1941, Hitler reaffirmed to the Japanese that he would join them in a war against the United States. The time had come to engage 'world Jewry' on all fronts.

On 7 December, the Japanese launched a surprise attack on the US Pacific Fleet in Pearl Harbor. Roosevelt now had the wrong war. He was rescued by Hitler, who was determined to deliver on his commitment to Tokyo. The German dictator was convinced that the United States needed to be engaged in a 'two-ocean war' to forestall a rapid Japanese collapse which would allow Roosevelt to concentrate all his energies on Europe. On 11 December, Hitler declared war on America, to the relief and jubilation of the German high command, especially the navy, which welcomed the chance to wage what had become a debilitating shadow conflict openly. In effect, Hitler had provoked the very global encirclement of the *Reich* which he had always feared. His pre-emptive strike against world Jewry created the Judaeo-Bolshevik-plutocrat alliance which the German dictator had sought for so long to put off, before he had secured the *Lebensraum* in the east which would enable Germany to weather the challenge. It remains one of the great unanswerable counter-factuals of history: what would have happened if Hitler had not risen to Roosevelt's bait, and the United States had taken no active part in the European war.

From late 1941, two great coalitions, the 'Grand Alliance' – a phrase which Churchill borrowed from his ancestor Marlborough – of Britain, the Soviet Union and the United States, and the Axis of Germany, Italy and Japan, together with their various satellites and allies, locked horns across the globe. In January 1942, the Allied powers issued their 'Declaration by the United Nations', pledging to employ their 'full resources' to 'the struggle for victory over Hitlerism'.[153] Like its predecessor, the League, the United Nations was conceived as an answer to the German problem. For nearly six months it seemed possible that the Axis would prevail. The Japanese ran riot against the Americans and the European colonial empires. Hong Kong, Singapore, Malaya and the Dutch East Indies fell in quick succession. Meanwhile, the German U-boats massacred unprotected US shipping off the American coasts; the *Wehrmacht* resumed its advance in Russia, reaching Stalingrad on the Volga and pushing south towards the crucial oil fields of the Caucasus; and, in North Africa, Rommel's *Afrikakorps* seemed close to capturing Egypt and pushing on into Palestine. In the summer of 1942, as German troops converged on the Middle East from the north and west, and as the Japanese navy raided Ceylon and the Indian Ocean, a 'link-up' between the two Axis powers seemed possible.

The contending coalitions engaged in a massive domestic mobilization to generate the necessary resources and manpower.[154] The entire US economy was now devoted to the war effort and soon began to outproduce the Axis. Here the driving force was the president himself, and his New Dealers who defied the advice of business leaders so as to set ambitious targets which were not only met but far exceeded in reality. These weapons not only equipped the growing US army, navy and air force, but were sent to help the British and Russians. In 1942, Hitler put Albert Speer in charge of the war economy. Through innovation, organization and the ruthless use of slave labour he achieved a massive increase in armament production. Early in the following year, the propaganda minister, Joseph Goebbels, increased the sense of psychological mobilization by declaring 'total war'. The Soviet war economy, too, depended heavily on the forced labour in the Gulag. Very soon, Russia was also outproducing the Third Reich in most key categories of armaments. Perhaps the most remarkable mobilization, however, was that of Britain. Despite being cut off from vital European trade and raw materials by Hitler's domination of the continent, she managed to produce armaments in greater quantity – if not always of better quality – than Germany. Britain was able to sustain not only her own effort against Germany, but also had enough to spare considerable supplies for the Soviet Union after June 1941. Millions of men were recruited and sent to serve overseas. All the while, parliament continued to sit and most basic civil liberties continued to be respected. Once again, the British 'warfare state' showed that democracy and mass military mobilization were not only entirely compatible but a more efficient combination than dictatorship.

Germany, by contrast, relied on the exploitation and settlement of conquered territories. The native population was to be subjugated, deported and often simply murdered. '*Generalplan Ost*', which was drafted in January 1941 and went through several versions over the next two years, involved the colonization of large tracts of Poland, the Baltic, White Russia and the Ukraine. About 30 million of its inhabitants were to be expelled into western Siberia and replaced by about half that number of German settlers who would double as a garrison and strategic military reserve for the *Reich*. The idea was to turn the Ukraine into the 'breadbasket' of the *Reich* , 'so that', as Hitler put it, 'no one is able to starve us again'.[155] Inside Germany, the Nazis promoted the concept of the *Volksgemeinschaft*, an exclusionary national community purged of Jews, Gypsies and other 'undesirable' elements, which would be strong enough to hold out against the encircling Judaeo-Bolshevik-plutocratic coalition. They conceived this as a more egalitarian society, breaking with the corporate rigidities and setting free the energies of the people. In reality, social inequalities largely persisted, but old caste barriers were broken down in the armed forces, where high casualties among the traditional officer corps provided candidates from the lower middle classes and working classes with openings. Some gender distinctions were also relaxed in the interests of greater mobilization of women for the war effort.[156] There was also a distinct political bias – particularly in the later years of the war – in favour of commanders, often from quite humble backgrounds, who openly supported National Socialist ideology. After the war, Hitler hoped to reward the *Volk* with a welfare state of autobahns, guaranteed employment, social housing and package holidays; in that sense, his vision blended racial utopia with 'modernity'.

In the democratic powers, by contrast, the war hastened the emergence of an inclusive welfare state. In 1941, the British coalition government – at the instigation of the Labour Party – commissioned a report designed to map out a full-scale transformation of British society. The resulting document – the 'Beveridge report' – was published in late 1942. It contained proposals for a National Health Service, improved public housing and a comprehensive system of social welfare. The main aim was to promote the social cohesion and demographic strength necessary to support Britain's great-power position, not only during the war but also in times to come. This came across very clearly in the report's attitude to the family and women's health, where the emphasis was on increasing the birth rate through maternity benefits. 'In the next thirty years,' Beveridge wrote, 'housewives as mothers have vital work to do in ensuring the adequate continuance of the British race and of the British ideal in the world.'[157] More generally, the report was designed to hold out to the soldiers and the home front a tangible reward for their exertions against Hitler. A similar process took place in the United States, where the 'warfare state' grew to an unprecedented size.[158] Across the Atlantic, welfare and warfare were inextricably intertwined. The logic was inescapable: if Britons and Americans were to be mobilized in defence of hearth and home, it made sense to give those who had neither, hearths and homes to defend.

The war effort also had a profoundly integrative and emancipatory effect in the United States. In the American army, men from diverse backgrounds across the Union served together and found themselves welded into a more cohesive nation.[159] African-Americans were still kept in segregated units for fear of reducing the effectiveness of Caucasian formations, but they served in combat units in large numbers for the first time, demonstrating their patriotism and making a substantial contribution to the war effort. Millions of American women were drafted into the factories and on to the farms. Because many of them had families, the state was forced for the first time to provide, as General Louis McSherry of the War Production Board put it, 'adequate facilities for the children of working mothers'. All this was expensive because unpaid home labour had to be replaced; in the numerous shipyards where work nurseries existed, for example, the cost was integrated into the price of the vessel. The struggle against Hitler, in other words, transformed the lives of women on both sides of the Atlantic. Norman Rockwell's famous depiction of Rosie the Riveter, in the *Saturday Evening Post* of May 1943, which shows a formidable female war worker with her foot firmly on a copy of *Mein Kampf*, summed up this process.

On the other hand, the war also gave a powerful impetus to exclusionary forces within belligerent societies. In Britain, governmental paranoia and popular xenophobia led to the internment of thousands of central European refugees – many of them Jewish – as potential fifth columnists. Likewise, after Pearl Harbor, Roosevelt ordered the internment of Americans of Japanese descent. In part, this policy reflected the anti-Asian prejudice prevalent on the western seaboard, but the main motivation was a strategic desire to forestall attempts at espionage or sabotage. Stalin resorted to much more extreme measures, deporting whole populations either in anticipation of disloyalty or as a punishment for collaboration. Germans, Chechens, Kalmyks and various other suspect ethnic groups were transplanted in conditions of great hardship.

Hitler's campaign against the Jews was also strategically motivated but otherwise of a completely different order. He regarded them as the directing mind behind a vast international coalition directed against Germany. Their containment and eventual physical destruction were thus an integral part of the Nazi war effort. Until late 1941, Hitler held off exterminating western European Jews in order to keep them as hostages for the behaviour of the United States. Now the gloves were off. Only a few days after the declaration of war on America, Hitler made his intentions plain to the Nazi leadership. 'With regard to the Jewish Question,' Goebbels noted in his diary, 'the Führer is determined to make a clean sweep. He prophesied that if they brought about a new world war, they would experience their annihilation. This was no empty talk. The world war is here. The annihilation of the Jews must be the necessary consequence.'[160] In January 1942, the administrative details were worked out at a much-postponed conference in the Berlin suburb of Wannsee. Over the next three years, another 5 million Jews – about a million had already been murdered by the *Einsatzgruppen* in Russia – were either shot locally or deported from central, southern and western Europe to death camps such as Auschwitz and Lublin-Majdanek in Poland and killed.[161] In a speech to SS leaders in Posen in October 1943, Heinrich Himmler explained that the programme of annihilation was necessary to maintain German racial superiority. This, he argued, was 'the foundation, the precondition of our historical existence. A people which lies in the centre of Europe, which is surrounded by enemies on all sides . . . such a people only survives thanks to its quality, its racial value.'[162] The 'final solution' was thus an extreme interpretation of the classic German doctrines of 'encirclement' and the *Mittellage*.

There were serious disagreements between the Russians, Americans and British over war aims and the conduct of the war. These differences reflected a wider discordance about how Europe should be ordered and international relations conducted after the war was over. Right from the start, Roosevelt spoke in favour of a global condominium of the 'Four Horsemen' – the United States, the Soviet Union, Great Britain and China – who would dominate the new international organization to replace the League of Nations. Churchill sought to guard against domination by the two 'superpowers' by adding France to the list. Stalin liked the idea of a post-1815 style 'Concert of Europe', but insisted that the security of the Soviet Union required the annexation of substantial adjacent territories and the establishment of Moscow-dominated buffer states between her and Germany. Roosevelt, by contrast, was adamant that there should be no division of Europe into 'spheres of influence', a policy which he believed had substantially contributed to the outbreak of war in the past, and American public opinion strongly supported this view. A European Advisory Commission of the three foreign ministers was therefore established to work out a compromise.

The real sticking point, however, was Germany. Stalin demanded its partition into an independent Rhineland, Bavaria and a rump state encompassing the rest (including Pomerania and Silesia); East Prussia was to be ceded to Poland. 'Germany', as Molotov put it, 'must be rendered harmless for the future.'[163] Roosevelt proposed an even more drastic split into six states of Hesse, Hanover–North West Germany, Saxony, Baden–Württemberg–Bavaria, Prussia (Brandenburg, Silesia and Pomerania) and East Prussia; the vital war-making potential of the Saar and the Ruhr were to be placed under international administration. Only partition, the Secretary of State, Sumner Welles, suggested 'would possibly have an effect on the German psychology' and cure them of aggressive tendencies.[164] Churchill instinctively inclined towards more extreme measures: he periodically spoke of the need to 'castrate' German men to prevent future aggression, or hoped that Germans would become 'fat and impotent'. On the other hand, the prime minister worried that Stalin might fill the resulting vacuum. He warned the cabinet not to 'weaken Germany too much – we may need her against Russia'.[165] Most British planners, however, supported partition schemes of one sort or another, even at the cost of Soviet hegemony in central Europe.[166]

Central to the containment of a post-war Germany, and the exclusion of the Soviet Union, were the revival and unification of Europe, or at least its western half. In October 1942, Churchill 'look[ed] forward to a United States of Europe ... which would possess an international police and be charged with keeping Prussia disarmed'.[167] The Americans, in particular, were highly sympathetic to European unity. State Department planners favoured economic integration of the continent accompanied by a free trade regime with the rest of the world, especially the United States. In theory, this would both serve American economic interests and secure the global balance by converting the war-making potential into peaceful production. The danger, though, was that a future Hitler would gain control of this customs union and use it against the United States.[168]

For the moment, the only thing the Allies could agree on was that no separate peace with Hitler was possible. At the Casablanca Conference in January 1943, Britain and the United States announced a policy of 'unconditional surrender', to which Stalin subscribed a few months later.[169] First, however, Hitler had to be defeated. In the United States there was general agreement – despite grumbling from some US 'Asia-Firsters' – that the priority was to crush Hitler;[170] only then would the coalition devote all its attention to Japan. The British needed no persuading. 'Germany', a joint Anglo-American communiqué announced in January 1942, was 'the prime enemy and her defeat is the key to victory. Once Germany is defeated, the collapse of Italy and the defeat of Japan must follow.'[171] Washington and London were bitterly divided, however, about the timing of the cross-Channel assault which would be necessary to defeat Hitler. The British preferred to 'wear down' Hitler through operations in the Mediterranean and other marginal fronts first, while US commanders favoured delivering an early 'knock out' blow in northern France.[172]

These disagreements climaxed at the Casablanca Conference of 1943 when the British succeeded in beating back US demands for an early invasion of France, agreeing a Mediterranean strategy instead. For the moment, therefore, the Allies would depend on the massive use of air power. Once again, however, London and Washington were divided on the best strategy. The Royal Air Force, which flew by night to reduce losses, tried to compensate for its inaccuracy by bombing residential areas in order to break German morale. By contrast, the Americans favoured pin-point bombing of key industries such as ball-bearing factories and synthetic fuel plants. Taken together, these operations opened a whole new front over Germany itself. Hundreds of thousands of German civilians were killed, war production was seriously disrupted, morale at home and at the front plummeted, and, perhaps most importantly of all, 800,000 German servicemen were diverted to air defence, as were thousands both of the *Reich*'s most modern aircraft and of her best pilots; the *Luftwaffe*'s capacity to deploy in the east was greatly curtailed.[173]

The resources which Hitler could bring to bear in Europe were unprecedented and formidable, but they were far exceeded by the combined might of the British Empire, the Soviet Union and the United States.[174] In the course of 1942, the imbalance began to tell. Rommel's advance on the Nile Delta was checked; a few months later, Montgomery's Eighth Army launched an offensive at El Alamein which was ultimately to drive the Axis out of North Africa altogether. In the Pacific, the Japanese were first checked at the battle of the Coral Sea and then suffered the catastrophic loss of most of their aircraft carriers at Midway in May 1942. The United States now began the slow reconquest of the Pacific, 'island-hopping' ever closer to Japan itself. Hitler's attempt to capture the oil fields of the Caucasus failed when his summer offensive of 1942 ran out of steam. By the end of the year, the German Sixth Army had been surrounded at Stalingrad, where it surrendered in February 1943. A few months later, Hitler suffered a disaster of similar proportions at 'Tunisgrad' when almost his entire North African army surrendered to the Allies. He now made overtures to Stalin for a separate peace, but without success. The attempt to starve out Britain through submarine warfare nearly succeeded, but by the spring of 1943 the Battle of the Atlantic had been lost with terrible losses among the U-boat crews. A massive armoured attack at Kursk also failed that same summer. Not long after, the Allies occupied Sicily and then landed in southern Italy. This final indignity provoked a revolt against Mussolini's foreign policy in the Fascist Grand Council, which soon led the country to switch sides. All Hitler could do now was to turn Europe into a fortress within which the *Reich* could weather the storm.

German strategy hinged on mobilizing the continent against the United Nations. 'Whoever controls Europe,' Hitler explained to his regional party bosses, the *Gauleiter*, in early May 1943, 'will thereby seize the leadership of the world.' 'It must therefore remain the objective of our struggle,' he continued, 'to create a unified Europe, but Europe can only be given a coherent structure through Germany.'[175] Nazi propaganda tirelessly proclaimed the idea of a 'European crusade against Bolshevism'. Like Napoleon, Hitler could rely not only on occupied Europe, but also on a slew of satellite states whose attitude to the New Order ranged from enthusiastic cooperation to conditional support: Ante Pavelić's New Croatian State, Milan Nedić's Serbia, Monsignor Jozef Tiso's Slovakia, Admiral Miklós Horthy's Hungary, General Ion Antonescu's Romania, Marshal Carl Mannerheim's Finland, and Bulgaria. In purely extractive terms, the results were impressive. The economy of occupied Europe, especially the two powerhouses of France–Belgium and Bohemia–Moravia, kept the *Wehrmacht* equipped; their output far exceeded that of the lands pillaged in the east, and gave the lie to the concept of *Lebensraum*. Millions of slave-workers were deported to the *Reich*. Nor was it all coercion. A heterogeneous array of volunteer formations from across the continent was deployed to defend the 'Atlantic Wall' against the Anglo-Americans, and to repel the 'Asiatic hordes' of the Red Army. What Hitler was unable even to imagine, however, was a strategy to bring the peoples of Europe into a collaborative political project, albeit under German hegemony. When the foreign office produced plans for a European Confederation in September 1943, Hitler rejected them. He conceived of Europe as a subordinate, not a partner.[176]

In early June 1944 – on 'D-Day' – the British, Americans and Canadians hurled themselves into northern France. Two weeks later, the Red Army launched a shattering offensive against the German Army Group Centre in what was to be the largest land battle of the war. Within a short period of time, the Soviet forces were well inside the pre-war Polish border. In order to forestall a Stalinist occupation, the non-communist Polish Home Army launched a rising in Warsaw in August 1944. The Russians stood aside, and the rising was crushed; shortly afterwards they resumed their advance. After six weeks of fierce fighting the western allies broke through the German lines in Normandy and raced towards Paris. The catastrophic military situation added new vigour to the activities of the German resistance against Hitler, but its most spectacular operation – the July bomb plot of 1944 – narrowly failed to kill the Führer. By the end of the year, a last desperate gamble in the Ardennes had failed. The vision of *Lebensraum* and German hegemony was dead. Instead, a vacuum was opening up in central Europe. The second war against Germany was almost over, another battle for Germany was about to begin.

The clash of the three Utopias, democratic, communist and National Socialist, left no continent untouched. Its principal focus, however, was always Europe, especially Germany. The *Reich* was the prize in the struggle between communists and democrats after 1917. German leaders reacted to this predicament by seeking to offset the power of the global empires, through the quest for *Mitteleuropa* in the First World War, economic dominance during the Weimar Republic and Hitler's genocidal *Lebensraum* project. This strategy almost succeeded. The consolidated power of the European centre twice came close to achieving continental and thus global hegemony in 1917–18 and 1939–42. In the end, however, the combined might of the 'American Union', the British Empire and the other powers of the United Nations proved too much for the *Reich*. The Nazi Utopia was utterly defeated. A new European geopolitics would now pit the democratic and communist blocs against each other, in a conflict which was primarily fought over the ruins of their erstwhile foe.

7
Partitions, 1945–73

With the defeat of the Reich and pending the emergence of the Asiatic, the African, and perhaps the South American nationalisms, there will remain in the world only two great powers capable of confronting each other – the United States and Soviet Russia. The laws of both history and geography will compel these two powers to a trial of strength, either military or in the fields of economics and ideology. These same laws make it inevitable that both powers should become enemies of Europe. And it is equally certain that both these powers will sooner or later find it desirable to seek the support of the sole surviving great nation in Europe, the German people.

Adolf Hitler, April 1945

If there is no real European federation and if Germany is restored as a strong and independent country, we must expect another attempt at German domination. If there is no real European federation and if Germany is not restored as an independent country, we invite Russian domination . . . This being the case, it is evident that the relationship of Germany to the other countries of western Europe must be so arranged as to provide mechanical and automatic safeguards against any unscrupulous exploitation of Germany's pre-eminence in population and in military-industrial potential.

George Kennan, 1948[1]

Germany and Berlin overshadowed everything; Germany was, of course, the historic balance at the center of Europe, as well as our historic enemy, the cause of two world wars, and now the main battleground of the Cold War, with Berlin, literally, as the front line.

Anatoly Dobrynin, Soviet ambassador to Washington, 1962–86[2]

Partition was the central fact of the post-1945 world. The globe was ideologically divided between a democratic west and a communist east. Key areas, such as Korea, Palestine and Vietnam were partitioned. Europe itself was divided between the North Atlantic Treaty Organization (NATO) and the Warsaw Pact. At the heart of the conflict, however, lay the partitioned Germany: a divided country in the middle of a divided continent, at the centre of a divided world. The struggle for that space dominated international politics. Both sides sought to win over the Germans, or at least to deny them to the other side. They were also determined to prevent the re-emergence of German power. The parallel projects of NATO and European integration were designed with this twin purpose in mind; so was the permanent US military presence, making Washington a guarantor of the European settlement. The German Question also drove domestic politics in France, Britain, the Soviet Union and, of course, Germany herself, which sought to regain her sovereignty and transform herself back into an independent actor.

The Third Reich died hard. Hitler's armies fought bitterly all the way back from Normandy, from Italy and from their positions in Poland, the Baltic and the western Ukraine. After a headlong retreat across northern France in August 1944, the line was stabilized in Alsace-Lorraine and the Low Countries. In September an attempt by British, American and Polish parachutists to secure the bridges over the Meuse, Waal and Lower Rhine at Arnhem was repulsed with heavy loss of life. In the east, the Red Army advance came to a temporary halt on the Vistula. Not long after, however, the Allies surged forward again on all fronts. One by one, Germany's eastern allies jumped ship: Romania switched sides in late August, Bulgaria in early September, and a week later even the Finns were forced into an armistice. Hungary's attempt to follow suit was halted by energetic German action in December 1944; Admiral Horthy was replaced in Budapest by a more pliable figure. By the end of the year, though, Allied forces were on German soil: the Russians had penetrated into East Prussia and the Anglo-Americans had gained a toehold near Aachen. It would not be long before the Grand Alliance overran the rest of the *Reich* and put an end to Hitler's rule.

The question of the post-war order now became acute. Despite two decades of mutual suspicion, Stalin and Churchill agreed to divide south-eastern Europe into spheres of influence. In the 'percentages agreement' of October 1944, Romania and Bulgaria fell to the Soviet Union. By contrast, Greece was assigned to the Anglo-Americans, while both sides would share influence in Yugoslavia and Hungary equally. The withdrawal of German troops led to mayhem in Yugoslavia – where Tito's partisans battled it out with various right-wing and centrist forces – and Greece, where British troops promptly found themselves embroiled in fighting with the communist KKE in December 1944. Stalin, however, honoured his commitments and left the Greek party to its fate. Nor did the Allies fall out, yet, over eastern Europe. Here Stalin, on the other hand, was determined to prevent the re-creation of the interwar '*cordon sanitaire*' on his western border. In particular, he refused point-blank to countenance any potentially hostile government in Warsaw. At the Yalta Conference of 1945, the three powers agreed that the Polish eastern border should be moved closer to Warsaw according to the old 'Curzon Line', which more or less reflected the linguistic boundary between Polish and Ukrainian or White Russian; in return she would gain 'substantial accession of territory in the north and west'.[3]

Overshadowing everything, of course, was the question of what to do with Germany.[4] Roosevelt believed Germany should be punished, partitioned and crippled with reparations. In the view of the Treasury, this was not only the most just but the cheapest way of administering the area. The 'Morgenthau Plan', named after the Secretary to the Treasury, Henry Morgenthau, and adopted by the Americans and British in late 1944, argued that Germany should be de-industrialized so as to destroy its capacity for making war. At around the same time, the American military authorities ordered that Germany was to be treated as a defeated rather than a liberated country, and its elite subjected to a thoroughgoing process of 'denazification'. It also recommended the partition of Germany 'as a measure for the prevention of German rearmament and renewed aggression'. This was the stated policy of the western powers as the final defeat of Germany approached.

The State Department, on the other hand, favoured the rehabilitation of Germany. The Secretary of State, Cordell Hull, drew on the experience of the Civil War – when 'it gradually took people 75 years to get back again' – as a model for 'uproot[ing]' the strain of Nazism in the German people.[5] The best way of preventing another round of aggression, the argument went, was the creation of strong democratic structures. A punitive peace in the style of Versailles – or worse – would only complicate this. Moreover, like Keynes in 1919, the State Department believed that the health of the European economy as a whole was dependent on the engine of German growth. The 'pastoralization' suggested by Morgenthau, and the huge reparations payments demanded by almost everyone else, would not only make Germany but the entire continent dependent on long-term US economic aid. It would also reduce the potential market for American goods. The experts warned that the partition of Germany would be a 'disaster' which would delay economic recovery, encourage the growth of extremism, and tempt the victors to squabble among themselves over the spoils.[6] Britain took a broadly similar view. It saw 'Prussian militarism' as the primary threat to European stability. Likewise, Churchill repeatedly warned of the danger of 'inflicting severities upon Germany, which is ruined and prostrate ... open[ing] to the Russians in a very short time to advance if they chose to the waters of the North Sea and the Atlantic'. The best way of preventing this, of course, was to create a strong Germany.

Stalin was keeping his options open. He argued that while the Hitlers came and went, the German people would remain. 'We are now smashing the Germans, and many people now assume that the Germans will never be able to threaten us again,' he exploded in March 1945. 'Well, that's simply not true. I HATE THE GERMANS! ... It's impossible to destroy the Germans for good, they will still be around. But we must bear in mind that our allies will try to save the Germans and conspire with them ... That is why we, the Slavs, must be ready in case the Germans can get back on their feet and launch another attack.'[7] On the one hand, this made him fearful about the re-emergence of Weimar-style revanchism. For this reason, Stalin initially hoped for a longer-term American presence in or at least engagement with Europe. To be on the safe side, however, he concluded a series of alliances designed to contain the threat:

a Soviet treaty with the Czech government-in-exile in late 1943, a Franco-Soviet treaty with the Free French Leader, General Charles de Gaulle, in December 1944, and treaties with Poland and Yugoslavia in April of the following year. On the other hand, Stalin was quick to spot the potential accretion of power which control of Germany would bring him. In 1943, he set up the *Nationalkomitee Freies Deutschland*, made up of captured senior officers, including the commander at Stalingrad, Friedrich Paulus. This and subsequent initiatives were designed to revive traditional Prusso-Russian friendship and harness the power of German nationalism for Soviet ends. Stalin also kept the cadres of the powerful German Communist Party – or at least those who had survived Hitler and the Moscow purges – in reserve in order to effect the communist transformation of as much of Germany as required. Finally, Stalin deliberately left open the question of whether the Polish gains in the west would be confirmed or returned to Germany on terms acceptable to him.[8]

The Yalta Conference sought to reconcile these conflicting views on Germany.[9] Germany was divided into four occupation zones: Soviet, American, British and French. She was to pay extensive reparations, mainly in kind of such items as 'equipment, machine tools, ships, rolling stock ... these removals to be carried out chiefly for the purpose of destroying the war potential of Germany'. The British, Americans and Russians promised to 'take such steps, including the complete disarmament, demilitarization and dismemberment of Germany as they deem[ed] requisite for future peace and security'.[10] A joint Allied Control Council of Germany would administer the country after victory had been achieved. Finally, there was to be a broader global organization, which would rally the world behind the containment of Germany. The protocol announced the convening of a 'United Nations Conference' to be made up of the existing coalition powers and 'such of the Associated Nations as have declared war on the common enemy by 1 March 1945'.[11] This would create a 'General International Organization for the maintenance of international peace and security'. In short, the United Nations – even more so than the League of Nations – had its origins as a wartime alliance against Germany.

All this was to be embedded in a profound ideological transformation across the continent. This reflected the US belief that the only way to prevent the outbreak of another war was to ensure a fair distribution of economic resources and 'the right of all peoples to choose the form of government under which they will live'. The declaration laid down precisely how this was to be achieved. Once 'internal peace' had been established, and 'emergency measures for the relief of distressed peoples' had been undertaken, states were expected 'to form interim governmental authorities broadly representative of all democratic elements in the population' to be followed by the 'establishment through free elections of governments responsible to the will of the people'.[12] In other words, far from openly selling out eastern Europe to Stalin, the new order agreed at Yalta was supposed to inaugurate a pan-continental democratic revolution in governance.

Despite this impressive display of Allied unity, Hitler believed that he could repeat the achievement of Frederick the Great by fighting on until the encircling coalition fell apart. When President Roosevelt died suddenly in April 1945, the Führer was convinced that just as Peter III had made peace with Prussia after the death of the Empress Elizabeth in 1762, so the new president would lead the United States out of the coalition. This hope was dashed when Harry Truman pledged to carry on the struggle. The final dramatic confrontation in Berlin pitted *Wehrmacht*, *Volkssturm*, French, Flemish, Scandinavian, Russian and many other auxiliaries against the Red Army.[13] Its outcome was never in doubt. On 30 April, Hitler committed suicide, bequeathing what was left to Admiral Dönitz. On 8 May, the new German government surrendered. It had taken nearly six years, and the combined effort of the United States, the Soviet Union, the British Empire and all the other members of the United Nations, to bring the Third Reich and its European allies to heel. The war had shown, as the US Under-Secretary of State, Dean Acheson, wrote in 1945, 'that the Germans were able to fight all the rest of the world'.[14] The experience was to shape European geopolitics for decades to come.

Two months after the German capitulation, the victorious Grand Alliance conferred at Potsdam to agree 'the measures necessary to assure that Germany never again will threaten her neighbours or the peace of the world'.[15] The four zones of occupation now took definite shape: a Soviet one in Mecklenburg, Thuringia, the central Prussian provinces around Brandenburg and in Saxony; an American zone in south-western Germany; a British zone in north-western Germany; and a French zone carved out of the Anglo-American share in the southern Rhineland, the Palatinate, Baden and southern Württemberg. Berlin – which lay deep in the Soviet Zone – was also split into four sectors, one for each of the powers. Austria was likewise divided into four zones of occupation: the Soviet one in Lower Austria, an American around Salzburg and Linz, a British one in the south including Carinthia and Styria, and a French one in the west centred on Innsbruck. The capital, Vienna – which lay in the middle of the Soviet Zone – was also divided into four sectors. Eupen-Malmedy was returned to Belgium, Alsace-Lorraine to France and northern Schleswig to Denmark. These decisions essentially restored the settlement of 1919, but in the east the changes were far more radical. Pomerania and Silesia were ceded to Poland – although the 'final limitation of the western frontier of that country should await the peace settlement' – while East Prussia was divided between Poland and the Soviet Union. All three regions had been ruled by German princes for centuries, and with the exception of Upper Silesia, where the Germans were a bare majority, they had been inhabited almost exclusively by Germans for hundreds of years. In total, Germany lost about one third of her pre-war territory.

There were substantial boundary changes elsewhere in Europe. Stalin held on to his gains of 1939–40: the formerly Finnish Karelia, the formerly Romanian Bessarabia, the Baltic states and of course eastern Poland. As Stalin explained at Yalta, the annexation of Polish territory was not just driven by concern about her neighbour. 'The essence of the problem,' he stressed, 'lies much deeper. Throughout history Poland was always a corridor through which the enemy has come to attack Russia . . . the Germans have twice come through Poland in order to attack our country.'[16] It was the German Question, in other words, which drove the new territorial settlement in the east. In ethnographic terms, the scale of the transformation was even more breathtaking.[17] Virtually the entire Jewish population between the Don and the Bay of Biscay had been murdered. The Germans of Pomerania, Silesia and East Prussia – all 7.5 million of them – were expelled *en masse* westwards into the occupation zones; so were the 3 million Sudeten Germans. The Germans, the restored Czech president, Edvard Beneš, argued, had 'ceased to be human in the war, and appeared to us as a single, great, human monster. We have decided that we have to liquidate the German problem in our republic once and for all.'[18] The Polish populations of Pinsk, Lvov and Brest-Litovsk were also deported westwards, and settled in the regions vacated by Germans. There were still a few substantial pockets of national minorities – especially Hungarians and Germans in Romanian Transylvania and Hungarians in southern Slovakia – but the ethnic diversity that had characterized central and eastern Europe for hundreds of years was no more.

The geopolitical implications of these changes were seismic. The European centre had been destroyed. Germany had ceased to exist as an independent state. The resulting vacuum was filled by the French, British, American and Soviet armies of occupation. In territorial terms, Russia had moved almost as far west as Alexander had by 1815, but in practice Stalin's reach extended much further. The Red Army was physically present in large numbers in Poland, central Germany and eastern Austria. It was more thinly spread across Czechoslovakia, Hungary and Romania, but all three countries were now firmly in Stalin's orbit. No less significant, in the long term, were the ethnographic shifts. Not only was the area of German settlement now largely confined to the area between the Oder–Neisse and Rhine rivers, but the uprooting of her traditional East Elbian ruling elite profoundly changed the composition of German society and politics, and thus potentially of her strategic orientation. The Holocaust also had a profound geopolitical effect. European Jewry had largely been destroyed, but European anti-semitism still flourished. Holocaust survivors were discriminated against, expelled and in extreme cases murdered, for example during the Kielce pogrom in Poland shortly after the war. All this meant only one thing to the victims: Jews had no future in Europe. They would only be secure in their own state, defended by their own weapons. A flood of Jewish refugees now began to leave for their new Zionist homeland. In the mandate itself, Zionist guerrillas in the *Irgun*, *Haganah* and the 'Stern Gang' stepped up their campaign to force out the British.

With Germany subdued, the international architecture designed in the last year of the war came into its own. The San Francisco Conference of May–June 1945 brought the United Nations (UN) into being. It consisted of a General Assembly and a Security Council made up of representatives of the victorious wartime coalition: Great Britain, France, the United States, the Soviet Union and China. Flanking the new world organization was an array of other international institutions designed to facilitate global economic prosperity and thus, Washington believed, to keep the international peace. 'Nations which are enemies in the marketplace,' a US Assistant Secretary of State remarked in 1945, 'cannot long be friends at the council table.' By extension, economic interdependence would prevent disputes from ever reaching the battlefield. At Stalin's insistence, the permanent members of the Security Council were granted a veto. As the British civil servant and historian Charles Webster, who was intimately involved in drafting the Charter remarked, this made the UN 'an alliance of the Great Powers embedded in a universal organization'.[19] Most of those assembled at San Francisco, however, also had profound ideological expectations.

The original conception of the United Nations as a democratic club found expression in its treatment of Franco's Spain, regarded with extreme distaste by both Washington and Moscow. Spain was therefore specifically barred from membership of the UN so long as it remained a dictatorship. Matters came to a head in August 1945 over the future of Tangier. The port had been seized by Franco five years earlier; now he was not only told to hand it back, but informed that Spain's participation in a new international authority there was contingent on 'the re-establishment of a democratic regime' in Madrid.[20] Stalin now tried to mobilize the United Nations as a whole against Franco. In particular, Franco was accused of sheltering Nazi refugees and allowing German scientists to work on an atomic bomb in Spain. A special committee reported to the Security Council that while the Spanish dictatorship was undoubtedly a 'fascist regime' which had helped Hitler and Mussolini, and remained a 'source of international friction', there was no evidence that it was 'preparing for an act of aggression'. All the same, the commission recommended that the General Assembly present Franco with an ultimatum to give up power within fifteen months or face the breaking off of diplomatic relations by the General Assembly. Nothing came of this, but it is clear that at its creation the United Nations was a highly interventionist body. The fetishization of state sovereignty for which it later became known was a subsequent re-invention by Third-Worldist dictators and unworldly international lawyers.

The Allies were far apart on the promotion of democracy in eastern Europe and the extra-European world. His commitments at Yalta notwithstanding, Stalin made clear at Potsdam that he had no intention of allowing central and eastern Europeans to decide their own destiny. 'A freely elected government in every one of these countries,' he announced, 'would be anti-Soviet and we cannot permit that.'[21] For the moment, however, Stalin only interfered directly in the strategically vital areas of

Poland and Germany. He allowed elections in Czechoslovakia, Hungary and Romania to go ahead. Likewise, the European imperial powers were in no rush to organize elections in their overseas colonies, on the grounds that the populations there were 'not ready' to make an informed choice about whether they wished to remain part of their respective empires. There were also widespread fears that broader political participation would spark fresh rounds of traditional communal blood-letting in religiously or ethnically mixed parts of Africa, the Middle East, Asia and the Indian subcontinent.

In the autumn of 1945, the centre of military and diplomatic attention switched briefly to the Far East, where the Japanese still offered determined resistance to the Americans as they 'island-hopped' across the Pacific. Britain sent substantial forces partly to assert her imperial interests, partly to impress the increasingly sceptical Australians and New Zealanders, but mainly to build up goodwill in Washington which could be parlayed into American engagement with European post-war security. In early August, the US dropped a devastating atomic bomb on the Japanese city of Hiroshima and then another on Nagasaki, killing around 200,000 Japanese instantly, nearly all of them civilians.[22] The introduction of this new and devastating weapon radically changed the nature of international politics, at least in the short term. 'Hiroshima has shaken the whole world,' Stalin remarked shortly afterwards. 'The balance has been broken.'[23] The United States was certainly determined to maintain its nuclear monopoly: in August 1946 Congress passed the Atomic Energy Act, which prohibited the US administration from transferring nuclear technology to any other power, including close allies. There were in fact serious ethical, political and operational obstacles to the use of the atomic bomb for purposes of strategic coercion. This threat was used only once by the Americans during their four-year nuclear monopoly, in order to hasten the Soviet withdrawal from Iran. The key thing, as Stalin repeatedly said, was to keep one's nerve. He now instructed his scientists to build a Soviet bomb without delay. It was not only the Soviet Union, but America's allies who felt threatened by the new nuclear geopolitics. The British chiefs of staff were adamant that they needed to have 'every club in the bag' and began to adapt the bomber force for the delivery of the atomic bomb even before they had the technology itself. In short, the development of the atomic bomb simply led to an extreme form of the 'Dreadnought-style' arms races familiar in years past. As we shall see, nuclear weapons certainly interacted with the traditional concerns of European geopolitics – especially the German Question – but they did not fundamentally change them.

The terrible experience of war and the uncertainty of its immediate aftermath served to promote the idea that Europe should collectively assert its separate cultural, spiritual, economic and political identity. During the conflict two Italian anti-fascists, Altiero Spinelli and Ernesto Rossi, had drawn up their manifesto 'For a free and united Europe'. They condemned the tendency of 'capitalist imperialism' and 'totalitarian states' to unleash destructive wars. The only way of breaking this vicious cycle, Spinelli and Rossi argued, was to break with the classic balance of power and to create a completely new system of coexistence in Europe through 'the definitive abolition of the division of Europe into national, sovereign states', and the creation of a 'European Federation'. This 'United States of Europe' was to be 'based on the republican constitution of federated countries'. The authors knew that the best moment to realize their scheme would be in the turbulent aftermath of the German defeat, 'when the States will lie broken, when the masses will be anxiously waiting for a new message, like molten matter, burning, and easily shaped into new moulds capable of accommodating the guidance of serious internationalist minded men'.[24] The continent would be a *tabula rasa*, and could thus be shaped into a new system designed not to deal with an external enemy but to prevent Europe from tearing itself apart.

The near-universal experiences of war and occupation fundamentally shaped domestic politics after the end of hostilities. They did not, however, lead to a groundswell movement for political union or integration. Instead, the first post-war elections were dominated by an inquest into the causes and conduct of the war, the containment of Germany, the pressing question of reconstruction, and the economics of demobilization. In Britain, Churchill suffered a surprise defeat in the July 1945 election, a reflection not so much on him personally, or of any irresistible tide of popular radicalism, as a withering judgement on the Conservative policy of appeasement and the fall of France. 'It was not Churchill who lost the 1945 election,' Harold Macmillan later remarked, 'it was the ghost of Neville Chamberlain.'[25] Likewise, the French Assembly elections of October 1945 were dominated by a settling of accounts with the defeat of 1940, the Vichy regime and concern about a possible German revival. These issues were far more important than fear of Stalin, or the unification of Europe. The results were a conclusive rejection of the interwar right and its subsequent association with Marshal Pétain and national humiliation. The communists secured just over a quarter of the vote, and became the largest party; the socialists and the Christian democratic Popular Republican Movement of Maurice Schumann polled almost as many votes. Charles de Gaulle was re-elected president on an independent ticket, his immense personal standing as leader of the Resistance outweighing suspicion of his domestic conservatism. In Britain, the peace led to the immediate termination of the American Lend-Lease programme, precipitating a financial crisis. The costs of reconstruction and the continuing defence of the empire would have to be borne alone.[26] It was far from clear where the new Labour government would find the resources to fund not only the domestic 'New Jerusalem' it had promised but Britain's enormous strategic ambitions and obligations.[27]

The experience of the war, their continued international ambitions, and the post-war financial squeeze had profound implications for the European colonial empires.[28] To the British and French, the retention of overseas possessions and the reassertion of imperial control over territories occupied by the Axis were essential, not only to make up for resources missing back home, but also in order to increase their weight on the European and world stage. It was vital, de Gaulle announced a day after the German capitulation, that 'our Indochina' be regained and France's grandeur thereby 'increased'. 'It is in union with the overseas territories,' de Gaulle declared, 'that France is a great power. Without these territories she would no longer be one.'[29] Likewise, the Labour Foreign Secretary, Ernest Bevin, spoke of the need to 'mobilize the resources of Africa in support of a western European Union ... [to] form a bloc which, both in populations and productive capacity, could stand on an equality with the western hemisphere and the Soviet blocs', a task all the more important after the end of Lend-Lease.[30]

The United States initially regarded the attempt of the European powers to re-establish their colonial empires with disdain. Not least thanks to their own revolutionary origins, most American politicians and statesmen were initially sympathetic to the aspirations of Vietnamese, Indonesian and other nationalists. With British help – and to the fury of de Gaulle – they eased the French out of Syria and Lebanon in 1945. They also put pressure on London to withdraw from Palestine after mediating a compromise between Jews and Arabs. Washington also discouraged the Dutch from trying to recover Indonesia from Sukarno, who had repudiated colonial rule. The Americans warned that they were not prepared to support western European powers economically so long as they squandered scarce resources on pursuing their imperial pretensions. More generally, the United States was anxious not to appear to be supporting colonialism partly to appease domestic public opinion, which was strongly anti-imperialist, and partly in order to remain on the right side of sentiment in the United Nations.

Meanwhile, relations between Stalin and the west deteriorated sharply in Europe and its Middle Eastern periphery. He ruthlessly crushed all independent political expression in Poland – thus violating the letter of the Yalta Agreement – and in his zone of occupation in Germany.[31] In Hungary, Romania and Czechoslovakia, on the other hand, the Soviet dictator was inclined, for the moment, to allow some room for democratic politics, so long as those states remained strategically firmly within his orbit.[32] Finland was permitted to choose her own domestic orientation so long as she maintained a strict neutrality in foreign policy, thus serving as a buffer in the north-west. Stalin was also well pleased with the new territorial dispensation, which gave him the Slavic solidarity he needed to guard against a revival of German power. Looking at the Caucasus, however, Stalin announced: 'I don't like our border here.'[33] For this reason, encouraged by local Azeri and Kurdish nationalists, the Soviet Union welched on her wartime agreement to evacuate Iran after the end of hostilities, and put pressure on Turkey to grant her joint administration in the Straits. Meanwhile, by early 1946 Greece was wracked by a full-scale civil war between communists and the British-backed royalist government. London and Washington were convinced – wrongly – that Stalin was the driving force behind the communist advance there. In fact, the Greek guerrillas drew most of their logistical support from Tito, who hoped to draw the Slavophone Macedonians into the Yugoslav orbit.

The breakdown in trust between Soviet Union and the western allies was increasingly reflected in public statements and secret memoranda. In late February 1946, a young US diplomat at the embassy in Moscow, George Kennan, responded to a State Department request for an analysis of Soviet policy with a brutal confidential memorandum, which later became famous as the 'Long Telegram'. Reviewing Stalin's recent moves and communist ideology, Kennan warned that 'We have here a political force committed fanatically to the belief that with the United States there can be no permanent *modus vivendi*, that it is desirable and necessary that the internal harmony of our society be disrupted, our traditional way of life be destroyed, the international authority of our state be broken, if Soviet power is to be secure.' The Soviet Union, in other words, was not just a strategic threat but an ideological threat; indeed, it was a strategic menace *because* it was an ideological challenge.[34] At the beginning of the following month, Winston Churchill, now out of office, summed up the new mood in a famous speech entitled 'Sinews of Peace' at Fulton, Missouri. He began by announcing that the right to 'free and unfettered elections' and all the other liberties enjoyed by Britons and Americans had universal applicability and 'should lie in every cottage home'. The reality, however, was that 'from Stettin in the Baltic to Trieste in the Adriatic an iron curtain has descended across the continent'. The defence of European liberty was synonymous in Churchill's mind with the prevention of another European war.

The sense of a growing strategic and ideological confrontation was shared in Moscow. In September 1946, the Soviet diplomat Nikolai Novikov was asked for a memorandum on US policy by the foreign minister, V. Molotov. His memorandum warned that 'The foreign policy of the United States, which reflects the imperialist tendencies of American monopolistic capital, is characterized in the postwar period by a striving for world supremacy.' Against the background of 'broad plans for expansion', the establishment of a 'system of naval and air bases stretching far beyond the boundaries of the United States', not to mention 'the creation of ever newer types of weapons', looked decidedly sinister. The aim of the United States, in short, was to 'limit' and 'dislodg[e] the influence of the Soviet Union from neighbouring countries' and more generally to 'impose' her will on Moscow.

All this both reflected and was reflected in the breakdown of the Allied consensus over central Europe. Ideally, both sides would have preferred to win over Gemany in its entirety, but failing that both the Soviet Union and the western allies were determined to secure as much of its huge economic and military potential as possible, or at the very least to deny it to their rivals. Here Stalin had a head start. Right at the end of the war he signalled his willingness to cut a deal with German nationalism by delaying the handover of Stettin to the Poles as long as possible. He stalled on western demands for the formal abolition of Prussia. Stalin also authorized the German communists to take a strong stand against French ambitions. In late April 1946, he merged the old German Communist and Social Democratic parties in his zone with the intent of using the new Socialist Unity Party to extend Soviet influence throughout the western areas of occupation as well.[35] Three months later, Molotov appealed directly to the German people in a speech offering them a united and independent Germany. Stalin made less headway than he hoped, however, partly because the behaviour of Soviet forces – which was characterized by killings, mass rape and the systematic dismantling of German industry – antagonized the local population, and partly because communism was itself inherently antipathetic to most of the population, even the working class.[36] It was not just that Stalin's right hand in Germany did not know what his left hand was doing: the Soviet dictator himself does not seem to have made up his mind whether he was aiming for a single Soviet-dominated country, a militarily defanged neutral state or some combination of the two possibilities.[37]

The western allies, for their part, fundamentally reassessed their German policy in the light of perceived Soviet actions. Washington wanted to co-opt German nationalism. In May 1946, the Americans abolished reparations in their zone unilaterally. In a widely discussed speech in Stuttgart that autumn the Secretary of State, James F. Byrnes, announced not only that the US would remain committed to Europe, but that it favoured German self-determination and even the revision of the Oder–Neisse line. Washington was determined, however, that the new Germany, or at least the parts under western control, should be democratic. Under the direction of General Lucius D. Clay, the US military governor, a fundamental transformation of the American zone of occupation, and increasingly of the two other western zones, was got underway. Working closely with the West German elites Clay oversaw the restoration of participatory political structures, bringing the British along with him. In June 1946, the Anglo-American occupation authorities held elections for regional assemblies; the former mayor of Cologne, Konrad Adenauer, performed particularly well. They also laid particular emphasis on the 're-education' of Germans away from Nazism towards western values.[38] Later that year, the British and Americans announced that they intended to merge their areas of occupation to create 'Bizonia'. Clay believed that although a permanently divided Germany would be 'catastrophic', a Soviet-dominated united Germany represented 'an even greater threat to the security of western civilization and to world peace'.[39]

Britain and France, by contrast, were sceptical of the prospects for German democracy and deeply hostile to German unity. 'A reunited Germany will join one side or the other,' Bevin cautioned, 'and will almost inevitably start serious trouble.'[40] So London was happy to go along with American plans to democratize Germany, and combine the western zones, but as a means towards entrenching the division of Germany, not of overcoming it. France, of course, was strongly opposed to anything which restored German unity and sought to keep her neighbour down by controlling and exploiting her resources.[41] On the other hand, the French feared that Germany might be sucked into an eastern orientation. So, in March 1946, the French reluctantly dropped their demand that the Rhineland and the Ruhr be separated from Germany. They began to think, however, of new ways of containing German power through some form of European integration. General de Gaulle, then on one of his periodic 'retirements', even wrote that France was 'destined by her geography to promote a European Union', primarily as a solution to the German problem.

Against this background, British commitments in the eastern Mediterranean became an expensive luxury. In February 1947, London suddenly announced that it wished to transfer the costly task of defending Greece to the Americans. The baton being passed from London to Washington was not just responsibility for the eastern Mediterranean but the defence of the European balance as a whole. George Kennan glossed the new policy in a famous article in *Foreign Affairs* in June 1947. This reprised the arguments from his confidential 'Long Telegram', and stressed once again the importance of communism to Soviet foreign policy. 'Ideology,' Kennan argued, taught the men in the Kremlin 'that the outside world was hostile and that it was their duty eventually to overthrow the political forces beyond their borders'. 'A permanent and peaceful coexistence' was thus not possible. At the same time, however, Kennan pointed out that ideology was also a restraining force, because since the victory of communism over capitalism was inevitable, it could be awaited rather than brought about. The Kremlin would therefore avoid 'adventurism', and would have 'no compunction about retreating in the face of superior force'. The correct approach, therefore, was not reflexive 'toughness' but 'a long-term, patient but firm and vigilant containment of Russian expansive tendencies'.[42]

The main front in the 'containment' of Stalin was Europe. A paper of the Joint Chiefs of Staff of April 1947 listed US allies and theatres of activity in order of importance: Great Britain, France and Germany came first. Japan, China, Korea and the Philippines came last, behind Belgium. The danger was that the Soviet Union, which already dominated a large chunk of Europe, would bring the all-important areas of central and western Europe under her control as well.[43] Washington therefore needed to rally the continent – or at least its western half – against Stalin, militarily, politically, economically, culturally and spiritually. This was a tall order, because European economies recovered far more slowly than had been expected, and by the beginning of 1947 the situation was still dire across the continent;[44] unemployment was rife and rationing was still in place. Faith in capitalism, and even in democracy, was low. The Americans feared that this socio-economic vacuum would be filled by communism, especially in France and Italy, where the national parties were strong, and in Germany, where the misery was greatest.

So, in June 1947, the US Secretary of State, George Marshall, announced a plan for the economic regeneration of Europe. The United States offered a massive transfusion of funds to bridge the 'dollar gap' not only to France, Britain and Germany (the principal beneficiaries), Italy and other countries to the west of the 'iron curtain', but also to the eastern European countries as well, including the Soviet Union itself. Germany, however, was the key. 'The restoration of Europe,' Marshall told Congress, 'involves the restoration of Germany. Without a revival of German production there can be no revival of Europe's economy.' The principal motivation here was not commercial – scarcely 5 per cent of US GDP came from exports – but strategic. The United States was vitally concerned both to neutralize the threat of German revanchism and to secure central Europe against Soviet penetration. Even the commitment to open markets was primarily driven by the belief that free trade reduced the risk of war.[45]

The onset of open confrontation with the Soviet Union inspired moves towards greater western European unity.[46] In March 1948, the

Brussels Pact brought together Britain, France, Belgium, Holland and Luxemburg in a Western European Union partly to hedge against the revival of German power, but primarily to contain the Soviet Union. The signatories committed themselves to mutual defence in the event of external aggression, and in September 1948 military planning on how to repel the Red Army began: air defences were integrated and a joint high command was established. To many Europeans, a new system of alliances was not enough, however. They had come out of the war convinced that some form of federalism or shared sovereignty would be essential to prevent a relapse into barbarism, and the threat from Stalin only reinforced this view. Washington, wanting to contain Germany and mobilize the continent against the Soviet Union, was strongly supportive: Truman indicated that he 'favoured a United States of Europe'.[47] In early May 1948, hundreds of European politicians, trade unionists, intellectuals and other representatives of civil society met at The Hague under the chairmanship of Churchill and at the invitation of the International Committee of the Movements for European Unity. It was attended by the Conservative grandee Harold Macmillan, François Mitterrand (then a minister in the French government), the former French prime minister Édouard Daladier, the future West German chancellor Konrad Adenauer, the Italian statesman Altiero Spinelli and many others. The Hague Congress therefore had the potential to develop into the European equivalent to the Philadelphia Convention of 1787, when the United States gave herself a central government and a constitution in order to forestall internal division and to deter external attack.

Unlike the founding fathers, however, the men and women assembled at The Hague failed to achieve a European political, economic and currency union. They could not agree whether the unity of Europe should be generated on supra-national or intergovernmental lines. At this point the French, and many other western European governments, were sympathetic to the idea of a European federation. Britain, too, was sympathetic to much closer European cooperation, which it hoped would give it the weight to act on the world stage on terms of equality with the United States and the Soviet Union.[48] London resisted, however, any attempt to merge its sovereignty into a larger whole, partly because of its Commonwealth links but mainly because, not having experienced defeat and occupation, British opinion regarded European political unification as an attempt to repair something that was not broken in the first place. The Foreign Secretary, Ernest Bevin, therefore signalled: cooperation and even 'spiritual confederation' – yes; complete political union – no.[49] Washington's hope that the administration and distribution of Marshall Aid would lead to the establishment of federal European structures was disappointed.

The shift to a policy of 'containment' had profound implications for the link between US strategic interests and democracy promotion. On the one hand, there was now much less pressure on right-wing dictatorships in southern Europe and Latin America to reform, and within a few years the United States would negotiate a deal with Franco on the use of naval and air bases in Spain.[50] On the other hand, the decision to confront the Soviet Union had profound implications for the future of the western zones of occupation in Germany. 'It is not overstating the matter,' the Deputy Under-Secretary of State at the Foreign Office, Sir Orme Sargent, argued, 'to say that if Germany is won this may well decide the fate of liberalism throughout the world.'[51] It was therefore vital to establish a political order capable of resisting Soviet infiltration, strong enough to contribute to the defence of the west as a whole and yet incapable of or uninterested in dominating the rest of Europe. In effect, this meant the introduction of some form of federal democracy. The first step here was the formal abolition of the state of Prussia in 1947, which, the occupying powers claimed, had 'always represented the elements of militarism and reaction in Germany'. At the London accords in April–June 1948, the French reluctantly agreed to the creation of an independent albeit federal Germany.

Democracy and self-determination were useful weapons against Stalin in Europe, but they could be turned on the western powers overseas. In India, Mahatma Gandhi's policy of non-violent resistance ground down the authorities, leading to partition and independence in 1947. The Muslim-majority areas in the west and in Bengal became Pakistan; the land in between became India. The strategic consequences of Indian independence were huge: Britain forfeited the military hub from which the defence of empire east of Suez had been funded and manned for generations. London hoped to make good this loss by developing, as Bevin put it in early 1948, 'the material resources in the [remaining] Colonial Empire', and by intensifying cooperation with the white settler dominions. Australia, for example, agreed to support the British position in the Middle East. Canada, for her part, remained committed to the defence of the European balance. Increasingly, however, the dominions were going their own way in grand strategy. This was reflected in the creation of ANZUS, an alliance between the Antipodes and the United States which bypassed the British Empire.

In September 1947, under pressure from Zionist terrorists and Arab nationalists, the British announced their intention to relinquish the mandate in Palestine, hand the problem over to the United Nations and withdraw. When the UN proclaimed the division of the territory into an Arab state and the state of Israel in late November 1947, the Jewish settlers agreed to abide by the resolution. It was furiously rejected, however, both by the Arab population and by neighbouring Arab states. In 1948, a full-scale war between the Zionists and the Arabs resulted in the total defeat of the latter within a few months. This led to an attack on Israel in May 1948 by Iraq, Syria, Lebanon, Egypt and Jordan. Once again, Israel prevailed, despite an international arms embargo in which the US and all western powers participated. Hundreds of thousands of Palestinian Arabs either fled or were expelled by the Zionists, an experience which became known as the '*Nakba*', or catastrophe; the West Bank of the Jordan was annexed by the Kingdom of Jordan. The new state was a European transplant in the heart of the Middle East. Its leadership was mostly German or eastern European in origin. Although vastly outnumbered, the Jewish settlers adopted European forms of organization, recruitment and extraction with the result that they were able to field a slightly larger army than the Palestinians with about half the population. Israel was militarized without being militaristic.[52] 'It is no secret,' the minister of labour, Mordechai Bentov, remarked shortly after the end of hostilities, 'that success in war hinges not only on success at the front, but also success at the home front; and mobilization under modern wartime conditions must approach total mobilization.'[53]

Faced with a concerted western attempt to contain him in Europe, Stalin reacted by consolidating his hold on central and eastern Europe.[54] When eastern European governments showed a keen interest in Marshall Aid in the summer of 1947, however, Stalin feared that they would be drawn into the western orbit and forced them to decline the American offer. In September 1947, Stalin founded the Cominform – a successor organization to the old Comintern – to keep the eastern European parties in line and to ensure that the activities of international communism conformed with the interests of Moscow. Its headquarters were located in the Yugoslav capital, Belgrade. Single-party communist rule was imposed on all of eastern and central Europe by the end of 1948. Stalin did not, however, attempt to promote communist revolution in France or Italy,[55] on the grounds that this would be premature and give the capitalists a pretext to crush the parties there. The Soviet dictator particularly wished to avoid unnecessary provocations in what he regarded as peripheral areas. He made clear his intention to honour the 'percentages agreement' with Churchill and to refrain from supporting the Greek communists. This led to a confrontation with the independent Yugoslav leader, Marshal Tito. In June 1948, Stalin's patience snapped, not least because he did not want to be dragged into a Balkan quagmire while he was engaged over Berlin. Tito was denounced, Yugoslavia was expelled from the Cominform and the two dictators henceforth became sworn enemies. As Tito moved closer to the west in order to contain Stalin, he cut off support to the Greek communists, whose resistance soon collapsed.

The really crucial arena, of course, was Germany. In March–April 1947, a meeting of the Council of Foreign Ministers in Moscow failed to reach a consensus. The Americans, in particular, were no longer willing to countenance Russian demands for reparations from the western zones, which would – as the senior Republican John Foster Dulles argued – 'in effect make the Soviets master of all Germany – including the Ruhr – and with that all Europe will go under'.[56] Stalin regarded the creation of Bizonia, the currency reform and the Marshall Plan, rightly, as steps preparatory to the creation of a West German state and ultimately to the reunification of Germany under the Allied aegis. Determined to forestall such a mortal threat to his European position, Stalin withdrew his representative on the Four Power Allied control council in late March 1948. Towards the end of June, immediately after the currency reform, he imposed a blockade – cutting off water, electricity and all land routes into the city – on the Allied sectors of Berlin. This was designed not so much to drive the Allies out of the former German capital, as to force them to desist from moves to draw Germany into their camp. The struggle for mastery in central Europe was entering a new and more intense phase.

The west responded by stepping up 'containment', particularly in central Europe. Allied transport planes supplied Berlin by air throughout the winter of 1948–9, forcing Stalin to lift the blockade.[57] In early

April 1949, the United States, Canada, Britain, France, Belgium, the Netherlands, Luxemburg, Norway, Denmark, Iceland, Portugal and Italy came together to form the North Atlantic Treaty Organization. The signatories agreed that 'an armed attack against one or more of them in Europe or North America shall be considered an attack against them all' and would trigger a 'collective self-defence' by all members of the treaty. This amounted to nothing less than a peacetime geopolitical revolution in Europe: not only was the United States (and Canada) now a guarantor of the post-1945 territorial order, but the long-existing community of fate between Europe and North America had been given international legal expression. The treaty was primarily directed against the Soviet Union, but for many of the signatories it also helped to guard against the revival of German power. As the British General 'Pug' Ismay, the first Secretary General, famously quipped, NATO was designed to keep the Americans in, the Russians out and the Germans down.

Shortly afterwards, the western allies decided to risk democracy in Germany as the best strategy of denying the area to Stalin and integrating it into the common front against communism. In late May 1949, the American, British and French zones of occupation were merged to form the Federal Republic of Germany, or West Germany, as it soon became known. The resulting German constitution was drawn up, as one American liaison officer remarked, 'primarily for international purposes'.[58] It established a federation of regions with considerable autonomy, much closer to the old German Confederation and Second Empire than the more centralized Weimar Republic and Third Reich. This reflected partly the survival of strong federal traditions in Germany and partly the desire of the occupying powers, especially the French, to prevent the development of a strong state. For the same reason, the new Federal Republic remained disarmed for the time being. In order to ensure that the Soviet Union would not dominate the new state by stealth, the Basic Law enshrined the right to private property, which effectively excluded any move towards a planned economy, and included a strong defence of basic individual rights. Likewise, the invitation to join the new General Agreement on Trade and Tariffs (GATT) ensured that West Germany would not succumb to economic protectionism, but remain integrated into the global economic system. As always, the domestic structure of Germany and the European balance were intimately connected.

In the face of widespread scepticism, democracy flourished in West

Germany.[59] Chancellor Konrad Adenauer and his economics minister, Ludwig Erhard, presided over an economic boom, the party system stabilized, and under the 'social market economy' labour relations and wealth redistribution functioned so well that the kind socio-economic unrest which had bedevilled the Weimar Republic, and which threatened to return after the war, became a thing of the past. Left and right were united in an anti-totalitarian consensus against communism and, retrospectively at least, Nazism.[60] The really critical issue facing the new democracy, however, was the Soviet threat and reconciliation with her European neighbours. For this reason, Adenauer urgently sought a rapprochement between France and the Federal Republic, a diplomatic revolution which endured to become a principal pillar of European geopolitics.[61]

The confrontation between Stalin and the west, and to a much lesser degree persisting fears of German revanchism, was the dominant factor in European and American domestic politics. The US presidential elections of 1948 were shaped by debates over America's place in the world, and their implications for society and economy. For Harry Truman, the contest was essentially a referendum on his management of containment. By contrast, the principal concern of the leader of the new Progressive Party, Henry Wallace, was a more conciliatory policy towards the Soviet Union. The Republicans were deeply divided between isolationists such as Robert Taft, who opposed the Marshall Plan as an expensive folly, and their eventual candidate, Thomas Dewey, an internationalist supporter of containment. During the campaign they failed either to land any significant blows on Truman or to pin on him what Dewey called 'policies which resulted in surrendering 200,000,000 people in middle Europe into the clutches of Soviet Russia'.[62] To everyone's surprise, Truman won re-election, a victory at least partly due to his perceived firmness on foreign policy especially during the Berlin crisis.

In France, on the other hand, the principal preoccupation was the revival of German power. In July 1948, a popular outcry over Georges Bidault's agreement to the creation of a (west) German state led to the fall of his administration, and his replacement by Robert Schuman. The Italian elections of 1948 went badly for the communists, partly because of their association with Stalin and partly because of direct US support for the rival Christian Democrats. In Britain, both the Labour government and the Conservative opposition were preoccupied with the preservation of

British power; one prominent Labour tract claimed that 'the maintenance of Britain as a world power is . . . the precondition of a socialist foreign policy'.[63] Grand strategy was furiously contested not only between the parties, but within them. The ruling Labour Party, in particular, was divided between those who wanted rapprochement with Moscow and supporters of containment. Opinion was shifting against Moscow, however. In 1947, the party's International Secretary, Denis Healey, published *Cards on the table*, an impassioned plea to come off the fence and to oppose Soviet advances in eastern and central Europe. Likewise Bevin argued that communism should not just be 'disparag[ed] on material grounds' but by comparison with 'a positive ideology . . . of civil liberty and human rights'.[64] British socialists might maintain an ideological equidistance between capitalism and communism, but they could not remain neutral between freedom and dictatorship.

The emerging Cold War also shaped European governmental structures. In 1945, the British set up the Joint Intelligence Committee to coordinate the flow of strategically important information to the prime minister. This was the first step in the creation of a 'secret state' geared to counter Soviet subversion and prepare Britain for the worst.[65] Similar structures were either established or restored in France. In both countries, conscription was retained even after the end of the war. All these developments paled, however, by comparison with those taking place on the far side of the Atlantic. The policy of containment was underpinned by a programme of domestic mobilization designed to maximize American power for the struggles which lay ahead. The National Security Act of 1947 established the National Security Council, to advise the president on foreign affairs and international security, the Central Intelligence Agency, the Joint Chiefs of Staff and many other features now loosely, and often pejoratively, described as the 'National Security State'. The draft by which young male Americans served was maintained. For the first time in its history the United States was undergoing a peacetime militarization. Big government, which had begun during the New Deal and expanded massively during the war, was there to stay. The United States had effectively become a European state not only in terms of its geopolitical orientation, but also with regard to domestic structure and mindset.

Many despaired of the ability of western polities to withstand the centralized structures of the Soviet Union. Denis Healey, for example, warned of the 'inestimable advantage' which Moscow had of dispensing with public opinion. This gave the Soviet Union the 'freedom to fit policy closely to the scientific calculation of a fluctuating national interest'.[66] The National Security Act and the Joint Intelligence Committee were attempts to address this deficiency in Washington and London, but they did not mean that either the United States or Britain came to resemble the enemy they were fighting. In America, especially, popular and parliamentary hostility to the state remained strong. Congressional committees maintained strict oversight over expenditure, which may have cramped the style of the executive and the national security apparatus in the short term, but made the United States a more efficient and vibrant defender of its values and interests over the long haul.[67]

In previous eras, substantial external challenges had driven programmes of profound social change to increase national resilience. This did not happen in the early Cold War. Most western European states were too concerned with the problems of reconstruction to think of preparing society for the next war. In the United States, however, there were some who argued that the challenge of the Soviet Union required a fresh look at the position of African-Americans, especially in the South, where they were still heavily discriminated against. This was partly driven by fear that the Communist Party would exploit their grievances to undermine the home front, and partly by the desire to rally all sectors of society for the struggle ahead. As the black American Roy Wilkins, the executive director of the National Association for the Advancement of Colored People, argued, 'the survival of the American democratic system in the present global conflict of ideologies depends upon the strength it can muster from the minds, hearts and spiritual convictions of all its people'. 'The Negro,' he explained, 'wants change . . . not only to preserve and strengthen the standard [of rights] here at home, but to guarantee its potency in the world struggle against dictatorship.'[68] The Soviets routinely used racial discrimination to attack the United States, and it was particularly embarrassing in Germany, where black servicemen made up more than 10 per cent of the garrison, and where they were supposed to serve as ambassadors for democracy against communism and Nazi racial hatred.[69] A segregated military, Jacob Javits, a senator on the European Study Mission of the Foreign

Affairs Committee, seriously hampered US efforts in Germany, 'the main front of the cold war'.[70] The emancipation of the American blacks and the struggle for mastery in central Europe were thus closely linked.

Globally, the rights of men and women were now very firmly in contention. In early December 1948, scarcely a month after the US election, the United Nations issued its Universal Declaration of Human Rights. The preamble asserted that recognition of the 'equal and inalienable rights of all members of the human family' was 'the foundation of freedom, justice and peace in the world'. This was because 'contempt for human rights' had 'resulted in barbarous acts which have outraged the conscience of mankind' – a clear reference to defeated Nazism – and because 'rebellion against tyranny and oppression' would otherwise result. Either way, the promotion of human rights was seen not only as a good in itself, but as a strategy for the avoidance of international and civil war. Right at the top of the list was the right to freedom from discrimination on the basis of 'race, colour, sex, language, religion, political or other opinion, property, birth or other status'. Slavery, the slave trade, arbitrary arrest, detention and exile were to be abolished. The international implications of this move were complex. On the one hand, the Declaration strengthened the hand of the west against Stalin in Europe. The European Convention on Human Rights, which was agreed two years later, was certainly driven by such Cold War imperatives.[71] Moreover, as Roosevelt's widow, Eleanor, pointed out, the Soviet Union – which effectively imprisoned its own and subject populations – was particularly vulnerable to the idea that emigration was a fundamental human right.[72] On the other hand, the Universal Declaration, particularly its commitment to 'self-determination', could be used by colonial peoples to challenge the European imperial powers.

The international developments of 1947–8 had a profound impact on Soviet domestic politics. Many of the freedoms permitted during the war were curtailed by a regime which felt itself under attack from without by the west, and subverted by internal dissidence. Tito's apostasy sparked off a fresh round of party purges, as Stalin sought to root out potential deviationists. By the end of the decade, his Gulag contained more prisoners than ever before. The most striking domestic political shift, however, came in response to the triumph of Zionism in Palestine in 1948. Stalin had supported the creation of Israel in order to embarrass the British, but the enthusiastic welcome Soviet Jews afforded

Golda Meir, the first Israeli ambassador to Moscow, and his own paranoia caused him to fear a Zionist-American plot against his person. 'Every Jew is a nationalist and agent of American intelligence,' Stalin claimed.[73] Over the next four years or so, the Soviet Union was gripped by a wave of anti-semitism: Jewish doctors were accused, without a shred of evidence, of trying to poison Stalin; Jewish communists were murdered or imprisoned.[74] Similar events took place in eastern Europe, especially in Czechoslovakia, where Jewish party-leader Rudolf Slansky was charged with 'Trotskyite Zionism' and other crimes more or less explicitly linked to his racial background.[75] International anti-semitism was firmly back on the agenda. This was the Jewish security dilemma: the establishment of Israel had fuelled the very anti-semitism which it was designed to guard against.

Stalin responded to the creation of West Germany with the establishment of the German Democratic Republic later in 1949. In keeping with his existing policy, the Soviet dictator was not trying to set the partition of Germany in stone, quite the opposite. The creation of the GDR was meant to signal an alternative for the whole of the country. 'This is not the creation of an East German state or an East German government,' its founding proclamation announced, 'but of a government for all of Germany.' For the moment, however, the GDR was to remain disarmed, at least ostensibly. Its chief value to Stalin lay in its capacity to disrupt the re-militarization of the Federal Republic. 'West' and 'East' Germany thus became two experiments as to which model of society and government could best satisfy the material, spiritual and national needs of the German people. Stalin also pressed ahead with his nuclear programme. In August 1949, the Soviet Union exploded its first atomic bomb, and although her arsenal was to remain markedly inferior to that of the United States for many years, the spectre of being blackmailed by the American nuclear monopoly had been banished.

At the same time, the Russians – who had until recently regarded the rest of the world largely as an unwelcome distraction from European matters – sought to put the pressure on the United States globally in order to force the Americans to relax their grip in Europe, and especially Germany. In March 1949, with defeat over Berlin looming, Stalin finally agreed to supply North Korea's communist leader, Kim Il Sung, with large quantities of modern armaments.[76] That same year, Mao finally triumphed in the longstanding Chinese Civil War and drove his rival, Chiang, to seek refuge on the island of Formosa (Taiwan). The desire to restore China's global position – and thus to avenge a century of 'humiliation' at the hands of outside powers – was a crucial motivating force for the communists. Equally important, however, was a mission to implement and export the tenets of Marxism. Mao aimed at the revolutionary transformation of Chinese society, and to spread the word into neighbouring countries, partly for its own sake and partly because he believed that there was no other way of keeping the revolution at home safe. For this reason Mao, who yielded to none in his resentment of foreigners, nevertheless deferred to Stalin as the ideological leader of world communism.[77] He inherited all the European communist conceptions of 'encirclement' and external threats.[78] A Sino-Soviet Treaty duly followed in 1950, and Mao announced that he would 'lean to one side' in the struggle between the Soviet Union and the west. The new People's Republic of China, in other words, was driven by a combination of local concerns and a revolutionary agenda first set out in Germany nearly a hundred years before. Central Europe had come to the Far East with a vengeance.

Taken together, Stalin's bomb, his German policy and the emergence of militant communism in east Asia led to a much broader programme of western military re-mobilization. In January 1950, Truman authorized the construction of a still more deadly nuclear weapon – the hydrogen bomb. A few months later, the United States government issued National Security Directive 68 (NSC 68), which called – in often apocalyptic terms – for much greater investment in armaments in order to meet the global communist challenge. Implicitly invoking the experience of 'appeasement', the memorandum warned of 'gradual withdrawals under pressure' until the Soviet Union had achieved 'domination of the Eurasian landmass'.[79] The echoes of Mackinder were unmistakable.

The main battlefield remained Europe. The 'coordinated' Kremlin offensive feared for Asia was refracted through European lenses. In northern and east Asia, this anxiety dictated a policy of support for governments such as Chiang's Kuomintang in Taiwan and Syngman Rhee's dictatorship in South Korea, to help them resist communist subversion from within and aggression from without. Washington would very much have preferred to have backed similar local forces in the European colonies of Indochina, Indonesia and Malaya, believing that they enjoyed a legitimacy which the imperial authorities lacked. In spite of this, the United States supported the British, French and Dutch attempts to hold on to their colonial empires, because they needed European cooperation on the central front against Stalin. 'The Netherlands,' the State Department explained, 'is a strong proponent of US policy in Europe ... the stability of the present Dutch government would be seriously undermined if the Netherlands fails to retain a very considerable stake [in Indonesia] and the political consequences of failure of the present Dutch government would in all likelihood be prejudicial to the US position in Western Europe'.[80] Europe, and especially Germany, trumped everything else.

Matters came to a head in late June 1950, when Kim Il Sung launched a surprise attack on South Korea, with Stalin's foreknowledge and approval though not at his instigation. What shook Washington, and especially the western European capitals, was the belief that the attack on South Korea heralded a much broader assault on the west, particularly in Europe. The new West German chancellor, Konrad Adenauer, was fervently of this opinion. It was for this reason that the United States immediately sent troops to shore up the collapsing South Korean defences. The French foreign minister and avid European integrationist Robert Schuman responded to news of the American intervention with visible emotion, saying, 'Thank God, this will not be a repetition of the past',[81] that is of the 1930s. Shortly afterwards, the United States persuaded the United Nations to support the war against Kim's Democratic People's Republic of Korea, the first operation of the new international organization. Britain and Australia sent substantial forces; France, Belgium, the Netherlands, Greece and Turkey also sent troops. West Germany had, as yet, none to send. They were all there not to protect the South Korean dictator, Syngman Rhee, but to fight a global battle against world communism which would soon engulf Europe if not stopped in the Far East.

With the majority of US forces now engaged in Asia, more troops were required to deter the Soviet Union along the Rhine and Elbe. Some form of permanent European defence integration, which would harness the resources of Britain, France, the Low Countries and Italy, or the rearmament of West Germany, or some combination of the two approaches, was required. For the next five years or so, European geopolitics and domestic politics were dominated by these interrelated issues. Should there be a strong Germany to deter the Soviet Union, with all the potential dangers to her neighbours, or should German strength be diluted through some form of supra-national European political integration in which the Germans gave up their sovereignty along with everyone else? As the German economy boomed in the early 1950s in the famous *Wirtschaftswunder* – by late 1951 onwards, growth outstripped that of Great Britain – the issue of how soon this financial muscle would be converted into political and military power, and whether those capabilities could be harnessed to the wider western cause, became increasingly pressing.

Washington's preference was clear.[82] Only a politically and militarily united Europe – or at least a concerted western European effort – could mobilize the economic, moral and military energies to stop Stalin, and relieve the burden on the Americans. Central to this programme on the military side was German rearmament, either unilaterally or as part of a broader process of political integration. 'You cannot have any sort of security in western Europe,' the Secretary of State, Dean Acheson, argued, 'without using German power.' The only question was whether it would 'be integrated into western European power or grow up to be a power of its own'.[83] In September 1950, therefore, the US made the dispatch of more troops to Europe contingent on British and French acceptance of the creation of a large West German force within NATO. At the same time, Washington saw the European project as crucial to the management of German power. In April 1950, John McCloy, former US high commissioner to Germany, warned that 'no permanent solution of the German problem seems possible without an effective European Union'.[84] European unification, in short, was intended to serve the 'double containment' of Germany and the Soviet Union.

The United States gave not only strong diplomatic backing, but also extensive covert financial assistance to the European project. The new Central Intelligence Agency, and to a lesser degree the British Secret Intelligence Service, funded a broad range of political and cultural activities in support of European unification – or at least greater European unity.[85] These included the anti-Moscow trade unions, anti-communist liberals and leftists, the Congress of Cultural Freedom (1950) for intellectuals, Radio Free Europe in Munich (founded 1951),[86] the secretive 'Bilderberg' group (founded 1952) and publications such as Melvin Lasky's *Der Monat* (founded in 1948), which was edited in the iconic frontline city of Berlin, and the very widely read *Encounter* magazine (founded

1953). More modestly, the Information Research Department in the British Foreign Office clandestinely subsidized *Animal Farm*, George Orwell's devastating critique of Soviet communism.[87] Conservatives, leftists and liberals came together to defend not so much capitalism – many still clung to the idea of a 'third way' between the American and Soviet economic extremes – as 'European values' such as democracy, freedom of speech and civil rights. The European Convention on Human Rights, which was championed by European conservatives as much as by liberals and the non-communist left, was signed in 1950 specifically to strengthen the west morally in the Cold War.[88] The fight for the soul of Europe, and especially of Germany, was on.

In May 1950, the French foreign minister, Robert Schuman, proposed a joint administration of French and German coal and steel resources. Ostensibly a form of economic rationalization, the scheme was really a device to bring the war-making potential of Germany under multilateral control. 'A United Europe was not achieved [before 1939],' Schuman argued in his declaration, 'and we had war.' In effect, Paris wanted to Europeanize Germany, before it Germanized Europe. Britain, predictably, was highly sceptical, partly because she refused to pool the necessary sovereignty, and partly because the British economy was still largely geared towards the Commonwealth and Empire, which took more than half of British exports in 1951, with the balance being shared between western Europe and the United States.[89] The West German government under Konrad Adenauer supported the Schuman Plan, partly as a vehicle for the return of their country to the diplomatic top table, but also out of genuine belief in a common European destiny. Washington had some initial reservations about what was effectively a European cartel in competition with US industry, but the political and strategic advantages of greater European cooperation were so compelling that it endorsed the plan; indeed, US negotiators worked closely with Schuman in drawing up the scheme.[90] In 1951, the European Coal and Steel Community (ECSC) came into being, the first major step towards political unification.

The core of the project, however, was always common defence. Economic self-interest and a common European 'civilization' were not enough. Only fear of Soviet domination and – to a lesser but still substantial extent – of German revanchism would drive well-established states such as France, Belgium, the Netherlands, Italy and perhaps even

Britain to give up or at least share their sovereignty. In late October 1950, the French prime minister, René Pleven, responded to US pressure for German rearmament with a proposal for a European Defence Community (EDC). This was to be 'the complete merger of men and equipment under a single European political and military authority', integrating Germans in smaller formations to operate on the crucial central front. In late May 1952, with strong US encouragement, France, Italy, West Germany, the Netherlands, Belgium and Luxemburg signed the European Defence Community Treaty.[91] At first, only Britain stood aloof, rejecting the project as an unacceptable dilution of her sovereignty. In March 1953, the signatories to the EDC concluded a draft treaty for a matching European supra-national authority – the European Political Community (EPC) – to govern the defence community and the ECSC. This was to include not only an Executive Council of national prime ministers, a Court of Justice and an Economic and Social Council, but also a two-chamber European parliament, one made up of deputies directly elected from the peoples of the community and another of senators representing the 'peoples' of all the participating states. The EDC, and the political integration it spawned, was effectively a European government-in-waiting.[92] Within a very short period of time, parliaments in Bonn and the Benelux countries had ratified the treaty, and that of Italy, though delayed, was expected to follow. Continental western Europeans appeared to be on the verge of creating a mighty union to banish discord between them and to present a common front against Soviet communism.

Moscow watched these developments with mounting alarm. Ever since Napoleon and Hitler's 'crusades' against Russia, it had regarded the political and military union of the continent as a potential threat, and the prospect of German rearmament under its umbrella as a mortal danger.[93] 'The Americans will draw West Germany into the Atlantic Pact,' Stalin warned the East German communists in early April 1952. 'They will create West German troops. Adenauer is in the pocket of the Americans. All ex-fascists and generals also are there. In reality there is an independent state being formed in West Germany.'[94] The Soviets now strained every nerve to disrupt western European defence integration. They played on British and French fears of German rearmament. They instructed European communists, especially the French and Italian parties, to stop the necessary legislation from passing parliament. On the diplomatic front, Moscow opened a peace offensive, designed to show that the waning threat of war rendered the EDC redundant. Finally, as the French military effort in Indochina foundered, the Soviets explicitly linked their support for a face-saving withdrawal formula at the Geneva peace talks to the rejection of the defence community.

The main target, however, was the Federal Republic. If it could be prised loose from the west, the EDC would be dealt a severe blow. There was some urgency to this, because the Soviet Union had begun to despair of using the GDR as a magnet to rally nationalist opinion to her side. On the contrary, the regime of Walter Ulbricht in East Berlin conspicuously failed to satisfy the materialist appetites of Germans bewitched by the 'economic miracle' in the west. Nor was he able to slake their spiritual thirst as the dictatorial nature of communist rule, backed up by Soviet tanks, became increasingly clear. Millions of Germans fled westwards; only a trickle made the journey in the other direction. What had once been thought of as a porous border to infiltrate the western zones of occupation had become an open wound through which the GDR was being demographically bled dry. In order to deprive Adenauer and the Americans of a pretext for West German rearmament, Ulbricht was permitted only a small number of clandestine paramilitary police formations. These were fully engaged in internal repression and were too weak to be of much use to the Red Army. Ulbricht, in short, had become a liability, the more so as he was more and more open about his preference for a smaller GDR under his control, rather than merging into a united neutral and democratic state.[95] The basis on which Stalin's German policy had rested since the closing stages of the Second World War was being rapidly undermined.

So in early March 1952, the Soviet dictator made one last attempt to break the deadlock. In a series of communiqués – which have gone down in history as the 'Stalin Notes' – he offered the west a deal. In return for the demilitarization and neutralization of Germany, the Soviet Union would withdraw its own forces of occupation and permit reunification. This was very much less than the optimal solution he had canvassed after 1945, but it had the merit of shedding a liability – Ulbricht's regime – while forcing the Allies to sacrifice the burgeoning West Germany. Ostensibly, the notes were directed at the three occupying powers, but the real addressee was the government in Bonn, and the wider West German public; he was still trying to trade on their nationalistic instincts.

Adenauer, however, refused to be drawn.[96] Instead, he forced the pace on German rearmament and the Federal Republic's alignment with the west – the *Westbindung* as it came to be known. This involved persuading the Allies that German militarism had died with Hitler and the *Junker* class, but that German military traditions could be placed in the service of the western cause.[97] In April 1951, for example, he asserted that the *Wehrmacht* had come through the war with its 'honour' unbesmirched, and he played up the importance of the German resistance at every turn. This might have been bad history, but it was good politics from Adenauer's point of view. At the same time, he tried to repair Germany's image as far as possible with world and especially Jewish opinion. The German chancellor thus made a point of trying to establish good relations with Israel, and in 1952 he came to an agreement about restitution payments for Nazi crimes against the Jews.[98] Against this background, Adenauer rejected the Soviet offer, thus signalling his rejection of a policy of oscillation between the two camps, in favour of a wholehearted commitment to the integration with the west.

Frustrated, Stalin now moved to the other extreme. He had held the GDR back from the crash programme of industrialization, state ownership, and one-party rule which he had imposed on the other European satellites in order to appease West German nationalist opinion, but now he ordered Ulbricht to proceed with the 'Construction of Socialism' in July 1952. Announced with much fanfare by his Socialist Unity Party, this involved the building of more factories, further expropriations of 'bourgeois' enterprises, suppression of the churches, and the creation of formal East German military formations, though not yet a separate army. The effect of all this was the exact opposite of what Stalin had hoped. Rather than strengthening Ulbricht's grip, the exodus of refugees actually doubled, as East Germans fled westwards for economic and political reasons. Desertion from the security forces was rife. As for using Ulbricht's republic as a showcase, that was now quite out of the question. Soviet intelligence candidly reported that the GDR no longer held 'even the slightest attraction for citizens of West Germany'.[99]

The sharp increase in international tension due to the Korean War, the process of European military integration and developments in Germany had a profound impact on domestic politics in Europe and the United States.[100] It dominated the 1952 American presidential campaign. The decision of the former wartime Allied Supreme Commander and NATO Supreme Commander Europe, Dwight Eisenhower, to run was strongly driven by his belief that the Republican frontrunner, Robert Taft, a prominent 'Asia-Firster', was unsound on collective security and rearmament, that only he could save NATO, and that Germany – 'the prize for which the international game is being played', as he put it in March 1952 – was being neglected.[101] Eisenhower promised to 'go to Korea' and end the conflict, increasingly seen as 'the wrong war, at the wrong place, at the wrong time and with the wrong enemy', as the chairman of the Joint Chiefs of Staff, General Omar Bradley, had described it.[102] Instead, Eisenhower undertook to 'roll back' Soviet power in Europe. He won the election comfortably. In the Soviet Union, the question of how to deal with the deteriorating situation in Germany was right at the top of the high political agenda after the death of Stalin in early March 1953.[103] The troika which succeeded him – made up of Georgi Malenkov, Lavrenti Beria and Nikita Khrushchev – sharply changed course on the GDR and forced Ulbricht to relax his policies of repression. They ordered an immediate halt to the 'Socialist Construction Programme', including a reversal of collectivization in the countryside. This about-face, which was initiated by the police chief Beria, was designed to reduce the flow of refugees to the west. It backfired spectacularly within a few months. The new line from Moscow divided the German party between those such as Rudolf Herrnstadt, who supported unification with the west, and Ulbricht, who feared that he was about to be sacrificed for Soviet strategic gain. On 17 June 1953, East German workers took advantage of the new freedoms to demonstrate in favour of better working conditions, and even German unification. In the end, Ulbricht was forced to beg the Soviets to intervene, which they did with heavy loss of life, and further loss of reputation. Moscow's German policy was once again in tatters. At the end of that month, Beria was arrested on trumped-up charges and executed. There were many reasons for his fall, especially fear that he was planning to murder his comrades, but it was the failure of Beria's German strategy which made it so easy for his enemies to assemble a conspiracy against him. Two years later, Khrushchev crushed his principal (post-Beria) rival, Malenkov, who was forced to resign as prime minister. The chief charge against him at the Central Committee was his past support for Beria's more liberal policy in the GDR. Khrushchev's rise to power in the Soviet Union, in other words, was on the strength of his status as vindicator of Russia's vital national interests, especially in Germany.

In West Germany, foreign policy was also at the heart of domestic political polarization. The governing coalition parties – the moderately conservative Christian Democratic Union (CDU) and the Free Democrats (FDP) – supported German rearmament and the western orientation. There were some dissidents, however, such as Adenauer's interior minister, Gustav Heinemann, who resigned in 1950 over the prospect of German rearmament, partly because he feared another war but also because it would damage the prospects for German unification. The other large party, the still notionally Marxist Social Democrats (SPD), were strongly opposed to Adenauer's foreign policies, which they blamed for entrenching the partition of Germany. Their leader, the fiery First World War veteran Kurt Schumacher, roundly condemned Adenauer as the 'chancellor of the Allies'. The German public respected Schumacher, and there was also a groundswell of opinion that Stalin's offers on reunification should at least have been considered. Many were sceptical about rearmament, which often provoked the response, 'count me out' (*ohne mich*). In the end, however, most backed the chancellor on foreign policy, and accepted that Germany would have to contribute militarily to its own security. In early September 1953, Adenauer romped to victory in the federal elections with a greatly increased majority. This was, of course, primarily a tribute to his economic stewardship, but it was also an endorsement of his unswerving commitment to the west.

British politics were also profoundly shaped by the new sense of international crisis after 1950. The spiralling costs of defence (about 12 per cent of GNP) associated with the maintenance of an overseas empire, the prosecution of war in Korea, the development of the atom bomb (achieved by 1950) and defensive measures against a possible Soviet invasion of Europe forced the government into painful cuts to domestic spending. When in the spring of the following year, the Chancellor of the Exchequer, Hugh Gaitskell, proposed to introduce charges on dental and eye treatment in order to pay for increased armaments the minister for labour, Aneurin Bevan, resigned in protest. He was supported by left-wingers such as Michael Foot and Harold Wilson. The Labour Party was now deeply split. Gaitskell's cuts were to n avail, in any case, because in September 1951 Britain suffered a balance-of-payments crisis largely caused by massive defence expenditure, not least the huge currency cost of the British Army of the Rhine.[104] At around the same time, Britain officially fell behind West Germany in terms of economic performance.[105] In October 1951, the Labour Party went down to a narrow defeat in a general election in which foreign policy – the unpopular Korean War, the cost of rearmament, and the shaky British position in the Middle East – were central issues. Labour portrayed itself as the 'peace' party which would rescue the nation from Tory warmongers; the Conservatives condemned the slide in Britain's international standing, and the 'appeasement' of her enemies. 'Whose finger on the [nuclear] trigger?' the press asked. From late 1951, it would once again be that of the Conservative prime minister, Winston Churchill.

The polarization of British domestic politics around foreign and defence policy gathered pace in the early 1950s. A full-scale battle erupted within Labour over Germany.[106] The dominant anti-communists, such as Healey and Gaitskell, strongly supported NATO and were prepared to tolerate German rearmament within a system of multilateral constraints. They pointed out that the EDC corresponded to the old socialist principle of transcending narrow national boundaries and preoccupations. Thus Gaitskell warned a group of trade unionists in 1952 that if the democracies were 'divided' in the face of Stalin, they would 'fall one by one as Hitler's victims did'.[107] The 'Gaitskellites' went along with the Americans, not because they had been bought by the CIA, but because they were persuaded that Washington was still the best defence of 'free institutions'. A significant minority in the Labour Party, however, was highly suspicious of what they saw as American warmongering and materialism. They were also deeply opposed to the creation of a new German army under the auspices of the EDC or any other umbrella. And whereas opinion on the United States tended to divide on ideological lines, the question of what to do about Germany transcended the left–right split: two of the most strident opponents of German rearmament were the left-winger Bevan and Hugh Dalton, who was firmly on the right of the party.[108] In 1954, the Labour Party Conference narrowly endorsed German rearmament, but only by using the trade union 'block vote' to overrule the rank-and-file sceptics.

Eisenhower's election victory led to the announcement of a new

American foreign and defence policy. In a dramatic televised address shortly after taking office in 1953, his Secretary of State, John Foster Dulles, pointed to a map demonstrating the 'vast area' from Germany to east Asia, including the Soviet bloc and China, which the 'Russian communists completely dominate[d]'.[109] He warned that not only was Moscow pursuing a policy of 'encirclement' against the west, but that the population of the communist world had quadrupled from 200 million to 800 million since the Second World War. Most of the resources of Eurasia were in hostile hands. This was effectively Mackinder's 'heartland' theory in a new guise. Containment, therefore, was not enough: an active policy to 'roll back' Soviet power was necessary to prevent the slow strangulation of the free world. The ideological and strategic here were closely linked: the National Security Council argued that a permanent Soviet domination of eastern Europe 'would represent a serious threat to the security of western Europe and the United States'. For this reason, Washington reiterated her 'traditional policy to recognize the right of all people to independence and to governments of their own choosing. The elimination of Soviet domination of the satellites is, therefore, in the fundamental interest of the United States.'[110] A barrage of speeches, radio broadcasts and psychological warfare directed against the eastern bloc followed. This approach even extended to Islamism, which Washington regarded as a lever against the Soviet Union in central Asia and the Caucasus. The CIA began to cultivate activists such as Said Ramadan, effectively the Muslim Brotherhood's foreign minister, and sponsored the construction of a mosque in Munich which would serve as a focal point for stateless Muslims opposed to Godless communism.[111]

In the 'Third World', on the other hand, the Eisenhower administration and the western European powers were potentially confronted by a sharp contradiction between ideology and *Realpolitik*. There, the weapons of self-determination and human rights, which could be used so effectively to rally opinion at home and to prise open the Soviet position in eastern Europe, tended to boomerang. In Africa and Asia, local nationalists now used these arguments against European imperialists. Moreover, as the US administration began a systematic alignment with authoritarian regimes in Latin America, the Middle East and Asia against popular movements which were believed to tilt towards Soviet or Chinese communism, it became vulnerable to similar charges. The empires, once European assets, had become liabilities in Europe, while Washington's global commitments weakened not only her military commitment to but also her moral standing in Europe.

The other plank of Eisenhower's grand strategy was the need to reduce the budget deficit in order to safeguard the long-term economic health on which US security depended. Like many Republicans and libertarians, he was also fearful that the machinery of the military-industrial complex – as he later christened it – would slowly swallow the freedoms it was supposed to defend. To this end, the new president moved quickly to end the costly war in Korea, which was finally achieved in late July 1953. Eisenhower also reduced spending on conventional forces, seeking to make up the missing firepower through reliance on massive nuclear force. This strategy – the 'New Look' announced in NSC 162/2 – was enshrined in NATO's MC 48, which threatened to respond to a Soviet attack with 'massive retaliation'. His various disarmament proposals were public relations gambits, designed to wrong-foot the Soviet Union. Central to this policy of nuclear reliance and fiscal retrenchment, however, was Europe, and especially Germany. It would only be possible if NATO or the EDC picked up the resulting slack, in terms both of conventional and, if possible, of nuclear capability. For this reason, the Eisenhower administration was a staunch supporter of European integration, and especially military cooperation; his Secretary of State, Dulles, had been a sponsor of Jean Monnet, the president of the High Authority of the ECSC and one of the continent's leading integrationists since the Second World War. The European Defence Community seemed the solution both to the Soviet threat and to the president's enduring 'grave anxieties about German rearmament involving the recreation of a German national army and a German general staff'. Eisenhower therefore told the British and French in December 1953 that the EDC was 'not only the best, but also the only hope of a solution to the problem of a German contribution, without which NATO would fall down'.[112]

The course of French domestic politics, however, ultimately frustrated Eisenhower's efforts. In June 1954, the forces of Ho Chi Minh, the North Vietnamese nationalist and communist leader, vanquished the French at Dien Bien Phu. Eisenhower rejected French appeals to save their cause through direct military intervention. The government of Pierre Mendès France came to power shortly afterwards with a mandate to end the war, and in late July the Geneva accords ended this phase of the conflict. France abandoned her empire in Indochina. Laos and Cambodia became independent states. Vietnam was divided into a communist north, backed by the Soviet Union and Red China, and a US-supported right-wing regime in the south, the Republic of Vietnam.

It was in Europe, however, where the impact of French politics was most keenly felt. The withdrawal from Indochina greatly lessened interest in following the American lead in Europe, especially German rearmament and military integration. Moreover, Stalin's death had reduced the sense of a Soviet threat. During a passionate debate in the French National Assembly, critics lined up to attack the EDC for failing to provide sufficient guarantees against the revival of German militarism,[113] not least because the British refused to participate. In a subsequent vote right at the end of August 1954, the treaty was rejected by a clear, though not massive, majority. This was the decisive '*non*'. The European Defence Community, and with it the military integration of Europe, was dead. Whatever else it would be, 'Europe' would not be a mighty union on the lines agreed by the thirteen American states in the late 1780s.

The defeat of the EDC shaped European geopolitics for the rest of the decade. Britain moved into the resulting political vacuum and seized control of the European project.[114] In late October 1954, Britain, France, Germany, Greece, Italy, Luxemburg, the Netherlands, Portugal and Spain came together under the leadership of the British Foreign Secretary, Anthony Eden, to agree to 'promote the unity and to encourage the progressive integration of Europe'; in May of the following year, this pact was formally christened the Western European Union (WEU). Unlike the supra-national EDC and EPC, however, this was an intergovernmental organization acceptable to London. Germany was once again an actor on the European scene, and thus consoled for the failure of the EDC. Her sovereignty was still highly conditional, however, in deference to French demands. Adenauer was obliged to make a unilateral declaration abjuring any interest in atomic and chemical weapons, or in the construction of guided missiles, and large naval and aerial capabilities, without the permission of the WEU. The German troop commitment was to be capped, and Allied forces were to remain in Germany on a permanent basis not only to deter the Soviet Union, but also to prevent German aggression in the future. They reserved the right to intervene in defence of the democracy in West Germany, to stop the independent development of nuclear or chemical armaments, or in the event of an attempt by Bonn to achieve unification by force. The future of political freedom in West Germany, in other words, was integral to the security of western Europe.

Jean Monnet was so scarred by the French parliamentary rejection of the EDC that he came to believe that unity could only be achieved through stealthy cooperation between the major European governments, beginning with the economy. In 1955, he founded the Action Committee for a United States of Europe – which was made up of leading Christian Democrat, socialist, liberal and labour leaders. That same year, the ECSC countries met in the Sicilian city of Messina in early June 1955 to deepen their supra-national economic ties. The foreign ministers of France, Germany, Italy and the Benelux countries agreed to form a customs union – known as a 'common market' – and to integrate the transport and civil atomic energy sectors. Britain, which was not a member of the Coal and Steel Community, tried in vain to push a much looser free trade association. It argued that further economic union would divide western Europe and, far from containing Bonn, would actually, in the words of one official, provide 'a means of re-establishing the hegemony of Germany'.[115] This signalled the beginning of a separation of what all previous successful unions – from England and Scotland, through the American Constitution to the creation of the second German Empire – had combined: of economic union on the one hand, and defence integration on the other.

Washington now pressed ahead with the rearmament of West Germany within NATO. In early May 1955, the German Basic Law was abandoned to allow the creation of armed forces. Not long after, Dulles made a substantial concession to German nationalist opinion, and dealt the French a stinging rebuke, when he reiterated American support for the unification of Germany 'under conditions which will neither "neutralize" nor "de-militarize" a united Germany, nor subtract it from NATO'.[116] A complex system of financial transfers and 'offsets' was established to share the burden of the US military presence between Bonn and Washington. At around the same time, EURATOM was set up to manage the European acquisition of nuclear expertise, and thus prevent Bonn from developing atomic weapons independently. One way or the other, the principal provider of military security was now NATO, rather than any European organization. It had relieved western Europeans of the need for further political-military integration.[117]

*

The EDC controversy subsided, but the unresolved underlying tensions erupted in a European double crisis in the middle of the decade. Overlapping and interlocking developments in Moscow, London, Paris, Cairo and Tel Aviv led the continent to the edge of a general conflagration. The trail began in Moscow, where West German rearmament had shocked Soviet policy makers to the core. In mid-May 1955, only a week after the final announcement from Bonn, Khrushchev responded with the creation of the Warsaw Pact, which rallied the entire eastern bloc, including the GDR, in a formal military alliance with the Soviet Union. The day after, the Russian leader approved the Austrian state treaty. This agreement to end the four-power presence in the country in return for its neutralization was not about Austria. It was a clear signal to all Germans that a similar arrangement was on offer for them. Once again, Adenauer did not take the bait; West Germany would rearm. She immediately became more assertive: in December 1955, Walter Hallstein, the State Secretary, announced that West Germany would no longer recognize any state that recognized the GDR, apart from the Soviet Union (the 'Hallstein Doctrine').[118]

Moscow was deeply alarmed by all this. 'The West Germans are the only ones who might bring about a new war in Europe,' Khrushchev remarked to his son.[119] This fact drove domestic politics in the Warsaw Pact: all member states were characterized by one-party systems, state ownership of the principal means of production, militarization of all levels of society and the emergence of a *nomenklatura*, a new party aristocracy who were rewarded for their service to communism and Moscow with economic privileges. Like the North Atlantic Treaty Organization its strategic operational horizon was Germany and the Rhine. Unlike NATO, which was led by the United States but was also a genuine alliance, the Warsaw Pact was completely dominated by Moscow. Right at the end of May 1955, Khrushchev and Marshal Bulganin visited Belgrade to patch up relations with Tito. Two months later, Khrushchev sought an understanding with Eisenhower at a summit in Geneva where the future of Germany was the main issue. The United States, however, was not prepared for any solution which did not involve free elections, which would lead to the immediate collapse of the GDR, and it was not prepared to allow Germany to cut loose as a neutral, either. Eisenhower warned that 'There was no possibility of having 80 million hard-working people in the center of Europe as neutrals.'[120]

This precipitate decline of Russian influence in Germany drove Khrushchev to abandon the traditional Soviet reticence about intervening in the Third World. In a famous speech in early 1956 the Soviet leader hailed the arrival of the 'new period in world history predicted by Lenin when the peoples of the East will play an active part in deciding the destinies of the world and become a new and mighty factor in international relations'.[121] This required an ideological recalibration: 'anti-imperialist' cooperation with diverse anti-western regimes rather than pan-Marxist solidarity was now the watchword. In particular, Moscow pursued a relationship with the Egyptian leader, Colonel Gamal Nasser, in order to embarrass Paris and London, and to frustrate Washington's attempts to complete the encirclement of the Soviet Union from the south. The local communists were left to the tender mercies of the Egyptian secret police.

At the same time, Khrushchev sought to strengthen the Soviet system by making the European satellites more viable, and releasing the domestic energies sapped by years of Stalinist terror. In his remarkable 'secret' speech to the Twentieth Party Congress in Moscow in late February 1956, Khrushchev announced a new policy of de-Stalinization. Millions of prisoners were released from the Gulag; attempts were made to wrestle control from the bureaucracy back to the party. Stalin's body was removed from his mausoleum on Red Square. A few months later, the Soviet leader authorized the removal of the hardline Hungarian party leader Mátyás Rákosi and his replacement by a more moderate figure. Not long after that, Khrushchev permitted the return of the independent-minded Polish communist leader, Wladylsaw Gomulka, from internal exile. As was so often the case, however, these reforms merely whetted the appetite for more freedoms. By late October 1956, a full-scale crisis had erupted in both countries. In Poland, the riots were largely directed against shortages, albeit with a strongly Russophobic undertone. In Hungary, on the other hand, matters quickly escalated beyond the control of the local party and the Russian garrison. It soon became clear that the reformist leader, Imre Nagy, encouraged by the Austrian precedent, was planning to take his country out of Moscow's immediate control, and perhaps out of the Warsaw Pact altogether. Hungarian workers and students – pumped up not least by US 'rollback' propaganda – prepared for a showdown with the Red Army. A year after the announcement of German rearmament, the Soviet position in central and eastern Europe was locked in a perilous downward spiral.

Meanwhile, the British and French were grappling with Egypt's Colonel Nasser, who not only took delivery of a Czechoslovak – effectively a Soviet – arms shipment, but also nationalized the Suez Canal. London and Paris believed not just Egypt and the wider Middle East were at stake, but 'Europe' itself. Paris was rocked by the start of a nationalist revolt in Algeria in 1954, which among other things threatened the testing grounds for the French nuclear programme. Britain, for her part, was alarmed by the outbreak of a Greek Cypriot rebellion, which threatened the crucial base areas in thc eastern Mediterranean. Moreover, dealing with the Egyptian challenge was seen as vital to the success of the 'Eurafrican' project of collectively mobilizing the continent in support of European power.[122] For this reason, the West German chancellor, Konrad Adenauer, strongly supported military intervention on the grounds of 'European *raison d'état*'.[123] In early September the French prime minister, Guy Mollet, secretly proposed a Franco-British union of states – a revival of the Churchill scheme of 1940 – in order to present a united front to the world. London rejected these overtures as a dilution of national sovereignty, but it did agree to approach Tel Aviv to concert joint action against Nasser. The Israelis – having failed to secure an American arms deal to deter the Arabs – welcomed these approaches with open arms. French weapons now flowed instead. In late October, the British, French and Israelis agreed a secret protocol in the Paris suburb of Sèvres by which the Israelis agreed to attack Egypt, after which the two European powers would step in to 'separate' the combatants and restore international control over the Canal.

Everything now happened very quickly, as the eastern European and Middle Eastern crises climaxed simultaneously.[124] Right at the end of October the Israelis attacked Egypt. A day later, fearful that the new Hungarian government was about to leave the Warsaw Pact – which it did shortly afterwards – Khrushchev sent Soviet tanks into Budapest. By contrast, the Poles – who were prepared to stay within the direct Soviet sphere of influence – were appeased with vague assurances of domestic autonomy. That very same day, the British and the French began 'Operation Musketeer', the military intervention promised at Sèvres.[125] The WEU powers – the Belgians, Dutch, Germans and Italians (with fingers firmly crossed behind their backs) offered unequivocal support. Egyptian resistance collapsed quickly; the Hungarians put up a desperate fight in their capital. In the UN and at the bar of world opinion, London and Paris were mercilessly pilloried for their 'colonialist' adventure. The Hungarians were largely forgotten. The (cold) war of European unification, which Washington had expected to take place against the Soviet Union, was now taking place in Egypt.

Eisenhower was furious, partly because the crisis cut across his desire to cooperate with Arab nationalism wherever possible, partly because he shared the global distaste at Anglo-French 'imperialism', partly because he was standing for re-election in the following month, but mainly because the crisis in Egypt shifted the spotlight from Hungary and allowed Khrushchev to restore Soviet control in eastern Europe. The Hungarians were crushed; the United States stood aside. Eisenhower straight away sponsored a UN resolution demanding an immediate ceasefire in Egypt. When that failed due to an Anglo-French veto in the Security Council, Eisenhower turned to tougher measures. Using massive economic pressure – through the International Monetary Fund and the crash sale of sterling bonds – the United States sought to compel the two European powers to withdraw. The French, who had prepared themselves for the intervention much better financially, were relatively untroubled, but London – confronted by a run on the pound – soon buckled.[126] Britain and France backed down, and they had completely withdrawn from the Canal Area by the end of the year. It was a devastating blow to the Anglo-French position in the Middle East, and thus to their condominium in Europe.

In France, the US intervention in support of Nasser was taken to show that Washington could never be trusted. The French redoubled their efforts to secure a nuclear weapon and clung on grimly to their installations and testing grounds in Algeria. The British, on the other hand, took away from Suez a powerful sense that they must never find themselves on the wrong side of an argument with the Americans again. Moreover, there was now a widespread realization in London that the empire, once a major bulwark of the British position in Europe, was now a liability which complicated attempts to rally the world against communism.[127] Britain could no longer stand for both the defence of democracy in Europe and imperialism overseas, even if the former plausibly required the latter. In 1957, Britain wound down its war in Cyprus, and released the Greek Cypriot leader, Archbishop Makarios. Three years later, after securing the continued use of the base areas, London released the island into independence, albeit with the national tensions between Turks and the majority Greeks still unresolved. Britain also abandoned most of her African and Asian empire, which had become a distraction from her European destiny, and a cause of suspicion to friendly capitals on both sides of the Atlantic. She had built up her colonial empire largely for strategic purposes, and it was for the same reason that she relinquished it: in deference to US wishes, to strengthen the argument against Soviet human rights abuses, and to ease Britain's path back into 'Europe'.

Suez shifted the balance between the western European powers. As the British Chancellor of the Exchequer remarked in early January 1957, the Achilles heel of Britain at Suez had been the 'weakness of [its] post-war economy'.[128] That summer, London was rocked by another sterling crisis: wages were high, inflation was on the increase, and speculation against the pound resumed. Public expenditure was too high. Something would have to give: it would have to be either guns or butter. Britain chose butter. The population was appeased with throwaway budgets: Macmillan told them in 1957 that 'You have never had it so good.' The price was paid in terms of Britain's European standing. In the late 1950s, financial pressures became so great that the government was forced to cut the RAF and the Army of the Rhine. National service was abolished for cost reasons; ever greater reliance was placed on the independent nuclear deterrent. As Britain fell, Germany rose with her booming economy and began to demand more military equality, especially with regard to nuclear weapons.

Most importantly of all, the events of 1956 gave a decisive new impulse to the European project. 'Europe will be your revenge,' Adenauer told the French prime minister, Guy Mollet, just after news of the US ultimatum over Suez came through. London – especially the Foreign Secretary, Selwyn Lloyd – shared the view that Europe would have to be economically united in order to balance both Russia and the Americans. For now, however, the British still refused to compromise their sovereignty and antagonize the Commonwealth by participating in an economic union. Moreover, the British feared that Germany would use the resulting agreement as a vehicle for the return to great-power status. Macmillan warned that it would lead to 'western Europe dominated in fact by Germany and used as an instrument for the revival of power through economic means. It is really giving them on a plate what we fought two wars to prevent.'[129] Paris shared these concerns, but now believed that political and economic – but not military – integration with Bonn was the best way to guard against them.

In late March 1957, with strong American backing, the Messina countries concluded the 'Treaty on the Functioning of the European Union', better known as the Treaty of Rome. France, Germany, Italy and the Benelux countries – the 'Six' – agreed to create a common economic market, as of the beginning of the following year. At the Stresa Conference of July 1958, the Six also agreed a Common Agricultural Policy (CAP) designed to manage surpluses and prevent the flight from the land. This European Economic Community (EEC) was a customs and economic union explicitly designed, like the more modest nineteenth-century *Zollverein*, to achieve 'ever closer' European political union. Britain remained aloof; London would liaise with the EEC via the Western European Union. The European project inaugurated by the Treaty of Rome differed from the original EDC and EPC in two crucial respects, however. There was no military dimension – that now rested entirely with NATO – and there was very little direct democratic accountability. Unlike the Anglo-Scottish and American unions, moreover, European integration would not be a single act, but a process. 'Europe will not be made in one fell swoop, nor in one joint construction,' Robert Schuman remarked, 'it will be made by concrete steps creating first a solidarity of fact.'

The Hungarian and Suez crises also fundamentally recast Moscow's relationship with the independent communist world. The treatment of Hungary, and the subsequent execution of Imre Nagy, who had taken refuge in the Yugoslav embassy, wrecked the Soviet rapprochement with Tito. Relations with Mao were also deteriorating badly. This was partly due to local factors: Chinese resentment about Russia's unjust treaties, refusal to share nuclear technology, and other real or imagined slights. The real problem, however, was ideological: how best to promote world revolution and under whose leadership? Mao had been content to follow Stalin – whose revolutionary credentials stretched back beyond 1917 – but he regarded himself as Khrushchev's senior in the world of international communism. After the 'secret' break with Stalinism, Bejing lambasted the Soviet Union for 'revisionism', that is deviating from the common party line. Central to this argument was the fate of communist regimes in central and eastern Europe. Mao now began to intervene in European affairs, sometimes criticizing the Soviet Union for its heavy-handedness, more often attacking its weakness, always seeking to maximize the embarrassment for Moscow. He laid the unrest in Poland and the fiasco in Hungary – both direct results of de-Stalinization – at Khrushchev's door. First Mao claimed that Soviet measures against the Poles reflected their 'big-power chauvinism', then he demanded that the Hungarian revolutionaries be crushed without further ado. He made thinly veiled accusations of cowardice against the Soviet leader, promising to pick up the torch of global revolutionary communism dropped by Moscow. East European leaders were quick to appeal to Peking in order to carve out some independence from Moscow. In November 1955, for example, the GDR party ostentatiously adopted the Chinese rather than the Soviet method of taking over the remaining large private enterprises.[130] More spectacularly the senior Chinese party leader, Chou En-lai, famously announced that he was not afraid of nuclear war, and that month Mao was the dominant presence at an international communist summit in Moscow. The overall effect of all this Red Chinese activism was to limit Khrushchev's room for manoeuvre in central and eastern Europe.

As the decade drew to a close, a fresh trail was laid which would lead to another round of multiple European and global detonations. President Charles de Gaulle aimed to restore French 'grandeur' by reducing costly colonial commitments, pressing ahead with the development of a nuclear capability, and striking an independent pose in Europe. In 1958, de Gaulle demanded the creation of a Franco-British-US 'Tripartite Directorate' in NATO, partly with a view to controlling Germany and partly in order to stake a claim to complete equality in military matters. When this was rejected by Washington, the general showed his displeasure by taking France out of NATO's Mediterranean Command in 1959. That same year, the Cuban revolutionary Fidel Castro took power in Havana, ousting a pro-American dictator. A year later, the French exploded their first atomic bomb, greatly increasing their strategic confidence. In 1961 – against the backdrop of Algerian riots in Paris itself and furious resistance from generals and *pied noir* colonists – de Gaulle pulled out of Algeria. This enabled him to reorient French policy more fully towards Europe.[131]

Khrushchev, for his part, was grappling with the continued rise of West Germany. In the spring of 1957, the Bonn government officially notified Moscow that it was about to embark on a military nuclear programme. Soviet analysts expected that within a few years the *Bundeswehr* would not only number around half a million men but would also be armed with atomic bombs. It is hardly surprising, therefore, that diplomats and journalists in Moscow reported Khrushchev's increasing sense of paranoia, his repeated references to the German surprise attack of 1941, to the revival of German 'revanchism' and to Konrad Adenauer, whom he regarded as a Hindenburg-style figure likely to facilitate a Nazi revival.[132] What drove Khrushchev to utter despair, however, was the progressive collapse of East Germany. Since 1949, more than 2 million refugees had fled the country and the flood was showing no signs of abating. Yet Khrushchev dared not remove Ulbricht, or even remonstrate with him too strongly, because Mao was in the background demanding the defence of socialism against imperialist aggression. The East German leader was now effectively the tail wagging the Russian dog, and in 1959–60 – egged on by Red China – Ulbricht pushed through the collectivization of agriculture. This had the predictable effect of reducing the food supply further, though Mao – in order to underline his support for the 'frontline' German communists – sent Ulbricht food which his own peasantry so desperately needed. In short, by the end of the decade, the Soviet leader was faced with the unbearable prospect of a demographic and economic collapse of the GDR, followed by German reunification on Bonn's terms, leading to the accession of the whole country armed with nuclear weapons into NATO.

Khrushchev still had one ace to play: Berlin. That city, he famously said, was 'the testicles of the west. Every time I want to make the west scream, I squeeze on Berlin.'[133] In November 1958, the Soviet leader issued an ultimatum. Either Washington, London and Paris agreed a mutually acceptable final settlement for Germany, or the Soviet Union would conclude a separate peace treaty with the GDR and return its territory to Ulbricht's full control. The clear implication was that the GDR would close the access routes to Berlin and thus precipitate another blockade. Against this background, the Soviet leader approached the western powers in turn over the next two years. In January 1959, he made overtures to Washington, bypassing Bonn, but when that did not bring instant results, Khrushchev tried Adenauer. The German chancellor, however, rejected all offers of a confederation of the two German states – and the option of a conference possibly leading to unification – in return for a recognition of the GDR and the Oder–Neisse border with Poland. Khrushchev now turned back to de Gaulle, but by the time the two met in Paris in March–April 1960 it was clear that the Frenchman wanted to maintain the partition of Germany, rather than explore Soviet schemes for a neutralist confederation. At the same time, Khrushchev was determined to increase the Soviet nuclear arsenal, to achieve parity with the United States as soon as possible. He was convinced that only this would induce Washington to deal with him on a basis of equality. If there were to be another showdown over Berlin, the Soviet Union would this time be better prepared than Stalin in 1948, when the US had enjoyed an atomic monopoly. Resources were diverted from the army, navy and air force towards the Strategic Missile Forces, which were constituted as a separate service in 1959.

London took a ringside seat throughout the early stages of the second Berlin crisis, and showed no appetite for a confrontation with Moscow. While Dulles was prepared to go to the 'brink', Macmillan warned Eisenhower in November 1958 that Britain was 'not prepared to face obliteration for the sake of 2 million Berlin Germans, their former enemies'.[134] Britain was also in the throes of a fundamental strategic rethink. Throughout the late 1950s, the extent to which Britain was falling behind financially and technologically became painfully clear. A bilateral agreement on nuclear weapons cooperation with the United States reached at Bermuda in 1957 underlined this inferiority. It surfaced again in 1960, when technical problems forced the cancellation of the much-vaunted independent British missile system, 'Blue Streak'. Moreover, the costs of maintaining an 'imperial' presence now threatened Britain's ability to fulfil her obligations in Europe, the main battleground. Only by joining the European Economic Community, Macmillan felt, could the nation hope to regain the weight she had lost on the international stage. In July 1961, Britain made a formal application to be admitted to the EEC. All the same, Britain's stated view of the primacy of Europe led to a deepening estrangement with Australia and New Zealand.[135]

The international turbulence around the turn of the decade also left its mark on domestic politics. In the United States the perceived Soviet advances in space – they sent the first *Sputnik* satellite into orbit in October 1957 – and the nuclear field caused a widespread crisis of confidence in her own capacity to innovate. The creation of the National Aeronautics and Space Administration (NASA) in late July 1958 and the passing of the National Defense Education Act that same year were attempts to address this problem. There was also a widespread elite feeling that the administration was not doing enough to prop up the friendly government in Saigon against communist aggression from within and without. All these factors – the *Sputnik* crisis, Vietnam and especially the 'missile gap' – were issues which John Fitzgerald Kennedy, the Democratic candidate for the presidency, mercilessly exploited in the election campaign. In November 1960, Kennedy was narrowly elected – with some help from his late father's friends in Chicago – on a hawkish platform in foreign policy.

It soon turned out that the 'missile gap' he had laid at the door of the Republican candidate – Richard Nixon – did not in fact exist. That said, national security was at the heart of the vision for a 'new frontier' which the Kennedy administration unfolded. It believed that the key to the defence of the United States lay in the socio-economic modernization of the world along western lines. The new National Security Advisor, Walt Rostow, was an academic economist who believed passionately that US aid, especially judicious state infrastructural investment, could stimulate capitalist 'take-off' across the developing world, and by reducing poverty bring it gradually into the western fold. Kennedy had much less interest in Germany – which his predecessor regarded as 'the central bastion in Europe' – and sought to bypass Bonn in the search for an early thaw in the Cold War. The New Frontiersmen initially saw Germany – as the influential Under-Secretary of State, George Ball, recalled – as 'an irritating footnote' to the broader confrontation.[136] They were about to be rudely awakened.

If socio-economic 'modernization' was one plank of Kennedy's new grand strategy, a departure from Eisenhower's emphasis on the immediate use of nuclear weapons in the event of a major crisis was the other. The new administration rejected 'massive retaliation' as too constraining, forcing Washington to use an atomic sledgehammer to crush a conventional nut, and increasingly unrealistic as Soviet nuclear forces approached parity with those of the United States. Instead, the United States now pursued a policy of 'flexible response', which according to Kennedy's chief military adviser, General Maxwell Taylor, involved 'a capability to react across the entire spectrum of possible challenge, for coping with anything from general atomic war to infiltrations and aggressions'. In Europe, this meant an increase in NATO conventional forces in order to hold the Soviet Union before a nuclear showdown became unavoidable. In the rest of the world, 'flexible response' involved not only a greater willingness to deploy regular ground forces, but also the development of more substantial capabilities in intelligence and 'counter-insurgency'. The testing ground for the new doctrine was increasingly Indochina, where more and more US civil and military advisers, and eventually combat troops, were deployed. Washington feared that a communist victory in Saigon would unleash a 'domino effect', as Soviet-inspired revolutions rippled down through Thailand and Malaysia to link up with Sukarno's radical regime in Indonesia.

The Kennedy administration was soon in difficulty. Large-scale economic programmes failed to reconcile the South Vietnamese population or reduce widespread support for the Viet Cong. Moreover, the general perception was that despite the best efforts of the military mission, the South Vietnamese army would never be able to defeat the insurgency. There were now growing calls in Washington for the removal of the unpopular Ngo Dinh Diem regime, and the dispatch of large US forces to finish the job.[137] For the moment, however, the president resisted further escalation in Vietnam, and rejected demands for intervention in Laos.[138] This was primarily because unlike George Ball he regarded Indochina as a distraction from the main battlefront in Germany.[139]

Meanwhile, the Berlin crisis had reached boiling point; the city, as the black civil rights leader Martin Luther King told its citizens, had become 'the hub around which turns the wheel of history'.[140] The Soviet leader now expected an immediate collapse of the GDR and its swift absorption by West Germany. Then, Khrushchev feared, 'The *Bundeswehr* would advance to the borders of Poland and Czechoslovakia and therefore nearer to our borders.'[141] In June 1961, Khrushchev told the Politburo that Germany was 'the key issue'.[142] His demand that the United States recognize the boundaries of the satellite states, especially those of the GDR, was rejected. Worse still, Kennedy vowed to defend Berlin, even at the cost of war. Mao was still on Khrushchev's back, demanding tougher action. Drastic measures were required. In mid-August 1961, therefore, Moscow finally permitted Ulbricht to build a large barrier along the zonal border in Berlin to prevent further emigration. Those attempting to escape were mown down without warning. As one historian has put it, the East German leader drove the Soviets 'up the wall'.[143] The main function of the NVA, the East German army, was no longer to defend against capitalist aggression, but to incarcerate its own population. The last gap in the 'iron curtain' had been plugged, but at the price of admitting the inferiority of the communist system in the central theatre of the strategic and ideological conflict.

Humiliated over Berlin, Khrushchev began to look around for ways, as he put it to his defence minister in April 1962, of 'throw[ing] a hedgehog down Uncle Sam's pants'.[144] He therefore authorized the dispatch of medium- and intermediate-range nuclear missiles to Castro's Cuba a month later. Khrushchev wanted to put pressure on Washington's southern flank and thus weaken her in Germany; at the very least, he hoped that he could force the withdrawal of American missiles deployed along his own southern border with Turkey. In mid-October 1962, however, US reconnaissance spotted the deployment before it was complete. President Kennedy demanded the immediate withdrawal of the missiles, which could reach American cities with almost no warning and represented a flagrant breach of the Monroe Doctrine, and imposed a naval blockade on Cuba. He saw the connection to Germany at once. 'I need not point out to you,' he told the British prime minister at the height of the crisis, 'the possible relation of this secret and dangerous move on the part of Khrushchev to Berlin.'[145] The world now moved rapidly towards a nuclear confrontation. Moreover, unbeknown to Washington, Soviet 'advisers' in Cuba were authorized to use the tactical missiles already on the island at their discretion. An American attack – even a purely conventional one – might have provoked an instant atomic exchange. Castro and Che Guevara, the charismatic Latin American revolutionary, pressed for war, which would expose the Americans as paper tigers and precipitate a broader struggle for the liberation of Latin America. Khrushchev, however, rejected their demands for a pre-emptive strike. He informed Castro that if Moscow had been 'the first to launch a nuclear strike against the territory of the enemy [this] would have been the start of a thermonuclear world war'. '[W]e are not struggling against imperialism in order to die,' he reminded the Cuban leader.[146] Within a few days, Khrushchev had backed down, the missiles were withdrawn in return for a promise to remove the Jupiter missiles in Turkey quietly, and war was averted.

The Berlin and Cuban crises shaped world geopolitics over the next three years. Mao finally lost patience with Khrushchev. He accused the Soviets of 'bluffing' over Germany, where they had backed away from their 'deadline',[147] and especially in the Caribbean. Fortunately for Moscow, the consequences of this in Europe were containable. The defection of Albania to the Red Chinese camp in late 1961 remained an isolated incident in an isolated country, though it cost Moscow some valuable port facilities on the Adriatic. In the Far East, however, Mao's hostility was a more serious matter. All Soviet advisers were withdrawn, Moscow continued to refuse all nuclear cooperation, and Mao accused the Russians of failing to support Ho Chi Minh adequately. In October–November 1962, taking advantage of Khrushchev's preoccupation with Cuba, Mao launched a surprise attack on India, which the Soviet Union was backing in its border disputes with China. And when Khrushchev folded over Cuba, Mao's derision knew no bounds. The Sino-Soviet split – which US policymakers had dreamed of since 1949 – burst into the open. Mao would not 'lean to one side' much longer. Two years later, Red China tested its first atomic device at Lop Nor in the Gobi desert. The Soviet Union was now encircled west and east by hostile nuclear powers. The bi-polar system which had dominated geopolitics since the late 1940s had become tri-polar.

In western Europe, and especially in Germany, the Berlin and Cuban crises also had a lasting impact. On the one hand, Kennedy's firm stance over the missiles gave heart to western publics and statesmen, particularly the inhabitants of Berlin, who perceived Khrushchev's move as an attempt to renew the pressure on their city; 'it's about us,'[148] they said, even though the events were taking place on the other side of the Atlantic. On the other hand, many Germans, including Chancellor Adenauer, had been deeply disappointed that the American president had not taken a harder line over the construction of the wall. They suspected him – and the British – of wishing to perpetuate the partition of their country. The Germans were also unsettled by the military implications of 'flexible response', which deprived them of automatic American nuclear protection while exposing their country to the ravages of a conventional war between NATO and the Warsaw Pact. To make matters worse, Washington had not bothered to consult with her allies over Cuba: not just Bonn, but London and especially Paris were outraged at how close they had come to nuclear obliteration over a remote island in the Caribbean.

The stage was set for an intense round of European diplomacy, as the Germans searched to escape their military inferiority, while the western powers sought to draw Germany over to their own side, or at least to keep Bonn from becoming more deeply committed to the rival camp.[149] In late 1961 and early 1962, the senior French diplomat Christian Fouchet launched plans for a European Political Union (EPU). This was designed to compensate for the loss of Algeria and to make up for the waning effectiveness of the US nuclear deterrent in Europe, through greater diplomatic cooperation between western European states under French leadership. The Fouchet plan finally collapsed in April 1962 because some states, such as Italy and the Netherlands, rejected French intergovernmentalism in favour of a supra-national union, while most other members of the EEC were wary of de Gaulle's hostility to the US and his determination to keep out the British. All this aroused intense anxiety in Washington about the state of the western alliance in general, and the future of Germany in particular. President Kennedy responded with a 'Grand Atlantic Design' to renew NATO, bind Germany even more closely to the west, meet their demands for consultation halfway, and mobilize more European energies for the common struggle against the Soviet Union.[150] He also took up a scheme for a Multi-Lateral (nuclear) Force (MLF), which Eisenhower had conceived in the final months of his presidency. This involved a shared shipborne atomic deterrent, which would be under NATO rather than national US command. Full West German participation was envisaged. Kennedy hoped that all this would be accompanied by a new wave of political integration, preferably supra-national rather than intergovernmental. Britain was expected to play an important role in driving this process forward, for which reason Washington strongly supported London's second bid for EEC membership in late 1962. Kennedy, in turn, promised Macmillan at the Nassau Summit at the very end of that year to supply Britain with Polaris nuclear missiles on the understanding that these would eventually be deployed under the MLF umbrella. In mid-January 1963, however, de Gaulle unilaterally vetoed Britain's admission to the EEC. 'If Britain were admitted,' he announced, 'Europe would eventually be absorbed into a colossal Atlantic community dependent on America and under American control, and this France could not permit.'

The MLF plan and the associated programme of political integration dominated European geopolitics over the next two years. To France, the prospect of nuclear weapons under any sort of German control was deeply alarming.[151] De Gaulle therefore used the same press conference at which he rejected Britain's EEC application to rule out any French participation in the scheme. In late January 1963, a week after the rejection of Britain's EEC application, his overtures culminated in the Franco-German Élysée Treaty. This was designed to drive a wedge between Bonn and Washington, derail US-sponsored European defence and political integration, and inaugurate a European alliance under French leadership. De Gaulle seems to have planned to expand this agreement into a much deeper dual union with common institutions, foreign policy and possibly even joint citizenship. Within a very short time, however, US pressure and a revolt within Adenauer's own administration led the *Bundestag* to add a qualifying preamble. This reaffirmed Germany's support for the transatlantic link and the MLF, the commitment to admit Britain to the EEC, and the vision of supra-national European integration, and generally emptied the Élysée Treaty of any content beyond the symbolic expression of Franco-German friendship. The United States now began to regard European integration – which could potentially be directed against them as much as against Moscow – with ambivalence,[152] but de Gaulle was back where he started.

Kennedy remained preoccupied by the German Question generally and Berlin in particular; it was the need for large-scale conventional forces to defend the city which underlay the whole concept of 'flexible response'.[153] In late June 1963, Kennedy famously announced in the former German capital that he was a 'Berliner' – literally: a doughnut – and called upon its citizens to look beyond the city to 'the advance of freedom everywhere'. He also invited anybody in the outside world who was uncertain of what was at stake to 'come to Berlin' and observe the two systems at first hand: freedom and prosperity in the west, and backwardness and oppression in the east. Like Eisenhower, he made every effort to spur the west Europeans and especially the West Germans to greater military efforts on the central front. Like his predecessor, however, the president was also profoundly wary of the revival of German power. In the summer of 1963, the administration forced Bonn to sign the Nuclear Partial Test Ban Treaty (NPT), which effectively scotched the prospect of an independent German deterrent. Bonn feared that the treaty would lock her into a permanent position of atomic inferiority; Franz Josef Strauss, a senior conservative politician and former defence minister, famously spoke of a 'nuclear Versailles'. It was for this reason that the PTBT was accompanied by a US–West German agreement that 'As long as the German government and people are convinced that the United States will defend Germany, Germany does not need nuclear weapons.'[154] In short, the NPT – like many other forms of international organization and governance – had its origins in the containment of Germany.

All this made progress on the MLF even more urgent. President Lyndon Johnson – who had succeeded Kennedy after his assassination in November 1963 – was keen to proceed partly because the rising costs of the war in Vietnam made him eager to spread the burden of defence more evenly in Europe. His main concern, however, was Germany: 'The object,' the president remarked, 'was to keep the Germans with us and keep their hand off the trigger.'[155] Moreover, the European and especially the German issues and the war in Vietnam were closely linked in the administration's mind. If the United States failed to hold Saigon, they reasoned, the West Germans might doubt their ability to defend Berlin and seek a rapprochement with Moscow. In this sense, the Under-Secretary for Political Affairs, Eugene Rostow, claimed, the bombing of North Vietnam 'should greatly fortify our system of alliances'. The German government itself accepted this argument. The new chancellor, Ludwig Erhard, explained in June 1965 that he was asking the Americans to remain in Vietnam because otherwise 'the Germans would say to themselves, that just as the Americans were not able to hold South Vietnam, they would not be able to hold onto . . . Berlin if it were seriously threatened'.[156]

In 1963–4, US efforts merged with those of Jean Monnet to revive the process of European integration. In early November 1964, the German government finally invited its European partners to explore the outlines of what Monnet was proposing: a deeper political union, centred on common defence through the MLF, in cooperation with Washington; Bonn hoped that Paris might be reconciled through concessions on agriculture. Later that month, the European parliament called upon the states of the EEC to convene a conference to agree a common foreign and defence policy, to create a federation and to establish an equal partnership of equals with the United States. The continent was on the move again: a democratic European superstate was back on the agenda.

De Gaulle now pulled out all the stops to rein in Bonn, pre-empt German nuclear armaments, reduce the American security dominance on the continent, and sabotage any European political cooperation which was not strictly intergovernmental or at least under French leadership. He berated the Bonn government during a disastrous state visit in early July 1964: they were bluntly told to choose between Paris and Washington. If the West Germans failed to work together with him on security matters on the intergovernmental basis envisaged in the Élysée Treaty, de Gaulle added, then he would withdraw from all economic cooperation. Thus, far from being persuaded to shelve his security objections for concessions on agriculture, de Gaulle used economic cooperation for strategic ends. In order to show that he was in earnest, de Gaulle now also made overtures to Moscow from mid-1964. This French *Ostpolitik* was driven primarily by the need to intimidate Germany rather than any yearning for an east–west détente. Some German observers – including Adenauer – began to speak of a return of 'encirclement'.

In Moscow, the MLF revived the nightmares which had led to the second Berlin crisis at the end of the previous decade. In the summer of 1964, Khrushchev sent his son-in-law on a special mission to the West Germans to dissuade them from going ahead.[157] At the same time, he authorized the supply of tactical nuclear weapons to the East German army, which he planned to withdraw in the event of an agreement with Bonn. In late April 1965, the French and Soviet governments issued a joint communiqué stating that Germany must permanently renounce nuclear weapons. Shortly afterwards, de Gaulle made good his threats against the EEC: from July 1965, he paralysed the community through his policy of the 'empty chair', when the French representatives boycotted meetings of the Council of Ministers. This was ostensibly a protest against its policies on finance and agriculture, but his real aim was to bring Bonn to heel and to block the introduction of majority voting in the Council on economic matters as a dilution of French sovereignty. The British were also deeply concerned that the MLF would give the Germans nuclear parity with them.[158] In the end, President Johnson, worn out by French objections, anxious to avoid provoking the Soviet Union more than necessary, and increasingly distracted by Vietnam, allowed the MLF initiative to peter out. And as east–west tensions declined from their peak in 1961–2 so did the pressure for greater security cooperation. Bonn abolished its ministry for atomic affairs.

With the MLF died not only German nuclear ambitions but also all hopes for supra-national European defence integration and thus of full political union.

Domestic politics in Europe and across the Atlantic were profoundly influenced by all this international turbulence. Defence issues dominated West German internal affairs, from the controversies about the Starfighter – an expensive and apparently unreliable jet, whose initial deployment was plagued by crashes which caused heavy loss of life among German pilots – to the '*Spiegel* Affair' of 1962, when the defence minister, Franz Josef Strauss, ordered the arrest of investigative journalists who had questioned the military readiness of the *Bundeswehr.* The first to pay the price for foreign policy failure was the veteran German chancellor, Adenauer. Mainstream 'Atlanticist' opinion in his governing coalition, especially the foreign minister, Gerhard Schröder, his economics minister, Ludwig Erhard, and the defence minister, von Hassel, was outraged that he had put Bonn's relationship with Washington and London through the Élysée accord. Adenauer's position was so weakened that he was forced to resign soon after and was succeeded by Ludwig Erhard, a firm Atlanticist.

In the Soviet Union, the foreign policy failures of the early 1960s destroyed Khrushchev. The charge sheet against him at the party's plenary meeting in mid-October 1964 was long and included his ridiculously inflated targets in agriculture, his confused bureaucratic 'reforms' and his generally boorish, undignified behaviour. At the heart of the critique, however, was national security. Khrushchev's obsession with atomic weapons had not saved the Soviet Union from humiliation over Berlin and Cuba. Many felt that Cuba had not been worth fighting for in any case. The Soviet leader was also accused of mismanaging the relationship with Mao, who had not only worsted Moscow's Indian friends, but had just brought a nuclear programme to fruition on the Soviet Union's eastern border. What really did for Khrushchev, however, was Germany. When Alexei Adzhubei went to Bonn, his father-in-law's apparent willingness to sacrifice Ulbricht in a deal over MLF alarmed both Peking and a Soviet establishment which now regarded the GDR as the best guarantee against German revanchism. They were particularly outraged by German press reports that Adzhubei had offered to 'talk to papa about . . . tear[ing] down [the Berlin] wall'. Buckling under an avalanche of criticism, Khrushchev was forced to resign. 'Why was Khrushchev removed,' the Soviet foreign minister, Andrei Gromyko, remarked, 'because he sent Adschubei to Bonn, of course.'[159] Soviet German policy, the very issue which had propelled him to the top in Moscow, was the subject which had brought him down.

Foreign policy also played a crucial role in the 1964 US presidential election. The Republican candidate, Barry Goldwater, alienated many, including many moderate conservatives, with his support for the right of states to resist the imposition of civil rights legislation. What really wrecked his candidature, though, was his perceived volatility on foreign policy. Goldwater had already supported the use of tactical nuclear weapons in Vietnam, and joked about 'lob[bing]' a nuclear bomb 'into the men's room of the Kremlin'. Democratic television commercials repeatedly suggested that his trigger-happiness might lead to a nuclear conflagration; the media routinely questioned his sanity. By contrast, the Democratic candidate, the sitting president, Lyndon Baines Johnson, came across as robust but measured in foreign policy.[160] When they elected Johnson by a landslide in November 1964, the American people believed they were getting the best of both worlds: more butter for those who needed it, and enough guns to protect their values and prosperity.

The international strains of the mid-1960s also shaped social and economic developments on both sides of the Cold War divide. In the United States, President Johnson aimed to create a 'Great Society' at home to match, and ultimately to support, US great-power ambitions abroad. He not only enacted sweeping bills for health, welfare and education provision, but also tackled the cancer at the heart of American society: race. The treatment of Southern blacks had long been a matter of moral outrage to liberal opinion. With the advent of the Cold War, however, racial discrimination also proved a liability on the world stage: it embarrassed America's friends, and gave her Soviet enemies a stick to beat her with.[161] The demands of the international system now required that the United States heal the racial divide, bring her domestic record into line with her external rhetoric, mobilize all sections of the population for the global contest with communism, and reward those who were already serving in the front line. To this end, the president pushed through the Civil Rights Act of July 1964, which enshrined the civil equality of all races, made segregation illegal and abolished registration practices designed to disenfranchise blacks. The Johnson administration in short, embarked on a thoroughgoing domestic transformation designed not only to enable Americans to live in peace with each other, but also to vindicate their destiny abroad.

In Moscow, the new General Secretary, Leonid Brezhnev, reversed Khrushchev's cuts in military expenditure. Instead, he embarked on a fresh round of armaments production designed to achieve the much-desired parity with the United States. Soviet domestic structures appeared uniquely configured to sustain this effort: according to conventional wisdom the command economy allowed Moscow to allocate vast resources to the goal of national security without, as in the west, permitting the market to introduce distorting elements of competition and demands for consumer goods. A huge proportion of the economy was thus devoted to military purposes.[162] The Soviet Union, in short, did not have a military-industrial complex like the United States, it *was* a military-industrial complex.[163] It was true that the French, British, Germans and some other European peoples remained willing to make great sacrifices to defend themselves against aggression; peacetime conscription remained the order of the day in most countries. But they had for the most part lost their appetite for national greatness and thus the imperative to order society accordingly. The long uncoupling of western European state and society from the project of making war had begun.[164] Just as the interminable wars of past centuries had left their mark on European society, so now would the long peace shape domestic structures. The tradition of the primacy of foreign policy passed to the remaining European great powers, the Soviet Union and the United States.

No sooner had the controversy over the MLF subsided than the international scene was roiled by three separate but interlocking developments. The crisis began in Europe where de Gaulle took advantage of two major shifts in the international climate to articulate an even more independent 'European' foreign policy under French leadership. Not only had West German nuclear ambitions finally been shelved, but the immediate Russian threat was receding also. In March 1966, de Gaulle took France out of the NATO command structure: its headquarters were moved from Fontainebleau outside Paris to Mons, near Brussels. Three months later, he embarked on an ostentatious state visit to Moscow, and in subsequent years he also undertook trips to Poland and

Romania. Even though France remained part of NATO itself, and was expected to stand alongside the alliance in the event of a Russian attack, de Gaulle's initiative was a terrible shock to the political and strategic cohesion of the organization. There was uncertainty about how the French troops deployed in Baden-Württemberg and the Palatinate would behave. A hole had been blown in the defences of the west on its most central front: Germany.[165]

Normally, these events would have provoked a massive US response, but they came at a time when the escalating war in Vietnam meant that President Johnson was unable to give Europe his full attention. The new regime in Saigon proved even less able than Diem to stop the communist advance, which was massively supported by Hanoi and its Sino-Soviet backers. President Johnson now decided to escalate the US commitment.[166]

As south-east Asia burned, the Middle East exploded once more. From the mid-1960s onwards, the Israelis began to feel ever more pressure on their borders, north, east and south. The Palestine Liberation Organization (PLO) was founded in 1964 under the leadership of the charismatic Yassir Arafat, after which guerrilla operations intensified. Jordan and especially Egypt were busy importing arms in preparation for the final showdown with Israel. In May 1967, Nasser ordered the UN buffer force in the Sinai to leave, and closed the straits of Tiran once more. A month later, Israel launched a surprise pre-emptive strike on Egypt, Jordan and Syria. The Arab armies were crushed in a *Blitzkrieg* lasting less than a week. The German-Jewish financier Siegmund Warburg approvingly compared Israel, with its capacity to punch above its weight and pre-empt threats, to eighteenth-century Prussia. Israel occupied the Gaza Strip, the Sinai peninsula, the West Bank of the Jordan, and the formerly Syrian Golan Heights. The war transformed not only the Middle East, but also the region's position in world geopolitics. On the one hand, Israel had become the regional hegemon, largely through her own efforts, and thus became a valuable partner for the United States in containing Soviet influence. On the other hand, Israel was now an occupying power and as such came under increasing international scrutiny not just at the United Nations, but also in Europe.

The French withdrawal from NATO's command structure, the Vietnam War and – to a lesser but still important extent – the Six Day War in the Middle East dominated global geopolitics and domestic politics until the beginning of the next decade. The United States now sought to enlist the military backing of her allies in Vietnam, especially – as the Secretary of State, Dean Rusk, put it – 'to get some Germans into the field'.[167] This 'more flags' campaign secured Australian, South Korean and Taiwanese support, but Johnson drew a complete blank in Europe, where he completely failed to persuade, or bully, the British prime minister, Harold Wilson. In 1965, the German chancellor, Ludwig Erhard, had refused to send a battalion of *Bundeswehr* troops. Instead, Washington now began look for ways to reduce its commitments in Europe.[168] In March 1966, 30,000 men were withdrawn from Germany without consulting Bonn. Some Congressional voices, such as the Democratic Senate Majority leader, Mike Mansfield, even called for US troops to be pulled out of Germany altogether.

As the United States sank deeper and deeper into the south-east Asian morass, Britain turned back towards her European destiny, and more specifically Germany and the British Army of the Rhine.[169] The 1966 sterling crisis and the defence cuts showed just how precarious her position in the world had become. In May 1967, Britain made a renewed attempt to join the EEC, primarily for strategic reasons. London was hopeful that this time US support, West German favour and de Gaulle's isolation within Europe over NATO and the 'empty chair' crisis would count in London's favour. The urgency of putting the British economy on an even keel was underlined six months later, when a sustained speculative attack led to another sterling crisis. Only a week after that, however, the second application was vetoed by de Gaulle. Once again, the French president argued that British membership would simply serve as a Trojan horse for US domination of the Community.[170] Britain simply redoubled her efforts. In January 1968, she announced her decision to withdraw from 'east of Suez', and signalled to the white dominions that the preferential tariffs they enjoyed would be wound down. The Commonwealth now ceased to have much strategic or economic meaning; the defence relationship with Canada ran through NATO headquarters in Brussels, not London.

West Germany also regarded the shifting international situation with concern. Bonn felt left out of de Gaulle's Franco-Russian flirtation, which made her more conscious of her historic *Mittellage*. She also felt discriminated against by the NPT process – which she condemned as 'atomic complicity' in her permanent inferiority – and the collapse of the MLF. At the same time, though, Bonn was anxious about the reduction in the British Army of the Rhine, the steady transfer of American troops from Germany to Vietnam, and the increased cost of those remaining. It was disagreements about how the American garrison should be paid for – through tax increases or cuts in government spending – which brought down the Erhard government in early November 1966. The new Christian Democrat 'Grand Coalition' under Chancellor Kurt Kiesinger came in committed to exploring whether the east–west divide, and thus the partition of Germany, could be overcome. 'Germany, a reunited Germany,' the new chancellor remarked in June 1967, 'is too big to play no role in the balance of forces, and too small to keep the forces around it in balance by itself', and because if united it could not simply join one side or the other, 'one can only see the growing together of the separated parts of Germany bedded into the process of overcoming the East–West conflict in Europe'.[171] A first step in this direction was the abandonment of the Hallstein Doctrine by which the FRG refused to maintain diplomatic relations with any country – except the Soviet Union – which recognized the GDR.

In short, all the major powers, with the exception of Red China, were for one reason or another desirous of reducing tensions, at least in Europe. Towards the end of June 1967, President Johnson and the Soviet prime minister, Alexei Kosygin, met at Glassboro, New Jersey. The general atmosphere of mutual goodwill was widely commented upon. Six months later, the NATO powers adopted the 'Harmel report'. There would be no reduction in military security, but every effort should be made to explore a policy of détente with the Soviet Union to make war less likely.[172] The failure of the MLF added new urgency to the negotiations on nuclear proliferation. Here the established atomic powers, east and west, were determined to prevent the dilution of their monopoly. In particular, they were concerned to stop the Germans from developing an independent capability. The principal non-nuclear states, on the other hand – Germany foremost among them – were anxious to avoid an international regime which cast their inferiority in stone for all time. The Non-Proliferation Treaty agreed in 1968 was a compromise between these two positions. Signatories committed themselves to the principle that there should be no new nuclear powers. Peaceful use of atomic energy, however, was expressly permitted.

The Vietnam War, the Sino-Soviet split and the Six Day War caused an earthquake in domestic politics in Europe and around the world. In the course of 1968–9, the cities of western Europe and the United States erupted as students hurled themselves against the police, the political and educational establishment, and increasingly against society as a whole. The 'Sixty-Eighters', as they came to be known, were a diverse coalition of feminists, civil rights workers, student activists and Maoists, motivated by a broad antipathy to western modernity, which appropriated and transcended existing class and racial divides. They constructed a 'counter-culture' of communal living, sexual experimentation, rock music and recreational narcotics to counter the prevailing 'patriarchal' and 'exploitative' societal norms of western capitalist democracies. At the heart of this global critique, however, was a rage against US 'imperialism' – and its supporters – in Indochina and across the world. Its demonology embraced not only the American military-industrial complex, and its western European, Latin American and Asian lackeys, but increasingly Israel and her occupation of Arab lands. All these themes had come together in 1967 with the escalation in Vietnam, and the resulting nightly carnage on the television screens, the CIA-sponsored killing of the iconic revolutionary Che Guevara in Bolivia, and what was regarded as Israeli swaggering after its crushing victory over Egypt, Jordan and Syria.[173]

The shock troops of this revolution would not be the proletariat of North America and western Europe. According to the radicals, western workers had not only gone soft but slipped into various forms of false consciousness, lulled by the 'repressive tolerance' of the system – to use a phrase coined by the 'Frankfurt School' professor Herbert Marcuse in 1965 – into believing that they enjoyed real democracy. Instead, the charge would be led by a vanguard of educated and aware student activists, who would provoke governments into counter-measures which would radicalize the population. At the same time, the revolution would cooperate with 'national liberation movements' in the Third World, partly to divert the resources of the imperialists but also to allow the re-importation of revolution from Che Guevara and what the writer Frantz Fanon called 'the wretched of the earth'. Reversing Marx, they expected that the great transformation would begin in the shanty towns of the new global south, before spreading to the industrialized west. This was the reason why the avowedly 'international' 'Sixty-Eighters' supported nationalist struggles in Palestine, Ireland and, of course, Vietnam.

Throughout 1968–9, waves of popular and often insurrectionary violence beat against western governments. In the United States, rioters and policemen turned the 1968 Democratic Convention in Chicago into a battlefield. Along the Hudson River in New York, patriotic longshoremen, often of east European descent, attacked student protesters whom they suspected of selling the country out to communism. The nation – which had just weathered the civil rights turbulence – was now back at war with itself. In Paris, the *évènements* of 1968 were so dramatic that President de Gaulle either was forced to flee to the French garrison in Baden-Baden or made a flying visit there in order to discuss military intervention with the local commander, just as the royalist émigrés had once sought sanctuary in Koblenz. In Northern Ireland, large sections of the Catholic population – appropriating the language of US civil rights and student protest – rose in protest and barricaded themselves into their communities. The separatist Irish Republican Army seized the opportunity to renew its 'armed struggle' against the British state in pursuit of a United Ireland. All this had momentous strategic implications for the west: the United States was tearing itself apart at home while fighting in the paddy fields of Vietnam, France seemed on the verge of another revolutionary takeover, while Britain was in danger of being bundled out of the strategically important Ulster naval bases.

The key, however, was Germany. Many of the most prominent revolutionaries, as de Gaulle observed with asperity, were German, especially the French student leader Daniel Cohn-Bendit ('Danny the Red') and the German student leader Rudi Dutschke, a refugee from the GDR who had never come to terms with partition. 'It was in Berlin,' one of the French protesters later remarked, 'that we learned how to demonstrate in the streets.'[174] Dutschke saw the struggle in Germany both as a 'second front' against the imperialist war in Vietnam, and a cause in its own right; some German protestors even saw themselves as a colonized people.[175] In the summer of 1967, he speculated in a pseudonymous article whether the creation of a 'Free City of Berlin' – like so many others east and west, he regarded the former capital as an Archimedean point at the centre of the world – might serve as 'a strategic transmission belt for a future re-unification of Germany'. This would generate the kind of 'focus' – following the French revolutionary theorist Régis Debray – through which 'an armed vanguard of the people, can create the objective conditions for the revolution through subjective activity'. Indeed, if the movement could bring down the Bonn government and force the withdrawal of NATO forces perpetuating the division of their country – 'an instrument for suppressing revolutions in Europe',[176] as Dutschke described them – then the whole capitalist system in Europe might give way, and some sort of deal with the Soviet Union on unification and withdrawal from the system of armed alliances might be possible. Foreign policy was thus at the heart of the revolutionary project in Germany, even more than elsewhere. From 1966, exhibitions, articles and demonstrations convinced students that Washington was waging a 'colonialist war' in Indochina, or, as the Socialist Student League put it, a 'genocide emanating from imperialist political and economic interest'. American bases – which were already in the public eye after the offset crisis – were the next targets of the demonstrators, who often made common cause with Black Power conscript activists. 'USA-SA-SS,' they chanted, neatly aligning Washington with their 'perpetrator' parents.[177] A year later, as the war in Indochina reached its climax, the Middle Eastern conflict served to further inflame German students. On their reckoning, Zionism was simply a bridgehead for western imperialism in the Middle East.

The international situation also provoked turbulence inside the Soviet bloc. Just as Stalin had been taken aback by the enthusiasm of Russian Jews for the creation of Israel in 1948, the euphoria with which they greeted the victory of the Jewish state over the Kremlin's Arab allies in 1967 gave renewed offence. A new wave of anti-semitic propaganda against 'Zionist elements', at home and abroad, was unleashed. There were no new 'doctors' plots', but Soviet Jews were now increasingly subjected to systematic discrimination. At the same time, Moscow looked anxiously on developments in Czechoslovakia, where liberal elements in the party took advantage of the new spirit of détente to challenge hardliners. In January 1968, the reliable Antonín Novotný was replaced as First Secretary of the party by the reformist Alexander Dubček. Over the next months, he introduced a series of liberalizing measures, such as the abolition of censorship and confirmation of the right to criticize the government, which became known as the 'Prague

Spring'. Throughout the summer Dubček – mindful of the Hungarian experience – repeatedly assured the Soviet Union that he had no intention of leaving the Warsaw Pact, but Moscow remained deeply worried that – as in the west – the spark of subversion would leap across national boundaries and create a conflagration it could not control.

In the end, none of the protest movements succeeded in toppling a government. The Soviet Union crushed the Prague Spring by force in August 1968; after intensive 'fraternal consultations', the Czech party withdrew its reform programme. Three months later, the Soviet Union issued what has become known as the 'Brezhnev Doctrine', announcing that it would never allow any 'socialist' state to abandon socialism. The inspiration here was largely strategic, of course, but the claim also reflected a deeply ideological belief that the onward march of socialism was inevitable, and ought therefore to be irreversible. The protesters did not get anywhere in the west, either. French workers were stirred by the *évènements*, but the much-hoped-for collaboration with the students did not take place. De Gaulle won the subsequent election comfortably. The West German system was also shaken, but it survived. Northern Ireland was convulsed, but British troops managed to keep the situation under some kind of control. In the west, the protestors were stopped with ballot boxes; in the east, by bullets, or the threat of them. A small minority of the protestors – in particular the Italian 'Red Brigades' and the German '*Rote Armee Fraktion*' – now launched a campaign of armed resistance against 'the system'.

That said, the international situation did lead to immediate domestic changes in the west, which in turn led to important geopolitical shifts. These were effected through elections rather than revolutionary violence. In November 1968, the Republicans won the US presidential elections, not least because the Indochina War had caused the public to lose confidence in the ability of the Democratic administration to manage foreign policy. The new administration of Richard Nixon, and his National Security Advisor, Henry Kissinger, came to power with clear views on how the United States should rebuild her global position. In late April 1969, de Gaulle resigned after a referendum defeat, an event which may not have been inspired by foreign policy, but which had considerable strategic consequences as France began to retreat from the general's policy of 'grandeur'. Six months later, the West German elected the SPD leader, Willy Brandt, partly because he promised 'to risk more democracy', but also because he seemed to have the most coherent programme for reducing Cold War tensions and if not overcoming the partition of Germany, then at least making it more bearable.

The tasks the incoming Nixon government set itself in 1969 were formidable: to withdraw from Vietnam 'with honour', leaving behind a regime in Saigon capable of surviving the renewed communist onslaught; to rebuild the frayed alliances with her European partners; and to find a new equilibrium with Moscow and Peking, however unstable, in a world in which the United States could no longer count on retaining an indefinite primacy. Military sticks – or the threat of them – were central to this strategy, if only to maintain 'credibility'. The core of the project, however, was diplomacy. By establishing cooperative relationships with the Russians across a range of subjects, some of them more important to them than to Washington, Nixon and Kissinger sought to create a 'linkage' which could be used to advance their interests, especially extrication from Indochina. Moreover, by exploiting the Sino-Soviet split, Kissinger hoped to 'triangulate' between Moscow and Peking. When the tensions on the Sino-Soviet border exploded in the spring and summer of 1969, and Chinese fears of a Russian 'pre-emptive' nuclear strike mounted, Washington made clear that it regarded any attack on Mao as an unacceptable threat to the global balance of power.[178]

Kissinger's model was Otto von Bismarck, whom he lauded as a 'white revolutionary'. There was certainly something Bismarckian about the way in which he ensured that the United States would always be one of two in a world of three superpowers: America, the Soviet Union and Red China. Like the German chancellor, the new National Security Advisor had a difficult relationship with representative institutions, and his domestic policy was driven by the need to enable the United States to act with 'authoritarian purposefulness' in the world.[179] In truth, though, the closer analogy was with Metternich, because what Kissinger was trying to do was to delay what he believed to be US decline, rather than create a new dynamic power. One way or the other, by liberating 'geopolitics' – here Kissinger essentially meant *Realpolitik* – from ideological distractions, such as global commitment to democracy and human rights, Washington was free to establish more fruitful relationships with potentially friendly regional hegemons. In late July 1969, the president announced this new doctrine in a famous speech at Guam.

The central thesis of what became known as the 'Nixon Doctrine', he reminded Congress a year later, was that 'the United States will participate in the defence and development of allies and friends, but that America cannot and will not conceive all the plans, all the programs, execute all the decisions and undertake all the defence of the free nations of the world'.[180]

To the new chancellor in Bonn, Willy Brandt, the American retrenchment was both a threat and an opportunity. With the United States bogged down in Vietnam, strained transatlantic relations and low troop morale within NATO it was clear that the alliance was incapable of guaranteeing the security of West Germany. Reaching an accommodation with Moscow was therefore imperative. On the other hand, Brandt hoped to exploit the American preoccupation with Vietnam to pursue an independent policy designed to bring the two German states, and east and west generally, closer together. The long-term goal of this *Ostpolitik* was certainly reunification, but for the moment the chancellor was content to make the lives of ordinary Germans easier through the lifting of travel restrictions and other 'small steps'.[181] West German diplomats spoke of 'overcoming partition by accepting it'. In the process, Brandt expected that the two systems – capitalism and communism – would become increasingly alike. The core of *Ostpolitik*, however, was a new geopolitics. Overtures were to be made to all eastern European leaders, especially those in Moscow. At the same time, Bonn needed to keep its NATO allies, especially France and the United States, onside. To this end, West Germany made considerable concessions on EEC agricultural policy, which benefited French farmers. At first, the Americans feared that Germany would leave the NATO alliance and attempt to strike a unilateral 'Rapallo'-style deal with Moscow.[182] As time passed, however, Nixon and Kissinger were persuaded that *Ostpolitik* actually complemented their efforts to reach an accommodation with Moscow.[183]

In Moscow, the American and German détente projects were received in an atmosphere of acute strategic alarm. As Russian and Chinese forces faced each across the Ussuri River, and Mao forged ahead with nuclear and conventional arms construction, the encirclement of the Soviet Union by NATO in the west and Red China in the east became ever more painfully clear. This made it important to reach rapprochement with the Americans and the Germans, and absolutely essential to prevent Nixon and Mao from coming together at their expense. Moscow was also becoming anxious that Brandt's *Ostpolitik* would soften up the defences so painfully erected in the GDR and lead sooner or later to German unification. In these circumstances, the best course of action was to try to capitalize on Moscow's current position of strength to secure recognition by Bonn of the territorial settlement in Europe, or at least to manage the absorption of the GDR in such a way as to ensure – as the KGB chief, Yuri Andropov, put it – that the rampant West Germany would 'understand' Soviet needs.[184]

Meanwhile, Brandt pressed ahead with *Ostpolitik*. In mid-August 1970, he concluded the Treaty of Moscow with the Soviet Union, in which he effectively recognized the GDR and the disputed Oder–Neisse border with Poland; Germany explicitly renounced any attempt to seek revision through the use of force. A similar agreement with Poland was signed in early December, and a few days later Brandt fell to his knees at the memorial for the Warsaw Ghetto uprising as a gesture of German national contrition for the crimes of Nazism. In early September of the following year, the four powers finally settled the status of Berlin. Then, right at the end of 1972, once the geopolitical groundwork had been laid, the German Democratic Republic and the Federal Republic of Germany signed a Basic Treaty to regulate relations between the two halves of a single people. Despite intense Soviet and East German pressure, however, Bonn refused to recognize the GDR and send a fully fledged ambassador. Instead, it agreed to establish a 'permanent representation' only and set up a ministry devoted solely to 'Inter-German' affairs. In return, the GDR regime undertook to permit some carefully controlled travel between the two states, especially between West and East Berlin and within a defined border zone. A year after that, Bonn signed a treaty with Czechoslovakia in which it agreed to drop its support for the Sudeten Germans. The two Germanies were admitted to the United Nations. Without challenging a single boundary, indeed by confirming the territorial status quo, Brandt had changed the east–west dynamic and thus wrought a fundamental geopolitical shift at the heart of Europe.

The Soviet Union was, for now, well satisfied with these events. 'For the first time since the war,' Gromyko told the Supreme Soviet in June 1972, 'a large capitalist state – the legal successor of Hitler-Germany to boot, has recognized by treaty the western border of the People's Republic of Poland and the order between the GDR and the FRG.' This meant, he continued, 'the strengthening of the western borders of the socialist community of states'.[185] Moscow could face Peking in the east with much greater confidence. At the same time, Russia would benefit from western investment and the purchase of surplus grain at bargain rates, 'sweeteners' which Nixon threw in to appease them (and the agricultural lobby back home). Yet it was not Mao or economic actors but Germany which was the primary Soviet concern. 'Kissinger thinks it was China that played the decisive role in getting us to feel the need to preserve our relationship with the USA,' the Soviet expert on American affairs, Georgy Arbatov, recalls, 'but Berlin actually played a much bigger role, almost a decisive one. Having the East German situation settled was most important to us, and we did not want to jeopardise that'.[186] The Russians, in short, supported détente because they believed that it solved the German Question for them.

If international rivalries had fundamentally shaped domestic politics since the war, the relaxation of those tensions after 1969–70 created a new and complex internal dynamic. In the GDR, détente led to a high-political shift when Walter Ulbricht was forced to make way for Erich Honecker, not so much because of differences over détente but because the latter had shown himself to be more subservient to Moscow.[187] Similarly, *Ostpolitik* dominated party politics in the Federal Republic.[188] The renunciation of German territorial claims to Silesia, Pomerania and East Prussia, and of the right of return for the Sudeten Germans, proved extremely controversial, among nationalists generally and especially the millions of refugees from Poland and Czechoslovakia. The conservative parties, led by Franz Josef Strauss, battered the 'eastern' treaties relentlessly. There were several high-level defections from the SPD, and its coalition partner, the FDP, throughout 1970–71. Eventually, though, the treaties made it through parliament and, in November 1972, Brandt cruised to victory at the general election in a popular endorsement not only of his domestic policies but also of *Ostpolitik*, which had been a major issue in the campaign. By late July of the following year, Brandt had weathered a serious legal challenge to the treaties in the Federal Constitutional Court.

Among Palestinians, the defeat of 1967 and the subsequent failure of

Arab states to lay a glove on Israel drove the PLO not only to rely more on its own efforts, but to 'globalize' the Middle Eastern conflict through terrorism. This tendency merged with the steady drift of European – and particularly German – radicals towards armed action. Palestine began increasingly to replace Vietnam as the main concern of European leftists, especially in Germany. In the summer of 1969, a German student delegation visited Palestinian training camps in Jordan. On 9 November of that year, the anniversary of *Kristallnacht*, German radicals attempted to bomb a Jewish community centre in West Berlin; Jewish cemeteries were desecrated. The subsequent statement of responsibility explained that such actions were not 'far right excesses, but rather . . . a crucial part of international socialist solidarity'. The authors stressed the 'historical illegitimacy of the Israeli state', and proclaimed their 'clear and simple solidarity with the fighting *fedayeen*'.[189] International anti-semitism, in other words, was coming home to Europe.

In the United States, the battle increasingly shifted from the streets and student campuses to a restive Congress, weary of the expense and the human cost of stopping – or failing to stop – the spread of communism in south-east Asia. In September 1970, Nixon saw off an attempt by senators George McGovern and Mark Hatfield to force the withdrawal of all US troops from Indochina before the end of the year. In January 1971, however, Congress repealed the Gulf of Tonkin resolution which had originally authorized Johnson to become more engaged in Vietnam. Six months after that, the former marine, defence analyst and sometime Vietnam War supporter Daniel Ellsberg finally succeeded in persuading the *New York Times* to publish the 'Pentagon Papers', a brutally frank documentary record of how the war in Indochina was being lost. Nixon's need to maintain credibility abroad now drove his administration to increasingly extreme, and often illegal, measures against opponents at home, including burglary, wire-tapping and other 'dirty tricks'. The focal point here was not so much party politics as national security. In order to discredit Daniel Ellsberg, and to prevent him from embarrassing the government during a critical moment in the negotiations with China, the White House had ordered the theft of his psychiatric record in 1971. When the same gang was arrested a year later breaking into the Democratic National Committee's offices in Washington's Watergate Complex, Nixon was forced to launch a desperate, and initially successful, cover-up. This was designed not to obscure the partisan burglary, of which he had no prior knowledge, but to prevent the trail from leading back to the original crime carried out for reasons of foreign policy.

In January 1972, several years of careful 'back channel' diplomacy by Henry Kissinger resulted in a breakthrough when Nixon met Mao in Peking. The Chinese leader, concerned that détente in Europe would lead to an increase of Soviet pressure on his western border, was anxious to begin normalizing relations with Washington. Four months later, the president held a resoundingly successful summit with Brezhnev in Moscow. The first Strategic Arms Limitation Agreement (SALT I) was signed. An 'anti-ballistic missile agreement' limited the use of defensive weapons, thus ensuring that 'mutual assured destruction' remained guaranteed. It was on the strength of this brilliant record abroad, as much as the left-wing programme of his opponent, George McGovern, that Nixon swept to an overwhelming victory in the November 1972 presidential election.

The success of détente caused France, which had taken something of a back seat after the resignation of de Gaulle in 1969, to fear a US–Soviet 'condominium' globally, but especially in Europe. In response, Paris moved to mobilize other European states, especially the Federal Republic, to coordinate their policies more closely and thus balance both Moscow and Washington. Contrary to French hopes, 'Europe' did not fill the vacuum left by declining American power. It seemed there was no longer a German threat to contain, or a Soviet threat to mobilize against. Moreover, US policy had now changed. The recession had destroyed her economic confidence and she feared European economic competition. Psychologically, Nixon was wary of his allies 'ganging up' on him, and Kissinger was intellectually sympathetic to a European 'concert', or even an 'Executive Committee' of the larger powers, but not a union on American lines.[190] Instead, Washington now placed a new emphasis on bilateral relations with individual capitals. Détente, in short, stalled European integration.

The only major advance during this period was the accession of Great Britain.[191] With de Gaulle out of the way, London launched a third campaign to join the EEC in 1969. This was partly driven by concern over Britain's low economic growth rates. The main purpose of the bid, however, was political and strategic: to regain the nation's historic pivotal role in Europe. A furious argument erupted across the country. At the start of the debate, opinion polls suggested that about 70 per cent of the population were opposed to membership, with fewer than a fifth actively in favour. All the same, there was widespread resentment at Labour for Britain's botched 1967 application, and in the closely fought 1970 election – in which Europe played an important though not decisive part – Britain elected a strongly pro-EEC Conservative prime minister, Edward Heath.[192] Moreover, thanks to the efforts of the European Movement, the Information Research Department of the Foreign Office, various MPs, elements of the BBC and the force of the argument itself, most Britons were persuaded over the next two years to change their minds.[193] On the very first day of 1973, Britain was duly admitted to the EEC without a referendum; Ireland joined at the same time. Given London's strong 'intergovernmental' instincts, however, this represented a 'widening' rather than a 'deepening' of the Community. One way or the other, the question of 'finding a role' continued to dominate British domestic politics and foreign policy.

As 1973 dawned, it seemed as if Nixon and Kissinger would be able to extricate the United States from Vietnam, and devote more energies to shoring up her shaky position in Europe. At the end of January, Kissinger and the North Vietnamese finally agreed the Paris Accord. The United States agreed to withdraw her forces and work towards a peaceful reunification of Vietnam.

Nixon and Kissinger now turned to the much neglected European stage, where the United States had taken more and more of a supporting role from 1966. Kissinger's 'Year of Europe' in 1973 was designed to reform NATO, and move through a series of ritual affirmations of common purpose towards a new Atlantic Charter.[194] At the beginning of the following year, there were NATO–Soviet talks at Vienna to achieve 'Mutual Balanced Force Reductions' (MBFR) in order to curb the arms race in central Europe. The hoped for renewal of ties between Washington and the European capitals did not come to pass, however. There were many reasons for this failure, not least western European resentment at what they regarded as Kissinger's Machiavellianism and patronizing undertone, but the principal bone of contention was a fresh Middle Eastern conflict launched by the new Egyptian president, Anwar al-Sadat. This was the more disconcerting as Kissinger had made determined attempts to lure Cairo into the western fold in early 1970; by 1971 he had opened another 'back channel' of communication. For the moment, however, Sadat was having none of it. In October 1973, taking advantage of the Jewish festival of Yom Kippur, the Egyptians launched a surprise attack across the Suez Canal, while the Syrians took the offensive against Israel's northern flank.

Sadat and Hafez al-Assad's coup caught the Jewish state completely off guard. Within a few days, however, not least thanks to a swift transfusion of US weaponry, the Israelis were able to turn the tables militarily by smashing the Syrians in the Golan Heights and pinning large Egyptian forces against the Suez Canal. This turned a regional crisis into a global and a European one. The Soviet Union, desperate to avoid the complete destruction of her allies, began to make nuclear threats.[195] In response, Washington went on atomic alert. The Organization of Petroleum Exporting Countries (OPEC) retaliated against US arms supplies to Israel by announcing a reduction in overall oil production and an embargo on the United States and all European states collaborating in the deliveries. Prices quadrupled; queues formed at the pumps. European governments panicked, and sought to dissociate themselves from Israel and the United States. The Belgians refused their airfields for the resupply effort, Britain was rumoured to have temporarily banned the use of Cyprus, and even the usually helpful West Germans complained about the use of their ports to ship war material to Israel. US–European relations plummeted. 'I do not care what happens to NATO,' Kissinger was widely quoted as saying, 'I am so disgusted.'[196] One way or the other, the geopolitics of the Middle East, Europe and the United States had intersected with consequences which were to become clear over the next thirty years.

The three decades since 1945 were dominated by the Cold War between east and west. In some parts of the world this conflict led to direct military confrontation. The United States twice went to war in east Asia, for example, fighting Soviet allies in Korea and Vietnam, and was almost embroiled in a nuclear conflict over Cuba. The real prize, however, was always Germany. It was there, especially in Berlin, that nuclear Armageddon was closest and it was there that a conventional war would first be fought. Control of that space and its resources would decide the conflict; all other fronts were therefore interpreted within an essentially Germano-centric framework. The winners and losers in this struggle were not yet clear. Britain and France had lost most of their overseas empires and much of their European weight, but they were still nuclear powers, held permanent seats on the United Nations Security Council, and kept their role as guarantors of the German settlement. West Germany had made great strides since the end of the war, and the eastern treaties marked its return to the international system, but the country remained in a state of 'semi-sovereignty' and was no nearer achieving reunification with the east. The United States and the Soviet Union, of course, dominated their respective camps, albeit in very different ways, but the question of which of the two systems they represented would prevail in Europe was still very much open.

8

Democracies, 1974–2011

The Germans must be careful because they have grown relatively stronger in the course of the last ten or fifteen years . . . We have to be careful to avoid the danger that one day others will regard our country as having become too big and too important.

Helmut Schmidt, German chancellor, at a closed party meeting, February 1979[1]

Around the world today, the democratic revolution is gathering new strength . . . From Stettin on the Baltic to Varna on the Black Sea, the regimes planted by totalitarianism have had more than thirty years to establish their legitimacy. But none – not one regime – has yet been able to risk free elections. Regimes planted by bayonets do not take root. We must be staunch in our conviction that freedom is not the sole prerogative of a lucky few, but the inalienable and universal right of all human beings.

Ronald Reagan, June 1982[2]

What is more important to the history of the world? The Taliban or the collapse of the Soviet Empire? Some stirred-up Moslems or the liberation of central Europe and the end of the Cold War?

Zbigniew Brzezinski, former US National Security Advisor, January 1998[3]

The resolution of the German Question through détente did not last. Within a few years, Europe was convulsed by a Soviet attempt to leverage its global gains for European advantage. Germany, in particular, became the cockpit of a bitter 'Second Cold War'. The struggle was decided by a new transatlantic democratic geopolitics which ultimately brought down the Warsaw Pact, shattered the Soviet Union and led to the unification of Germany. Contrary to widespread predictions, this territorial revolution at the heart of Europe did not upset the balance of power, partly because the Germans themselves demonstrated no hegemonic ambitions and partly because the process of European integration was speeded up in order to constrain the new giant. It was only with the revival of Russian power in the east, the onset of the euro sovereign debt crisis and the Arab Spring that Germany began to flex its muscles.

In the mid-1970s, the Soviet Union had good reason to feel satisfied.[4] The United States had been humiliated in Vietnam, and she was deeply divided at home; so were the societies of the larger western European states. In the Vladivostok Agreement in November 1974, Moscow finally achieved nuclear parity while retaining superiority in conventional capabilities. Most importantly of all, the German Question had been resolved through détente, or so it seemed. The priority now was to secure a general NATO agreement to the inviolability of the Potsdam settlement. To that end, Soviet diplomats pressed for the establishment of a Conference on Security and Cooperation in Europe (CSCE), which would be based on the integrity of existing borders and provide a forum for the peaceful resolution of differences between the blocs. In order to add weight to this demand, and also to widen the cracks in the western alliance, the Soviet Union sought to exploit her powerful military position in central Europe. There was a massive increase in deployments of conventional forces on the territory of the GDR. Towards the end of 1974, moreover, Moscow approved the testing of the SS-20, a mobile intermediate-range weapon which would nullify the perceived NATO advantage in forward-based systems. Its secret deployment over the next few years was intended to compel the withdrawal of US forward-based systems from West Germany, and to increase the military pressure on Bonn, now perceived as the weakest link in the western chain. 'Under the roof of the SS-20 it was possible to think about deep [conventional] operations,' General Danilevich of the Soviet central staff recalls. 'We were immediately able to hold all of Europe hostage.'[5] The point was not lost on Bonn, which, as one West German defence paper noted, 'will be affected first and hit hardest by any attack in Central Europe'.[6]

Meanwhile, the Soviet Union stepped up its support for subversive groups in Europe, especially Germany,[7] and intervened ever more confidently in the Third World, greatly encouraged by the American withdrawal from Indochina.[8] A cascade of events, partly inspired by Moscow, partly the result of independent initiatives by her allies and partly driven by local dynamics, now upset the uneasy equilibrium established by détente. The pro-western government of King Zahir Shah in Afghanistan was toppled by a leftist cabal of army officers who not only sought closer ties to Moscow, but resurrected old territorial claims on America's close ally Pakistan. In April 1974, the Portuguese right-wing dictatorship was toppled by a group of army officers determined to end the costly colonial war in Africa. The Soviet Union now hoped for a communist election victory or at least a coup, thus weakening the western hold on the Mediterranean, and casting NATO's presence in the vital Azores into question. Shortly afterwards, the Turks invaded Cyprus to forestall an attempt by radical Greek nationalists to exterminate the Turkish population. This led to the immediate fall of the junta in Athens and an outburst of popular anti-Americanism; Greece left the NATO command structure in protest against the alliance's failure to discipline Turkey, another alliance member. Even more worryingly, from the western point of view, the Italian communists were making steady inroads in the polls and looked likely to join a government in Rome at some point in the near future; there was talk that 'Eurocommunism' might prevail at the ballot box, not just in Italy.[9] In November 1975, the Spanish dictator Franco died, and the decision of King Juan Carlos to call elections seemed certain to result in a government hostile to Washington, leaving Gibraltar hopelessly exposed; Spain pulled out of the Western Sahara, creating a vacuum. By the end of 1975, in other words, the whole southern flank of NATO was in crisis.

The sense of strategic instability produced by this unprecedented surge of Soviet power globally provoked contrasting reactions in Washington, the capitals of western Europe and the US Congress. Convinced that US power globally was waning, Henry Kissinger – now Secretary of State – was determined to uphold US credibility, to confront Soviet advances across the board, and to use American regional strengths to gain the 'leverage' to compel Moscow to respect Washington's interests elsewhere. Regional allies were cultivated even more assiduously than before: Israel; South Africa, which acquired renewed importance over Angola; Indonesia, whose brutal invasion of East Timor in 1974 was tolerated; and Morocco, which was permitted to seize the Western Sahara in 1975. In the Middle East, Kissinger 'shuttled' between the capitals in 1973–4 trying to mediate the disengagement of the Arab and Israeli armies. At stake in all these cases was not so much the regional balance as the global 'credibility' of the United States. Kissinger worried that 'the Europeans [would] say to themselves if they can't hold [the Angolan capital of] Luanda, how can they defend Europe?'[10]

The biggest challenge, though, remained Germany, where the central front was buckling. Thanks to the withdrawal from Indochina, US forces there were increased by nearly 10 per cent in the first years of the decade. This was not nearly enough, however, to match the massive Soviet advantage in conventional weaponry.[11] Besides, the quality of the Vietnam-era army left much to be desired. 'Alcoholism and drug abuse were serious and widespread,' recalls General Al Haig, who took over as Supreme Commander of NATO in 1974. 'Our state of readiness was way below acceptable standards.' As if all this were not bad enough, transatlantic relations were in profound crisis, partly due to the determination of the western Europeans not to allow the superpower confrontation in Africa and the Middle East to destroy the hard-won détente in Europe, and partly due to fears that the US was no longer completely committed to their defence. In order to underline the American determination to hold the line in central Europe, thousands of additional forces were deployed before Hamburg.

Throughout all this, the United States was in the grips of a domestic crisis, which heavily distracted the executive. The break-in at the Democratic Party headquarters had finally been traced to the White House, leading to impeachment proceedings against President Nixon, and his resignation in August 1974. His successor, former Vice-President Gerald Ford, continued the policy of détente; Kissinger remained as Secretary of State. Meanwhile, the legislature arm tightened its grip on the machinery of foreign policy. In November 1974, the mid-term elections produced a Congress of doveish Democrats committed to reducing American involvement overseas. Early in the following year, Congress voted to cut off all aid to the Saigon government, rendering it effectively defenceless against a renewed North Vietnamese onslaught.

*

If all of this was very much within the tradition of the classic 'balance of power', a new geopolitics was about to emerge which sought to transcend it. The intellectual driving force here was the 'human rights' revolution which burst on to the western political scene in the early 1970s.[12] After decolonization and the US withdrawal from Vietnam, the Soviet treatment of domestic opposition was thrown into sharper relief. Lobbyist groups such as Amnesty International, and parliamentary committees across the western world, reflected and promoted this new global morality. Soviet dissidents, such as the writer Alexander Solzhenitsyn, were lionized across the west. The sentiment was taken up by the Democratic senator Henry 'Scoop' Jackson, a defence expert deeply unhappy about what he regarded as Kissinger's capitulation to Soviet demands under détente. Invoking Solzhenitsyn, he told Congress that 'mankind's sole salvation lies in everyone making everything his business, in the people in the east being vitally concerned with what is thought in the west, the people of the west being vitally concerned with what goes on in the east'.[13] From the mid-1970s, this discourse began to have a profound effect on the international system.

In 1974, Jackson persuaded Congress to pass the Jackson–Vanik Amendment. This rider to the Nixon administration's Trade Bill with the USSR called for 'the continued dedication of the United States to fundamental human rights', and denied 'most-favoured nation' status to any non-market economy country which 'denies its citizens the right or opportunity to emigrate'. It was a direct blow at Kissinger's attempt to create 'linkage' with the Soviet Union through economic ties. As a convinced 'realist', he bitterly resisted any attempts to suggest that the promotion of human rights was in the American national interest. 'And if they put Jews into gas chambers in the Soviet Union,' he told Nixon, 'it is not an American concern. Maybe a humanitarian concern.'[14] The bill did not in fact specify any religious group, but the legislation took place against the background of Moscow's refusal to allow Soviet Jews to leave the country. Not long after, the Ford administration was compelled by Congress to set up a Bureau of Human Rights in the State Department. The US legislature, in other words, was breaking with the idea of non-intervention in the internal affairs of another state.

Jackson was a strong supporter of Israel, and of the right of Soviet Jews to emigrate, but the amendment was not primarily driven by

Middle Eastern concerns.[15] Jackson planned to use the issue to cripple détente, which he regarded as a betrayal of US values and interests, and as part of a broader propagandistic attack on Soviet tyranny. Moscow's Achilles heel – most graphically demonstrated by the construction of the Berlin Wall – was its refusal to allow free movement of its citizens. Putting the spotlight on this fact damaged the regime internationally and gave heart to those groups trying to undermine it from within. More generally, Jackson believed that states which were oppressive at home would tend towards aggression abroad, so that the spread of human rights and democracy would serve to promote world peace.[16] The Jackson–Vanik Amendment, in other words, was not about what the US Congress could do for Soviet Jews, but about what Soviet Jews could do for American grand strategy.

In Europe, the increased Soviet threat also led to a new geopolitics. Western Europeans returned to the question of how to make their collective voice heard in the world, or at least on their own continent. In 1974, they established the European Council, consisting of the prime ministers or presidents of the member states. In practice, this was dominated by Paris, Bonn and London and provided a forum at which a common European strategy could be articulated. Many felt that this intergovernmental cooperation did not go nearly far enough. Towards the end of 1974, the EEC tasked the Belgian prime minister, Leo Tindemans, with investigating how the commitment to 'European Union' could be advanced. He reported that Europeans generally felt 'vulnerable and powerless'; it was essential, therefore, that they 'present a united front to the outside world' and use the 'collective strength' of the continent 'in support of law and justice in world discussions'.[17] He argued that the 'European Union will not be complete until it has drawn up a common defence policy'. Tindemans proposed to achieve this by strengthening institutions, the adoption of common policies, cooperation on arms production and the extension of the powers of the European Commission. A particular emphasis was placed throughout on democracy, both as a criterion for cooperation with other European states and as a mode of proceeding within the Community. The president of the Commission should be appointed by the European Council, but – crucially – approved by the European parliament. This meant that the parliament, hitherto a mere consultative assembly, would have to be elected by universal suffrage; the first pan-European elections were scheduled to take place at the end of the decade. Europe, in other words, needed to acquire democratic legitimacy in order to defend its interests.

This new European voice immediately made itself heard in the negotiations with the Soviet Union at Helsinki and Geneva on the recognition of borders and the establishment of the CSCE. Britain, in particular, used the forum to continue – to quote the young British diplomat George Walden – the 'Cold War by other, more subtle means'. This was to be done, he explained, by 'securing genuine improvements in reducing barriers within Europe and "generally to spread the contagion of liberty"'.[18] Kissinger rejected this approach: he drew a clear distinction between the interests of states and of peoples. His refusal to engage seriously in these talks gave the Europeans a free hand to pin the Soviet Union down to at least formal commitments to respect human and religious rights. A new Westphalian settlement now became possible.

The Helsinki Final Act, which was made public in June 1975 and signed later that year by the United States, the Soviet Union and all member states of NATO and the Warsaw Pact reflected both the old and the new geopolitics. On the one hand, the agreement committed all parties to respect the sanctity of existing borders and to work together in the new Conference on Security and Cooperation in Europe. This guarantee of her territorial gains since 1945 and recognition of her parity with the United States was a major victory for the Soviet Union. So was the article stipulating 'non-intervention in internal affairs'. This was contradicted, however, by the European-inspired clauses which committed the signatories to respect 'human rights and fundamental freedoms, including the freedom of thought, conscience or belief'. The agreement also guaranteed the freer movement of ideas and people, a clear gesture towards the right of migration. Even though the Soviet Union had agreed to these clauses under duress, and had no intention of honouring them, she had made a public international commitment with fateful consequences.[19] For the moment, this did not matter much – there was no enforcement mechanism – but over time it became clear to Moscow that the thread with which it had hoped to sew up the territorial settlement, would actually unravel the whole Soviet system.

Kissinger paid little attention to the Helsinki Final Act, which he said might as well have been written in 'Swahili'. He was more concerned about the continuing global advance of communism. In April 1975,

Saigon fell to the advancing North Vietnamese armies amid humiliating scenes of chaos at the American embassy. Kissinger embarked on intensive diplomacy to pre-empt the spread of communism across the Mediterranean. The Turks and Greeks were forced if not to patch up their quarrel over Cyprus, then at least to desist from going to war against each other. With regard to Italy, President Ford warned that the United States would 'vigorously oppose any communist participation' in government.[20] Otherwise, however, the Americans decided to let the democratic process run its course. In Greece, the junta was followed not by a left-wing takeover, but by a moderate and pro-European ministry. The march of communism in Portugal came to an abrupt end when the party secured a pathetic one fifth of the vote in the 1975 elections; a subsequent attempt at a coup petered out. Portugal remained a committed member of the Atlantic alliance.[21] In Spain, the transition to democracy produced a moderate socialist government and opened the way for the country's admission to NATO. The democratization of southern Europe, in short, strengthened rather than undermined the western alliance.[22]

The international events of 1974–6 had a profound effect on domestic politics across the globe. Britain erupted in an acrimonious debate about Europe and the implications of the deepening economic crisis for foreign policy. In early June 1975, the Labour government put her membership in the EEC to a popular referendum. The resulting debate divided the country, the parties and even families. In the end, just over two thirds of the electorate voted to stay in the EEC; support in England was higher than in any other part of the United Kingdom, substantially so in the cases of Scotland and Northern Ireland. The dire international situation – the poll took place in the shadow of the fall of Saigon and the apparently irresistible advance of world communism – substantially contributed to the outcome. A year later, the country was convulsed by economic problems which culminated in a sterling crisis and a bailout by the International Monetary Fund. The implications for Britain's strategic position were profound: there were plans to repair the public finances by reducing troop presence in Germany and withdrawing from Cyprus.[23] This was the context in which Margaret Thatcher, the new leader of the opposition Conservative Party, launched her powerful critique of British decline. 'The first duty of any government,' she warned the Labour prime minister, Jim Callaghan, in mid-January

1976, 'is to safeguard its people against external aggression; to guarantee the survival of our way of life.' She charged that Labour was 'dismantling our defence at a moment when the strategic threat to Britain and her allies from an expansionist power is graver than at any moment since the end of the last war'.[24] This strongly anti-communist speech earned Thatcher the sobriquet 'Iron Lady' from the Soviet press.

In West Germany, foreign policy remained at the centre of domestic politics. Chancellor Willy Brandt was forced to resign when it was revealed in May 1974 that his key adviser, Günter Guillaume, had been a Soviet spy. He was succeeded by Helmut Schmidt; the new foreign minister was Hans-Dietrich Genscher. Both men were committed to continuing détente and *Ostpolitik*, albeit with more emphasis on 'stability' over human rights. Meanwhile, the *Rote Armee Fraktion*, also known as the Baader–Meinhof Group after its two most prominent members, continued its attack on the state. In 1975, the leaders were brought to trial and sentenced. In 1976, Palestinian and Baader–Meinhof guerrillas hijacked an Air France jet, diverted it to Entebbe and demanded the release of prisoners in Israeli jails. They segregated the Jewish passengers (including those not holding Israeli passports), and released the rest. A year later, the escalating violence in the Federal Republic culminated in the 'German autumn', when the influential industrialist Hanns-Martin Schleyer was kidnapped, and Palestinian operatives – acting independently of the PLO – took a Lufthansa aircraft hostage, demanding the release of prisoners in German and Turkish jails. Not long after, German special forces stormed the plane and freed the captives, leading to the murder of Schleyer and the suicide of the Baader–Meinhof detainees. The events of 1976–7 thus demonstrated the threads connecting the Federal Republic to the radical global struggle against the west, Israel and the Jews.

The international developments of the mid-1970s also had a profound impact on domestic politics in the Soviet bloc, where the Helsinki Accords – which all signatory states were obliged to publish – provoked a passionate debate in the Kremlin, the capitals of eastern Europe and in society at large. The KGB chief, Yuri Andropov, argued that while the 'principle of inviolability of borders [was] of course good, very good', he was concerned that the borders would become transparent as a result of 'the flow of information' and 'the expansion of contacts'.[25] As Andropov feared, Helsinki was promptly invoked by dissident groups claiming political, religious and human rights. From the mid-1970s, the domestic affairs of the eastern bloc were progressively internationalized, embarrassing the Soviet Union and making the task of repression much more difficult. In 1975, the prominent dissident Andrei Sakharov was awarded the Nobel Peace Prize, a huge public slap in the face for the regime. That same year, a US Congressional delegation visited Russia and met with another prominent critic of the regime, Yuri Orlov. In May 1976, Sakharov and Orlov set up the Public Group to Assist the Implementation of the Helsinki Accords in the USSR. A year later, Czechoslovak dissidents appealed to the Final Act in their famous Charter 77. The 'contagion of liberty', which Walden had spoken of, was well and truly at large.

The decline of détente and the Helsinki process also changed the course of American politics. Foreign policy dominated the primaries in both parties during the 1976 election. Critics on both sides of the partisan divide lamented the global retreat of the United States, demanded a tougher line on nuclear weapons, and dismissed the Helsinki Final Act as a betrayal by which the Soviet Union secured its aims in return for meaningless assurances on human rights. In 1976, Henry Jackson, his principal aide, Richard Perle, and the arms control expert Paul Nitze, who resigned in 1974 in protest over SALT II, founded the Committee on the Present Danger to warn against a rampant Soviet Union.[26] Jackson mounted a strong campaign for the Democratic nomination, but was defeated by Jimmy Carter, who combined a fervent commitment to human rights with a more optimistic view of the chances of an understanding with the Soviet Union. US foreign policy was also under attack in the Republican Party. With some difficulty, President Ford saw off a powerful primary challenge from the charismatic and ferociously anti-Soviet governor of California, Ronald Reagan, who blamed him for the fall of Saigon and retreating more generally in the face of Russian aggression. A terrible gaffe during one of the televised debates, when Ford suggested that the Soviet Union did 'not dominate' eastern Europe, cost him vital Polish and other ethnic votes in the industrial heartlands and thus the election. In January 1977, Jimmy Carter was inaugurated President of the United States.

The new administration was committed to a twin-track strategy, which soon became schizophrenic. On the one hand, Carter promised to 'return to moral principles and human rights' in US foreign policy, which signalled a confrontational course against communist and right-wing dictatorships alike. 'Human rights', indeed, became the watchword of his presidency. On the other hand, Carter sought to reduce international tension through reaching an understanding with the Soviet Union on arms control and mediating an end to regional conflicts, especially in the Middle East.

Carter's emphasis on human rights, and on the growing nuclear imbalance, caused a deep split with the western Europeans. The Federal Republic, in particular, was deeply uneasy with the escalating US rhetoric on Soviet and east European treatment of dissidents.[27] Chancellor Helmut Schmidt – who made no secret of the fact that he considered Carter 'naïve' – worried that the president would jeopardize recent hard-won 'practical' cooperation with the Soviet Union on travel, emigration and trade. What really drove Washington and the Europeans apart, however, was the fear that Carter was unsound on the question of nuclear deterrence and not committed to holding the central front in Germany. The president's known desire to abolish all atomic weapons threatened to leave the Europeans exposed to the full force of Soviet conventional superiority. More immediately, Bonn was angered by well-founded rumours that the Americans were thinking about abandoning the forward regions of Germany in the event of a Soviet attack. In particular, the Germans were disturbed at the American failure to respond adequately to the Soviet deployment of the SS-20 missiles, which was detected in early 1977.

The need for physical and moral rearmament, and the apparent weakness of Washington, now drove the western Europeans further together.[28] The first European elections were held in early June 1979, with a substantial turnout of more than 60 per cent. That same year saw the creation of the European Monetary System in order to prepare the participating states – led by Germany and France, with Britain opting out – to meet the necessary 'convergence criteria' for currency union. Its real purpose, however, was political: another step on the road to 'ever closer union'. Schmidt, especially, was anxious about Germany's 'unintended and dangerous rise to the second global power of the west in the perception of other governments ... particularly the Soviet leadership'.[29] He even feared 'potential ... cooperation between the Soviet leadership and political factors in western Europe against the interests of the Federal Republic of Germany'. Schmidt therefore sought to embed West Germany in broader European structures. The European project, in other words, remained an instrument to maximize the power of the continent and bind that of Germany.

At the Guadeloupe Summit of January 1979, the Europeans finally pushed Carter into the 'dual-track decision'. NATO proclaimed itself willing to conduct further nuclear arms limitation talks with the Soviet Union, but committed itself to the deployment of hundreds of Cruise and Pershing II intermediate-range missiles by 1983 in the event of no satisfactory agreement being reached. More important even than the waving of sticks to complement the carrots of détente was the renewed sense of American engagement with the Atlantic alliance. At the same time, in July 1979, the Carter administration – at Brzezinski's urging – sent military aid to Afghans opposed to the communist government in Kabul. Brzezinski's plan was to provoke a Soviet intervention, thus creating a Vietnam-style ulcer on the Russian border which would cause Moscow to loosen its grip on central and eastern Europe.[30]

In 1979, a series of crises erupted which were to shape world and European geopolitics until the end of the Cold War and beyond. In mid-January 1979, the Shah of Iran fled into exile after many months of protests by demonstrators opposed to his oppressive domestic policy and to his diplomatic alignment with the United States and Israel. The new Islamic Republic of Iran was an avowedly revolutionary force, whose constitution undertook to 'exert continuous effort until political, economic and cultural unity is realized in the Islamic world'.[31] Not long after, a group of students stormed the US embassy and took more than sixty diplomats hostage. A month later, the Chinese – with US encouragement – launched a limited but large-scale military assault on the North Vietnamese border as a warning to Hanoi and Moscow.[32] There was also heightened tension along the Sino-Soviet border. In July, Saddam Hussein seized absolute power in Iraq, with a programme for regional dominance; a year later, he attacked Iran. In mid-November 1979, the US ally and oil-rich state of Saudi Arabia was rocked by the occupation of the Grand Mosque in Mecca by an international group of Wahabis protesting against the impiety of the ruling monarchy and its alleged subservience to Washington. The House of Saud called in French mercenaries as advisers (briefly converting them to Islam for the purpose), ordered the storming of the mosque and beheaded the surviving terrorists.[33] A simultaneous Shiite rising along the coast in the oil-producing areas was also suppressed.

The cumulative effect of these events on the geopolitics of the Middle East and the overall global balance was seismic. Tehran began to support Islamist forces in neighbouring Iraq and Afghanistan, as well as as far afield as Lebanon. In Saudi Arabia, the monarchy's use of foreigners to suppress the Grand Mosque rising drove many into opposition, and some – such as the young Osama bin Laden – towards armed resistance to the United States and its local allies. Riyadh reacted to these threats by demonstrating its Muslim credentials through supporting fundamentalist preachers at home and Islamist causes abroad. All this provoked deep alarm in Moscow. The Islamic Revolution in Iran and the spread of Wahabi doctrines from Saudi Arabia were beginning to make an impact in the central Asian republics. Most worrying of all, however, was the situation in communist Afghanistan, which was exposed to infiltration from Tehran, Islamabad and CIA agents based in Pakistan. 'We see the Islamic resurgence as terribly important,' Brzezinski remarked in mid-March 1979. 'It marks the rebirth of Arab vitality, which is the best bulwark against communism.'[34] In March 1979, the western city of Herat saw a brief but bloody revolt which Moscow and the Afghan government blamed on Iranian and Pakistani interference. The situation escalated throughout the year, and by November the Soviet Union was terrified that the regime of Hafizullah Amin would collapse within months, or worse still defect to the Americans.[35] Right at the end of the year, therefore, the Soviet Union invaded Afghanistan, assassinated the errant Amin and installed the more pliable Babrak Karmal in his place. The operation was conceived as a pre-emptive strike to keep Afghanistan within the socialist system rather than as an overture to further expansion towards the Indian Ocean. Moscow, however, had walked straight into the trap which Brzezinski had set for it. On the day the Soviets officially crossed the border, he wrote to Carter that the United States now had the opportunity to inflict a Vietnam War on them.

In January 1980, the president proclaimed what has become known as the 'Carter Doctrine'. Carter defined the 'region which is now threatened by Soviet troops in Afghanistan' as of 'great strategic importance' because it 'contains more than two-thirds of the world's exportable oil'. He therefore declared that 'an attempt by any outside force to gain control of the Persian Gulf region will be regarded as an assault on the vital interests of the United States', which would be 'repelled by any means necessary, including military force'.[36] That same month he withdrew SALT II from the Senate, short-circuiting the ratification process and thus effectively killing off the agreement. A large-scale programme of conventional military expansion, already underway, was speeded up. More than 30,000 additional troops were permanently deployed to Europe. NATO members were put under considerable pressure to increase their defence spending. After some debate, the decision was taken to launch 'Operation Cyclone', the full-scale arming of the Afghan Mujahedin resistance against the Soviet Union through the offices of the Pakistani intelligence agency, ISI. Its real aim was not so much to keep the Soviets out of Afghanistan or even the Gulf, but to wear them down globally and especially in the main European battleground.

The shocks of 1979 widened the gulf between Washington and the western Europeans, who wanted to keep the United States focused on the Soviet threat to Germany, but to maintain global détente as long as possible. When the US, along with Red China, Egypt, Iran, Israel, Turkey, Saudi Arabia and a number of other states boycotted the Moscow Olympics of 1980 in protest at the invasion of Afghanistan, Bonn followed suit grudgingly, but the rest of NATO (with the exception of Norway) did not. The divide over the Middle East also grew wider, when the 'second oil shock' of 1979 – a spike in petrol prices caused by the Iranian Revolution – reminded Europeans of their vulnerability on the energy front. In June 1980, the EEC called for the creation of a Palestinian homeland and the inclusion of the Palestinian Liberation Organization in all future Arab–Israeli talks.

The collapse of détente and developments in the Middle East shaped domestic politics. In early May 1979, the Conservative Party leader, Margaret Thatcher, won a comfortable election victory in Britain. She had campaigned largely on economic issues, but her triumph was also a mandate for a harder line against the Soviet Union. The positions were, moreover, linked: Thatcher's Churchillian stance abroad was matched by a liberal free-market economic policy designed to reverse British decline. After the invasion of Afghanistan at the end of the year, and the sharp increase in east–west tensions, European politics polarized further. Whereas on the right and in the centre there was a tendency among Europeans to close ranks with Washington, the left divided between those who remained committed to NATO and a neutralist, anti-American constituency. The prospective deployment of Cruise and Pershing II missiles, which had to be ratified by various national parliaments, now dominated domestic politics.[37] In Germany, Schmidt came under increasing pressure from the left wing of the SPD, and in January 1980 the founding of the Greens, an ecological party committed to making Germany a nuclear-free zone, signalled that the old consensus was fragmenting. At the end of that year, the bitter Labour leadership election saw the narrow victory of the unilateral disarmer Michael Foot over the NATO stalwart Denis Healey.

Across western Europe, in fact, party activists and civil groups mobilized against the increased threat of an atomic conflagration. In April 1980, the appeal for European Nuclear Disarmament (END) was launched in London by a coalition of MPs, intellectuals, artists, Church leaders and trade union leaders. The appeal to halt deployment of SS-20s, Cruise and Pershing II missiles was theoretically directed at both superpowers, but in practice the absence of any traction in the Soviet Union meant that NATO was being called upon to exercise unilateral restraint. Moscow, sensing the opportunity to detach western Europe, or parts of it, from the NATO alliance, embarked on a systematic campaign of infiltration and covert funding of nuclear disarmament groups.

In the United States, foreign policy continued to dominate domestic politics.[38] The 'Scoop' Jackson Democrats – though not the senator himself – now began to align themselves with the Republicans, whom they considered 'sounder' on questions of national security. The collapse of détente was – together with the economy – the greatest single issue in the 1980 election campaign. Carter's attempts to portray Reagan as a dangerous and inexperienced extremist largely failed to dent his chal lenger's infectious optimism and stated determination to rebuild the foundations of American economic and military power. The Republi cans duly won the poll with a comfortable margin of the popular vote and a landslide in the Electoral College.[39]

If the collapse of détente – *per se* – had relatively little domesti impact on the Soviet bloc, the Helsinki Accords were another matter. I July and August 1980, Poland was rocked by unrest beginning in th Gdansk shipyards, leading to the founding of the trade union 'Solida ity' in September under the leadership of the charismatic dockyar worker Lech Walesa. It received strong covert support not only fro

Washington, where the National Security Advisor was of Polish origin, but from the Vatican, under a Polish pope. For the rest of the decade, the country was in a state of latent national-religious insurrection against the communist regime and its Russian sponsors. This posed a mortal threat to Moscow. The country was a vital strategic buffer for the Soviet Union, contributed crucial forces towards the first strategic echelon of the Warsaw Pact, hosted numerous tactical nuclear missiles, and above all constituted an essential link to the Group of Soviet Forces in the German Democratic Republic. Without Poland, the Soviet position in Germany would collapse.[40] In the end, the Soviet Union encouraged the Polish General Jaruzelski to impose martial law in mid-December 1981, which kept the lid on the situation for the time being.

The changes of government in Britain and the United States in 1979–80 led to a new strategic approach. At his first press conference in late January 1981, the new president signalled the abandonment of détente as 'a one-way street that the Soviet Union has used to pursue its own aims'.[41] Convinced that Moscow had taken advantage of US weakness after Vietnam, Reagan would negotiate only from a position of strength. Indeed, the president was determined to use the long-term economic superiority of the United States to put the Soviet system under unbearable pressure, and therefore force Moscow into a 'realistic' arms control agreement. So the president massively increased spending on both conventional and nuclear weaponry. It was in this spirit that the president entered into the negotiations on Theater Nuclear Forces – intermediate- and short-range missiles – at Geneva in November 1981. Eighteen months later, he announced plans to develop a space-based missile defence system – the Strategic Defense Initiative (SDI), quickly dubbed 'Star Wars' – which would be able to prevent Soviet warheads from reaching their targets in the United States.

Even more important than military and economic pressure, however, was the concerted ideological offensive Reagan unleashed against the communist bloc. The Soviet Union was roundly condemned as an 'evil empire'. Above all, the president championed religious and political dissidents, and put the promotion of democracy at the heart of his grand strategy. The administration believed that democracies were reliable bulwarks against Soviet expansionism. It was also convinced that a shared democratic political culture would prevent countries from going to war with each other; in political science literature, this has come to be known as the 'democratic peace' theory. 'Free people,' Reagan argued, 'where governments rest upon the consent of the governed, do not wage war on their neighbours. Free people, blessed by economic opportunity and protected by laws that respect the dignity of the individual, are not driven towards the domination of others.' 'Freedom and democracy are the best guarantors of peace,' he remarked on another occasion. 'History has shown that democratic nations do not start wars.'[42]

Rhetoric was important, but the administration also took active measures to promote democracy. Captive Nations Day – in which the United States remembered the peoples of eastern Europe under communist domination – was revived in 1982. At around the same time, in accordance with Reagan's demand to foster 'the infrastructure of democracy – the system of a free press, unions, political parties, universities', the administration oversaw the establishment of the National Endowment for Democracy in 1983, with its brief to encourage the spread of representative government around the world. Reagan was determined to use democracy and human rights to unravel the entire Soviet satellite system. In April 1981, the CIA concluded a clandestine agreement with the Israeli secret service, which put its extensive network in eastern Europe, especially in Poland, at the service of the new strategy. When Jaruzelski declared martial law, Reagan saw his opportunity. By early June 1982, Reagan had met with the pope to coordinate joint secret assistance for Solidarity. He also enlisted the collaboration of the strongly anti-communist US labour leaders of the AFL–CIO (American Federation of Labor–Confederation of Industrial Organizations). While the Soviet Union was being 'bled' militarily in Afghanistan, it would also be forced on the defensive politically in eastern Europe.

The centrality of Europe was further affirmed by the two local crises which rocked the state system in 1982. In early April 1982, the Argentine junta, desperate to shore up its shaky domestic position and determined to vindicate longstanding national claims to 'Las Malvinas', invaded the Falkland Islands and expelled the tiny British garrison. London believed that backing down in the face of aggression by a dictatorship would seriously damage British prestige and very probably encourage further attacks closer to home. 'Resolute defence of freedom in the South Atlantic,' the Minister of State for the Armed Forces, Lord Blaker, argued, 'is directly relevant to the defence of freedom in Europe. Our action will have encouraged our NATO allies and enhanced the prospects of peace by showing that when the chips are down the British are prepared to fight for what they believe in.'[43] For this reason, there was widespread parliamentary and popular support – especially from the Labour leader, Michael Foot – when the prime minister, Margaret Thatcher, resolved to send a naval task force to evict the Argentinians.[44] Shortly afterwards, in early June 1982, Israel responded to a rising tide of Palestinian attacks inside and outside the Middle East by invading the Lebanon, to destroy PLO bases there and establish a buffer zone in the south. After a rapid advance to the outskirts of Beirut, the Israeli army began to shell suspected enemy positions in the city, causing widespread civilian casualties. In the Bekaa Valley, the air force battled it out with Syrian jets, and there were also scattered tank and artillery exchanges. Inside the Lebanese capital the most gruesome incident was the massacre of Palestinian women and children by Christian militias allied to Israel. Yassir Arafat finally agreed to withdraw to Tunis, but the Jewish state did not achieve the hoped-for security. The Shiite population of the south and north-east flocked to join the new Iranian-sponsored Hezbollah militia, which vowed to drive the Israelis out of all Lebanon before liberating Palestine.

Both wars had powerful implications for the superpowers. The invasion of the Falklands, and Britain's determination to recapture them, provoked initial embarrassment in Washington. Argentina was a valued partner against Soviet subversion in Latin America, and the junta provided useful training for Nicaraguan 'Contras', rebels opposed to the Moscow-leaning Sandinista government in Nicaragua. Some of Reagan's advisers, in particular his UN ambassador, Jeane Kirkpatrick, counselled against being too closely associated with British 'imperialism'. In the end, however, London was a far closer ally than Buenos Aires: her support in Europe was essential. The president therefore quickly came down on Thatcher's side, authorizing the dispatch of the vital military aid which facilitated the recapture of the islands in the summer of 1982; France, too, provided Britain vital intelligence assistance. Likewise, the United States supported Israel in the Lebanon because it was a key ally in the defence of the eastern Mediterranean. It was the *European* strategic rather than any Middle Eastern imperative which was decisive here. When the United States set up a new unified command for the Middle East – CENTCOM – in 1983, Israel remained, along with Egypt, Turkey, Syria and Lebanon, part of the old US European Command (USEUCOM). Moreover, the figures for US aid to Israel, which was only about 10 per cent of that sent to West Germany during the Cold War, told their own tale about American priorities.[45]

Moscow now saw itself, as Gromyko warned the Warsaw Pact foreign ministers in early April 1983, as 'encircled' by enemies in Europe, the Far East and the Indian Ocean. It was particularly worried by the growing power of the German *Bundeswehr*. For this reason it was agreed at the Berlin meeting of the Pact in mid-October 1983 'to use all available means to prevent the [achievement] of military superiority by NATO'.[46] Moscow deployed ever greater numbers of intermediate-range nuclear missiles on the central front. It dangled closer economic ties and a return to détente before the eyes of west European governments, particularly Helmut Schmidt's embattled coalition in Bonn. Any force likely to weaken western cohesion, such as the British National Union of Miners, the Labour Party, various left-wing politicians, nuclear disarmament campaigners, and German Green Party luminaries such as Petra Kelly and Gert Bastian, was supported with covert funding.[47] SDI, however, filled the Soviet elite with despair. If successful, the project would completely transform the timeframe within which a nuclear confrontation would take place. The attack, one Soviet general feared, 'could come in nanoseconds. Consequently, the Soviet General Staff would have no time to make key decisions.' It also threatened to encircle the Soviet Union, which was already surrounded by NATO and the Chinese, from the direction of space as well.[48]

All this widened existing splits in the western alliance. Just as Carter had been, Reagan was often dismissed by European leaders in private – and sometimes in public – as 'naïve'. This time, though, the concern was not so much that the US president would be gulled by the Soviet Union but rather that his robust anti-communism might provoke a global conflagration. At the very least, many Europeans, the Germans most of all feared that Reagan's moral absolutism jeopardized the 'practical' gain of détente. Schmidt, in particular, was appalled by Reagan's ignorance of European affairs, and feared the president's early disdain for fresh arms limitation talks exposed him to anti-nuclear protestors at home. There was further tension over the building of a pipeline designed to transport Soviet natural gas to western Europe. This was a project which the Americans – citing the strategic dangers of energy dependence on Russia – wanted to see terminated, even as they sold subsidized excess wheat to Moscow at reduced prices. More importantly, Bonn clashed with Washington over its support for Solidarity, a movement which the West Germans regarded as a threat to détente. SDI was a further shock: the Europeans had not been consulted on the programme, and there was no mention of extending the missile shield to Europe.[49] The Germans, especially, worried that SDI – by protecting only the American homeland – might 'decouple' US security from that of Europe and thus leave them more vulnerable to attack.

The 'Second Cold War' and the transatlantic differences over how to handle it inspired a fresh round of western European integration and cooperation. Greece was admitted to the EEC in 1981, expanding the Community into the eastern Mediterranean; Spain and Portugal joined five years later. The Soviet threat also stimulated a new phase in Franco-German military and political collaboration. In 1983, Paris pushed for a European [space] Defence Initiative (EDI), christened 'EUREKA', designed to balance Reagan's SDI. In February 1984, the European parliament adopted a Draft Treaty on European Union, designed to reform the institutions of the Community and thus 'preserve peace and liberty by an ever closer union'. Four months later, the French launched an initiative to breathe fresh life into the Western European Union, the largely defunct military arm of the European integration process. Margaret Thatcher, for her part, sought to use the Community to promote the vision of a free-market Europe. At the European Council at Milan in June 1985, she supported plans for 'political cooperation' – 'which in normal English means foreign policy' – because of 'the need for western solidarity in dealing with the eastern bloc',[50] especially with regard to the defence of Germany. The resulting Single European Act was agreed in late 1985 and signed in February of the following year. It simplified economic decision-making in the EEC, a gesture towards London, and strengthened European Political Cooperation, in accordance with the wishes of Paris and Bonn.

Neo-liberal economics at home and the robust defence of freedom abroad proved to be winning formulas for Thatcher and Reagan. The Labour Party opposition tore itself apart on the question of defence. Here it was not so much its patriotism which was in doubt – the leader, Michael Foot, had taken a tough line with the Argentine junta over the Falklands – as its understanding of European security. The Labour manifesto in the election campaign of 1983, which committed the party to unilateral nuclear disarmament and to withdrawal from the European Economic Community, was described by the Labour MP Gerald Kaufman as the 'longest suicide note in history'. Thatcher duly won in a landslide. In the United States, Reagan made defence a central issue in his successful 1984 re-election campaign. The Anglo-American alliance for democratic geopolitics was set fair to continue for another four years.

It was in Germany, however, where the real domestic battle over grand strategy was fought out. Until the *Bundestag* ratified the twin-track decision, Cruise and Pershing could not be deployed, and the whole NATO strategy hung in the balance. Schmidt battled to convince his party and the public. Popular opposition to the deployment, however, grew steadily. In October 1981, some 300,000 protestors converged on Bonn; during the 'Easter Marches' of 1982, about half a million people turned out to demonstrate. Schmidt gradually lost control of his own party, which increasingly tended towards the unconditional resumption of détente and unilateral nuclear disarmament. Younger Social Democrats such as Oskar Lafontaine rejected the whole concept of deterrence and argued that Germany was obliged for historic reasons to pursue an exclusively peaceful policy. In 1982, Schmidt's liberal coalition partners, the Free Democrats (FDP), concerned at the general leftward drift of the government and particularly about defence policy, jumped ship and entered into an arrangement with the opposition. The incoming chancellor, Helmut Kohl, was strongly committed to the deployments, as were most of his Christian Democratic Union, and the liberal leader, Hans-Dietrich Genscher, who stayed on as foreign minister. In March 1983, the new coalition won a convincing election victory, although the country remained deeply polarized on defence. By November 1983, the *Bundestag* had agreed to the stationing of Cruise and Pershing II if negotiations did not produce a satisfactory compromise. The Soviet attempt to uncouple Bonn from the NATO alliance had failed.

In the Soviet Union, the international turbulence of the early 1980s had initially favoured the 'hawks'. When Brezhnev died, he was replaced in November 1982 by the hardline former KGB leader Yuri Andropov. When he expired in February 1984, his successor, Konstantin Chernenko, persisted with the existing strategy, until he in turn was replaced by Mikhail Gorbachev just over a year later. Beneath the surface, however, there was considerable elite and popular anxiety across the Warsaw Pact. Moreover, for all the upbeat public production figures, the Soviet economy had been stagnating for about a decade; the Russian population had been reduced by communism to shiftless, work-shy alcoholics.[51] The gap between capitalism and communism, which had appeared to narrow in the 1960s, was growing again. It was not clear how long the huge cost of armaments could be met. Moreover, the deterioration of relations with the west meant that Soviet citizens spent much of the early 1980s in a state of war psychosis, further undermining domestic morale.

By the middle of the decade, Brezhnev's grand strategy was a cul-de-sac. The Red Army remained bogged down in Afghanistan, which had become – as the new leader, Gorbachev, put it in February 1986 – a 'bleeding wound'.[52] There was widespread discontent among conscripts drafted to fight there, and their families; a backwash of Islamic fundamentalism was visible in the Soviet central Asian republics.[53] In Europe, western technological superiority was becoming ever more painfully obvious, in the 'smart weapons' of NATO conventional forces, the Strategic Defense Initiative and more generally in the 'microchip revolution' which invigorated the advanced industrial economies. Determined attempts to decouple Europe from Washington had failed. The dreaded Cruise and Pershing II missiles were deployed and by 1985 the German government had even signed up to SDI. Solidarity and other dissident groups were a running sore in eastern Europe, and increasingly in the Soviet Union itself. Above all, the Soviet economy was crippled by inefficient central planning, low oil prices (thanks to the Saudis), widespread corruption and incompetence.[54] The Soviet Union was therefore no longer economically in a position to support the demands of the Red Army and a whole array of needy allies in eastern Europe and the Third World.[55] A fresh approach was needed.

The Soviet Union reacted to strategic decline, as competitive European states always had, through a programme of domestic reform.[56] In his first speech as leader Gorbachev announced his intention to maintain 'military-strategic parity with the aggressive NATO'.[57] Like the tsarist modernizers of old, Gorbachev's first concern was not economic liberalization, popular standards of living or democratization but technological backwardness and low economic growth. What was innovative about his approach, however, was that it did not just conceive of internal change as a means to increasing external power through greater military mobilization. Instead, Gorbachev sought to expose and reform abuses in what he regarded as a basically just system. He also hoped that a more conciliatory attitude towards dissidents would reduce the terrible international battering the Soviet Union had received over human rights since the mid-1970s.[58] Gorbachev now proclaimed a policy of reconstruction ('*Perestroika*') – a 'revolution[ary] . . . acceleration of the socio-economic and cultural development of Soviet society' – and openness ('*Glasnost*'). Greater freedom of expression, Gorbachev believed, would mobilize the intelligentsia and reduce incompetence and corruption. Dissidents were released, police repression was greatly eased, civil rights groups emerged, there was a revival of the Russian Orthodox Church and a vibrant public sphere moved from the underground into the open. The structure of ministries was simplified and made more efficient. Longstanding, sclerotic and venal party leaders were sacked and replaced by dynamic reformers. As yet, however, there was no talk of democracy. Rather like the old Leninist NEP, Gorbachev was promoting economic modernization to strengthen the state without accompanying political participation.

On the international scene, Gorbachev spoke a new language not just of détente, but of interdependence. The new Soviet leader invited the west to resume negotiations on arms control, on condition that the US shelved SDI, and began to withdraw from the Third World. In key theatres, though, Gorbachev's initial strategy reflected traditional Soviet geopolitics. He stepped up the campaign in Afghanistan. In Europe, the Soviet leader increased the deployment of theatre nuclear weapons. He sought to split the western alliance by visiting Paris on his first trip abroad as General Secretary in October 1985. The principal concern of Gorbachev's strategy, however, was that the GDR and perhaps the whole of the Comecon was on the verge of economic collapse. It therefore became a matter of urgency to spread *Perestroika* to the eastern bloc, particularly East Germany, in order to make it more resistant to pressure from below. At the same time, Moscow had to grapple with the increasing importance of Bonn. 'West Germany, . . . like it or not – and whether its allies in NATO like it or not,' Gorbachev argued, 'is a massive weight in the balance of world power, and its role in international affairs will grow.' 'Without Germany,' he repeated over and over again 'we can have no real European policy'.[59] A 'rapprochement' between Bonn and Moscow was thus necessary, holding the 'trump card' of German unification in reserve.[60]

At the same time, Gorbachev believed that the growth of a new collaborative European political culture rendered traditional fears of German power less acute. In April 1989, Vyacheslav Dashichev, a reformer and foreign policy expert, penned a memorandum entitled 'The concept of the "Common European Home" and the German Question', which conceded that the GDR was on its last legs, and looked to Bonn to fund its radical economic and political reform, before it was toppled through mass protests. 'One thing is clear,' Aleksandr Yakovlev, the most powerful reforming voice on the Politburo, argued a few months later, 'democratic and peaceful states must exist in the heart of Europe, on the German territories, not states that are increasing their armaments'. European integration, or at least cooperation, was a key part of this process. 'The European countries,' Yakovlev predicted, 'will have a common parliament, common affairs and trade relations; the borders will be open.' If a 'Common European Home' could be built, he continued, and 'succeeded in creating [a] functioning economic association, if it succeeds in following the social interests of the workers, then it deserves our interest, and we are prepared to cooperate with Europe'.[61] Russia was bidding, in effect, to rejoin a Europe which had solved the German Question.

In central Europe, *Glasnost* enabled the emergence of a new popular geopolitics. The German public was soon gripped by 'Gorbymania' – a messianic faith in the Soviet leader's ability to deliver an end to the Cold War which so dominated their lives.[62] His concept of a Common European Home resonated widely. German historians, for their part, began to speak more openly about the importance of the *Mittellage*, the central location of Germany, for the understanding of its traumatic history.[63] Hungarian, Polish, Czech, Romanian, Slovenian, Croatian and even Lithuanian intellectuals began a lively exchange with their Austrian and German counterparts about the concept of *Mitteleuropa*.[64] In eastern and south-eastern Europe, by contrast, the decline of communism as an integrative ideology led to the revival of nationalism. Estonians, Latvians, Lithuanians, Georgians, Azeris, Armenians, central Asians and even the Ukrainians began to stir. At the same time, *Glasnost* let the Russian nationalist genie out of the bottle.[65] Balkan communist regimes even co-opted nationalism as a new legitimating ideology. In Romania,

Nicolae Ceauşescu sought confrontation with the substantial Hungarian minority, whose Transylvanian and Banat villages were singled out for particular attention in the campaign of rural 'systemization'. In Bulgaria, the regime turned on the local Turkish population in late 1984 and forced them to change their names, restricted their use of the Turkish language, and closed down mosques, all in the name of stamping out an alleged 'fifth column' of 'terrorists' and 'separatists'. In Yugoslavia, the Serb leader, Slobodan Milošević, rose to power through the articulation of a Serb nationalist agenda.

It soon became clear that the first phase of *Perestroika* had largely failed to meet its objectives at home and abroad. The economic reforms were not radical enough to increase productivity. Thanks to the success of *Glasnost*, moreover, these failures could no longer be concealed and were widely discussed. Hopes that the Warsaw Pact allies, especially Honecker, would embrace *Perestroika* were disappointed. On the international front, Gorbachev struck up a good working relationship with France's President François Mitterrand and Thatcher, who had already proclaimed him a man she could do business with. Crucially, however, he made little headway with his main quarry, Chancellor Kohl, who initially dismissed the Soviet leader as a propagandist 'like Goebbels'. Reagan, too, was initially sceptical, not least because of Gorbachev's intensification of the war in Afghanistan. In 1986, Washington authorized the dispatch of sophisticated 'Stinger' hand-held anti-aircraft missiles to the Mujahedin. Moreover, Reagan steadfastly refused to shelve the dreaded SDI as a precondition for an arms limitation agreement. The Soviet leader was forced to acknowledge that he was losing the arms race. Worse still, West Germany had yet to realize its full military capability. In October 1986, Gorbachev warned the Politburo that the Soviet Union 'will be pulled into an arms race that is beyond our capabilities, and we will lose it, because we are at the limit of our capabilities. Moreover, we can expect that Japan and the FRG [Federal Republic of Germany] could very soon join the American potential ... If a new round begins, the pressure on our economy will be unbelievable.'[66]

Gorbachev now embarked on still more radical domestic reforms and diplomatic initiatives. He began to speak of the need for a thoroughgoing democratization of the Communist Party and the Soviet Union. 'We need democracy as we need air,' he repeatedly stated.[67] Gorbachev was not at this stage planning a democracy in the western sense:

his plan was to return to Bolshevik first principles by revitalizing the Soviets and injecting electoral mechanisms into the Communist Party.[68] All the same, Gorbachev was widening domestic political participation to save the state from continued stagnation and make it stronger on the international scene. In foreign policy, Gorbachev – desperate to reach agreement before he was swamped by a new generation of NATO weaponry – dropped his insistence that Reagan should abandon SDI. Rapid agreement was reached with the United States at the Washington Summit in early December 1987 on the abolition of all intermediate-range nuclear weapons in Europe (INF Treaty). Gorbachev also resolved to withdraw from Afghanistan, a decision already taken in principle but announced publicly early the following year.[69] None of this, however, solved the real problem, which was the progressive collapse of the Soviet position in eastern Europe, most obviously in Poland, but most dangerously in East Germany. From 1987, Soviet experts were predicting the imminent collapse of their ally.

It was not just in Moscow, however, that the re-emergence of the German Question was causing concern. Having grown up in the shadow of the Second World War, Margaret Thatcher shared the concerns of many of her compatriots about Germany in general, and the growth of the Federal Republic in particular. She was not reassured by the revival of the Paris–Bonn axis under Kohl and Mitterrand, and their creation of a joint 'Eurocorps'. This anxiety fused in her mind with hostility to the increasingly activist – and in her view *dirigiste* – president of the European Commission, Jacques Delors.[70] British ministers began to refer to Britain's 'island status' and the Shakespearian 'moat' of the Channel in ways not seen for decades.[71] Thatcher feared the loss of British sovereignty and the prospect of German domination either directly or by European proxy. By the end of the decade, therefore, Thatcher had come to see the Soviet Union as the guarantor of the European balance. 'We do not want a united Germany,' she told Gorbachev. 'This would lead to a change to post-war borders, and we cannot allow that because such a development would undermine the whole international situation and endanger our security.'[72]

In Bonn, the relaxation of tensions with the Soviet Union caused new stresses within the NATO alliance. The West Germans were offended by Reagan's failure to consult on the INF Treaty, and concerned that the abolition of intermediate-range weapons would lead to greater emphasis on the remaining short-range theatre missiles, such as Lance. The old spectre of 'decoupling' returned. This was an issue around which left-wingers and the right wing alike could rally. 'The shorter the range,' the national conservative stalwart Alfred Dregger memorably remarked, 'the deader the German.' It seemed as if Germany could not escape the implications of the *Mittellage*. More generally, the growth of 'Gorbymania' among the public made the militarization of West German society increasingly difficult to sustain. The population began to grumble more and more about low-flying NATO aircraft on exercise, the treatment of locals during military manoeuvres, and the conversion of huge swathes of the North German Plain into tank training grounds. The very success of the organization in keeping the Warsaw Pact and communist dictatorship at bay seemed to have rendered it redundant.

The summer of 1988 saw the start of series of interlocking domestic and geopolitical transformations which would completely transform the European territorial and ideological landscape.[73] As the Soviet withdrawal from Afghanistan began, jihadists debated their next move. In August 1988, the most influential international fighters came together to form what would later be called 'al-Qaeda' ('the base'), which was dedicated to resurrecting the caliphate and fighting the Zionist-American alliance.[74] Some members, such as Abdullah Azzam, argued that the time had now come to take the fight to Israel herself, using Afghanistan as a 'solid base' for jihadist operations.[75] The dominant faction, led by Ayman al-Zawahiri, insisted on the need to consolidate their position in Afghanistan. Rather than confronting the Jews directly, al-Qaeda decided to help the various Mujahedin factions to subdue the Afghan communist Najibullah regime in order to create a 'base' from which to assault America's Middle Eastern allies, and ultimately the 'far enemy', the United States itself.[76] In Palestine, growing signs that the PLO was planning some sort of accommodation with Israel led to the creation of Hamas, an offshoot of the Muslim Brotherhood. Its charter – published in mid-August 1988 – fused traditional Islamic Judaeophobia, Palestinian irredentism and modern European-style anti-semitism. 'Our struggle against the Jews [sic],' the introduction announced, 'is very great and very serious.' Specifically drawing on the 'Protocol of the Elders of Zion', Hamas claimed that the Jews were behind the French Revolution, the Russian Revolution, the Balfour Declaration, the destruction of the caliphate after the First World War, the creation of the League of Nations, 'through which they could rule the world', and the Second World War. 'There is no war going on anywhere,' the charter suggested, 'without their having a finger in it.'

For the moment, however, all eyes were on Gorbachev. The Soviet leader knew that he could simply no longer afford to sustain the required global military posture. It would have to be reduced, especially in central and eastern Europe, which was the greatest single item of expenditure. The punitive cost of keeping up with Reagan's armament programmes forced Moscow to start releasing its grip. In December 1988, therefore, Gorbachev announced that the Soviet Union would unilaterally cut its forces by half a million men, mostly in eastern Europe, and withdraw all short-range nuclear missiles. Gorbachev also hinted publicly that he would allow the Warsaw Pact countries to go their own way. The Brezhnev Doctrine was dead. That same month, Gorbachev embarked on a programme of still more radical reforms to mobilize the population in support of *Perestroika*, by establishing a Congress of People's Deputies, two thirds of which was to be elected by secret ballot. Independent candidates could stand provided that their platform did not 'contradict the constitution or the laws of the Soviet Union', but this stipulation proved unenforceable in practice.[77] In Poland, renewed unrest forced the government to agree to 'round-table' talks with Solidarity, and consent to free elections not long after.

The ideological and geopolitical vacuum which now opened up in central and eastern Europe was quickly filled by a democratic revolution which rippled across the Warsaw Pact in the course of 1989. In late March 1989, the elections to the Soviet Congress of People's Deputies brought in a raft of radical representatives determined to carry on the work of *Perestroika*. Nationalists swept the board in the Baltic, where henceforth even local communist leaders found themselves locked into a confrontational stance with Moscow. At around the same time, the Hungarian communists agreed to elections. In June 1989, Solidarity utterly destroyed the party at the polls, leading to negotiations about the handover of power in Poland. That same month, alarmed by the growth of democratic activism at home and the global retreat of communism, the Chinese government launched a brutal crackdown on protestors in Tiananmen Square. In East Germany, Czechoslovakia, Romania and Bulgaria, party leaders were unsure whether the new wind from Moscow represented a permanent shift in policy or just a temporary 'deviation' – of which they had seen many in the past. Honecker announced that the Berlin Wall would remain for another fifty and even one hundred years. Ceauşescu, who was in any case a law unto himself, also battened down the hatches. The question now was: with the Red Army no longer at their disposal, and Poland effectively 'lost', would the eastern European leaderships give way or attempt a 'Chinese' solution?

In late June 1989, the Hungarian authorities brought matters to a head by opening their border with Austria. Because Warsaw Pact citizens could travel to Hungary freely on holiday, thousands of East German tourists used the opportunity to flee to the west. Thousands of others sought sanctuary in the West German embassy in Prague. When the Honecker regime allowed them to emigrate via the GDR, thousands of desperate men and women attempted to board the trains as they headed westwards. In October 1989, huge crowds took to the streets of Leipzig, East Berlin and other cities to demand reforms. A last-minute reshuffle of the East German party leadership, replacing Honecker by Egon Krenz, did not appease the protestors. In early November, the regime opened the Wall to scenes of mass jubilation, and soon entered into dialogue with the opposition.[78] Hundreds of thousands of East Germans emigrated to West Germany. Shortly afterwards, the communist governments in Czechoslovakia and Bulgaria also threw in the towel, and right at the end of the year Ceauşescu was lynched in a palace revolt which ultimately led to the collapse of dictatorship in Romania as well. The logic of the Jackson–Vanik Amendment had worked its way through the Soviet Empire. Once the principle of free emigration had finally been conceded, the system unravelled of its own accord. Brzezinski had been vindicated too: the Soviet commitment to Afghanistan had weakened her hold on the Warsaw Pact states. 'It was not so much thinkers in the corridors of the Kremlin,' the Russian democratic activist and strategic analyst Andrei Piontkovsky wrote, 'as the Mujahedin in the hills of Afghanistan who were the real liberators of Eastern Europe.'[79]

Now the democratic-nationalist virus began to mutate through the communist body politic. In March 1990, the conservative Christian Democrats won a handsome victory in the East German elections, effectively ending any chance that the GDR could survive as an independent state. There were huge demonstrations in favour of German unity: 'We are one people,' the crowds chanted. At around the same time, the Lithuanians made a unilateral declaration of independence, followed not long after by Latvia and Estonia. Soviet military intervention put an abrupt end to these aspirations, but only briefly. The Red Army was already in the grips of a profound ideological crisis of identity which rendered it an extremely uncertain instrument for the maintenance of Soviet power at home and abroad.[80] In June of that year, the Soviet Communist Party was disestablished as the official party of government. A month later, key radicals such as Boris Yeltsin and Anatoly Sobchak resigned from the organization. By mid-July 1990, both the Ukraine and Russia itself had declared their sovereignty, putting the whole Union in doubt. Meanwhile, the Communist Party in Yugoslavia had split into its constituent parts in 1990, and the first free elections brought nationalists to power in Slovenia and Croatia in April, while in Serbia Slobodan Milošević rode the nationalist ticket to victory at the polls in December 1990. Only in Bosnia and Macedonia were there substantial elements committed to keeping some sort of federation intact.

The democratic revolution of 1989–90 precipitated a crisis in the European state system. Right at the top of the agenda was Germany.[81] Chancellor Kohl seized the initiative in late November 1989, with the announcement of a 'ten point' programme for 'Overcoming the division of Europe and the division of Germany'. He envisaged a confederation of the two German states 'with the aim of creating a federation', and in due course a unified Germany. This was to be 'embedded' in the east–west dialogue and the process of European integration. 'The EC,' Kohl argued, 'must not end at the Elbe; rather it must also maintain openness towards the east' in order to 'serve as the foundation for a truly comprehensive European unification'. Kohl's urgency was dictated by two factors. First of all, the wave of refugees from East Germany needed to be addressed: there was a real danger that all Germans would be reunited on the soil of the Federal Republic. Secondly, the chancellor was acutely conscious of Gorbachev's precarious domestic position and the fact that his changes might be reversed any minute, just as those of earlier reformers had been. He therefore sought to take advantage of what might only be a very small window of opportunity.

The collapse of the GDR and Kohl's initiative provoked consternation across the capitals of Europe. A day after the Wall came down, Gorbachev warned George Bush that the 'emotiona[al]' statements coming from West Germany represented an 'implacable rejection of the post-war realities, that is the existence of two German states', threatening a 'destabilization ... not only in Central Europe, but on a larger scale'.[82] The British and French governments were also firmly opposed to German unification, which they believed would upset the European balance of power. So were the new democratic governments of Poland and Czechoslovakia, who were anxious about German demands for border revision and the return of refugees. Over the next months or so, these powers searched for ways to prevent, or at least slow, the unification of East and West Germany. Gorbachev repeatedly stated that he would not accept it. The French president even made a separate trip to the GDR in order to strengthen the government of Hans Modrow in its resistance to rapid absorption into the Federal Republic. The Poles tried to insist on being consulted on any solution. Perhaps the most sustained opposition, however, came from Margaret Thatcher, who believed that Germany 'would, once again, dominate the whole of Europe'.[83] She summoned a special conference of experts to the prime minister's country residence of Chequers to brief her on whether a united Germany could be 'trusted'.

The American attitude proved decisive.[84] Washington came down early and clearly in favour of German unification in the hope of establishing a good working relationship with the new state. The main concern of the US administration after the barriers were lifted, in fact, was to ensure that unity did not shatter the cohesion of the Atlantic alliance, and thus enable a major Soviet aim to be realized by the back door. For this reason the State Department indicated in mid-November that 'the United States should support German self-determination without endorsing a specific outcome', stipulating only that 'unification should be peaceful and gradual', that it should respect all other existing boundaries, and should be 'consistent with German membership of NATO and the European Community'.[85]

In late May 1990, the Soviet leader finally gave way on German unity. Moscow remained desperate, however, to 'solve' the German Question, and lock the new giant into a constraining European framework. For the Kremlin, 'Europe' and the German Question were one and the same; 'they cannot be divorced from each other,' Gorbachev emphasized to Bush.[86] Private assurances were given that NATO would not expand any further eastwards.[87] France also rolled over, and so eventually did Thatcher. The Federal Republic and the GDR proclaimed a currency union in early July. That same month Kohl and Gorbachev sorted out the details of unification, not least substantial West German financial aid for the ailing Soviet economy, at the famous Caucasus Summit. The Oder–Neisse boundary with Poland was explicitly recognized after some hesitation caused by Kohl's electoral courtship of the expellees. In early October 1990, Germany was united, remaining a NATO member. A month later, the Soviet Union, the United States and the European powers agreed the Conventional Forces Europe Treaty (CFE), within the CSCE framework. This hugely reduced the number of American and Soviet forces deployed in Europe. All Russian troops were to be out of Germany by 1994.[88] After more than forty years of partition, the European centre had been reconstituted and pacified.

German reunification, the reorganization of central and eastern Europe, and the consequent surge in European integration had a profound impact on domestic politics across the continent. Margaret Thatcher was already under fire for her unpopular domestic policies – especially the poll tax – but what turned the Conservative Party establishment against her was her policy on Europe, and especially her steadfast refusal to join the European Exchange Rate Mechanism (ERM). The Foreign Secretary, Geoffrey Howe, a strong supporter of the Community, resigned amid great controversy on 1 November, and Thatcher herself was replaced a few weeks later by John Major. Gorbachev also came under attack on foreign policy, in his case for permitting the unification of Germany and the loss of the Soviet Empire in Europe.[89] Yegor Ligachev, influential Second Secretary of the Soviet Communist Party, warned the Politburo of 'a new Munich'.[90] In the August following unification, a group of disgruntled hawks attempted to depose Gorbachev, as the first step in a programme for the reassertion of Soviet power; they were frustrated by the prompt intervention of Boris Yeltsin, chairman in the Praesidium of the Supreme Soviet and a leading reformer, and the unwillingness of the army to risk a civil war. The principal beneficiary of German unity, of course, was Chancellor Kohl, who coasted to a third successive election victory in early December 1990.

The years 1989–90 marked an obvious watershed in European geopolitics. The costs of German unification had a profound impact on the European Exchange Rate Mechanism,[91] by which most currencies in the Community were supposed to fluctuate only within predetermined 'bands', in order to achieve the harmonization necessary for subsequent Monetary

Union. After some hesitation, Britain finally joined the ERM in October 1990 at the time of German unification. The problem was that German interest rates were high in order to balance the huge inflationary threat from the massive costs of reunification. This put pressure on other European economies, especially the British one, which was forced to intervene to support the pound against the German mark, at huge cost to the Treasury at a time when a lower rate was desperately necessary for exports as the country slipped into recession. Within two years, in fact, the British had been forced to withdraw from the ERM in a humiliating manner after a brutal run on the pound during 'Black Wednesday'. Anglo-German relations plummeted as the two capitals engaged in a 'blame game'; London felt that strong hints in mid-September 1992 from the *Bundesbank*'s powerful president, Helmut Schlesinger, that the pound was overvalued had unleashed the speculators.[92] To some it was an omen of how the European framework designed to dilute and constrain German power actually increased it.

Otherwise, however, the new Germany showed few signs of domestic radicalization, strategic adventurism or constructive leadership in Europe.[93] There was a brief eruption of popular xenophobia against immigrants after unification which soon petered out. Extreme right-wing parties fared no better at the polls in the united Germany than they had beforehand; there was no surge in anti-semitism.[94] German democracy proved resilient.[95] Moreover, the sheer economic cost of unification – which proved to be much higher than forecast – absorbed much of the country's attention during the early 1990s.[96] German politicians showed no interest in acquiring nuclear weapons, and the political culture of the Federal Republic was notably averse to foreign policy activism and military engagement. It saw itself essentially as a 'civilian power'. At the same time, the sincere commitment of the elite to working through the multilateral structures of the NATO alliance and the European Union remained unchanged. The claim to membership of the Security Council, which Washington, London and Paris supported as a way of involving the new power more closely in the management of global problems, was not advanced with any vigour after it was blocked by the Italians.[97] The whole country, as one historian put it, was 'afraid of power', and indeed of military conflict.[98] 'War – that is something we leave to the Americans' was the prevailing view for most of the decade to come.[99]

*

In early August 1990, Saddam Hussein invaded Kuwait and announced the annexation of the Emirate. Worse still, from the western point of view, Saddam appeared on the verge of pushing further south into Saudi Arabia, a move which would put him in control of a huge proportion of world oil supplies. The Saudi royal family, rejecting offers of assistance from Osama bin Laden and other returning veterans of the Afghan jihad, turned to the Americans for help. At around the same time, Yugoslavia fell apart. In the summer and autumn of 1990, Serb paramilitaries backed by Belgrade clashed with Croatian police. In June of the following year, Slovenia and Croatia declared independence, leading to a war between the Yugoslav People's Army and Slovene territorial forces. In the late summer and autumn of 1991, hundreds of thousands of Croats were expelled from their homes by the People's Army and Serb paramilitaries. In April 1992, however, Serb militias and the People's Army began their assault on Bosniak Muslim and Croat communities in eastern Bosnia, soon extending their reach throughout the republic. By the autumn, they had killed tens of thousands of Muslims and Croats, expelled hundreds of thousands, surrounded the capital, Sarajevo, and controlled more than half the territory of Bosnia-Herzegovina.[100] The most spectacular development, however, was the disintegration of the Soviet Union itself. Gorbachev's authority never recovered from the coup attempt and he found himself increasingly outmanoeuvred by a Boris Yeltsin determined to rule an independent Russia.[101] In early December 1991, the people of Ukraine voted for independence in a referendum. A week later, the heads of the constituent republics agreed to dissolve the Soviet Union. Russia, Belarus, Ukraine, Lithuania, Latvia, Estonia, the central Asian republics and the Caucasian republics all became sovereign states. Faced with a *fait accompli*, Gorbachev resigned at the end of the month.

The debate on how these three crises should be handled dominated European geopolitics in the new decade. After some hesitation, President Bush resolved that Saddam Hussein should be forced to withdraw from Kuwait. Thanks to Gorbachev's support, the United Nations Security Council issued an ultimatum to Iraq to withdraw by the middle of January 1991, or face ejection by 'all necessary means'. France and Britain sent substantial contingents; the Turks provided bases. Germany refused to send troops, citing constitutional difficulties.[102] After a short air campaign, and a lightning ground war, Saddam Hussein was totally defeated by the coalition in operation 'Desert Storm'.[103] There was no such consensus on how to fill the vacuum in central and eastern Europe left by the departure of the Russians.[104] To many Europeans, the end of the Cold War was an opportunity to break with the old alliance system and move to a new collaborative relationship with the Soviet Union – and then with its Russian successor. They also hoped that an increasingly integrated Europe would be able to take on many of the functions of the old Atlantic alliance and thus gradually emancipate itself from American tutelage.

Most members of the European Community were therefore initially opposed to the eastward expansion of NATO. There was a widespread view that the alliance was now 'redundant'. France, in particular, sought to replace the existing US-dominated hierarchy with a 'two-tier' NATO in which all but the gravest threats to western Europe would be dealt with by the Europeans.[105] This effectively relegated the security of the old Soviet Empire to the second tier. London also rejected the extension of the alliance, because the Defence Secretary, Malcolm Rifkind, believed that it could not deliver collective security in eastern Europe. The Germans, by contrast, called for the eastern enlargement of NATO, for the obvious reason that it would secure their own flank and relieve them from the frontline status they had enjoyed since the Second World War. They were also determined that foreign forces, especially American ones, stayed in Germany to guarantee its security and western orientation. The security of central Europe remained inseparable from that of the continent as a whole.

On European integration, the key debate was between those who wanted to respond to the collapse of communism and the unification of Germany by 'widening' the Community, through the admission of new members, and those who wanted to 'deepen' it, by strengthening the bonds between the existing members. The British, who feared being dominated by Germany through Europe and were determined to safeguard their national sovereignty, were ardent 'wideners' in the hope of slowing down further integration.[106] The French, no less anxious to contain the growing power of a united Germany, were staunch 'deepeners', in particular with respect to political and military matters. Mitterrand was opposed to eastwards enlargement of the Community and expressed the view that it would be 'decades and decades' before it happened; he proposed an interim 'European confederation' instead. The

Germans themselves favoured both widening and deepening, partly in the spirit of compromise, partly because their security and prosperity were better guaranteed by a larger and more cohesive 'Europe', and partly because they understood that their own unification would only be accepted as part of a broader process of European integration.[107] Just a month after the fall of the Wall, therefore, the European Council met at Strasbourg in early December 1989 to address the changes in central and eastern Europe, and especially the growth of German power.[108] They agreed to speed up the process of creating a single currency by establishing an intergovernmental conference on European Monetary Union, which began its work at the Dublin Council in late June 1990. In effect, the German Mark was to be sacrificed as the price for ending the partition of Germany.

The continental European powers now pressed ahead with not only economic but also political integration. In October 1991, Paris persuaded Bonn to create a multinational corps 'answerable to the European Union' – the Eurocorps.[109] A few months later, the European Community summit at Maastricht in 1992 established the European Union, at the heart of which was to be the forthcoming currency union and the new Common Foreign and Security Policy. The member states agreed 'to support the Union's external and security policy actively and unreservedly in a spirit of loyalty and mutual solidarity'. Once agreement had been reached member states were pledged 'to ensure that their national policies conform to the common positions'. Decisions were to be taken by qualified majority voting except where one state objected; the requirement for consensus effectively created a *liberum veto*, paralysing 'Europe's' ability to act coherently on the international scene. Many Europeans now hoped that the Community would no longer be what the Belgian foreign minister, Mark Eyskens, had called it during the Gulf War: 'an economic giant, but a political dwarf and a military worm'.[110]

Yugoslavia was the first test.[111] The Luxemburgian foreign minister, Jacques Poos, famously proclaimed it 'The hour of Europe'. A 'troika' of ministers set off to negotiate a ceasefire between Croatia and her Serb assailants. Their efforts and all subsequent initiatives were subverted by the complete lack of consensus among EU member states. Initially, all agreed that it would be best to keep Yugoslavia together in preparation for her eventual incorporation into the Union; some even saw Milošević as a Balkan Lincoln, attempting to stop secession. Once his ambition to create a 'Greater Serbia' had become clear, however, strategies diverged widely. The British government saw no pressing 'national interest' at stake in stopping ethnic cleansing in the Balkans, feared being drawn into an interminable guerrilla war, and generally exhibited a scepticism about the prospects for intervening for ethical rather than pragmatic reasons.[112] France was determined to prevent the extension of German influence southwards, to forestall the creation of a Bonn-dominated *Mitteleuropa*.[113] At the end of 1991, the Germans browbeat the Community into recognition of Slovenia and Croatia, a move which helped to bring the war in Croatia to an end, and had no real bearing on subsequent events in Bosnia,[114] but convinced Paris that Bonn harboured secret ambitions in the region. The Greeks openly sympathized with the Serbs.[115] By the time the Bosnian War exploded in the spring of 1992, therefore, the only thing that all European states agreed on was the need to prevent the conflict from spreading, especially southwards into the former Yugoslav Republic of Macedonia, where the new state was locked in a standoff with Greece which had the potential to draw in regional powers as far away as Turkey.

What gave the common European policy the *coup de grâce* was its complete lack of any collective enforcement capacity. Britain and France, as we have seen, had the military capability, but refused to intervene against Milošević. Germany cited constitutional barriers to intervention out of the NATO area, and also pleaded the 'Kohl Doctrine' by which Germany was forbidden from undertaking military action in any country which had suffered Nazi occupation during the Second World War. Auschwitz became an argument for allowing ethnic cleansing. One way or the other, 'Europe' proved to be completely toothless. As a result of this painful collective military impotence, EU mediators were simply humiliated by Slobodan Milošević and the Serb militias. The baroque town of Vukovar in eastern Slavonia was completely levelled, the architecturally remarkable port city of Dubrovnik was repeatedly shelled in a televised siege. A UN arms embargo, imposed in the autumn of 1991 and initially policed by the Europeans through the WEU, increased the imbalance in favour of the Serbs, who already had access to the weaponry of the Yugoslav People's Army. By the beginning of 1992, the European Union was forced to admit defeat. The United Nations was drafted in to oversee the distribution of humanitarian aid and mediate a settlement. It too failed to make any headway. The war in Bosnia continued to rage unchecked.

Meanwhile, the European Union expanded eastwards. Association agreements with central and eastern European countries were set up in 1991–2, and in 1993 the European Council announced that 'the associated countries' would be welcomed into the Union as soon as they satisfied the political and economic conditions. The former Soviet bloc countries themselves were eager, indeed desperate, to join the European project to end their isolation from the mainstream, and in 1994 the presidents of the Czech Republic, Hungary, Poland, Slovenia and Slovakia all assembled in Prague to make a formal request for membership, with strong German backing. A year later Austria, Sweden and Finland all joined the Union, with the prospect of further accessions in due course. Germany appeared well on the way to surrounding herself with friendly democratic states while simultaneously diluting her national power through ever greater pooling of sovereignty.

The US administration welcomed the expansion of the EU to the former Warsaw Pact states. It was also enthusiastic about the Maastricht Treaty because a stronger Europe would be better placed to assume a larger share of the burden of upholding the new World Order. Bush also agreed with the Europeans that the Soviet Union should be kept together as long as possible. Washington was strongly opposed, however, to any weakening of NATO. It resented the Eurocorps as a dilution of the alliance. The establishment of an EU military planning cell was a further slap in the face, which was compounded by the exclusion of NATO, and thus Washington, from the all-European WEU naval force monitoring the arms embargo on the former Yugoslavia. By the end of 1991, relations with the allies had reached rock bottom.

When the new US president, Bill Clinton, was inaugurated in January 1993, he was confronted by Congressional and popular pressure to reduce spending on European security. This was accompanied by a sense of the growing commercial and strategic importance of Asia, where the 'Tiger Economies' were powering ahead. In particular, Washington was mesmerized by the rise of China, whose spectacular economic expansion and apparent strategic ambitions seemed to threaten not only the regional but the global balance.[116] In fact, however, the new president soon not merely reaffirmed the primacy of Europe in US grand strategy, but made it the centrepiece of a new democratic geopolitics.

The policy of 'democratic enlargement', conceived by his National Security Advisor, Tony Lake, posited that the security of the United States was best served by the spread of western-style democracy. The strategy of democratic enlargement was globally conceived, but its principal application was to be in central and Eastern Europe. To this end, Clinton was favourable to the expansion of the European Union, which he described in January 1994 as essential to 'lock in democratic and market' reforms in the former Soviet bloc. He was determined, moreover, to complement this with the enlargement of NATO, which, as he told an alliance summit at the beginning of 1994, 'would reach to democratic states to our east as part of an evolutionary process'. The first step was the 'Partnership for Peace' programme, where the emphasis was not just on military cooperation but also on the democratic reforms, economic liberalization and respect for the rights of minorities necessary to avert another European war. 'If democracy in the east fails,' Clinton warned, 'then violence and disruption from the east will once again harm us and other democracies.'[117]

Russia, too, was wrestling with the question of how the vacuum on her western flank should be filled. Under the influence of Gennady Burbulis, Yeltsin's principal adviser on foreign policy, Russia toyed with the idea of joining the EU and even NATO in 1991–2. The dire economic situation and low price of oil also reduced her effectiveness on the world stage; some spoke of a 'Weimar on the Volga'.[118] By the mid-1990s, however, the feeling that the west was taking advantage of Russian weakness, and a general sense of imperial loss over the collapse of the Soviet Union, was making itself felt in the Kremlin and among the national security establishment. As far they were concerned, they were being pushed out of the Common European Home which Gorbachev had envisaged.[119] In particular, Moscow was bitterly opposed to the expansion of NATO.[120] To lose control of eastern Europe was one thing, but to see a potentially hostile alliance established there was quite another. Yeltsin himself had initially accepted the enlargement of NATO, at least into Poland, but soon reversed course. 'Those who insist on an expansion of NATO are making a major political mistake,' he cautioned, 'The flames of war could burst out across the whole of Europe.'[121] Yeltsin therefore embarked on a more activist foreign policy. In Bosnia, Russia became increasingly assertive on behalf of the Serbs, not so much out of any intrinsic sympathy with their cause, but in order to underline Moscow's right to be consulted. At the same time, Moscow became more involved in what it called its 'near' or 'inner' abroad. In December 1995, Yeltsin finally decided to reassert Russian authority in Chechnya. The operation was a complete fiasco which soon mired the Russian army in a bitter guerrilla war.[122]

Meanwhile, Clinton's strategy of democratic enlargement was foundering on the shoals of Bosnia, where first the European Union and then the UN had proved powerless to stop the creation of an ethnically pure 'Greater Serbia'. 'Bold tyrants and fearful minorities,' the US Secretary of State, Warren Christopher, warned in February 1993, 'are watching to see whether "ethnic cleansing" is a policy the world will tolerate.'[123] At an ill-tempered meeting of the Conference on Security and Cooperation in Europe in Budapest in December 1994, Václav Havel reminded his audience that 'Europeans continue to suffer and die in the former Yugoslavia, and with them is dying the hope that Europe will be able to bring these horrors to an end.'[124] Yet NATO, which was drawn in to provide air support to the humanitarian mission, found itself hamstrung by micro-management from UN headquarters in New York, and the British and French governments concerned for the safety of their troops and aid workers on the ground. 'I am the head of the most powerful military organization in world history,' the NATO Secretary General, Manfred Wörner, lamented, 'and I can do nothing.'

So from 1993 onwards, Washington began to press for military intervention by NATO in support of the Bosnian government. Britain and France, however, resisted American initiatives on the grounds that they constituted unwarranted interference in a civil war, were unlikely to work militarily and would merely lead to an escalation in the fighting. In the spring of 1993, they frustrated a mission by Warren Christopher to persuade the Europeans to pursue a policy of lifting the arms embargo on the Bosnian government and NATO air strikes on the Bosnian Serb army – 'lift and strike'. Meanwhile, the ethnic cleansing continued, culminating in the Srebrenica massacre of July 1995, when thousands of Muslim men and boys were murdered under the nose of the UN in the eastern enclave of Srebrenica. The Clinton administration now decided to strong-arm the Europeans, over Bosnia and NATO more generally. US diplomats mediated an end to the war between the Sarajevo government and Bosnian Croat separatists; covert military support was sent to the Bosnian Muslims while the regular Croat forces of President Franjo

Tudjman were trained by retired US army personnel. In December 1994, Washington finally forced NATO foreign ministers to begin planning the eastward enlargement. From now on, the question was not 'whether' the states of the old Soviet bloc would be admitted, but 'when' the process would begin.[125] In September–October 1995, NATO retaliated against Serb shelling of Sarajevo with a massive air campaign. The Bosnian army and Croatian regulars surged forward. Within weeks, their defences crumbling, President Milošević had forced the Bosnian Serbs to accept a ceasefire and compromise peace at Dayton. NATO had fought, and won, its first European war 'not' under American leadership.

Most European societies, eager to cash in on the 'peace dividend' and unwilling to take on additional defence burdens, scarcely registered these events. To be sure, there were mass demonstrations against the use of force to eject Saddam Hussein from Kuwait, particularly in Germany, and smaller protests against the killing in Bosnia. It is also true that the Conservative administration of John Major in London was under constant attack from 'Eurosceptics' within his own Conservative Party determined to defend British sovereignty against 'Brussels' and 'German domination' by stealth. This culminated in a leadership challenge in the summer of 1995 which he only survived with his authority badly damaged.[126] Yet the international upheavals of 1991–5 did not affect the 1994 federal election in Germany, Chancellor Kohl's fourth and final victory. Nor did they have much impact on John Major's unexpected triumph in April 1992, or his defeat by the Labour Party candidate, Tony Blair, five years later.[127] Other factors were dominant in both cases, usually the stewardship of the economy or more general questions of probity and competence. The primacy of foreign policy, which had so long determined European domestic politics, was no more. On the other side of the Atlantic, foreign policy also lost its domestic importance. George Bush proved unable to capitalize on his victory over Saddam Hussein in the US election campaign of 1992. 'It's about the economy, stupid,' Clinton famously remarked. The position of their country in the world did not much concern American voters in the 1990s, despite or perhaps because of the fact that the United States was the undisputed global hegemon.

In Russia, on the other hand, the impact of foreign policy on domestic politics in the early and mid-1990s was immense. The vast majority of Russian citizens regarded the break-up of the Soviet Union as a blow to their standing in the world. Western intervention in Yugoslavia, the prospect of NATO expansion and a general sense of national humiliation powered a bitter popular and elite critique of the Kremlin. The foreign minister, Andrei Kozyrev, the 'Mr Yes' who had pursued a pro-western policy after the failed coup of August 1991, was a particular target. Elite and educated circles experienced a revival of Eurasianism and Panslavism; a small number of volunteers set off to fight for the Bosnian Serbs. In the December 1993 parliamentary elections, nationalist parties and communists swept the board, capitalizing on widespread discontent not only with Yeltsin's economic performance but also with the retreat of Russian power. The need to play a greater role on the world stage and the desire for a return of 'strong government' are, in Russia, an aspiration known as *derzhavnost*. When the parliament under Ruslan Khasbulatov defied Yeltsin in late September and early October 1993, the president sent in the tanks. Two months later, Yeltsin pushed through a new constitution which strengthened his executive powers. By the mid-1990s, the westernizing rhetoric of the first part of the decade, in which the regions had been told to seize as much sovereignty as they could 'digest', had been replaced by an emphasis on an indivisible 'Great Russia'. It was thus no surprise that Yeltsin won re-election in 1996.

In western Europe, the strategic legacy of the Bosnian War was immense. Despite the hopes that the Yugoslav crisis would prove to be the 'Hour of Europe', the EU and the European states collectively had manifestly failed to diagnose the problem, let alone master it.[128] So had the United Nations, which lost much of its credibility among western and Muslim states. By contrast, the United States, which had initially hoped to scale down its military commitment to Europe after the Cold War, was confirmed as the dominant power on the continent. The new US Secretary of State, Madeleine Albright – a fervent interventionist who as Clinton's representative at the UN had repeatedly clashed with the British and French over Bosnia – even spoke of America as 'the indispensable nation'. In the end, however, Washington had persuaded as much it had compelled. The concept of 'humanitarian intervention' now gained wide acceptance on both sides of the Atlantic, not just in order to relieve the suffering of the population, but also to defend the values on which western security ultimately depended. The strict division between the national interest and humanitarian concerns, which realists had insisted on over Bosnia, was no longer sustainable. 'Realism', in other words, was not enough; it was not even realistic.

The new US National Security Strategy promulgated in February 1995 reflected these concerns. Based on the assumption that 'democratic states are less likely to threaten our interests and more likely to cooperate with the United States', President Clinton promised to address the shifting threats to the ideals and habits of democracy, through the 'enlargement of the community of market democracies', 'especially in areas of greatest strategic interest, as in the former Soviet Union' and communist bloc.[129] Clinton also undertook to support the growth of participatory government in the Far East – where the administration specifically rejected the idea that 'democracy is somehow unsuited for Asia' – Africa and Latin America. The only exception to this strategy of democratic enlargement was the Middle East. Here the document referred only to the 'dual containment' of Iran and Iraq, supporting the 'peace process', 'assuring the security of Israel and our Arab friends, and maintaining the free flow of oil at reasonable prices'. There was no reference to the promotion of democracy, which policy-makers feared would simply unleash a tsunami of popular anti-western and anti-Israeli aggression.

Within the European Union, Bosnia led to crucial strategic shifts in Britain and Germany. The new British prime minister, Tony Blair, had attacked the Major government's failure in Yugoslavia during the 1997 election campaign, stressed the link between morality and foreign policy and reaffirmed the idea of British exceptionalism. 'Century upon century, it has been the destiny of Britain to lead other nations,' he announced in his famous Bridgwater House Speech in Manchester. Blair argued that 'Europe is today the only route through which Britain can exercise power and influence. If it is to maintain its historic role as a global player, Britain has to be a central part of the politics of Europe.'[130] It soon became clear, however, that Britain's ability to play a leading role in Europe would be hampered by its unwillingness to subscribe to the planned single currency. In October 1997, the new government announced that any decision to join the euro was dependent on the outcome of five economic 'tests' set by the Chancellor of the Exchequer, Gordon Brown, to determine the long-term compatibility between the British economy and those of the projected eurozone. This put a particular premium on military integration as the principal vehicle of British influence in Europe. The stage was set for a radical increase in British activism in Europe and around the world.

An even more spectacular transformation took place in Germany. After an early activist stance over Croatia, Bonn had been shamed into near silence on Bosnia on account of her inability, or unwillingness, to participate in military measures herself. As the war continued, and the civilian casualties mounted, German popular and elite opinion became increasingly reconciled to the idea of putting the country's own forces in harm's way for humanitarian purposes. The government itself was anxious to become more involved in order to reduce the growing instability on its southern flank, restore the credibility of the Atlantic alliance and underline Germany's claim to a permanent seat on the UN Security Council. In 1994, the question of military action could no longer be avoided, when NATO required the cooperation of German crews on the AWACS early-warning aircraft supporting the maintenance of the Bosnian no-fly zone. In a piece of political schizophrenia which underlined the explosive nature of the issue, Kohl's FDP coalition partner agreed to the deployment but then took the government – that is, itself – to the Federal Constitutional Court to test the legality of the measure. This ruled the decision constitutional, and a year later German aircraft participated in the NATO aerial armada which helped to bring the war to an end. In the subsequent parliamentary debate, intervention was strongly opposed by the Greens and Social Democrats, but supported by a number of influential voices within those parties. One of those was the Green Joschka Fischer, who entered government as foreign minister after the election victory of the Red–Green coalition in 1998. The Bosnian War, in other words, began the re-militarization of German foreign policy.

Once Bosnia had been settled, NATO enlargement proceeded apace, with strong support from the United States, Britain and Germany. In September 1995, two days after the outline of a post-war settlement had been agreed, NATO published its study on enlargement. The emphasis was on increasing security across the Euro-Atlantic area through the promotion and protection of democracy. The spread of representative government to the east would help to protect it in the west. All candidate countries therefore had to demonstrate that they had a functioning democratic political system based on a market economy; that they treated minorities fairly; were committed to the peaceful resolution of conflicts;

and were able to make a military contribution to NATO operations, out of area if necessary. In early July 1997, the Madrid Summit of NATO invited Poland, the Czech Republic and Hungary to begin accession talks; their admission was scheduled to take place before the end of the decade.

The great beneficiary of all this was the enlarged Federal Republic, with its new capital in Berlin from 1994. 'For the first time in its existence,' Hans-Friedrich von Ploetz, the State Secretary at the foreign office, pointed out in November 1997, 'Germany is surrounded by allies, not enemies , who don't see us as a threat any more.' This did not, as yet, lead to strategic complacency in Berlin, on the contrary. Invoking the old German maxim that 'Politics is the daughter of history and history is the daughter of geography', Ploetz argued that Germans needed further European integration in order to embed their security in an 'irreversible peace order' on the continent.[131] 'Germany,' Federal President Roman Herzog warned, 'belongs to the concert of the great democracies whether it likes it or not, and if one of these democracies stands aside she inevitably damages not only the others, but in the last analysis herself as well . . . We see ever more clearly that risk-averse inaction can in the long run be more risky than potentially risky action. If we do not confront risks locally, they will come to us.'[132]

The collective failure of the EU in the former Yugoslavia, and to a lesser extent related anxieties over US power, also led to a major leap in European integration. Humiliated by the need for American intervention in 1995, and determined never to be found wanting on their own continent again, European leaders made strenuous efforts to give themselves the necessary political cohesion and military muscle. They no longer feared either the Germans or the Russians, or any other outside enemy. There was no coherent 'other' to rally against. Instead, European leaders feared the past: the capacity of the continent to tear itself apart with the revival of old demons. Bosnia was a prime example – and European leaders were determined never to let it happen again.[133] To do this, they had to address the 'capability–expectations gap': the fact that Europeans wanted to be able to sort out problems on their doorstep but lacked the means to do so.[134] For this reason, the Treaty of Amsterdam in 1997 sought to address the central weaknesses of the Union: the problem of unanimity in the Council of Ministers and the lack of continuity resulting from the rotating presidency. A new High Representative for the Common Foreign and Security Policy was created. It was decided to open membership negotiations with Poland, the Czech Republic, Hungary, Slovenia, Estonia and Cyprus. 'Enlargement,' the EU presidency announced, 'will add to Europe's weight in the world, will provide the Union with new neighbours and make Europe a peaceful, more united and stable area.'[135] In June 1998, the European Central Bank was established under the presidency of the Dutchman Wim Duisenberg.

In the Muslim world, the slaughter of their co-religionists in Bosnia contributed substantially to the emergence of a common consciousness on foreign policy.[136] According to this global discourse, Muslims were now on the defensive across the world: in Palestine, Bosnia, Kashmir, Chechnya and elsewhere. A large number of Arab, Turkish, Caucasian, central Asian and other Mujahedin – in search of a new jihad after Afghanistan – went to Bosnia to fight. It was among European Muslims, however, that the Bosnian experience resonated most forcefully.[137] 'It doesn't really matter whether we perish or survive,' the Grand Mufti of Bosnia-Herzegovina remarked in May 1994, 'the lesson will always be there. And it is a simple one: that the Muslim community must always be vigilant and must always take their destiny in their own hands. They must never rely on anyone or anybody to solve their problems or come to their rescue.'[138] This 'Zionist' message echoed across the immigrant communities in western Europe, especially Britain. 'Bosnia Today – Brick Lane tomorrow' warned the banners in one East London demonstration.[139] Some of the most prominent subsequent British jihadists – such as Omar Sheikh, who masterminded the kidnapping and murder of the journalist Daniel Pearl, and the Guantanamo detainee Moazzam Begg – were radicalized by Bosnia. In other words, the new Muslim geopolitics of the mid-1990s was a reaction not to western meddling but to non-intervention in the face of genocide and ethnic cleansing.

At the same time, global Islamism was undergoing a strategic transformation. Most foreign fighters left Afghanistan shortly after the Russians pulled out: Osama bin Laden returned to Saudi Arabia, others went to Egypt, North Africa or Bosnia in search of greener pastures. In 1994, a group of Afghan religious students (*Talebs*) founded the Taliban, which was dedicated to eliminating the warlords tearing their country apart. Two years later, thanks to extensive support from Pakistan, which sought 'strategic depth' in Afghanistan against India, they swept into Kabul. Osama bin Laden now moved back to Afghanistan in order to support the Taliban's campaign to subdue the rest of the country, and then to use it as a base from which to launch a devastating offensive on the United States, the Jews and their allies. In late August 1996, he issued a 'Declaration of Jihad against the Americans occupying the land of the two Holy Sanctuaries' from the mountains of the Hindu Kush.[140]

The result of all this was a new geo-religious faultline across Europe and the Middle East to central and south Asia. It did not pass, as one might have thought, through the Balkans. To be sure, local Bosnian and Albanian Muslims were determined to protect themselves, but they saw the United States and NATO as their ultimate guarantors. They were also highly resistant to religious radicalism, especially the kind of Wahabism which the Saudis tried to introduce by banning pork and alcohol and by rebuilding destroyed baroque and Renaissance mosques in Middle Eastern style. Al-Qaeda therefore failed to make much impression on native European Muslims in the Balkans. In the immigrant communities of western Europe, on the other hand, a fresh front in the confrontation between Islam and the west was opening up. Activists from across the Muslim world converged on the British capital and mingled with local Islamists.

In 1998, the strategy of democratic enlargement was tested by the outbreak of open war between Serbia's Slobodan Milošević and the Kosovo Liberation Army. In Washington and the European capitals, the conflict was seen as test for NATO and the EU. If Milošević was not stopped, so the argument ran, then ethnic cleansing would return to the Balkans with incalculable consequences not only for the region itself, but also for the credibility of western institutions. The growing flow of refugees into Macedonia threatened the fragile balance between Slavs and Albanians there. A civil war there would probably draw in outside powers and trigger a wider conflagration involving Greece and Turkey. When the Serbian leader ignored an ultimatum to cease attacks on the civilian population, NATO – including Germany – launched a massive air campaign in March 1999 designed to bring him to heel. Eventually, the cumulative effect of relentless bombardment from the air, the belated start of NATO preparations for a ground war and Moscow's mediation persuaded Milošević to back down in June 1999, withdraw from Kosovo and accept the entry of a NATO-led international force. The

European Union launched a Stability Pact to promote the transition of the region as a whole to the free market, human rights and representative government.

The millennium thus seemed to presage a new era. It was generally accepted that the promotion of democracy increased stability, served to protect minorities and reduced the threat of armed conflict.[141] By 2000, 60 per cent of the world's population lived in democracies, a far higher figure than in 1974. In eastern and central Europe autocracy was almost entirely a thing of the past. The remaining dictatorships, especially Red China, appeared to be swimming against the tide. History seemed finally to have come to an end, albeit ten years later than Fukuyama had announced. The optimistic new consensus was summed up by Tony Blair in his 'Chicago Speech' of April 1999. He proclaimed a doctrine of 'international community', in which global interdependence and the increasing reach of communication technologies made every state a neighbour of every other. Breaking with what he understood to be the Westphalian insistence on sovereignty, Blair argued that the abuse of human rights was not merely a moral outrage, but threatened the security of the developed world through the spread of instability. 'In the end,' Blair argued, 'values and interest merge. If we can establish and spread the values of liberty, the rule of law, human rights and an open society then that is in our national interests too. The spread of our values makes us safer.'

In Germany, the concept of 'humanitarian intervention' became the vehicle by which the country accepted the responsibilities of great-power status.[142] 'At last,' the Social Democrat defence minister, Rudolf Scharping, noted in his diary at the height of the Kosovo war, 'we appear not, as so often before 1945, as aggressor, but rather as a defender of human rights.'[143] It was this determination 'not to look away', as Scharping put it, which persuaded the federal government to set aside its longstanding insistence on the sanctity of international law. If the Kohl Doctrine stipulated that German troops should never serve in any region where the *Wehrmacht* had committed crimes, the new 'Fischer Doctrine' proclaimed that it was precisely the existence of the Nazi crimes which made Germany peculiarly responsible for preventing them from happening again.[144] The new German chancellor put a rather different spin on the greater strategic activism of the Federal Republic, however. 'Germany', Gerhard Schröder announced in mid-September 1999, was now 'a great power in Europe'; this transition was underlined by the move of the parliament from Bonn to Berlin that same year. For all Schröder's insistence that the Federal Republic remained 'anchored . . . in Europe, for Europe and of Europe', it was clear that Germany was beginning to slip her moorings in the centre of the continent.

The impact of the Balkan crises on European integration was immense. The former European commissioner for external relations, Chris Patten, spoke of them 'as the lowest point in Europe's post-war history, exposing the gap between our pretensions as Europeans and our ability to act decisively together'.[145] The first EU High Representative for foreign affairs described the area as 'the birthplace of EU foreign policy'.[146] Never again did the Union want to be humiliated as it had been over Bosnia, and although the Kosovo war had been a much happier experience, many European leaders were still shocked at just how dependent they had been on US military power during that campaign.[147] The turn of the century therefore saw a huge surge in European political-military integration and NATO enlargement led by Germany.[148] In a speech to the European parliament in Strasbourg, the German foreign minister, Fischer, suggested that it might be necessary to establish a 'core Europe' of states committed to further integration in order to maintain the momentum as the Union expanded, and to make it capable of action to confront the challenges ahead. In order to do so, however, Fischer argued, it would need to become more transparent and democratic through provision of greater powers for the European parliament, greater accountability for EU institutions and the creation of a directly elected presidency. Fischer hoped that this deepening integration would 'overcome the risks and temptations objectively inherent in Germany's dimensions and central situation'. European Union, in other words, would transcend the *Mittellage*.[149]

There were bitter divisions, however, about what kind of united Europe it should be. Many felt that the continent had pioneered a new form of 'civilian' power, transcending traditional geopolitics, and should therefore not attempt to turn itself into a superpower on American lines.[150] They wanted Europe to become, or remain, something more resembling the old Holy Roman Empire, a legal order rather than a great power. On this reading, European integration was a solution to war, and especially to German aggression; it therefore made no sense to endow the Union with military capabilities. Instead, Europeans should play to their economic, political and cultural strengths in the areas of conflict prevention, post-war reconstruction, and spreading their values through peaceful enlargement.[151] This interpretation appealed to the Germans, in particular, because it released them from the obligation to deploy troops in support of European interests. At the same time, the bitter experiences with the former Yugoslavia and fears about the spread of weapons of mass destruction persuaded most Europeans that a more robust approach was needed.

The first step was taken at the EU's Council meeting at Cologne in June 1999, just after the end of the Kosovo war. This defined the Union's objective as the establishment of a European Security and Defence Policy. The next nine months were spent setting up a Political Security Committee, a European Military Committee, and a European military staff. That same year, the Union finally appointed Javier Solana High Representative for the Common Foreign and Security Policy. Two months later, the EU Council session at Helsinki laid down 'headline goals', and committed itself to the creation of a 60,000 strong 'Rapid Reaction Force' which would be capable of undertaking humanitarian interventions in complex civil conflicts. At the same time, the political broadening and deepening of the Union proceeded apace. The Balkan states were offered a Stability Pact and the prospect of joining once they had satisfied the demanding criteria laid down by Brussels. In December 1999, the Union decided at Nice to open accession negotiations with Malta, Romania, Slovakia, Latvia, Lithuania and Bulgaria beginning in mid-January 2000; this treaty, and thus the whole enlargement, was subject to ratification by member states.[152]

All this went hand in hand with the enlargement of NATO. In March 1999, the Czech Republic, Hungary and Poland joined the alliance, consolidating its grip on central Europe. A month later, the Washington Summit launched the Membership Action Plan for Romania, Bulgaria, Slovakia, Slovenia, Estonia, Latvia and Lithuania, which was designed not only to close up the gaps in central Europe, but to bring forward NATO's perimeter line to the Baltic and Black Sea. Membership or prospective membership of the NATO alliance had a powerful stabilizing effect on fragile new democracies in eastern Europe; so did the prospect of 'joining Europe'.[153] In the autumn of 2001, the Europeans – led by Germany – conducted their first successful military operation by leading a NATO force into Macedonia to keep the peace between the Albanian minority and the Slav-dominated government. The European Union also began to flex its muscles, when the extreme right-wing Austrian 'Freedom Party' won second place in the Austrian general elections and thus a place in government. Early in the following year, the other fourteen members of the Union imposed diplomatic and cultural sanctions on Austria, including the suspension of normal bilateral links, joint military exercises, isolation of Austrian ambassadors and opposing the candidature of Austrians for international posts. Jörg Haider was compelled to make a humiliating public declaration in support of European values such as tolerance and was ultimately forced to resign as leader of the Freedom Party.[154]

All the while, however, a number of explosive charges built into the European project were ticking away at its centre. The European Union had created a Monetary Union, and was attempting to establish a Common Foreign and Security Policy, without first creating a parallel single political authority. The establishment of Monetary Union in January 1999 was accompanied by an agreement that states which got into financial difficulties would not automatically be 'bailed out' by the Union or any other members. The new European Central Bank (ECB) in Frankfurt, however, only had the power of setting interest rates and controlling the money supply. It could not superintend the economic policies or budgets of the member states, and nor did the European parliament or any other institution have that authority.

Above all, the 'democratic deficit', which Fischer had identified at the heart of the European project, remained unresolved. To be sure, the sharing of sovereignty was agreed by elected governments, but there was no direct involvement of the peoples.[155] Early in the new millennium, the whole integration process now hit a series of democratic and electoral roadblocks. In September 2000, the Danes rejected the euro in a referendum; like Britain, Denmark would retain her own currency. Nine months later, in June 2001, the Union was convulsed by the unexpected defeat of the Nice Treaty referendum in Ireland, where in a low turnout voters rejected a process which seemed to set them on the path towards an expanded European superstate with a large army and less money to spend on them. Because the enlargement of the EU required ratification by all member states, Brussels put considerable pressure on Dublin to vote again; the signal, however, was clear. As the memory of the Second World War and the Soviet threat faded, peoples of Europe were becoming increasingly suspicious of EU 'bureaucracy', and sceptical of the need to sacrifice their national sovereignty. There was no sign that the common currency would lead inexorably to a common state, just as the *Zollverein* had not in and of itself set Germany on the path to political unification in the nineteenth century.

So if the external challenges of the 1990s had created a demand for 'more Europe', they had not yet led to the consultation and participation of the European peoples in their own collective defence or economic management. Nor had the European public – as a whole – asserted a claim to such involvement. The elections to the European parliament in 1999 were a non-event.[156] A European 'public sphere' hardly existed, let alone a vigorous pan-European popular debate on security matters. What little discussion did exist was ill-informed, parochial, fragmented and highly elite-driven. There were already signs of trouble ahead, particularly with regard to NATO expansion. The huge enlargements of the 1990s and those planned for the new decade threatened to create a two-tier alliance in which the central, south-eastern and eastern European members enjoyed a less credible security guarantee than the original 'core' western states. There were no alliance nuclear or conventional forces deployed east of the former German Federal Republic and, as yet, no active war planning for the defence of the new perimeter line. Moreover, the absorption of much of the former Soviet Empire automatically made the remaining successor states such as Belarus and Ukraine less secure: Moscow was now more anxious that they would be next in line for NATO membership, and no longer concerned about driving their western neighbours into the alliance, which they had already joined, by intimidating them.[157] The logic of all this, in short, was that NATO's eastward enlargement must continue indefinitely, until the alliance either bordered or incorporated Russia.

This, of course, was exactly what the Kremlin feared. As the decade progressed, Russian strategists had become increasingly concerned about 'encirclement' by China to east, by Islamic fundamentalism in Afghanistan, central Asia, Iran and the Caucasus (notably Chechnya) to the south and especially by NATO in the west. Russian intellectuals now began to resurrect Halford Mackinder and his 'heartland' theories, in the belief that the west sought to dominate the Eurasian 'World Island' and thus the world. When NATO pushed aside the UN Security Council – where Russia laid particular stress on its right of veto – over

Kosovo and ignored Moscow's objections, these anxieties multiplied. What, the Kremlin asked, was to stop the Atlantic alliance from applying the new concept of 'humanitarian intervention' or 'international community' to Chechnya or even Russia itself?

The domestic impact of the Kosovo war, and foreign policy generally, in Europe and on the other side of the Atlantic, varied considerably. In the US general election of November 2000, foreign policy was not a major issue, but after a decade of strategic bi-partisanship there was a clear divide between the Democratic candidate, former Vice-President Al Gore – who had been a prominent supporter of military action in Bosnia, and who proposed to carry on the Clinton administration's policy of intervention – and the victorious Republican candidate, George Bush, Jnr, who, by contrast, was profoundly sceptical of American involvement in 'nation-building efforts', and expressed the hope that the United States would become a 'more humble country'. Likewise, Kosovo played virtually no role in Tony Blair's resounding second election victory in June 2001, although it is clear that his strong advocacy of humanitarian intervention enjoyed widespread popular support. In Russia, on the other hand, the Kosovo war and the relentless advance of NATO led to a change of government. Just two months after the hostilities ended, in August 1999, a weary Yeltsin anointed the unknown Vladimir Putin as his successor. The new president had served as a middle-ranking intelligence officer in Germany, where the collapse of Soviet power in 1989 made a deep impression on him. He was respected as a German expert, spoke the language well and was convinced of Berlin's central geopolitical importance.[158] In late March 2000, Putin won the presidential election with more than 50 per cent of the vote, and without the need to go to a second round, but with the help of the 'administrative reserve', in other words manipulation by the security services and local authorities. His mandate was clear: to stamp out corruption at home, halt the encroachment of NATO, seek to divide the alliance through approaches to the Germans and French, sort out the Chechens and generally re-establish Russia as a great power.[159]

Throughout the next decade, the Russian government embarked on a thoroughgoing domestic transformation to make the state more effective on the international scene. A fresh service class redistribution led to a redistribution of power towards the *Siloviki*, the security apparatus of the interior ministry and Federal Security Service (successor to the

KGB). The country was transformed into a 'sovereign democracy', a concept which had little to do with political participation and everything to do with preserving the integrity of the state. Now control of natural resources was wrested back from foreign corporations; local 'oligarchs' had their wings clipped through legislation, harassment and in some cases imprisonment. More generally, the state re-nationalized, or exerted more direct control over, all domestic sectors relevant to foreign policy: transportation, telecommunications, finance and of course the defence industry. In part, all this was a response to Chechen-driven domestic Islamist terrorism, which was used to justify the curtailment of civil liberties and extensive media censorship; many prominent journalists critical of the Kremlin were mysteriously murdered. More importantly, Moscow sought to guard against western manipulation through the democratic revolutions which had toppled Milošević and were engulfing Russia's neighbours. Putin's main aim, however, was to reassert Russian power more generally, especially against Washington, and make the nation respected abroad once again.

Early in the morning of 11 September 2001, al-Qaeda operatives hijacked four American civilian passenger aircraft and used them as human missiles against the twin World Trade Towers and the Pentagon. The perpetrators all came from the Middle East, mainly Saudi Arabia, and the operation had been inspired by Osama bin Laden and planned by his al-Qaeda out of Afghanistan. It was an attack not merely on the symbols of US political, military and economic power but on the whole western world. President Bush declared a 'Global War on Terror'. The prime minister, Tony Blair, immediately committed Britain in support; the German leader, Gerhard Schröder, promised 'unlimited solidarity' with the US; and the French newspaper *Le Monde* even proclaimed that 'we are all Americans (now)'. NATO declared the al-Qaeda attacks an assault on its territory, and therefore activated article 5 of the charter, which committed members to its collective defence. In Berlin, the defence minister proclaimed that Germany was being 'defended at the Hindukusch', and sent troops. 'By making this contribution,' Chancellor Schröder argued, 'the unified and sovereign Germany will be meeting its growing responsibilities.'[160] The geopolitics of the Middle East, of radical Islamism, of Afghanistan and of Europe had finally fused into a single battle space. A process of radicalization which had begun with the Muslim defeat before the walls of Vienna in 1683, and which had been encouraged by Washington in the 1980s in order to protect central Europe from Soviet attack, had now come full circle.

In Europe, the attacks of September 11 provoked a fresh push for further political and military integration. The 'Global War on Terror' was not, as it might have been in the past, explicitly waged as a war of European unification, although there was some self-definition against the Muslim and Arab 'other' to be sure.[161] It was widely accepted, however, that the threat of Islamist terrorism from without and from radicalized immigrant Muslim communities from within required more European unity and coordination. Some hoped that the new danger might even induce the nation states to pool their sovereignty for the sake of common security. The German foreign minister, Joschka Fischer, made this connection when he remarked in December 2001 that 'Europe has only grown because of crisis and pressure, and not because of papers, and not out of conviction.'[162] The allusion to Bismarck's famous claim that German unity would be achieved not by 'speeches and resolutions' but by 'blood and iron' was unmistakable. Fischer now argued that 'the weight of the major European states is, pure and simple, no longer sufficient'. At the very end of 2001, the states of the European Union convened at Laeken to agree a European [military] Capabilities Action Plan. It adopted, moreover, a very wide definition of Europe: the preamble announced that 'The only boundary that the European Union draws is defined by democracy and human rights.' In February 2002 the Brussels convention on the future of Europe met to draft a Constitution for Europe.

Beneath the surface, however, huge strategic differences were alread tearing the Union apart. There was no consensus on priorities: Spair France and Italy were firmly focused on the Mediterranean, with its bel of unstable North African dictatorships to the south, threatening t spew out a tidal wave of economic or political migrants in their direc tion; the Maghreb was also the source of most domestic Islami terrorism. The eastern Europeans, by contrast, primarily feared Russia power and looked to the EU and especially the Atlantic alliance to con tain it. In accordance with its new strategic concept, NATO obliged a its Prague Summit in November 2002 by opening accession talks wit Bulgaria, Estonia, Latvia, Lithuania, Romania, Slovakia and Sloveni they joined in late March 2004. At around the same time, Preside

Leonid Kuchma signalled his desire to bring Ukraine into the alliance. Paris and Berlin, on the other hand, were increasingly sceptical of eastward expansion, which in the latter case was no longer necessary to safeguard German security, and threatened to antagonize Moscow still further.

It was the differences between European states over the next steps in the 'War on Terror', however, which really paralysed the Union. To some Americans, and most Europeans, the best way of dealing with al-Qaeda and Islamist terrorism generally was through coordinated police action across the world. They called for careful, painstaking 'realist' diplomacy, which often involved accommodations with repressive regimes themselves grappling with 'terrorism'. On their reading, it was necessary to meet these states – such as Egypt, Syria and Saudi Arabia – halfway in their need to pacify their restive populations by taking a tougher line on Israel. The idea that the question of Palestine was at the core of al-Qaeda's strategy, and at the root of global unpopularity of the west, particularly America, was in widespread circulation among western politicians, strategists and publics. Influential 'neoconservatives', such as the Deputy Defense Secretary, Paul Wolfowitz, on the other hand, argued that the most important casualty of 9/11 was the 'realist' paradigm in the Middle East. For many decades, western governments – especially the United States – had maintained a Faustian bargain with 'moderate' repressive regimes in the Middle East. The United States provided security and stifled its concerns about human rights; the regimes kept the oil flowing and their populations in check. The alternative, so the argument ran, would be either Islamic fundamentalism or anarchy of the sort that engulfed Algeria shortly after the army annulled elections in 1992. But on 12 September, the neoconservatives argued, it became clear that 'realism' did not work. Far from keeping the lid on a seething cauldron of anti-western sentiment, the policy had perpetuated it. The hijackers, after all, came mainly from two 'allied' states, Saudi Arabia and Egypt, not Palestine. The solution, the neoconservatives suggested, was to break with the traditional US reliance on repressive regimes and democratize the Middle East, by force if necessary.

President Bush now adopted this analysis. Once again, the notion of the 'democratic peace' underpinned US strategy.[163] His new 'National Security Strategy' now extended the doctrine of democratic enlargement to the Middle East; far from singling the area out for special treatment, President Bush removed its exceptional status. This discourse fused with a growing sense that the United States should not wait until it was attacked again, but act more preventively to neutralize potential threats. The administration announced that 'pre-emptive' action would be taken not only against al-Qaeda, and jihadism generally, but also against sovereign states with access to weapons of mass destruction. Here Washington targeted the Iraq of Saddam Hussein, the most dictatorial government in the region, with a long record of external aggression and of trying to develop a chemical, biological and nuclear arsenal. So rather than putting pressure on the only democracy in the Middle East, Israel, the United States now confronted its least democratic state.

The European elite agreed with much of the new American strategy. In 2003, the Union published its first *European Security Strategy*, reflecting a consensus across the continent. 'Our traditional concept of self-defence – up to and including the Cold War,' the document warned, 'was based on the threat of invasion. With the new threats, the first line of defence will often be abroad.' It was not enough, in other words, simply to sit back and patrol the European perimeter line: the security of the Union required engagement and buffers well beyond its own borders. 'Even in an era of globalization,' the document argued, 'geography is still important. It is in the European interest that countries on our borders are well governed.'[164] For this reason, the Union not only wished to extend its boundaries but also proclaimed a new European Neighbourhood Policy, to create what Romano Prodi, president of the European Commission, described as a 'ring of friends' which would serve as a bulwark for the inner core.[165] In short, Europe should expand not only territorially but ideologically: the spread of its values, so the argument ran, would render the Union more secure.

The decision to remove Saddam Hussein, however, bitterly divided the Europeans from Washington and from each other. Tony Blair strongly supported it, not least because Saddam Hussein had featured in the Chicago Speech of 1999, delivered while George Bush was still a mere candidate for the Republican nomination. More generally, Blair saw the shock of September 11 as an opportunity to create a more just and secure world: 'The kaleidoscope has been shaken, the pieces are in flux, let us reorder this world around us.'[166] In his view dictators such as Saddam Hussein provoked terrorism by repressing their own people and trying to divert popular hostility against the west. The Italian prime minister, Silvio Berlusconi, the Spanish leader, José María Aznar, the Baltic states and most of the former Soviet bloc – which the US Defense Secretary, Donald Rumsfeld, dubbed 'New Europe' – followed the Anglo-American lead on Iraq. Paris and Berlin, on the other hand, did not believe Saddam Hussein to be a serious threat to the west, and feared that a war to unseat him would be a costly distraction from the struggle against terrorism. They were also determined to wrest leadership of Europe back from London and to mobilize the Union as a counterweight to American unilateralism. At the United Nations Security Council, where France enjoyed a veto, Chirac frustrated Anglo-American attempts to mobilize that body to enforce the disarmament clauses of the 1991 ceasefire agreement.

Chancellor Schröder of Germany went a step further, assuring the population during the general election campaign of 2002 that Germany would not support an attack on Iraq, even if it was authorized by the United Nations. This decision was part and parcel of a much broader determination to pursue a separate 'German path' from that of the United States. 'The era in which we look to America and others as a model for our economy is over,' Schröder told a large crowd at the Opernplatz in Hanover. 'The way things are in the United States, with bankruptcies and the exploitation of the little people who now have to worry about who will take care of them when they are old – I say to you, that is not the German Way that we want for our people.' On Iraq, he warned against 'playing around with war and military intervention . . . We won't be part of it.'[167] For the first time in the history of the transatlantic alliance, the German government had broken publicly and acrimoniously with Washington on a matter of critical importance to the US administration.[168]

In March 2003, the allied coalition invaded Iraq, deposed Saddam Hussein, and enjoyed a brief honeymoon among the Shia majority glad to be rid of the dictator and Sunni dominance. Unlike Bosnia and Kosovo, however, the opposition to military action did not subside with the end of major combat operations. This was partly because no weapons of mass destruction were actually found. The continuing controversy was also fuelled by the outbreak of a sustained 'insurgency' of Syrian-backed former Baathists, Iranian-sponsored Shia militants, Sunnis fearful of losing their old privileges and assorted international jihadists against the Allied occupation. Throughout late 2003 and 2004, the

Americans struggled to get the situation under control. The prospect of democracy in Iraq, and through it a transformation of the wider region, seemed remote. Meanwhile, Europe's eastern periphery was in turmoil. It soon became clear that President Putin's 'sovereign democracy' meant not only very qualified sovereignty for Russia's neighbours, but rather limited their democratic prospects as well.[169] In September 2003, the Russians set up the 'Single Economic Space', a wide-ranging cooperation agreement with Belarus, Kazakhstan and Ukraine, which was intended to replace the defunct Commonwealth of Independent States. This was so bitterly attacked by Ukrainian nationalists and democrats under the charismatic leadership of Viktor Yuschenko that it was only ratified with difficulty by the parliament in Kiev. Moscow began to intervene ever more openly in Ukraine in support of its favoured candidate, Viktor Yanukovich, whose power base lay in the Russian-speaking east of the country. In Belarus, tension flared in 2005 between the 'Union of Poles', who looked to Warsaw for protection, and the Moscow-backed autocracy of President Lukashenko.

The cumulative consequences of the Iraq crisis and Russia's renewed great-power ambitions for European geopolitics were immense. At the diplomatic level, Paris and Berlin sought closer cooperation with Moscow to balance what they regarded as US pretensions to global hegemony and in order to safeguard the supply of Russian energy, especially gas, on which so much of Europe depended. A joint declaration of the three powers in March 2003 showed, the German chancellor argued, that they could stand up to the Americans if they stuck together. Just after the end of the Iraq War, the EU powers opposed to the Anglo-American operation convened at Luxemburg under Franco-German leadership. At the end of the year, Schröder visited China, mainly in order to secure trade deals for German industry as it emerged from the recession; scornful of human rights issues, he called for a relaxation of the EU arms embargo on Beijing. France and Germany agreed temporarily to waive their own stability and growth convergence criteria set down by the Maastricht Treaty, and to turn a blind eye to violations elsewhere in the Union. Unlike generations of German leaders, who had stressed transatlantic ties, Schröder increasingly spoke of Germany's European mission and distinctive 'German path'. He and his French colleagues now pressed ahead with further integration in order to give Europe the weight it needed to balance the United States. The battle for

Europe was entering a new phase: there was a widespread hope and expectation among elites that the continent would find the unity to become a decisive actor on the world stage.[170]

In mid-April 2003, the Czech Republic, Estonia, Cyprus, Latvia, Lithuania, Hungary, Malta, Poland, Slovenia and Slovakia signed accession protocols; a total of another 100 million people were scheduled to join the Union within a year. In June 2004, Croatia was given candidate status. Six months later, negotiations began with Bulgaria and Romania, whose accession was agreed in late April 2005. At the same time, the Union moved to strengthen its political coherence and military reach. The Naples Summit of 2003 established an operational planning cell in EU military headquarters in Brussels. Preliminary drafts from the European Convention were circulating in public not long after the Iraq War ended. By late October 2004, the governments had signed the Treaty for the Constitution of Europe. This envisaged both a quantitative and qualitative shift in the powers to be transferred from national to Union level. The number of areas subject to qualified majority voting, which diluted national sovereignty, nearly doubled, especially in Justice and Home Affairs. More powers were given to the European parliament, in the hope of increasing democratic legitimacy.[171] It was in defence and foreign policy, however, that the greatest innovations were envisaged. The Constitution would create two new offices of foreign minister and president of the Union. Nor were these to be the last steps. The preamble reaffirmed the commitment to 'an ever closer union'.[172] All that now remained was to ratify the Constitution and make it law.

Where this depended on governmental action, for example in Germany, Britain and in most other European states, the Constitution sailed through more or less unopposed. In those countries where a popular vote was required, however, the treaty was soon in deep water. Unlike the United States, the European Union was established by governments, not by the people, or even by the peoples.[173] French voters rejected the Constitution in late May 2005, and the Dutch electorate followed suit shortly afterwards. The 'democratic deficit' underlying the whole integration project was starkly exposed: the Union was attempting to export democracy without being one itself. When asked, European publics saw no compelling economic or strategic reason to give up their sovereignty, and the 'European' ideal as such did not have sufficient traction to provide the missing dynamic.[174] In the short term, the French and Dutch votes simply drove the framers of the Constitution to repackage their proposals and try again. The deeper issue therefore remained unresolved. How was the great power being amassed at the heart to be made accountable to the peoples it was supposed to serve? Conversely, how could these populations be brought to participate in the great union project, thereby setting free the even greater energies which still lay dormant at the heart of the continent?

There were also continuing divisions about how far Europe should be expanded. In Germany, the expansion of the Union eastwards completed the process set in motion by NATO enlargement. 'It's a historic moment,' the German foreign minister remarked of the accession of the Baltic states, Bulgaria, Romania, Slovakia and Slovenia. 'It will be the first time in modern history that Germany will be at the centre of Europe without direct threats to our border and without us threatening anybody.'[175] For many Germans 'Europe' had now served its purpose and, rather than extend the battlements further south and east, they preferred to raise the drawbridge and rest secure in their fortress. This sentiment also affected further eastward expansion of NATO. Paris and Berlin, themselves now militarily secure, wanted to appease the Kremlin and to safeguard their energy supplies from Russia; the British, together with the Poles, Balts and other powers directly in the firing line, sought to fill the vacuum between themselves and the Russians. Matters came to a head over Ukraine. In late April 2005, Kiev finally began a dialogue with NATO about accession. Right at the end of that year, the country was thrown into crisis over a disputed general election, in which Moscow made no secret of its support for the party accused of falsifying the results. In the ensuing 'Orange Revolution', Democratic protestors gained the upper hand and a pro-western government under Viktor Yuschenko took power, determined to bring Ukraine closer to Europe.

The Iraq conflict and the 'Global War on Terror' also had a profound effect on domestic politics. After 2001, the United States was a country at war, in which the home front remained in a state of heightened anxiety and preparedness, putting a political premium on resilience. The Democratic candidate for the presidency in November 2004, the war veteran John Kerry, failed to persuade the American people that he was more capable of dealing with the terrorist threat; it is widely accepted that national security considerations decided the outcome. George W. Bush was therefore re-elected for a second term, with a mandate to continue the 'Global War on Terror' and the democratic transformation of the Middle East. In Europe, on the other hand, the Iraq War radicalized publics, embarrassed governments who had supported it, and benefited those who had come out in opposition. Chancellor Schröder unexpectedly won the 2002 general election in Germany, partly because he had shown firm leadership during floods in the eastern provinces, but mainly because he had terrified voters with talk of being dragged into a Middle Eastern war. In London, party politics was often dominated by foreign affairs; there were even plans to impeach Blair for 'High crimes and misdemeanours in relation to the invasion of Iraq'. The political consequences of all this were more limited, however. In the May 2005 election, Tony Blair secured an unprecedented third Labour term in office, though disaffection over the Iraq War, and his perceived subservience to Washington, cost him part of his reduced majority. Moreover, opposition to George Bush did not save the German chancellor from subsequent election defeat at the hands of Angela Merkel in 2005, and Nicolas Sarkozy's more favourable view of Washington was no barrier to his succession to the French presidency.

Among European Muslims the 'Global War on Terror' – in which Iraq was often not the most salient issue – was widely perceived as an attack on Islam itself.[176] The question of making foreign policy in a multicultural society now became acute, as the children of immigrants took aim at the strategies of their 'host' countries.[177] The spate of Islamist terrorism which rocked European societies in the middle of the decade was driven by a strategic and ideological programme strongly influenced by, but predating, the 'Global War on Terror'. Jihadist strategists had long argued that all former Muslim lands, including southern Spain and much of the Balkans, should be regained, and many radicals born or based in Britain regarded England, too, as there for the taking. In March 2004, Islamist bombs caused carnage on the Madrid metro system, in early July 2005 London was attacked by British-born radicals, causing heavy loss of life, and similar plots were uncovered in the nick of time in a number of other European countries. A new battlefront had opened up between the caliphate and the west. More than 500 years after the *Reconquista*, and 400 years after the Ottomans had been repulsed at Vienna, militant Islam once more had Europe in its sights; this time, moreover, Muslims were already within the gates.

Central to the radical Muslim world view was anti-semitism. This was now re-imported into Europe as part of an anti-western critique, which saw the United States and the European Union as either allies or pawns of the forces of global Zionism and Jewry. On their reading, and indeed in the eyes of many westerners, the 'Global War on Terror', the invasion of Iraq and the (pretended) export of democracy were part of a vast conspiracy directed by neoconservative American Jews and their puppet-masters in Israel. 'Today the Jews rule the world by proxy,' the Malaysian prime minister, Mahathir Mohamad, told the Organization of Islamic Conference in 2003. 'They get others to fight and die for them.'[178] The 'Protocols of the Elders of Zion', an old forgery instigated by the tsarist secret police, enjoyed a renaissance.[179] Holocaust denial became widespread. Many western European countries saw a sharp increase in physical and verbal attacks on Jews, especially the visible Orthodox community. Some of these were carried out by the 'traditional' extreme right, but most stemmed from Muslim immigrant communities. This wave fed the political, legal and cultural 'de-legitimization' of Israel – which commanded the support of many Europeans who were not, or did not think of themselves as, anti-semitic.

The 'Global War on Terror' had the potential to reshape European domestic politics as deeply as external and internal threats had in the past.[180] As they scrambled to contain the terrorist threat and the challenge of hostile immigrant communities, polities were forced to confront the classic balance between freedom and security.[181] There was, however, no systematic attempt to recast society and economy. Outside of Russia, and Putin's recast of socio-economic relations to protect the country's sovereignty against western encroachment, the old primacy of foreign policy, which had lapsed in the course of the late twentieth century, was not revived. Unlike the United States after 2001, Europe in the new millennium was still a society at peace even while her young men and women fought and died in unprecedented numbers since the end of the Second World War: in Iraq, Afghanistan and elsewhere.

Meanwhile the expansion of NATO and the European Union continued apace. In January 2007, Bulgaria and Romania joined the Union; Ukraine was scrambling to reform economics and civil society to prepare a membership bid in due course. At the very end of that year, European governments agreed to a slightly revised Constitution at Lisbon, which reaffirmed the intention to transform the Union into a military alliance.

The ratification process now began anew. In late September 2006, an 'intensified dialogue' was offered by NATO to the Caucasian state of Georgia. This was furiously resisted by Paris and Berlin – in this respect Merkel followed Schröder's lead – on the grounds that it would provoke Russia and over-extend the alliance. Two months later, Albania and Croatia were invited to begin formal accession talks, and were admitted two years later. At a tempestuous NATO summit at Bucharest in early April 2008, Macedonia was assured that an invitation would follow once her dispute with Greece had been resolved, while Bosnia and Montenegro were called upon to start 'intensified dialogues'. Most controversially of all, and over the objections of France and Germany, Ukraine and Georgia were informed that future membership was possible, though contingent on resolving their minority problems.

In 2008, however, Europe was rocked by an escalating series of crises. The Kosovo Assembly unilaterally declared its independence from the former Yugoslavia in February, exposing deep divisions in the Union. Twenty-two EU members – including Britain, France and Germany – recognized the new state, but Greece (with one eye on Macedonia and its Slavophone citizens), Cyprus (with its Turkish population), Spain (with its Basques and Catalans), Romania and Slovakia (both with large Hungarian minorities) refused to do so. A European parliament resolution demanding recognition was simply ignored. Not long afterwards, in June 2008, the Irish people rejected the Lisbon Treaty in a referendum. The outcome of the vote was determined by a range of factors: a low turnout, fear of being drawn into 'Europe's wars' in spite of Ireland's traditional neutrality, anxieties that EU structural funds would be diverted to new entrants in the east, a general sense of alienation from a 'bureaucratic' and 'undemocratic' Brussels, and above all the belief that the Lisbon Treaty threatened Irish sovereignty. Because of the principle of unanimity, and because the EU had no mechanism for expelling a member state, further integration was stalled until the Irish changed their minds.

Two months later, Europe was shaken by another crisis. After NATO had announced that Ukraine and Georgia could be admitted in principle, Russia had stepped up the pressure on the Caucasian state through the breakaway regions of Abkhazia (which had formerly had a Georgian majority population) and South Ossetia (where there was still a substantial Georgian minority). Georgia's President Mikhail Saakashvili, determined to join NATO, bolstered by the support of more than three quarters of the vote in a referendum on membership, and desperate to 'solve' the territorial disputes which the alliance had set as a condition of membership now made a fateful decision. In August 2008, he launched a full-scale attack on South Ossetia, giving Moscow the pretext to respond with a 'humanitarian intervention' to protect the civilian population. Russian tanks rolled southwards and began to threaten not only the integrity of Georgia itself but also the east–west oil pipeline. Europe was still reeling, when the western financial system suddenly collapsed in September 2008. The crisis began on Wall Street with the failure of the investment bank Lehman Brothers, engulfed the whole of the United States, and crossed the Atlantic. European banks began to go under across the continent, especially in Britain, Ireland, Spain and even in Germany. In the wake of the financial crisis came a sharp general economic downturn, as the United States and many European states tipped into recession, mild in Britain, but severe in Ireland, Greece and Spain. Housing markets, retail and many other sectors went into sharp decline.

Washington and the European capitals scrambled to respond to the Russian intervention. President Bush, now at the very end of his tenure, still stuck in Iraq and Afghanistan and deeply unpopular, lacked the power to act. In London, there was a bi-partisan consensus between the Labour government and the new Conservative leader, David Cameron, in favour of robust action against Moscow. The Bulgarians, Czechs, Danes, the Balts, Poles – all fearful of Russia – also came out in favour of strong action. Latvia suggested boycotting the 2014 Winter Olympic Games in the Russian resort of Sochi, and even sending military aid to Georgia. Europe failed to support anything beyond token measures against Moscow, however, largely because the French and Germans were opposed. President Sarkozy hastily arranged a ceasefire which not only failed to restore Georgian sovereignty over the disputed territories, but left Russian troops on the soil of Georgia proper.

There was also no consensus on how to react to the financial crisis. In the last months of his administration, George Bush and the British prime minister pushed through packages to stabilize the financial system and stimulate the economy, largely through 'quantitative easing' – printing more money. In the Eurozone, however, governments had surrendered monetary sovereignty to the ECB, so that the instruments available to them were limited. Germany – whose economy required low inflation, which was strongly opposed to taking on additional debt to finance deficit spending, and to whose interests the ECB largely deferred – prevented more radical action. Indeed, the Federal Republic continued to enjoy strong exports and a hefty balance-of-payments surplus. Germany, which had been economically somewhat eclipsed over the past fifteen years, was once again the industrial and financial powerhouse of Europe. Nearly twenty years after the fall of the Berlin Wall and the start of the Wars of the Yugoslav Succession, ten years after the Kosovo war and the establishment of the euro, and eight years into the 'Global War on Terror', the Union was still deeply divided on foreign, security and economic policy.

The cumulative domestic consequences of these crises were profound. Foreign policy did not dominate the 2008 presidential election – which was decided by the dire state of the economy – but the American people were asked to choose between two fundamentally different strategic approaches to the outside world. John McCain, the Republican contender, promised to continue the work of democratic enlargement, appealed to 'democratic solidarity', called for a 'worldwide League of Democracies', and roundly condemned Russian 'brutality' in the Caucasus.[182] The Democratic candidate for the presidency, Barack Obama, accused the Republicans of plunging the United States into an unnecessary and illegal war in Iraq, of neglecting the 'necessary' war in Afghanistan, of ignoring Pakistan's complicity with the Taliban and generally causing a precipitate decline in America's standing in the world; he conspicuously did not target Russia over its invasion of Georgia. The Democrat also expressed scepticism about the morality, wisdom and viability of exporting democracy as an instrument of national security. In early November, Obama – born of a Kenyan father and a white mother – won election comfortably, making him the first mixed-race president of the United States.

The new administration embarked on a radical departure in foreign policy. The US Secretary of State, Hillary Clinton, pointedly dropped any mention of human rights on her first visit to China in 2009. President Obama refused to see the Dalai Lama when he visited Washington, a practice which had deeply irritated Peking during the Bush years. The United States also undertook to press the 'reset' button with the Russians, by abandoning plans for a land-based system of missile interceptors in eastern Europe. More generally, the new administration signalled its intention to break with the policy of democratic transformation, to rely more closely on local authoritarian allies, and yet at the same time to improve America's image in the Muslim world. In Europe, the new president concentrated on Germany. Turning his back on Bush's celebration of the 'special relationship' with Britain, Obama made Berlin the centrepiece of his European tour, delivering a rousing speech under the Brandenburg Gate during the election campaign. The new importance of Germany was underlined by James Rubin, former Democratic Assistant Secretary of State to President Clinton, during the election campaign. 'Germany, not the United States', he noted, was the 'power broker' in NATO, at least as far as further eastern enlargement was concerned. 'The United States,' Rubin wrote, 'must make Germany its primary focus in rebuilding the NATO alliance.'[183] The administration had high hopes that Berlin would contribute more troops to a 'surge' in Afghanistan.

It was not long, however, before the new US grand strategy was in difficulty. The decision to abandon the missile shield in deference to Moscow provoked a furious response across eastern Europe, and especially in Poland. With the exception of Britain, European governments – who had already refused to send more troops to Afghanistan under Bush – also refused to oblige Obama. The brief transatlantic honeymoon had been based on a misunderstanding: the new president thought that the Europeans would give more, while the Europeans expected him to ask for less.[184] In the Federal Republic, in particular, the Afghan War was coming under intense scrutiny; public opinion and many politicians called for the withdrawal of the substantial *Bundeswehr* contingent. Despite the fact that they were stationed in a relatively quiet part of the country, and geared towards reconstruction rather than combat, the Germans had suffered dozens of fatalities, many fewer than the Americans, and British, of course, but still an unimaginably high number for a largely pacifist public. The Green Party, which had been won over to humanitarian intervention by Fischer and Cohn-Bendit in the 1990s, now voted against sending more Tornado aircraft. Chancellor Merkel repeatedly refused to dispatch the additional forces which Washington demanded, or to agree to more robust rules of engagement. Clearly, Germany was no longer being defended on the 'Hindukusch'.

Meanwhile, Europe returned to the ratification of the Lisbon Treaty with renewed vigour. The Irish were cajoled into voting again in 2009.

This time – against the background of the dire economic situation and larger turnout – the treaty was passed. The Lisbon Treaty duly came into force: the positions of President of the European Council and High Representative of the Union for Foreign and Security Policy were officially established. This did not lead, however, to a substantial increase in the power and authority of the Union, quite the opposite. Instead of choosing high-profile figures such as Tony Blair – strongly tipped by some, but too controversial after Iraq – or Joschka Fischer, the presidency went to the little-known Belgian prime minister, Herman van Rompuy, and the foreign policy brief to the virtually unknown Catherine Ashton, the British trade commissioner. Moreover, the European elections of 2009 were characterized by neither the triumph of Euroscepticism – parties hostile to the Union fared uniformly badly – nor an extensive engagement by the populations of Europe with the great economic and strategic threats facing their continent, but instead, by widespread apathy. Not only had the integrationist elites made little effort to bring the *demos* with them, the European peoples had failed – even in this hour of crisis – to assert their right to participate in the defence of their common prosperity and security. Either way, the 'democratic deficit' continued to gnaw away at the entire European project. The Union remained a 'compound democracy',[185] an association of representative systems, but it was not a democracy itself. It was configured not for the mobilization, but for the diffusion of power.

The Union was therefore ill-equipped to deal with a fresh set of crises, which exploded in 2010–11.[186] In the spring of 2010, the cumulative effect of the financial crisis, governmental incompetence, lower tax yields, systematic tax evasion, and huge euro-dominated debts run up thanks to the low interest rates spawned by Monetary Union combined to put the finances of Portugal, Ireland, Italy, Greece and Spain – the 'PIIGS' – under unbearable pressure. That spring, Athens erupted in civil unrest as the government sought to balance the books through reducing expenditure. A year later, Greeks took to the streets again to protest at a further round of austerity measures. In Ireland, the state's takeover of the huge banking debt threatened to capsize the whole fiscal system, with default a real possibility. Here the population acquiesced more willingly to the cuts, in the hope and expectation that 'Europe' would come to their rescue. Meanwhile, the public finances of Portugal, Italy and Spain also teetered on the brink of collapse, and there were even question marks against 'core' countries such as Belgium. International investors, many of them heavily exposed to government bonds in Ireland and the Mediterranean, pondered whether to 'dump' their holdings in favour of more stable assets, such as German securities. By early 2011, Europe was on the verge of financial meltdown.

At the same time the Middle East suddenly erupted into revolt. In January 2011, the Tunisian dictator, President Zine El Abidine Ben Ali, was driven out by protestors demanding an end to corruption and autocratic rule. A month later, the long-established Egyptian dictator, Hosni Mubarak, was toppled by a similar movement. Not long after, eastern Libya rose in armed insurrection against the equally long-serving dictator Muammar Gaddafi, although his security forces soon regained control in the west and began to march on the rebel stronghold of Tripoli. From March 2011, protests also broke out in Syria. This Arab Spring left few areas of the Middle East untouched and reached as far afield as the Gulf State of Bahrain, where the Shia majority demanded more rights from the Sunni royal family. It had many different local cultural, political and sectarian roots, and embraced currents as diverse as women's groups and Islamists, but what united them all was a call for western-style political participation and accountability. Highly unusually, and completely unlike the events which led to the fall of the Shah, foreign policy played almost no role in these revolutions. There was widespread criticism of US and European support for Middle Eastern dictators, but the demonstrators showed little appetite for confrontation with Israel and the west generally. All in all, therefore, the Arab Spring seemed to resemble the popular democratic protests of 1989 in central and eastern Europe more than the Islamist Iranian Revolution of 1979, but by the middle of 2011 it was still far too early to tell for sure.

Europe and the United States were caught unawares. They had long regarded the Middle Eastern dictators, in particular Mubarak, as forces for stability in the region and valued partners in the 'Global War on Terror'. Gaddafi had only just been wooed into the western camp by Tony Blair, and some capitals were even looking with favour on Bashar al-Assad's Syria. The Arab Spring thus dislodged old and new friends in Egypt, Tunisia and Libya, and threatened others in Yemen, Bahrain and possibly Saudi Arabia, the ultimate nightmare. Western leaders now feared that the rise of popular politics would lead to the triumph of Islamism, especially the Muslim Brotherhood, and a more aggressive policy towards them and Israel, spewing out a stream of economic migrants and extremists northwards across the Mediterranean. For this reason, Washington and the European capitals were at first slow to embrace the transformations in Tunisia and Egypt. Once the changes were perceived as not only inevitable but sustainable, though, there was widespread agreement that the democratic transformation of the region would increase western security. What President Bush had tried so hard to achieve now seemed to fall unbidden into President Obama's lap.

What really changed the dynamic was Libya, where in March 2011 the rebels stood on the brink of annihilation by Gaddafi, who threatened to 'hunt them down like rats'. President Obama initially refused to intervene, leaving it to the French and British to push for an air operation in defence of Benghazi. Thanks to pressure from within the US national security establishment, Washington came round to supporting the initiative from the back seat, and so did the Arab League. Germany, on the other hand, unexpectedly abstained on UN authorization, arguing that military intervention was unjustified under international law, and likely to endanger the democratic transformations in Tunisia, Egypt and elsewhere by rallying opinion against the west. Many Europeans agreed with this assessment, although few cared to state this publicly. The air campaign soon stopped Libyan government forces in their tracks and eventually brought the Colonel's regime down. This intervention was justified in 'humanitarian' terms, but it was also driven by the fear that a victory for Gaddafi would cause democrats across the region to lose heart, and by a sense that there could otherwise be a prolonged Bosnia-style crisis on the southern periphery of the Union. The connection between 'humanitarian intervention', the defence of democracy abroad and *Realpolitik* was thus re-established.

It was the euro debt crisis, however, which most preoccupied western leaders. If Greece or Ireland actually defaulted, this would cast doubt on the value of previously sacrosanct government bonds and precipitate a general collapse in Spain, Portugal and Italy as investors fled the state bond market. It might even destroy the entire euro-system itself, and tip the whole continent and thus probably the entire world into recession. For this reason, the EU and the IMF sought to prop up Irish and Greek finances through a series of largely German-funded 'bail-outs', which lent money – often at high interest rates – to cover the shortfall, in return for a commitment to further austerity measures to bring the national finances in order. The central actor here was Germany, where a struggle erupted between the establishment, which feared that a Greek or Irish default would destroy their own banking system, which was heavily invested in the relevant bonds, and the population at large, which was increasingly weary of funding yet another 'bailout' for improvident peripheral economies and was registering that fact in the regional elections. By the middle of 2011, in order to avoid further electoral losses, Chancellor Merkel had retreated from her original joint position with Paris in defence of the bondholders, towards an insistence that international investors would have to share some of the losses. This stance, however reasonable in itself, not only infuriated the French, whose banks were even more exposed to Greek debt, but also increased the chance of an escalating sovereign default across substantial parts of the Union.

Taken together, all this amounted to a severe and possibly terminal challenge to the European project. As of the time of writing, Europe remains in one of its deepest crises since the Second World War. The European divisions over Libya made a mockery of the vaunted Common Foreign and Security Policy, as did the fact that the intervention could not have been mounted without extensive US logistical support. This dependency was skewered in a scornful speech by the departing US Defense Secretary. If Europe had made such heavy weather of dealing with a comparatively puny foe, many wondered, how could it hope to match a much larger power such as a resurgent Russia? Above all, European states have still not been able to master the Euro debt crisis. The supposedly absolute and all-mighty ECB was shown not only to be ultimately dependent on national government support, especially from Germany, but also to lack the financial muscle to defy the international money markets. Europe was exposed as wanting in solidarity, machinery and capability. One way or the other, the years 2010–11 proved, once again, a turning point at which the history of Europe resolutely refused to turn towards political unity. The external challenges confronting the Union continued to divide Europeans rather than weld them more closely together.

Underlying everything was the fracture at the core of the European project. Germany, long the mainstay of integration and its paymaster of last resort, was slowly turning its back on the Union. In 2009, the respected Constitutional Court determined that Germany could not engage in further integration without the consent of the people. At the same time, the German people revolted at the idea of a 'transfer union' by which they subsidized the chronic mismanagement of other states. More generally, Germany was becoming a more 'normal' and thus more 'assertive' nation, as it left the past behind it. Unlike the early twentieth century, however, this process did not lead to greater activism on the European or world stage, quite the contrary. It was German military abstinence, not ambition, which disabled the Union strategically. Now secure in a bubble of democratic market economies on every side, Germany began to absent itself from the world, concentrating ever more on the promotion of its prosperity, and thus inadvertently of the colossal economic power which destabilized the rest of the continent. Political leaders were becoming less and less inclined to risk the wrath of the public by supporting military intervention in the Middle East, or the wrath of Russia over eastern enlargement and thus energy reprisals, and German regional elections were becoming as important to Europe as a whole as the successions to obscure principalities in the Holy Roman Empire had been in centuries past. A 'central secession' from the EU, by which Germany simply washed its hands of Europe, and reintroduced the Deutschmark, could no longer by completely excluded. All this caused consternation in capitals across the Union, and provoked a popular anti-Germanism unknown since the late 1980s. In short, at the start of the second decade of the second millennium, Europeans were no less preoccupied by how the vital space at the heart of the continent was to be organized than they had been in times gone by. The German Question, eclipsed for more than a decade after unification, was back.

Conclusion

History is not ... a cookbook offering pretested recipes. It teaches by analogy, not by maxims. It can illuminate the consequences of actions in comparable situations, yet each generation must discover for itself what situations are in fact comparable.

Henry Kissinger, 1979[1]

This book has covered more than 500 years of European history. It has discussed dozens of wars, interventions, reform movements and their associated debates. We have been introduced to very different polities, personalities and cultures, starting with the Holy Roman Empire, progressing through absolutism, parliamentary government, the Third Reich, and ending with the European Union. Despite all the differences of time and place, however, we have seen that there are recurring geopolitical themes in the history of the European states. It is to these patterns, and the question of where – if anywhere – they might point in the future, that we now turn.

The fundamental issue has always been whether Europe would be united – or dominated – by a single force: the Universal Monarchy attributed to Charles V, Philip II (for whom the world was 'not enough') and Louis XIV; the caliphate of Suleiman the Magnificent and his successors; the continental bloc which Napoleon so nearly achieved; the *Mitteleuropa* of Imperial Germany; Hitler's 'Thousand Year' *Reich*; the socialist Utopia espoused by the Soviet Union; and the democratic geopolitics of NATO and the European Union today. In each case the central area of contention was Germany: because of its strategic position at the heart of Europe, because of its immense economic and military potential and – in the Early Modern period – because of the political legitimacy which its imperial title conferred. In the late nineteenth century, this latent power was realized under Bismarck's leadership and dominated European politics until the fall of Hitler. During the subsequent Cold War, the struggle for control of Germany was at the heart of the rivalry between the Soviet Union and the west. After the fall of the Berlin Wall, German power surged again with reunification – albeit more slowly than many had expected – and now dominates the European Union. Again and again, from the Treaty of Westphalia, through the Vienna Settlement, to the establishment of the Western European Union, and the new surge in European integration after the fall of the Wall, the link between the internal order in Germany and the peace of Europe has been made explicit. Some of the most important international institutions – the League of Nations, the United Nations, the project of European integration, the Non-Proliferation Treaty and (in part) NATO – were originally designed to contain Germany or to mobilize her energies in the common cause.

Germany has also been the cockpit of the European ideological struggle. The south-eastern flank of the Holy Roman Empire was the most important front against Islam: the Turks penetrated twice as far as Vienna. It was also the fulcrum of the battle between Catholic and Protestant, which culminated in the Thirty Years War and continued to roil relations within and between states for a long time after. It was in Germany where the confrontation between conservative autocrats and liberal constitutionalists was sharpest in the nineteenth century. Germany was the birthplace of Marxism and home to the most powerful socialist party before the First World War. It was Germany which produced Nazism. Finally, the clash between communist dictatorship and democracy was nowhere stronger than in Germany, and particularly in Berlin, which took on a crucial symbolic importance as a divided former capital, in a divided Germany, in a divided Europe, in a divided world. The Cold War started and ended there. Today, the question of whether Europe will go forward into a closer union or will remain a confederation of nation states will primarily be decided in and by Germany.

The European balance of power – and especially the future of Germany – was also crucial to the most important extra-European power, the United States. North America was settled as part of the contest between Britain, France and Spain; this struggle both drove the colonists to seek independence and made it possible. Despite periodic attempts at isolation, the security of the new republic was always primarily dependent on the policies of the European states. They were rivals for influence in the western hemisphere and posed a mortal threat when they sought to establish themselves on the flanks of the United States. Washington slowly learned to live with the British presence in Canada, but it strenuously resisted any European penetration of Latin America: by Britain over slavery in Cuba, Napoleon III's attempt to establish a satellite empire in Mexico, Imperial Germany's links with Mexico and finally the Soviet gambit in Cuba. More generally, American strategists were fearful that were any one power to become predominant in Europe, this would soon be followed by an attempt to impose its authority and ideology on them. They therefore followed the Napoleonic Wars, the early-nineteenth-century clash between liberalism and autocracy, and the ambitions of both Imperial Germany and the Third Reich with profound concern. After the Second World War, Washington was determined not to allow the central European landmass to fall into the hands of a rival power, for the same reason. The United States thus originated as part of the European state system and has become increasingly central to it ever since.

It would be tempting to end with a list of prognostications and recommendations. Instead, I will conclude with a series of questions.

This book goes to press during a period of exceptional European uncertainty. Nobody knows whether the Franco-German-led Eurozone will survive the onslaught of the markets or whether it will be pulverized by the outside world as surely as the Continental System, *Mitteleuropa* and 'Fortress Europe' were crushed in their time. Will Europe find a common position on the challenges and opportunities of the Arab Spring, Russian ambitions in the east and the growth of Chinese power, or will it fragment into its component parts? Will Europeans persist in regarding the EU as a modern-day Holy Roman Empire, which enables them to coexist more easily than ever before but is incapable of effective collective action, or will they conclude that all these problems can only be mastered by establishing a new constitutional settlement on the lines pioneered by the Anglo-Americans in the eighteenth century: a mighty union based on a common debt, strong central institutions responsible to a directly elected parliament and a common defence against common enemies?

Only two states have the power to unlock this door to deeper integration: Britain, because she possesses the most credible fighting force on the continent at the moment; and Germany, because her economic strength is vital to the functioning of the Single Market and the Euro. Will they turn the key together? Will Britain serve as the Prussia of the European project, driving forward security integration and providing it with the military credibility it so desperately needs? Will it embrace the European destiny which Englishmen have pursued since Henry VIII, Marlborough and Castlereagh if not earlier? Will it at least support the continent in its quest for union, even if it supports the project only as a buttress from outside. Or will Britain turn her back on Europe and destroy all hopes for a mighty union for the defence of western values at home and their projection abroad? Will Germany, for her part, return to the traditions of 'Rapallo', permanently blocking NATO expansion, and pursue a policy of narrow fiscal advantage, by seceding from the common currency? Or will Berlin accept that the alternative to a democratically controlled European currency is a German economic hegemony which will in the long run destroy the European Union, thereby greatly increasing the economic and strategic insecurity of the Federal Republic? Will Germany therefore concede the logic that she is 'too small for the world and too large for Europe', by seeking through democratic union the critical weight which had eluded her leaders from Bismarck to Hitler?

This book began with the call to rally 'Christendom' in the mid fifteenth century as it struggled to meet the Ottoman challenge. It argues that Europeans have only ever experienced that unity in the face of an external or internal threat, for example against Louis XIV, Napoleon, Hitler or Stalin. It follows that only a major external threat will unite Europeans today. Will this take the form of a confrontation with Mr Putin's Russia, perhaps over the Baltic states, Belarus or Ukraine? Will it be a showdown with the Islamist caliphate in the Middle East or on the 'home front' of western societies? Or will it be a clash with China as it expands into areas of vital interest to Europe and becomes an ever more severe ideological challenge? Will the Union meet these threats by expanding east and south until it hits natural geographical or impermeable political borders. Will the 'lands between', in Ukraine and Belarus, be absorbed to end instability and pre-empt their subversion by Moscow? Above all, will the European Union become a more cohesive international actor, particularly in the military sphere. Will its army and navy serve as the 'school of the Union'? Or will Europeans duck these challenges, retreat into themselves and even split apart? If that happens, history will judge the European Union an expensive youthful prank which the continent played in its dotage, marking the completion rather than the starting point of a great-power project.

References

PREFACE

1. Quoted in D. M. Schreuder, 'Gladstone and Italian unification, 1848–70: the making of a Liberal?', *The English Historical Review*, LXXXV, 336 (1970), p. 477.
2. Halford Mackinder, *Democratic ideals and reality* (London, 2009 [1919]), p. 23.

INTRODUCTION: EUROPE IN 1450

1. See Robert Bartlett, *The making of Europe. Conquest, colonisation and cultural change, 950–1350* (London, 1993), pp. 269–91, especially p. 291.
2. Thus Thomas N. Bisson, 'The military origins of medieval representation', *American Historical Review*, 71, 4 (1966), pp. 1199–1218, especially pp. 199 and 1203.
3. There are overviews in A. R. Myers, *Parliaments and estates in Europe to 1789* (London, 1975), and H. G. Koenigsberger, 'Parliaments and estates', in R. W. Davis (ed.), *The origins of modern freedom in the west* (Stanford, Calif., 1995), pp. 135–77. For England, Germany and Sweden see Peter Blickle, Steven Ellis and Eva Österberg, 'The commons and the state: representation, influence, and the legislative process', in Peter Blickle (ed.), *Resistance, representation, and community* (Oxford, 1997), pp. 115–54. For a parliamentary critique of grand strategy and the flashing of fiscal teeth see J. S. Roskell, *The history of parliament. The House of Commons, 1386–1421* (Stroud, 1992), pp. 89, 101, 101–15, 126, 129 and 137.
4. See Samuel K. Cohn Jr, *Lust for liberty. The politics of social revolt in medieval Europe, 1200–1425. Italy, France and Flanders* (Cambridge, Mass., and London, 2006), pp. 228–42.
5. See Richard Bonney (ed.), *The rise of the fiscal state in Europe, c. 1200–1815* (Oxford, 1999), and Philippe Contamine (ed.), *War and competition between states* (Oxford, 2000).

6. See Michael Wintle, *The image of Europe. Visualizing Europe in cartography and iconography throughout the ages* (Cambridge, 2009), pp. 58–64.
7. For an overview see Alfred Kohler, *Expansion and Hegemonie. Internationale Beziehungen 1450–1559* (Paderborn, 2008).
8. Thus Peter Blickle, *Obedient Germans? A rebuttal. A new view of German history* (Charlottesville, and London, 1997), especially pp. 44–52. See also Martin Kintzinger and Bernd Schneidmüller, *Politische Öffentlichkeit im Spätmittelalter* (Darmstadt, 2011).
9. For the intense English interest in the Empire see Arnd Reitemeier, *Aussenpolitik im Spätmittelalter. Die diplomatischen Beziehungen zwischen dem Reich und England, 1377–1422* (Paderborn, 1999), pp. 14–15, 474–81 and passim.
10. See Marie Tanner, *The last descendant of Aeneas. The Hapsburgs and the mythic image of the emperor* (New Haven, 1993); Martin Kintzinger, *Die Erben Karls des Grossen. Frankreich und Deutschland im Mittelalter* (Ostfildern, 2005); and Alexandre Y. Haran, *Le lys et le globe. Messianisme dynastique et rêve impérial en France à l'aube des temps modernes* (Seyssel, 2000). For the strategic dimension see Duncan Hardy, 'The 1444–5 expedition of the dauphin Louis to the Upper Rhine in geopolitical perspective', *Journal of Medieval History*, 38, 3 (2012), pp. 358–87 (especially pp. 360–70).
11. See Bernd Marquardt, *Die 'europäische Union' des vorindustriellen Zeitalters. Vom Universalreich zum Staatskörper des Jus Publicum Europaeum (800–1800)* (Zurich, 2005).
12. See Thomas A. Brady, *German histories in the age of Reformations, 1400–1650* (Cambridge, 2009), pp. 90–98.
13. See Eberhard Isenmann, 'Reichsfinanzen und Reichssteuern im 15. Jahrhundert', *Zeitschrift für die historische Forschung*, 7 (1980), pp. 1–76 and 129–218 (especially pp. 1–9).
14. See Tom Scott, 'Germany and the Empire', in Christopher Allmand (ed.) *The New Cambridge Medieval History*. Vol. VII: *c.1415–c.1500* (Cambridge, 1998), pp. 337–40.

1. EMPIRES, 1453–1648

1. Quoted in Hugh Thomas, *Rivers of gold. The rise of the Spanish Empire* (London, 2003, 2010 edition), p. 494.
2. Quoted in Andreas Osiander, *The states system of Europe, 1640–1990. Peacemaking and the conditions of international stability* (Oxford, 1994), p. 79.
3. See Jonathan Harris, *The end of Byzantium* (New Haven and London, 2010), pp. 178–206.
4. Thus Daniel Goffman, *The Ottoman Empire and Early Modern Europe* (Cambridge, 2002), pp. 2–3, 9–10, 13 (re the prophet Muhammed),

222 and passim; and Osman Turan, 'The ideal of world domination among the medieval Turks', *Studia islamica*, IV (1955), pp. 77–90, especially pp. 88–9.

5. See Steven Runciman, *The fall of Constantinople, 1453* (Cambridge, 1966), pp. 160–80, and W. Brandes, 'Der Fall Konstantinopels als apokalyptisches Ereignis', in S. Kolditz and R. C. Müller (eds.), *Geschehenes und Geschriebenes. Studien zu Ehren von Günther S. Henrich und Klaus-Peter Matschke* (Leipzig, 2005), pp. 453–69.
6. Quoted in Iver B. Neumann and Jennifer M. Welsh, 'The other in European self-definition: an addendum to the literature on international society', *Review of International Studies*, 17, 4 (1991), pp. 327–48 (p. 336).
7. Quoted in Peter O'Brien, *European perceptions of Islam and America from Saladin to George W. Bush. Europe's fragile ego uncovered* (London, 2009), p. 75. See also Rhoads Murphey, 'Süleyman I and the conquest of Hungary: Ottoman manifest destiny or a delayed reaction to Charles V's universalist vision', *Journal of Early Modern History*, 5 (2001), pp. 197–221.
8. Theodore Spandounes, *On the origin of the Ottoman emperors*, trans. and ed. Donald M. Nicol (Cambridge, 1997), p. 5.
9. See Wim Blockmans and Nicolette Mout (ed.), *The world of emperor Charles V* (Amsterdam, 2004), and Alfred Kohler, *Karl V. 1500–1558. Eine Biographie* (Munich, 1999).
10. John Lynch, *Spain under the Habsburgs*. Vol. I: *Empire and absolutism* (Oxford, 1981), quotation p. 38. On Charles V and 'Universal Monarchy' see Franz Bosbach, *Monarchia universalis. Ein politischer Leitbegriff der Frühen Neuzeit* (Göttingen, 1988), pp. 35–64.
11. See Geoffrey Parker, *The grand strategy of Philip II* (New Haven and London, 1998), p. 4.
12. Thus Gábor Ágoston, 'Information, ideology, and limits of imperial policy: Ottoman grand strategy in the context of Ottoman–Habsburg rivalry', in Virginia H. Aksan and Daniel Goffman (eds.), *The Early Modern Ottomans: remapping the empire* (Cambridge, 2007), pp. 75–103.
13. On Suleiman and the German princes see Goffman, *Ottoman Empire and Early Modern Europe*, p. 111.
14. The Sultan's instructions to the Moriscos and his envoy to Flanders are cited in Andrew C. Hess, 'The Moriscos: an Ottoman fifth column in sixteenth-century Spain', *American Historical Review*, 74, 1 (1968), pp. 19–20.
15. See Esther-Beate Körber, *Habsburgs europäische Herrschaft. Von Karl V. bis zum Ende des 16. Jahrhunderts* (Darmstadt, 2002), p. 20 and passim.
16. Quoted in Lynch, *Spain under the Habsburgs*, pp. 74–5.
17. This watershed is stressed by Aurelio Espinosa, 'The grand strategy of Charles V (1500–1558): Castile, war, and dynastic priority in the

Mediterranean', *Journal of Early Modern History*, 9 (2005), pp. 239–83, especially pp. 239–41 and 258–9.

18. See Federico Chabod, '"¿Milán o los Países Bajos?" Las discusiones en España sobre la "alternativa" de 1544', in *Carlos V (1500–1558). Homenaje de la Universidad de Granada* (Granada, 1958), pp. 331–72, especially pp. 340–41. I thank Miss Carolina Jimenez Sanchez for translating this article for me.
19. Volker Press, 'Die Bundespläne Karls V und die Reichsverfassung', in Heinrich Lutz (ed.), *Das römisch-deutsche Reich im politischen System Karls V.* (Munich, 1982), pp. 55–106.
20. Thus Alfred Kohler, *Expansion und Hegemonie. Internationale Beziehungen, 1450–1559* (Paderborn, Munich, etc., 2008), pp. 371–84.
21. Olivares on Flanders is cited in Jonathan I. Israel, *Conflicts of empires. Spain, the Low Countries and the struggle for world supremacy, 1585–1713* (London, 1997), pp. 67–8. For projected Spanish military expenditure in 1634 see the figures in J. H. Elliott, 'Foreign policy and domestic crisis: Spain, 1598–1659', in J. H. Elliott, *Spain and its world, 1500–1700. Selected essays* (New Haven and London, 1989), p. 130.
22. Randall Lesaffer, 'Defensive warfare, prevention and hegemony: the justifications of the Franco-Spanish war of 1635', *Journal for International Law*, 8 (2006), pp. 91–123 and 141–79. Richelieu on gateways is cited in J. H. Elliott, *Richelieu and Olivares* (Cambridge, 1984), p. 123.
23. Quoted in Derek Croxton, *Peacemaking in Early Modern Europe. Cardinal Mazarin and the Congress of Westphalia, 1643–1648* (Selinsgrove, Pa, and London, 1999), p. 271.
24. Quoted in Stuart Carroll, *Martyrs and murderers. The Guise family and the making of Europe* (Oxford, 2009), p. 68.
25. Quoted in Alison D. Anderson, *On the verge of war. International relations and the Jülich-Kleve succession crises (1609–1614)* (Boston, 1999), p. 51.
26. For Richelieu's Germany policy see Anja Victorine Hartmann, *Von Regensburg nach Hamburg. Die diplomatischen Beziehungen zwischen dem französischen König und dem Kaiser vom Regensburger Vertrag (13. Oktober 1630) bis zum Hamburger Präliminarfrieden (25. Dezember 1641)* (Münster, 1998).
27. Richelieu is quoted in Hermann Weber, 'Richelieu und das Reich', in Heinrich Lutz, Friedrich Hermann Schubert and Hermann Weber (eds.), *Frankreich und das Reich im 16. und 17. Jahrhundert* (Göttingen, 1968) pp. 36–52 (pp. 39 and 41).
28. Quoted in Osiander, *States system of Europe*, p. 28.
29. This paragraph is largely based on James D. Tracy, *The founding of the Dutch Republic. War, finance, and politics in Holland, 1572–1588* (Oxford, 2008), pp. 5–7, 143–5, 238–41 and passim. For the connections between

the Netherlands and the Empire see Johannes Arndt, *Das heilige Römische Reich und die Niederlande 1566 bis 1648. Politisch-Konfessionelle Verflechtung und Publizistik im Achtzigjährigen Krieg* (Cologne, 1998).

30. Rory McEntegart, *Henry VIII, the League of Schmalkalden and the English Reformation* (Woodbridge, 2002), pp. 11–12 and 217–18 (quotation p. 17).
31. Cited in R. B. Wernham, *Before the Armada. The growth of English foreign policy, 1485–1588* (London, 1966), p. 292.
32. See J. Raitt, 'The Elector John Casimir, Queen Elizabeth, and the Protestant League', in D. Visser (ed.), *Controversy and conciliation. The Reformation and the Palatinate, 1559–1583* (Allison Park, Pa, 1986), pp. 117–45.
33. For Elizabeth's reservations about territorial expansion into the Low Countries see Simon Adams, 'Elizabeth I and the sovereignty of the Netherlands, 1576–1585', in *Transactions of the Royal Historical Society*, Sixth Series, XIV (2004), pp. 309–19.
34. See Michael Roberts, *Gustavus Adolphus* (London and New York, 1992), pp. 59–72, and 'The political objectives of Gustav Adolf in Germany, 1630–2', in Roberts, *Essays in Swedish History* (London, 1967), pp. 82–110. The quotations from Gustavus Adolphus and the *Rijkstag* are in Erik Ringmar, *Identity, interest and action. A cultural explanation of Sweden's intervention in the Thirty Years War* (Cambridge, 1996), p. 112. Oxenstierna is quoted in Peter H. Wilson (ed.), *The Thirty Years War. A Sourcebook* (Basingstoke and New York, 2010), p. 133.
35. 'Swedish Manifesto. 1630', in Wilson (ed.), *Thirty Years War. A Sourcebook*, p. 122. The concerns about the Habsburgs 'drawing nearer to the Baltic provinces' are clearly spelled out on pp. 123–4. The 'liberty of Germany' is invoked in the final paragraph, p. 130.
36. See Sigmund Goetze, *Die Politik des schwedischen Reichskanzlers Axel Oxenstierna gegenüber Kaiser und Reich* (Kiel, 1971), pp. 75–90.
37. Quoted in Michael Roberts, 'Oxenstierna in Germany', in Roberts, *From Oxenstierna to Charles XII. Four studies* (Cambridge, 1991), p. 26.
38. On Spanish perceptions of the importance of Germany to the Dutch see Charles Howard Carter, *The secret diplomacy of the Habsburgs, 1598–1625* (New York and London, 1964), p. 58.
39. Quoted in Osiander, *States system of Europe*, p. 79.
40. See Gülru Necipoğlu, 'Süleyman the Magnificent and the representation of power in the context of Ottoman–Habsburg–Papal rivalry', *The Art Bulletin*, 71 (1989), pp. 401–27, especially pp. 411–12.
41. On Suleiman and the imperial crown, see Goffman, *Ottoman Empire and Early Modern Europe*, pp. 107–8. The importance of central Europe and the Mediterranean is stressed in Metin Kunt and Christine Woodhead (eds.), *Süleyman the Magnificent and his age. The Ottoman Empire in the Early Modern world* (London, 1995), pp. 24 and 42–3.

42. Quoted in Karl Brandi, *Kaiser Karl V. Wenden und Schicksal einer Persönlichkeit und eines Weltreiches* (Munich, 1959), p. 78.
43. Quoted in John M. Headley, 'Germany, the Empire and Monarchia in the thought and policy of Gattinara', in Lutz (ed.), *Das römisch-deutsche Reich*, p. 18.
44. See Henry J. Cohn, 'Did bribes induce the German electors to choose Charles V as emperor in 1519?', *German History*, 19, 1 (2001), pp. 1–27.
45. For the centrality of Germany to the imperial vision of Charles V see Headley, 'Germany, the Empire and Monarchia', in Lutz (ed.), *Das römisch-deutsche Reich*, pp. 15–33, especially pp. 18–19 (quotations pp. 16 and 22).
46. On the importance of 'imperial Italy' see Matthias Schnettger and Marcello Verga (eds.), *Das Reich und Italien in der Frühen Neuzeit* (Berlin and Bologna, 2000). On the imperial clash between Maximilian and Charles see Hermann Wiesflecker, *Kaiser Maximilian I. Das Reich, Österreich und Europa an der Wende zur Neuzeit* (Munich, 1975) (quotation p. 50). For Charles's 'messianic' imperial ambitions see Haran, *Le lys et le globe*, pp. 39–40.
47. Quoted in Heinrich Lutz, 'Kaiser Karl V., Frankreich und das Reich', in Lutz et al., *Frankreich und das Reich im 16. und 17. Jahrhundert*, pp. 7–19 (quotation p. 13).
48. Quoted in William F. Church, *Richelieu and reason of state* (Princeton, NJ, 1972), p. 287.
49. Stella Fletcher, *Cardinal Wolsey. A life in Renaissance Europe* (London and New York, 2009), pp. 61–2.
50. See C. S. L. Davies, 'Tournai and the English crown, 1513–1519', *Historical Journal*, 41 (1998), pp. 1–26, especially pp. 11–12.
51. See generally Euan Cameron, *The European Reformation* (Oxford, 1991) pp. 99–110.
52. See John W. Bohnstedt, *The infidel scourge of God. The Turkish menace as seen by German pamphleteers of the Reformation era* (Philadelphia, 1968), pp. 12–13 and 23–5.
53. On the link between nation, Reformation and participation see Dieter Mertens, 'Nation als Teilhabeverheissung: Reformation und Bauernkrieg', in Dieter Langewiesche and Georg Schmidt (eds.), *Föderative Nation. Deutschlandkonzepte von der Reformation bis zum Ersten Weltkrieg* (Munich, 2000), pp. 115–34, especially pp. 117–18 and 125–32. See also Klaus Arnold, '". . . damit der arm man vnnd gemainer nutz iren furgang haben" . . . Zum deutschen "Bauernkrieg" als politischer Bewegung: Wendel Hiplers und Friedrich Weigandts Pläne einer "Reformation" des Reiches', in *Zeitschrift für historische Forschung*, 9 (1982), pp. 257–31[illegible] especially pp. 296–307 on imperial reform plans.

54. See Andrew Pettegree, *The Reformation and the culture of persuasion* (Cambridge, 2005), especially pp. 185–210; R. W. Scribner, *For the sake of simple folk. Popular propaganda for the German Reformation* (Cambridge, 1981); and Peter Lake and Steven Pincus (eds.), *The politics of the public sphere in Early Modern England* (Manchester and New York, 2007), especially pp. 1–30.
55. See Diarmaid MacCulloch, *Reformation. Europe's house divided, 1490–1700* (London, 2003), especially pp. 124–5. On the increased sense of insecurity, internally and externally, produced by the Reformation see Robert von Friedeburg, *Self-defence and religious strife in Early Modern Europe. England and Germany, 1530–1680* (Aldershot, 2002).
56. See Claus-Peter Clasen, *The Palatinate in European history, 1555–1618* (Oxford, 1963), especially pp. 10–11; and Volker Press, 'Fürst Christian I. von Anhalt-Bernburg, Statthalter der Oberpfalz, Haupt der evangelischen Bewegungspartei vor dem Dreissigjährigen Krieg (1568–1630)', in Konrad Ackermann and Alois Schmid (eds.), *Staat und Verwaltung in Bayern* (Munich, 2003), pp. 193–216.
57. D. J. B. Trim, 'Calvinist internationalism and the shaping of Jacobean foreign policy', in Timothy Wilks (ed.), *Prince Henry revived. Image and exemplarity in Early Modern England* (London, 2007), pp. 239–58. For one of the most interesting agents of the 'Calvinist International' see Hugh Trevor-Roper, *Europe's physician. The various life of Sir Theodore de Mayerne* (New Haven, 2006).
58. Cecil on the German princes is cited in David Trim, 'Seeking a Protestant alliance and liberty of conscience on the continent, 1558–85', in Susan Doran and Glenn Richardson (eds.), *Tudor England and its neighbours* (Basingstoke, 2005), pp. 139–77 (p. 157).
59. See Peter H. Wilson, 'The Thirty Years War as the Empire's constitutional crisis', in R. J. W. Evans, Michael Schaich and Peter H. Wilson (eds.), *The Holy Roman Empire, 1495–1806* (Oxford, 2010), pp. 95–114.
60. See Heinz Duchhardt, *Protestantisches Kaisertum und altes Reich. Die Diskussion über die Konfession des Kaisers in Politik, Publizistik und Staatsrecht* (Wiesbaden, 1977), pp. 326–30.
61. R. A. Stradling, *Spain's struggle for Europe, 1598–1668* (London, 1994).
62. Zúñiga and Onate are quoted in Eberhard Straub, *Pax et imperium. Spaniens Kampf um seine Friedensordnung in Europa zwischen 1617 und 1635* (Paderborn and Munich, 1980), pp. 116–17.
63. See Brennan C. Pursell, *The Winter King. Frederick V of the Palatinate and the coming of the Thirty Years War* (Aldershot, 2003).
64. Thomas Brockmann, *Dynastie, Kaiseramt und Konfession. Politik und Ordnungsvorstellungen Ferdinands II. im Dreissigjährigen Krieg* (Paderborn, 2009).

65. See Heinz Duchhardt, 'Das Reich in der Mitte des Staatensystems. Zum Verhältnis von innerer Verfassung und internationaler Funktion in den Wandlungen des 17. und 18. Jahrhunderts', in Peter Krüger (ed.), *Das europäische Staatensystem im Wandel. Strukturelle Bedingungen und bewegende Kräfte seit der Frühen Neuzeit* (Munich, 1996), pp. 1–9; and Christoph Kampmann, *Europa und das Reich im Dressigjährigen Krieg. Geschichte eines europäischen Konflikts* (Stuttgart, 2008).
66. Quoted in R. J. Knecht, *The Valois. Kings of France, 1328–1589* (London, 2004), p. 144.
67. For an overview see Maurice Keen, 'The end of the Hundred Years War: Lancastrian France and Lancastrian England', in Michael Jones and Malcolm Vale (eds.), *England and her neighbours, 1066–1453* (London and Ronceverte, W. Va, 1989), pp. 297– 311, especially pp. 299–301.
68. For the existence of a 'political sphere' before print and the centrality of the English wars see Clementine Oliver, *Parliament and political pamphleteering in fourteenth-century England* (Woodbridge, 2010), p. 4 and passim.
69. Cited in Helen Castor, *Blood and roses* (London, 2004), p. 60.
70. See G. L. Harriss, 'The struggle for Calais: an aspect of the rivalry between Lancaster and York', *The English Historical Review*, LXXV, 294 (1960), pp. 30–53, especially pp. 30–31.
71. Alexandra Gajda, 'Debating war and peace in late Elizabethan England', *Historical Journal*, 52 (2009), pp. 851–78.
72. See Noel Malcolm, *Reason of state, propaganda, and the Thirty Years' War. An unknown translation by Thomas* Hobbes (Oxford, 2007), especially pp. 74–8, and Robert von Friedeburg, '"Self-defence" and sovereignty: the reception and application of German political thought in England and Scotland, 1628–69', *History of Political Thought*, 23 (2002), pp. 238–65.
73. See Almut Höfert, *Den feind beschreiben. Türkengefahr und europäisches Wissen über das Osmanische Reich 1450–1600* (Frankfurt, 2003), and Robert Schwoebel, *The shadow of the crescent. The Renaissance image of the Turk (1453–1517)* (Nieuwkoop, 1967).
74. See Caspar Hirschi, *Wettkampf der Nationen. Konstruktionen einer deutschen Ehrgemeinschaft an der Wende vom Mittelalter zur Neuzeit* (Göttingen, 2005), pp. 12, 159, and passim.
75. See Alfred Schröcker, *Die deutsche Nation. Beobachtungen zur politischen Propaganda des ausgehenden 15. Jahrhunderts* (Lübeck, 1974), pp. 116–45, and Joachim Whaley, *Germany and the Holy Roman Empire, 1493–1806*, 2 vols. (Oxford, 2011).
76. For the travails of Lerma see Elliott, 'Foreign policy and domestic crisis', in Elliott, *Spain and its world*, especially, pp. 118–19.
77. See Sharon Kettering, *Power and reputation at the court of Louis XIII. The career of Charles d'Albert, duc de Luynes (1578–1621)* (Manchester and New York, 2008), pp. 217–42.

78. For the vital European context see Jonathan Scott, *England's troubles. Seventeenth-century English political instability in European context* (Cambridge, 2000), and John Reeve, 'Britain or Europe? The context of Early Modern English history: political and cultural, economic and social, naval and military', in Glenn Burgess (ed.), *The new British history. Founding a modern state, 1603–1715* (London and New York, 1999), pp. 287–312.
79. 'Resolutions on religion drawn by a sub-committee of the House of Commons', 24 February 1629, in S. R. Gardiner, *Constitutional documents of the Puritan revolution*, 3rd rev. edn (Oxford, 1906), p. 78. On the rise of Calvinist internationalism in England see David Trim, 'Calvinist internationalism and the shaping of Jacobean foreign policy', in Timothy Wilks (ed.), *Prince Henry revived. Image and exemplarity in Early Modern England* (London, 2007), pp. 239–58.
80. See Alfred Kohler, 'Karl V., Ferdinand I. und das Königreich Ungarn', in Martina Fuchs, Teréz Oborni and Gábor Újváry (eds.), *Kaiser Ferdinand I. Ein mitteleuropäischer Herrscher* (Münster, 2005), pp. 3–12.
81. Quoted in Hans Sturmberger, 'Türkengefahr und österreichische Staatlichkeit', *Südostdeutsches Archiv*, X (1967), pp. 132–45.
82. See Winfried Schulze, *Reich und Türkengefahr im späten 16. Jahrhundert. Studien zu den politischen und gesellschaftlichen Auswirkungen einer aüsseren Bedrohung* (Munich, 1978), especially pp. 270–97.
83. The declaration of 1575 is cited in Geoffrey Parker, *The Dutch Revolt* (Harmondsworth, 1990), p. 146. M. C. 't Hart, *The making of a bourgeois state. War, politics and finance during the Dutch revolt* (Manchester, 1993), pp. 216–17, makes the point that war and state formation do not necessarily lead to absolutism.
84. On the sealing of England's northern border see Jane E. A. Dawson, 'William Cecil and the British dimension of early Elizabethan foreign policy', *History*, 74 (1989), pp. 196–216 (Cecil quotation p. 209). For the English conception of Scotland in the broader European rather than 'British' context see Roger A. Mason, 'Scotland, Elizabethan England and the idea of Britain', *Transactions of the Royal Historical Society*, Sixth Series, 14 (2004), pp. 279–93 (especially p. 285). See also William Palmer, *The problem of Ireland in Tudor foreign policy 1485–1603* (Woodbridge, 1995), p. 79 and passim, and Brendan Bradshaw and John Morrill (eds.), *The British problem, c. 1534–1707. State formation in the Atlantic archipelago* (Basingstoke, 1996).
85. Philip's representative's comments to the Moriscos are cited in Lynch, *Spain under the Habsburgs*, p. 227.
86. This paragraph is largely based on Hess, 'The Moriscos: an Ottoman fifth column', pp. 1–25.
87. Már Jónsson, 'The expulsion of the Moriscos from Spain in 1609–1614: the destruction of an Islamic periphery', *Journal of Global History*, 2 (2007), pp. 195–212, stresses the security dimension, especially p. 203.

88. On the link between toleration and the need to mobilize against the Ottomans see M. A. Chisholm, 'The *Religionspolitik* of Emperor Ferdinand I (1521–1564)', *European History Quarterly*, 38, 4 (2008), p. 566.
89. Niccolò Machiavelli, *The discourses*, ed. Bernard Crick (Harmondsworth, 1970), with quotations (in order of appearance) on pp. 98, 100–102, 152, 168, 300, 252, 255, 130, 124, 259 and 122–3. See also Mikael Hörnqvist, *Machiavelli and empire* (Cambridge, 2004).
90. On the English inquest into the fall of France see Catherine Nall, 'Perceptions of financial mismanagement and the English diagnosis of defeat'. I thank Dr Nall for allowing me to see this unpublished text.
91. A point made by Steven Gunn, David Grummitt and Hans Cools, *War, state, and society in England and the Netherlands, 1477–1559* (Oxford, 2007), pp. 329–34.
92. See Wallace MacCaffrey, 'Parliament and foreign policy', in D. M. Dean and N. L. Jones (eds.), *The parliaments of Elizabethan England* (Oxford, 1990), pp. 65–90, especially pp. 65–7.
93. On the link between a strong monarchy and success in foreign policy see Emmanuel Le Roy Ladurie, *The royal French state, 1460–1610*, trans. Judith Vale (Oxford and Cambridge, Mass., 1994). See also Steven Gunn, 'Politic history, New Monarchy and state formation: Henry VII in European perspective', *Historical Research*, 82 (2009), pp. 380–92.
94. John Guy, 'The French king's council, 1483–1526', in Ralph A. Griffiths and James Sherborne (eds.), *Kings and nobles in the later Middle Ages* (Gloucester and New York), pp. 274–87. See also Emmanuel Le Roy Ladurie, *Royal French state*, especially pp. 54–78.
95. Lynch, *Spain under the Habsburgs*, pp. 50–51, 59, 63–4, 92–3 and 97.
96. Quoted in James D. Tracy, *The founding of the Dutch Republic. War, finance, and politics in Holland, 1572–1588* (Oxford, 2008), p. 26.
97. The Middle Volga peasants are cited in Valerie Kivelson, 'Muscovite "Citizenship": rights without freedom', *Journal of Modern History*, 74, 3 (2002) pp. 465–89 (citation p. 474). See also Hans-Joachim Torke, *Die staatsbedingte Gesellschaft im Moskauer Reich. Zar und Zemlja in der altrussischen Herrschaftsverfassung, 1613–1689* (Leiden, 1974).
98. George William is cited in Christopher Clark, *Iron kingdom. The rise and downfall of Prussia, 1600–1947* (London, 2006), p. 26.
99. A. S. Piccolomini, *Secret memoirs of a Renaissance pope. The* Commentaries *of Aeneas Sylvius Piccolomini, Pius II. An abridgement*, trans. Florence A. Gragg and ed. Leona C. Gabel (London, 1988), p. 62. I thank Anastasia Knox for this reference.
100. Quoted in Karl Nehring, *Matthias Corvinus, Kaiser Friedrich III. und das Reich. Zum hunyadisch-habsburgischen Gegensatz im Donauerraum* (Munich, 1975), p. 130.

101. On the famous Diet of July 1489 see Gerhard Benecke, *Maximilian I 1459–1519. An analytical biography* (London, Boston, Melbourne and Henley, 1982), pp. 141–6.
102. See Peter Schmid, *Der gemeine Pfennig von 1495. Vorgeschichte und Entstehung, verfassungsgeschichtliche, politische und finanzielle Bedeutung* (Göttingen, 1989).
103. See Whaley, *Germany and the Holy Roman Empire*, pp. 67–80 and passim.
104. Cited in Branka Magaš, *Croatia through history* (London, 2008), p. 90. On the initial response of the German Diet to the Ottoman threat see Stephen A. Fischer-Galati, *Ottoman imperialism and German Protestantism, 1521–1555* (New York, 1972 repr.), pp. 10–17. I am very grateful to Miss Andrea Fröhlich for sharing her expertise on early sixteenth-century Hungary with me.
105. See Thomas Nicklas, *Um Macht und Einheit des Reiches. Konzeption und Wirklichkeit der Politik bei Lazarus von Schwendi (1522–1583)* (Husum, 1995), with quotations on pp. 113–14, 116 and 121.
106. Quoted in Weston F. Cook, *The hundred years war for Morocco. Gunpowder and the military revolution in the Early Modern Muslim world* (Boulder, San Francisco and Oxford, 1994), p. 83.
107. On Columbus and the crusade see Felipe Fernández-Armesto, *Columbus* (Oxford, 1991), pp. 46 and 153–5.
108. The description of Bartolomé de las Casas, whose father and uncle sailed with Columbus, in Abbas Hamdani, 'Columbus and the recovery of Jerusalem', *Journal of the American Oriental Society*, 99, 1 (Jan.–Mar. 1979), pp. 39–48 (p. 43). For the Turkish response see Andrew Hess, 'The evolution of the Ottoman seaborne empire in the age of the oceanic discoveries, 1453–1525', *American Historical Review*, 75, 7 (1970), pp. 1892–1919, especially pp. 1894 and 1899 (encirclement), 1905 and 1908 (Indian Ocean).
109. The ideological and strategic agenda is stressed by Robert Finlay, 'Crisis and crusade in the Mediterranean: Venice, Portugal, and the Cape Route to India (1498–1509)', in Robert Finlay, *Venice besieged. Politics and diplomacy in the Italian wars 1494–1534* (Aldershot, 2008), pp. 45–90.
110. Hugh Thomas, *Rivers of gold. The rise of the Spanish Empire* (London and New York, 2003), pp. 540–54.
111. On the impact of New World bullion see Patrick Karl O'Brien and Leandro Prados de la Escosura, 'Balance sheets for the acquisition, retention and loss of European empires overseas', *Itinerario*, XXIIII (1999), p. 28 and passim. The quotation is in Lynch, *Spain under the Habsburgs*, p. 38.
112. For the centrality of Europe in Charles's thinking see Hans-Joachim König, 'Plus ultra – Ein Weltreichs- und Eroberungsprogramm? Amerika und Europa in politischen Vorstellungen im Spanien Karls V.', in Alfred Kohler,

Barbara Haider and Christine Ottner (eds.), *Karl V. 1500–1558. Neue Perspektiven seiner Herrschaft in Europa und Übersee* (Vienna, 2002), pp. 197–222, especially pp. 203–4.

113. Contrary to the claims of Hugh Thomas, *The golden empire. Spain, Charles V and the creation of America* (New York, 2011), pp. 362–3, 370–72 and passim (figures for distribution of gold p. 511).

114. The English parliamentarians are cited in Thomas Cogswell, *The Blessed revolution. English politics and the coming of war, 1621–1624* (Cambridge, 1989), pp. 72–3. Rudyerd is cited in J. H. Elliott, *The Old World and the New 1492–1650* (Cambridge, 1992) pp. 90–91.

115. For the importance of the contest with Spain to control the tobacco trade see Thomas Cogswell, '"In the power of the state": Mr Anys's project and the tobacco colonies, 1626–1628', *The English Historical Review*, CXXIII, 500 (2008), pp. 35–64.

116. On the two-way traffic across the Atlantic generally see Susan Hardman Moore, *Pilgrims. New World settlers and the call of home* (New Haven and London, 2007).

117. On the importance of the Palatinate, the Protestant cause in Europe and 'Christendom' generally see Francis J. Bremer, *Puritan crisis. New England and the English Civil Wars, 1630–1670* (New York and London, 1989), pp. 27–32, 36–42, 45–50, 55–60, 63–4, 84–7 and 237–9 (quotations pp. 63 and 137). Perry Miller, *The New England mind. From colony to province* (Harvard, 1953), p. 25, stresses that Winthrop's hill was to be visible in Europe. Winthrop on Bohemia is cited in Francis J. Bremer, *John Winthrop. America's forgotten founding father* (New York and Oxford, 2003), p. 137.

118. On this see Christoph Kampmann, 'Peace impossible? The Holy Roman Empire and the European state system in the seventeenth century', in Olaf Asbach and Peter Schröder (eds.), *War, the state and international law in seventeenth-century Europe* (Farnham, 2010), pp. 197–210.

119. See Michael Rohrschneider, *Der gescheiterte Frieden von Münster. Spaniens Ringen mit Frankreich auf dem Westfälischen Friedenskongress (1643–1649)* (Münster, 2007), pp. 90 and 307–11.

120. Karsten Ruppert, *Die kaiserliche Politik auf dem westfälischen Friedenskongress (1643–1648)* (Münster, 1979), pp. 39–42 and 115–16.

121. Quoted in Andreas Osiander, *The state system of Europe, 1640–1990. Peacemaking and the conditions of international stability* (Oxford, 1994), p. 74.

122. See Lothar Höbelt, *Ferdinand III. Friedenskaiser wider Willen* (Graz, 2008), pp. 224–9.

123. Thus K. J. Holsti's hugely influential *International politics. A framework for analysis*, 4th edn (Englewood Cliffs, 1983), pp. 4 and 83–4. For a more recent enunciation of this view see Thomas G. Weiss, *Humanitarian intervention. Ideas in action* (Cambridge, 2007), p. 14.

124. Article 8. The text of the treaty can be found in Clive Parry (ed.), *The consolidated treaty series* (New York, 1969), pp. 198–356.
125. On this see Joachim Whaley, 'A tolerant society? Religious toleration in the Holy Roman Empire, 1648–1806', in Ole Grell and Roy Porter (eds.), *Toleration in Enlightenment Europe* (Cambridge, 2000), pp. 175–95, especially pp. 176–7.
126. See Derek Croxton, 'The Peace of Westphalia of 1648 and the origins of sovereignty', *International History Review*, 21, 3 (1999) pp. 569–91 (quotations pp. 589–90).
127. See Andreas Osiander, 'Sovereignty, international relations, and the Westphalian myth', *International Organization*, 55 (2001), pp. 251–87; Stéphane Beaulac, 'The Westphalian legal orthodoxy – myth or reality?', *Journal of the History of International Law*, 2 (2000), pp. 148–77; and Stephen D. Krasner, 'Westphalia and all that', in Judith Goldstein and Robert O. Keohane (eds.), *Ideas and foreign policy. Beliefs, institutions and political change* (Ithaca and London, 1993), p. 235. For a sociological view of the settlement see Benno Teschke, *The myth of 1648. Class, geopolitics, and the making of modern international relations* (London and New York, 2003).
128. For a sense of the trauma and destruction see Peter Englund, *Die Verwüstung Deutschlands. Eine Geschichte des dreissigjährigen Krieges* (Stuttgart, 1998), especially pp. 343–63, and Thomas Robisheaux, *Rural society and the search for order in Early Modern Germany* (Cambridge, 1989), pp. 201–26.
129. See Ian Roy, 'England turned Germany? The aftermath of the Civil War in its European context', *Transactions of the Royal Historical Society*, Fifth Series, 28 (1978), pp. 127–44 (especially pp. 127–30).
130. For a differentiated view see David Lederer, 'The myth of the all-destructive war: afterthoughts on German suffering, 1618–1648', *German History*, 29, 3 (2011), pp. 380–403.

2. SUCCESSIONS, 1649–1755

1. Quoted in Klaus Malettke, 'Europabewusstsein und europäische Friedenspläne im 17. und 18. Jahrhundert', *Francia*, 21 (1994), pp. 63–94 (p. 69).
2. Quoted in Sven Externbrink, *Friedrich der Grosse, Maria Theresia und das alte Reich. Deutschlandbild und diplomatie Frankreichs im Siebenjährigen Krieg* (Berlin, 2006), pp. 89–90.
3. See now David Onnekink (ed.), *War and religion after Westphalia, 1648–1713* (Farnham, 2009), pp. 1–15.
4. See Bernd Marquardt, 'Zur reichsgerichtlichen Aberkennung der Herrschergewalt wegen Missbrauchs: Tyrannenprozesse vor dem Reichshofrat am Beispiel des südöstlichen schwäbischen Reichskreises', in Anette Baumann, Peter Oestmann, Stephan Wendehorst and Siegrid Westphal (eds.),

Prozesspraxis im alten Reich. Annäherungen – Fallstudien – Statistiken (Cologne, Weimar and Vienna, 2005).

5. Karl Härter, 'Sicherheit und Frieden im frühneuzeitlichen Alten Reich: zur Funktion der Reichsverfassung als Sicherheits- und Friedensordnung 1648–1806', *Zeitschrift für historische Forschung*, 30 (2003), pp. 413–31.
6. On the 'humanitarian intervention' over Savoy see D. J. B. Trim, "If a prince use tyrannie towards his people": interventions on behalf of foreign populations in Early Modern Europe', in Brendan Simms and D. J. B. Trim (eds.), *Humanitarian intervention. A history* (Cambridge, 2011), pp. 54–64.
7. Thomas Gage's remarks of about 1654 are cited in Charles P. Korr, *Cromwell and the New Model foreign policy. England's policy toward France, 1649–1658* (Berkeley, Los Angeles and London, 1975) p. 89. Article 42 of the Treaty of the Pyrenees is cited in Peter Sahlins, 'Natural frontiers revisited. France's boundaries since the seventeenth century', *American Historical Review*, 95, 5 (1990), pp. 1423–51 (p. 1430).
8. See Robert I. Frost, *The northern wars. War, state and society in northeastern Europe, 1558–1721* (Harlow, 2000), pp. 198–200.
9. The Great Elector is cited in Richard Dietrich (ed.), *Die politischen Testamente der Hohenzollern* (Cologne and Vienna, 1986), p. 188.
10. Thus Paul Sonnino, *Mazarin's quest. The Congress of Westphalia and the coming of the Fronde* (Cambridge, Mass., and London, 2008), pp. 168–71.
11. See the various remonstrances of the *parlements*, printed in Richard Bonney, *Society and government in France under Richelieu and Mazarin 1624–61*(Basingstoke, 1988), pp. 21–5.
12. Cited in Christopher Clark, *Iron kingdom. The rise and downfall of Prussia, 1600–1947* (London, 2006), p. 55.
13. See Christoph Fürbringer, *Necessitas und libertas. Staatsbildung und Landstände im 17. Jahrhundert in Brandenburg* (Frankfurt, 1985), passim (quotations pp. 56, 67 and 162–3).
14. See F. L. Carsten, 'The resistance of Cleves and Mark to the despotic policy of the Great Elector', *The English Historical Review*, LXVI, 259 (1951), pp. 219–41, especially pp. 223–4 and 232 on the foreign policy link.
15. See Ferdinand Grönebaum, *Frankreich in Ost- und Nordeuropa. Die französisch-russischen Beziehungen von 1648–1689* (Wiesbaden, 1968), especially pp. 32–3.
16. Thus Peter Burke, *The fabrication of Louis XIV* (New Haven, 1992).
17. On Louis's policy towards the Empire see Georges Livet, 'Louis XIV and the Germanies', in Ragnhild Hatton (ed.), *Louis XIV and Europe* (London and Basingstoke, 1976), pp. 60–81, especially pp. 62–3.
18. Quoted in Andrew Lossky, *Louis XIV and the French monarchy* (New Brunswick, NJ, 1994), p. 129.
19. See Guy Rowlands, *The dynastic state and the army under Louis XIV. Royal service and private interest, 1661–1701* (Cambridge, 2002).

20. The strategic motivation is highlighted by Leslie Tuttle, *Conceiving the old regime. Pronatalism and the politics of reproduction in Early Modern France* (Oxford, 2010), p. 7.
21. Thus John A. Lynn, *Giant of the Grand Siècle. The French army, 1610–1715* (Cambridge, 1997), especially pp. 595–609.
22. See William Beik, *Absolutism and society in seventeenth-century France. State power and provincial aristocracy in Languedoc* (Cambridge, 1985), pp. 150–51 and 156–7, and Bailey Stone, *The genesis of the French Revolution. A global-historical interpretation* (Cambridge, 1994), p. 58. The quotations range from the 1630s to the 1690s.
23. Writing in 1673, quoted in Klaus Malettke, *Frankreich, Deutschland und Europa im 17. und 18. Jahrhundert. Beiträge zum Einfluss französischer politischer Theorie, Verfassung und Aussenpolitik in der Frühen Neuzeit* (Marburg, 1994), p. 311.
24. On the link between external pressure and the permanence of the Diet see Anton Schindling, *Die Anfänge des immerwährenden Reichstags zu Regensburg. Ständevertretung und Staatskunst nach dem Westfälischen Frieden* (Mainz, 1991), pp. 53–5, 68–90 and 229–30.
25. See Wout Troost, '"To restore and preserve the liberty of Europe". William III's ideas on foreign policy', in David Onnekink and Gijs Rommelse (eds.), *Ideology and foreign policy in Early Modern Europe (1650–1750)* (Farnham, 2011), pp. 283–304 (German context pp. 288–9).
26. On the centrality of the Low Countries and Germany to Spanish strategy in the late seventeenth century see Christopher Storrs, *The resilience of the Spanish monarchy, 1665–1700* (Oxford, 2006), pp. 14 and 113–14. For the annexation of the Franche-Comté see Darryl Dee, *Expansion and crisis in Louis XIV's France. Franche-Comté and absolute monarchy, 1674–1715* (Rochester, NY, and Woodbridge, 2009).
27. See Sonja Schultheiss-Heinz, 'Contemporaneity in 1672–1679: the Paris *Gazette*, the *London Gazette*, and the *Teutsche Kriegs-Kurier* (1672–1679)', in Brendan Dooley (ed.), *The dissemination of news and the emergence of contemporaneity in Early Modern Europe* (Farnham, 2010), pp. 115–36.
28. On the huge surge in English pamphleteering on foreign policy see Tony Claydon, *Europe and the making of England, 1660–1760* (Cambridge, 2007), pp. 220–25. For Germany see Erich Everth, *Die Öffentlichkeit in der Aussenpolitik von Karl V. bis Napoleon* (Jena, 1931), pp. 155–7.
29. See Alexander Schmidt, 'Ein französischer Kaiser? Die Diskussion um die Nationalität des Reichsoberhauptes im 17. Jahrhundert', *Historisches Jahrbuch*, 123 (2003), pp. 149–77, especially pp. 150, 156–8 and 174.
30. See Gabriel Glickman, 'Conflicting visions: foreign affairs in domestic debate, 1660–1689', in William Mulligan and Brendan Simms (eds.), *The primacy of foreign policy in British history, 1660–2000. How strategic concerns shaped modern Britain* (Basingstoke, 2010), pp. 15–31.

31. Quoted in Brendan Simms, *Three victories and a defeat. The rise and fall of the first British Empire, 1714–1783* (London, 2007), p. 32.
32. For the centrality of the strategic critique see Annabel Patterson, *The Long Parliament of Charles II* (New Haven and London, 2008), pp. 178–208, especially pp. 179–80.
33. On the critical importance of the War of Devolution for German views of Louis see Martin Wrede, *Das Reich und seine Feinde: politische Feindbilder in der reichspatriotischen Publizistik zwischen Westfälischem Frieden und Siebenjährigem Krieg* (Mainz, 2004), pp. 330–407.
34. See Leonard Krieger, *The German idea of freedom. History of a political tradition* (Chicago and London, 1957), pp. 6, 19 and passim.
35. Quoted in Peter Schröder, 'The constitution of the Holy Roman Empire after 1648: Samuel Pufendorf's assessment in his *Monzambano*', *Historical Journal*, 42 (1999), pp. 961–83 (quotation p. 970).
36. See Wolfgang Burgdorf, *Reichskonstitution und Nation. Verfassungsreformprojekte für das Heilige Römische Reich deutscher Nation im politischen Schrifttum von 1648 bis 1806* (Mainz, 1998), W. H. Pufendorf quotations pp. 70–73.
37. See Sophus Reinert, *Translating Empire. Emulation and the origins of political economy* (Cambridge, Mass., 2011).
38. For the link between the effects of Westphalia and the Peace of the Pyrenees and Spanish overseas policy see Stanley H. Stein and Barbara H. Stein, *Silver, trade and war. Spain and America in the making of Early Modern Europe* (Baltimore and London, 2000), pp. 57–105.
39. Louvois's remark of June 1684 is cited in Livet, 'Louis XIV and the Germanies'.
40. See Wouter Troost, 'William III, Brandenburg, and the construction of the anti-French coalition, 1672–88', in Jonathan Israel (ed.), *The Anglo-Dutch moment. Essays on the Glorious Revolution and its world impact* (Cambridge, 1991), pp. 299–333.
41. Quoted in G. Symcox, 'Louis XIV and the outbreak of the Nine Years War', in Ragnhild Hatton (ed.), *Louis XIV in Europe* (London, 1976), p. 187.
42. Quoted in John A. Lynn, *The wars of Louis XIV, 1667–1714* (London and New York, 1999), p. 197.
43. Quotations in Claydon, *Europe and the making of England*, pp. 56 and 239.
44. Charles II is quoted in ibid., p. 237.
45. See Tony Claydon, *William III and the godly revolution* (Cambridge, 1996), pp. 138–40 and passim.
46. On the centrality of the Low Countries to Spanish strategy even as late as the Nine Years War see Christopher Storrs, 'The army of Lombardy and the resilience of Spanish power in Italy in the reign of Carlos II (1665–1700)', in *War in History*, Part I, 4 (1997), pp. 371–97, and Part II, 5 (1998), pp. 1–22.

47. Quoted in Wout Troost, 'Ireland's role in the foreign policy of William III', in Esther Mijers and David Onnekink (eds.), *Redefining William III. The impact of the King-Stadholder in international context* (Aldershot, 2007), pp. 53–68 (quotation p. 53).
48. Quoted in Everth, *Öffentlichkeit in der Aussenpolitik*, p. 147.
49. Steve Pincus, *1688. The first modern revolution* (New Haven and London, 2009), pp. 475–7 and passim.
50. David Stasavage, *Public debt and the birth of the democratic state. France and Great Britain, 1688–1789* (Cambridge, 2003).
51. Philip J. Stern, *The company-state. Corporate sovereignty and the Early Modern foundations of the British Empire in India* (Oxford, 2011).
52. See Robert D. McJimsey, 'A country divided? English politics and the Nine Years' War', *Albion*, 23, 1 (1991), pp. 61–74.
53. Quoted in Miles Ogborn, 'The capacities of the state: Charles Davenant and the management of the excise, 1683–1698', *Journal of Historical Geography*, 24 (1998), pp. 289–312.
54. See A. F. Upton, *Charles XI and Swedish absolutism* (Cambridge, 1998), pp. 71–89.
55. See Peter H. Wilson, *War, state and society in Württemberg, 1677–1793* (Cambridge, 1995), especially pp. 247–8.
56. Thus Andre Wakefield, *The disordered police state. German cameralism as science and practice* (Chicago and London, 2009).
57. See Owen Stanwood, 'The Protestant moment: anti-popery, the Revolution of 1688–1689, and the making of an Anglo-American empire', *Journal of British Studies*, 46 (2007), pp. 481–508 (quotations pp. 488, 491, 501 and 491).
58. Quoted in Christian Greiner, 'Das "Schild des Reiches". Markgraf Ludwig Wilhelm von Baden-Baden (1655–1707) und die "Reichsbarriere" am Oberrhein', in Johannes Kunisch (ed.), *Expansion und Gleichgewicht. Studien zur europäischen Mächtepolitik des ancien régime* (Berlin, 1986), pp. 31–68 (quotation p. 47).
59. Linda and Marsha Frey, *A question of empire. Leopold I and the War of Spanish Succession, 1701–1705* (Boulder, 1983), pp. 15–17, 47 (quotation) and passim.
60. Peter Baumgart, 'Die preussische Königskrönung von 1701, das Reich und die europäische Politik', in Oswald Hauser (ed.), *Preussen, Europa und das Reich* (Cologne and Vienna, 1987), pp. 65–86, especially pp. 72–4.
61. The Admiralty instructions are quoted in Simms, *Three victories*, p. 50.
62. Quoted in Frey and Frey, *Question of empire*, p. 77.
63. Charles Spencer, *Blenheim. Battle for Europe. How two men stopped the conquest of Europe* (London, 2004).
64. The Prussian envoy Hoverbeck and Elector Frederick III are quoted in Martin Schulze-Wessel, *Russlands Blick auf Preussen. Die polnische Frage*

in der Diplomatie und der politischen Öffentlichkeit des Zarenreiches und des Sowjetstaates, 1697–1947 (Stuttgart, 1995), pp. 35 and 37.

65. Peter's ambassador to Vienna, Golitsyn, is quoted in Andrew Rothstein, *Peter the Great and Marlborough. Politics and diplomacy in converging wars* (Basingstoke, 1986), p. 37.
66. Marlborough is cited in Rothstein, *Peter the Great and Marlborough*, pp. 63 and 65–6.
67. Quoted in J. M. Dunn, '"Bright enough for all our purposes". John Locke's conception of a civilized society', *Notes and Records of the Royal Society London*, 43 (1989), p. 134.
68. See Michael Kwass, 'A kingdom of taxpayers: state formation, privilege and political culture in eighteenth-century France', *Journal of Modern History*, 70, 2 (1998), pp. 295–339, especially pp. 301 and 303.
69. For the primacy of foreign policy and the way in which it underpinned domestic transformation in Petrine Russia see Simon M. Dixon, *The modernisation of Russia, 1676–1825* (Cambridge, 1999), pp. 42–9 and 61–7.
70. See Christopher Storrs, 'The Union of 1707 and the War of the Spanish Succession', in Stewart J. Brown and Christopher A. Whatley (eds.), *The Union of 1707. New dimensions* (Edinburgh, 2008), pp. 31–44, and Allan I. Macinnes, *Union and empire. The making of the United Kingdom in 1707* (Cambridge, 2007), pp. 243–76.
71. The Council of State's protest to Philip is in Henry Kamen, *The war of succession in Spain, 1700–1715* (London, 1969), p. 91.
72. Albert N. Hamscher, *The Parlement of Paris after the Fronde, 1653–1673* (Pittsburgh, 1976), pp. 89–90, 122–3 and 198.
73. 'Erste Ermahnung Kurfürst Friedrichs III. an seinen Nachfolger', in Richard Dietrich (ed.), *Die politischen Testamente der Hohenzollern* (Cologne and Vienna, 1986), p. 218.
74. Quoted in Charles Ingrao, *In quest and crisis. Emperor Joseph I and the Habsburg monarchy* (West Lafayette, 1979), p. 58. On the increasing divisions between Habsburg and Hohenzollern see Christiane Kauer, *Brandenburg-Preussen und Österreich, 1705–1711* (Bonn, 1999), pp. 85–6, 159 and passim.
75. Marlborough is quoted in Rothstein, *Peter the Great and Marlborough* p. 112.
76. Louis's appeal is quoted in James B. Collins, *The state in Early Modern France* (Cambridge, 1995), p. 162.
77. St John is quoted in Simms, *Three victories*, p. 65.
78. See Ragnhild Hatton, *George I. Elector and king* (London, 1978).
79. Leibniz is quoted in Rothstein, *Peter the Great and Marlborough*, p. 124.
80. See David Kirby, 'Peter the Great and the Baltic', in Lindsey Hughe (ed.), *Peter the Great and the West. New perspectives* (Basingstoke, 2001) pp. 177–88.

81. Quoted in Karl A. Roider, *Austria's Eastern Question, 1700–1790* (Princeton, 1982), p. 40.
82. These two paragraphs are closely based on my remarks in '"A false principle in the law of nations". Burke, state sovereignty, [German] liberty, and intervention in the age of Westphalia', in Brendan Simms and D. J. B. Trim (eds.), *Humanitarian intervention. A history* (Cambridge, 2011), pp. 89–110 (quotations p. 95), and on the unpublished dissertation work of Patrick Milton on intervention in early-eighteenth-century central Europe.
83. Benedict Wagner-Rundell, 'Holy war and republican pacifism in the early-eighteenth-century Commonwealth of Poland–Lithuania', in David Onnekink and Gijs Rommelse (eds.), *Ideology and foreign policy in Early Modern Europe (1650–1750)* (Farnham, 2011), pp. 163–80, especially pp. 172–3.
84. Speaking in 1721, quoted in Simms, *Three victories*, p. 169.
85. Huxelles is quoted in Jörg Ulbert, 'Die Angst vor einer habsburgischen Hegemonie im Reich als Leitmotiv der französischen Deutschlandpolitik unter der Regentschaft Philipps von Orleans (1715–1723)', in Thomas Höpel (ed.), *Deutschlandbilder – Frankreichbilder. 1700–1850. Rezeption und Abgrenzung zweier Kulturen* (Leipzig, 2001), pp. 57–74 (p. 67).
86. Quoted in Simms, *Three victories*, p. 183.
87. Townshend is quoted in Simms, *Three victories*, p. 197.
88. See Lucian Hölscher, *Öffentlichkeit und Geheimnis. Eine begriffsgeschichtliche Untersuchung zur Entstehung der Öffentlichkeit in der Frühen Neuzeit* (Stuttgart, 1979), and Andreas Gestrich, *Absolutismus und Öffentlichkeit. Politische Kommunikation in Deutschland zu Beginn des 18. Jahrhunderts* (Göttingen, 1994).
89. The *Friedens-Courier* is quoted in Gestrich, *Absolutismus und Öffentlichkeit*, p. 222.
90. The First Commissioner of the French foreign ministry is quoted in Externbrink, *Friedrich der Grosse*, pp. 89–90.
91. The Austrian instructions are quoted in Arthur M. Wilson, *French foreign policy during the administration of Cardinal Fleury, 1729–1743. A study in diplomacy and commercial development* (New York, 1972), p. 169.
92. See Maren Köster, *Russische Truppen für Prinz Eugen. Politik mit militärischen Mitteln im frühen 18. Jahrhundert* (Vienna, 1986).
93. See Colin Jones, *The great nation. France from Louis XV to Napoleon, 1715–99* (London, 2007), p. xxi and passim.
94. Thus Paul Bushkovitch, *Peter the Great. The struggle for power, 1671–1725* (Cambridge, 2001), passim, especially pp. 270–80 (on Poland p. 444).
95. See James Cracraft, *The revolution of Peter the Great* (Cambridge, Mass., 2003), pp. 29–37 and 54–74 (Table of Ranks p. 35).
96. Thus Hanna Schissler, *Preussische Agrargesellschaft im Wandel. Wirtschaftliche, gesellschaftliche und politische Transformationsprozesse von 1763 bis 1847* (Göttingen, 1978).

97. Lars Atorf, *Der König und das Korn. Die Getreidehandelspolitik als Fundament des brandenburgisch-preussischen Aufsteigs zur europäischen Grossmacht* (Berlin, 1999), pp. 86–139.
98. Frederick William's warning is quoted in Helmut Neuhaus, 'Kronerwerb und Staatskonsolidierung. Der Aufstieg Brandeburg-Preussens im 18. Jahrhundert als Forschungsproblem', in Christiane Liermann, Gustavo Corni and Frank-Lothar Kroll, *Italien und Preussen. Dialog der Historiographien* (Tübingen, 2005), pp. 27–37 (p. 29).
99. On the persistence of representative systems in the face of princely absolutism see D. W. Hayton, James Kelly, and John Bergin (eds.), *The eighteenth-century composite state. Representative institutions in Ireland and Europe, 1689–1800* (Basingstoke, 2010), especially pp. 4–5.
100. Michael G. Müller, *Polen zwischen Preussen und Russland. Souveränitätskrise und Reformpolitik, 1736–1752* (Berlin, 1983), especially pp. 253–4 and 152–200.
101. On the Dutch debate see Herbert H. Rowen, *The princes of Orange. The Stadholders in the Dutch Republic* (Cambridge, 1988).
102. Ministerial critiques of frequent elections, and the trenchant views of William Shippen, MP, are quoted in Simms, *Three victories*, pp. 103–4.
103. Thus John Brewer, *The sinews of power. War, money, and the English state, 1688–1783* (London, 1989).
104. Hasan Kurdi is quoted in Virginia H. Aksan, *Ottoman wars 1700–1870. An empire besieged* (Harlow, 2007), p. 92.
105. See Suraiya Faroqhi, *The Ottoman Empire and the world around it* (London, 2007), pp. 27–8.
106. On Ottoman moral panic see Daniel Goffman, *The Ottoman Empire and Early Modern Europe* (Cambridge, 2002), pp. 117–18, and George S. Rentz, *The birth of the Islamic reform movement in Saudi Arabia. Muhammad b.'Abd al-Wahhāb (1703/4–1792) and the beginnings of Unitarian empire in Arabia* (London, 2004).
107. The Abbé de Saint-Pierre is quoted in Wilson, *Fleury*, p. 42. Frederick William's remarks on colonies are to be found in Clark, *Iron kingdom*, p. 93.
108. Münnich is quoted in Lavender Cassels, *The struggle for the Ottoman Empire, 1717–1740* (London, 1966), p. 100.
109. The Ottoman observer (a *Kadi*, or senior legal figure) is quoted in Cassels, *Struggle for the Ottoman Empire,* p. 154.
110. The British envoy is quoted in ibid., p. 24.
111. Lord Bathurst is quoted in Simms, *Three victories*, p. 259.
112. Philip Woodfine, *Britannias glories. The Walpole ministry and the 1739 war with Spain* (London, 1998).
113. Quoted in Simms, *Three victories*, p. 275.
114. Quoted in ibid., p. 251.
115. Quoted in ibid., p. 274.

116. Johannes Kunisch, *Friedrich der Grosse. Der König und seine Zeit* (Munich, 2004), pp. 159–84.
117. *The history of my times* is quoted in Neuhaus, 'Kronerwerb und Staatskonsolidierung', in Liermann et al. (eds.), *Italien und Preussen*, pp. 27–37 (quotation p. 27).
118. Tim Blanning, 'Frederick the Great', in Brendan Simms and Karina Urbach (eds.), *Die Rückkehr der 'Grossen Männer'. Staatsmänner im Krieg – ein deutsch-britischer Vergleich 1740–1945* (Berlin and New York, 2010), pp. 11–20 (quotation p. 12).
119. Newcastle is quoted in Simms, *Three victories*, p. 288.
120. Frederick's remarks of June 1742 are quoted in Peter Baumgart, 'The annexation and integration of Silesia into the Prussian state of Frederick the Great', in Mark Greengrass (ed.), *Conquest and coalescence. The shaping of the state in Early Modern Europe* (London, 1991), p. 160.
121. See P. G. M. Dickson, *Finance and government under Maria Theresia, 1740–1780*, 2 vols. (Oxford, 1987), especially vol. I, pp. 1, 266–7 and 270–71.
122. Baruch Mevorach, 'Die Interventionsbestrebungen in Europa zur Verhinderung der Vertreibung der Juden aus Böhmen und Mähren, 1744–1745', *Jahrbuch des Instituts für deutsche Geschichte*, IX (1980), pp. 15–81 (quotations pp. 34 and 54).
123. The quotations are in Simms, *Three victories*, p. 289.
124. For the quotation see Rowen, *The princes of Orange*, p. 163.
125. Gyllenborg is quoted in John P. LeDonne, *The Russian Empire and the world, 1700–1917. The geopolitics of expansion and containment* (New York and Oxford, 1997), p. 35.
126. See Francine-Dominique Liechtenhan, *La Russie entre en Europe. Elisabeth Ière et la succession de l'Autriche (1740–1750)* (Paris, 1997), especially pp. 46–9.
127. Stainville is quoted in Rohan Butler, *Choiseul.* Vol. 1: *Father and son, 1719–1754* (Oxford, 1980), p. 700. For French fears of the advancing Russians see ibid., pp. 724–6 (Sandwich quotation p. 724).
128. See Thomas E. Kaiser, 'The drama of Charles Edward Stuart, Jacobite propaganda, and French political protest, 1745–1750', *Eighteenth-Century Studies*, 30 (1997), pp. 365–81.

3. REVOLUTIONS, 1756–1813

1. Quoted in Hagen Schulze, *The course of German nationalism. From Frederick the Great to Bismarck, 1763–1867* (Cambridge, 1990).
2. Quoted in T. C. W. Blanning, 'The Bonapartes and Germany', in Peter Baehr and Melvin Richter (eds.), *Dictatorship in history and theory. Bonapartism, Caesarism, and totalitarianism* (Cambridge and New York, 2004), p. 54.

3. Cited in Daniel A. Baugh, 'Withdrawing from Europe: Anglo-French maritime geopolitics, 1750–1800', *International History Review*, 20, 1 (1998), pp. 14–16.
4. Quoted in Externbrink, *Friedrich der Grosse, Maria Theresia und das alte Reich. Deutschlandbild und Diplomatie Frankreichs im Siebenjährigen Krieg* (Berlin, 2006), p. 316.
5. Quoted in L. Jay Oliva, *Misalliance. A study of French policy in Russia during the Seven Years' War* (New York, 1964), p. 9.
6. Newcastle is cited in Reed Browning, *The Duke of Newcastle* (Cambridge, Mass., 1975), p. 182.
7. See Reed Browning, 'The Duke of Newcastle and the imperial election plan, 1749–1754', *Journal of British Studies*, 7 (1967–68), pp. 28–47.
8. On this see Richard L. Merritt, 'The colonists discover America: attention patterns in the colonial press, 1735–1775', *William and Mary Quarterly*, Third Series, XXI, 2 (April 1964), pp. 270–87, especially pp. 270–72.
9. Cited in Max Savelle, 'The appearance of an American attitude toward external affairs', *American Historical Review*, 52, 4 (1947), pp. 655–66 (quotation p. 660).
10. Quoted in Brendan Simms, *Three victories and a defeat. The rise and fall of the first British Empire, 1714–1783* (London, 2007), p. 393.
11. Ibid., p. 391.
12. A. G. Olson, 'The British government and colonial union, 1754', *William and Mary Quarterly*, Third Series, XVII, 1 (1960), pp. 24–6 (quotation p. 26).
13. See Fred Anderson, *Crucible of war. The Seven Years War and the fate of empire in British North America, 1754–1766* (New York, 2000).
14. Frederick the Great, *The history of my own times (1746). Posthumous works of Frederic II. King of Prussia* (London, 1789), Vol. I, p. xx. I thank Ilya Berkovich for this reference.
15. Quoted in Tim Blanning, 'Frederick the Great', in Brendan Simms and Karina Urbach (eds.), *Die Rückkehr der 'Grossen Männer'. Staatsmänner im Krieg – ein deutsch-britischer Vergleich 1740–1945* (Berlin and New York, 2010), p. 18.
16. Frederick the Great, *History of my own times*, Vol. I, pp. 214–15.
17. On the deportation of the Acadians as 'ethnic cleansing' see Geoffrey Plank, *An unsettled conquest. The British campaign against the peoples of Acadia* (Philadelphia, 2001), pp. 140–57.
18. Quoted in H. M. Scott, *The emergence of the eastern powers, 1756–1775* (Cambridge, 2001), p. 26.
19. See Erich Everth, *Die Öffentlichkeit in der Aussenpolitik von Karl V. bis Napoleon* (Jena, 1931), pp. 355–60 (quotation p. 360).
20. See now D. A. Baugh, *The global Seven Years War, 1754–1763. Britain and France in a great power contest* (Harlow, 2011).

21. Helmut Neuhaus, 'Das Problem der militärischen Exekutive in der spätphase des Alten Reiches', in Johannes Kunisch (ed.), *Staatsverfassung und Heeresverfassung in der europäischen Geschichte der Frühen Neuzeit* (Berlin, 1986), pp. 297–346 (quotations pp. 297 and 299).
22. Philip Carter, 'An "effeminate" or "efficient" nation? Masculinity and eighteenth century social documentary', *Textual Practice*, 11 (1997), pp. 429–43 (quotation p. 429).
23. Matthew McCormack, 'The new militia: war, politics and gender in 1750s Britain', *Gender & History*, 19 (2007), pp. 483–500 (quotation p. 497).
24. Thus Erica Charters, 'The caring fiscal-military state during the Seven Years War, 1756–1763', *Historical Journal*, 52 (2009), pp. 921–41, especially pp. 937–40 (quotation p. 939).
25. For the broader picture see H. M. Scott, 'The decline of France and the transformation of the European states system, 1756–1792', in Peter Krüger and Paul W. Schroeder (eds.), *The transformation of European politics, 1763–1848. Episode or model in modern history?* (Oxford, 1996), pp. 105–28 (Voltaire quotation p. 114).
26. See John Shovlin, *The political economy of virtue. Luxury, patriotism and the origins of the French Revolution* (Ithaca and London, 2006), pp. 54–5.
27. Quoted in Bailey Stone, *The genesis of the French Revolution. A global-historical interpretation* (Cambridge, 1994), p. 55. See also T. C. W. Blanning, *The French Revolutionary Wars, 1787–1802* (London, 1996).
28. See Brendan Simms, 'William Pitt the Elder. Strategic leadership at home and abroad during the great war for the empires (1756–1763)', in Simms and Urbach (eds.), *Die Rückkehr der 'Grossen Männer'*, pp. 29–48, especially pp. 32–4.
29. Brendan Simms, 'Pitt and Hanover', in Brendan Simms and Torsten Riotte (eds.), *The Hanoverian dimension in British history, 1714–1837* (Cambridge, 2007), pp. 28–57 (quotation p. 55).
30. See Gary Savage, 'Favier's heirs: the French Revolution and the *secret du roi*', *Historical Journal*, 41 (1998), pp. 225–58.
31. Hamish Scott, 'The Seven Years War and Europe's *ancien régime*', *War in History*, 18 (2011), pp. 419–55.
32. Quoted in Hugh Ragsdale, 'Russian projects of conquest in the eighteenth century', in Ragsdale (ed.), *Imperial Russian foreign policy* (Cambridge, 1993), p. 76.
33. Quoted in Externbrink, *Friedrich der Grosse,* p. 339.
34. For the crisis of the French nobility after the Seven Years War see William Doyle, *Aristocracy and its enemies in the Age of Revolution* (Oxford, 2009), pp. 57, 83 and passim.
35. See Gabriel B. Paquette, *Enlightenment, governance and reform in Spain and its empire, 1759–1808* (Basingstoke, 2008).

36. On the secret committee on the Indies see J. H. Elliott, *Empires of the Atlantic World. Britain and Spain in America, 1492–1830* (New Haven and London, 2006), p. 299.
37. See D. R. Murray, 'Statistics of the slave trade to Cuba, 1790–1867', *Journal of Latin American Studies*, 3, 2 (1971), pp. 131–49. I am grateful to Carrie Gibson and Felicitas Becker for very useful conversations on this subject.
38. Thus Evelyn Powell Jennings, 'War as the "forcing house of change": state slavery in late-eighteenth-century Cuba', *William and Mary Quarterly*, Third Series, LXII (2005), 411–40.
39. See Scott, *Emergence of the eastern powers*, pp. 76 and 79.
40. See Manfred Schort, *Politik und Propaganda. Der Siebenjährige Krieg in den zeitgenössischen Flugschriften* (Frankfurt am Main, 2006), p. 463.
41. Thus Hans-Martin Blitz, *Aus Liebe zum Vaterland. Die deutsche Nation im 18. Jahrhundert* (Hamburg, 2000), pp. 160–67 (quotation p. 165).
42. Quoted in Neuhaus, 'Das Problem der militärischen Exekutive', p. 301.
43. 'The Instructions to the Commissioners for Composing a New Code of Laws', Moscow, 30 July 1767, in William F. Reddaway (ed.), *Documents of Catherine the Great. The correspondence with Voltaire and the Instruction of 1767 in the English text of 1768* (Cambridge, 1931), pp. 216–17.
44. Quoted in Scott, *Emergence of the eastern powers*, p. 99.
45. See Franz A. J. Szabo, *Kaunitz and enlightened absolutism, 1753–1780* (Cambridge, 1994), p. 76. I am grateful to Daniel Robinson for this reference.
46. See Kathleen Wilson, *The sense of the people. Politics, culture and imperialism in England, 1715–1785* (Cambridge, 1995), pp. 215–16.
47. See Michael Roberts, *Splendid isolation, 1763–1780* (Reading, 1970).
48. Quoted in Simms, *Three victories*, p. 536. See also P. J. Marshall, *The making and unmaking of empires. Britain, India and America, c. 1750–1783* (Oxford, 2005), pp. 1–3, 59–60, 273–310, and passim.
49. Quoted in Norman Davies, *God's playground. A history of Poland*. Vol. I: *The origins to 1795* (Oxford, 1981), p. 511.
50. See T. C. W. Blanning, *The culture of power and the power of culture. Old regime Europe, 1660–1789* (Oxford, 2003).
51. On this see Ron Chernow, *Washington, a life* (London, 2010), pp. 59–62.
52. On the 'expansionist' settler faction see Marc Egnal, *A mighty empire. The origins of the American Revolution* (Ithaca and London, 1988). The most recent account of colonists as English imperialists is Robert Kagan, *Dangerous nation* (New York, 2006), pp. 12–16 and 18.
53. See Jerzy Lukowski, *The partitions of Poland, 1772, 1793, 1795* (London and New York), pp. 52–81 (Frederick is quoted on p. 55).
54. Cited in D. B. Horn, *British public opinion and the First Partition of Poland* (Edinburgh, 1945), pp. 26 and 36–7.

55. See Bernd Marquardt, 'Zur reichsgerichtlichen Aberkennung der Herrschergewalt wegen Missbrauchs. Tyrannenprozesse vor dem Reichshofrat am Beispiel des südöstlichen schwäbischen Reichskreises', in Anette Baumann, Peter Oestmann, Stephan Wendehorst and Siegrid Westphal (eds.), *Prozesspraxis im Alten Reich. Annäherungen – Fallstudien – Statistiken* (Cologne, Weimar and Vienna, 2005), p. 53.
56. See Jennifer Pitts, 'The stronger ties of humanity: humanitarian intervention in the eighteenth century'. I thank Dr Pitts for letting me have sight of her excellent unpublished paper.
57. See Robin A. Fabel, *Colonial challenges. Britons, Native Americans and Caribs, 1759–1775* (Gainesville, 2000), pp. 158–60.
58. On Americans and Corsica see George P. Anderson, 'Pascal Paoli: an inspiration to the Sons of Liberty', *Publications of the Colonial Society of Massachusetts*, 26 (1924–6), pp. 180–210, especially pp. 189–91 and 202–3 (for quotations).
59. See Richard B. Sheridan, 'The British credit crisis of 1772 and the American colonies', *Journal of Economic History*, 20 (1960), pp. 161–86.
60. John Adams to Mercy Warren, 20 July 1807, in *Collections of the Massachusetts Historical Society*, Fifth Series, IV (1878), p. 338. I thank Daniel Robinson for drawing this letter to my attention.
61. See Richard Middleton, *The War of American Independence, 1775–1783* (Harlow, 2012), pp. 15–36.
62. Hamish Scott, *British foreign policy in the age of the American Revolution* (Oxford, 1990), and Donald Stoker, Kenneth J. Hagan and Michael T. McMaster (eds.), *Strategy in the American War of Independence. A global approach* (London and New York, 2010).
63. Cited in Robert Rhodes Crout, 'In search of a "just and lasting peace": the treaty of 1783, Louis XVI, Vergennes, and the regeneration of the realm', *International History Review*, 5, 3 (1983), p. 374.
64. Quoted in Kagan, *Dangerous nation*, p. 47.
65. Thus Jonathan R. Dull, *A diplomatic history of the American Revolution* (New Haven and London, 1985), p. 47.
66. David M. Fitzsimmons, 'Tom Paine's new world order: idealistic internationalism in the ideology of early American foreign relations', *Diplomatic History*, 19 (1995), pp. 569–82 (quotations p. 579).
67. See Mlada Bukovansky, *Legitimacy and power politics. The American and French Revolutions in international political culture* (Princeton and Oxford, 2002), pp. 110–64 and 216–20, and Walter McDougall, *Promised land, crusader state. The American encounter with the world since 1776* (New York, 1997).
68. Ben Baack, 'Forging a nation state: the Continental Congress and the financing of the War of American Independence', *Economic History Review*, 54, 4 (2001), pp. 639–56, especially pp. 639–40.

69. Quoted in Munro Price, *Preserving the monarchy. The Comté de Vergennes, 1774–1787* (Cambridge, 1995), p. 22.
70. Sandwich remarks to cabinet, 19 January 1781, Queens' House, in the presence of the king, in John G. R. Barnes and J. J. Owen (eds.), *The Private Papers of John, Earl of Sandwich, 1771–1782* (London, 1932–8), Vol. 4, p. 24.
71. See Stephen Conway, *The British Isles and the War of American Independence* (Oxford, 2000), pp. 16, 350 and 17.
72. Cited in Scott, *Emergence of the eastern powers*, p. 1.
73. Quotations in Crout, 'A "just and lasting peace"', p. 398, and Maya Jasanoff, *Liberty's exiles. American loyalists in the revolutionary world* (New York, 2011), p. 87.
74. Quoted in Stone, *Genesis of the French Revolution*, p. 142.
75. Quoted in Claus Scharf, '"La Princesse de Zerbst Catherinisée". Deutschlandbild und Deutschlandpolitik Katharinas II.', in Dagmar Herrmann (ed.), *Deutsche und Deutschland aus russischer Sicht. 18. Jahrhundert: Aufklärung* (Munich, 1992), p. 320.
76. Quoted in Jeremy Black, *The rise of the European powers* (London, 1990), p. 130.
77. Quoted in Brendan Simms, *The struggle for mastery in Germany, 1779–1850* (Basingstoke, 1998), p. 45.
78. See Vincent T. Harlow, *The founding of the second British empire*, 2 vols. (London, 1952–64), and C. A. Bayly, *Imperial meridian. The British Empire and the world, 1780–1830* (London, 1989).
79. Quoted in Jeremy Black, *British foreign policy in an age of revolutions, 1783–1793* (Cambridge, 1994), p. 13.
80. See P. G. M. Dickson, 'Count Karl von Zinzendorf's "new accountancy": the structure of Austrian government finance in peace and war, 1781–1791', *International History Review*, 29, 1 (2007), pp. 22–56.
81. See Ernst Wangermann, *Die Waffen der Publizität. Zum Funktionswandel der politischen Literatur unter Joseph II.* (Vienna, 2004), pp. 168–84.
82. Thus Karl Härter, 'Möglichkeiten und Grenzen der Reichspolitik Russlands als Garantiemacht des Teschener Friedens (1778–1803)', in Claus Scharf (ed.), *Katharina II., Rußland und Europa. Beiträge zur internationalen Forschung. Veröffentlichungen des Instituts für Europäische Geschichte*, Supplement 45 (Mainz, 2001), pp. 133–81.
83. See Hugh Ragsdale, 'Evaluating the traditions of Russian aggression: Catherine II and the Greek Project', *Slavonic and East European Review*, 66 (1988), pp. 91–117, especially pp. 95–6.
84. Quoted in Virginia H. Aksan, *Ottoman wars 1700–1870. An empire besieged* (Harlow, 2007), p. 161.
85. Quoted in Karl A. Roider, *Austria's Eastern Question, 1700–1790* (Princeton, 1982), p. 180.

86. Alexander Hamilton, Federalist Paper no. 34, 5.1.1788, in J. R. Pole (ed.), *The Federalist. Alexander Hamilton, James Madison, John Jay* (Indianapolis and Cambridge, 2005), p. 178.
87. See James R. Sofka, 'The Jeffersonian idea of national security. Commerce, the Atlantic balance of power, and the Barbary War, 1786–1805', *Diplomatic History*, 21 (1997), pp. 519–44, especially pp. 519, 522 and 527.
88. Quoted in Doris A. Graber, *Public opinion, the president, and foreign policy. Four case studies from the formative years* (New York, Chicago etc., 1968), p. 133.
89. See Deborah Allen, 'Acquiring "knowledge of our own continent": geopolitics, science, and Jeffersonian geography, 1783–1803', *Journal of American Studies*, 40 (2006), pp. 205–32 (Jay is quoted on p. 216). For the importance of the west see François Fürstenberg, 'The significance of the trans-Appalachian Frontier in Atlantic history, c.1754–1815', *American Historical Review*, 113 (2008), pp. 647–77.
90. Alexander Hamilton, Federalist Paper no. 25, 21.12.1787, in Pole (ed.), *Federalist*, p. 133.
91. Federalist Paper no. 7, 17.11.1787, in Pole (ed.), *Federalist*, pp. 28–9.
92. On the colonists' fear of fragmention and repeating the experience of Italian city states see David C. Hendrickson, *Peace pact. The lost world of the American founding* (Lawrence, Kan., 2003), p. 63.
93. Federalist Paper no. 8, 20.11.1787, in Pole (ed.), *Federalist*, p. 37.
94. Federalist Paper no. 19, 8.12.1787, in Pole (ed.), *Federalist*, pp. 99–102. For the impact of the Polish partition on the constitutional convention see Frederick W. Marks, *Independence on trial. Foreign affairs and the making of the constitution* (Baton Rouge, 1973), pp. 3–51, especially p. 33.
95. Federalist Paper no. 5, 10.11.1787, in Pole (ed.), *Federalist*, pp. 17–18.
96. See George William van Cleve, *A slaveholders' union. Slavery, politics, and the constitution in the early American Republic* (Chicago and London, 2010), p. 9.
97. The centrality of the international context to the framing of the constitution is stressed by Michael Schwarz, 'The great divergence reconsidered. Hamilton, Madison, and U.S.–British relations, 1783–89', *Journal of the Early Republic*, 27 (2007), pp. 407–36, especially pp. 419–21.
98. Quoted in Doyle, *Aristocracy and its enemies*, p. 99. See also Markus Hünemörder, *The Society of the Cincinnati. Conspiracy and distrust in early America* (New York and Oxford, 2006).
99. Roy Weatherup, 'Standing armies and armed citizens: an historical analysis of the Second Amendment', *Hastings Constitutional Law Quarterly*, 2 (1975), pp. 961–1001, especially p. 995.
100. See Wolfgang Burgdorf, *Reichskonstitution und Nation. Verfassungsreformprojekte für das Heilige Römische Reich Deutscher Nation im politischen Schrifttum von 1648 bis 1806* (Mainz, 1998), pp. 328–35.

101. Munro Price, 'The Dutch Affair and the fall of the *ancien régime*, 1784–1787', *Historical Journal*, 38 (1995), pp. 875–905 (quotation p. 904).
102. My understanding of the relationship between the diplomatic decline of the *ancien régime* and the outbreak of the French Revolution has been heavily influenced by Gary J. Savage, 'The French Revolution and the *secret du roi*. Diplomatic tradition, foreign policy and political culture in later eighteenth-century France (1756–1792)' (unpublished Ph.D. dissertation, University of Cambridge, 2005).
103. See Thomas Kaiser, 'Who's afraid of Marie-Antoinette? Diplomacy, Austrophobia and the Queen', *French History*, 14, 3 (2000), pp. 241–71.
104. Quoted in Price, *Vergennes*, p. 234.
105. Montmorin is quoted in Jeremy J. Whiteman, *Reform, revolution and French global policy, 1787–1791* (Aldershot, 2003), p. 103.
106. Munro Price, 'The court nobility and the origins of the French Revolution', in H. Scott and B. Simms (eds.), *Cultures of power in Europe during the Long Eighteenth Century* (Cambridge, 2007), pp. 278–9.
107. Thus chapter 2 of the *Cahiers*, quoted in John Hall Stewart (ed.), *A documentary survey of the French Revolution* (New York, 1951), p. 59.
108. Quotation in Stone, *Genesis of the French Revolution*, p. 207.
109. See David A. Bell, *The cult of the nation in France. Inventing nationalism, 1680–1800* (Cambridge, Mass., and London, 2001), pp. 14–17 and passim (Sieyes is quoted on p. 14).
110. Quoted in Michael Hochedlinger, 'Who's afraid of the French Revolution? Austrian foreign policy and the European crisis, 1787–1797', *German History*, 21, 3 (2003), pp. 293–318 (quotation p. 303).
111. *Reflections on the Revolution in France*, in Paul Langford (ed.), *The writings and speeches of Edmund Burke*. Vol. VIII: *The French Revolution, 1790–1794* (Oxford, 1989), pp. 131 and 60.
112. Richard Bourke, 'Edmund Burke and international conflict', in Ian Hall and Lisa Hill (eds.), *British international thinkers from Hobbes to Namier* (Basingstoke, 2009), pp. 91–116.
113. P. J. Marshall and John A. Woods (eds.), *The correspondence of Edmund Burke*. Vol. VII: *January 1792–August 1794* (Cambridge, 1968), p. 383; R. B. McDowell (ed.), *The writings and speeches of Edmund Burke*. Vol. IX: *I The Revolutionary War. II Ireland* (Oxford, 1991), pp. 195 and 250 (vicinage); Brendan Simms, '"A false principle in the Law of Nations". Burke, state sovereignty, [German] liberty, and intervention in the age of Westphalia', in Brendan Simms and D. J. B. Trim (eds.), *Humanitarian intervention. A history* (Cambridge, 2011), p. 110.
114. Quoted in T. C. W. Blanning, *The origins of the French Revolutionary Wars* (Harlow, 1986), p. 132.

115. Thus Horst Möller, 'Primat der Aussenpolitik: Preussen und die französische Revolution, 1789–1795', in Jürgen Voss (ed.), *Deutschland und die französische Revolution* (Munich, 1983), pp. 65–81.
116. See Adam Hochschild, *Bury the chains. The first international human rights movement* (London and New York, 2005), p. 137, and William Hague, *William Wilberforce. The life of the great anti-slave trade campaigner* (London, 2007), pp. 149–50.
117. See Jeremy Popkin, *You are all free. The Haitian Revolution and the abolition of slavery* (Cambridge, 2010), p. 276. See also John Thornton, '"I am the subject of the King of Congo": African political ideology and the Haitian Revolution', *Journal of World History*, 4, 2 (1993), pp. 181–214, especially p. 183.
118. See Michael Hochedlinger, '"La cause de tous les maux de la France". Die "Austrophobie" im revolutionären Frankreich und der Sturz des Königtums, 1789–1792', *Francia*, 24 (1997), pp. 73–120.
119. Thus Eckhard Buddruss, *Die französische Deutschlandpolitik, 1756–1789* (Mainz, 1995).
120. Quotations in Savage, 'The French Revolution and the *secret du roi*', p. 211.
121. See Sidney Seymour Biro, *The German policy of Revolutionary France. A study in French diplomacy during the War of the First Coalition, 1792–1797*, 2 vols. (Cambridge, Mass., 1957).
122. The Padua Circular and Declaration of Pillnitz are printed in Hall Stewart (ed.), *Documentary survey*, pp. 221–4.
123. Quoted in Patricia Chastain Howe, *Foreign Policy and the French Revolution. Charles-François Dumouriez, Pierre LeBrun, and the Belgian Plan, 1789–1793* (Basingstoke, 2008), p. 47.
124. Quoted in Whiteman, *Reform, revolution and French global policy*, p. 130.
125. Thus Linda and Marsha Frey, '"The reign of the charlatans is over". The French Revolutionary attack on diplomatic practice', *Journal of Modern History*, 65, 4 (1993), pp. 706–44, especially pp. 714–17.
126. The Brunswick Manifesto, 25.7.1792, in Hall Stewart (ed.), *Documentary survey*, pp. 307–8.
127. See Munro Price, *The fall of the French monarchy. Louis XVI, Marie Antoinette and the Baron de Breteuil* (London, 2002).
128. Declaration of the National Assembly, in Hall Stewart (ed.), *Documentary survey*, p. 285.
129. Decree of Fraternity and Help to Foreign Peoples, 19.11.1792, in Hall Stewart (ed.), *Documentary survey*, p. 381.
130. Quoted in T. C. W. Blanning, *The French Revolution in Germany. Occupation and resistance in the Rhineland, 1792–1802* (Oxford, 1983), p. 64.
131. See Erwin Oberländer, '"Ist die Kaiserin von Russland Garant des Westfälischen Friedens?" Der Kurfürst von Trier, die Französische Revolution

und Katharina II. 1789–1792, *Jahrbücher für Geschichte Osteuropas*, New Series, 35 (1987), pp. 218–31.

132. See Jerzy Lukowski, *Liberty's folly. The Polish–Lithuanian Commonwealth in the eighteenth century, 1697–1795* (London and New York, 1991), p. 265.

133. See David Pickus, *Dying with an enlightening fall. Poland in the eyes of German intellectuals, 1764–1800* (Lanham etc., 2001), pp. 36–45, 54–9 and 126–31 (quotation pp. 126–7).

134. Moser's warning is quoted in Burgdorf, *Reichskonstitution und Nation*, p. 343.

135. See Thomas Hippler, *Citizens, soldiers and national armies. Military service in France and Germany, 1789–1830* (London and New York, 2008).

136. Quoted in Reynald Secher, *A French genocide. The Vendée* (Notre Dame, Ind., 2003), pp. 250–51.

137. Quoted in Richard Whatmore, '"A gigantic manliness". Paine's republicanism in the 1790s', in Stefan Collini, Richard Whatmore and Brian Young (eds.), *Economy, polity and society. British intellectual history, 1750–1950* (Cambridge, 2000), p. 150. For the strategic context of Paine's thought see pp. 136, 138–40, 149 and passim.

138. Decree of 15.12.1792, in Hall Stewart (ed.), *Documentary survey*, p. 383.

139. Thus David A. Bell, *The first total war. Napoleon's Europe and the birth of modern warfare* (London, 2007).

140. Quoted in Howe, *Foreign policy and the French Revolution*, pp. 119 and 151.

141. Quoted in Jörg Ulbert, 'France and German dualism, 1756–1871', in Carine Germond and Henning Türk (eds.), *A history of Franco-German relations in Europe. From 'hereditary enemies' to partners* (Basingstoke, 2008), pp. 41–2.

142. Quoted in Biro, *German policy of Revolutionary France*, Vol. II, p. 624.

143. T. C. W. Blanning, *Reform and revolution in Mainz, 1743–1803* (Cambridge, 1974).

144. See, for example, the case of Friedrich Cotta in Monika Neugebauer-Wölk, *Revolution und Constitution. Die Brüder Cotta. Eine biographische Studie zum Zeitalter der Französischen Revolution und des Vormärz* (Berlin, 1989), especially pp. 141–3.

145. See Blanning, *Reform and revolution in Mainz*.

146. The quotations of Duke Frederick and the Bavarian envoy are in Simms, *Struggle for mastery in Germany*, pp. 60–61.

147. The Senckenberg quotation is in Burgdorf, *Reichskonstitution und Nation*, p. 411.

148. Thus Philip Dwyer, *Napoleon. The path to power, 1769–1799* (London, 2007), passim.

149. Quoted in Blanning, 'Frederick the Great', in Simms and Urbach (eds.), *Die Rückkehr der 'Grossen Männer'*, p. 23.

150. On the prevalence of 'glory' and 'destiny' in Napoleon's thinking see Philip G. Dwyer (ed.), 'Napoleon and the drive for glory: reflections on the

making of French foreign policy', in Philip G. Dwyer (ed.), *Napoleon and Europe* (London, 2001), p. 129.

151. See Javier Cuenca Esteban, 'The British balance of payments, 1772–1820: India transfers and war finance', *Economic History Review*, 54, 1 (2001), pp. 58–86, especially pp. 58 and 65–6.

152. Quoted in Gunther E. Rothenberg, 'The origins, causes, and extension of the wars of the French Revolution and Napoleon', *Journal of Interdisciplinary History*, 18 (1988), p. 789.

153. On this see Daniela Neri, 'Frankreichs Reichspolitik auf dem Rastatter Kongress (1797–1799)', *Francia*, 24 (1997), pp. 137–57, especially pp. 155–6.

154. Quoted in Hochedlinger, 'Who's afraid of the French Revolution?', p. 310.

155. See Geoffrey Symcox, 'The geopolitics of the Egyptian expedition, 1797–1798', in Irene A. Bierman (ed.), *Napoleon in Egypt* (Reading, 2003).

156. Quoted in Edward James Kolla, 'Not so criminal: new understandings of Napoleon's foreign policy in the east', *French Historical Studies*, 30, 2 (2007), p. 183. For Napoleon's general tendency to conceive of Asia in terms of the European balance of power see Iradji Amini, *Napoleon and Persia. Franco-Persian relations under the First Empire, within the context of the rivalries between France, Britain and Russia* (Richmond, 1999), pp. 47–54.

157. Quoted in Karl A. Roider, *Baron Thugut and Austria's response to the French Revolution* (Princeton, 1992), pp. 283–4.

158. See Manfred Hellmann, 'Eine Denkschrift über Russland aus dem Jahre 1800', in Heinz Dollinger, Horst Gründer and Alwin Hanschmidt (eds.), *Weltpolitik. Europagedanke. Regionalismus* (Münster, 1962), pp. 135 and 156 (quotation p. 139).

159. James Livesey, 'Acts of Union and disunion: Ireland in Atlantic and European contexts', in Dáire Keogh and Kevin Whelan (eds.), *Acts of Union. The causes, contexts and consequences of the Act of Union* (Dublin, 2001), pp. 95–105 (Cooke is quoted on p. 97).

160. Quoted in Erwin Hölzle, *Das alte Recht und die Revolution. Eine politische Geschichte Württembergs in der Revolutionszeit, 1789–1806* (Munich and Berlin, 1931), p. 273.

161. Quoted in Friedrich Wilhelm Kantzenbach, *Politischer Protestantismus. Von den Freiheitskriegen bis zur Ära Adenauer* (Saarbrücken, 1993), p. 310. (Herder was writing in 1802.)

162. Thus Brendan Simms, *The impact of Napoleon. Prussian high politics, foreign policy and the crisis of the executive, 1797–1806* (Cambridge, 1997).

163. See John Ferling, *John Adams. A life* (Knoxville, 1994), p. 341. For an account of how foreign political issues shaped US domestic politics down to the lowest level see Maurice J. Bric, *Ireland, Philadelphia and the re-invention of America, 1760–1800* (Dublin, 2008), pp. xvi, 117 and 246–7.

164. Quoted in Michael Duffy, 'Britain as a European ally, 1789–1815', in *Diplomacy and Statecraft*, 8, 3 (1997), p. 28. On the centrality of uniting the continent against Britain to Napoleon's strategy see Charles Esdaile, *The wars of Napoleon* (London, 1995), pp. 75–6 and 106.
165. James E. Lewis Jr, *The American Union and the problem of neighborhood. The United States and the collapse of the Spanish Empire, 1783–1829* (Chapel Hill, 1998), pp. 25–7.
166. Jon Kukla, *A wilderness so immense: the Louisiana Purchase and the destiny of America* (New York, 2003), pp. 229–34 (Jefferson is quoted on p. 231).
167. Gentz's remark of August 1806 is cited in Alexander von Hase, 'Das konservative Europa in Bedrängnis: zur Krise des Gleichgewichtspublizisten Friedrich (von) Gentz (1805–1809)', *Saeculum*, 29 (1978), pp. 385–405 (p. 393).
168. Philip G. Dwyer, 'Napoleon and the foundation of the Empire', *Historical Journal*, 53 (2010), pp. 339–58.
169. Quoted in Ulrike Eich, *Russland und Europa. Studien zur russischen Deutschlandpolitik in der Zeit des Wiener Kongresses* (Cologne and Vienna, 1986), p. 59.
170. Quoted in Krüger and Schroeder (eds.), *Transformation of European politics*, p. 237.
171. Quoted in Roider, *Baron Thugut*, p. 372.
172. See Helmuth Rössler, *Napoleons Griff nach der Karlskrone. Das Ende des alten Reiches 1806* (Munich, 1957).
173. See Philip G. Dwyer, *Talleyrand* (London, 2002), pp. 98–100 and 108–9.
174. See Tim Blanning, 'Napoleon and German identity', *History Today*, 48 (1998), pp. 37–43.
175. Quoted in John P. LeDonne, *The Russian Empire and the world, 1700–1917. The geopolitics of expansion and containment* (New York and Oxford, 1997), p. 303. See also Dominic Lieven, *Russia Against Napoleon* (London, 2009).
176. Quoted in Enno E. Kraehe, *Metternich's German policy.* Vol. II: *The Congress of Vienna, 1814–1815* (Princeton, 1983), p. 6.
177. Quoted in Simms, *Struggle for mastery in Germany*, p. 92.
178. See Rafe Blaufarb, 'The *ancien régime* origins of Napoleonic social reconstruction', *French History*, 14, 4 (2000), pp. 408–23, especially pp. 416–20.
179. See Donald Stoker, Frederick C. Schneid and Harold D. Blanton (eds.), *Conscription in the Napoleonic era. A revolution in military affairs?* (London and New York, 2009), pp. 6–23 and 122–48.
180. See Stuart Woolf, *Napoleon's integration of Europe* (London and New York, 1991).

181. Thus Stuart Woolf, 'French civilization and ethnicity in the Napoleonic Empire', *Past and Present*, 124 (1989), pp. 96–120, especially pp. 106–7.
182. Quoted in Biancamaria Fontana, 'The Napoleonic Empire and the Europe of nations', in Anthony Pagden (ed.), *The idea of Europe. From antiquity to the European Union* (Cambridge, 2002), pp. 116–28 (quotation p. 120).
183. Martyn P. Thompson, 'Ideas of Europe during the French Revolution and Napoleonic Wars', *Journal of the History of Ideas*, 55 (1994), pp. 37–58 (quotation p. 39).
184. Biro, *German policy of revolutionary France*, vol. 2, p. 62.
185. Quoted in David Lawday, *Napoleon's master. A life of Prince Talleyrand* (London, 2007), p. 116.
186. Quoted in Brendan Simms, 'Reform in Britain and Prussia, 1797–1815: confessional fiscal-military state and military-agrarian complex', in *Proceedings of the British Academy*, 100 (1999), pp. 82–3.
187. Thus Ute Frevert, 'Das jakobinische Modell: allgemeine Wehrpflicht und Nationsbildung in Preussen-Deutschland', in Ute Frevert (ed.), *Militär und Gesellschaft im 19. und 20. Jahrhundert* (Stuttgart, 1997), pp. 17–47 (quotation p. 20).
188. See Heinz Duchhardt, *Stein. Eine Biographie* (Münster, 2007), pp. 164–235.
189. Quotations in Simms, 'Reform in Britain and Prussia', pp. 83–4.
190. See Brendan Simms, 'Britain and Napoleon', in Dwyer (ed.), *Napoleon and Europe*, pp. 189–203.
191. See, for example, Otto Johnston, 'British espionage and Prussian politics in the Age of Napoleon', *Intelligence and National Security*, 2 (1987), especially p. 238.
192. On the link between external threat and domestic transformation see Karl Roider, 'The Habsburg foreign ministry and political reform', *Central European History*, 22 (1989), especially pp. 162 and 172.
193. Quoted in Henry A. Kissinger, *A world restored. Metternich, Castlereagh, and the problems of peace, 1812–1822* (London, 1957), p. 20.
194. Thus Geoffrey Ellis, *Napoleon's continental blockade. The case of Alsace* (Oxford, 1981).
195. On this see Maya Jasanoff, *Liberty's exiles. American loyalists in the Revolutionary world* (New York, 2011).
196. Quoted in Simms, *Struggle for mastery in Germany*, p. 99.
197. Quoted in Krüger and Schroeder (eds.), *Transformation of European politics*, p. 460.
198. Alexander's remarks are quoted in John P. LeDonne, *The grand strategy of the Russian Empire, 1650–1831* (Oxford, 2004), p. 206.
199. Quoted in Eich, *Russland und Europa*, p. 150.
200. For the figures see Blanning, 'The Bonapartes and Germany', p. 59.

4. EMANCIPATIONS, 1814–66

1. Quoted in H.-O. Sieburg, *Deutschland und Frankreich in der Geschichtsschreibung des neunzehnten Jahrhunderts* (Wiesbaden, 1954), p. 108.
2. Quoted in James Chastain, 'Privilege versus emancipation: the origins of Franco-Austrian confrontation in 1848', *Proceedings of the Consortium on Revolutionary Europe* (1987), p. 247
3. Quoted in Anselm Doering-Manteuffel, *Vom Wiener Kongress zur Pariser Konferenz. England, die deutsche Frage und das Mächtesystem, 1815–1856* (Göttingen and Zurich, 1991), pp. 137–8.
4. See Peter Hofschroer, *1815. The Waterloo campaign. The German victory* (London, 1999).
5. The Massachussetts Senate is quoted in James G. Wilson, *The imperial republic. A structural history of American constitutionalism from the colonial era to the beginning of the twentieth century* (Aldershot, 2002), pp. 130–32.
6. Quoted in Hermann Wentker, 'Der Pitt-Plan von 1805 in Krieg und Frieden: zum Kontinuitätsproblem der britischen Europapolitik in der Ära der napoleonischen Kriege', *Francia*, 29, 2 (2002), pp. 129–45 (quotation p. 137).
7. See Enno E. Kraehe, *Metternich's German policy*. Vol. II. *The Congress of Vienna, 1814–1815* (Princeton, 1983).
8. On the Russian parade see John P. LeDonne, *The grand strategy of the Russian Empire, 1650–1831* (Oxford, 2004), p. 208.
9. Quoted in Ulrike Eich, *Russland und Europa. Studien zur russischen Deutschlandpolitik in der Zeit des Wiener Kongresses* (Cologne and Vienna 1986), p. 172.
10. Quoted in Wentker, 'Der Pitt-Plan', p. 141.
11. Quoted in John Bew, *Castlereagh. Enlightenment, war and tyranny, 1769–1822* (London, 2011), p. 377.
12. Quoted in Brendan Simms, *The struggle for mastery in Germany, 1779–1850* (Basingstoke, 1998), p. 105.
13. Quoted in Henry A. Kissinger, A *world restored* (London, 1957), p. 33.
14. See Betty Fladeland, 'Abolitionist pressures on the Concert of Europe 1814–1822', *Journal of Modern History*, 38, 4 (1966), pp. 355–73 (quotation p. 363).
15. See Paul Kielstra, *The politics of the slave trade suppression in Britain and France, 1814–48* (Basingstoke, 2000), pp. 26–9 (quotation p. 28).
16. See Thomas Neve, *The Duke of Wellington and the British army of occupation in France, 1815–1818* (Westport and London, 1992), pp. 93–103.
17. Cited in Wolf Gruner, 'Der deutsche Bund und die europäische Friedensordnung', in Helmut Rumpler (ed.), *Deutscher Bund und deutsche Frage 1815–1866* (Munich, 1990), p. 248.

18. For the internal 'German' functions and purposes of the German Confederation see Jürgen Müller, *Der deutsche Bund, 1815–1866* (Munich, 2006).
19. Thus Anselm Doering-Manteuffel, *Vom Wiener Kongress zur Pariser Konferenz. England, die deutsche Frage und das Mächtesystem, 1815–1856* (Göttingen and Zurich, 1991), pp. 57–72.
20. See David Laven, 'Austria's Italian policy reconsidered: revolution and reform in Restoration Italy', *Modern Italy*, 2, 1 (1997), pp. 1–33, which places particular emphasis on the geopolitical dimension.
21. See Kenneth Bourne, *Britain and the balance of power in North America, 1815–1908* (London, 1967), pp. 53–119.
22. See Philip Harling and Peter Mandler, 'From "fiscal-military state" to "laissez-faire state", 1760–1850', *Journal of British Studies*, 32 (1993), pp. 44–70.
23. Quoted in Jonathan Parry, *The politics of patriotism. English liberalism, national identity and Europe, 1830–1886* (Cambridge, 2006), p. 46.
24. Frank Lawrence Owsley Jr and Gene A. Smith, *Filibusters and expansionists: Jeffersonian Manifest Destiny, 1800–1821* (Tuscaloosa, 1997).
25. See Edward Howland Tatum, *The United States and Europe, 1815–1823. A study in the background of the Monroe Doctrine* (New York, 1936), pp. 186–7.
26. Thus John M. Belohlavek, *'Let the eagle soar!' The foreign policy of Andrew Jackson* (Lincoln, Nebr., 1985), pp. 9–10.
27. See Gary P. Cox, *The halt in the mud. French strategic planning from Waterloo to Sedan* (Boulder, San Francisco and Oxford, 1994), p. 97.
28. See Michael Stephen Partridge, *Military planning for the defence of the United Kingdom* (New York, 1989), pp. 4–21, 147–8 and passim.
29. On Russian restraint see Henry A. Delfiner, 'Alexander I, the Holy Alliance and Clemens Metternich: a reappraisal', *East European Quarterly*, XXXVII, 2 (2003), especially pp. 138–50.
30. Quoted in Derek Beales and Eugenio F. Biagini, *The Risorgimento and the unification of Italy* (Harlow, 2002), pp. 213–14.
31. See Daniel Moran, *Toward the century of words. Johann Cotta and the politics of the public realm in Germany, 1795–1832* (Berkeley, 1990).
32. Brendan Simms, 'Napoleon and Germany: a legacy in foreign policy', in David Laven and Lucy Riall (eds.), *Napoleon's legacy. Problems of government in Restoration Europe* (Oxford and New York, 2000), pp. 97–112 (Görres is quoted on p. 101).
33. See Lucy Riall, *The Italian Risorgimento. State, society and national unification* (London, 1994), especially pp. 11–28.
34. Thus Maurizio Isabella, 'Mazzini's internationalism in context: from the cosmopolitan patriotism of the Italian Carbonari to Mazzini's Europe of the nations', in *Proceedings of the British Academy*, 152 (2008), p. 50.
35. See Jaime E. Rodríguez O., *The independence of Spanish America* (Cambridge, 1998), pp. 169–92.

36. For the 'teamwork' between individuals of many differing nationalities engaged in the slave trade see Joseph C. Dorsey, *Slave traffic in the age of abolition. Puerto Rico, West Africa, and the non-Hispanic Caribbean, 1815–1859* (Gainesville, 2003), pp. 83–100.
37. Maeve Ryan, 'The price of legitimacy in humanitarian intervention: Britain, the right of search, and the abolition of the West African slave trade, 1807–1867', in Brendan Simms and D. J. B. Trim (eds.), *Humanitarian intervention. A history* (Cambridge, 2011), pp. 231–55. Nearly 400,000 African slaves were trafficked to Cuba alone after the trade was made illegal: for figures see D. R. Murray, 'Statistics of the slave trade to Cuba, 1790–1867', *Journal of Latin American Studies*, 3, 2 (1971), pp. 131–49 (pp. 134, 136, 141, 142, 144, 147 and especially 149).
38. See Paul W. Schroeder, *Metternich's diplomacy at its zenith, 1820–1823* (Austin, 1962), especially pp. 237–66.
39. Quoted in D. L. Hafner, 'Castlereagh, the balance of power, and "non-intervention"', *Australian Journal of Politics and History*, 26, 1 (1980), p. 75.
40. Quoted in Rafe Blaufarb, 'The Western Question: the geopolitics of Latin American independence', *American Historical Review*, 112, 3 (2007), pp. 742–63 (quotation p. 746).
41. Quoted in John Bew, '"From an umpire to a competitor". Castlereagh, Canning and the issue of international intervention in the wake of the Napoleonic Wars', in Simms and Trim (eds.), *Humanitarian intervention*, p. 130.
42. See Günther Heydemann, *Konstitution gegen Revolution. Die britische Deutschland und Italienpolitik, 1815–1848* (Göttingen and Zurich, 1995), pp. 47–9 (quotation p. 49).
43. Ibid., p. 108.
44. See Theophilius C. Prousin, *Russian society and the Greek Revolution* (DeKalb, Ill., 1994), pp. 26–54.
45. See Davide Rodogno, *Against massacre. Humanitarian intervention in the Ottoman Empire, 1815–1914* (Princeton, 2011).
46. See David T. Murphy, 'Prussian aims for the Zollverein, 1828–1833', *Historian*, 53 (1991), pp. 287, 291 and passim.
47. Quoted in F. R. Bridge, *The Habsburg monarchy among the great powers, 1815–1918* (New York, Oxford and Munich, 1990), p. 34.
48. Quoted in Barbara Jelavich, *Russia's Balkan entanglements, 1806–1914* (Cambridge, 1991), p. 62.
49. Quoted in Frank Lorenz Müller, *Britain and the German Question. Perceptions of nationalism and political reform, 1830–63* (Basingstoke, 2002), p. 29
50. Quoted in Heydemann, *Konstitution gegen Revolution*, pp. 239–40 and 347.
51. Quoted in Robert Tombs, *France 1814–1914* (London and New York 1996), p. 37.

52. Matthew Rendall, 'Restraint or self-restraint of Russia: Nicholas I, the Treaty of Unkiar Skelessi, and the Vienna System, 1832–1841', *International History Review*, 24, 1 (2002), pp. 37–63, especially pp. 38 and 57.
53. Quoted in Beales and Biagini, *Risorgimento and the Unification of Italy*, pp. 26–7.
54. See Jürgen Angelow, *Von Wien nach Königgrätz. Die Sicherheitspolitik des deutschen Bundes im europäischen Gleichgewicht, 1815–1866* (Munich, 1996), p. 81.
55. Quoted in Simms, *Struggle for mastery in Germany*, pp. 116 and 112.
56. Thus Manfred Meyer, *Freiheit und Macht. Studien zum Nationalismus süddeutscher, insbesondere badischer Liberaler 1830–1848* (Frankfurt, 1994), pp. 117–30, 132, 137 and passim.
57. On this see Simms, *Struggle for mastery in Germany*, pp. 128–31 and passim (quotation p. 131).
58. 'Prince Joseph zu Salm-Dyck an den General-Gouverneur Prinzen Wilhelm. Memorandum on the Constitutional Question', 28.1.1831, Aachen, in Joseph Hansen (ed.), *Rheinische Briefe und Akten zur Geschichte der politischen Bewegung, 1830–1850*. Vol. 1: *1830–1845* (Essen, 1919), p. 5.
59. Quoted in John M. Knapp, *Behind the diplomatic curtain. Adolphe de Bourqueney and French foreign policy, 1816–1869* (Akron, 2001), p. 60.
60. Quoted in Parry, *Politics of patriotism*, p. 149.
61. Lawrence C. Jennings, *French anti-slavery. The movement for the abolition of slavery in France, 1802–1848* (Cambridge, 2000), pp. 50–53.
62. See Lacy K. Ford, *Deliver us from evil. The Slavery Question in the Old South* (Oxford, 2009), pp. 199–200.
63. See Christopher Schmidt-Nowara, *Empire and anti-slavery. Spain, Cuba and Puerto Rico, 1833–74* (Pittsburgh, 1999), p. 15.
64. See now Seymour Drescher, *Abolition. A history of slavery and anti-slavery* (Cambridge, 2009), pp. 294–306.
65. Quoted in Oscar J. Hammen, 'Free Europe versus Russia, 1830–1854', *The American Slavic and East European Review*, XI (1952), pp. 27–41 (p. 29).
66. Quoted in Roger Bullen, 'France and the problem of intervention in Spain, 1834–1836', *Historical Journal*, 20, 2 (1977), pp. 363–93 (quotation p. 381).
67. Thus Anthony Howe, 'Radicalism, free trade, and foreign policy in mid-nineteenth century Britain', in William Mulligan and Brendan Simms (eds.), *The primacy of foreign policy in British history, 1660–2000. How strategic concerns shaped modern Britain* (Basingstoke, 2010), pp. 167–80.
68. See Letitia W. Ufford, *The Pasha. How Mehmet Ali defied the west, 1839–1841* (Jefferson, 2007).
69. Quoted in Abigail Green, 'The British Empire and the Jews: an imperialism of human rights?', *Past and Present*, 199 (2008), pp. 175–205.
70. Quoted in Tombs, *France*, p. 365.

71. The Duc d'Orléans is quoted in H. A. C. Collingham (with R. S. Alexander), *The July monarchy. A political history of France, 1830–1848* (London and New York, 1988), p. 232.
72. Quoted in Simms, *Struggle for mastery in Germany*, pp. 159 and 162.
73. Quoted in David H. Pinkney, *Decisive years in France, 1840–1847* (Princeton, 1986), p. 133.
74. Quoted in Simms, *Struggle for mastery in Germany*, p. 165.
75. Quoted in John P. LeDonne, *The Russian Empire and the world, 1700–1917. The geopolitics of expansion and containment* (New York and Oxford, 1997), p. 125.
76. Quoted in Cemil Aydin, *The politics of anti-westernism in Asia. Visions of world order in pan-Islamic and pan-Asian thought* (New York, 2007), p. 20.
77. Quoted in Robert Kagan, *Dangerous nation* (New York, 2006), p. 218.
78. See Donald Bruce Johnson and Kirk H. Porter (eds.), *National party platforms, 1840–1972* (Urbana, Chicago and London, 1956), pp. 12, 31, 36 and passim.
79. Quotations are in Abigail Green, 'Nationalism and the "Jewish International". Religious internationalism in Europe and the Middle East, c.1840–c.1880', *Comparative Studies in Society and History*, 50 (2008), pp. 548 and 546.
80. Ibid., pp. 535 and 547.
81. Quoted in Abigail Green, 'Intervening in the Jewish Question, 1840–1878', in Simms and Trim (eds.), *Humanitarian intervention*, p. 143.
82. See Jon Elster (ed.), *Karl Marx. A reader* (Cambridge, 1986), pp. 171–86. The *German ideology* was not published until 1932, by the Marx-Engels Institute in Moscow (quotation p. 182).
83. Quoted in Michael Stephen Partridge, *Military planning for the defense of the United Kingdom* (New York, 1989), p. 9.
84. Quoted in Parry, *Politics of patriotism*, pp. 159–60. My thinking on this subject has been heavily influenced by Howe, 'Radicalism, free trade and foreign policy', in Mulligan and Simms (eds.), *Primacy of foreign policy in British history*, pp. 167–80.
85. Quoted in Tombs, *France*, p. 38.
86. Harald Müller, 'Zu den aussenpolitischen Zielvorstellungen der gemässigten Liberalen am Vorabend und im Verlauf der bürgerlichen-demokratischen Revolution von 1848/49 am Beispiel der "Deutschen Zeitung"', in H. Bleiber (ed.), *Bourgeoisie und bürgerliche Umwälzung in Deutschland 1789–1871* (Berlin, 1977), p. 233.
87. Quoted in Simms, *Struggle for mastery in Germany*, p. 171.
88. Ibid.
89. This account is based on the very useful analytical chronology in Jonathan Sperber, *The European revolutions, 1848–1851*, 2nd edn (Cambridge, 2005), especially pp. viii–xx.

90. Quoted in Harry Hearder, 'The making of the Roman Republic, 1848–1849', *History* 60 (1975), p. 181.
91. Drouyn de Lhuys is quoted in Martin Stauch, *Im Schatten der heiligen Allianz. Frankreichs Preussenpolitik von 1848 bis 1857* (Frankfurt, 1996), p. 78.
92. Lamartine and Bastide are quoted in James G. Chastain, 'France's proposed Danubian federation in 1848', *Proceedings of the Consortium on Revolutionary Europe* (Tallahassee, 1978), p. 103.
93. Quoted in Tombs, *France*, p. 385.
94. See Stauch, *Im Schatten der heiligen Allianz*, pp. 41–3 (quotations pp. 11 and 47).
95. Karl Marx and Friedrich Engels, *The communist manifesto*, ed. David McLellan (Oxford, 1992), pp. 2, 17 and 23.
96. Quoted in Alan Sked, *Metternich and Austria. An evaluation* (Basingstoke and London, 2008), p. 65.
97. Quoted in Parry, *Politics of patriotism*, p. 196.
98. Milbanke made similar comments throughout 1848–9, as the records in the National Archives show (letters to Palmerston of 8.5.1848, 6.6.1848 and 31.3.1849 in NA F09/10; NA F09/101 and NA F09/103). I am most grateful to Frank Lorenz Müller for supplying me with these references.
99. Ibid., p. 39.
100. Quoted in Martin Schulze Wessel, *Russlands Blick auf Preussen. Die polnische Frage in der Diplomatie und der politischen Öffentlichkeit des Zarenreiches und des Sowjetstaates, 1697–1947* (Stuttgart, 1995), p. 120.
101. See Randolf Oberschmidt, *Russland und die Schleswig-holsteinische Frage, 1839–1853* (Frankfurt am Main, 1997), pp. 281, 289 and passim.
102. Quoted in Mathias Schulz, 'A balancing act: domestic pressures and international systemic constraints in the foreign policies of the great powers, 1848–1851', *German History* 21, 3 (2003), pp. 319–46 (quotation p. 326).
103. Quoted in A. J. P. Taylor, *The struggle for mastery in Europe, 1848–1918* (Oxford, 1971 [1954]), p. 37.
104. Quoted in Schulz, 'A balancing act', p. 328.
105. See Schulz, pp. 335–6, for quotations.
106. Quoted in Frank Lorenz Müller, *Britain and the German Question. Perceptions of nationalism and political reform, 1830–63* (Basingstoke, 2002), p. 153.
107. Lamartine's 'Manifesto to Europe', in Alphonse de Lamartine, *History of the French Revolution of 1848* (London, 1849), pp. 283–5
108. The *Gazette de France* is quoted in Stauch, *Im Schatten der heiligen Allianz*, p. 73; Bastide is quoted in Jörg Ulbert, 'France and German dualism, 1756–1871', in Carine Germond and Henning Türk (eds.), *A history of Franco-German relations in Europe. From 'hereditary enemies' to partners* (Basingstoke, 2008), p. 44.

109. See Manfred Kittel, 'Abschied vom Völkerfrühling? National- und aussenpolitische Vorstellungen im konstitutionellen Liberalismus 1848/49', *Historische Zeitschrift*, 275 (2002), pp. 333–83.
110. Quoted in Tombs, *France*, p. 398.
111. See R. J. W. Evans, 'From confederation to compromise: the Austrian experiment, 1849–1867', *Proceedings of the British Academy*, 87 (1995), pp. 135–67 (especially pp. 138–40).
112. Quoted in Nikolaus Buschmann, *Einkreisung und Waffenbruderschaft. Die öffentliche Deutung von Krieg und Nation in Deutschland, 1850–1871* (Göttingen, 2003), p. 191. See also Kevin Cramer, *The Thirty Years War and German memory in the nineteenth century* (Lincoln, Nebr., and London, 2007), pp. 51–93 and 141–77.
113. See Christian Jansen, *Einheit, Macht und Freiheit. Die Paulskirchenlinke und die deutsche Politik in der nachrevolutionären Epoche, 1849–1867* (Dusseldorf, 2000), pp. 510–20 and 530–64.
114. Quoted in Otto Pflanze, *Bismarck and the development of Germany. The period of unification, 1815–1871* (Princeton, 1963), p. 72.
115. Quoted in Efraim Karsh, *Islamic imperialism. A history* (New Haven, 2006), p. 97.
116. See Taylor, *Struggle for mastery in Europe*, p. 61: 'The real stake in the Crimean war was not Turkey. It was central Europe; that is to say Germany and Italy.'
117. Quoted in Doering-Manteuffel, *Vom Wiener Kongress zur Pariser Konferenz*, p. 215.
118. Quoted in Müller, *Britain and the German Question*, p. 162.
119. Quoted in Kagan, *Dangerous nation*, p. 234.
120. See Robert E. May, *The Southern dream of a Caribbean empire, 1854–1861*, 2nd edn (Gainesville, 2002), pp. 46–76. The link between territorial expansion and the Southern interest in Congress is described on pp. 11–12.
121. Paul W. Schroeder, *Austria, Great Britain and the Crimean War. The destruction of the European Concert* (Ithaca and London, 1972), especially, pp. 423–4.
122. These fascinating figures are in David Saunders, *Russia in the age of reaction and reform, 1801–1881* (London and New York, 1992), p. 207.
123. Quoted in Saunders, *Russia in the age of reaction and reform*, pp. 223–4.
124. On the centrality of foreign policy in British domestic politics throughout the 1850s see Adrian Brettle, 'The enduring importance of foreign policy dominance in mid-nineteenth-century politics', in Mulligan and Simms (eds.), *Primacy of foreign policy in British history*, pp. 154–66.
125. Quoted in Parry, *Politics of patriotism*, p. 68.
126. See Denis Mack Smith, *Cavour* (New York, 1985), p. 111 and passim.
127. Quoted in Derek Beales, *England and Italy, 1859–1860* (London, Edinburgh, etc., 1961), pp. 3–4.

128. See Mack Walker (ed.), *Plombières. Secret diplomacy and the rebirth of Italy* (New York, London and Toronto, 1968), pp. 27–37, especially pp. 28–9.
129. On the centrality of Germany during the Italian war see Franco Valsecchi, 'European diplomacy and the expedition of the thousand. The conservative powers', in Martin Gilbert (ed.), *A century of conflict, 1850–1950. Essays for A. J. P. Taylor* (London, 1967), pp. 49–72, especially pp. 54–65.
130. See Michael J. Salevouris, *'Riflemen form'. The war scare of 1859–1860 in England* (New York and London, 1982), pp. 152–95.
131. See D. M. Schreuder, 'Gladstone and Italian unification, 1848–70: the making of a Liberal?', *The English Historical Review*, LXXXV (1970), p. 475.
132. See Mark Hewitson, *Nationalism in Germany, 1848–1866* (Basingstoke, 2010), pp. 76–7.
133. Andreas Biefang, *Politisches Bürgertum in Deutschland, 1857–1868. Nationale Organisationen und Eliten* (Dusseldorf, 1994), pp. 66–79.
134. Quoted in Knapp, *Behind the diplomatic curtain*, p. 270.
135. Quoted in Frank Lorenz Müller, 'The spectre of a people in arms: the Prussian government and the militarisation of German nationalism, 1859–1864', *The English Historical Review*, CXXII, 495 (2007), pp. 82–104 (quotation p. 85).
136. The two positions are discussed in Hans-Christof Kraus, 'Militärreform oder Verfassungswandel? Kronprinz Friedrich von Preussen und die "deutschen Whigs" in der Krise von 1862/63', in Heinz Reif (ed.), *Adel und Bürgertum in Deutschland*. Vol. I: *Entwicklungslinien und Wendepunkte im 19. Jahrhundert* (Berlin, 2000), pp. 207–32.
137. See Andreas Kärnbach, 'Bismarcks Bemühungen um eine Reform des Deutschen Bundes 1849–1866', in Oswald Hauser (ed.), *Preussen, Europa und das Reich* (Cologne and Vienna, 1987), pp. 199–221, especially pp. 207–8.
138. This remarkable exchange is cited in Jonathan Steinberg, *Bismarck. A life* (Oxford, 2011), p. 174.
139. Quoted in May, *The Southern dream of Caribbean empire*, p. 237. In general May is too modest about the extent to which the question of territorial expansion led to the Civil War: pp. 242–3.
140. On the Southern pre-emptive strike see Matthew Flynn, *First strike. Pre-emptive war in modern history* (New York and London, 2008), pp. 41–2.
141. Quoted in Kagan, *Dangerous nation*, p. 91.
142. See John Dunn, 'Africa invades the new world: Egypt's Mexican adventure, 1863–1867', *War in History*, 4 (1997), pp. 27–34.
143. Quoted in Henry Blumenthal, *France and the United States. Their diplomatic relations, 1789–1914* (Chapel Hill, 2009), p. 109.
144. Quoted in James Chambers, *Palmerston, the people's darling* (London, 2004), p. 495.

145. See David F. Krein, *The last Palmerston government. Foreign policy, domestic politics, and the genesis of 'splendid isolation'* (Ames, 1978), pp. 174–9.
146. See Jacques Freymond and Miklós Molnár, 'The rise and fall of the First International', in Milorad Drachkovitch (ed.), *The revolutionary Internationals, 1864–1943* (Stanford, 1966).
147. R. J. W. Evans, 'From confederation to compromise: the Austrian experiment, 1849–1867', *Proceedings of the British Academy*, 87 (1995), pp. 135–67 (quotation p. 164).
148. Quoted in Schulze Wessel, *Russlands Blick auf Preussen*, p. 130.
149. Quoted in Tombs, *France*, p. 414.
150. Quoted in Sked, *Metternich and Austria*, p. 63.
151. For the internal causes of the war on Vienna's side see Geoffrey Wawro, 'The Habsburg *Flucht nach vorne* in 1866: domestic political origins of the Austro-Prussian War', *International History Review*, 17, 2 (1995), pp. 221–48, especially pp. 221 and 229.

5. UNIFICATIONS, 1867–1916

1. Quoted in Christopher Clark, *Iron kingdom. The rise and downfall of Prussia, 1600–1947* (London, 2006), p. 557.
2. Quoted in Michael Howard, 'A thirty years' war? The two world wars in historical perspective', *Transactions of the Royal Historical Society*, Sixth Series, Vol. III (1993), p. 171.
3. For the connection between the wars of American and German unification see C. A. Bayly, *The birth of the modern world, 1780–1914* (Oxford, 2004), p. 163; Michael Geyer and Charles Bright, 'Global violence and nationalizing wars in Eurasia and America: the geopolitics of war in the mid-nineteenth century', *Comparative Studies in History and Society*, 38 (1996), pp. 619–57, especially p. 621; and Stig Förster and Jörg Nagler (eds.), *On the road to total war. The American Civil War and the German wars of unification, 1861–1871* (Cambridge, 1997).
4. Quoted in Robert Kagan, *Dangerous nation* (New York, 2006), p. 276.
5. See Bruce Cumings, *Dominion from sea to sea. Pacific ascendancy and American power* (New Haven and London, 2009), pp. 55–125.
6. Quoted in John Dunn, 'Africa invades the new world. Egypt's Mexican adventure, 1863–1867', *War in History*, 4, 1 (1997), p. 32.
7. Quoted in Clark, *Iron kingdom*, p. 546.
8. Frank Becker shows that German nationalist acceptance of Prussian leadership was a product not a cause of the Franco-Prussian War of 1870–71: Frank Becker, *Bilder von Krieg und Nation. Die Einigungskriege in der bürgerlichen Öffentlichkeit Deutschlands, 1864–1913* (Munich, 2001), pp. 488–9 and passim.

9. Quoted in F. R. Bridge, *The Habsburg monarchy among the great powers, 1815–1918* (New York, Oxford and Munich, 1990), p. 95.
10. Quoted in Florian Buch, *Grosse Politik im neuen Reich. Gesellschaft und Aussenpolitik in Deutschland 1867–1882* (Kassel, 2004), p. 351.
11. Geoffrey Hicks, '"Appeasement" or consistent conservatism? British foreign policy, party politics and the guarantees of 1867 and 1939', *Historical Research*, 84 (2011), pp. 520–21 and 525–6 (Stanley quotation pp. 526–7). Augustus Loftus, *The diplomatic reminiscences of Lord Augustus Loftus, 1862–1879*, Vol. I (London, 1894), p. 99.
12. Quoted in Jonathan Parry, *The politics of patriotism. English liberalism, national identity and Europe, 1830–1886* (Cambridge, 2006), p. 243.
13. J. M. Hobson, 'The military extraction gap and the wary titan: the fiscal sociology of British defence policy, 1870–1913', *Journal of European Economic History*, 222 (1993), pp. 461–506.
14. Quoted in Bridge, *Habsburg monarchy*, p. 84.
15. Quoted in Hans A. Schmitt, 'Count Beust and Germany, 1866–1870: reconquest, realignment, or resignation?', *Central European History*, 1, 1 (1968), pp. 20–34.
16. See Dietrich Beyrau, 'Der deutsche Komplex: Russland zur Zeit der Reichsgründung', in Eberhard Kolb (ed.), *Europa und die Reichsgründung. Preussen-Deutschland in der Sicht der grossen europäischen Mächte, 1860–1880* (Munich, 1980), p. 87.
17. See M. Katz, *Mikhail N. Katkov. A political biography, 1818–1887* (The Hague and Paris, 1966), pp. 112–17.
18. The quotation is in Dietrich Geyer, *Russian imperialism. The interaction of domestic and foreign policy, 1860–1914* (Leamington Spa, 1987), p. 94.
19. Quoted in Elisabeth Fehrenbach, 'Preussen-Deutschland als Faktor der französischen Aussenpolitik in der Reichsgründungszeit', in Kolb (ed.), *Europa und die Reichsgründung*, p. 124.
20. Quoted in Tombs, *France*, p. 417.
21. Quoted in Clark, *Iron kingdom*, p. 548.
22. Quoted in Tombs, *France*, p. 423.
23. Alexander Seyferth, *Die Heimatfront 1870/71. Wirtschaft und Gesellschaft im deutsch-französischen Krieg* (Paderborn, 2007), pp. 76–8, stresses fear of French aggression over patriotic enthusiasm.
24. These figures are in A. J. P. Taylor, *The struggle for mastery in Europe, 1848–1918* (Oxford, 1971 [1954]), p. xxv.
25. Quoted in Detlef Junker, 'Die manichäische Falle: das deutsche Reich im Urteil der USA, 1871–1945', in Klaus Hildebrand (ed.), *Das deutsche Reich im Urteil der grossen Mächte und europäischen Nachbarn (1871–1945)* (Munich, 1995), pp. 141–58 (quotation p. 142).
26. Peter Krüger, 'Die Beurteilung der Reichsgründung und Reichsverfassung von 1871 in den USA', in Norbert Finzsch et al., *Liberalitas. Festschrift für*

Erich Angermann zum 65. Geburtstag (Stuttgart, 1992), pp. 263–83 (quotations pp. 271 and 273).

27. See Paul W. Schroeder, 'The lost intermediaries: the impact of 1870 on the European system', *International History Review*, 6, 1 (1984), pp. 1–27, especially pp. 2–3, 8 and 11–12.
28. See Sudhir Hazareesingh, 'Republicanism, war and democracy: the *Ligue du Midi* in France's war against Prussia, 1870–1871', *French History*, 17, 1 (2003), pp. 48–78, especially pp. 50–51.
29. Bertrand Taithe, *Defeated flesh. Welfare, warfare and the making of modern France* (Manchester, 1999), pp. 71–98, and *Citizenship and wars: France in turmoil, 1870–1871* (London and New York, 2001).
30. Quoted in Jacques Bariety, 'Das deutsche Reich im französischen Urteil, 1871–1945', in Hildebrand (ed.), *Das deutsche Reich im Urteil der grossen Mächte*, pp. 203–18 (quotation p. 208).
31. See Allan Mitchell, *Victors and vanquished. The German influence on Army and Church in France after 1870* (Chapel Hill, 1984), especially pp. 41–8, and Rachel Chrastil, *Organising for war. France, 1870–1914* (Baton Rouge, 2010), pp. 157–8 and passim.
32. Heinrich Lutz, 'Zur Wende der österreichisch-ungarischen Aussenpolitik 1871. Die Denkschrift des Grafen Beust für Kaiser Franz Joseph vom 18. mai', in *Mitteilungen des österreichischen Staatsarchivs* 25 (1972), pp. 169–84, especially pp. 177–8 ('Mitteleuropa', p. 180).
33. Quoted in Bridge, *Habsburg monarchy*, p. 94.
34. See W. E. Mosse, *The European powers and the German Question*, Appendix C: 'The Russian national press and the "German Peril", 1870–71', pp. 391–2.
35. Deryck Schreuder, 'Gladstone as "Troublemaker": Liberal foreign policy and the German annexation of Alsace-Lorraine, 1870–1871', *Journal of British Studies*, 17 (1978), pp. 106–35 (quotation p. 119). I am grateful to Eddie Fishman for conversations on the subject.
36. Quoted in Karina Urbach, *Bismarck's favourite Englishman. Lord Odo Russell's mission to Berlin* (London, 1999), p. 208.
37. Thus Klaus Hildebrand, *No intervention. Die Pax Britannica und Preussen 1865/66–1869/70. Eine Untersuchung zur englischen Weltpolitik im 19. Jahrhundert* (Munich, 1997), pp. 393–4 and passim.
38. See Scott W. Murray, *Liberal diplomacy and German unification: the early career of Robert Morier* (Westport and London 2000), pp. 91–138.
39. Thus William Mulligan, 'Britain, the "German Revolution", and the fall of France, 1870/1', *Historical Research*, 84, 224 (2011), pp. 310–27.
40. Quoted in ibid., p. 324.
41. Quoted in Thomas Schaarschmidt, *Aussenpolitik und öffentliche Meinung in Grossbritannien während des deutsch-französischen Krieges von 1870/71* (Franfurt am Main, Berne, etc., 1993), p. 132.

42. See Michael Pratt, 'A fallen idol: the impact of the Franco-Prussian War on the perception of Germany by British intellectuals', *International History Review*, 7, 4 (1985), pp. 543–75.
43. Quoted in Mulligan, 'Britain, the "German Revolution", and the fall of France'.
44. On the importance of the empire to Britain's great power standing see Edward Ingram, *The British Empire as a world power* (London, 2001), especially pp. 25–45. See also James Belich, *Replenishing the earth. The settler revolution and the rise of the Anglo-World, 1783–1939* (Oxford, 2009).
45. My view of Imperial Federation has been strongly influenced by conversations with Daniel Robinson, James Rogers and Duncan Bell. See Duncan Bell, *The idea of greater Britain. Empire and the future of world order, 1860–1900* (Princeton, 2007).
46. Thus Max Beloff, *Imperial sunset: Britain's liberal empire, 1897–1921* (London, 1969), p. 37.
47. Quoted in Parry, *Politics of patriotism*, p. 293.
48. See William Mulligan, 'British anti-slave trade and anti-slavery policy in East Africa, Arabia, and Turkey in the late nineteenth century', in Brendan Simms and D. J. B. Trim (eds.), *Humanitarian intervention. A history* (Cambridge, 2011), pp. 257–82, especially p. 273.
49. See Jacques Freymond and Miklós Molnár, 'The rise and fall of the First International', in Milorad Drachkovitch (ed.), *The revolutionary Internationals, 1864–1943* (Stanford, 1966), p. 33.
50. Articles 60 and 63 of the constitution are quoted in Christopher Clark, *Kaiser Wilhelm II. A life in power* (London, 2009), p. 94.
51. Margaret Lavinia Anderson, *Practicing democracy. Elections and political culture in imperial Germany* (Princeton, 2000). See also Gerhard A. Ritter, 'Die Reichstagswahlen und die Wurzeln der deutschen Demokratie im Kaiserreich', *Historische Zeitschrift*, 275 (2002), pp. 385–403.
52. Thus Prince Hohenlohe-Schillingsfürst, as quoted in W. N. Medlicott and Dorothy K. Coveney (eds.), *Bismarck and Europe* (London, 1971), p. 138.
53. Quoted in Lothar Gall, *Bismarck. Der weisse Revolutionär* (Frankfurt, 1980), p. 623.
54. Quoted in Detlef Junker, *The Manichean Trap: American perceptions of the German empire, 1871–1945* (Washington, DC), p. 14.
55. See the text of the agreement (6.6.1873) in Bridge, *Habsburg monarchy*, Appendix I, p. 381.
56. Quoted in Medlicott and Coveney (eds.), *Bismarck and Europe*, pp. 87–8.
57. Quoted in Klaus Hildebrand, *Das vergangene Reich. Deutsche Aussenpolitik von Bismark bis Hitler* (Stuttgart, 1995), p. 33. For perception and reality of the French threat see Johannes Janorschke, *Bismarck, Europa und die 'Krieg in Sicht' Krise von 1875* (Paderborn, 2010), pp. 146–56, and 192–4.

58. The importance of the *caesura* is stressed by T. G. Otte, 'From "War-in-sight" to nearly war: Anglo-French relations in the age of high imperialism, 1875–1898', *Diplomacy and Statecraft*, 17, 4 (2006), pp. 693–714, especially pp. 695–7.
59. For the importance of the war for development of newspapers see Louise McReynolds, *The news under Russia's old regime. The development of a mass-circulation press* (Princeton, 1991), pp. 73–92.
60. Quoted in Matthias Schulz, 'The guarantees of humanity: the Concert of Europe and the origins of the Russo-Ottoman War of 1877', in Simms and Trim (eds.), *Humanitarian intervention*, pp. 184–204 (quotation p. 184).
61. Quoted in Medlicott and Coveney (eds.), *Bismarck and Europe*, pp. 96–7 and 102–3.
62. Carole Fink, *Defending the rights of others. The great powers, the Jews and international minority protection, 1878–1938* (Cambridge, 2004). The British diplomat, speaking in the late 1860s, is quoted in Abigail Green, 'Intervening in the Jewish Question, 1840–1878', in Simms and Trim (eds.), *Humanitarian intervention*, pp. 139–58 (quotation p. 139).
63. Quoted in Medlicott and Coveney (eds.), *Bismarck and Europe*, p. 99.
64. Quoted in Geyer, *Russian imperialism*, p. 82. See also S. Lukashevich, *Ivan Aksakov, 1823–1886. A study in Russian thought and politics* (Cambridge, Mass., 1965), pp. 140–41.
65. Quoted in Geyer, *Russian imperialism*, p. 78.
66. Thus Barry Bascom Hayes, *Bismarck and Mitteleuropa* (London and Toronto, 1994), pp. 302–3, 353, 391 and passim (quotations pp. 303 and 357).
67. Quoted in Bridge, *Habsburg monarchy*, p. 135.
68. Quoted in Medlicott and Coveney (eds.), *Bismarck and Europe*, p. 126.
69. Quoted in Hugh Seton-Watson, *The decline of Imperial Russia, 1855–1914* (New York, 1960), p. 494.
70. For the 'defensiveness' of early Zionism see Anita Shapira, *Land and power. The Zionist resort to force, 1881–1948* (Oxford, 1992), pp. 3–52. See John Klier, *Russians, Jews, and the pogroms of 1881–1882* (Cambridge, 2011), pp. 1 (Ignatiev quotation) and 234–54 (for the foreign policy implications).
71. David Foglesong, *The American mission and the 'Evil Empire'. The crusade for a 'Free Russia' since 1881* (New York, 2007), pp. 7–33.
72. See Wolfgang Schivelbusch, *The culture of defeat. On national trauma, mourning, and recovery*, trans. Jefferson Chase (New York, 2003), pp. 179–80 (Bert quotation), and Peter Grupp, *Deutschland, Frankreich und die Kolonien. Der französische 'parti colonial' und Deutschland, 1890 bis 1914* (Tübingen, 1980), pp. 75–9.
73. Edward E. Morris, *Imperial Federation. A lecture* (Melbourne, 1885), quotations pp. 8–9.

74. See Georgios Varouxakis, '"Great" versus "small" nations: scale and national greatness in Victorian political thought', in Duncan Bell (ed.), *Victorian visions of global order. Empire and international relations in nineteenth-century political thought* (Cambridge, 2007), pp. 136–59.
75. Quoted in John Darwin, *The Empire project. The rise and fall of the British world-system, 1830–1970* (Cambridge, 2009), p. 79.
76. See generally Humphrey J. Fisher, *Slavery in the history of Muslim Black Africa* (London, 2001), pp. 98–137.
77. See Mulligan, 'British anti-slave trade and anti-slavery policy', in Simms and Trim (eds.), *Humanitarian intervention*, pp. 257–82.
78. Thus W. J. Mommsen, 'Bismarck, the Concert of Europe, and the future of West Africa, 1883–1885', in Stig Förster, Wolfgang Mommsen and Ronald Robinson (eds.), *Bismarck, Europe and Africa. The Berlin Africa conference 1884–1885 and the onset of partition* (Oxford, 1988), pp. 151–70, especially pp. 165–6.
79. Sönke Neitzel, '"Mittelafrika". Zum Stellenwert eines Schlagwortes in der deutschen Weltpolitik des Hochimperialismus', in Wolfgang Elz and Sönke Neitzel (eds.), *Internationale Beziehungen im 19. und 20. Jahrhundert. Festschrift für Winfried Baumgart zum 65. Geburtstag* (Paderborn, Munich, etc., 2003), pp. 83–103.
80. See Benedikt Stuchtey, *Die europäische Expansion und ihre Feinde. Kolonialismuskritik vom 18. bis in das 20. Jahrhundert* (Munich, 2010).
81. Quoted in Gregory Claeys, *Imperial sceptics. British critics of empire, 1850–1920* (Cambridge, 2010), p. 111.
82. Quoted in Schivelbusch, *Culture of defeat*, p. 181.
83. Quoted in Hildebrand, *Das vergangene Reich*, p. 109.
84. But see Terence Zuber, *Inventing the Schlieffen Plan. German war planning, 1871–1914* (Oxford, 2002), pp. 135–219, who sees the plan as a bid for increased defence funding rather than a fully worked-out strategy.
85. Quoted in Hildebrand, *Das vergangene Reich*, p. 156.
86. On the importance of the *Mittellage* for Caprivi's thinking see Rainer Lahme, *Deutsche Aussenpolitik 1890–1894. Von der Gleichgewichtspolitik Bismarcks zur Allianzstrategie Caprivis* (Göttingen, 1990), pp. 34–5 and passim.
87. Quoted in Hildebrand, *Das vergangene Reich*, p. 168.
88. Quoted in Clark, *Kaiser Wilhelm II*, p. 83.
89. See Francis W. Wcislo, *Tales of Imperial Russia. The life and times of Sergei Witte, 1849–1915* (Oxford, 2011), pp. 138–88, especially pp. 140–42.
90. See Moshe Zimmermann, 'Muscle Jews vs. nervous Jews', in Michael Brenner and Gideon Reuveni (eds.), *Emancipation through muscles. Jews and sports in Europe* (Lincoln, Nebr., 2006), pp. 15–28.
91. On the German character of Zionists see David Aberbach, 'Zionist patriotism in Europe, 1897–1942: ambiguities in Jewish nationalism', *International*

History Review, 31, 6 (2009), pp. 268–98, especially pp. 274–81 (quotation p. 278).

92. Moshe Zimmermann, 'Jewish nationalism and Zionism in German-Jewish students' organisations', *Publications of the Leo Baeck Institute*, Year Book XXVII (1982), pp. 129–53 (quotations p. 153).
93. Quoted in Otte, 'From "War in sight"', p. 703.
94. Quoted in Hildebrand, *Das vergangene Reich*, p. 202.
95. See Sönke Neitzel, *Weltmacht oder Untergang. Die Weltreichslehre im Zeitalter des Imperialismus* (Paderborn, 2000).
96. See Sönke Neitzel, 'Das Revolutionsjahr 1905 in den internationalen Beziehungen der Grossmächte', in Jan Kusber and Andreas Frings (eds.), *Das Zarenreich, das Jahr 1905 und seine Wirkungen* (Berlin, 2007), pp. 17–55 (quotation p. 21).
97. Quoted in Hildebrand, *Das vergangene Reich*, p. 187.
98. See Harald Rosenbach, *Das deutsche Reich, Grossbritannien und der Transvaal (1896–1902)* (Göttingen, 1993), pp. 309–314.
99. Matthew S. Seligmann, *Rivalry in Southern Africa, 1893–99. The transformation of German colonial policy* (Basingstoke, 1998), pp. 16–17, 58–61 and 128–31 (quotation p. 16).
100. Quoted in Darwin, *Empire project*, p. 110.
101. Quoted in Kagan, *Dangerous nation*, p. 357.
102. See Mike Sewell, 'Humanitarian intervention, democracy, and imperialism: the American war with Spain, 1898 and after', in Simms and Trim (eds.), *Humanitarian intervention*, pp. 303–22 (quotation p. 303), and Paul T. McCartney, *Power and progress. American national identity, the war of 1898, and the rise of American imperialism* (Baton Rouge, 2006), quotation p. 272.
103. Quoted in Tony Smith, *America's mission. The United States and the worldwide struggle for democracy in the twentieth century* (Princeton, 1994), p. 41.
104. See Keith Wilson (ed.), *The international impact of the Boer War* (Chesham, 2001).
105. Quoted in Warren Zimmermann, *First great triumph. How five Americans made their country a world power* (New York, 2002), p. 446. I am grateful to Charles Laderman for this reference. See also T. G. Otte, *The China Question. Great power rivalry and British isolation, 1894–1905* (Oxford, 2007).
106. Quoted in Gordon A. Craig, *Germany, 1866–1945* (Oxford, 1978) p. 313.
107. See Phillips Payson O'Brien, *British and American naval power. Politics and policy, 1900–1936* (London, 1998), pp. 26–7.
108. Quoted in William Mulligan, 'From case to narrative: the Marquess of Landsdowne, Sir Edward Grey, and the threat from Germany, 1900–1906' *International History Review*, 30, 2 (2008), p. 292.

109. Matthew Seligmann, 'Switching horses: the Admiralty's recognition of the threat from Germany, 1900–1905', *International History Review*, 30, 2 (2008), pp. 239–58, and Matthew Seligmann, 'Britain's great security mirage: the Royal Navy and the Franco-Russian naval threat, 1898–1906', *Journal of Strategic Studies*, 35 (2012), pp. 861–86.
110. Quoted in Christopher Ross, 'Lord Curzon, the "Persian Question", and geopolitics, 1888–1921' (Ph.D. dissertation, University of Cambridge, 2010).
111. Matthew Seligmann, 'A prelude to the reforms of Admiral Sir John Fisher: the creation of the Home Fleet, 1902–3', *Historical Research*, 83 (2010), pp. 506–19, especially pp. 517–18.
112. See G. R. Searle, *The quest for national efficiency* (Berkeley, 1971). For the role of foreign policy in British electoral politics see T. E. Otte, '"Avenge England's dishonour" By-elections, parliament and the politics of foreign policy in 1898', *The English Historical Review*, CXXI, 491 (2006), pp. 385–428.
113. Quoted in Mathew Johnson, 'The Liberal War Committee and the Liberal advocacy of conscription in Britain, 1914–1916', *Historical Journal*, 51. (2008), who cites the *National Service Journal* of November 1903.
114. On the centrality of foreign policy to Chamberlain's conception of tariff reform see Paul Readman, 'Patriotism and the politics of foreign policy, *c.* 1870–*c.* 1914', in William Mulligan and Brendan Simms (eds.), *The primacy of foreign policy in British history, 1660–2000. How strategic concerns shaped modern Britain* (Basingstoke, 2010), especially, pp. 264–5.
115. See Richard H. Collin, *Theodore Roosevelt, culture, diplomacy and expansion. A new view of American imperialism* (Baton Rouge and London, 1985), pp. 101–2. I thank Quinby Frey for this and many other references on US history.
116. See James Ford Rhodes, *The McKinley and Roosevelt administrations, 1897–1909* (New York, 1922), p. 249.
117. Thus Frederick Marks III, *Velvet on iron. The diplomacy of Theodore Roosevelt* (Lincoln, Nebr., and London, 1979), pp. 6–10, 38–47 and 172–3. For a different view see Nancy Mitchell, *The danger of dreams. German and American imperialism in Latin America* (Chapel Hill and London, 1999), pp. 216–28 passim (quotations pp. 75–6).
118. James R. Holmes, *Theodore Roosevelt and world order. Police power in international relations* (Washington, DC, 2006), passim, especially pp. 70 and 110. For a case study see Stephen Wertheim, 'Reluctant liberator: Theodore Roosevelt's philosophy of self-government and preparation for Philippine independence', in *Presidential Studies Quarterly*, 39, 3 (2009), pp. 494–518.
119. For US attacks on Prussianism and German 'autocracy' in the early 1900s see Marks, *Velvet on iron*, p. 8. For the emergence of an anti-German

'generation' in Britain and the United States around the turn of the century see Magnus Brechtken, *Scharnierzeit, 1895–1907. Persönlichkeitsnetze und internationale Politik in den deutsch-britisch-amerkanischen Beziehungen vor dem Ersten Weltkrieg* (Mainz, 2006), pp. 374–6.

120. Stuart Anderson, *Race and rapprochement. Anglo-Saxonism and Anglo-American relations, 1895–1904* (London and Toronto, 1981), pp. 66–9 (quotation p. 67).

121. On the Copenhagen Complex see Jonathan Steinberg, 'The Copenhagen Complex', *Journal of Contemporary History*, 1, 3 (1966), pp. 23–46, especially pp. 29–30.

122. Quoted in Howard K. Beale, *Theodore Roosevelt and the rise of America to world power* (Baltimore, 1956), p. 236 I thank Charles Laderman for this reference.

123. Quoted in Geyer, *Russian imperialism*, p. 221.

124. Josh Sanborn, *Drafting the Russian nation. Military conscription, total war and mass politics, 1905–1925* (DeKalb, Ill., 2003), pp. 25–9.

125. Jan Rüger, *The great naval game. Britain and Germany in the Age of Empire* (Cambridge, 2007), pp. 234–40.

126. On this strategy see William Philpott, 'Managing the British way in warfare: France and Britain's continental commitment, 1904–1918', in Keith Neilson and Greg Kennedy (eds.), *The British way in warfare. Power and the international system, 1856–1956. Essays in honour of David French* (Farnham, 2010), pp. 83–100.

127. Thus T. G. Otte, '"Almost a law of nature"? Sir Edward Grey, the Foreign Office, and the balance of power in Europe, 1905–12', in Erik Goldstein and B. J. C. McKercher (eds.), *Diplomacy and Statecraft. Special Issue on Power and Stability. British Foreign Policy, 1865–1965*, 14, 2 (2003), pp. 77–118 (pp. 80–81).

128. See Neitzel, 'Das Revolutionsjahr 1905', in Kusber and Frings (eds.), *Das Zarenreich, das Jahr 1905 und seine Wirkungen*, pp. 43–4.

129. Quoted in Annika Mombauer, 'German war plans', in Richard F. Hamilton and Holger H. Herwig (eds.), *War planning 1914* (Cambridge, 2010), pp. 48–79 (quotation p. 54).

130. Albrecht Moritz, *Das Problem des Präventivkrieges in der deutschen Politik während der ersten Marokkokrise* (Berne and Frankfurt am Main, 1974), pp. 144 and 280–84.

131. See Michael Epkenhans, *Die wilhelminische Flottenrüstung, 1908–1914 Weltmachtstreben, industrieller Fortschritt, soziale Integration* (Munich 1991). On the capacity of the British state for massive military mobilization even in peacetime see G. C. Peden, *Arms, economics and British strategy From Dreadnoughts to hydrogen bombs* (Cambridge, 2007), pp. 1–16.

132. Balfour was speaking in 1906, 'Navy estimates, 1906–1907', Hansard vol. 162, col. 112. (1906)

133. Quoted in John Albert White, *Transition to global rivalry. Alliance diplomacy and the Quadruple Entente, 1895–1907* (Cambridge, 1995), p. 288. Another work which, unlike this book, stresses the primacy of imperial over European considerations is Keith Wilson, *The limits of eurocentricity. Imperial British foreign and defence policy in the early twentieth century* (Istanbul, 2002).
134. Quoted in Hildebrand, *Das vergangene Reich*, p. 245.
135. See Frank Boesch, '"Are we a cruel nation?" Colonial practices, perceptions, and scandals', in Dominik Geppert and Robert Gerwarth (eds.), *Wilhelmine Germany and Edwardian Britain. Essays in cultural affinity* (Oxford, 2008), pp. 115–40, especially pp. 121–3.
136. Quoted in Hildebrand, *Das vergangene Reich*, p. 249.
137. On the link between foreign policy and domestic reform see Uwe Liszkowski, *Zwischen Liberalismus und Imperialismus. Die zaristische Aussenpolitik vor dem Ersten Weltkrieg im Urteil Miljukovs und der Kadettenpartei, 1905–1914* (Stuttgart, 1974), pp. 56–77.
138. Quotations in Geyer, *Russian imperialism*, pp. 295–6.
139. See Matthew Seligmann, 'Intelligence information and the 1909 naval scare: the secret foundations of a public panic', *War in History*, 17, 1 (2010), pp. 37–59, and Phillips Payson O'Brien, 'The 1910 elections and the primacy of foreign policy', in Mulligan and Simms (eds.), *Primacy of foreign policy in British history*, pp. 249–59.
140. Thus Christopher Andrew, *The defence of the realm. The authorized history of MI5* (London, 2009), pp. 3–18.
141. David Lloyd George, Limehouse Speech, 30 July 1909.
142. See Jean H. Quataert, 'Mobilising philantropy in the service of war: the female rituals of care in the new Germany, 1871–1914', in Manfred F. Boemeke, Roger Chickering and Stig Förster (eds.), *Anticipating total war. The German and American experiences, 1871–1914* (Cambridge, 1999); Roger Chickering, '"Casting their gaze more broadly": women's patriotic activism in imperial Germany', *Past and Present*, 118 (1988), pp. 156–85, especially pp. 172, 175 and 182–3.
143. Quoted in Sheila Rowbotham, *A century of women. The history of women in Britain and the United States* (London, 1997), p. 82.
144. Quoted in Hildebrand, *Das vergangene Reich*, p. 240.
145. See Friedrich Katz, *The secret war in Mexico. Europe, the United States and the Mexican Revolution* (Chicago and London, 1981), quotation p. 88, and Reiner Pommerin, *Der Kaiser und Amerika. Die USA in der Politik der Reichsleitung, 1890–1917* (Cologne, 1986).
146. Quoted in John Lamberton Harper, *American visions of Europe. Franklin D. Roosevelt, George F. Kennan and Dean G. Acheson* (Cambridge, 1994), p. 31. See Matthew S. Seligmann, 'Germany and the origins of the First World War in the eyes of the American diplomatic establishment', *German History*, 15, 3 (1997), pp. 307–32.

147. Quoted in Mark Hewitson, 'Germany and France before the First World War: a reassessment of Wilhelmine foreign policy', *The English Historical Review*, 115, 462 (2000), pp. 570–606 (quotation pp. 594–5).
148. Writing in 1913, quoted in Hartmut Pogge von Strandmann, 'Germany and the coming of war', in R. J. W. Evans and Hartmut Pogge von Strandmann (eds.), *The coming of the First World War* (Oxford and New York, 1988), p. 111.
149. Quoted in Fritz Fischer, *War of illusions. German policies from 1911 to 1914* (London, 1975), p. 180.
150. See Keith Jeffery, *Field Marshal Sir Henry Wilson. A political soldier* (Oxford, 2006), pp. 99–100 and passim.
151. See P. P. O'Brien, 'The Titan refreshed: imperial overstretch and the British navy before the First World War', *Past and Present*, 172 (2001), pp. 145–69, especially pp. 154–5.
152. Quoted in Darwin, *Empire project*, p. 306.
153. Thomas Meyer, *'Endlich eine Tat, eine befreiende Tat.' Alfred von Kiderlen-Wächters 'Panthersprung nach Agadir' unter dem Druck der öffentlichen Meinung* (Husum, 1996), pp. 295–302.
154. Quoted in Groh, p. 432
155. Quoted in Hildebrand, *Das vergangene Reich*, p. 266.
156. Thus Niall Ferguson, 'Public finance and national security: the domestic origins of the First World War revisited', *Past and Present*, 142 (1994).
157. Quoted in Geyer, *Russian imperialism*, p. 306.
158. Quoted in Seton-Watson, *Decline of Imperial Russia*, p. 676.
159. Quoted in Smith, *America's mission*, p. 69.
160. Quoted in Mustafa Aksakal, *The Ottoman road to war: The Ottoman Empire and the First World War* (Cambridge, 2008), p. 21.
161. Quoted in Aksakal, *Ottoman road to war*, p. 76.
162. Quoted in Sean McMeekin, *The Russian origins of the First World War* (Cambridge, Mass., 2011), p. 6.
163. Quoted in Smith, *America's mission*, p. 70.
164. See now Christopher Clark, *The sleepwalkers. How Europe went to war in 1914* (London, 2012), pp. 367–403.
165. Bridge, *Habsburg monarchy*, p. 335.
166. According to the testimony of Count Forgach. See Annika Mombauer, 'The First World War: inevitable, avoidable, improbable or desirable? Recent interpretations on war guilt and the war's origins', *German History*, 25, 1 (2007), pp. 78–95 (quotation p. 84).
167. See Samuel R. Williamson, *Austria-Hungary and the origins of the First World War* (Basingstoke and London, 1991), pp. 191, 197 and passim.
168. Quoted in Fischer, *War of illusions*, p. 224.
169. Quoted in Geyer, *Russian imperialism*, p. 314.

170. See K. M. Wilson, 'The British cabinet's decision for war, 2 August 1914', *British Journal of International Studies*, I (1975), pp. 148–59 (quotation p. 153).
171. Martin Ceadel, *Living the great illusion. Sir Norman Angell, 1872–1967* (Oxford, 2009), especially pp. 104–14. On this failure of 'liberal peace' see also Ralph Rotte, 'Global warfare, economic loss and the outbreak of the Great War', *War in History*, 5 (1998), pp. 481–93, especially p. 483.
172. In November 1914, quoted in Bridge, *Habsburg monarchy*, p. 346.
173. See Fritz Fischer, *Germany's aims in the First World War* (London, 1967), pp. 103–4.
174. Quoted in McMeekin, *The Russian origins of the First World War*, p. 92.
175. A. L. Macfie, 'The Straits Question in the First World War, 1914–18', *Middle Eastern Studies*, 19,1 (1983), pp. 43–74 (quotations pp. 50 and 58).
176. Figures are in William Mulligan, *The origins of the First World War* (Cambridge, 2010), pp. 181–4.
177. Taylor, *Struggle for mastery in Europe*, p. xxv.
178. Quoted in J. W. B. Merewether and Frederick Smith, *The Indian Corps in France* (London, 1917), pp. 1–20. I am very grateful to Tarak Barkawi for this reference.
179. See Hew Strachan, *The First World War. Vol. I: To arms* (Oxford, 2001).
180. Robert T. Foley, *German strategy and the path to Verdun: Erich von Falkenhayn and the development of attrition, 1870–1916* (Cambridge, 2005).
181. See Elizabeth Peden, *Victory through coalition. Britain and France during the First World War* (Cambridge, 2005).
182. Thus A. L. Macfie, 'The Straits Question in the First World War, 1914–18', *Middle Eastern Studies*, 19, 1 (1983), pp. 43–74, and Graham T. Clews, *The real story behind the origins of the 1915 Dardanelles campaign* (Santa Barbara, 2010), pp. 66–7 and 293–4.
183. See Robert A. Doughty, *Pyrrhic victory. French strategy and operations in the Great War* (Cambridge, Mass., 2006), pp. 2, 109, 169–71 and passim.
184. Thus the revisionist argument of William Philpott, *Bloody victory. The sacrifice on the Somme* (London, 2009), pp. 96–7, 624–9 and passim (Joffre is quoted on p. 96).
185. See Donald McKale, *War by revolution. Germany and Great Britain in the Middle East in World War I* (Kent, Ohio, 1998), pp. 46–68 (quotation p. 48). See also Sean McMeekin, *The Berlin–Baghdad Express. The Ottoman Empire and Germany's bid for world power, 1898–1918* (London, 2010).
186. See Kris Manjapra, 'The illusions of encounter: Muslim "minds" and Hindu revolutionaries in First World War Germany and after', *Journal of Global History*, 1 (2006), pp. 363–82, especially pp. 372–7.

187. See Mark von Hagen, *War in a European borderland. Occupations and occupation plans in Galicia and Ukraine, 1914–1918* (Seattle and London, 2007).
188. Quoted in Hildebrand, *Das vergangene Reich*, p. 359.
189. Thus Friedrich Katz, *The life and times of Pancho Villa* (Stanford, 1998), pp. 554–5 (quotation p. 555).
190. See Hugh and Christopher Seton-Watson, *The making of a new Europe. R. W. Seton-Watson and the last years of Austria-Hungary* (London, 1981).
191. Quoted in Branka Magaš, *Croatia through history* (London, 2008), p. 462.
192. See Matthew S. Seligmann, 'Germany and the origins of the First World War in the eyes of the American diplomatic establishment', *German History*, 15, 3 (1997), pp. 307–32, especially pp. 312, 315 and 323.
193. See Martin Horn, *Britain, France and the financing of the First World War* (Montreal and Kingston, 2002), pp. 142–65.
194. Quoted in Nancy Mitchell, *The danger of dreams. German and American imperialism in Latin America* (Chapel Hill and London, 1999), p. 1.
195. Quoted in Katz, *Secret war in Mexico*, p. 302.
196. Frank McDonough, *The Conservative Party and Anglo-German relations, 1905–1914* (Basingstoke, 2007), p. 143.
197. Thus Paul Bridgen, *The Labour Party and the politics of war and peace, 1900–1924* (Woodbridge, 2009), p. 51.
198. See John Turner, *British politics and the Great War. Coalition and conflict, 1915–1918* (New Haven and London, 1992).
199. Quoted in Alistair Horne, *The French army in politics* (London, 1984), p. 39.
200. Thus Keith Robbins, 'The Welsh Wizard who won the war: David Lloyd George as war leader', in Brendan Simms and Karina Urbach (eds.), *Die Rückkehr der 'Grossen Männer'. Staatsmänner im Krieg – ein deutsch-britischer Vergleich 1740–1945* (Berlin and New York, 2010), pp. 96–107, especially p. 105.
201. See Axel Jansen, 'Heroes or citizens? The 1916 debate on Harvard volunteers in the "European War"', in Christine G. Krüger and Sonja Levsen (eds.), *War volunteering in modern times. From the French Revolution to the Second World War* (Basingstoke, 2011), pp. 150–62.
202. For Russia see Peter Holquist, *Making war, forging revolution: Russia's continuum of crisis, 1914–1921* (Cambridge, Mass., 2002), pp. 18–19 and 38–9 (on the need to imitate the Germans).
203. On the balance between conscription and volunteering see Alexander Watson, 'Voluntary enlistment in the Great War: a European phenomenon?', in Krüger and Levsen (eds.), *War volunteering in modern times*, pp. 163–88.
204. Quoted in Matthew Johnson, 'The Liberal War Committee and the Liberal advocacy of conscription in Britain, 1914–1916', *Historical Journal*, 51, 2 (2008), pp. 402 and 414–15.

205. See Laurence V. Moyer, *Victory must be ours: Germany in the Great War, 1914–1918* (Barnsley, 1995), pp. 102–33.
206. Marc Michel, *L'appel à l'Afrique. Contributions et réactions à l'effort de guerre en A.O.F (1914–1919)* (Paris, 1982). I am grateful to Christopher Andrew for this reference.
207. Quoted in Darwin, *Empire project*, p. 333.
208. I base this paragraph on Darwin, *Empire project*, pp. 324–5.
209. See Bridge, *Habsburg monarchy*, pp. 353–4.
210. Quoted in ibid., p. 358.
211. Thus Jo Vellacott, *Pacifists, patriots and the vote. The erosion of democratic suffragism in Britain during the First World War* (Basingstoke, 2007), pp. 21 and 45.
212. See William C. Fuller, *The foe within. Fantasies of treason and the end of Imperial Russia* (Ithaca, 2006), pp. 172–83.
213. See Donald Quataert, *The Ottoman Empire, 1700–1922*, 2nd edn (Cambridge, 2005), pp. 187–8.
214. Quoted in Rowbotham, *Century of women*, p. 67.
215. See Frances M. B. Lynch, 'Finance and welfare: the impact of two world wars on domestic policy in France', *Historical Journal*, 49 (2006), pp. 625–33, especially pp. 628–29; and Paul V. Dutton, *Origins of the French welfare state. The struggle for social reform in France, 1914–1947* (Cambridge, 2002), pp. 14–19.
216. Quoted in Hildebrand, *Das vergangene Reich*, p. 336.
217. Thus Jürgen Kocka, *Facing total war. German society, 1914–1918* (Leamington Spa, 1984).
218. See Ernst-Albert Seils, *Weltmachtstreben und Kampf für den Frieden. Der deutsche Reichstag im Ersten Weltkrieg* (Frankfurt, 2011), pp. 194–7.
219. Quoted in Seton-Watson, *Decline of Imperial Russia*, p. 712.
220. Quoted in ibid., p. 723. For the parliamentary critique of 'German dominance' within Russia in the early war years see M. M. Wolters, *Aussenpolitische Fragen vor der vierten Duma* (Hamburg, 1969), pp. 122–34.

6. UTOPIAS, 1917–44

1. Quoted in Klaus Schwabe, *Woodrow Wilson, revolutionary Germany and peacemaking, 1918–1919. Missionary diplomacy and the realities of power* (Chapel Hill and London, 1985), p. 256.
2. Quoted in Klaus Hildebrand, *Das vergangene Reich. Deutsche Aussenpolitik von Bismarck bis Hitler* (Stuttgart, 1995), p. 781.
3. Halford Mackinder, *Democratic ideals and reality* (London, 2009 [1919]), p. 70.

4. Quotations in John Darwin, *The Empire project. The rise and fall of the British world system, 1830–1970* (Cambridge, 2009), pp. 335 and 348.
5. See Charles Seymour (ed.), *The intimate papers of Edward House arranged as a narrative by Charles Seymour* (Boston and New York, 1926–8), p. 323. President Wilson Flag Day address, 14 June 1917. I thank Charles Laderman for these references.
6. Quotations in Tony Smith, *America's mission. The United States and the worldwide struggle for democracy in the twentieth century* (Princeton, 1994), pp. 92 and 84.
7. Indeed, German critics of Wilson argued that Allied policy was 'not the democratization or subjection of Germany but rather the subjection of Germany through its democratization': Peter Stirk, 'Hugo Preuss, German political thought and the Weimar Constitution', *History of Political Thought*, 23, 3 (2002), pp. 497–516 (quotation p. 515).
8. The State Secretary (Kühlmann) to the foreign ministry liaison officer at general headquarters, 3 December 1917, Berlin, in Z. A. B. Zeman (ed.), *Germany and the revolution in Russia, 1915–1918. Documents from the archives of the German foreign ministry* (London, 1958), p. 94.
9. 'Decree on peace', 8.11.1917, in Jane Degras (ed.), *Soviet documents on foreign policy* (London, 1951), pp. 1–2.
10. See Michael A. Reynolds, 'Buffers not brethren: Young Turk military policy in the First World War and the myth of Panturanism', *Past and Present*, 203 (2009), pp. 137–79.
11. Cited in John Thompson, *Woodrow Wilson* (Harlow, 2002), p. 170.
12. Quoted in Darwin, *Empire project*, pp. 313–14.
13. Jonathan Schneer, *The Balfour Declaration. The origins of the Arab–Israeli conflict* (London, 2010), pp. 343–5 (quotation p. 343).
14. See David Aberbach, 'Zionist patriotism in Europe, 1897–1942. Ambiguities in Jewish nationalism', *International History Review*, 31, 2 (2009), pp. 268–98, especially pp. 277–9 (quotations pp. 281 and 287). On British fears of Jewish sympathies for Germany see John Ferris, 'The British Empire vs. The Hidden Hand: British intelligence and strategy and "The CUP–Jew–German–Bolshevik combination", 1918–1924', in Keith Neilson and Greg Kennedy (eds.), *The British way in warfare: power and the international system, 1856–1956. Essays in honour of David French* (Farnham, 2010), p. 337. For French belief in the international power and German sympathies of Jews see David Pryce-Jones, *Betrayal. France, the Arabs, and the Jews* (New York, 2006), pp. 28–32.
15. Balfour note, 25.4.1918, in James Bunyan (ed.), *Intervention, civil war, and communism in Russia, April–December 1918. Documents and materials* (Baltimore, 1936), p. 73. For fears that Germany would take over Russia and its resources see Benjamin Schwartz, 'Divided attention. Britain's perceptions of a German threat to her eastern position in 1918', *Journal*

of Contemporary History, 28, 1 (1993), pp. 103–22 (quotation pp. 118–19).

16. For the general background see Caroline Kennedy-Pipe, *Russia and the world, 1917–1991* (London and New York, 1998), pp. 18–23.
17. See John Plamenatz, *German Marxism and Russian communism* (London, 1954).
18. Quoted in R. Craig Nation, *Black earth, red star. A history of Soviet security policy, 1917–1991* (Ithaca, 1992), pp. 2, 120 and 15.
19. See for example Timothy Snyder, *The red prince. The fall of a dynasty and the rise of modern empire* (London, 2008).
20. Here the Bolsheviks were able to capitalize on the preceding mobilization against the central powers: Peter Holquist, *Making war, forging revolution. Russia's continuum of crisis, 1914–1921* (Cambridge, Mass., and London, 2002), pp. 285–6 and passim.
21. Ibid., p. 121.
22. Quoted in J. F. McMillan, *Twentieth-century France. Politics and society 1898–1991* (London, 1992), p. 73.
23. For American domestic propaganda against Germany see Alan Axelrod, *Selling the Great War. The making of American propaganda* (Basingstoke, 2009), pp. 63–5, 143–4 and passim.
24. See C. Cappozzola, *Uncle Sam wants you. World War I and the making of the modern American citizen* (Oxford, 2008), especially pp. 207–14; Adriane Lentz-Smith, *Freedom struggles. African Americans and World War I* (Cambridge, Mass., 2009), pp. 3–5.
25. See Wilhelm Deist, 'The military collapse of the German Empire: the reality behind the stab-in-the-back myth', *War in History*, 3 (1996), 186–207.
26. See Gary Sheffield's rehabilitation of Lord Haig, *Forgotten victory. The First World War: myths and realities* (London, 2001). For the American contribution to the defeat of Germany see John Mosier, *The myth of the Great War. A new military history of World War I* (London, 2002), pp. 327–36 and passim.
27. On the greater resilience of the 'liberal-democratic states' see John Horne (ed.), *State, society and mobilisation in Europe during the First World War* (Cambridge, 1997), p. 16 and passim.
28. Quoted in Hildebrand, *Das vergangene Reich*, p. 390.
29. Clemens King, *Foch versus Clemenceau. France and German dismemberment, 1918–1919* (Cambridge, Mass., 1960).
30. Quoted in Patrick O. Cohrs, *The unfinished peace after World War I. America, Britain and the stabilisation of Europe, 1919–1932* (Cambridge, 2008), p. 213.
31. Quoted in Stefan Berger, 'William Harbutt Dawson: the career and politics of an historian of Germany', *The English Historical Review*, 116, 465 (2001), pp. 76–113 (quotation p. 91).

32. Lenin is quoted in John Riddell (ed.), *The German Revolution and the debate on Soviet power. Documents: 1918–1919. Preparing the Founding Congress* (New York, 1986), pp. 27–8 and 3.
33. Quoted in Klaus Schwabe, *Woodrow Wilson, revolutionary Germany and peacemaking, 1918–19. Missionary diplomacy and the realities of* power (Chapel Hill and London, 1985), pp. 395–9 (quotation p. 46).
34. John Ramsden, 'Churchill and the Germans', *Contemporary British History*, 25, 1 (2011), pp. 125–39 (quotations pp. 129–30n).
35. Manfred F. Boemeke, Gerald D. Feldman and Elisabeth Glaser (eds.), *The Treaty of Versailles. A reassessment after 75 years* (Cambridge, 1998).
36. Margaret Pawley, *The watch on the Rhine. The military occupation of the Rhineland, 1918–1930* (London and New York, 2007), pp. 16–18. Over the next two decades Germany continued to be the British army's main potential enemy: David French, *Raising Churchill's army. The British army and the war against Germany, 1919–1945* (Oxford, 2000).
37. On the centrality of the League to the containment of Germany and locking the *Reich* into collaboration against Bolshevism see Peter J. Yearwood, *Guarantee of Peace. The League of Nations in British policy, 1914–1925* (Oxford, 2009), pp. 149–50.
38. The phrase is quoted in Thompson, *Woodrow Wilson*, p. 199.
39. Quoted in Maurice Vaïsse, 'Security and disarmament: problems in the development of the disarmament debates, 1919–1934', in R. Ahmann, A. M. Birke, and M. Howard (eds.), *The quest for stability. Problems of West European security, 1918–1957* (Oxford, 1993), p. 175.
40. See Mark Levene, *War, Jews and the new Europe. The diplomacy of Lucien Wolf, 1914–1919* (Oxford, 1992).
41. See for example Antoine Prost, 'The impact of war on French and German political cultures', *Historical Journal*, 37 (1994), 209–17.
42. Thus William Lee Blackwood, 'German hegemony and the Socialist International's place in inter-war European diplomacy', *European History Quarterly*, 31 (2001), pp. 101–40 (quotation pp. 108–9).
43. Quoted in William Mulligan, 'The Reichswehr, the Republic and the primacy of foreign policy, 1918–1923', *German History*, 21, 3 (2003), p. 356.
44. See William Mulligan, 'Civil–military relations in the early Weimar Republic', *Historical Journal*, 45, 4 (2002), pp. 819–41.
45. On the centrality of demographic-military concerns see Paul V. Dutton, *Origins of the French welfare state. The struggle for social reform in France, 1914–1947* (Cambridge, 2002), pp. 22–3.
46. John Maynard Keynes, *The economic consequences of the peace*, in *Collected writings of John Maynard Keynes*, Vol. 2 (London, 1920), p. 226.
47. Thus John Milton Cooper Jr, *Breaking the heart of the world. Woodrow Wilson and the fight for the League of Nations* (Cambridge, 2001), p. 119.
48. Quoted in Thompson, *Woodrow Wilson*, pp. 224 and 229.

49. Lloyd Ambrosius, 'Wilson, the Republicans, and French security after World War I', *Journal of American History*, 59 (September 1972), pp. 341–52.
50. See Stephen Wertheim, 'The league that wasn't. American designs for a legalist-sanctionalist League of Nations and the intellectual origins of international organisation, 1914–1920', *Diplomatic History*, 35, 5 (2011), pp. 797–836. The Wilson quotation is in Stephen Wertheim, 'The Wilsonian chimera: why debating Wilson's vision hasn't saved American foreign relations', *White House Studies*, 10 (2011), p. 354.
51. See Gerhard Weinberg, 'The defeat of Germany in 1918 and the European balance of power', *Central European History*, 2, 3 (1969), pp. 248–60.
52. See Lucian M. Ashworth, 'Realism and the spirit of 1919: Halford Mackinder and the reality of the League of Nations', *European Journal of International Relations* (online, 2010), pp. 1–23, especially pp. 9–10.
53. See Norman Davies, *White eagle, red star: the Polish–Soviet war, 1919–1920* (New York, 1972).
54. Robert Himmer, 'Soviet policy toward Germany during the Russo-Polish War, 1920', *Slavic Review*, 35, 4 (Dec. 1976), pp. 665–82, especially pp. 666–7.
55. For the centrality of Germany in French thinking on Poland in 1920 see Michael Jabara Carley, 'Anti-Bolshevism in French foreign policy: the crisis in Poland in 1920', *International History Review*, 2, 2 (1980), pp. 410–31, especially pp. 411–12 and 428.
56. See Shelley Baranowski, *Nazi Empire. German colonialism and imperialism from Bismarck to Hitler* (Cambridge, 2011), pp. 116–71.
57. See Werner T. Angress, *Stillborn revolution. The communist bid for power in Germany, 1921–1923* (Princeton, 1963).
58. Stephanie C. Salzmann, *Great Britain, Germany and the Soviet Union: Rapallo and after, 1922–1934* (Rochester, 2003), emphasizes that while the treaty caused a sensation, it did not lead to panic in the Foreign Office.
59. Mussolini is quoted in MacGregor Knox, 'Conquest, foreign and domestic, in Fascist Italy and Nazi Germany', *Journal of Modern History*, 56, 1 (1984), pp. 1–57 (quotation p. 19), and in 'The Fascist regime, its foreign policy and its wars: an "anti-anti-Fascist" orthodoxy?', in Patrick Finney (ed.), *The origins of the Second World War* (London, New York, etc. 1997), p. 159
60. See Charlotte Alston, '"The suggested basis for a Russian Federal Republic". Britain, anti-Bolshevik Russia and the border states at the Paris Peace Conference, 1919', *History*, 91 (2006), pp. 24–44, especially pp. 33–4.
61. Thus Andrew Orr, '"We call you to holy war". Mustafa Kemal, communism, and Germany in French intelligence nightmares, 1919–1923', *Journal of Military History*, 75 (2011), pp. 1095–1123.
62. Margaret Pawley, *The watch on the Rhine. The military occupation of the Rhineland, 1918–1930* (London and New York, 2007), pp. 77–88.
63. Quoted in Degras (ed.), *Soviet documents on foreign policy*, p. 287.

64. See M. D. Lewis, 'One hundred million Frenchmen. The "assimilation" theory in French colonial policy', *Comparative Studies in Society and History*, 4 (1962), pp. 129–53.
65. Quoted in Robert C. Reinders, 'Racialism on the left. E. D. Morel and the "Black Horror on the Rhine"', *International Review of Social History*, XIII (1968), pp. 1–28 (quotation p. 8).
66. Keith L. Nelson, 'The "Black Horror on the Rhine". Race as a factor in post-World War I diplomacy', *Journal of Modern History*, 42, 4 (1970), pp. 606–27 (quotations pp. 613 (Mangin) and 616 (Müller)).
67. Jonathan Wright, *Gustav Stresemann. Weimar's greatest statesman* (Oxford, 2002).
68. Carole Fink, 'German *Revisionspolitik*, 1919–1933', in *Historical papers/Communications historiques. A selection from the papers presented at the annual meeting [of the Canadian Historical Association] held at Winnipeg, 1986* (Ottawa, 1986), pp. 134–45 (quotation p. 143). On Stresemann's use of economic power for strategic purposes see Gottfried Niedhart, *Die Aussenpolitik der Weimarer Republik* (Munich, 1999), pp. 63–99.
69. On all this see Peter Jackson, 'France and the problems of security and disarmament after the First World War', *Journal of Strategic Studies*, 29, 2 (2006), pp. 247–80.
70. See Richard Coudenhove-Kalergi, *Paneuropa* (Vienna, 1923).
71. Ina Ulrike Paul, 'In Kontinenten denken, paneuropäisch handeln. Die Zeitschrift *Paneuropa* 1924–1938', *Jahrbuch für europäische Geschichte*, 5 (2004), pp. 161–92, especially pp. 182–3.
72. Quoted in Cohrs, *Unfinished peace after World War I*, pp. 105 and 135.
73. Quoted in Darwin, *Empire project*, p. 365.
74. See Melvin P. Leffler, *The elusive quest. America's pursuit of European stability and French security, 1919–1933* (Chapel Hill, 1979), pp. 41–3 (quotation p. 41).
75. See Gaynor Johnson (ed.), *Locarno revisited: European diplomacy 1920–1929* (London and New York, 2004), quotation p. 103.
76. Quoted in Cohrs, *Unfinished peace after World War I*, pp. 215 and 225.
77. Adolf Hitler, *Mein Kampf*, trans. Ralph Manheim (Boston, 1971), pp. 645, 642–3, 646, 649 and 651.
78. Quoted in Teddy J. Uldricks, 'Russia and Europe: diplomacy, revolution, and economic development in the 1920s', *International History Review*, 1, 1 (1979), p. 74.
79. Quoted in Cohrs, *Unfinished peace after World War I*, p. 372.
80. Andrew Webster, 'An argument without end: Britain, France and the disarmament process, 1925–34', in Martin S. Alexander and William J. Philpott (eds.), *Anglo-French defence relations between the wars* (Basingstoke, 2002), pp. 49–71.

81. See John Keiger, 'Wielding finance as a weapon of diplomacy: France and Britain in the 1920s', *Contemporary British History*, 25, 1 (2011), pp. 29–47, especially pp. 40–43.
82. Quoted in Nation, *Black earth, red star*, pp. 61 and 63.
83. This point is made very effectively in Richard Hellie, 'The structure of Russian imperial history', *History and Theory*, 44, 4 (2005), pp. 88–112 (pp. 102–3); despite its title, much of the article deals with the Soviet period.
84. For Hitler's knowledge of and keen interest in the United States see Klaus P. Fischer, *Hitler and America* (Philadelphia, 2011), pp. 9–46.
85. Quotations in Adolf Hitler, *Second book* [*Aussenpolitische Standortbestimmung nach der Reichtagswahl Juni–Juli 1928*], ed. Gerhard L. Weinberg, in Institut für Zeitgeschichte (ed.), *Hitler. Reden, Schriften, Anordnungen, Februar 1925 bis Januar 1933* (Munich, New Providence, London and Paris, 1995), pp. 15, 88–90.
86. For Germany and the Young Plan see Michael Wala, *Weimar und Amerika. Botschafter Friedrich von Prittwitz und Gaffron und die deutsch-amerikanischen Beziehungen von 1927 bis 1933* (Stuttgart, 2001), pp. 12–151.
87. Quoted in Hildebrand, *Das vergangene Reich*, pp. 524–5.
88. Quoted in ibid., p. 525.
89. Jürgen Elvert, *Mitteleuropa! Deutsche Pläne zur europäischen Neuordnung (1918–1945)* (Stuttgart, 1999).
90. See Andreas Rödder, *Stresemann's Erbe. Julius Curtius und die deutsche Aussenpolitik, 1929–1931* (Paderborn, 1996), quotations pp. 199 and 202.
91. See William L. Patch Jr, *Heinrich Brüning and the dissolution of the Weimar Republic* (Cambridge, 1998), pp. 213–19. (quotation p. 255)
92. See Irene Strenge, *Kurt von Schleicher. Politik im Reichswehrministerium am Ende der Weimarer Republik* (Berlin, 2006).
93. See Enrico Syring, *Hitler. Seine politische Utopie* (Frankfurt am Main, 1994), pp. 234–7.
94. See Kiran Klaus Patel, *Soldiers of labor. Labor service in Nazi Germany and New Deal America, 1933–1945* (Cambridge and New York, 2005), pp. 4, 72 and 228–9.
95. See Wolfram Wette, 'Ideology, propaganda and internal politics as preconditions of the war policy of the Third Reich', in Militärgeschichtliches Forschungsamt (ed.), *Germany and the Second World War.* Vol. I. *The build-up of German aggression* (Oxford, 1990).
96. Thus Patrizia Albanese, *Mothers of the nation. Women, families and nationalism in twentieth century Europe* (Toronto, Buffalo and London, 2006), pp. 32–44 (quotation p. 36).
97. Quoted in Zach Shore, 'Hitler's opening gambit. Intelligence, encirclement, and the decision to ally with Poland', *Intelligence and National Security*, 14, 3 (1999), quotation p. 112.

98. For British misconceptions see R. J. Overy, 'German air strength 1933 to 1939: a note', *Historical Journal*, 27, 2 (1984), pp. 465–71.
99. Thus Jonathan Haslam, *The Soviet Union and the struggle for collective security in Europe, 1933–39* (London, 1984), pp. 1–226, especially p. 2.
100. Thus Wesley K. Wark, *The ultimate enemy. British intelligence and Nazi Germany, 1933–1939* (Ithaca, 1985).
101. Quoted in Ramsden, 'Churchill and the Germans', p. 131. For the mainstream view see Philip Towle, 'Taming or demonising an aggressor: the British debate on the end of the Locarno system', in Gaynor Johnson (ed.), *Locarno revisited: European diplomacy, 1920–1929* (London and New York), pp. 178–98 (pp. 190–91).
102. See Bret Holman, 'The air panic of 1935: British press opinion between disarmament and rearmament', *Journal of Contemporary History*, 46, 2 (2011), pp. 288–307 (quotation p. 295).
103. See Arnold A. Offner, *American appeasement. United States policy and Germany, 1933–1938* (Cambridge, Mass., 1969), pp. 12, 59 and passim, and Alonzo L. Hamby, *For the survival of democracy. Franklin Roosevelt and the world crisis of the 1930s* (New York, 2009).
104. Thus Mary E. Glantz, *FDR and the Soviet Union. The president's battles over foreign policy* (Lawrence, Kan., 2005), pp. 17–35.
105. Quoted in Nation, *Black earth, red star*, p. 117.
106. For the link between the (exaggerated) fear of encirclement, Polish subversion and repressive policies in the Ukraine and Belarus see Timothy Snyder, *Bloodlands. Europe between Hitler and Stalin* (New York, 2010), pp. 30–31, 37, 42, 71 and 89.
107. R. Heller, 'East Fulham revisited', *Journal of Contemporary History*, 6, 3 (1971), pp. 172–96; C. Stannage, 'The East Fulham by-election, 25 October 1933', *Historical Journal*, 14, 1 (1971), pp. 165–200. See also Philip Williamson, *Stanley Baldwin* (Cambridge, 1999).
108. See Mona Siegel, '"To the Unknown Mother of the Unknown Soldier". Pacifism, feminism, and the politics of sexual difference among French *institutrices* between the wars', *French Historical Studies*, 22, 3 (1999), pp. 421–51, especially pp. 428–9.
109. See Benedikt Stuchtey, '"Not by law but by sentiment". Great Britain and imperial defense, 1918–1939', in Roger Chickering and Stig Förster (eds.), *The shadows of total war. Europe, East Asia, and the United States, 1919–1939* (Cambridge, 2003), pp. 255–70 (quotation p. 263).
110. Quoted in Darwin, *Empire project*, p. 457.
111. Thus Michaela Hoenicke Moore, *Know your enemy. The American debate on Nazism, 1933–1945* (Cambridge, 2010), pp. 78–93 and 341–2.
112. Quoted in Alan Bullock, *Hitler. A study in tyranny* (London, 1952), p. 315.

113. Both Göring and Hitler are quoted in Hildebrand, *Das vergangene Reich*, p. 623.
114. Quoted in Pierre-Henri Laurent, 'The reversal of Belgian foreign policy, 1936–1937', *The Review of Politics*, 31, 3 (July 1969), p. 370.
115. See Nicole Jordan, *The Popular Front and central Europe. The dilemmas of French impotence, 1919–1940* (Cambridge, 1992).
116. See Antony Beevor, *The battle for Spain. The Spanish Civil War, 1936–1939* (London, 2006).
117. See David Patterson, *A genealogy of evil. Anti-semitism from Nazism to Islamic Jihad* (Cambridge, 2011).
118. On the link between encirclement and Stalin's 'total security state' see Silvio Pons, *Stalin and the inevitable war, 1936–1941* (London and Portland, 2002).
119. Quoted in John Lamberton Harper, *American visions of Europe. Franklin D. Roosevelt, George F. Kennan and Dean G. Acheson* (Cambridge, 1994), p. 67.
120. See J. Noakes and G. Pridham (eds.), *Nazism. A history in documents and eyewitness accounts, 1919–1945*. Vol. II: *Foreign policy, war and racial extermination* (New York, 1988), quotation p. 685.
121. Quoted in David Dilks, '"We must hope for the best and prepare for the worst". The prime minister, the Cabinet and Hitler's Germany, 1937–1939', *Proceedings of the British Academy*, LXXIII (1987), p. 325.
122. Quoted in B. J. C. Roi and M. L. McKercher, '"Ideal" and "punchbag": conflicting views of the balance of power and their influence on interwar British foreign policy, diplomacy and statecraft', *Diplomacy and Statecraft*, 12, 2 (2001), pp. 47–78 (quotation, p. 53).
123. Daniel Hucker, 'French public attitudes towards the prospect of war in 1938–1939', *French History*, 21, 4 (2007), pp. 431–4; Jerry H. Brookshire, 'Speak for England, act for England: Labour's leadership and British national security under the threat of war in the late 1930s', *European History Quarterly*, 29, 2 (1999), pp. 251–87.
124. Thus Maurice Cowling, *The impact of Hitler. British politics and British policy, 1933–1940* (Chicago and London, 1975).
125. Quoted in Tobias Jersak, 'A matter of foreign policy: "Final Solution" and "Final Victory" in Nazi Germany', *German History* 21, 3 (2003), pp. 369–91 (quotation p. 378).
126. Quoted in John Thompson, 'Conceptions of national security and American entry into World War II', *Diplomacy and Statecraft*, 16, 4 (2005), pp. 671–97 (quotations pp. 673–4).
127. Quoted in Thompson, 'Conceptions of national security', p. 674.
128. See Barbara Rearden Farnham, *Roosevelt and the Munich Crisis. A study of decision-making* (Princeton, 1997), p. 159.

129. Quoted in Nation, *Black earth, red star*, p. 98.
130. On the rhetorical duel between the two see David Reynolds, *From world war to Cold War. Churchill, Roosevelt and the international history of the 1940s* (Oxford, 2006), pp. 18–19.
131. See Jochen Thies, *Archtekt der Weltherrschaft. Die 'Endziele' Hitlers* (Dusseldorf, 1976).
132. Thus Rolf-Dieter Müller, *Der Feind steht im Osten. Hitlers geheime Pläne für einen Krieg gegen die Sowjetunion im Jahr 1939* (Berlin, 2001), pp. 251–61.
133. Quoted in Albert L. Weeks, *Stalin's other war. Soviet grand strategy, 1939–1941* (Lanham, Boulder, etc., 2002), pp. 172–3.
134. For the prehistory of these Anglo-French tergiversations see A. J. Prazmovska, 'War over Danzig? The dilemma of Anglo-Polish relations in the months preceding the outbreak of the Second World War', *Historical Journal*, 26 (1983), pp. 177–83.
135. Thus Jonathan Haslam, 'Soviet war aims', in Ann Lane and Howard Temperley (eds.), *The rise and fall of the Grand Alliance, 1941–45* (Basingstoke and New York, 1995), pp. 24–5.
136. For the contrast between the British and French war economies in this respect see Talbot C. Imlay, *Facing the Second World War. Strategy, politics and economics in Britain and France, 1938–1940* (Oxford, 2003).
137. Jan T. Gross, *Revolution from abroad. The Soviet conquest of Poland's western Ukraine and western Belorussia* (Princeton, 1988).
138. See David Reynolds, '1940: fulcrum of the twentieth century?', *International Affairs*, 66 (1990), pp. 325–50.
139. See Robert O. Paxton, *Vichy France. Old guard and new order, 1940–1944* (London, 1970), pp. 51–62.
140. See Davide Rodogno, *Fascism's European empire. Italian occupation during the Second World War* (Cambridge, 2006).
141. See Richard Bosworth, 'War, totalitarianism and "deep belief" in Fascist Italy, 1935–43', *European History Quarterly*, 34, 4 (2004), pp. 475–505 especially pp. 492–93.
142. Thus Stanley G. Payne, *Spain, Germany and World War II* (New Haven and London, 2008), pp. 87–113.
143. Avi Shlaim, 'Prelude to downfall: the British offer of union to France, June 1940', *Journal of Contemporary History*, 9, 3 (1974), pp. 27–63.
144. See Anthony J. Cumming, 'Did the Navy win the Battle of Britain? The warship as the ultimate guarantor of Britain's freedom in 1940', *Historical Research*, 83 (2010), pp. 165–88.
145. See now David Edgerton, *Britain's war machine. Weapons, resources and experts in the Second World War* (London, 2011), especially pp. 47–8 and 124–5.

146. J. Lee Ready, *Forgotten allies. The military contribution of the colonies, exiled governments and lesser powers to the Allied victory in World War II. Vol. I: The European theatre* (Jefferson and London, 1985).
147. On this see Andrew Stewart, *Empire lost. Britain, the dominions and the Second World War* (London, 2008), p. 106.
148. See Norman J. W. Goda, *Hitler, northwest Africa, and the path toward America* (College Station, Texas, 1998).
149. Roosevelt's reported remarks of late September 1939 are quoted in Harper, *American visions of Europe*, p. 59.
150. Quoted in Reynolds, *From world war to Cold War*, p. 19.
151. Quoted in Nation, *Black earth, red star*, pp. 122–4.
152. See Steven Merritt Miner, *Stalin's holy war. Religion, nationalism, and alliance politics, 1941–1945* (Chapel Hill and London, 2003).
153. See Dan Plesch, *America, Hitler and the UN. How the Allies won World War II and forged a peace* (London, 2011), especially pp. 31–57 (quotation p. 34).
154. Mark Harrison, 'Resource mobilisation for World War II: the USA, UK, USSR and Germany, 1938–1945', *Economic History Review*, 41, 2 (1988), pp. 171–92.
155. Quoted in Snyder, *Bloodlands*, p. 161.
156. See Nicole Kramer, *Volksgenossinnen an der Heimatfront. Mobilisierung. Verhalten. Erinnerung* (Göttingen, 2011), pp. 164–5.
157. Quoted in Sheila Rowbotham, *A century of women. The history of women in Britain and the United States* (London, 1997), p. 247.
158. See James T. Sparrow, *Warfare state. World War II Americans and the age of big government* (Oxford and New York, 2011).
159. See Thomas Bruscino, *A nation forged in war. How World War II taught Americans how to get along* (Knoxville, 2010).
160. Quoted in Ian Kershaw, *Fateful decisions. Ten decisions that changed the world, 1940–1941* (London, 2007).
161. Christopher Browning, *The origins of the Final Solution. The evolution of Nazi Jewish policy, 1939–1942* (London, 2005). My interpretation here follows closely that of Jersak, 'A matter of foreign policy', pp. 369–89.
162. Quoted in Hildebrand, *Das vergangene Reich*, p. 752.
163. Speaking at the Moscow Conference in October 1943, quoted in Michael R. Beschloss, *The conquerors. Roosevelt, Truman and the destruction of Hitler's Germany* (New York, 2002), p. 21.
164. Quoted in Ilse Dorothee Pautsch, *Die territoriale Deutschlandplanung des amerikanischen Aussenministeriums, 1941–1943* (Frankfurt am Main, 1990), p. 122. For US fears of German post-war power even while the conflict raged see James McAllister, *No exit. America and the German problem, 1943–1954* (Ithaca and London, 2002), pp. 1–42.
165. Quoted in Klaus Larres, 'Churchill: flawed war leader or charismatic visionary?', in Brendan Simms and Karina Urbach (eds.), *Die Rückkehr der*

'Grossen Männer'. Staatsmänner im Krieg – ein deutsch-britischer Vergleich 1740–1945* (Berlin and New York, 2010), p. 154.

166. Quoted in Lothar Kettenacker, *Krieg zur Friedenssicherung. Die Deutschlandplanung der britischen Regierung während des Zweiten Weltkrieges* (Göttingen and Zurich, 1989), pp. 534 and 537–42.
167. Quoted in Larres, 'Churchill', p. 141.
168. See Patrick J. Hearden, 'Early American views regarding European unification', *Cambridge Review of International Affairs*, 19 (2006), pp. 67–78, especially pp. 74–5.
169. See Brian P. Farrell, 'Symbol of paradox: the Casablanca Conference, 1943', *Canadian Journal of History*, 28, 1 (1993), pp. 21–40, which puts the debate about the best strategy against Germany at the forefront.
170. See Steven T. Ross, *American war plans, 1941–1945* (London and Portland, 1997), pp. 9, 17, 21 and 47, and Mark Stoler, *Allies and adversaries. The Joint Chiefs of Staff, the Grand Alliance, and U.S. strategy in World War II* (Chapel Hill and London, 2000), p. 71.
171. Quoted in Reynolds, '1940: fulcrum of the twentieth century?', p. 344.
172. See now Reynolds, 'Churchill and allied grand strategy in Europe, 1944–1945: the erosion of British influence', in *From world war to Cold War*, pp. 121–36.
173. Thus Roger Beaumont, 'The bomber offensive as a second front', *Journal of Contemporary History*, 22, 1 (1987), pp. 3–19, especially pp. 13–15, and Stephan Glienke, 'The Allied air war and German society', in Claudia Baldoli, Andrew Knapp and Richard Overy (eds.), *Bombing, states and peoples in western Europe, 1940–1945* (London, 2011), pp. 184–205.
174. See Mark Harrison (ed.), *The economics of World War II: six powers in international comparison* (Cambridge, 1998).
175. Quoted in Hildebrand, *Das vergangene Reich*, p. 781.
176. See Sönke Neitzel, 'Hitlers Europaarmee und der "Kreuzzug" gegen die Sowjetunion', in Michael Salewski and Heiner Timmermann (eds.), *Armeen in Europa – europäische Armeen* (Münster, 2004), pp. 137–50.

7. PARTITIONS, 1945–73

1. Quoted in Mary N. Hampton, *The Wilsonian impulse. U.S. foreign policy, the alliance, and German unification* (Westport, 1996), p. 18.
2. Anatoly Dobrynin, *In confidence: Moscow's ambassador to America's six Cold War presidents (1962–1986)* (New York, 1995), p. 63.
3. 'The Yalta Protocol of Proceedings', in T. G. Paterson, *Major problems in American foreign policy since 1914*, Vol. II, 3rd edn (Lexington, Mass., 1989), pp. 243–4.

4. Thus Melvyn Leffler, *The struggle for Germany and the origins of the Cold War* (Washington, DC, 1996).
5. Quoted in Carolyn Woods Eisenberg, *Drawing the line. The American decision to divide Germany, 1944–49* (Cambridge, 1996), p. 38.
6. See John Lewis Gaddis, 'Repression versus rehabilitation: the problem of Germany', in Gaddis, *The United States and the origins of the Cold War, 1941–1947* (New York, 1972), pp. 94–132 (quotations pp. 98–9).
7. Mark Kramer, 'The Soviet Union and the founding of the German Democratic Republic: 50 years later. A review article', *Europe–Asia Studies*, 51 (1999), pp. 1093–1106 (quotation pp. 1097–8).
8. See R. C. Raack, *Stalin's drive to the west, 1938–1945. The origins of the Cold War* (Stanford, 1995), pp. 133–4 and passim.
9. See Fraser J. Harbutt, *Yalta 1945. Europe and America at the crossroads* (Cambridge, 2010).
10. 'Yalta Protocol', p. 242.
11. Ibid., pp. 239–40.
12. Ibid., p. 241.
13. For an epic account see Antony Beevor, *Berlin. The downfall* (London, 2002).
14. Quoted in Leffler, *Struggle for Germany*, p. 13.
15. Quoted in Charles Mee, *Meeting at Potsdam* (New York, 1975), p. 320.
16. Quoted in Jonathan Haslam, 'Soviet war aims', in Ann Lane and Howard Temperley (eds.), *The rise and fall of the Grand Alliance, 1941–45* (Basingstoke and New York, 1995), p. 27.
17. See now Jessica Reinisch and Elizabeth White (eds.), *The disentanglement of populations. Migration, expulsion and displacement in post-war Europe, 1944–9* (Basingstoke, 2011), especially pp. 3–50.
18. Quoted in Zbyněk Zeman and Antonín Klimek, *The life of Edvard Beneš, 1884–1948. Czechoslovakia in peace and war* (Oxford, 1997), p. 247. See also Eagle Glassheim, 'The mechanics of ethnic cleansing: the expulsion of Germans from Czechoslovakia, 1945–1947', in Philipp Ther and Ana Siljak (eds.), *Redrawing nations. Ethnic cleansing in east-central Europe, 1944–1948* (Lanham, 2001), pp. 197–200.
19. Quoted in Mark Mazower, *No enchanted palace. The end of empire and the ideological origins of the United Nations* (Princeton and Oxford, 2009), p. 7.
20. See David J. Dunthorn, 'The Paris Conference on Tangier, August 1945. The British response to Soviet interest in the "Tangier Question"', *Diplomacy and Statecraft*, 16, 1 (2005), pp. 117–37 (quotation p. 123).
21. Quoted in Andreas Hillgruber, *Die Zerstörung Europas. Beiträge zur Weltkriegsepoche, 1914 bis 1945* (Frankfurt am Main and Berlin, 1988), p. 363.
22. Andrew J. Rotter, *Hiroshima. The world's bomb* (New York, 2008), pp. 177–228.

23. Caroline Kennedy-Pipe, *Russia and the world, 1917–1991* (London and New York, 1998), p. 84. Hiroshima had 'destroyed the equilibrium of the world'.
24. Altiero Spinelli and Ernesto Rossi, 'For a free and united Europe. A draft manifesto', in Mette Eilstrup-Sangiovanni (ed.), *Debates on European integration. A reader* (Basingstoke, 2006), pp. 37–42.
25. See Scott Kelly, '"The ghost of Neville Chamberlain". Guilty Men and the 1945 election', *Conservative History Journal*, 5 (Autumn 2005), 18–24, especially, 21–2 (quotation p. 18).
26. See Correlli Barnett, *The audit of war. The illusion and reality of Britain as a great nation* (London, 1986).
27. See Jim Tomlinson, 'Balanced accounts? Constructing the balance of payments problem in post-war Britain', *The English Historical Review*, CXXIV, 509 (2009), pp. 863–84.
28. See generally, Martin Thomas, Bob Moore and L. J. Butler, *Crises of empire. Decolonisation and Europe's imperial states, 1918–1975* (London, 2008), especially pp. 47–72.
29. Quoted in Pablo de Orellana, *Implications of the Cold War for the maintenance of colonialism in Indochina, 1945–1954* (M.Phil. dissertation, University of Cambridge, 2009), p. 23. I am most grateful to Mr de Orellana for extremely interesting conversations on this subject.
30. Anne Deighton, 'Entente neo-coloniale? Ernest Bevin and the proposals for Anglo-French Third World power, 1945–1949', in Glyn Stone and T. G. Otte (eds.), *Anglo-French relations since the late eighteenth century* (London and New York, 2008), pp. 200–218 (Bevin quotation p. 208).
31. See Kevin McDermott and Matthew Stibbe (eds.), *Stalinist terror in eastern Europe. Elite purges and mass repression* (Manchester and New York, 2010), p. 5 and passim for the crucial international context.
32. Thus Norman Naimark and Leonid Gibianskii (eds.), *The establishment of communist regimes in eastern Europe, 1944–1949* (Boulder and Oxford, 1998).
33. Quoted in Fernande Scheid Raine, 'Stalin and the creation of the Azerbaijan Democratic Party in Iran, 1945', *Cold War History*, 2, 1 (2001), pp. 1–38 (quotation p. 1).
34. Compare George F. Kennan, 'Containment: 40 years later. Containment then and now', *Foreign Affairs*, 65, 4 (Spring 1987).
35. See Dirk Spilker, 'The Socialist Unity Party of Germany (SED) and the German Question, 1944–1953', dissertation abstract, compiled by Cornelie Usborne, *German History*, 17, 1 (1999), pp. 102–3.
36. Thus Norman Naimark, *The Russians in Germany. A history of the Soviet zone of occupation, 1945–49* (Cambridge, Mass., 1995).
37. Hannes Adomeit, *Imperial overstretch. Germany in Soviet policy from Stalin to Gorbachev* (Baden-Baden, 1998).

38. Richard L. Merritt, *Democracy imposed: US occupation policy and the German public, 1945–1949* (New Haven, 1995). I am grateful to my student Ross J. Tokola for this and many other references.
39. Wolfgang Krieger, 'Was General Clay a revisionist? Strategic aspects of the United States occupation of Germany', *Journal of Contemporary History*, 18, 2 (1983), pp. 165–84 (quotation p. 180).
40. See Josef Foschepoth, 'British interest in the division of Germany after the Second World War', *Journal of Contemporary History*, 23, 3 (1986), pp. 391–411. For a broader overview of the post-war British preoccupation with Germany see Daniel Gossel, *Briten, Deutsche und Europa. Die deutsche Frage in der britischen Aussenpolitik, 1945–1962* (Stuttgart, 1999).
41. William I. Hitchcock, *France restored: Cold War diplomacy and the quest for leadership in Europe, 1944–1954* (Chapel Hill, 1998), pp. 74–7 and passim.
42. 'X' [George Kennan], 'The sources of Soviet conduct', *Foreign Affairs*, 25, 4 (July 1947), pp. 566–82.
43. See John Lewis Gaddis, *The long peace. Inquiries into the history of the Cold War* (New York and Oxford, 1987), pp. 41–2.
44. See Tony Judt, *Postwar. A history of Europe since 1945* (London, 2005).
45. For the centrality of Germany to Truman's thinking see Arnold A. Offner, *Another such victory. President Truman and the Cold War, 1945–1953* (Stanford, 2002), pp. 157–67.
46. See Klaus Schwabe, 'The Cold War and European integration, 1947–63', *Diplomacy and Statecraft*, 12, 4 (2001), pp. 18–34.
47. Quoted in Robert E. Ferrell, 'The Truman era and European integration', in Francis H. Heller and John R. Gillingham (eds.), *The United States and the integration of Europe. Legacies of the postwar era* (New York, 1996), p. 28.
48. See Avi Shlaim, *Britain and the origins of European unity* (Reading, 1978), pp. 114–42.
49. See John W. Young, *Britain, France and the unity of Europe, 1945–1951* (Leicester, 1984), pp. 77–9 and passim.
50. See Mark Byrnes, 'Unfinished business: the United States and Franco's Spain, 1944–47', *Diplomacy and Statecraft*, 11, 1 (2000), pp. 153–6.
51. Cited in Anne Deighton (ed.), *Britain and the First Cold War* (Basingstoke, 1990), p. 58.
52. See Moshe Zimmermann, 'Militär, Militarismus und Zivilgesellschaft in Israel – eine europäische Erbschaft?', in Ute Frevert (ed.), *Militär und Gesellschaft im 19. und 20. Jahrhundert* (Stuttgart, 1997), pp. 342–58.
53. Quoted in Moshe Naor, 'Israel's 1948 war of independence as a total war', *Journal of Contemporary History*, 43, 2 (2008), pp. 241–57 (quotation p. 246).
54. See Scott Parrish, 'The Marshall Plan and the division of Europe', in Naimark and Gibianskii (eds.), *Establishment of communist regimes in eastern Europe*, pp. 267–90, especially pp. 286–7.

55. Silvio Pons, 'Stalin, Togliatti, and the origins of the Cold War in Europe', *Journal of Cold War Studies* 3, 2 (2001), pp. 3–27, especially pp. 5 and 12.
56. For the centrality of Germany at the Moscow conference see Robert H. Van Meter, 'Secretary of State Marshall, General Clay, and the Moscow Council of Foreign Ministers meeting of 1947: a response to Philip Zelikow', *Diplomacy and Statecraft*, 16, 1 (2005), pp. 139–67, especially pp. 142–3, 145 and 152 (Dulles quotation p. 151).
57. Roger G. Miller, *To save a city. The Berlin airlift, 1948–49* (College Station, Texas, 2000), pp. 36–86.
58. See Edmund Spevack, 'American pressures on the German constitutional tradition: basic rights in the West German constitution of 1949', *International Journal of Politics, Culture and Society*, 10, 3 (1997), pp. 411–36 (quotation p. 424). For the US role in the party-political democratization of Germany see Daniel E. Rogers, 'Transforming the German party system. The United States and the origins of political moderation, 1945–1949', *Journal of Modern History*, 65, 3 (1993), pp. 512–41.
59. Paul Fritz, 'From defeat and division to democracy in Germany', in Mary Fran T. Malone (ed.), *Achieving democracy. Democratization in theory and practice* (New York and London, 2011), pp. 169–94.
60. See Abbott Gleason, *Totalitarianism. The inner history of the Cold War* (Oxford, 1995), pp. 157–66, for anti-totalitarianism as the 'quasi-official ideology of the West German state' (p. 157).
61. Thus Ulrich Lappenküper, 'Primat der Aussenpolitik! Die Verständigung zwischen der Bundesrepublik Deutschland und Frankreich, 1949–1963', in Eckart Conze, Ulrich Lappenküper and Guido Müller (eds.), *Geschichte der internationalen Beziehungen. Erneuerung und Erweiterung einer historischen Disziplin* (Cologne, Weimar and Vienna, 2004), pp. 45–63.
62. See Robert A. Divine, 'The Cold War and the election of 1948', *Journal of American History*, 59 (1972), pp. 90–110, especially pp. 91, 95 and 98–9 (Dewey quotation p. 100).
63. Quoted in John Callaghan, 'The Cold War and the march of capitalism, socialism and democracy', *Contemporary British History*, 15, 3 (2001), pp. 1–25 (quotation p. 4).
64. Quoted in Dianne Kirby, 'Divinely sanctioned. The Anglo-American Cold War alliance and the defence of western civilisation and Christianity, 1945–48', *Journal of Contemporary History*, 35, 3 (2000), pp. 385–412 (quotation p. 405).
65. See Peter Hennessy, *The secret state. Whitehall and the Cold War* (London, 2002), and now Christopher Andrew, *The defence of the realm. The authorized history of MI5* (London, 2010).
66. Quoted in Peter Clarke, 'Labour's beachmaster', *London Review of Books* 23.1.2003, p. 25.

67. Thus Aaron L. Friedberg, *In the shadow of the garrison state. America's anti-statism and its Cold War grand strategy* (Princeton, 2000), especially pp. 340–45.
68. Quoted in Mary L. Dudziak, *Cold War civil rights. Race and the image of American democracy* (Princeton and Oxford, 2000), p. 29.
69. Thus ibid., pp. 2–3 and passim.
70. Quoted in Maria Höhn and Martin Klimke, *A breath of freedom. The civil rights struggle, African American GIs and Germany* (Basingstoke, 2010), pp. 56 and 76.
71. Geoffrey Marston, 'The United Kingdom's part in the preparation of the European Convention on Human Rights, 1950', *International and Comparative Law Quarterly*, 42 (1993), pp. 796–826.
72. I thank Thomas Probert for drawing this fact to my attention.
73. Speaking in December 1952 as quoted in Timothy Snyder, *Bloodlands. Europe between Hitler and Stalin* (New York, 2010), p. 366.
74. Jonathan Brent and Vladimir P. Naumov, *Stalin's last crime. The plot against the Jewish doctors, 1948–1953* (London, 2003), especially pp. 183–4.
75. See Kevin McDermott, 'Stalinist terror in Czechoslovakia: origins, processes, responses', in McDermott and Stibbe (eds.), *Stalinist terror in eastern Europe*, pp. 98–118, especially pp. 101–11.
76. See Kathryn Weathersby, *The Soviet aims in Korea and the origins of the Korean War, 1945–1950. New evidence from Russian archives*, Cold War International History Project, Working Paper No. 8 (Washington, DC, 1993).
77. See Michael M. Sheng, *Battling western imperialism. Mao, Stalin, and the United States* (Princeton, 1997), pp. 187–96, which is based on Red Chinese archives, and Lorenz M. Luethi, *The Sino-Soviet split. Cold War in the communist world* (Princeton, 2008), pp. 345–52.
78. On this general complex see Tony Smith, *Thinking like a communist. State and legitimacy in the Soviet Union, China, and Cuba* (New York, 1987), pp. 191–2.
79. Quoted in Walter Lafeber, *America, Russia and the Cold War, 1945–1996*, 8th edn (New York, 1997), p. 96.
80. See Robert J. McMahon, 'The Cold War comes to south-east Asia', in McMahon and Thomas G. Paterson (eds.), *The origins of the Cold War* (Boston, 1999), pp. 227–43.
81. Quoted in William Stueck, *The Korean War. An international history* (Princeton, 1995), p. 373.
82. See John Gillingham, *European integration, 1950–2003. Superstate or new market economy?* (Cambridge, 2003) p. 27.
83. Christopher Gehrz, 'Dean Acheson, the JCS and the "single package": American policy on German rearmament, 1950', *Diplomacy and Statecraft*,

12, 1 (2001), pp. 135–60, especially pp. 137 and 141–3 (Acheson quotation p. 141).

84. Quoted in Kai Bird, *The chairman. John J. McCloy and the making of the American establishment* (New York, 1992), p. 337.
85. Thus Richard J. Aldrich, 'OSS, CIA and European unity: the American Committee on United Europe, 1948–60', *Diplomacy and Statecraft*, 8, 1 (1997), pp. 184–227. I thank David Gioe for this reference.
86. See Arch Puddington, *Broadcasting freedom. The Cold War triumph of Radio Free Europe and Radio Liberty* (Lexington, 2001), pp. 73–4, on the importance on the Munich location, and Scott Lucas, *Freedom's war. The American crusade against the Soviet Union* (Manchester, 1999), especially p. 81 on Germany as the hub of psychological warfare.
87. Volker R. Berghahn, *America and the intellectual cold wars in Europe. Shepard Stone between philanthropy, academy, and diplomacy* (Princeton and Oxford, 2001), pp. 108–51.
88. See Samuel Moyn, *The last Utopia. Human rights in history* (Cambridge, Mass., and London, 2010), pp. 78–9 on this.
89. Alan S. Milward, *The United Kingdom and the European Community.* Vol. I: *The rise and fall of a national strategy* (London, 2002).
90. See A. W. Lovett, 'The United States and the Schuman Plan. A study in French diplomacy, 1950–1952', *Historical Journal*, 39, 2 (1996), pp. 425–55.
91. See Kevin Ruane, *The rise and fall of the European Defence Community. Anglo-American relations and the crisis of European defence, 1950–55* (Basingstoke, 2000).
92. Thus Gillingham, *European integration*, pp. 29–30.
93. See Vladislav Zubok, 'The Soviet Union and European integration from Stalin to Gorbachev', *Journal of European Integration History*, 2, 1 (1996), pp. 85–98, especially pp. 85–8.
94. Quoted in Christoph Bluth, *The two Germanies and military security in Europe* (Basingstoke, 2002), p. 13.
95. Thus Dirk Spilker, *The East German leadership and the division of Germany: patriotism and propaganda, 1945–53* (Oxford, 2006).
96. See Hans-Peter Schwarz, *Konrad Adenauer. A German politician and statesman in a period of war, revolution and reconstruction.* Vol. I: *From the German Empire to the Federal Republic, 1876–1952* (Providence and Oxford, 1995), pp. 649–63.
97. For these Cold War imperatives see Ronald Smelser and Edward J. Davies *The myth of the eastern front. The Nazi–Soviet war in American popular culture* (Cambridge, 2008), pp. 46–89.
98. Jeffrey Herf, *Divided memory. The Nazi past in the two Germanys* (Cambridge, Mass., 1997).

99. Quoted in Mark Kramer, 'The early post-Stalin succession struggle and upheavals in east central Europe: internal–external linkages in Soviet policy making', *Journal of Cold War Studies*, 1, 1 (1999), p. 12.
100. Thomas J. Christensen, *Useful adversaries. Grand strategy, domestic mobilization, and Sino-American conflict, 1947–1958* (Princeton, 1996).
101. See William B. Pickett, *Eisenhower decides to run. Presidential politics and Cold War strategy* (Chicago, 2000), pp. 213–15 (quotation p. 182).
102. Quoted in Steven Casey, *Selling the Korean War. Propaganda, politics and public opinion in the United States, 1950–1953* (New York, 2008), p. 251.
103. For the role of foreign policy in Soviet high politics see Kramer, 'Early post-Stalin succession struggle', pp. 3–55. (Kramer seems to me too modest on the importance of foreign policy, p. 9, when his own evidence seems to suggest the opposite.) Jeremy Smith and Melanie Ilic (eds.), *Khrushchev in the Kremlin. Policy and government in the Soviet Union, 1953–1964* (London and New York, 2011).
104. See Hubert Zimmermann, 'The sour fruits of victory: sterling and security in Anglo-German relations during the 1950s and 1960s', *Contemporary European History*, 9, 2 (2000), pp. 225–43.
105. On the centrality of Germany to British economic strategy see Geoffrey Owen, *From Empire to Europe. The decline and revival of British industry since the Second World War* (London, 1999), pp. 30–56 and passim.
106. On this see Lawrence Black, '"The bitterest enemies of communism": Labour revisionists, Atlanticism and the Cold War', *Contemporary British History*, 15, 3 (2001), pp. 26–62, especially pp. 27–8.
107. Quoted in ibid., p. 34.
108. Martin Ceadel, 'British parties and the European situation, 1952–1957', in Ennio di Nolfo (ed.), *Power in Europe? II. Great Britain, France, Germany and Italy and the origins of the EEC, 1952–1957* (Berlin and New York, 1992), pp. 309–32.
109. Quoted in John Lewis Gaddis, *The United States and the end of the Cold War. Implications, reconsiderations, provocations* (Oxford, 1992), p. 73.
110. Quoted in László Borhi, 'Rollback, liberation, containment or inaction? U.S. policy and Eastern Europe in the 1950s', *Journal of Cold War Studies*, 1, 3 (1999), pp. 67–110 (quotations p. 68).
111. See Ian Johnson, *A mosque in Munich. Nazis, the CIA, and the rise of the Muslim Brotherhood in the west* (New York, 2010).
112. See Kevin Ruane, 'Agonizing reappraisals: Anthony Eden, John Foster Dulles and the crisis of European defence, 1953–54', *Diplomacy and Statecraft*, 13, 4 (2002), pp. 151–85 (quotations pp. 151, 153, 156–7 and 172).
113. The importance of anti-German sentiment is emphasized by Arnold Kanter, 'The European Defense Community in the French National Assembly:

a roll call analysis', *Comparative Politics*, 2, 2 (1970), pp. 206, 212 and passim.

114. See Anne Deighton, 'The last piece of the jigsaw: Britain and the creation of the western European Union, 1954', *Contemporary European History*, 7, 2 (1998), pp. 181–96.
115. See Martin Schaad, 'Plan G – a "counterblast"? British policy towards the Messina countries, 1956', *Contemporary European History* 7, 1 (1998), pp. 39–60, passim (quotation p. 46).
116. Quoted in Lafeber, *America, Russia and the Cold War*, p. 178.
117. Thus Dieter Krüger, *Sicherheit durch Integration? Die wirtschaftliche und politische Integration Westeuropas 1947 bis 1957/58* (Oldenbourg, 2003), p. 514 and passim.
118. See William Glenn Gray, *Germany's Cold War. The global campaign to isolate East Germany, 1949–1969* (Chapel Hill and London, 2003).
119. Quoted in Sergei N. Khrushchev, *Nikita Khrushchev and the creation of a superpower* (University Park, Pa, 2000), p. 63.
120. Quoted in Ira Chernus, *Apocalypse management. Eisenhower and the discourse of national insecurity* (Stanford, 2008), p. 141.
121. Quoted in Mohamed Heikal, *Sphinx and commissar. The rise and fall of Soviet influence in the Arab world* (London, 1978), p. 65.
122. See Robert W. Heywood, 'West European Community and the Eurafrica concept in the 1950s', *Journal of European Integration*, 4, 2 (1981), pp. 199–210.
123. Quoted in Ralph Dietl, 'Suez 1956: a European intervention?', *Journal of Contemporary History*, 43, 2 (2008), pp. 259–78 (quotation p. 261).
124. See John C. Campbell, 'The Soviet Union, the United States, and the twin crises of Hungary and Suez', in William Roger Louis and Roger Owen (eds.) *Suez 1956. The crisis and its consequences* (Oxford, 1989), pp. 233–53.
125. See Simon C. Smith (ed.), *Reassessing Suez 1956. New perspectives on the crisis and its aftermath* (London, 2008).
126. See Diane B. Kunz, *The economic diplomacy of the Suez crisis* (Chapel Hill and London, 1991), especially pp. 113–14 and 192–3.
127. See W. R. Louis, 'Public enemy number one: the British Empire in the dock at the United Nations, 1957–1971', in Martin Lynn (ed.), *The British Empire in the 1950s. Retreat or revival?* (Basingstoke, 2006).
128. Quoted in Kenneth O. Morgan, *Britain since 1945. The people's peace* (Oxford, 1990), p. 158.
129. Quoted in Schaad, 'Plan G – a "counterblast"?', p. 50.
130. See Yinghong Cheng, 'Beyond Moscow-centric interpretation: an examination of the China connection in eastern Europe and North Vietnam during the era of de-Stalinisation', *Journal of World History*, 15, 4 (2004), pp. 487–518, especially pp. 489, 492–3 and 496 (quotation p. 489).

131. Thus Martin Thomas, *The French North African crisis. Colonial breakdown and Anglo-French relations, 1945–1962* (Basingstoke, 2000).
132. See Vladislav Zubok, *Khrushchev and the Berlin crisis (1958–1962)*, Cold War International History Project, Working Paper No. 6 (Washington, DC, 1993), p. 8. For the centrality of Germany to Khrushchev see p. 3.
133. Quoted in Nicholas Thompson, *The hawk and the dove. Paul Nitze, George Kennan and the history of the Cold War* (New York, 2009), p. 175.
134. Quoted in Richard Immerman, *John Foster Dulles. Piety, pragmatism, and power in U.S. foreign policy* (Wilmington, 1999), p. 188.
135. See Andrea Benvenuti, *Anglo-Australian relations and the turn to Europe, 1961–1972* (Woodbridge, 2008), pp. 26–41.
136. Quoted in Frank A. Mayer, *Adenauer and Kennedy. A study in German–American relations, 1961–1963* (Basingstoke, 1996), p. 96.
137. For an upbeat revisionist view of the military situation in the early 1960s see Mark Moyar, *Triumph forsaken. The Vietnam War, 1954–1965* (Cambridge, 2006).
138. Lawrence Freedman, *Kennedy's wars. Berlin, Cuba, Laos and Vietnam* (Oxford, 2000).
139. Thus David Kaiser, 'Men and policies', in Diane B. Kunz (ed.), *The diplomacy of the crucial decade* (New York, 1994), pp. 11–41, especially pp. 23–9.
140. Höhn and Klimke, *A breath of freedom*, p. 95.
141. Quoted in Zubok, *Khrushchev and the Berlin crisis*, p. 25.
142. Quoted in Gordon S. Barrass, *The Great Cold War. A journey through the hall of mirrors* (Stanford, 2009), p. 131.
143. See Hope M. Harrison, *Driving the Soviets up the wall. Soviet–East German relations, 1953–1961* (Princeton, 2005).
144. Quoted in Robert Cottrell, 'L'homme Nikita', *New York Review of Books*, 1.5.2003, pp. 32–5 (quotation p. 33).
145. Quoted in Tony Judt, 'On the brink', *New York Review of Books*, 15.1.1998, quotation p. 55.
146. Quoted in John Lewis Gaddis, *We now know. Rethinking Cold War history* (Oxford, 1997), p. 277. On the crisis more generally see Aleksandr Fursenko and Timothy Naftali, *'One hell of a gamble'. Khrushchev, Castro, Kennedy, and the Cuban missile crisis, 1958–1964* (London and New York, 1997).
147. See Hope M. Harrison, *Ulbricht and the concrete 'Rose'. New archival evidence on the dynamics of Soviet–East German relations and the Berlin crisis, 1958–61*, Cold War International History Project, Working Paper No. 5 (Washington, DC, 1993), p. 59.
148. According to the former US diplomat W. R. Smyser quoted in Gregor Peter Schmitz, 'The day Berlin was divided', *Spiegel International*, 30.10.2009:

http://www.spiegel.de/international/world/the-day-berlin-was-divided-kennedy-surprised-by-such-strong-american-outrage-to-the-wall-a-658349.html.

149. See Frédéric Bozo, *Two strategies for Europe. De Gaulle, the United States, and the Atlantic alliance* (Lanham and Boulder, 2001), and Jeffrey Glen Giauque, *Grand designs and visions of unity. The Atlantic powers and the reorganization of western Europe, 1955–1963* (Chapel Hill and London, 2002).

150. See Frank Costigliola, 'The failed design: Kennedy, de Gaulle, and the struggle for Europe', *Diplomatic History*, 8, 3 (1984), pp. 227–52.

151. See Matthias Schulz, 'Integration durch eine europäische Atomstreitmacht? Nuklearambitionen und die deutsche Europa-Initiative vom Herbst 1964', *Vierteljahreshefte für Zeitgeschichte*, 53, 2 (2005), p. 286.

152. See Eckart Conze, 'Hegemonie durch Integration? Die amerikanische Europapolitik und ihre Herausforderung durch de Gaulle', *Vierteljahreshefte für Zeitgeschichte*, 43 (1995), pp. 297–340.

153. Thus Francis J. Gavin, 'The myth of flexible response: United States strategy in Europe during the 1960s', *International History Review*, 23, 4 (2001), 847–75, especially pp. 848, 862–5.

154. Ibid., p. 869. See also Marc Trachtenberg, *A constructed peace. The making of the European settlement, 1945–1963* (Princeton, 1999) pp. 382–98, which sees the atomic inferiority of West Germany through the NPT as the completion of the post-war settlement.

155. Quotations in Thomas Alan Schwartz, *Lyndon Johnson and Europe. In the shadow of Vietnam* (Cambridge, Mass., 2003), p. 44.

156. Quotations in Frank Costigiola, 'The Vietnam War and the challenges to American power in Europe', in Lloyd C. Gardner and Ted Gittinger (eds.), *International perspectives on Vietnam* (College Station, Texas, 2000), pp. 146–7 and 151.

157. Daniel Kosthorst, 'Sowjetische Geheimpolitik in Deutschland? Chruschtschow und die Adschubej-Mission 1964', *Vierteljahreshefte für Zeitgeschichte*, 44 (1996), pp. 257–94.

158. See Susanna Schrafstetter, *Die dritte Atommacht. Britische Nichtverbreitungspolitik im Dienst von Statussicherung und Deutschlandpolitik, 1952–1968* (Munich, 1999), pp. 224, 234–6.

159. See Paul du Quenoy, 'The role of foreign affairs in the fall of Nikita Khrushchev in October 1964', *International History Review*, 25, 2 (2003), pp. 334–56 (quotations pp. 339 and 351), and James G. Richter, *Khrushchev's double bind. International pressures and domestic coalition politics* (Baltimore and London, 1994).

160. See R. D. Johnson, *All the way with LBJ. The 1964 presidential election* (Cambridge, 2009), pp. 77–90 and 124–5. I am very grateful to Andrew Preston for this reference.

161. Thomas Borstelmann, *The Cold War and the color line. American race relations in the global arena* (Cambridge, Mass., 2001).
162. See Clifford G. Gaddy, *The price of the past. Russia's struggle with the legacy of a militarized economy* (Washington, DC, 1997).
163. Thus Martin Malia, *The Soviet tragedy. A history of socialism in Russia, 1917–1991* (New York, 1994).
164. See James Sheehan, *The monopoly of violence. Why Europeans hate going to war* (London, 2008).
165. See Thomas A. Schwartz, 'The de Gaulle challenge: the Johnson administration and the NATO crisis of 1966–1967', in Helga Haftendorn, Georges-Henri Soutou, Stephen F. Szabo and Samuel F. Wells Jnr (eds.), *The strategic triangle. France, Germany, and the United States in the shaping of the new Europe* (Baltimore, 2006), p. 133.
166. See Fredrik Logevall, *Choosing war. The lost chance for peace and the escalation of war in Vietnam* (Berkeley, 1999), especially pp. 375–498.
167. See Mark Atwood Lawrence, *Assuming the burden. Europe and the American commitment to war in Vietnam* (Berkeley, 2007). Quotation in Costigiola, 'Vietnam War and the challenges to American power in Europe', p. 148.
168. See Thomas Alan Schwartz, *Lyndon Johnson and Europe. In the shadow of Vietnam* (Cambridge, Mass., 2003).
169. See Saki Dockrill, *Britain's retreat from east of Suez. The choice between Europe and the world?* (Basingstoke, 2002), pp. 196–7 and 218–19.
170. Helen Parr, 'Saving the community: the French response to Britain's second EEC application in 1967', *Cold War History*, 6, 4 (2006), pp. 425–54.
171. Quoted in Timothy Garton Ash, *In Europe's name. Germany and the divided continent* (London, 1993), p. 54.
172. See Frédéric Bozo, 'Détente versus alliance: France, the United States and the politics of the Harmel Report (1964–1968)', *Contemporary European History*, 7, 3 (1998), pp. 343–60.
173. On the international nature of 1968, and the centrality of the Vietnam War, see Carole Fink, Philipp Gassert and Detlef Junker (eds.), *1968. The world transformed* (Cambridge, 1998), pp. 8–18 and passim, and R. Gildea, James Mark and Niek Pas, 'European radicals and the "Third World": imagined solidarities and radical networks, 1958–73', *Cultural and Social History*, 8 (2011), pp. 449–72.
174. Quoted in Hans Kundnani, *Utopia or Auschwitz. Germany's 1968 generation and the Holocaust* (London, 2009), p. 64.
175. On the link between the German and American movements see Martin Klimke, *The other alliance. Student protest in West Germany and the United States in the global sixties* (Princeton, 2010).
176. Quoted in Kundnani, *Utopia or Auschwitz*, pp. 42 and 45.

177. Thus Dan Diner, *America in the eyes of the Germans. An essay on anti-Americanism* (Princeton, 1996), pp. 105–50.
178. See William Burr, 'Sino-American relations, 1969: the Sino-Soviet border war and steps towards *rapprochement*', *Cold War History*, 1, 3 (2001), pp. 73–112, especially pp. 87 and 104.
179. I follow here the analysis of John Lewis Gaddis, 'Rescuing choice from circumstance. The statecraft of Henry Kissinger', in Gordon A. Craig and Francis L. Loewenheim (eds.), *The diplomats, 1939–1979* (Princeton, 1994), pp. 564–92 (the phrase 'authoritarian purposefulness' is on p. 571).
180. Quoted in G. R. Sloan, *Geopolitics in United States strategic policy, 1890–1987* (Brighton, 1988), p. 173.
181. See Carole Fink and Bernd Schaefer (eds.), *Ostpolitik, 1969–1974. European and global responses* (Cambridge, 2009).
182. Quoted in Henry Kissinger, *Diplomacy* (New York, 1994), p. 735.
183. See Jussi Hanhimäki, *The flawed architect. Henry Kissinger and American foreign policy* (Oxford, 2004), pp. 85–90.
184. Quoted in Gordon S. Barrass, *The Great Cold War. A journey through the hall of mirrors* (Stanford, 2009), p. 169.
185. Quoted in H. G. Linke (ed.), *Quellen zu den deutsch-sowjetischen Beziehungen*. Vol. II: *1945–1991* (Darmstadt, 1999), p. 146.
186. Quoted in William Bundy, *A tangled web. The making of foreign policy in the Nixon presidency* (New York, 1998), p. 321.
187. Thus Mary E. Sarotte, *Dealing with the devil. East Germany, détente, and Ostpolitik, 1969–1973* (Chapel Hill, 2001), pp. 109–11.
188. Thus Garton Ash, *In Europe's name*.
189. Quoted in Kundnani, *Utopia or Auschwitz*, p. 90.
190. See Jeremy Suri, *Henry Kissinger and the American century* (Cambridge, Mass., 2007), pp. 171–2.
191. Niklas H. Rossbach, *Heath, Nixon and the rebirth of the special relationship. Britain, the US and the EC, 1969–74* (Basingstoke, 2009).
192. See Jenna Phillips, 'Don't mention the war? History suggests foreign policy can swing voters', *History and Policy*, 22.4.2010, pp. 2–3.
193. Brian Harrison, *Finding a role? The United Kingdom, 1970–1990* (Oxford, 2010), pp. 20–38.
194. See Keith Hamilton, 'Britain, France, and America's year of Europe, 1973', in Stone and Otte (eds.), *Anglo-French relations*, pp. 237–62.
195. For an inside view from the Kremlin see Victor Israelyan, 'The October 1973 war: Kissinger in Moscow', *Middle East Journal*, 49 (1995), pp. 248–68.
196. Quoted in 'Z', 'The year of Europe? ', *Foreign Affairs*, 52, 2 (January 1974).

8. DEMOCRACIES, 1974–2011

1. Quoted in A. James McAdams, 'The new diplomacy of the West German *Ostpolitik*', in Gordon A. Craig and Francis L. Loewenheim (eds.), *The diplomats, 1939–1979* (Princeton, 1994), p. 559.
2. Quoted in Tony Smith, *America's mission. The United States and the worldwide struggle for democracy in the twentieth century* (Princeton, 1994), p. 266.
3. Interview with Zbigniew Brzezinski, *Le Nouvel Observateur*, 15–21.1.1998.
4. See Norman Stone, *The Atlantic and its enemies. A personal history of the Cold War* (London, 2010), chapter 19, 'The Kremlin consolations', pp. 353–81.
5. Quoted in Jonathan Haslam, *Russia's Cold War. From the October Revolution to the fall of the Wall* (New Haven and London, 2011), p. 304.
6. Quoted in Jonathan Haslam, *The Soviet Union and the politics of nuclear weapons in Europe, 1969–87. The problem of the SS-20* (Basingstoke, 1989), p. 76.
7. See Michael Ploetz, 'Mit RAF, Roten Brigaden und Action Directe – Terrorismus und Rechtsextremismus in der Strategie von SED und KPdSU', *Zeitschrift des Forschungsverbundes SED-Staat*, 22 (2007), pp. 117–44.
8. See Christopher Andrew, *The world was going our way. The KGB and the battle for the Third World* (New York, 2005).
9. See Paolo Filo della Torre, Edward Mortimer and Jonathan Story (eds.), *Eurocommunism. Myth or reality?* (Harmondsworth, 1979).
10. Quoted in Odd Arne Westad, *The global Cold War. Third World interventions and the making of our times* (Cambridge, 2005), p. 245.
11. The centrality of the Soviet *conventional* threat is stressed in Christoph Bluth, *The two Germanies and military security in Europe* (Basingstoke, 2002), pp. 99–106, 227 and passim. For contemporary perceptions of the crushing Soviet conventional superiority see Jack L. Snyder, *The Soviet strategic culture. Implications for limited nuclear options* (Santa Monica, 1977), pp. 23–4.
12. See Aryeh Neier, *Taking liberties. Four decades in the struggle for rights* (New York, 2003), and Samuel Moyn, *The last Utopia. Human rights in history* (Cambridge, Mass., and London 2010).
13. See Thomas J. W. Probert, 'The innovation of the Jackson–Vanik amendment', in Brendan Simms and D. J. B. Trim (eds.), *Humanitarian intervention. A history* (Cambridge, 2011), pp. 323–42 (quotation p. 323). I have also benefited immensely from discussions with my doctoral student Jonathan Cook, who is writing a dissertation on Jackson.

14. Quoted in Clyde Haberman, 'Decades later, Kissinger's words stir fresh outrage among Jews', *The New York Times*, 16.12.2010, which reviews the latest release of tapes from the Oval Office.
15. See Noam Kochavi, 'Insights abandoned, flexibility lost: Kissinger, Soviet Jewish emigration, and the demise of détente', *Diplomatic History*, 29, 3 (2005), pp. 503–29, especially pp. 521–2.
16. Thus Robert G. Kaufman, *Henry M. Jackson. A life in politics* (Seattle and London, 2000), pp. 251–3.
17. 'Report by Mr Leo Tindemans, Prime Minister of Belgium, to the European Council', *Bulletin of the European Communities*, supplement 1/76 (1975), pp. 3, 5 and 11.
18. Quotations in Keith Hamilton, 'Cold War by other means: British diplomacy and the Conference on Security and Cooperation in Europe, 1972–1975', in Wilfried Loth and Georges-Henri Soutou (eds.), *The making of détente. Eastern and western Europe in the Cold War, 1965–75* (New York and London, 2008), pp. 169 and 172. See also Roger Beetham, 'Observations on British diplomacy and the CSCE process', *British Scholar*, III, 1 (2010), pp. 127–32. I thank Thomas Probert for this reference.
19. See William Korey, *The promises we keep. Human rights, the Helsinki process, and American foreign policy* (New York, 1993), p. xvii.
20. Quoted in Olav Njølstad, 'The Carter administration and Italy: keeping the communists out of power without interfering', *Journal of Cold War Studies*, 4, 3 (2002), pp. 56–94 (quotation p. 64).
21. Kenneth Maxwell, *The making of Portuguese democracy* (Cambridge, 1997).
22. See Donald Sassoon, *One hundred years of socialism. The west European left in the twentieth century* (London, 1996), especially chapter 21.
23. See Douglas Wass, *Decline to fall. The making of British macro-economic policy and the 1976 IMF crisis* (Oxford and New York, 2008).
24. Robin Harris (ed.), *The collected speeches of Margaret Thatcher* (London, 1997), p. 39. I am grateful to Matthew Jamison for this reference.
25. Quoted in Svetlana Savranskaya, 'Human rights movement in the USSR after the signing of the Helsinki Final Act, and the reaction of Soviet authorities', in Leopoldo Nuti (ed.), *The crisis of détente in Europe. From Helsinki to Gorbachev, 1975–1985* (London and New York, 2009), p. 29.
26. On Jackson's role in influencing a later generation of 'neo-conservatives' see Justin Vaïsse, *Neoconservatism. The biography of a movement* (Cambridge, Mass., 2010).
27. See Klaus Wiegrefe, *Das Zerwürfnis. Helmut Schmidt, Jimmy Carter und die Krise der deutsch-amerikanischen Beziehungen* (Berlin, 2005).
28. For the Cold War context see Maria Eleonora Guasconi, 'Europe and the EMS challenge: old and new forms of European integration in the 1970s', in Nuti (ed.), *Crisis of détente in Europe*, pp. 177–89, especially pp. 177–8 and 181.

29. Quoted in Oliver Bange, '"Keeping détente alive": inner-German relations under Helmut Schmidt and Erich Honecker, 1974–1982', in Nuti (ed.), *Crisis of détente in Europe*, pp. 233–4.
30. See interview with Zbigniew Brzezinski, *Le Nouvel Observateur*, 15–21. 1.1998.
31. See Ray Takeyh, *Guardians of the revolution. Iran and the world in the age of the ayatollahs* (Oxford and New York, 2009), especially pp. 11–33 (quotations pp. 28, 18, 20 and 21). I thank my student Roseanna Ivory for many interesting discussions on the Iranian Revolution and its international ramifications.
32. See Enrico Fardella, 'The Sino-American entente of 1978–1979 and its "baptism of fire" in Indochina', in Max Guderzo and Bruna Bagnato (eds.), *The globalization of the Cold War. Diplomacy and local confrontation. 1975–85* (London and New York, 2010), pp. 154–65, especially pp. 158–9.
33. Yaroslav Trofimov, *The siege of Mecca. The forgotten uprising* (London, 2007).
34. Quoted in Lloyd C. Gardner, *The long road to Baghdad. A history of U.S. foreign policy from the 1970s to the present* (New York and London, 2008), p. 56.
35. See Odd Arne Westad, 'The road to Kabul: Soviet policy on Afghanistan, 1978–1979', in Odd Arne Westad (ed.), *The fall of détente. Soviet–American relations during the Carter years* (Oslo, 1997), especially pp. 134–5 on concerns that Amin might 'turn to the west'.
36. Quoted in G. R. Sloan, *Geopolitics in United States strategic policy, 1890–1987* (Brighton, 1988), p. 191.
37. See Jeffrey Herf, *War by other means. Soviet power, West German resistance, and the battle of the Euromissiles* (New York, 1991), and Thomas Risse-Kappen, *Zero option. INF, West Germany, and arms control* (Boulder and London, 1988).
38. See David Skidmore, *Reversing course. Carter's foreign policy, domestic politics and the failure of reform* (Nashville and London, 1996), pp. 52–83.
39. For a sceptical view on the domestic importance of foreign policy see Richard Melanson, *American foreign policy since the Vietnam War. The search for consensus from Nixon to Clinton* (Armonk and London, 1996), p. 134.
40. See Mark A. Kramer, 'Poland, 1980–81. Soviet policy during the Polish crisis', *Cold War International History Project Bulletin*, issue 5 (Spring, 1995), pp. 118–23.
41. Quoted in Raymond L. Garthoff, *The great transition. American–Soviet relations and the end of the Cold War* (Washington, DC, 1994), p. 8.
42. Quoted in Smith, *America's mission*, p. 303.
43. Quoted in 'Obituary: Lord Blaker', *The Times*, 9.7.2009, p. 57.

44. See Lawrence Freedman, *The official history of the Falklands campaign*, 2 vols. (London, 2005).
45. Thus A. F. K. Organski, *The $36 billion bargain. Strategy and politics in US assistance to Israel* (New York, 1990), p. 204.
46. Quoted in Beatrice Heuser, 'The Soviet response to the Euromissiles crisis', in Nuti (ed.), *Crisis of détente in Europe*, p. 144. For Soviet concerns about the *Bundeswehr* see p. 143.
47. On Soviet penetration of the British Labour Party and trade union movement see the articles by Pavel Stroilov, 'Reaching through the Iron Curtain' (based on the diaries of the Soviet International Department official Antoly Chernyaev), and Gerald Kaufman, 'How my party was betrayed by KGB boot-lickers', in the section 'Labour and the Soviets', *Spectator*, 7.11.2009, pp. 14–17.
48. See Peter J. Westwick, 'The Strategic Offense Initiative? The Soviets and Star Wars', *Physics Today*, 61, 6 (June 2008), p. 45.
49. On the European response to SDI see Sean N. Kalic, 'Reagan's SDI announcement and the European reaction: diplomacy in the last decade of the Cold War', in Nuti (ed.), *Crisis of détente in Europe*, pp. 99–110.
50. Margaret Thatcher, *The Downing Street Years* (London, 1993), p. 548. For the centrality of security to Thatcher's view of Europe see Hugo Young, *The blessed plot. Britain and Europe from Churchill to Blair* (Basingstoke, 1998), pp. 306–74, especially pp. 310 and 358.
51. Thus the brutal summary of Richard Hellie, 'The structure of Russian imperial history', *History and Theory*, 44, 4 (2005), p. 107.
52. Quoted in Amin Saikal and William Maley (eds.), *The Soviet withdrawal from Afghanistan* (Cambridge, 1989), p. 13.
53. See now Rodric Braithwaite, *Afgantsy. The Russians in Afghanistan, 1979–89* (London, 2011), especially pp. 121–24.
54. On this see Stephen Kotkin, *Armageddon averted. The Soviet collapse, 1970–2000* (Oxford, 2001), and Mikhail Gorbachev, *Perestroika. New thinking for our country and the world* (London, 1987), p. 19 and passim.
55. Quoted in Vladislav M. Zubok, 'Why did the Cold War end in 1989? Explanations of "the turn"', in Odd Arne Westad (ed.), *Reviewing the Cold War. Approaches, interpretations, theory* (London, 2000), p. 347.
56. See Boris Meissner, *Vom Sowjetimperium zum eurasischen Staatensystem. Die russische Aussenpolitik im Wandel und in der Wechselbeziehung zur Innenpolitik* (Berlin, 1995), pp. 37–66.
57. Quoted in Vladimir Shlapentokh, 'A normal system? False and true explanations for the collapse of the USSR', *The Times Literary Supplement*, 15.12.2000, p. 12.
58. On this see Daniel Deudney and G. John Ikenberry, 'The international sources of Soviet change', *International Security*, 16, 3 (1991–2), pp. 105–6.

59. Quoted in Jonathan Haslam, '1989: History *is* rewritten', in S. Pons and F. Romero (eds.), *Reinterpreting the end of the Cold War. Issues, interpretations, periodizations* (London and New York, 2005), pp. 165–78 (quotations p. 167).
60. 'Memorandum from Anatoly Chernyaev to Aleksandr Yakovlev on Germany and eastern Europe', 10.3.1986, in Svetlana Savranskaya, Thomas Blanton and Vladislav Zubok (eds.), *Masterpieces of history. The peaceful end of the Cold War in Europe, 1989* (Budapest and New York, 2010), pp. 222–3.
61. See 'Record of conversation between Aleksandr Yakovlev and Zbigniew Brzezinski', 31.10.1989, in Savranskaya, Blanton and Zubok (eds.), *Masterpieces of history*, pp. 566–7.
62. On 'Gorbymania' see Thomas Risse-Kappen, 'Ideas do not float freely: transnational coalitions, domestic structures, and the end of the Cold War', *International Organization*, 48, 2 (1994), pp. 185–214 (pp. 206–7).
63. This formed an important sub-plot in the *Historikerstreit* of the mid-1980s. See Mark Bassin, 'Geopolitics of the *Historikerstreit*: the strange return of the *Mittellage*', in Jost Hermand and James Steakley (eds.), *Heimat, nation, fatherland. The German sense of belonging* (New York etc., 1996), pp. 187–228, especially pp. 191–4.
64. Erhard Busek and Emil Brix, *Projekt Mitteleuropa* (Vienna, 1986). For a discussion of the political significance see Robin Okey, 'Central Europe/eastern Europe: behind the definitions', *Past and Present*, 137 (1992), pp. 127–9.
65. Yitzhak M. Brudny, *Reinventing Russia. Russian nationalism and the Soviet state, 1953–1991* (Cambridge, Mass., 1998).
66. Quoted in Zubok, 'Why did the Cold War end in 1989?', p. 349.
67. See Richard Sakwa, *Gorbachev and his reforms, 1985–90* (New York and London, 1990), p. 9.
68. See here 'The new democratic revolution', in ibid., pp. 192–3.
69. Thus Eduard Schewardnadse, *Als der eiserne Vorhang zerriss. Begegnungen und Erinnerungen* (Duisburg, 2007), pp. 76–8.
70. See Stephen Wall, *A stranger in Europe. Britain and the EU from Thatcher to Blair* (Oxford, 2008).
71. See, for example, Baroness Young (Minister of State) at the Foreign and Commonwealth Office, Third Mackinder Lecture, printed in *Transactions of the Institute of British Geographers*, 12, 4 (1987), pp. 391–7, especially p. 393.
72. As quoted in the released Soviet record of a meeting in September 1989, before the fall of the Berlin Wall: Andrew Roberts, 'Why Thatcher feared Germany', *Sunday Telegraph*, 13.9.2009, p. 22.
73. Artemy M. Kalinovsky and Sergey Radchenko (eds.), *The end of the Cold War and the Third World. New perspectives on regional conflict* (London and New York, 2011).

74. Jason Burke, *Al-Qaeda. Casting a shadow of terror* (London, 2004).
75. Abdullah Azzam, 'The solid base', April 1988, extracts in Gilles Kepel and Jean-Pierre Milelli (eds.), *Al Qaeda in its own words* (Cambridge, Mass., 2008), pp. 140–43 (quotation p. 143).
76. Thus Fawaz A. Gerges, *The far enemy. Why jihad went global* (Cambridge, 2005).
77. Quoted in Sakwa, *Gorbachev and his reforms*, pp. 134–5.
78. See Charles S. Maier, *Dissolution. The crisis of communism and the end of East Germany* (Princeton, 1997).
79. Quoted in Douglas A. Borer, *Superpowers defeated. Vietnam and Afghanistan compared* (London and Portland, 1999), p. 220.
80. Thus William E. Odom, *The collapse of the Soviet military* (New Haven, 1998).
81. For the centrality of Germany see Jeffrey A. Engel (ed.), *The fall of the Berlin Wall. The revolutionary legacy of 1989* (Oxford, 2009), pp. 52–64, 69, 83–6, 140–41 and passim; and Harold James and Marla Stone (eds.), *When the Wall came down. Reactions to German unification* (London, 1993).
82. Quoted in Daniel Johnson, 'Seven minutes that shook the world', *Standpoint*, November 2009, p. 41.
83. Quoted in George R. Urban, *Diplomacy and disillusion at the court of Margaret Thatcher. An insider's view* (London and New York, 1996), pp. 118–50 (especially p. 136).
84. See Philip Zelikow and Condoleezza Rice, *Germany unified and Europe transformed: a study in statecraft* (Cambridge, Mass., 1995), and Robert L. Hutchings, *American diplomacy and the end of the Cold War: an insider's account of US policy in Europe, 1989–1992* (Washington, DC, Baltimore and London).
85. Quoted in Michael Cox and Steven Hurst, '"His finest hour?" George Bush and the diplomacy of German unification', *Diplomacy and Statecraft*, 13, 4 (2002), p. 135.
86. The centrality of Germany, and the Soviet desperation, is emphasized in George Bush and Brent Scowcroft, *A world transformed* (New York, 1998), pp. 182–203, 253, 280–81 (quotation) and passim.
87. See Michael R. Beschloss and Strobe Talbott, *At the highest levels. The inside story of the end of the Cold War* (Boston, 1993), pp. 185–6.
88. David Cox, *Retreating from the Cold War. Germany, Russia and the withdrawal of the Western Group of forces* (London, 1996).
89. Angela Stent, 'From Rapallo to reunification: Russia and Germany in the twentieth century', in Sanford R. Lieberman, David E. Powell, Carol R. Saivetz and Sarah M. Terry (eds.), *The Soviet Empire reconsidered. Essays in honour of Adam B. Ulam* (Boulder, San Francisco and Oxford, 1994).
90. Quoted in Cox and Hurst, '"His finest hour?"', p. 140.

91. Stephen F. Frowen and Jens Hölscher (eds.), *The German currency union of 1990. A critical assessment* (Basingstoke, 1997).
92. Anthony Glees, 'The diplomacy of Anglo-German relations: a study of the ERM crisis of September 1992', *German Politics*, 3 (1994), pp. 75–90.
93. See Ulrich Schlie, 'Die ersten fünf Jahre der Wiedervereinigung: von außen betrachtet – eine Bücherauslese', *Die neue Ordnung*, 49, 6 (1995), pp. 474–80; Manfred Görtemaker, *Geschichte der Bundesrepublik Deutschland. Von der Gründung bis zur Gegenwart* (Frankfurt am Main, 2004); Christian Hacke, *Die Aussenpolitik der Bundesrepublik Deutschland. Von Konrad Adenauer bis Gerhard Schröder*, 2nd edn (Berlin, 2004); and Eckart Conze, *Die Suche nach Sicherheit. Eine Geschichte der Bundesrepublik Deutschland von 1949 bis in die Gegenwart* (Munich, 2009).
94. See Arthur Hertzberg, 'Is anti-semitism dying out?', *New York Review of Books*, 24.6.1993, pp. 51–7, especially p. 56.
95. For the refusal of Germany to conform to the 'academic scare stories' see Jan Müller, 'The old questions and the German Revolution', *Contemporary European History*, 7, 2 (1998), pp. 271–84.
96. On the structural weakness of German federalism and the economy after 1990 see Helmut Wiesenthal, 'German unification and "Model Germany": an adventure in institutional conservatism', *West European Politics*, 26, 4 (2003), pp. 37–58.
97. See Christopher Hill, 'The European dimension of the debate on UN Security Council membership', *The International Spectator*, XL, 4 (2005), pp. 31–2. For the new Germany's 'internal culture of restraint and reticence' despite its 'enormous and increasing structural power' see Andrei S. Markovits and Simon Reich, *The German predicament. Memory and power in the new Europe* (Ithaca, 1997), pp. xiii and 3.
98. Gregor Schöllgen, *Angst vor der Macht. Die Deutschen und ihre Aussenpolitik* (Berlin, 1993).
99. The phrase is in a RAND study in the summer of 1990: Ronald D. Asmus, *German strategy and opinion after the Wall, 1990–1993* (Santa Monica, 1994), p. 61.
100. James Gow, *The Serbian project and its adversaries. A strategy of war crimes* (Montreal, 2003), and Gerard Toal and Carl T. Dahlman, *Bosnia remade. Ethnic cleansing and its reversal* (Oxford, 2011).
101. See Leon Aron, *Boris Yeltsin. A revolutionary life* (London, 2000), pp. 440–93.
102. See Karl Kaiser and Klaus Becher, 'Germany and the Iraq conflict', in Nicole Gnesotto and John Roper (eds.), *Western Europe and the Gulf. A study of West European reactions to the Gulf War* (Paris, 1992), pp. 39–69, especially pp. 39–43.
103. Lawrence Freedman and Efraim Karsh (eds.), *The Gulf conflict 1990–1991. Diplomacy and war in the New World Order* (London, 1993); Alex

Danchev and Dan Keohane (eds.), *International perspectives on the Gulf conflict, 1990–1991* (London, 1994).

104. For a contemporary survey of this debate, with particular emphasis on the centrality of Germany, see Josef Joffe, 'Collective security and the future of Europe: failed dreams and dead ends', *Survival*, 34, 1 (1992), pp. 36–50.
105. On the 'French alternative' see Kori Schake, 'NATO after the Cold War, 1991–1995: institutional competition and the collapse of the French alternative', *Contemporary European History*, 7, 3 (1998), pp. 379–407 (p. 380).
106. D. Allen, 'Wider but weaker or the more the merrier? Enlargement and foreign policy cooperation in the EC/EU', in J. Redmond and G. G. Rosenthal (eds.), *The expanding European Union. Past, present, future* (Boulder, 1998).
107. See Ludger Kühnhardt, 'The fall of the Berlin Wall and European integration', pp. 47–60; http://www.kas.de/upload/Publikationen/Panorama/2009/1/kuehnhardt.pdf.
108. As recollected by Helmut Kohl, *Ich wollte Deutschlands Einheit* (Berlin, 1996), pp. 194–201.
109. Quoted in Schake, 'NATO after the Cold War', p. 387.
110. Quoted in Jacques E. C. Hymans, 'Judgment at Maastricht', *The Harvard Crimson*, 4.12.1991.
111. See James Gow, *Triumph of the lack of will. International diplomacy and the Yugoslav war* (London, 1997), and Josip Glaurdić, *The hour of Europe. Western powers and the breakup of Yugoslavia* (New Haven and London, 2011).
112. See Brendan Simms, *Unfinest hour. Britain and the destruction of Bosnia* (London, 2001).
113. I base myself here on the unpublished thesis of Caoimhe ni Chonchuir, 'French policy towards Bosnia, 1992–1995' (Cambridge University M.Phil. dissertation, 2008).
114. See Richard Caplan, 'The European Community's recognition of new states in Yugoslavia: the strategic implications', *Journal of Strategic Studies*, 21, 3 (1998), pp. 24–45.
115. See Takis Michas, *Unholy alliance. Greece and Milošević's Serbia* (College Station, Texas, 2002).
116. For the 'China debate' of the mid-1990s see Richard Bernstein and Ross Munro, *The coming conflict with China* (New York, 1997). For the eastward turn in Washington and NATO see Philip H. Gordon, 'Recasting the Atlantic alliance', *Survival*, 38, 1 (1996), pp. 32–57.
117. Quoted in Smith, *America's mission*, p. 325. Clinton was speaking in January 1994.

118. See Niall Ferguson and Brigitte Granville, '"Weimar on the Volga". Causes and consequences of inflation in 1990s Russia compared with 1920s Germany', *Journal of Economic History*, 60, 4 (2000), pp. 1061–87.
119. Quoted in David Kerr, 'The new Eurasianism: the rise of geopolitics in Russia's foreign policy', *Europe–Asia Studies*, 47, 6 (1995), p. 986.
120. For fears about NATO enlargement in the Bosnian context see Hans-Joachim Hoppe, 'Moscow and the conflicts in former Yugoslavia', *Aussenpolitik*, 43, 3 (1997), pp. 267–77, especially p. 277.
121. Yevgeny Primakov, director of the Foreign Intelligence Service, and Yeltsin (speaking in September 1995) are quoted in Peter Truscott, *Russia First. Breaking with the west* (London and New York, 1997), pp. 48–9.
122. See John Dunlop and Anatol Lieven, *Chechnya. Tombstone of Russian power* (New Haven, 1998).
123. Quoted in Ivo H. Daalder, *Getting to Dayton. The making of America's Bosnia policy* (Washington, DC, 2000), p. 10.
124. Václav Havel, 'A new European order?' *New York Review of Books*, 2.3.1995, p. 43.
125. See James Goldgeier, *Not whether but when. The U.S. decision to enlarge NATO* (Washington, DC, 1999), and Ronald D. Asmus, *Opening NATO's door. How the alliance remade itself for a new era* (New York, 2002).
126. See John W. Young, *Britain and European unity, 1945–1999*, 2nd edn (Basingstoke, 2000), pp. 150–74.
127. Though the Conservative divisions over Europe played a role: see Christopher Stevens, 'Thatcherism, Majorism and the collapse of Tory statecraft', *Contemporary British History*, 16, 1 (2002), pp. 119–50, especially p. 139.
128. Sonia Lucarelli, *Europe and the breakup of Yugoslavia. A political failure in search of a scholarly explanation* (The Hague and London, 2000).
129. *A National Security Strategy of engagement and enlargement*, The White House, February 1995, pp. 1, 2, 22, 25 ,27, 30 and passim.
130. See also Oliver Daddow, *New Labour and the European Union. Blair and Brown's logic of history* (Manchester and New York, 2011), especially pp. 1 and 12.
131. Quoted in Paul Gillespie, 'History and geography rhyme for new Germany', *Irish Times*, 8.11.1997.
132. Quoted in Brendan Simms, 'From the Kohl to the Fischer Doctrine: Germany and the Wars of the Yugoslav Succession, 1991–1999', *German History*, 21, 3 (2003), pp. 393–414 (quotation p. 414).
133. Thomas Diez, 'Europe's others and the return of geopolitics', *Cambridge Review of International Affairs*, 17, 2 (2004), pp. 319–35 (quotation p. 327).
134. See Christopher Hill, 'The capability–expectations gap, or conceptualizing Europe's international role', in Simon Bulmer and Andrew Scott (eds.), *Economic and political integration in Europe. Internal dynamics and*

global context (Oxford, 1994), especially pp. 104 (on Bosnia) and 116–17 (on 'defence [as] the key to the development of the community's place in the world').

135. Quoted in Henrik Larsen, 'The EU: a global military actor?', *Cooperation and Conflict. Journal of the Nordic International Studies Association*, 37, 3 (2002), pp. 283–302 (quotation p. 293).
136. See Tariq Ramadan, *Islam, the west and the challenges of modernity* (Leicester, 2001), p. 277.
137. Gilles Kepel, *Allah in the west. Islamic movements in America and Europe* (Oxford, 1997).
138. Quoted in Jonathan Bronitsky, *British foreign policy and Bosnia. The rise of Islamism in Britain, 1992–1995*, published by the International Centre for the Study of Radicalisation and Political Violence (London, 2010), p. 9.
139. Thus Ed Husain, *The Islamist. Why I joined radical Islam in Britain, what I saw inside and why I left* (London, 2007), pp. 74–81 and passim.
140. Osama bin Laden, 'Declaration of Jihad against the Americans occupying the land of the two Holy Sanctuaries', in Gilles Kepel and Jean-Pierre Milelli (eds.), *Al Qaeda in its own words* (Cambridge, Mass., 2008), pp. 47–50.
141. There was, however, considerable doubt about this in the vast academic literature: Daniele Conversi, 'Demo-skepticism and genocide', *Political Studies Review*, 4 (2006), pp. 247–62, especially pp. 247 and 257.
142. Thus Gregor Schöllgen in Wolf-Dieter Eberwein and Karl Kaiser (eds.), *Deutschlands neue Aussenpolitik*. Vol. IV: *Institutionen und Ressourcen* (Munich, 1998), p. 217.
143. See Rudolf Scharping, *Wir dürfen nicht wegsehen. Der Kosovo-Krieg und Europa* (Munich, 2001), p. 114.
144. Simms, 'From the Kohl to the Fischer Doctrine'.
145. Chris Patten, 'No more roses', *The Times Literary Supplement*, 1.6.2007, p. 13.
146. Catherine Ashton, speech to European parliament, 3.3.2010.
147. For a contemporary analysis of this see Peter Riddell, 'Europe must learn to defend itself. Military muscle would give the EU more diplomatic clout', *The Times*, 28.6.1999, p. 20.
148. The centrality of Germany is stressed by Jolyon Howorth, 'Discourse, ideas and epistemic communities in European security and defence policy', *West European Politics*, 27 (2004), pp. 211–34 (p. 224).
149. Quoted in Hans Kundnani, *Utopia or Auschwitz. Germany's 1968 generation and the Holocaust* (London, 2009), pp. 254–5. Joschka Fischer, 'Vom Staatenbund zur Föderation: Gedanken über die Finalität der europäischen Integration'. Rede am 12. Mai 2000 in der Berliner Humboldt-Universität.

150. See James Rogers, 'From "civilian power" to "global power". Explicating the European Union's "Grand Strategy" through the articulation of discourse theory', *Journal of Common Market Studies*, 47, 4 (2009), pp. 831–62, and Jan Zielonka, *Explaining Euro-paralysis. Why Europe is unable to act in international politics* (Basingstoke and New York, 1998).
151. See Mette Eilstrup-Sangiovanni, 'Why a Common Security and Defence Policy is bad for Europe', *Survival*, 45, 4 (2003), pp. 193–206.
152. See Heinz Brill, 'Geopolitische Motive und Probleme des europäischen Einigungsprozesses', *Aus Politik und Zeitgeschichte*, 32 (2008), pp. 41–6.
153. For example, Svitlana Kobzar, 'The European Union's impact on democratisation of Ukraine', in David. Bosold, Petr Drulák and Nik Hynek (eds.), *Democratization and security in central and eastern Europe and the post-Soviet states* (Baden-Baden, 2012).
154. See Paul Lendvai, *Inside Austria. New challenges, old demons* (London, 2010), pp. 149–56.
155. See Giandomenico Majone, 'Europe's "democratic deficit": the question of standards', *European Law Journal*, 4, 1 (1998), pp. 5–28.
156. Deirdre Kevin, 'Coverage of the European parliament elections of 1999: national public spheres and European debates', *Javnost – The Public*, 8, 1 (2001), pp. 21–38.
157. See Philipp Borinski, 'NATO towards double enlargement: the case of the Balkans', *Journal of European Integration*, 24, 2 (2002), pp. 130–31.
158. See Alexander Rahr, *Wladimir Putin. Der 'Deutsche' im Kreml* (Munich, 2000).
159. See Bobo Lo, *Vladimir Putin and the evolution of Russian foreign policy* (London, 2003), pp. 72–3 and 83–6, and Stephen Blank, 'Russia's unending quest for security', in Mark Galeotti (ed.), *The politics of security in modern Russia* (Farnham, 2010), pp. 177–9.
160. Quoted in Kundnani, *Utopia or Auschwitz*, p. 268.
161. See from the perspective of 'critical security studies' J. Peter Burgess, *The ethical subject of security. Geopolitical reason and the threat against Europe* (London and New York, 2011), especially pp. 183 and 206–7.
162. 'Speech by Federal Foreign Minister Joschka Fischer during the European policy debate in the German *Bundestag* on 12 December 2001'.
163. For a critique see Tony Smith, *A pact with the devil. Washington's bid for world supremacy and the betrayal of the American promise* (New York, 2007), a *pentito* among the new Wilsonians.
164. *European Security Strategy*, pp. 7–8: http://europa.eu/legislation_summaries/justice_freedom_security/fight_against_organised_crime/r00004_en.htm.
165. See Romano Prodi, *A wider Europe. Proximity as the key to stability*, 6.12.02. For this new EU 'security perimeter' see Michael Smith, 'The European Union and international order: European and global dimen-

sions', *European Foreign Affairs Review*, 12, 4 (2007), pp. 437–56 (especially p. 449).

166. Blair speech 2.10.2001.
167. Quoted in Kundnani, *Utopia or Auschwitz*, p. 284.
168. See Gregor Schöllgen, *Der Auftritt. Deutschlands Rückkehr auf die Weltbühne* (Munich, 2003), and Joschka Fischer, *'I am not convinced.' Der Irak-Krieg und die rot-grünen Jahre* (Cologne, 2011), especially pp. 169–225.
169. Derek Averre, '"Sovereign democracy" and Russia's relations with the European Union', *Demokratizatsiya*, 15, 2 (2007), pp. 173–90, and Andrew Hurrell, 'Hegemony, liberalism and global order: what space for would-be great powers?', *International Affairs*, 82 (2006), pp. 1–19.
170. For example, Mark Leonard, *Why Europe will run the 21st century* (London and New York, 2005).
171. On this general issue see Andreas von Gehlen, 'Two steps to European party democracy', *European View*, 3 (2006), pp. 161–70.
172. http://europa.eu/legislation_summaries/justice_freedom_security/fight_against_organised_crime/r00004_en.htm.
173. Thus Thomas C. Fischer, 'An American looks at the European Union', *European Law Journal*, 12, 2 (2006), pp. 226–78, especially p. 227.
174. See Glyn Morgan, *The idea of a European superstate. Public justification and European integration* (Princeton, 2005).
175. Quoted in *International Herald Tribune*, 4.3.2004.
176. See Elizabeth Shakman Hurd, 'Political Islam and foreign policy in Europe and the United States', *Foreign Policy Analysis*, 3 (2007), pp. 345–67.
177. Christopher Hill, 'Bringing war home: making foreign policy in multicultural societies', *International Relations*, 21 (2007), pp. 259–83. For national cases see Sam Cherribi, *In the house of war. Dutch Islam observed* (Oxford, 2010), and Anthony McRoy, *From Rushdie to 7/7. The radicalisation of Islam in Britain* (London, 2006), pp. 50–67.
178. Barry Wain, *Malaysian maverick. Mahathir Mohamad in turbulent times* (Basingstoke, 2010).
179. See Menahem Milson, 'A European plot on the Arab stage: the Protocols of the Elders of Zion in the Arab media', *Middle East Research Institute, Inquiry and Analysis*, 20.5.2011.
180. Thus the diagnosis of Hanns W. Maull, the foremost theoretician of 'civilian power', that 'the new world situation requires a mobilization of society around a new primacy of foreign policy': 'Internationaler Terrorismus: die deutsche Aussenpolitik auf dem Prüfstand', *Internationale Politik*, 56, 12 (2001), pp. 1–10.
181. See Samy Cohen (ed.), *Democracies at war against terrorism. A comparative perspective* (Basingstoke, 2008).
182. John McCain, speech in Stanford, California, 2.5.2007.

183. James Rubin, 'Building a new Atlantic alliance: restoring America's partnership with Europe', *Foreign Affairs*, 87, 4 (2008), pp. 99–110 (quotations pp. 99 and 107). See also Andrew B. Denison, 'Amerika kommt auf Deutschland zu', *Aus Politik und Zeitgeschichte*, 37–8 (2008), pp. 3–5.
184. Thus George Friedman, 'The United States, Germany and beyond', *Stratfor Global Intelligence*, 30.3.2009.
185. See Sergio Fabbrini, *Compound democracies. Why the United States and Europe are becoming similiar* (Oxford, 2010).
186. See Richard Youngs, *Europe's decline and fall. The struggle against global irrelevance* (London, 2010).

CONCLUSION

1. Henry Kissinger, *White House years* (London, 1979), p. 54.

Acknowledgements

A great many people helped in the writing of this book and I cannot thank them all. I would, however, like to take this opportunity to express my gratitude to Doohwan Ahn, Ilya Berkovich, Tim Blanning, Arndt Brendecke, Christopher Clark, David Cooper, Nicola Craig, Geoffrey Dumbreck, Hazel Dunn, Liam Fitzgerald, Nick Guyatt, Bill Hamilton, Jonathan Haslam, Lara Heimert Christopher Hill, Rachel Hoffman, Charlie Laderman, the late Miranda Long, Roger Lovatt, Scott Mandelbrote, Heinrich Meier, Patrick Milton, William Mulligan, James Carleton Paget, Mateja Peter, Andrew Preston, Daniel Robinson, James Rogers, Christopher Ross, Liza Soutchek, Jan Vermeiren, Bob Wilkinson, Joachim Whaley, Simon Winder. To this list must be added the staff and students of the Department of Politics and International Studies at the University of Cambridge, the Master of Peterhouse, Adrian Dixon, and all the Fellows of that College not already individually mentioned. I am also deeply indebted to my family, especially my wife, Anita Bunyan, and my parents, David and Anngret Simms. Finally, I thank my children, Hugh, Katherine and Constance, the eldest, to whom this book is dedicated.

Index

Arabic names starting with the definite article (al-) are filed under the main element of the name; e.g. al-Assad is filed as Assad, Hafez al-.